SOCIAL INEQUALITY IN CANADA: PATTERNS, PROBLEMS, POLICIES

Third Edition

Edited by

JAMES CURTIS
University of Waterloo

EDWARD GRABB
University of Western Ontario

NEIL GUPPY
University of British Columbia

Prentice Hall Allyn and Bacon Canada Inc., Scarborough, Ontario

Canadian Cataloguing in Publication Data

Main entry under title:
Social inequality in Canada: patterns, problems, policies

3rd ed.
Includes index
ISBN 0-13-616632-6

1. Equality—Canada. 2. Social classes—Canada. 3. Canada—Social policy. I. Curtis, James E., 1943– . II. Grabb, Edward G. III. Guppy, L. Neil, 1949– .

HN110.Z9S6 1999a 305'.0971 C98-931018-3

Prentice-Hall, Inc., Upper Saddle River, New Jersey
Prentice-Hall International (UK) Limited, London
Prentice-Hall of Australia, Pty. Limited, Sydney
Prentice-Hall Hispanoamericana, S.A., Mexico City
Prentice-Hall of India Private Limited, New Delhi
Prentice-Hall of Japan, Inc., Tokyo
Simon & Schuster Southeast Asia Private Limited, Singapore
Editora Prentice-Hall do Brasil, Ltda., Rio de Janeiro

ISBN 0-13-616632-6

Acquisitions Editor: David Stover
Developmental Editor: Jean Ferrier
Production Editor: Matthew Christian
Copy Editor: Jim Zimmerman
Production Coordinator: Peggy Brown
Designer: Julia Hall
Page Layout: Carol Magee

Visit the Prentice Hall Canada web site! Send us your comments, browse our catalogues, and more at **www.phcanada.com**. Or reach us through e-mail at **phabinfo_pubcanada@prenhall.com.**

3 4 5 WEB 03 02 01

Printed and bound in Canada.

Contents

Section 3 Ascription and Social Inequality 159

Gender

Ethnicity, Race, and Ancestry

Age

Region

Section 4. Some Consequences of Social Inequality 293

Preface

Our purpose in this book is to introduce students to issues of social inequality in Canada. We do this by presenting a collection of 30 articles which address all of the major aspects of social inequality. The result is a book dealing with topics central to a range of courses, including Social Inequality, Social Class, Social Stratification, Social Issues, and Canadian Society.

This new edition begins from the same premise that guided the earlier versions of the book—that social inequality entails two broad components: *objective or structural conditions* of social inequality (power, poverty and wealth, occupations, and educational attainment, in particular) and *ideologies* that help support these differences. The ideologies—expressed in formal laws, public policies, dominant values, and so forth—provide justification for the objective patterns of inequality such as income differences by sex, region, or education level.

There are, of course, other, less influential ideologies in the society too—"counter-ideologies"—that often reflect the interests of the disadvantaged. These counter-ideologies, expressed, for example, by social movements promoting the interests of women, visible minorities, or Native people, frequently call for changes to existing conditions of inequality so as to better the lot of the disadvantaged. The proper study of social inequality involves the scrutiny of both these structural and ideological components.

In this revised edition we have sought, also, to retain other core strengths of the first two editions of the collection. As before, we have chosen articles with an eye to reflecting the range of theoretical perspectives and research approaches used to address issues of inequality. As well, we have retained our emphasis on papers that are imaginative and clear expositions of results and theories. Also, we have preserved our commitment in the earlier editions to the historical context of patterns of inequality. In addition, we have worked very hard to ensure that various dimensions of inequality, for example, gender and ethnicity, have not been confined exclusively to isolated sections. While separate sections for gender and race and ethnicity are maintained, we include several articles in other sections that deal with these dimensions as well (e.g., in the sections on education, income, and occupation). Finally, in keeping with the earlier editions, all sections of the book stress policies and ideologies related to inequality.

This new edition departs from its predecessors in some ways. Most importantly perhaps, only 3 of the 37 pieces in the second edition are retained in unaltered form. In this new edition, 10 of the pieces have never before been published. Each of the other 20 pieces reprinted here has been revised for inclusion, many of them substantially. Seven pieces were prepared especially for the second edition, and are now revised and up-dated for this edition. There was a similarly large proportion of changes from the first edition to the second edition. Substantial changes have been required to reflect the research that has been done since the previous edition. Over this period, the nature of social inequality in Canada has changed significantly in certain respects, and important research has continued to emerge.

Readers familiar with the other editions will note another substantial change. Although we were reluctant to do so, we have decreased somewhat the average length of articles.

While this made our selection of material even more difficult than before, there was little choice if we were to keep the book's price within reason, and still maintain a large number of selections and breadth of coverage of topics.

Space constraints have meant, again, that we have had to include some choices to the exclusion of many other fine works on the same topic. Our "Further Reference" sections, and the references in the selections themselves, only begin to suggest the amount of important research now available, and the difficulty we have had in making choices.

The study of social inequality in Canada has moved forward rapidly toward a much better understanding of the phenomenon. Those of us who would prefer to see our society changed to provide greater equality of opportunity and condition can take heart at this improved understanding. It is another matter, though, to turn our understanding into action and achieve social change. The following pages will show that many patterns of inequality are terribly resistant to change because they are maintained by formidable forces, especially by the *economic, political, and ideological control* of highly privileged groups. Much of this control operates through the apparatuses of the state, as some of the selections will emphasize.

This volume will show that there are inequalities that are becoming more marked over time—as is the case with the increased concentration of wealth and corporate control. There are also other forms of inequality that have considerably diminished—as with differences in the attainment of university degrees by women relative to men, and differences in earnings and occupations of some ethnic groups, especially those who are not visible minorities. And finally, there are other patterns, such as the distribution of income, that show little change in recent decades. Thus, those readers who would prefer a more egalitarian society than currently exists in Canada will find reasons for both optimism and pessimism in the research presented here.

We would like to thank many people for their help with this project. First, of course, are the contributors to the volume. The strengths of the book are largely their doing. Second, we are indebted to many people for helpful suggestions in improving our editions. In particular, we thank the many students, over several cohorts, who have given us valuable feedback on the volume in their courses. Also, those who have provided helpful suggestions include Bruce Arai, Gillian Creese, Dawn Currie, Brian Elliott, Dawn Farrough, and Martha Foschi from the University of British Columbia; Anton Allahar, Doug Baer, Paul Maxim and Jim Rinehart from the University of Western Ontario; Bill Johnston from the University of Alberta; Monica Boyd and John Myles, now at Florida State University; Lorne Tepperman from the University of Toronto; John Goyder, John Hirdes, and Ron Lambert from the University of Waterloo; and Tony Williams from Okanagan University College in B.C. Third, we appreciate the continuing support of Prentice Hall Canada personnel, including Laura Pearson, David Stover, David Jolliffe, Lisa Phillips, Matthew Christian and Jim Zimmerman. Fourth, the support staffs at our respective universities have been extremely helpful with each edition. For the present edition, we are particularly grateful to Terry Stewart for computing work, and Julie Dembski, Lois Wilbee, Joyce D'Souza, and Carol Wong for help with preparation of materials.

J.C.
E.G.
N.G.

General Introduction

CONCEPTUAL ISSUES IN THE STUDY OF SOCIAL INEQUALITY

Edward G. Grabb

That human beings are often very different from one another is one of those basic truths about life that we can all recognize. We need only observe the various sizes, shapes, and colours of other people, the different group affiliations they adopt, and the distinct goals or interests they pursue, to be reminded of the numerous differences that can be drawn between us. It is also true that many of these differences probably have little or no lasting influence on our existence. And yet it is clear that certain human differences regularly have significant consequences for the lives that we are able to lead in society.

The study of social inequality is really the study of these consequential human differences. In particular, inequality refers to differences that become socially structured, in the sense that they become a regular and recurring part of the ways in which people interact with one another on a daily basis. Structured inequality involves a process by which groups or individuals with particular attributes are better able than those who lack or are denied these attributes to control or shape rights and opportunities for their own ends. One major factor in this process is that the advantaged groups or individuals tend to obtain greater access to the various rewards and privileges that are available in society. These benefits, in turn, serve to reinforce the control over rights and opportunities enjoyed by the advantaged factions, in a cyclical process that structures and *reproduces* the pattern of inequality across time and place.

In general terms at least, this view of social inequality is held by most theorists and researchers in the social sciences, including many of those who study Canadian society. In this book we have brought together recent exemplary works by some noted Canadian writers, all of whom share an interest in understanding the consequential differences among people and the inequalities that they engender.

The main goal of this opening chapter is to provide an integrative background for the papers that have been selected, and a context within which the substance of our selections can be more easily located and comprehended. This is not an entirely straightforward task, since in the study of inequality, as in most vibrant and continuing areas of inquiry, there are clear divergences in theoretical orientations and research traditions.

Given these divergences, there is little possibility at present of establishing a single, universally accepted approach to analyzing the problem. In other words, a complete synthesis of existing thought and knowledge is currently not feasible. Nonetheless, we can arrive at a general understanding of the major theoretical issues and empirical questions that have held the attention of contemporary students of social inequality. This understanding should also help us to appreciate important areas of agreement and dispute among scholars in the field.

The central questions we shall address in this opening chapter are theoretical in nature. In particular, we will assess the two most important ideas in most theories of social inequality: the concept of *class* and the concept of *power*, or *domination*. In doing so, we will demonstrate that class and power are closely tied to questions of *economic control*, and also to questions of *ideological and political control*. The combined effects of these factors are what gives rise to the key bases for social inequality that operate in Canada and most modern societies. Our discussion here will provide the conceptual background for the selection and classification of papers in this volume.

SOCIAL INEQUALITY AND THE CONCEPT OF CLASS

If we were to ask most people what inequality is about, we would probably find that their responses put considerable stress on economic or material distinctions, on differences in economic rights, opportunities, rewards, and privileges between themselves and others. Although such differences might not be their sole focus, people do show a notable interest, for example, in whether or not they earn as much money as others in different occupations; they might wonder if their own share of society's wealth is growing or shrinking over time; they might even raise such questions as whether or not it is true that a small number of businesses increasingly control more and more of their country's economic resources.

In fact, until recently these same kinds of questions—about economic control and material privilege—have also been the predominant concern among most of the social scientists interested in the topic of inequality. Such a focus is understandable, of course, since economic differences involve the most immediate or fundamental inequality in social settings: people's relative access to the material necessities of life itself. Undoubtedly, this emphasis is at least partly responsible for the central role that the concept of economic class has always played in social analysis, particularly since the early writings of Karl Marx and Max Weber (see Marx 1867; Weber 1922).

Unfortunately, the concept of class has provoked long-standing and still unresolved questions about its precise meaning and significance. Of these questions, five in particular should be raised in this opening section. First, there is the question of whether classes are just categories of individuals who share similar economic circumstances, or whether the term *class* should refer only to an economic category which is also a real social group, a set of people with a shared sense of common membership or purpose. Second, analysts have debated whether classes are best thought of as simply the same as *strata*—ranked layers of people separated according to income or occupation level, for instance—or whether the dividing lines between classes are less arbitrary, less variable, and more fundamental than these stratum distinctions suggest. Third, some writers contend that classes are best understood as sets of *people*, while others say they are really sets of *places* or *positions*, like boxes or containers in which the people are located. Fourth, there is the question of whether classes should be defined principally by differences in the amount of material rewards *distributed* to them for consumption purposes, or whether such differences are secondary to, and largely derivative from, structured economic *relationships*, especially relationships which give sustained control over material life to some and not others. For some theorists, such control provides the real means by which classes are defined and delineated. Finally, many writers disagree about how many classes there are in modern societies. Are there just two, a small dominant one and a large subordinate one? Are there instead some intermediate classes between top and bottom and, if so, how many? Or is it the case that there are no easily identifiable classes, but a continuous hierarchy without clear class distinctions?

The difficulties inherent in any attempt to answer all of these questions are obvious from the volume of work that has been generated on the concept of class (for a review, see

Grabb 1997). These differing perspectives cannot be fully incorporated within a single conception or definition of class. Nevertheless, there is sufficient common ground for class to be viewed in a manner which, at least in general terms, is consistent with most major works in the field, including those of the key classical writers, Marx and Weber, and of subsequent writers broadly sympathetic to either or both of these theorists (for example, Poulantzas 1975; Carchedi 1977, 1987; Wright 1979, 1985, 1989, 1994; Wright et al. 1992; Parkin 1979; Giddens 1973, 1981a, 1981b, 1984, 1989, 1994).

Our approach to defining the concept of class involves the following answers to the five questions listed above:

1. Classes exist primarily as *categories* of people, and need not be defined as real *groups*. In other words, classes typically will not be sets of people having a common sense of group membership and capability to act in unison toward some collective goal. This is not to say that such united action is never possible; classes sometimes become groups, but only sometimes. As Giddens notes, for example, class systems exist on a national or even international scale in modern times, making such co-ordination and common purpose exceedingly difficult to generate, at least in the mass of the population (Giddens, 1973:84). In those rare instances where simple economic classes also develop these group-like characteristics, some writers find it useful, following Weber, to refer to such groups as social classes (Weber 1922:302–305; see also Giddens 1973:78–79; Grabb 1997:47).

2. While classes normally are not real groups, neither are they merely equivalent to strata, as certain writers seem to suggest (e.g., Johnson 1960:469; see Barber 1957:73; Parsons 1951:172). That is, strata are usually ranked statistical aggregates, for which the criteria used in ranking are quite variable (including such characteristics as income, education, occupation, and general prestige level) and for which the choice of boundaries is an arbitrary decision made by the researcher. In contrast, class divisions are traceable to more fundamental, deep-seated, and uniform cleavages than the ones implied by these stratum distinctions.

3. Classes are most completely comprehended if we recognize that they are neither just sets of people nor just structural categories, the containers that separate or encapsulate sets of people; they really are both of these things in combination. This double meaning of class is one aspect of a more general process that Giddens has called the "duality" of social structures (Giddens 1979, 1981b, 1984, 1989). Hence, classes exist as structural entities because certain enforceable rights or opportunities—such as the right to own and to exclude others from owning productive property—define them and distinguish them from each other. However, classes have almost no meaning if they are not also seen as real people, for it is people who create the rights or opportunities that define classes in the first place, it is people who enjoy or suffer the consequences of class inequalities, and it is people alone who are capable of changing or consolidating class structures through social action.

4. Classes are most readily defined as *economically-based* entities. However, as will be discussed later, they also have an important part to play in the *political* and *ideological* spheres of society, and can be said to exist, in a sense, within and across all social structures, not just the economic (see Wright 1978, 1980, 1989:343–345). In delineating classes, we can conform with Marx, Weber, and most leading contemporary theorists by

treating one distinction—between those who own or control society's productive property or resources and those who lack this attribute—as the initial and most fundamental division in modern class systems (e.g., Marx and Engels 1848a:58, 92; Weber 1922:927; Giddens 1973:100; Poulantzas 1975:14; Wright 1978:73; Parkin 1979:53).

While this basic division is the crux of most class structures, there are other forms of social inequality that can occur. The relations of domination and exploitation established by this division are the primary factors in class formation, but the distribution of material benefits such as income can also be significant for delineating classes, if only in an indirect way. Such benefits can enhance or blur the division between the dominant and the subordinate classes, depending on whether or not these benefits are distributed so that the two classes have markedly distinct consumption habits and qualities of life.

In addition, despite what some writers seem to suggest, the distribution of material benefits need not be an insignificant factor in the formation of classes. For example, some Marxist theorists tend to consider all wage and salary employees as simply members of the working class, or *proletariat*, because they depend for their livelihood on the sale of labour power to the propertied owning class, or *bourgeoisie*. However, wage and salary employees sometimes are paid sufficiently high incomes for them to be able to accumulate some surplus funds, over and above what they need for basic survival. These funds can be, and occasionally are, used to gain some control over productive resources, in the acquisition of such holdings as stocks, rental properties, interest-bearing bonds, annuities, pension plans, and so forth. To be sure, these are relatively minor forms of economic control or ownership, in most cases, somewhat like that of the *petty bourgeoisie*, who own small-scale businesses or farms but employ no workers themselves. Nonetheless, such resources provide a means by which distributive inequalities can give rise to economic categories that are distinct to some degree from both the bourgeoisie and the proletariat (see Wright 1989:325, 333; 1994:45–48).

A related point of note is that those with a distributive surplus have the opportunity to expend these funds in another manner: to help finance special educational qualifications or technical training for themselves or their children. Here again, distributive inequalities need not merely signify consumption differences. Some writers suggest that educational credentials themselves are another form of productive "property." This may be true to the extent that educational certificates are tangible possessions that can generate material dividends all their own and that, as a result, can provide a basis for economic control otherwise unattainable by those who lack similar credentials (Giddens 1973; Collins 1979; Parkin 1979). Hence, educational advantage or opportunity may be yet another basis on which divisions can arise in the class structure and be passed on or reproduced over generations. The important role of educational certification or "credential assets" in class formation has increasingly been acknowledged by recent Marxist scholars (e.g. Wright 1985, 1989, 1994), in contrast to some earlier Marxists who ignored or down-played the importance of this factor.

5. The final, and probably most controversial, question to address about class is how many classes actually exist in current capitalist societies. Again, complete agreement on this question is at present unattainable. Nevertheless, most writers now concur that modern class systems are more complex or pluralist in nature than the traditional Marxist division between bourgeoisie and proletariat alone is capable of representing. On the surface, this may seem to contradict standard Marxist accounts on the subject of class, espe-

cially those offered by Marx's early disciples. However, we should note that, on closer inspection, some allowance for a more complex portrayal of modern class systems is really quite consistent with Marx's own analysis and with more recent treatments by Marxist scholars.

At several points in his original writings, it is clear that Marx himself speaks of additional economic groupings that exist in real societies and that complicate the pure two-class model he believes will ultimately emerge in advanced capitalism. Marx refers to these complicating elements in various ways, calling them *Mittelstande* ("middle estates or strata"), *Mittelstufen* ("middle stages or ranks"), and *Mittelklassen* ("middle classes") (Marx and Engels 1848b:472; Marx 1862:368; 1867:673, 688, 784, 791; 1894:892). Most current Marxists describe similar complications in contemporary class structures, although they usually avoid referring to these additional elements as genuine classes (but see Carchedi 1977; Wright and Martin 1987; Wright 1989, 1994). Such elements may include the traditional petty bourgeoisie of small-scale owners, but also involve a diverse range of salaried personnel that, because of attributes such as educational training, technical knowledge, administrative authority, and so on, persist as "fractions," "contradictory class locations," or similar elements complicating the basic two-class structure of capitalism (Poulantzas 1975:23, 196–99, 297; Wright 1978:90–91; 1979:46–47; 1985:88–89; 1989:301–348; 1994:45–48, 252).

Among most non-Marxists, the existence of intermediate categories in the class structure is readily acknowledged. In fact, some non-Marxists argue that there are so many complexities and fine distinctions in today's economic structure that what we really have is a *continuous hierarchy* with no distinct classes at all (Nisbet 1959; Faris 1972). Other non-Marxists have tried to adhere to this notion of a continuum while simultaneously retaining the concept of class in their analyses. One approach is to conceive of a general social hierarchy that is continuous and yet can also be divided into identifiable class clusters. In contrast to Marxist writers, some non-Marxist analysts, especially the so-called "structural functionalist school," see classes as sets of *occupations* that share a similar level of *prestige* because they are similar in their supposed value to society as a whole (Parsons 1940, 1953; Barber 1957).

Among many recent non-Marxist scholars, however, it is common to reject this conception, primarily because it tends only to confuse classes with statistical categories or strata. Instead, leading contemporary writers outside the Marxist circle now conclude that it is essential to retain key aspects of Marx's original conception of class, provided these are revamped or supplemented to take account of subsequent developments in advanced class systems.

The latter approach is reminiscent of that adopted by Max Weber, the best known non-Marxist among major classical theorists in the field of inequality. Weber's work entails a constructive critique of Marx's writings. Weber envisions a class structure broadly similar to Marx's, involving a dominant bourgeoisie, or owning class at the top, a propertyless working class at the bottom, and a mix of "various middle classes" *(Mittelstandklassen)* in between (Weber 1922:303–305). There are several differences between the views of Marx and Weber, of course. Perhaps the most crucial difference concerns their expectations for the eventual fate of the middle categories in the class system. In contrast to Marx, Weber believes that the growing need for intermediate bureaucratic and technical personnel in modern societies means that the middle class will not fall into the proletariat with time, but will continue to endure as a significant force in the future; hence, Weber is far less convinced than Marx that a growing split will emerge between the top and the bottom classes, or that an ultimate revolt by the working class against capitalism is likely to occur.

Weber's approach to the study of class has had a notable influence on virtually all current non-Marxist theorists. For example, some recent writers see classes arising because some people are able to gain greater access to certain important "capacities" and "mobility chances" (Giddens 1973:101–103) or to special "resources and opportunities" (Parkin 1979:44–46) that serve to exclude other people from advantaged positions (see also Scott 1996). Certainly, these more recent approaches are not identical to one another, nor do they correspond precisely to the views of either Marx or Weber in their subtler details. Still, the class structures they portray are generally akin to one another and to the classical conceptions, for they also arrive at three key groupings: a *dominant class* composed mainly of those who own or control large-scale production; a *working class* made up of people who lack resources or capacities apart from their own labour power; and, in between, a *mixed intermediate range* that mainly includes professional, technical, or white-collar personnel who have some degree of special training or education (Giddens 1973:101–110; Parkin 1979:47–58, 102–110).

Thus, even a brief review of classical and contemporary conceptions of class indicates that what is really at issue among most theorists is not whether complications exist in the class system, but whether the complexities that do occur, especially those found in the centre of the structure, in fact constitute classes in their own right. Marxists usually say no, perhaps because they consider any middle segments as both transitional and heterogeneous, destined to fall eventually into the proletariat and to blur only temporarily the real two-class system that underlies capitalism. In contrast, non-Marxists routinely treat such central segments as a middle class (or set of middle classes), either because such writers use the term *class* differently or because they genuinely believe these intermediate categories are fundamental and persistent realities within modern class systems.

While no complete resolution of this debate is possible, the view put forth here is that, at least for the current stage of capitalist development, it is reasonable to use the term *middle class* to label these central categories. There are three reasons for taking this position.

First, there is nothing inherent in the word *class* that suggests that it must be reserved solely to refer to permanent and lasting social categories. Thus, while all Marxists treat the bourgeoisie as a real class within capitalism, Marxists also contend that this class is destined for eventual dissolution in future socialist societies. Similarly, then, whether or not the middle categories in the class system are destined to be transitional entities should not be a crucial concern for deciding whether or not they form a class at present. Marx clearly saw this himself since, as noted already, he sometimes spoke of the existence of a middle class even though he had no doubt that its days were numbered.

Second, it can be argued similarly that although the middle segments of the class structure are indeed heterogeneous, their diversity is insufficient grounds for denying that they form a distinct class. For, as leading Marxists and others acknowledge, the contemporary bourgeoisie and proletariat are also marked by considerable heterogeneity, but are deemed to be classes all the same (Poulantzas 1975:23, 139, 198).

Finally, between the proletarian or bourgeois classes, on the one hand, and the set of intermediate categories, on the other hand, there is some conceptual parity that suggests the latter also may be seen as a class. By *conceptual parity* we mean that the middle class is definable by means of the very same criteria used to delineate the bourgeoisie and proletariat.

These criteria are the measure of people's relative control over society's productive resources and the extent to which such control separates sets of individuals (and the positions they occupy) from one another. What is most distinct about the members of the middle class is their mixed, or hybrid, situation in the productive system relative to people from other classes. As suggested previously in point 4, middle-class incumbents are unlike those in the proletariat, and similar to people in the bourgeoisie, because they retain some control over productive resources or assets—the acquisition of property and investments or of educational credentials and skills, in particular. However, at the same time, middle-class members are unlike those in the bourgeoisie, and closer to people in the proletariat, because the resources they control are typically minor in scale and are often derived from a relatively small surplus fund accumulated from salaried or wage-based earnings. That these middle locations tend to commingle characteristics of the other two classes, and yet still remain marginal to both of them, is what most clearly identifies the middle class as a separate entity (see Wright 1989:333; Wright et al. 1992:41).

Given these considerations, we can deal with point 5 by provisionally suggesting that Canada, as well as most advanced capitalist countries, retains a class structure that, although highly complex and internally diverse, tends at its core to comprise three basic elements. The first is a predominant class of large-scale owners of productive property, the so-called *capitalist class* or *bourgeoisie* in classical Marxian terminology. The second element is a subordinate class of workers who live primarily through the sale of their labour power to the owning class and who are usually termed the *working class* or *proletariat*. The third major element is a mixed and more heterogeneous middle category of small-scale business people, educated professional-technical or administrative personnel, and various salaried employees or wage earners possessing some certifiable credentials, training, or skills. The latter grouping, while it is for some writers just a set of complicating fractions or fragments within a basic two-class model, can be considered a third or *middle class* for the reasons already outlined (see Grabb 1997:197–98).

Still, as has been pointed out from the beginning of this chapter, this provisional characterization cannot be presented as a universally acceptable conception of modern class structures. Rather, it can best be seen as an approximation, a compromise view with which the differing perspectives that are considered in this book can be compared and contrasted. Such an approximation allows us to recognize some level of agreement about how to think about the concept of class. Even so, other theoretical issues still remain to be addressed. In particular, we should be aware that many analysts believe a focus on class is too narrow to provide by itself a complete conceptualization of social inequality in all its forms. Such contentions move us beyond the problems of economic class and control over material or productive resources. They lead to a broader range of concerns that require us to consider the second key idea in most theories of social inequality—the concept of power or domination.

SOCIAL INEQUALITY AS POLITICAL AND IDEOLOGICAL CONTROL

In our opening remarks it was suggested that social inequality is primarily a question of consequential human differences, especially those that become structured and recurring features of our everyday lives. To this point, we have considered what many feel are the most familiar and fundamental illustrations of such differences: the inequalities that derive from differential *economic* control, or people's command over material and productive resources in society. In addition, however, many writers suggest at least two other major mechanisms that are crucial to the creation and continuation of social inequality. The first of these involves control over people and their conduct, over what some might call "human resources." This command over human resources is the essence of *political* control, as broadly defined by various analysts. The third major mechanism can be referred to as *ideological* control. It entails the control of ideas, knowledge, information, and similar resources in the establishment of structured inequality between groups or individuals (Mann 1986, 1993; Runciman 1989; Grabb 1997).

A basic premise of the current discussion is that these two additional forms of control, though they typically occur in conjunction with economic control (and with each other), are not simply reducible to nor a consequence of economic control, since both political and ideological control actually have their own distinct origins. In other words, it is possible to gain positions of dominance in society and to establish inequalities between factions without relying purely on control over material resources.

For example, inequality can result from political control when enforceable policies, statutes, or laws are invoked to ensure the compliance of subordinates with the will of others. The government or *state* is most commonly identified with the idea of political control, since it takes primary responsibility for creating the laws that govern the behaviour of people and can ensure compliance, if necessary, through the use of police or military force. However, political control in the broadest sense occurs whenever individuals' actions are constrained by rules of conduct established by others in authority over them in various organizations—when employees obey the work regulations of their jobs or when students comply with the academic regulations of their university, for example. The most extreme or blatant form that political control can take is one which is usually exercised by the state. This is the use of physical force by one faction on another, what Poulantzas quite literally calls the "coercion of bodies and the threat of violence of death" (Poulantzas 1978:28–29).

In addition to economic and political control, inequalities can also be created through or be reinforced by ideological forces. *Ideology* refers to the set of ideas, values, and beliefs that describe, explain, or justify various aspects of the social world, including the existence of inequality (Porter 1965, chs. 15, 16; Marchak 1988). Thus, for example, a belief in racial superiority or inferiority is central to the ideological system that helped create and justify the unequal treatment of Blacks by Whites in the nineteenth-century southern United States and in the old apartheid system in South Africa. Similarly, the belief in the divine right of kings was important in establishing and maintaining the rule of monarchs and nobles over other people in much of medieval Europe. Of course, it is also possible for ideologies to support *reductions* in inequalities among groups. For example, the Canadian Charter of Rights and Freedoms is one relatively recent attempt in Canada to implement the belief in equal rights and opportunities for all people, regardless of "race, national or ethnic origin, colour, religion, sex, age, or mental or physical disability." In each of these examples, ideas and beliefs about inequality were also converted by governments into official policy or formal laws. This illustrates the often close connection between politics and ideology in society.

We should also recognize, though, that ideology can be fundamental to the third major type of control we have been discussing, economic control. For example, the belief that it is acceptable for people to own private property is clearly an essential ideological prerequisite for the existence of economic inequalities based on such ownership. Similarly, the belief that people with unequal talents or motivation should also be unequal in the material rewards they receive can be used as both an explanation and justification for the economic differences that arise among individuals. In both of these examples, the extent to which people believe or reject ideas about themselves and their society will have an important bearing on how much inequality exists, and how likely it is to change with time.

POLITICAL AND IDEOLOGICAL FACTORS IN CLASS DIFFERENCES

The recognition of multiple mechanisms of control and the distinct resources they entail suggests that there is some degree of pluralism in the processes that generate social inequality. This, in turn, implies that any investigation based solely on economic class, especially if classes are conceived of only in conventional terms as groupings within the structure of material production, is not sufficient by itself to capture and express this pluralism.

Perhaps for this reason, some Marxists have sought to include in their conceptions of class the sense that not only economic control but also political and ideological control are crucial to the formation of class structures (Poulantzas 1975; Wright 1979, 1985, 1989, 1994). The incorporation of these additional elements into conventional conceptions of the class system is a significant innovation. Their inclusion permits us to recognize that classes, although they are primarily economic groupings, can also be important for other reasons and, in a way, may be fundamentally embedded within and across all social structures, both economic and noneconomic.

Here we should also note that, in addition to a revised notion of the class system, other complicating elements have come to be recognized in the multifaceted structure of inequality that characterizes most societies. As both Marxists and non-Marxists now generally acknowledge, various patterns of inequality exist that are at least partially independent of, and not reducible to, class inequality alone. The more prominent examples of these other bases for inequality include gender and race or ethnicity. Other important bases include age, region, and, in some cases, language and religion. Non-Marxists sometimes refer to these factors as different bases for "social closure" (Parkin 1979), while Marxists sometimes call them "multiple oppressions" (Wright 1985:57). Whatever label they are given, however, they represent important additional areas of inquiry for students of inequality and require a conceptual approach which is broader than that which the class concept by itself can provide.

SOCIAL INEQUALITY AS THREE FORMS OF POWER

It is primarily for this reason that some writers have recommended that the concept of power be used in conjunction with class theory, in an effort to move us toward a more general framework for analyzing and thinking about inequality in all its forms. Some Marxist scholars have been reluctant to take this approach, especially if it relegates class analysis to a secondary concern (Wright 1985:57; Clement, 1982:481). And, indeed, it is essential when analyzing other crucial problems in social inequality that we not ignore or downgrade the continuing importance of class in contemporary societies. Thus, although some now suggest that class may be "dying" as a significant issue or concept in sociology (e.g., Clark and Lipset 1991; Clark et al. 1993), existing research, including many of the studies presented in this book, make it clear that this suggestion is mistaken.

As noted already, however, it can be argued that class analyses are improved significantly by a fuller appreciation of the other forms of inequality and power relations in society. In other words, power can be used as a more generalizable, if not a more fundamental, concept than class, because it can be used to describe and analyze both class and nonclass forms of social inequality (Giddens 1981a; Grabb 1997:196–200). Those who adopt the latter perspective contend that class is pivotal in any complete understanding of social inequality, but that class differences represent one manifestation of the more general structure of power that is responsible for generating the overall system of inequality in most societies. Other crucial manifestations of inequality, such as those based on gender and race, can therefore be understood as the results of differential access to the different forms of power or domination in society (see, for example, Blalock 1989, 1991; Wilson 1973; Huber and Spitze 1983; Blumberg 1984; Milkman 1987; Connell 1987; Collins 1988; Li 1988; Mackie 1991; Chafetz 1990, 1997; Agger 1993; Andersen and Collins 1995).

However, even if power can serve this more general conceptual purpose, the question still remains: what precisely does the concept of power signify? This is not a simple question to answer since power, like class, is an idea that has stimulated numerous debates over its definition and meaning (see, for example, Lukes 1974; Wrong 1979; Mann 1986, 1993; Runciman 1989; Scott 1996). For our purposes, however, *power* can be defined briefly as the differential capacity to command resources and thereby to control social situations. We have already suggested that there are three major types of resources operating in social settings (material, human, and ideological) and three mechanisms of control corresponding to them (economic, political, and ideological). These three mechanisms can be seen as the key forms of power in society.

Whenever differences in economic, political, or ideological power are sufficiently stable and enduring that they promote regular, routinized relations of ascendance and subordination among people, the resulting pattern of interaction is a case of *structured power*, or what might be termed a *structure of domination* (Grabb 1997). Using abstract imagery, we can think of the overall system of inequality in a society as a kind of framework, involving all three forms of power and the three corresponding structures of domination. In more concrete terms, the structures of domination exist mainly as bureaucratic or corporate organizations: business enterprises in the economic sphere, departments of government in the political sphere, church hierarchies and institutions of higher learning in the ideological sphere, and so forth. It is within all these concrete settings that power differences among people (and among the positions they occupy) become manifest, thereby producing organized patterns of inequality.

Another point to note in this abstract imagery is that there is no perfect one-to-one linkage between each of the three forms of power and each set of concrete structures. These are just the *primary linkages,* since each of the means or forms of power can operate in at least a secondary fashion in any of the three structures. Thus, as noted earlier, political power (control over people or human resources) may indeed be the principal jurisdiction of the set of political or state organizations, but it is also exercised in the control imposed by owners on their workers in the economic structure. At the same time, the various political organizations composing the modern state do not derive all their power from the capacity to legislate or coerce human behaviour, for they also control material resources through their command over tax revenues, government ownership of some business enterprises, and so on. As for control of ideas or knowledge, this is most obviously identified with ideologically-oriented structures such as the mass media, the education system, and the church. However, as mentioned in a previous section, such ideological control is clearly a means for wielding power elsewhere too. This is illustrated by the policy-making, information-gathering, and surveillance capacities of the state and by the control over technical ideas and knowledge that occurs in the economic sphere (Giddens 1981b, 1985, 1989).

The combined operation of all the structures of domination, or rather the concrete organizations to which they correspond, establishes the major contours of the overall structure of inequality. The organizations themselves are patterned according to formal rules, laws, and rights of office, and their personnel exercise power in accordance with these formal guidelines. In addition, however, the inequalities that may develop within organizations, as well as the inequalities that organizations may engender for people outside them, are at least partly determined by informal practices or traditions, customs or habits, beliefs or prejudices. Not only formal rights or powers, but also informal privileges or advantages, tend to determine the nature and extent of inequality in society. Both act together to designate what the key bases of social inequality will be and how much each of them will matter.

THE BASES OF SOCIAL INEQUALITY IN CANADA

There is a final conceptual issue to consider. This involves the identification of the central bases of social inequality that arise from the exercise of power in Canada. As we have already suggested, the notion that there are several distinct bases for inequality in society is one that has achieved increasing acceptance by theorists and researchers in the field, among both non-Marxist and Marxist scholars. What has increasingly been argued is that there exists a multiple set of human characteristics or socially defined attributes that are consequential for determining the quality of life of most people. It will be recalled that this is the idea with which we began our introduction to the topic of social inequality in this chapter.

But what are these major bases for inequality, and why do these particular characteristics matter more than others? While it is difficult to provide answers to these questions that will satisfy all theoretical camps, we can see at least some common ground in the responses that most observers would give to both queries.

Perhaps the more difficult question to deal with is the second: why are some attributes of people more likely than others to lead to important inequalities? Why, for example, has colour of skin had such a sustained impact on the rights and rewards of people historically, but not colour of eyes or hair? In general terms, it is possible to conceive of this problem by looking once again at the idea of power, or domination, and by considering which factions within the population have historically been the most or the least successful in turning to their advantage the various economic, political, and ideological mechanisms of power that operate within social structures. That is, to the extent that those in positions of ascendancy are able to use the three forms of power to establish and routinize structures of domination, they will be relatively more successful in reproducing across time and place important advantages for themselves and others with similar backgrounds or characteristics. For example, within any capitalist society, those individuals who retain private ownership or control over productive property will clearly enjoy special advantages, and may well attempt to use their strategic position to encourage the further institutionalization of property rights in law, to foster belief systems favourable to such rights, and to employ other comparable means to help ensure that the privileges of property are maintained for themselves and succeeding generations of capitalists. In a similar fashion, those who have recognized training and skills, notably those who possess formal credentials or degrees in such areas as medicine and law, will themselves benefit from the advantages such exclusive accreditation brings, and will also tend to favour the continuation of the system of special certification (and attendant privileges) for themselves and the cohorts who follow.

In both of these illustrations, we have noted important bases for inequality—property and educational credentials—which also happen to correspond to two of the key types of economic or productive resources that are in demand in most societies. In the present context, however, these are not just resources but socially defined human attributes, or capacities of real people. In this form, they become recognized by others, as crucial characteristics for differentiating some individuals or factions from others, and for determining the rights, opportunities, rewards, and privileges of those who do or do not have them. We should note that this distinction, between resources, on the one hand, and human attributes, on the other hand, illustrates once again what has elsewhere been referred to as the duality of social structures. In addition to these attributes, though, there is a whole range of other consequential human differences that should be identified. Gender and race or ethnicity probably are the best contemporary examples. Inequalities based on gender and race or ethnicity are neither identical to nor reducible to class inequality. Nevertheless, like class inequality, these two bases of inequality can be conceived of as the product of long-standing factional antagonisms, struggles, or contests in which economic, political, and ideological mechanisms of power have played significant roles in establishing and structuring advantages for one grouping of people relative to others.

In fact, a full range of attributes or capacities can be delineated, comprising all the major bases of inequality. In the contemporary Canadian context, these include the set of class-related bases—property ownership, education, occupation, and possession of wealth or income—as well as the key non-class bases—gender, race, ethnicity, language, region, and age (see Grabb 1997). As the papers in this volume will show, there is evidence to indicate that social groupings that are distinguishable from others on these dimensions have often been able to maintain significant advantages within the system of social inequality in Canada, and that they have done so largely because of superior access to economic, political, and ideological power.

In considering such a list, of course, we should also be aware that not all of these factors will be equally influential in shaping the general patterns of inequality in Canadian society. It is also important to acknowledge that other factors may matter, in different historical periods or different places, and that there may be considerable variability over time in the importance or prevalence of some bases of inequality relative to others. One example is religious affiliation. This is one social characteristic that we have not listed here, but which in the past was probably a significant basis for inequality in Canada. Nevertheless, most analysts would agree that religion is now of relatively little consequence in influencing the power or rank of Canadians, especially compared to a century ago. At the same time, though, it is true that religious differences still play a major part in shaping the structure of inequality in other countries, in contemporary Northern Ireland or Iran, for example.

PLAN OF THE BOOK

The selections incorporated in this book reflect rather clearly the central role that the study of class and power has played in theory and research on inequality in Canada (see, in particular, Sections I and II). Various chapters also discuss the array of social characteristics that has arisen as important bases for inequality in this country (in particular, Sections II and III). As the title of the book suggests, we have attempted within each section to attend not only to the patterns of social inequality and to some of the problems these patterns pose for our society, but also to the policies and ideologies involved in inequality. Section IV traces out some of the varied consequences of inequality for individuals.

Our choice of "Power and Class" as the topic for our first section is meant to underscore that control over productive property provides a fundamental context within which the other bases for inequality operate in Canada and other capitalist societies. This section, therefore, provides necessary groundwork for understanding the patterns of inequality that are dealt with in the other sections.

We have said that certain key inherited or attained socio-economic characteristics are very important in defining the contours of inequality in our society. This issue is the principal focus of the second section of the book, which deals with the distribution of personal wealth or income, educational attainment, and occupational status. These are three bases for inequality that are distinct from each other and from the ownership factor itself, but which are also involved in shaping the system of economic classes. Ownership of productive property is the essential basis for class inequality, particularly that which exists between the owning class and the working class. At the same time, however, educational credentials and surplus wealth or income are, as we have seen, potentially important for distinguishing the "middle class," or comparable intermediate categories, from the two major classes. The reason for including occupation in the same section is perhaps less obvious, but follows from two considerations. First, occupation has long been used in social research as an approximate indicator of class location, although methodological problems associated with this have been of some concern to many writers, especially Marxists. Second, the analysis of occupational inequality is useful in a supplementary or residual sense, because occupation subsumes such phenomena as skill level, manual versus non-manual labour power, and so on, which are not fully captured in research that is restricted to the study of ownership, wealth or income, and education.

In Section III the central concern is with factors of social ascription. In Canada, these include gender, race, ethnicity, language, age, and region of residence. This third set of attributes is discussed separately from class and the socio-economic status characteristics for two reasons. First, these bases for inequality are independent of class distinctions, although, as we shall see, they may be correlated with class location and may give rise to important divisions *within* classes. Second, these attributes are ascriptive in nature, involving statuses that are not achieved or attained by people, but rather given to them. The ascriptive process is clearest in such characteristics as gender, race, and ethnicity, which are all essentially assigned to people at birth. Age is another social characteristic that, though constantly changing, is assigned and beyond the control of people. Language and region of residence are also assigned characteristics. For adults, there is some reason to dispute the ascriptive label for these last two attributes, because adults can elect to alter the language they speak or move to another place to live. However, even in adulthood, these attributes are more ascriptive than they appear, because of the pressures on many Canadians to retain the language and place of residence they are born into. Language barriers and regional divisions tend to reproduce themselves over time, in spite of any policy efforts to change or reduce them.

The first three sections of the volume concentrate on structural questions: the character of class divisions and the other key bases of social inequality, and the ways in which such inequalities have been developed and maintained. The final section serves a different purpose, by providing a broad sampling of evidence to show that all of the various bases of inequality can influence the quality of life enjoyed or endured by Canadians. Of course, the earlier parts of the book also deal with the consequences of inequality, to the extent that these sections examine the effects of class, gender, or ethnicity on education, occupation, or income, for example. Section IV, however, goes beyond the early sections to show the wide-ranging impact that social inequality can have on aspects of life as diverse as health and mortality, the incidence of domestic violence, and people's beliefs about the causes of inequality. Taken together, the collection of papers in this volume should give the reader a good sense of the array of important issues that Canadian researchers have addressed in the study of social inequality.

REFERENCES

Agger, Ben 1993 *Gender, Culture, and Power* Westport, Conn.: Praeger.

Andersen, Margaret and Patricia Collins (eds.) 1995 *Race, Class, and Gender* Belmont, California: Wadsworth.

Barber, Bernard 1957 *Social Stratification* New York: Harcourt Brace and World.

Blalock, H.M., Jr. 1989 *Power and Conflict: Toward a General Theory* Newbury Park: Sage.

Blalock, H.M., Jr. 1991 *Understanding Social Inequality* Newbury Park: Sage.

Blumberg, Rae Lesser 1984 "A general theory of gender stratification.'' In R. Collins (ed.), *Sociological Theory 1984*, pp. 23–101. San Francisco: Jossey-Bass.

Carchedi, Guglielmo 1977 *On the Economic Identification of Social Classes* London: Routledge.

Carchedi, Guglielmo 1987 *Class Analysis and Social Research* Oxford and New York: Basil Blackwell.

Chafetz, Janet Saltzman 1990 *Gender Equity: An Integrated Theory of Stability and Change* Newbury Park: Sage.

Chafetz, Janet Saltzman 1997 "Feminist theory and sociology: underutilized contributions for mainstream theory." *Annual Review of Sociology* 23:97–191.

Clark, Terry Nichols and Seymour Martin Lipset 1991 "Are social classes dying?" *International Sociology* 6:397–410.

Clark, Terry Nichols, Seymour Martin Lipset, and Michael Rempel 1993 "The declining political significance of class." *International Sociology* 8:293–316.

Clement, Wallace 1982 "Corporations, power, and class." In D.Forcese and S. Richer (eds.), *Social Issues: Sociological Views of Canada*, pp. 469–485. Scarborough: Prentice-Hall Canada.

Collins, Randall 1979 *The Credential Society* New York: Academic Press.

Collins, Randall 1988 *Theoretical Sociology* San Diego: Harcourt Brace Jovanovich.

Connell, R.W. 1987 *Gender and Power: Society, the Person and Sexual Politics* Cambridge: Polity Press.

Faris, Robert E. L. 1972 "The middle class from a sociological viewpoint." In G. Thielbar and S. Feldman (eds.), *Issues in Social Inequality,* pp. 26–32. Boston: Little Brown and Company.

Giddens, Anthony 1973 *The Class Structure of the Advanced Societies* London: Hutchinson.

Giddens, Anthony 1979 *Central Problems in Social Theory* Berkeley: University of California Press.

Giddens, Anthony 1981a "Postscript (1979)." In *The Class Structure of the Advanced Societies* (2nd ed.), pp. 295–320. London: Hutchinson.

Giddens, Anthony 1981b. *A Contemporary Critique of Historical Materialism Vol. 1, Power, Property, and the State* London: Macmillan.

Giddens, Anthony 1984 *The Constitution of Society* Berkeley and Los Angeles: University of California Press.

Giddens, Anthony 1985 *A Contemporary Critique of Historical Materialism Vol. 2, The Nation-State and Violence* Berkeley and Los Angeles: University of California Press.

Giddens, Anthony 1989 "A reply to my critics." In D. Held and J. Thompson (eds.), *Social Theory of Modern Societies*, pp. 249–301 Cambridge: Cambridge University Press.

Giddens, Anthony 1994 *Beyond Left and Right. The Future of Radical Politics* Stanford: Stanford University Press.

Grabb, Edward G. 1997 *Theories of Social Inequality: Classical and Contemporary Perspectives* (3rd ed.) Toronto: Harcourt Brace Canada.

Huber, Joan and Glenna Spitze 1983 *Sex Stratification: Children, Housework, and Jobs* New York: Academic Press.

Johnson, Harry M. 1960 *Sociology: A Systematic Introduction* New York: Harcourt, Brace and World.

Li, Peter S. 1988 *Ethnic Inequality in a Class Society* Toronto: Wall and Thompson.

Lukes, Steven 1974 *Power: A Radical View* London: Macmillan.

Mackie, Marlene 1991 *Gender Relations in Canada* Toronto: Butterworths.

Mann, Michael 1986. *The Sources of Social Power*, Vol.1 Cambridge: Cambridge University Press.

Mann, Michael 1993 *The Sources of Social Power,* Vol.2 Cambridge: Cambridge University Press.

Marchak, M. Patricia 1988 *Ideological Perspectives on Canada* Toronto: McGraw-Hill Ryerson.

Marx, Karl 1862 *Theories of Surplus Value,* Vol. 2 Moscow: Progress Publishers.

Marx, Karl 1867 *Capital,* Vol.1 New York: International Publishers.

Marx, Karl 1894 *Capital,* Vol.3 New York: International Publishers.

Marx, Karl and Friedrich Engels 1848a *The Communist Manifesto* New York: Washington Square Press.

Marx, Karl and Friedrich Engels 1848b. *The Communist Manifesto* (German version) In *Marx Engels Werke, Vol.4* Institut fur Marxismus-Leninismus Beim Zk Der Sed. Berlin: Dietz Verlag.

Milkman, Ruth 1987 *Gender at Work* Urbana and Chicago: University of Illinois Press.

Nisbet, Robert A. 1959 "The decline and fall of social class." *Pacific Sociological Review* 2:11–17.

Parkin, Frank 1979 *Marxism and Class Theory: A Bourgeois Critique* London: Tavistock.

Parsons, Talcott 1940 "An analytical approach to the theory of social stratification." In T. Parsons, *Essays in Sociological Theory*, pp. 69–88. New York: The Free Press.

Parsons, Talcott 1951 *The Social System* New York: The Free Press.

Parsons, Talcott 1953 "A revised analytical approach to the theory of social stratification." In T. Parsons, *Essays in Sociological Theory*, pp. 386–439. New York: The Free Press.

Porter, John 1965 *The Vertical Mosaic: An Analysis of Social Class and Power in Canada* Toronto: University of Toronto Press.

Poulantzas, Nicos 1975 *Classes in Contemporary Capitalism* London: New Left Books.

Runciman, W.G. 1989 *A Treatise on Social Theory, Vol. 2, Substantive Social Theory* Cambridge: Cambridge University Press.

Scott, John 1996 *Stratification and Power* Cambridge: Polity Press.

Weber, Max 1922 *Economy and Society,* Vols. 1–3 New York: Bedminster Press.

Wilson, William Julius 1973 *Power, Racism, and Privilege* New York: Macmillan.

Wright, Erik Olin 1978 *Class, Crisis, and the State* London: New Left Books.

Wright, Erik Olin 1979 *Class Structure and Income Determination* New York: Academic Press.

Wright, Erik Olin 1980 "Class and occupation." *Theory and Society* 9:177–214.

Wright, Erik Olin 1985 *Classes* London: Verso.

Wright, Erik Olin 1989 *The Debate on Classes* London: Verso.

Wright, Erik Olin 1994 *Interrogating Inequality: Essays on Class Analysis, Socialism, and Marxism* London: Verso.

Wright, Erik Olin, Andrew Levine, and Elliott Sober 1992 *Reconstructing Marxism* London: Verso.

Wright, Erik Olin and Bill Martin 1987 "The transformation of the American class structure, 1960– 1980." *American Journal of Sociology* 93:1–29.

Wrong, Dennis 1979 *Power: Its Forms, Bases and Uses* New York: Harper and Row.

FOR FURTHER REFERENCE: OVERVIEWS

Allahar, Anton, and James Cote 1998 *Richer and Poorer: The Structure of Inequality in Canada* Toronto: James Lorimer. The authors use a framework that centres on the role of dominant ideology to examine social inequality in Canada, with a special focus on issues of class, gender, age, and race/ethnicity. A key claim in this analysis is that Canadians are in a state of denial about the existence of major inequalities in their society.

Forcese, Dennis 1997 *The Canadian Class Structure* (4th ed.) Toronto: McGraw-Hill Ryerson. This text focuses on class-based inequalities in Canada, but also touches on other topics in social inequality, including gender, age, ethnicity, and race.

Grabb, Edward 1997 *Theories of Social Inequality: Classical and Contemporary Perspectives* (3rd ed.) Toronto: Harcourt Brace Canada. This book reviews and evaluates the major perspectives on social inequality that have emerged from classical and contemporary social theory.

Porter, John 1965 *The Vertical Mosaic: An Analysis of Class and Power in Canada* Toronto: University of Toronto Press. This book is now dated, but remains a classic work that provides an excellent analysis of social inequality in Canada's recent past, most notably the 1950s and 1960s. Porter considers such wide-ranging topics as class, power, ethnicity, language, region, and institutional elites and their relevance to the study of inequality in this country.

Section 1

POWER AND CLASS

We begin our look at social inequality in Canada with a series of papers dealing with the interplay of power and class structure in our society. This is a logical starting point because, as was discussed in the general introduction, the concepts of class and power are pivotal to any general understanding of social inequality. In this section, we are especially interested in the power that derives from ownership and control of productive property and resources, and the nature of the class structure that is defined by such power. Some of the selections also explore the connections between economic classes and the state, most notably the roles that government activities and policies play in shaping the pattern of both ownership and class inequality in Canada.

In capitalist countries like Canada, and perhaps in all societies, ownership of property is arguably the key defining criterion for those who wish to understand the nature of material inequality and the emergence of economic classes. But what is really meant by the notion of property ownership in this context? Most theorists agree that property does not refer to the simple possession of material resources that are used only for personal consumption, such as food, clothing, shelter, and the like. This is not to say that the distribution of these and other consumer items is unimportant to the study of inequality, nor is it to deny the tremendous significance of such items for those who experience a shortage or abundance of them in their daily lives. Rather, it is to recognize that the possession of material benefits or products is not only, or even primarily, what constitutes property ownership. Ownership of property, in its most crucial sense, entails the *right of disposition over the economic process in general.*

The essence of property ownership is having the capacity to command the various activities and organizational processes that are involved in producing, accumulating, investing, or expending society's material or economic resources. Ultimately, it is from this capacity that decisions are made about the distribution of economic benefits to people, and it is through this capacity that some groups and individuals can exclude others from economic control or influence. Perhaps the most important outcome of this process is that the class of people who own society's productive property is in a position to establish relations of domination and exploitation over the class of non-owners, who in turn must sell their labour in order to survive. The non-owners, or working class, may resist this pattern of relationships through political organization, unionization, and other forms of collective action. However, as both classical and contemporary social theorists have often pointed out, the owning class is typically able to override or limit the success of such opposition, given this class's rights to private productive property and the protection of these rights by the state or government.

The first chapter in this section, by Edward Grabb, assesses evidence on the concentration of economic power in Canada, in order to answer three related questions: has the share of Canada's economy that is controlled by private-sector corporations increased in recent decades; what part do foreign-controlled companies play in Canada's ownership structure; and how does the state's power and influence compare with that of private business interests when it comes to owning and directing the contemporary Canadian economy?

The second paper in this section, by Gordon Laxer, broadens the analysis of social inequality to include the important question of international class and power relations. His discussion of "globalization" and the global capitalist system underlines the importance of large-scale private-sector companies. Many of these large companies operate throughout the world as multinational or transnational enterprises, with business holdings in numerous countries. In some cases these individual enterprises actually rival or surpass the economic power of entire nations. A major issue that Laxer's analysis addresses is the prospect of democratic collective action and solidarity within the wider population of contemporary societies, given the increasing prominence of these globally-oriented businesses.

In the third article, James Conley considers the processes and forces that have been involved in the formation of the Canadian working class in the twentieth century. Beginning with Marx's and Weber's classical approaches to understanding capitalist class structures, the author then focuses on a review of Canadian evidence relating to four key topics. These include: the alleged tendency for increased class polarization in modern capitalism; the changing organization of the workplace and its possible effects on working-class solidarity; the likelihood of increasing class awareness or class consciousness within the working class; and the prospects for mobilization, formal organization, and collective action among workers in Canada today.

For many observers, the high concentration of economic control in relatively few hands is a potentially serious problem. The main concern is that far too much power has been wielded historically by the owners of productive property. Any further centralization of ownership only enhances the likelihood that such power could be abused, with the rest of the population facing increased exploitation and domination by the owning class. The final chapter in the section on Power and Class, by Julia O'Connor, reviews additional evidence of economic concentration in Canada, and examines some of the policies that the state might invoke to address the problems associated with economic concentration. In particular, this paper assesses the state's potential role in easing the effects of economic inequality in the population through policy options that deal with employment, social transfer expenditures, and taxation.

The overall message conveyed by this section of the book is that ownership of productive property or resources, especially through the mechanism of giant private-sector business enterprises, is perhaps the most fundamental force generating the overall pattern of social inequality, both in Canada and in the larger international context. Moreover, the available evidence suggests that this will continue to be true for some time in the future.

Chapter 1

CONCENTRATION OF OWNERSHIP AND ECONOMIC CONTROL IN CANADA: PATTERNS AND TRENDS IN THE 1990S

Edward Grabb

(An original chapter written for this volume.)

INTRODUCTION

For many years now, social scientists have been concerned with understanding the structure of economic ownership in Canada. In particular, investigators have sought to determine the extent to which the economy is controlled by a few powerful groups and organizations. Research on this question began in the early part of the twentieth century (e.g., Myers 1914; Creighton 1937), but it was John Porter's extensive analyses in the 1950s and 1960s that first provided detailed evidence of the high concentration of economic ownership and control in this country (Porter 1956, 1957, 1965). One of Porter's main conclusions from his research was that less than 200 large corporations and their directors appeared to dominate much of Canada's economic power structure at that time.

Porter's findings set the stage for most of the later attempts to understand Canadian patterns of ownership and control. The next influential series of studies arose from Wallace Clement's research on Canada's "corporate elite" (Clement 1975, 1977a, 1977b). Clement's findings suggested that, by the 1970s, economic control in Canada was probably even more concentrated than in the period Porter considered, with 113 powerful companies accounting for the majority of business activity.

Since Porter and Clement, numerous academics, commentators, and journalists have added to what is now a sizeable body of literature on the workings of the Canadian economy (e.g., Newman 1979, 1981; Marchak, 1979; Niosi 1978, 1981, 1985; Ornstein 1976; Carrol, Fox, and Ornstein 1982; Carrol 1982, 1984, 1986; Richardson, 1982; Brym 1985, 1989; Antoniou and Rowley 1986; Francis 1986; Veltmeyer 1987; Laxer 1989; Fox and Ornstein 1986; Grabb 1990; O'Connor 1993). Most of this research suggests that, by the 1980s, the concentration of economic power was still on the rise, with a shrinking group of large, often interconnected, and mainly private-sector corporations at the centre of Canada's ownership structure.

In the past, many of these powerful companies were owned or effectively controlled by a relatively small number of people. For much of our history, in fact, a few prominent and long-established families formed a major component of Canada's economic elite (see Newman 1979; Antoniou and Rowley 1986; Francis 1986). These included such well-known names as the Eatons, the Molsons, the Westons, and the McCains, to name just four examples. In more recent years, another component of our economic elite has involved less-established individual entrepreneurs who, through what are commonly called "conglomerates" or "holding companies," control interrelated sets of large and often quite diverse businesses. A prime illustration is Paul Desmarais who, through Power Corporation, has interests in major enterprises in such areas as forestry, oil and gas, newspaper publishing, and life insurance, among others. As the principal investors and shareholders in many of Canada's biggest businesses, these families and individual business leaders have tended to enjoy an inordinate amount of influence in determining the general nature and overall direction of our economy.

Apart from private-sector companies and their owners, most writers have identified two other principal components that are seen as integral to Canada's economic power structure. The first of these is foreign-owned private businesses, which have played a significant part in our economy for some time, but have been especially prominent in the latter half of the twentieth century. The degree to which our economy has been controlled by such outside interests has occupied the attention of numerous researchers and observers over the years (e.g., Levitt 1970; Clement 1977a; Laxer 1989).

The final key factor to consider when assessing who controls or directs the Canadian economy is the role of the government or state. Especially since the 1970s, contemporary social scientists in various countries have shown a sustained interest in the amount of state involvement in economic activity (e.g., Miliband 1973; Poulantzas 1978; Wright 1978; Friedman and Friedman 1980; Offe 1984). In Canada as well, observers have debated the extent of state intervention into business activity and its implications for shaping our system of economic power (e.g., Panitch 1977; Calvert 1984; Banting 1986; Fox and Ornstein 1986).

The goal of the present chapter is to build on previous research and analysis on these topics, by assessing the pattern of ownership and economic control in Canada during the 1990s. In this paper, we are primarily concerned with three related questions. First, what does the available evidence tell us about the trends in ownership concentration during the period between the 1970s and the 1990s, especially in regard to the role played by Canada's large-scale private-sector businesses and corporations? Second, what part do foreign or non-Canadian companies play in our economy, and has the level of involvement by foreign-controlled corporations changed from what it was in earlier years? Finally, how does the level of ownership by major private-sector companies compare to that of state-controlled agencies or enterprises? The answers to these questions will provide a clearer picture of the nature of economic power and ownership concentration in Canada in the contemporary period.

ANALYSIS

Trends in the Concentration of Corporate Assets

Our first concern is to assess the current degree of economic concentration among privately-owned corporate enterprises, and to determine if any major changes have occurred in this concentration in recent years. Research has shown that there was a high level of economic centralization in Canada in the recent past. For example, one study has reported that, although 400 000 companies were operating in Canada in 1987, the largest 25 enterprises by themselves accounted for over 41% of all corporate assets in that year (O'Connor 1993: 76). Previous research has also indicated that this level of ownership concentration was significantly greater in the mid-1980s than it had been just ten years before (e.g., Francis 1986: 3; Grabb 1990: 77).

More recent evidence suggests certain changes in the structure of corporate ownership. First of all, a number of the established family "dynasties," including the Eatons, McCains, and Reichmanns, among others, have experienced the loss or sale of some of their corporate holdings and a reduction in their overall influence (see Francis 1997: 38). Even so, other family-based enterprises continue to be very important. For example, the Westons, who are best known for their vast food empire, and the Thomsons, who have long dominated Canada's newspaper industry, continued to control two of the top ten corporations operating in Canada by the mid-1990s, and were still among the major decision-makers on the Canadian economic scene (Financial Post 1995). Similarly, while some individual entrepreneurs and their holding companies have fallen on harder times, others have seen their fortunes rise still further. Conrad Black's expansion into Canadian newspaper publishing through his interests in the Hollinger-Telegraph and Southam companies (which in turn are linked to his conglomerate, Argus Corporation) is but one example of this pattern (see Statistics Canada 1996b: 35, 43).

It may not be surprising, then, that government statistics show a continued trend toward even higher levels of economic concentration in the 1990s. From 1987 to 1993, for example, the share of Canada's corporate assets controlled by the largest 25 enterprises rose once again, from 41% to 46% of the national total (Statistics Canada 1995a: 50). Thus, almost half of Canada's corporate assets were held by the top 25 businesses, a trend which is also consistent with the numerous mergers and acquisitions involving major companies in recent years (Maclean's 1993: 34; Canadian Press 1996, 1997). In fact, 1997 was a record year for corporate takeovers, with 1274 mergers and acquisitions involving more than 100 billion dollars of assets. Some of these transactions were extremely large, with just 13 takeovers accounting for almost 30 billion dollars of the total (Greenwood 1998).

The high degree of concentration is apparent throughout most of the economy, but is especially pronounced in the financial sector, where only a handful of banks, trust companies, and insurance firms have consistently predominated (e.g., Francis 1986: 242). Recent mergers and acquisitions, including the 1997 purchase of National Trust Company by the Bank of Nova Scotia and the 1997 take-over of London Life Insurance by Great West Life Assurance (which in turn is controlled by the major conglomerate, Power Corporation), have only added to this centralization in the financial sphere (Statistics Canada 1996b: 35; see also Newman 1997: 54). If approved, the 1998 planned merger of the Royal Bank of Canada and the Bank of Montreal, which rank number one and number three in size among the nation's banks, will concentrate economic power further again. There is good reason to conclude, then, that the concentration of economic ownership in Canada is more pronounced now than it has ever been, at least in our recent history.

Changes in Foreign Economic Influence

Ever since Canada's beginnings as a colony, first of France and then of England, our economy has been marked by a considerable amount of foreign control and influence. While Canada in the modern era has evolved into one of the most prosperous and industrialized nations, we have continued to experience a relatively high level of foreign involvement in the economy, at least in comparison to the other developed societies of the world.

Much of the research on foreign ownership in Canada has focused on the influx of American-based transnational corporations during the twentieth century (e.g., Levitt 1970; Clement 1975, 1977a; Laxer 1989). Evidence indicates that this American involvement developed in a series of stages, but became especially important during a period of about 25 years after World War II. Between 1970 and the mid-1980s, however, Canada witnessed a decline in the general level of American and other foreign ownership (Niosi 1981: 31–33; Grabb 1990: 78).

The most recent available data indicate that foreign involvement is still a prominent feature of the Canadian economy, although it is less pronounced than in the peak period around 1970. For example, foreign companies accounted for 36% of the assets of non-financial companies operating in Canada in 1970, but this proportion had declined to about 22% by 1985, before rising marginally again to 24% by 1993 (Statistics Canada 1995a: 33). In the financial sector, where Canadian companies have always enjoyed government protection from external competition, the foreign presence is less prominent. Even so, the share of assets held by non-Canadian financial companies has risen somewhat in recent years, from 17% to 21% in the 1985–1993 period.

Perhaps the strongest evidence of foreign control in our economy can be found at the very top of the non-financial sector, where a few major non-Canadian corporations are predominant. In the mid-1980s, for example, six of the top ten companies operating in Canada were foreign-owned. These included the Canadian subsidiaries of the three American automotive giants (General Motors of Canada, Ford of Canada, and Chrysler Canada), as well as two American-owned oil subsidiaries (Imperial Oil and Texaco Canada) and one Dutch-controlled oil company (Shell Canada) (Financial Post 1985). By the mid-1990s, little had changed, with five foreign companies, all of them American-owned, among the top ten. These again included the three major automobile firms and Imperial Oil, along with IBM of Canada (Financial Post 1995). Such results illustrate a considerable amount of stability in the foreign presence at the top of our economy. These findings also reflect the tendency for American firms to dominate, especially in the transportation equipment, energy, and electronics industries (see Statistics Canada 1995a: 39; 1996a: 9). As of 1994, American companies still accounted for 67% of the total operating revenues going to foreign companies in Canada. This proportion was down slightly from the 73% that American companies received in 1975, but is similar to the share they have held since the mid-1980s. European nations (most notably Britain) accounted for another 19% of the foreign-controlled revenues in 1994, followed by 9% for the Pacific Rim countries (especially Japan), and about 5% for the rest of the world (see Statistics Canada 1991: 13; 1996a: 25–26).

The State and Economic Power

The next question to address is the role of Canada's various levels of government in the contemporary Canadian economy. Historically, business activities have often been influenced by state involvement, although sometimes in contradictory ways. At certain times, for example, governments have lent money to Canadian capitalists and imposed tariffs or other trade restrictions on foreign competitors, in order to promote and protect Canadian companies. At other times, however, governments have offered tax reductions and other incentives to encourage foreign business ventures in Canada, and have also established state-run enterprises that compete directly with Canada's private-sector firms (Clement 1975, 1977b; Traves 1979; Marchak 1979; Laxer 1989).

A good deal of the recent discussion on the role of the Canadian state has centred on whether or not government economic intervention has gone too far. Some researchers suggest that the state's role in the Canadian economy is actually rather small. Such analysts usually acknowledge that the state spends a considerable portion of the national wealth, with governments covering the costs of providing and maintaining public education, health care, a wide range of social services, transportation facilities, and the like. However, most of these writers also contend that, otherwise, the state has normally been a limited player in the Canadian economy, with private business interests still acting as the pre-eminent force (e.g., Calvert 1984; Fox and Ornstein 1986; Brym 1989; O'Connor 1993).

There are other observers, however, who allege that the various branches of the state have become exceedingly influential within our economic system. These writers argue that governments at all levels have too often used their considerable taxation and spending powers to fund a number of poorly-conceived endeavours, including expensive, loosely-administered social programs and unprofitable, inefficient government enterprises (see, e.g., Horry et al. 1992; Francis 1995: 13; Walker 1997). Similar views appear to be found among many private-sector capitalists, who see the government as an intruding competitor in the business arena (Ornstein 1985). Added to these perceptions is the belief that state-owned companies usually have an unfair advantage over private businesses, which need to turn a profit to survive and cannot rely on government financial assistance to bail them out of difficulty.

One direct means for measuring state economic power is to determine the proportion of major enterprises that are government-controlled. Previous research found that, in both 1975 and 1985, only four of the top 25 non-financial corporations operating in Canada were government-owned, and less than ten of the top 100 (Grabb 1990: 79). More recent business rankings reveal a similar picture. By the mid-1990s, there were three government-directed enterprises among the leading 25 companies operating in Canada, all of them in the areas of transportation and utilities. These three companies were Ontario Hydro, Hydro Quebec, and Canadian National. Within the top 100 enterprises, there were eleven government-controlled companies in 1995, including Petro-Canada (which has since been sold in part to private-sector interests), Canada Post, B.C. Hydro, and the Ontario Lottery Corporation, among others (Financial Post 1995; Canadian Business 1995). On this basis, then, it is difficult to argue that government enterprises dominate the Canadian economy.

Perhaps a more comprehensive gauge of government economic influence is to look at the share of the nation's total assets that is held by the various branches of the state. One earlier study, using government data on the "national balance sheet," estimated that, by the mid-1980s, less than 20% of Canada's total assets were owned by government entities of different kinds. These included state-run agencies, business enterprises, pension funds, and related organizations (Grabb 1990: 86–87). Such findings indicate that government economic control in Canada, though significant, was not as great as some observers have argued, and was far lower than that enjoyed by the private business sector, in particular.

Table 1-1 presents broadly similar data on the national balance sheet, for the years 1975, 1984, and 1993 (see Statistics Canada 1986: 32–33, 50–51; 1995b: 8–11). These figures suggest, as before, that the government or public sector accounts for a notable but again relatively minor segment of Canada's ownership structure. These data also reveal that the level of government control over assets has declined somewhat in the last two decades, to less than 14% of the total.

Although numerous factors probably account for this trend, one likely cause has been the changing policies of the federal government and some provincial administrations in recent years. In particular, state leaders have been increasingly motivated to encourage private sector economic expansion, and also to sell off various government-run enterprises to private interests. This pattern has been most notable since the election of the federal Progressive Conservatives in the mid-1980s. Similar initiatives to reduce state involvement in the economy have recently been put forward at the provinical level as well, especially by

TABLE 1-1 Estimated distribution of total assets held within Canada, 1975, 1984, and 1993

Year:	1975	1984	1993
Sector:			
I. Persons and Unincorporated Businesses	35.1%	37.0%	38.0%
II. Private Sector	38.3%	37.6%	39.0%
Non-financial enterprises	21.7	19.8	16.9
Financial institutions	16.6	17.8	22.1
III. Public Sector	20.1%	16.9%	13.9%
Non-financial enterprises	4.6	4.2	3.7
Financial institutions	2.4	2.0	1.7
Other (pensions, social security funds, other levels of government, etc.)	13.1	10.7	8.5
IV. Non-Residents	6.5%	8.4%	9.1%

Source: National Balance Sheet Accounts, 1961–1985 and 1984–1993. Catalogue 13-214.

the Conservative-led governments of Alberta and Ontario (see, e.g., Denis 1995).

As we would expect given the evidence reported earlier in this chapter, Table 1-1 also shows that private-sector corporations continue to hold the largest single portion of our national assets, with a 39% share as of 1994. This share remained relatively stable throughout the two decades considered in Table 1-1. One apparent change has been a steady increase in the share of assets held by private financial companies, from about 17% to 22% of the total. This pattern was counterbalanced by a decline in the assets of private non-financial companies, from 22% to 17%, during the same period.

The one sector that rivals private corporations in terms of assets share is the "persons and unincorporated businesses" category. This is a heterogeneous grouping that subsumes the personal possessions, savings, real estate, and private pension funds of individual citizens, as well as the assets of small businesses, farms, and non-profit organizations that are not officially constituted as corporate entities. The remaining 9% of assets held in 1994 were accounted for by non-residents, most notably in the financial holdings of foreign investors and business interests.

SUMMARY AND CONCLUSIONS

Our review of recent evidence on economic control and ownership in Canada has revealed that, by the 1990s, many of the same patterns of ownership that existed in previous decades are still in place. That is, we have found a relatively high concentration of economic power in a small group of giant private-sector corporations operating at the top of the ownership structure. Moreover, this level of concentration has continued to rise compared to the situations that obtained in the 1970s and 1980s. It seems clear, then, that large-scale financial and non-financial business enterprises, along with the major shareholders and directors that control them, are as powerful as they have ever been in the Canadian economy.

We have also considered the level of foreign involvement in Canada's ownership structure. In this case we determined that non-Canadian businesses play a substantial role in the economy, though significantly less so than they did in the peak years of foreign activity around 1970. Even so, the most powerful and profitable enterprises currently operating on the Canadian scene still show a notable foreign presence, with roughly half of the leading ten companies being subsidiaries of non-Canadian, most notably American, transnational corporations.

The final major issue we addressed was the degree of state control over Canada's economic affairs. In keeping with earlier research from previous decades, we have seen that the government role, though notable in some respects, is really quite minor in comparison to that played by private corporations. Moreover, the government's presence on the economic scene has declined somewhat in the past decade or more, especially in regard to its control over national assets, but also in its role as a director of large-scale business enterprises. In addition, during the 1990s we have seen concerted drives by the federal and provincial governments to cut back on services, in the interest of eliminating government deficits and reducing the nation's debt. These policies make it clear that there has been some curtailment of state economic activity in the spending area as well. The government strategy for the future appears to be one according to which political leaders look primarily to the private sector, and not to state-sponsored programs, to promote economic activity. Overall, then, the current climate is one in which private-sector businesses continue to determine the major contours and direction of Canada's economic power structure.

REFERENCES

Antoniou, Andreas and Robin Rowley 1986 "The ownership structure of the largest Canadian corporations, 1979." *Canadian Journal of Sociology* 11: 253–268.

Banting, Keith 1986 *The State and Economic Interests* Toronto: University of Toronto Press.

Brym, Robert (ed.) 1985 *The Structure of the Canadian Capitalist Class* Toronto: Garamond.

Brym, Robert 1989 "Canada." pp. 177–206 in T. Bottomore and R. Brym (eds.), *The Capitalist Class. An International Study* New York: New York University Press.

Calvert, John 1984 *Government, Limited* Ottawa: Canadian Centre for Policy Alternatives.

Canadian Business 1995 The Canadian Business 500 Vol. 68 (June).

Canadian Press 1996 "Mergers, acquisitions hit record in 1995." Reported in the London Free Press, January 6, Page B9.

Canadian Press 1997 "Can the merger mania last?" Reported in the London Free Press, December 30, Page D3.

Carroll, William 1982 "The Canadian corporate elite: financiers or finance capitalists?" *Studies in Political Economy* 8: 89–114.

Carroll, William 1984 "The individual, class, and corporate power in Canada." *Canadian Journal of Sociology* 9: 245–268.

Carroll, William 1986 *Corporate Power and Canadian Capitalism* Vancouver: University of British Columbia Press.

Carroll, William, John Fox, and Michael Ornstein 1982 "The network of directorship links among the largest Canadian firms." *Canadian Review of Sociology and Anthropology* 19: 44–69.

Clement, Wallace 1975 *The Canadian Corporate Elite* Toronto: McClelland and Stewart.

Clement, Wallace 1977a *Continental Corporate Power* Toronto: McClelland and Stewart.

Clement, Wallace 1977b "The corporate elite, the capitalist class, and the Canadian state." pp. 225–248 in L. Panitch (ed.), *The Canadian State* Toronto: University of Toronto Press.

Creighton, Donald 1937 *The Commercial Empire of the St. Lawrence* Toronto: Macmillan.

Denis, Claude 1995 "Government can do whatever it wants": moral regulation in Ralph Klein's Alberta." *Canadian Review of Sociology and Anthropology* 32: 365–383.

Financial Post 1985 The Financial Post 500. Summer 1985.

Financial Post 1995 The Financial Post 500. Summer 1995.

Fox, John and Michael Ornstein 1986 "The Canadian state and corporate elites in the post-war period." *Canadian Review of Sociology and Anthropology* 23, 4 (November): 481–506.

Francis, Diane 1986 *Controlling Interest* Toronto: Macmillan.

Francis, Diane 1995 "The need for laws to limit spending." *Maclean's*, February 13.

Francis, Diane 1997 "When famous families lose touch." *Maclean's*, March 17.

Friedman, Milton and Rose Friedman 1980 *Free to Choose* New York: Harcourt Brace Jovanovich.

Grabb, Edward 1990 "Who owns Canada? Concentration of ownership and the distribution of economic assets, 1975–1985." *Journal of Canadian Studies* 25: 72–93.

Greenwood, John 1998 "Corporate takeovers soar to record." Reported in the London Free Press, January 10, Page D8.

Horry, Isabella, Filip Palda, and Michael Walker 1992 *Tax Facts 8* Vancouver: The Fraser Institute.

Laxer, Gord 1989 *Open for Business* Toronto: Oxford University Press.

Levitt, Kari 1970 *Silent Surrender* Toronto: Macmillan.

Maclean's 1993 "The return of the big deal in mergers." October 25.

Marchak, Patricia 1979 *In Whose Interests? An Essay on Multinational Corporations in a Canadian Context* Toronto: McClelland and Stewart.

Miliband, Ralph 1973 *The State in Capitalist Society* London: Quartet Books.

Myers, Gustavus 1914 *A History of Canadian Wealth* Toronto: James Lewis and Samuel.

Newman, Peter 1979 *The Canadian Establishment* Toronto: McClelland and Stewart-Bantam.

Newman, Peter 1981 *The Acquisitors* Toronto: McClelland and Stewart-Bantam.

Newman, Peter 1997 "How Power trumped the Royal Bank." *Maclean's*, September 1.

Niosi, Jorge 1978 *The Economy of Canada* Montreal: Black Rose Books.

Niosi, Jorge 1981 *Canadian Capitalism: A Study of Power in the Canadian Business Establishment* Toronto: Lorimer.

Niosi, Jorge 1985 *Canadian Multinationals* Toronto: Garamond.

O'Connor, Julia 1993 "Ownership, class, and public policy." pp. 75–88 in J. Curtis, N. Guppy, and E. Grabb (eds.), *Social Inequality in Canada: Patterns, Problems, Policies* Scarborough: Prentice-Hall Canada.

Offe, Claus 1984 *Contradictions in the Welfare State* Cambridge, Mass.: MIT Press.

Ornstein, Michael 1976 "The boards and executives of the largest Canadian corporations: size, composition, and interlocks." *Canadian Journal of Sociology* 1: 411–437.

Ornstein, Michael 1985 "Canadian capital and the Canadian state: ideology in an era of crisis." pp. 129–166 in R. Brym (ed.), *The Structure of the Canadian Capitalist Class* Toronto: Garamond.

Panitch, Leo (ed.) 1977 *The Canadian State* Toronto: University of Toronto Press.

Porter, John 1956 "Concentration of economic power and the economic elite in Canada." *Canadian Journal of Economics and Political Science* 22: 199–220.

Porter, John 1957 "The economic elite and the social structure of Canada." *Canadian Journal of Economics and Political Science* 23: 377–394.

Porter, John 1965 *The Vertical Mosaic* Toronto: University of Toronto Press.

Poulantzas, Nicos 1978 *State, Power, Socialism* London: New Left Books.

Statistics Canada 1986 *National Balance Sheet Accounts, 1961–1985* Catalogue 13-214.

Statistics Canada 1995a *Corporations and Labour Unions Returns Act. Preliminary 1993* Catalogue 61-220.

Statistics Canada 1995b *National Balance Sheet Accounts, 1984–93* Catalogue 13-214.

Statistics Canada 1996a *Corporations and Labour Unions Returns Act Preliminary 1994* Catalogue 61-220.

Statistics Canada 1996b *Inter-Corporate Ownership 1996* Catalogue 61-517.

Veltmeyer, Henry 1987 *Canadian Corporate Power* Toronto: Garamond.

Walker, Michael 1997 "The law of diminishing returns applies to government." In the London Free Press, January 2, page B7.

Wright, Erik Olin 1978 *Class, Crisis, and the State* London: New Left Books.

Chapter 2

DEMOCRACY AND GLOBAL CAPITALISM

Gordon Laxer

(Revised from Gordon Laxer, "Social Solidarity, Democracy, and Global Capitalism." *Canadian Review of Sociology and Anthropology* 32, August 1995, pp. 287–313. Reprinted with permission.)

INTRODUCTION

If someone were to tabulate the top 40 words used today on the political newspeak charts, "globalization" would be at or near the top. "Globalization" is a short form for a cluster of related changes. Economic changes include the internationalization of production and the greatly increased mobility of capital and of transnational corporations (henceforth "transnationals"). Cultural changes involve trends toward a universal world culture and the erosion of the nation-state.

This paper challenges the globalization assumptions on three points. First, regarding the claim of greater global economic integration, is the relative level of transnational ownership and control higher now than in the past? Second, has globalization resulted from technological change or from the political project of the new right? Third, is democracy strengthened by global "market reforms"? The remainder of the paper examines the prospects for social solidarity in the future.

TRANSNATIONALS THEN AND NOW

In 1991 Robert Reich forecast a new age in which there would soon be no "national corporations" and no "national economies." In 1989 "over 7 per cent of the aggregate value of the world stock market was held by foreign investors" (138). Do Reich's claims of a higher level of global corporate integration withstand scrutiny?

Reich's figures do not impress. According to John Dunning (1988), the relative level of foreign direct investment (FDI) "was more significant" from 1900 to 1914 "than at any time before or since" (72). In contrast to Reich's 7% figure for 1989, Dunning estimates that FDI represented 35% of long-term international debt then. Although there were new waves of transnational investment after 1914, the World Wars, revolutions, decolonization, and repatriations weakened transnational control relatively from 1914 through the 1970s (Wilkins, 1974: 221; Dunning, 1993: 119, 126).

When foreign ownership was at its height before 1914, about three-fifths was located in what is now called the Third World. Its territorial compass was wider, much of it concentrated in Russia and China, areas to which it has only recently started returning.

Transnationals and foreign ownership are not new. Once entrenched they can be removed. It is their nature that is different. Before 1914 foreign ownership often involved freestanding companies and fairly autonomous subsidiaries (Dunning, 1993: 120). Global communications were difficult. Recent technological changes greatly enhance the ability of transnationals to move capital globally and to run subsidiaries and affiliates from afar. Computers, telephones, fax machines, high-resolution monitors, satellites, and modems allow corporations to link a global network of suppliers, designers, engineers, and dealers, and to develop flexible manufacturing processes. They can form alliances with companies anywhere to work on such things as research and development.

The recent upsurge in Japanese and European transnationals has restored the relative importance of transnationals globally to roughly that before 1914. According to Dunning (1993), transnationals "accounted for between 25% and 30% of the gross domestic product of the world's market economies in the mid-1980s. They were also responsible for around three-quarters of the world's commodity trade" (14). Stopford et al. (1991) add that transnationals control "80 per cent of the world's land cultivated for export crops, and the lion's share of the world's technological innovations" (15). Although there were up to 20 000 transnationals in 1988, the largest 300 "are thought to account for 70 percent of the total foreign direct investment stake" (15).

The technology is now at hand for global production that takes little account of borders, cultures, or democracy. The main barriers to transnationals' strategies have been the myriad social and political arrangements among governments, businesses, unions, and citizens in each polity. Current assumptions about the irreversibility of "globalization" and the decline of national sovereignty help to eliminate these barriers.

TECHNOLOGICAL DETERMINISM OR POLITICAL AGENCY

The inevitable direction of history has shifted recently. As late as the 1970s it was widely thought that history was inevitably moving toward international socialism. Now history has swung toward the globalization of the new right.

New technologies put much of the world in touch with common cultural products such as American films and English-language rock music and television programmes. The internet allows people in different countries to converse with one another. We have seen as great a revolution in transportation as in information. Everywhere on earth is quickly accessible for a price. Has the migration of labour across borders accelerated as has the international migration of corporations?

International labour migration has likely declined relatively since the great migration from Europe to the "New World" between the 1880s and 1914 (Hobsbawm, 1990: 91). No political revolution comparable to new right globalization has taken place to free labour mobility. Elites have been content to leave labour where it is. Exceptions have been made to allow managers, diplomats, businesspeople, investors, and certain professionals to migrate with the transnationals. But most wage-earners in the privileged countries have stayed put. Corporations can move from one labour market to another, playing off one set of wage-earners and one set of social citizenship rights against another. The smaller and weaker the polity, the easier it is to deploy economic blackmail strategies.

We can now see how peculiar the period between the 1940s and 1970s was for business and for the political right. The stark contrast between the 1930s depression under free-market conditions and the prosperity of the war years under government stimulus taught a lesson to many people outside war-torn areas. A positive state role was now widely thought to be necessary for economic growth. The prosperity of the thirty years after 1945 saw the expansion of the welfare state and the growing influence of unions and social democratic parties (Hobsbawm, 1994: 272). The right had been defeated, morally as well as militarily, in the war against fascism. Ideas with similarities to fascism were discredited (176–177).

In this unique context the power of organized workers and citizens grew. The ideas of renegade members of the establishment before World War II, Henry Ford and John Maynard Keynes among them, had highlighted underconsumption as the cause of economic crises. They challenged free-market capitalism, and their views became the ruling orthodoxy. Under "Fordism," corporations granted workers a share in productivity gains. Under "bastard" Keynesianism, governments stimulated demand through full-employment policies and public social services, and regulated economic cycles through fiscal and monetary policies (Lipietz, 1992: 5–7). A "great compromise" among capital, labour, and the state emerged in the advanced countries. It was sometimes forgotten that the consensus came only after major struggles by organized workers and in anti-Nazi resistance movements (7–8).

In the compromise, corporations acknowledged the legitimacy of unions and implicity recognized some obligation to workers and citizens. Labour accepted corporate control over production and investment and gave up its historic goal of overturning capitalism. There were different versions and levels of commitment to this compromise in each country (Esping-Andersen, 1990).

Seduced by these changes arising from a unique historical conjuncture, most Western socialists proclaimed old-style capitalism dead. It is curious to read their assertions now. All the state had to do, so they said, was regulate, not socialize, capital.

It went unnoticed that the great compromise was built on twin foundations: the politics of support for regulation and the embeddedness of corporations in communities. By the 1980s neither condition held.

Patricia Marchak (1991) has outlined the rise of the new right. Corporate leaders and their allies, organized institutes and business associations, aimed at undermining the ideological underpinnings of the Keynesian welfare state. The Trilateral Commission, founded in 1973 by David Rockefeller and other powerful leaders in North America, Europe, and Japan, was one of the most prominent of these (103). The "Trilateralists" identified an "excess of democracy" as a major problem in the advanced countries. Their solutions were to strengthen governments relative to citizens and to give transnationals greater freedom to make investments (Crozier et al., 1975: 162, 173).

The corporate agenda joined with two others to form the new right. One was a revived neoliberal economics that projected the image of championing the "little guy" against entrenched interests, especially in government. A third agenda, "neoconservatism," brought a popular base for the new right. Reaction to feminism was at the heart of the backlash (Eisenstein, 1982; Gilder, 1989). So too were reactions against rights for racial minorities, gays and lesbians, and immigrants. As unemployment and social benefits rose, the welfare state created a tax backlash (Esping-Andersen, 1990). Finally, there was a religious backlash, especially in the U.S., against secularism and the permissive values of the 1960s.

Intellectually the new right was a strange brew. The corporate agenda called for greater state authority, while libertarian economics wanted limited government. The latter allied with neoconservatives urging the state to legislate morality and enforce law and order (Nisbet, 1986: 102–103; Lipset, 1988). When it was all put together, freedom was for the corporations, and discipline for wage-earners and citizens.

The new right agenda had national and global components. The global component involved freeing corporations from obligations to wage-earners and citizens, and reducing the autonomy of countries. This was done through "trade" agreements. Although they invoked the image of "free trade," these agreements were concerned with granting citizen-like rights to transnationals and with using the state to entrench their monopoly positions.

The information revolution enhanced corporate mobility. New-right liberalism and its bedfellow "neoconservatism" provided the rationale and the popularity to allow corporations to cut their moorings. Have these changes strengthened democracy?

DEMOCRACY WITHOUT SOVEREIGNTY

Fukuyama (1992) embraces Lord Bryce's definition of political liberalism as exemptions from societal control over property rights, religion, and political matters unnecessary to the welfare of the whole community. Democracy, on the other hand, calls for citizens to share in political power (42–43). Transnationals make up 47 of the 100 largest economic entities in the world, while states make up the other 53 (Goldstein and Weiss, 1991). Shifting power from governments to "market forces" under these conditions means transferring power from democratic bodies to giant corporations. If neoliberalism exempts most societal spheres from democratic control and reduces the sovereignty of political communities, is real democracy still possible?

Global citizenship rights for corporations enables them to escape obligations to country. The implicit threat is: bring in strict antipollution regulations, promise public auto insurance or higher minimum wages, and we the corporation will move out. You the wage-earners and citizens who voted for such policies will be left hurting. Not us: we are mobile and responsible to shareholders, not communities. Global corporate-citizenship rights enhance the transnationals' ability to use blackmail to discipline democracies.

The global marketplace is the arena for transnationals, the rich, and some business professionals, where rights and power are based on unequal command of property. The arena for most wage-earners and most citizens is countries and regions where the principles of democracy and equality are widely recognized. Capital is mobile. Labour, by and large, is not. Most people do not want to roam the globe in search of a job. If most people are relatively immobile, then the sovereignty of their political communities to determine their destinies is fundamental to democracy.

PROSPECTS FOR SOCIAL SOLIDARITY IN THE GLOBAL ECONOMY

Are there alternatives to new right globalization?

What is new about the 1990s is that socialist alternatives to capitalism are, for the first time in over a century, not credible. This is not to say that new versions of democratic socialism cannot become credible as the bases for powerful movements. In place of the old socialisms, new language and concepts are needed that are more inclusive than that of class, and that place less emphasis on unity as uniformity.

Class is still with us. If anything, recent globalization has accentuated class inequalities. But, as feminist, racial, and national liberation movements have shown us, class is not the only form of domination and exploitation.

For democratic-egalitarian projects to succeed in challenging the power and unitary vision of the transnationals, they must be able to incorporate social movements that are class-based with those that are not. They must also be able to demonstrate that they, and not the elites, better represent the whole of the political community.

We know from historical experience that the mere socialization of work did not necessarily lead to the formation of communities of workers who rejected the logic and power of capitalism and campaigned for its replacement. The socialization of work created unfavourable as well as favourable conditions for the rise of such oppositional communities. Generally, circumstances favourable to union organizing were the ones with emancipatory potential.[1] Organized working-class power has been crucial to the development of social services, citizens' rights, and democracy.

What if we are now experiencing a historical reversal: the desocialization of work? The signs are not entirely clear. There is high real unemployment in all advanced countries, more part-time work, home-based work, self-employment, and contracting out from corporations and the state to small businesses in which employment is often temporary (Krahn and Lowe, 1993). These conditions are not conducive to building communities of wage-earners. The trends vary by country and are influenced by politics. Nevertheless, they seem to point to a reduction in the demand for labour and to the transference of work from the developed to the Third World.

Capitalism has been in crisis since 1973, recording lower productivity gains and lower profits. This crisis is at the heart of trends to end permanent jobs and to reduce wages and employment.

The 1990s have witnessed similar changes in the public sector. The 1990s recession and high-interest-rate policies led to a fiscal crisis of the state in most advanced countries.[2] The new right took advantage of this situation to demand major cutbacks in government services and the privatization of much that remained to be delivered (Osborne and Gaebler, 1992). The combined effect was massive cuts in public sector workforces and the weakening of public sector unions.

What are the emancipatory prospects for movements based outside communities of wage-earners? I am referring to feminist, civil-rights, transformative-nationalist, environmental, religious-reformist, and other bases for social movements.

Non-work-based movements are fragmented in their identities, in their issues of concern, and in the sites of their political actions. They lack an overarching vision.

Many things keep these movements apart, but several may bring them together. Shared democratic and egalitarian values are spreading into more and more spheres of life. National sovereignty and democracy are powerful rallying cries for citizens and wage-earners who are rooted in place and attached to their communities (Laxer, 1995a). The most powerful impetus for co-operation may be the new right's globalization project, which is totalizing in its ambitions and focuses on culture as much as on production.

The transnationals will not necessarily succeed in homogenizing world culture or in maintaining capital mobility. The scope of and opportunities for social movements are expanding. Many new social movements recruit mainly from the growing and diverse groups outside the traditional working class. Greater formal education, more leisure time, and better communications encourage a rich life of networking locally, nationally, and internationally.

Because environmentalists, feminists, economic nationalists, and others are all threatened by new right globalization, they can develop coalitions for common purposes. I use the word "can" rather than "must" because there is nothing inevitable about this. Non-work-based movements must develop means of dealing with the state, with elections, and with political parties.

Can such coalitions agree upon enough of a common vision, while respecting differences, to transform political communities into more egalitarian, democratic, communitarian societies? The answers will come from further research and thinking and from concrete attempts at coalition-building.

To pose alternatives to the transnationals, coalitions of labour and other social movements would have to be powerful and would have to occur in many countries. I am not optimistic that it is possible to build an effective, democratic internationalism from below to counter globalization from above, but it is worth trying. If popular democratic control is to be enhanced, there remains a major role for democratic states with sufficient sovereignty to represent immobile labour and territorially-based communities.

CONCLUSION

One element of relative continuity is that the values and aspirations of democratic-egalitarian social movements have remained similar. People want a sense of belonging, security, equality, respect, personal development, and freedom. These can best be fulfilled in socially supportive, democratic, and egalitarian communities. Globalization by the transnationals is not indifferent to these needs and aspirations; it is hostile to them.

NOTES

1. See Krahn and Lowe (1993: 247).
2. Of the 12 countries in the European Union in September 1994, only Ireland and Luxembourg had debt ratios of less than 60% of GDP and current deficits of 3% or less. Those were the convergence criteria for joining the European Monetary Union (*The European*, Sept. 23-29, 1994. p. 1).

REFERENCES

Crozier, M., S.P. Huntington, and J. Watanuki
1975 *The Crisis of Democracy: Report on the Governability of Democracies to the Trilateral Commission* New York: New York University Press.

Dunning, J.H. 1988 *Explaining International Production* London: Unwin and Hyman.

Dunning, J.H. 1993 *Multinational Enterprises and the Global Economy* Wokingham, England: Addison-Wesley.

Eisenstein, Z. 1982 "The sexual politics of the new right: understanding the 'crisis of liberalism' for the 1980s." *Signs*, Vol. 7, No. 3 (Spring), pp. 567–588.

Esping-Andersen, G. 1985 *Politics against Markets: The Social Democratic Road to Power* Princeton: Princeton University Press.

Esping-Anderson, G. 1990 *The Three Worlds of Welfare Capitalism* Princeton: Princeton University Press.

Fukuyama, F. 1992 *The End of History and the Last Man* Toronto: Maxwell Macmillan Canada.

Gilder, G. 1989 *Men and Marriage* Gretna: Pelican.

Goldstein, K. and M. Weiss 1991 "The Top 100." *Across the Board*, pp. 16–19.

Gonick, C. and J. Silver 1989 "Fighting free trade." *Canadian Dimension*, Vol. 23, No. 3 (April), pp. 6–14.

Hobsbawm, E. 1990 *Nations and Nationalism since 1780: Programme, Myth, Reality* Cambridge: Cambridge University Press.

Hobsbawm, E. 1994 *Age of Extremes: The Short Twentieth Century 1914–1991* London: Michael Joseph

Krahn, H. and G. Lowe 1993 *Work, Industry and Canadian Society* (2nd ed.) Scarborough, Ont: Nelson Canada.

Laxer, G. 1995 "Opposition to continental integration: Sweden and Canada." *Review of Constitutional Studies*, Vol. 2, No. 2, pp. 342–395.

Lipietz, A. 1992 *Towards a New Economic Order: Postfordism, Ecology and Democracy* New York: Oxford University Press.

Lipset, S.M. 1988 "Neoconservatism: Myth and reality." *Society*, Vol. 25, No. 5, pp. 30–37.

Marchak, P. 1991 *The Integrated Circus: The New Right and the Restructuring of Global Markets* Montreal and Kingston: McGill-Queen's University Press.

Nisbet, R. 1986 *Conservatism: Dream and Reality* Minneapolis: University of Minnesota Press.

Osborne, D. and T. Gaebler 1992 *Reinventing Government: How the Entrepreneurial Spirit is Transforming the Public Sector* New York: Plume.

Reich, R. 1991 *The Work of Nations: Preparing Ourselves for Twenty-First Century Capitalism* New York: Alfred A. Knopf.

Stopford, J.M., S. Strange, and J.S. Henley 1991 *Rival States, Rival Firms: Competition for World Market Shares* Cambridge: Cambridge University Press.

Wilkins, M. 1974 "Multinational enterprises." In *The Rise of Managerial Capitalism* H. Daems and H. van der Wee (eds.) The Hague: Martinus Nijhoff, pp. 213–235.

Chapter 3

WORKING-CLASS FORMATION IN TWENTIETH-CENTURY CANADA

James Conley

(An original chapter written for this volume.)

INTRODUCTION

On February 26, 1996, in Hamilton Ontario, 100 000 people marched and demonstrated in a protest organized by the labour movement and social activist groups against the provincial Conservative government's labour legislation and cuts to social spending. The day before, numerous factories, businesses, and public services in the city were closed by strikes and picketing. Three months previously, a similar protest was held in London, Ontario, and in the months to follow, "Days of Action" were held in other cities in the province. Similar protest campaigns led by organized labour have occurred in other provinces in the last few decades, including the "Operation Solidarity" protest campaign in British Columbia in the 1980s.

What is the relationship between a series of protests by unionized workers and others, and the sociological study of social inequality? Social conflicts such as these, and the social changes that sometimes result from them, are consequences of inequalities of power. Inequalities of power have always been central components of sociological inquiry into social inequality. "Who has power?" "What are its institutional bases?" "How is it used?" These are some of the many questions asked by sociologists, and treated in other chapters in this volume. The classical theories of class, which still define most theoretical debates and empirical research in this area, concentrated on identifying sources of power and conflicts of interest in the ownership of productive property (Marx) or in positions in markets and organizations (Weber).

The identification of inequalities of power and antagonistic interests in structured social relationships is only the first step to understanding social conflicts and social change, however. Intervening between structural inequalities of class power and class conflict are processes of class formation and mobilization. These involve consideration of: the sources of conflict and the resources available to classes; the existence of solidary relationships within classes; the awareness of class interests and dispositions to act on them by class members; the mobilization of classes by organizations; and the forms of collective action that class members undertake.

The resources, social organization, dispositions, and mobilization of dominant classes are often taken for granted, for their power is firmly institutionalized. Attention here will focus on the working class. Like most studies of working-class formation and collective action, this chapter starts from the ideas of Marx and Weber before turning to the dynamics of working-class formation in Canada.

CLASS FORMATION AND CLASS CONFLICT IN THEORY

The power of the capitalist class rests on its control over society's productive resources. Ownership of property gives businesses the right to exclude others from the use of those resources, to allocate them to different uses, to move them, to choose production technologies, and so on. These powers also give the capitalist class leverage on the state. But what are the bases for opposition to capitalist class power?

Marx

For Marx, the reasons for working-class opposition to the power of the capitalist class lie in workers' experiences of exploitative and alienating work, and in the consequences of capitalist profit-making strategies for working-class standards of life. The "general law of capitalist accumulation", Marx argues, is "that in proportion as capital accumulates, the lot of the labourer, be his pay high or low, must grow worse ... accumulation of wealth at one pole is, therefore, at the same time accumulation of misery, agony of toil, slavery, ignorance, brutality, mental degradation, at the opposite pole" (Marx, 1887: 604). Either in absolute terms, or relative to that of the capitalist class, the standard of living of workers falls as capitalism develops, and the conditions of work become more toilsome (Grabb 1997, Braverman 1974).

For Marx, capitalism created not only grievances among workers, but also the conditions of class formation and class power for workers to act to eliminate the sources of their distress. Specifically, Marx expected capitalism to create three conditions giving workers the organization and resources to resist capitalist power. First, changes in the production process would bring workers together in larger workplaces, and a more cooperative production process would lead to solidarity between workers. Unlike Durkheim (1893), who expected the increasing division of labour to lead (at least under certain circumstances) to organic solidarity between classes in modern societies, Marx expected that changes in production would obliterate skill differences, levelling workers to what are today called semi-skilled workers; mechanized production would also reduce the importance of physical strength, and gender differences between workers would cease to be significant. This process of homogenization would create mechanical solidarity within the working class (Sorenson 1994), and increase the possibility of and necessity for workers to organize on a broad, inclusive basis. The changing character of production also gave workers power: even as the demise of craft production and the introduction of machine-pacing deprived workers of control over the process of production as individuals, workers gained power as a collectivity.

Second, Marx emphasized the power that derives from class size. The capitalist class structure would polarize as the petty bourgeoisie of small owners disappeared, and the capitalist class would grow smaller or more concentrated as large capitalists swallowed up smaller capitalists. As a consequence, the working class would become the largest class in capitalist societies, confronting a small capitalist class in a conflict without any intermediaries.

However, structural tendencies in capitalism toward homogenization of the working class and polarization of the class structure only furnish preconditions for working-class power. The problem of collective action remains: individual workers do not have the resources to counter the power of capitalists,[1] and size is not enough for power unless it is organized. Marx expected that, in the course of conflict with capitalists, workers would develop increasingly broad levels of organization: unions would form on local, then on industrial, and finally on national levels, at the same time as political parties advancing the interests of workers would grow (Marx and Engels 1848). In other words, out of the experience of conflict, increasingly inclusive and politicized forms of organization of workers would result, and increasingly broad struggles would follow between workers, on the one hand, and capitalists and the state, on the other.

Weber

Weber is often described as involved in a debate with Marx's ghost. This certainly applies to Weber's thoughts on social inequality, which assume much of what Marx had to say, but which go on to add to and amend Marx's views (see Grabb 1997). Unlike Marx, who almost exclusively emphasized class, Weber considered classes, status groups, and parties as "phenomena of the distribution of power" within societies (Weber 1978: 927). Weber expected that, in addition to or instead of conflict occurring on class lines, there would also be organized conflict based on status groups and factions competing for power in organizations, especially the state.

Like Marx, Weber thought that property was central to the concept of class. However, unlike Marx, Weber conceived of classes as based on positions in markets, not in production. From this perspective, classes are distinguished by differences in the possession of marketable, income-producing goods and services. Thus, Weber's analysis points to possible lines of differentiation amongst workers based on possession of skills and other advantages in labour markets. Such differentiation in labour markets need not promote the general impoverishment of the working class that Marxian theory seems to suggest, because there would be distinct segments or strata within the working class, with different experiences, different interests, and different capacities for organization and collective action.

Weber's concept of *social classes*, "within which individual and generational mobility is easy and typical" (Weber 1978: 302), adds another layer of complexity to working-class formation. First of all, Weber believed that the development of a new middle class of white-collar employees, technical specialists, and professionals (due to the tremendous expansion of bureaucratic forms of administration in modern times) provides an avenue for mobility out of the working class (Weber 1978: 304). Because stability in class membership, both within and between generations, is positively associated with class formation, a high degree of mobility or fluidity between classes tends to weaken the formation of networks of solidarity or a strong sense of class identification. In addition, the existence of a middle class between the working class and the capitalist class works against the Marxian expectation that the capitalist class structure would become polarized over time.

Weber's concept of status is the second aspect of power that affects class formation. The existence of status groups that cut across different classes may also complicate or retard the increasing homogeneity of the working class that Marx envisioned. Moreover, rather than have group formation purely on the basis of class location, groups may form around status-related issues, including shared consumption patterns and styles of life. Thus, status groups based on gender, ethnicity, region, or education can divide members of one class, and create solidarity between members of different classes. Finally, relations of domination between such status groups may be more "transparent" than class relations and, therefore, may be a more readily available source of group identity than class.

Party is the third key aspect of power that Weber distinguishes. With respect to problems of class formation, Weber's insight here is that when groups organize to pursue power and its rewards in organizations, and above all in states, they may do so on bases other than class or status. The best example may be forms of political party organization. The history of party systems and of political cleavages in societies can thus be expected to have effects on working-class formation and the organization of class conflict.

Even today, the ideas of Marx and Weber continue to provide a basis for the way sociologists think about class formation and conflict. Marx tended to see working-class formation and collective action as a series of steps toward an end-point, a terminus on the road to a revolution that would overthrow capitalism. Weber, in contrast, presents a more complex and contingent view of class formation, as one of several possible lines along which groups in conflict might form.

CLASS FORMATION AND CLASS CONFLICT IN CANADA

What do we know about class formation and class conflict in late twentieth-century Canada? Evidence on working-class formation and conflict in Canada will be presented with respect to the following issues: i) the structural tendencies of class formation, with particular attention to the process of polarization expected by Marx; ii) the changes in social organization in workplaces and labour markets that have affected working-class solidarity; iii) the dispositions of members of different classes; iv) and levels of mobilization in unions and political parties, along with conflict in social movements and strikes.

Class Structure: Polarization?

As we have seen, Marxists have expected that working-class formation would be facilitated by a polarization of the class structure. This polarization has three aspects: decline of the petty bourgeoisie, polarization of incomes, and polarization of skills. While generally agreeing with Marxist theory on the demise of the petty bourgeoisie, Weber and his followers are less sure about the other two predictions. What does the Canadian evidence show?

Marx expected that the petty bourgeoisie, comprising self-employed artisans, farmers, shopkeepers, and the like, would disappear under the pressure of competition from larger, more efficient capitalist enterprises. The result would be a class structure polarized between workers on the one hand and capitalists on the other. Weber, in contrast, did not expect a polarization, because a new middle class of salaried employees with educational credentials would develop in tandem with bureaucratic organizations, and interpose itself between the capitalists and the workers.

In Canada, evidence on levels of self-employment over the course of the 1900s largely bears out Marxist expectations about the decline of the petty bourgeoisie.[2] The self-employed did decline from about 25 percent of the total labour force in 1931 to about 10 or 12 percent of all workers in the 1970s. Since then, however, the trend has reversed, both in Canada and in other countries. By the 1990s, close to 20 percent of Canada's work force was in the self-employed category.

Most of the historical decline of the petty bourgeoisie in Canada was due to falling employment in the agricultural sector, where levels of self-employment have always been, and continue to be, high.[3] Recent increases have occurred across all industries, but levels of self-employment have remained higher than average in the construction, business services and amusement, personal and household services industries; as Marx would have expected, the lowest level of self-employment is in manufacturing (Gardner 1995, Crompton 1993, Statistics Canada 1997a, Arai 1997).

Despite its recent growth, however, the petty bourgeoisie has in fact declined in prominence over the longer term, much as Marx expected. Has this polarized the class structure, making class conflict and working-class formation more likely? As noted earlier, Weberian understandings of the class structure point to the growth of a new middle class of employees characterized by authority within bureaucratic organizations and by the possession of educational credentials. Although the causes, characteristics, conceptualization, and future prospects of the new middle class have been the subject of considerable theoretical debate by neo-Marxist and neo-Weberian theorists (see Grabb 1997), there is agreement that the numbers of middle-level administrators, managers, professionals, and skilled technical employees constitute a significant and generally growing part of the post-industrial class structure, one which is relatively distinct from the bourgeoisie, the petty bourgeoisie, and the working class (Myles and Turegin 1994). In the only large-scale Canadian study to use neo-Marxist class categories, the new middle class, defined as lower-level managers and supervisors with authority to impose sanctions on other employees, was found to represent about 25 percent of the labour force in the early 1980s, compared to nearly 60 percent for the working class, over 10 percent for the petty bourgeoisie, and 6 percent for employers (Clement and Myles 1994). Since the early 1980s, however, it has been suggested that the middle class may have declined. This position was given some credibility by the wave of 'downsizing' that occurred in the 1980s, involving numerous well-publicized layoffs of middle managers in large corporations and reductions in employment in the public sector.

Nevertheless, based on census data on occupations, those occupations having the closest fit to what Marxists and Weberians consider to be the new middle class comprised slightly over a quarter of the labour force in both 1986 and 1991 (Table 3-1). This proportion, moreover, is little changed from those found in the 1971 and 1981 censuses (Pineo 1985). Thus, although the evidence cannot be considered definitive because of the rough occupational classification that is used, there appears to be little or no support in these data for the proposition that the new middle class has been in decline. On the contrary, this class has been growing faster than the labour force as a whole, with the only declining category being lower-level blue-collar supervisors (forewomen and foremen).

TABLE 3-1 Occupational change 1986–1991

Occupational Group	1986	1991	% Change
Middle Management	803 935	1 095 170	36.2
Employed Professionals	922 606	1 074 025	16.4
Semi-Professionals	819 170	1 008 825	23.2
Technicians	225 225	273 580	21.5
Supervisors	354 110	375 460	6.0
Foremen & Forewomen	325 235	289 545	-11.0
'New Middle Class'	3 450 281	4 116 605	19.3
Percentage	27.1	28.9	
All Occupations	12 740 225	14 220 230	11.6

Source: Statistics Canada 1993, Table 1. Occupational Classification: Revised Pineo-Porter-McRoberts Socioeconomic Classification of Occupations (Pineo 1985).

The economic restructuring that has occurred in both Canada and other advanced capitalist societies since the 1970s has spawned another debate about the new middle class. This debate concerns whether this class has declined, not in numbers, but in income and quality of working conditions. First of all, some writers suggest that the long-term processes of routinization, deskilling, and loss of autonomy that occurred with manual and clerical workers in previous stages of industrialization are now extending to professional employees and middle-level administrators in the post-industrial period. However, evidence from the early 1980s has not shown any decline in skill requirements in new middle class occupations; instead, the shift to a post-industrial service economy has created both skilled and unskilled jobs and, on balance, the former have grown more than the latter (Clement and Myles 1994).

The possible effects of further changes since the 1980s have yet to be determined. It may be that at least part of the recent increase in self-employment stems from members of the new middle class going into business for themselves, because of the reduced job security produced by large companies either downsizing or contracting out much of their work. Technological changes, especially computer technologies, make such arrangements possible, and also provide opportunities for self-employment in consulting work (Arai 1997, Statistics Canada 1997b).

The third possible pattern of class polarization to receive attention in recent decades concerns the polarization of earnings. In this case, the middle class is conceptualized in a gradational, distributive way, and is represented by those individuals in the middle categories of the income structure. Any shrinkage among middle-income earners could have important implications for class formation, because this group would include not only many members of the new middle class as defined in Marxist or Weberian terms, but also the 'affluent' part of the working class. In Canada, increases in real incomes for men, which began after World War II, actually stopped in the early 1980s, and have been largely stagnant since. Among women, both labour force participation and earnings have slowly risen, with the increasing prevalence of dual-income households helping to prevent declines in economic circumstances for many working-class families. Income polarization has occurred, but it is mainly on the basis of age and marital status, with declines in the earnings of younger workers relative to older workers, and lone-parent families (which are primarily female-headed) relative to two-parent families (Picot and Myles 1995, Morissette 1997).

What, then, can we conclude from the evidence on polarization in the class structure? First, Marx and Weber were broadly correct about the decline of the petty bourgeoisie, but its decline has not been uniform across all sectors of the economy, and the long-term trend has been reversed somewhat in the last two decades. Second, there has been growth in new middle class positions in the class structure, as Weber expected, and they have not been subject to the deskilling expected by many neo-Marxists. Moreover, although there has been a decline in job security for some middle class workers in both the private and public sectors since the 1980s, neither the absolute numbers nor the proportions of such jobs have decreased. Polarization of earned incomes has occurred, but it has not been clearly along class lines. Instead, polarization has involved falling incomes for workers in the most vulnerable labour market positions, with others in more secure positions being somewhat better protected. The result has been a more complex class structure than classical Marxism tends to suggest.

Social Organization: Homogenization of the Working Class?

Marx expected capitalism to facilitate working-class solidarity because of the concentration of workers in larger workplaces, the growth of a more cooperative labour process, and the decline in skill differences among workers. He also expected the significance of gender differences within the working class to decline. What has happened in Canada in regard to these issues?

Workplace Size

On average, workplace size has generally increased in this century (especially in manufacturing) although there is some evidence of a decline since the 1980s. Table 3-2 shows that, at least between 1930 and 1975, the proportion of manufacturing employees working in establishments with fewer than 100 workers dropped from 40 to 30 percent. At the same time, the proportion of employees in large establishments (500 and over) rose from less than 24 percent to more than 31 percent. Not all of this apparent shifting has involved blue-collar jobs. In fact, evidence from the 1986 Labour Market Activity Survey suggests that the proportion of professional and managerial em-

TABLE 3-2 Employees by size of establishment (manufacturing) 1925–1975

Year	Employees (%)			
	<50	50–99	100–499	500+
1925	27.3	13.5	35.4	23.8
1930	26.0	13.3	35.0	25.7
1940	23.9	11.4	34.5	30.2
1950	23.1	11.4	31.8	33.7
1960	23.1	12.6	32.4	31.9
1970	18.3	12.2	37.1	32.5
1975	18.1	12.0	38.6	31.3

Source: Historical Statistics of Canada, Revised Edition, Series R795-811, 812–825

ployees has generally risen with increases in workplace size (Morissette 1991: 37).

Outside of manufacturing, average workplace size in the private sector of the economy tends to be smaller. Between 1978 and 1988, in the Canadian commercial economy (excluding the agriculture, health, education, and government sectors) about 35 percent of employees worked for *companies* (not workplaces) with fewer than 50 employees, while 40 percent worked for companies with 500 or more employees. However, since large companies, in particular, may have more than one establishment or workplace, these figures overestimate the size of workplaces in Canada (Picot and Dupuy 1996).

As noted earlier, during the 1980s there was an increase in the share of private-sector employment accounted for by small companies and small establishments. This increase has potentially significant implications for working-class formation, since workers in small firms receive less pay and fewer benefits than workers in larger firms, and are also more likely to be laid off (Clement and Myles 1994: 57–59). Given these considerations, we might expect workers to be more class conscious in small firms. Nevertheless, as Stinchcombe (1990) points out, the social relations and employment relationships in small firms tend to reduce class solidarities. This is partly because the social distance between employer and employee is likely to be smaller than in larger firms, the employer is more likely to work alongside the employee, and employees can often perceive opportunities for themselves to move up into the role of small employer. In smaller firms, there are also likely to be more individualized labour contracts and less routinized production. By comparison, larger companies tend to have more bureaucratized labour relations, with internal labour markets, standardized employment conditions, and extensive quasi-judicial procedures for grievances. In recent years, some large employers have adopted new forms of workplace organization, such as the Japanese-style approaches to production management and flexible specialization. These forms of organization recreate, to some extent, the social relations of small firms, and are also supposed to empower workers through multi-tasking, job rotation, and reduction in status distinctions between workers and management. According to some analyses, however, these allegedly new forms of control are simply "old wine in new bottles," and have not reduced either workplace conflict or worker solidarity (Rinehart et al. 1997).

Class and Social Mobility

Social mobility refers to the movement of people into or out of different social groupings, including classes. The lower the amount of mobility between classes, of course, the more stable will be the composition of any one class over time. In turn, the more stable the composition of a class, the more likely it is that its members will develop a sense of class solidarity and identity. Table 3-3 provides evidence on patterns of class mobility or stability among Canadian males for the early 1980s, by comparing the class position of fathers with the class position of their adult sons. The data show that the employer, petty-bourgeois, and working classes were the most stable, with 38.1 percent, 47.4 percent, and 39.7 percent of respondents in these three groups having fathers with the same class locations. Class stability is particularly evident among the propertied classes, with nearly three-quarters of employer and petty-bourgeois respondents coming from either employer or petty-bourgeois backgrounds. As might be expected, the growing new middle class positions have much less stability than either the propertied or working classes, in

TABLE 3-3 Intergenerational class mobility of Canadian males, 1982 (Inflow percentages)

Class of Origin:	Employer	Petty-Bourg.	Expert Mgr.	Manager	Prof.	Semi-Prof.	Worker	N
Class of Destination:								
Employer	38.1	34.4	6.0	3.1	0.0	3.0	15.2	860
Petty-Bourgeoisie	24.5	47.4	8.7	3.5	0.6	1.3	14.0	1 354
Expert Manager	17.6	11.5	12.2	13.6	2.3	9.6	33.3	1 401
Manager	14.8	15.6	8.3	20.8	0.5	2.6	37.5	1 246
Professional	34.3	14.2	11.6	2.3	9.3	8.5	19.8	353
Semi-Professional	11.2	13.1	21.1	19.4	2.4	0.4	32.4	892
Worker	13.8	22.5	7.7	13.8	1.1	1.3	39.7	4 204
All	18.4	23.3	9.7	12.5	1.4	2.9	31.8	
	1 892	2 405	996	1 287	148	300	3 282	10 310

Source: Western and Wright 1994: 627, using data from the comparative class structure project (see Clement and Myles 1994).

that a third or more of expert managers, managers, and semi-professionals have worker backgrounds. In addition, a third of professionals have employer backgrounds. The tendency toward stability in the formation of social classes, therefore, appears to be strongest in the three 'oldest' classes: employers, the petty bourgeoisie, and workers.

Gender and Ethnicity

Two of the most important changes in the Canadian labour force in the last 50 years have been the increased participation of women in paid work, and the rise in immigration from non-European nations. Both of these processes are well documented in other chapters in this volume. Here our main concern is to consider their implications for working-class formation.

Although the importance of physical strength has declined in modern production, as Marx expected, the social significance of gender has not disappeared. Women are more likely than men to occupy working-class positions in the paid labour force, and are also more likely to be employed in the service sector than in the goods-producing sector of the economy (Clement and Myles 1994: 35). Not only is there gender segregation by industry, there is also segregation between women and men in individual occupations. Thus, women and men tend not to work in the same workplaces at the same jobs. Women's experiences at work are consequently different from men's. In addition, the continuing greater responsibility of women for household labour and child care further distinguishes their experience of the labour market and paid work from that of men. Women's average earnings are also lower than those of men. Consequently, despite the shared interests that working men and women may have as fellow employees, women's interests often diverge from those of their male co-workers over issues such as maternity leaves, child care, pay equity, and sexual harassment.

The changing gender composition of the Canadian working class has been accompanied by changes in its ethnic and racial composition, as immigration levels have increased from outside the traditional European sources. In the past, ethnic affiliations rooted in segregated residential communities and their institutions, and in exclusion from and competition for jobs, may have been a source of both ethnic and class solidarity (see, for example, Frager 1992). The assimilation of previous generations of European immigrants and their children has reduced the salience of ethnic differences within the working class. However, the linguistic-regional differences between anglophone and francophone workers have a long history in Canadian society. As well, differences in the occupation and income levels between those of European ethnic origin, on the one hand, and visible minority immigrants and Aboriginals, on the other hand, have continued to be significant.

As Weber long ago suggested, status differences involving gender, race, ethnicity, language, and region have often been features of working-class social organization, and have not disappeared with capitalist development. All of these differences tend to cut across class allegiances, reducing the sense of shared or common experience, especially among the working class. Located within different relations of power, status differences can be double-edged swords, contributing to working-class solidarities when class and status interests are congruent, but acting as sources of division at other times, as when males and females or Blacks and Whites must compete with each other for the same scarce employment opportunities.

Class Consciousness

Both class polarization and the changing social organization of workplaces and labour markets entail structural conditions that affect the broad patterns of social cleavage in capitalist societies, as well as the solidarity of workers within them. The third feature of class formation to consider is people's interpretations of these structural conditions, and the class-based perceptions or outlooks that follow from them. Despite some acknowledged methodological limitations, sample surveys of attitudes have provided a good deal of the evidence for assessing and measuring class consciousness in previous sociological research. These survey measures range from people's estimates of what their own class location is, to their attitudes about the role of corporations in the economy, to their feeling about unions and strikes, and so on. With this wide variety of attitude items, investigators seek to understand and study different dimensions of the class consciousness of members of the various classes. Conceptually, researchers influenced by Marx have generally used a typology involving three types or degrees of class consciousness: class awareness or identity, oppositional class consciousness, and revolutionary or counter-hegemonic class consciousness (Giddens 1973, Livingstone and Mangan 1996). Class identity has been defined as awareness of membership in a distinct class, class opposition as the belief that the interests of the workers and capitalists are opposed, and counter-hegemonic consciousness as a belief in the possibility and desirability of a society organized along non-capitalist lines.

Although assessment of the results of attitude surveys is complicated by the variety of measures that have been used for both class position and class consciousness, most studies suggest that the class identity adopted by the majority of respondents in all classes is "middle class." However, members of the working class and petty bourgeoisie are more likely than members of other classes to choose a working-class identity (Livingstone and Mangan 1996, Johnston and Baer 1993). The effects of the complex position of women in labour markets and households is shown in findings that married women's class identity is affected more by their husbands' class position than their own (Livingstone and Mangan 1996). This is perhaps a reflection of the persistence of the male "breadwinner" norm, and the traditional primacy accorded male jobs and male earnings in most households.

As for oppositional class consciousness, surveys have found that, on such issues as the rights of labour unions and the redistribution of income from the rich to the poor, the attitudes of workers and capitalists are indeed opposed: members of the capitalist class and the petty bourgeoisie express more pro-business and less pro-labour attitudes than do industrial and service workers. The findings for the new middle class are inconsistent, with some studies showing them to be little different from workers, and other studies showing them to have more pro-business attitudes. Gender further complicates this picture, for studies also show that women have less pro-labour attitudes than men. The organization of workers also has an effect on oppositional consciousness: most studies find that membership in a union is positively associated with pro-labour attitudes (Clement and Myles 1994, Livingstone and Mangan 1996).

Finally, little research has been conducted on hegemonic class consciousness, and what there is shows that most people in all class positions rarely see an alternative to a capitalist economy; members of the working class are somewhat more likely to do so, but even they are a tiny minority (Livingstone and Mangan 1996, Johnston and Baer 1993).[4]

Some ethnographic studies furnish additional insights into working-class consciousness. For example, a study of young white working-class men in Thunder Bay illustrates how people's consciousness or perceptions regarding class, gender, regional, and racial identities can be intertwined in complex and often inconsistent ways (Dunk 1991). The working-class 'boys' in this study expressed disdain for university-educated experts. They also promoted a cult of masculinity from which women were excluded, both at work and at leisure. Many were hostile toward and asserted moral superiority over Aboriginals, but also resented the dominant influence of corporations, governments, and outside experts in their region. Such attitudes suggest a mix of opposition to the interests of both the powerful and the powerless in Canadian society. These views may indicate a form of populist political culture, with possible roots in the traditional agrarian petty-bourgeois opposition to regional and capitalist dominance. Such cross-cutting outlooks also underscore the historical weakness of working-class mobilization and collective action in Canada, at least compared to Scandinavia and other places where class dispositions are stronger (Clement and Myles 1994, Johnston and Baer 1993).

Mobilization and Collective Action

For Marx and subsequent Marxists, class polarization, growing working-class solidarity based on changing workplaces, and oppositional and counter-hegemonic consciousness should all go hand-in-hand with increasing levels of working-class organization and, ultimately, power. In Canada, workers have become more organized, but power has not necessarily followed. This has had long-term effects on the other components of class formation.

Although it is not all that they do, labour unions exist to defend the economic interests of their members. These interests include wages and benefits, working conditions, decent treatment by employers, and job security. Unions have largely succeeded in protecting these interests, for union jobs typically have higher wages and better benefits than non-union jobs. This is not all that unions do, however. Many unions are also involved in movements and campaigns for broader objectives affecting working people more generally. Examples include support for the social programs of the welfare state, the organization of non-unionized workers, and support for social-democratic political parties, such as the New Democratic Party. As Marx expected, labour unions have grown from small local organizations, based mainly on skilled craft workers, to large, national or international bodies, often encompassing workers from a wide variety of different occupations. The growth of unions in Canada occurred in three major waves: the organization of craft unions in the late nineteenth and early twentieth centuries, the spread of industrial unions in manufacturing in the 1940s, and the rapid growth of public sector unionism in the 1960s. Union membership has expanded from 133 000 in 1911 to over 3.5 million in 1997. In Canada, union density, or the percentage of paid workers who belong to unions, has held steady at between 31 and 33 percent since the late 1960s. In the majority of other advanced capitalist societies, however, it has fallen, sometimes to very low levels. In the United States, for example, union density has declined from 23 to 16 percent in recent years (Galarneau 1996, Akeampong 1997, Western 1995).

Canadian unionization rates have not suffered such declines, largely because of the strength of unionism in the public sector. The union density in the public sector is 73 percent, with members of public sector unions making up 43 percent of all union members in Canada. However, even in Canada union growth has been rather stagnant in recent years, for several reasons. First, there is the shift of employment from goods-producing industries, in which union density is higher (but declining), to service industries, in which union density is lower. Second, there is the trend toward decreases in firm size, since unionization rates are generally lower in small firms. Third, there is the growth in part-time and temporary jobs, which are much less likely to be unionized (Galarneau 1995). Partly as a consequence of declining levels of unionization in goods-producing industries, union density has fallen among men in particular. Among women, despite the slowness of unions to take up women's concerns in the past, unionization has risen to nearly the same level as men. By 1997, women made up 45 percent of union members, up from approximately 33 percent in 1982 and only 16 percent in 1962 (Akcampong 1997, White 1993). One disturbing trend for the future of unions is a declining level of unionization among younger workers (Galarneau 1995). The average age of union members is rising because of slow job growth, and because of seniority protections in the manufacturing and public sectors, where union density is high.

Unions in Canada have often supported left-leaning political parties, in particular the New Democratic Party. Even so, such parties have never achieved more than third-party status in national politics, although they have formed several provincial governments. This has meant a relative lack of formal political power for workers at the national level, and so has made class a less important element in political discourse than might otherwise be the case. Instead, workers have been politically mobilized with reference to a variety of other issues or identities. Most of the opposition of workers to the power of capitalism or big business has been manifested in strike activity, workplace industrial conflict, and political protest campaigns.

Surges of union organization have corresponded historically to periods of heightened industrial conflict, with the two feeding off each other. The expansion of industrial unions in the 1940s and the rise of public sector unionism in the 1960s both occurred amid waves of strikes that, at times, gave Canada among the highest rates of industrial conflict in the world (Cruikshank and Kealey 1987). In recent times, strike levels have fallen to historically low levels, although there are some signs of an increase in the latter half of the 1990s (Akeampong 1997).

In addition to their role in collective bargaining, unions have also played prominent roles in protest campaigns against government cutbacks and attempts to restrict or eliminate union power. Some examples are the opposition to government-imposed wage controls in the 1970s, the Solidarity movement in British Columbia in the 1980s, and opposition to the Harris government's "Common Sense Revolution" in Ontario in the 1990s. At present, an important concern for unions, and working-class organization generally, is the threat of increasing capital mobility in today's "global economy." An example of this threat is the movement of companies and investments out of one nation or region and into another nation or region which is more friendly to big business interests. Such possibilities probably mean that both the federal and provincial governments will be more likely to adopt policies that favour business owners over workers and their unions, thereby increasing the likelihood of labour strife and protests in the future.

CONCLUSION

In this review, we have found that, although Marxist theory furnishes many of the key ideas for an understanding of class formation and class conflict, the history of these two processes, both in Canada and in many other countries, is more variable, contingent, and dependent on other issues than Marx may have fully anticipated (see Tilly 1992, Katznelson 1986). Certain modifications to the Marxian view, including some of those provided by Weber, are also required. These include the recognition that there is no inevitable progression toward class polarization, labour homogenization, working-class consciousness or organization, and proletarian revolution. Instead, the processes of class formation and class conflict appear to involve a complex pattern of rises and declines, with varying rates of class mobility, interactions between class and status-group identities and networks, and the persistent role of unions and other traditional organizational forms in the process of class mobilization.

NOTES

1. The power of individual and small-group 'resistance,' such as restriction of output, should not be ignored. This resistance has sometimes led to changing managerial strategies to deal with problems such as high rates of turnover.
2. The concept of self-employment does not correspond strictly to Marx's concept of petty bourgeoisie, as it includes both self-employed who do not employ paid help, and those who do, i.e., employers or capitalists. There is some debate in the literature about how many paid employees are required before a self-employed person becomes a member of the capitalist class (e.g., Clement and Myles 1994 use three as a threshold). Over 60% of the self-employed in Canada in 1996 did not have any paid employees. Of the remainder who were employers, more than a quarter had only one employee, and about two thirds had fewer than five employees (Statistics Canada 1997b: 39).
3. This pattern may be due less to capitalist competition than to technological changes, which have made possible larger scales of production, even for family farms. Although often feared, large-scale corporate farming has not been a major factor in Canadian agriculture. In fact, the rate of self-employment in agriculture has declined only marginally since 1931 (Gardner 1995).

4. This might be expected to vary according to the level of class conflict, but even in an industrial city such as Hamilton, in a period of high strike activity, Livingstone & Mangan (1996) found there was not much spontaneous recognition of class conflict. In his study of a postal workers' strike in the same city in the same time period, Langford (1994) found little enduring change in class consciousness as a result of participation in the strike.

REFERENCES

Akeampong, Ernest B. 1997 "A statistical portrait of the trade union movement." *Perspectives on Labour and Income* 9, 4: 45–54.

Arai, Bruce 1997 "The road not taken: The transition from unemployment to self-employment in Canada." *Canadian Journal of Sociology* 22: 365–82.

Braverman, Harry 1974 *Labor and Monopoly Capital* New York: Monthly Review Press.

Clement, Wallace and John Myles 1994 *Relations of Ruling: Class and Gender in Postindustrial Societies* Montreal and Kingston: McGill-Queen's University Press.

Crompton, Susan 1993 "The renaissance of self-employment." *Perspectives on Labour and Income* 5, 2: 22–32.

Cruikshank, Douglas and Gregory S. Kealey 1987 "Canadian strike statistics, 1891–1950." *Labour/Le Travail* 20: 85–145.

Dunk, Thomas W. 1991 *It's a Working Man's Town: Male Working-Class Culture in Northwestern Ontario* Montreal and Kingston: McGill-Queen's University Press.

Durkheim, Emile 1893 *The Division of Labor in Society* Translated by George Simpson. New York: The Free Press, 1933.

Frager, Ruth 1992 *Sweatshop Strife: Class, Ethnicity, and Gender in the Jewish Labour Movement of Toronto, 1900–1939* Toronto: University of Toronto Press.

Galarneau, Diane 1996 "Unionized workers." *Perspectives on Labour and Income* 8, 1: 43–52.

Gardner, Arthur 1995 "Their own boss: The self-employed in Canada." *Canadian Social Trends* 37: 26–29.

Giddens, Anthony 1973 *The Class Structure of the Advanced Societies* London: Hutchinson.

Grabb, Edward G 1997 *Theories of Social Inequality: Classical and Contemporary Perspectives* (3rd ed.) Toronto: Harcourt Brace and Company.

Johnston, William and Douglas Baer 1993 "Class consciousness and national contexts: Canada, Sweden and the United States in historical Perspective." *Canadian Review of Sociology and Anthropology* 30, 2: 271–95

Katznelson, Ira 1986 "Working-class formation: constructing cases and comparisons." In Ira Katznelson and Aristide Zolberg, (eds.) *Working-Class Formation* Princeton: Princeton University Press.

Langford, Tom 1994 "Strikes and class consciousness." *Labour/Le Travail* 34: 107–37.

Livingstone, David and J. Marshall Mangan, (eds.) 1996 *Recast Dreams: Class and Gender Consciousness in Steeltown* Toronto: Garamond.

Marx, Karl 1887 *Capital: A Critical Analysis of Capitalist Production,* Vol. 1 Moscow: Progress Publishers, 1953.

Marx, Karl and Frederick Engels 1848 "Manifesto of the Communist Party," In Marx and Engels, *Selected Works in Three Volumes,* Vol. 1 Moscow: Progress Publishers, 1969.

Morissette, René 1991 *Canadian Jobs and Firm Size: Do Smaller Firms Pay Less?* Research Paper No. 35, Analytical Studies Branch, Statistics Canada.

Morissette, René 1997 "Declining earnings of young men." *Canadian Social Trends* 46: 8–12.

Myles, John and Adnan Turegin 1994 "Comparative studies in class structure." *Annual Review of Sociology* 20: 103–24.

Picot, Garnett and Richard Dupuy 1996 *Job Creation by Company Size Class: Concentration and Persistence of Job Gains and Losses in Canadian Companies* Research Paper #93, Business and Labour Market Analysis Division, Statistics Canada.

Picot, Garnett, and John Myles 1995 "Social transfers, changing family structure, and low income among children." Statistics Canada, Analytical Studies Branch, Research Paper No. 82.

Pineo, Peter C. 1985 "Revisions of the Pineo-Porter-McRoberts socioeconomic classification of occupations for the 1981 Census." Research Report No. 125, Program for Quantitative Studies in Economics and Population, McMaster University.

Rinehart, James, Christopher Huxley, and David Robertson 1997 *Just Another Car Factory? Lean Production and Its Discontents* Ithaca: ILR Press.

Statistics Canada 1993 *Occupation: The Nation* Ottawa: Industry, Science & Technology.

Statistics Canada 1997a *The Daily*, October 24, 1997.

Statistics Canada 1997b *Labour Force Update 1, 3: The Self-employed* Ottawa: Minister of Industry.

Stinchcombe, Arthur L. 1990 *Information and Organizations* Berkeley: University of California Press.

Tilly, Louise 1992 *Politics and Class in Milan, 1881–1901* New York: Oxford University Press.

Wannell, Ted 1991 *Trends in the distribution of Employment by Employer Size: Recent Canadian Evidence* Research Paper No. 39, Analytical Studies Branch, Statistics Canada.

Weber, Max 1922 *Economy and Society* Guenther Roth and Claus Wittich (eds.) Berkeley: University of California Press. 1978.

Western, Bruce 1995 "A comparative study of working-class disorganization: Union decline in eighteen advanced capitalist countries." *American Sociological Review* 60: 179–201.

Western, Mark and Erik Olin Wright 1994 "The permeability of class boundaries to intergenerational mobility among men in the United States, Canada, Norway and Sweden." *American Sociological Review* 59: 606–29.

White, Julie 1993 *Sisters and Solidarity: Women and Unions in Canada* Toronto: Thompson Educational Publishing.

Chapter 4

OWNERSHIP, CLASS, AND PUBLIC POLICY

Julia S. O'Connor

(Revised from the previous edition of this volume.)

What thoughtful rich people call the problem of poverty, thoughtful poor people call, with equal justice, the problems of riches (R.H. Tawney [1913] as cited in Field [ed.] 1983: 1)

INTRODUCTION

It is a truism that capitalist economies are inherently unequal in the way they distribute wealth and income. However, comparative analysis indicates that there are vast differences in the policies chosen to deal with such inequalities. The policy choices are influenced not only by the level and distribution of economic resources, but also by the mobilization of power resources within the political structure and by the legacy of past policy choices. These patterns reflect the dual character of contemporary liberal democracies. The twin pillars of these societies are a capitalist economic system and a democratic political system. This duality means that economic and political power can constrain each other in important ways.

This chapter outlines recent studies on the size, concentration, cohesion, and political organization of the Canadian capitalist class. This provides the context for the analysis, in the second section, of key policy options chosen concerning employment, social expenditure, and taxation in Canada since World War II. The concluding section explains the pattern of policy-making in these different areas, with reference to the mobilization of economic and political power resources by social classes.

OWNERSHIP AND CONTROL IN CANADA

Discussion of ownership and control in Canada frequently centres on the small number of families that have accumulated large fortunes; for example, the Bronfman, Reichmann, Thomson, and Weston families. Evidence suggests that this group exercises enormous direct economic power through the ownership of huge conglomerates (Veltmeyer, 1987). Yet these families, whose fortunes illustrate well the role of inheritance in wealth accumulation, form only a minuscule element of the capitalist class, which in turn makes up a small percentage of the Canadian population and is almost exclusively White and male. The Canadian pattern is similar to that in other capitalist countries. In Canada we may be talking about less than four percent of the population, if we include only large and small employers in our definition of the capitalist class (Black and Myles, 1986: 162), or just over six percent of the total population if we include all those who control "production and the employment of others" (Clement, 1990: 468). Based on the broader definition, the capitalist class includes just under nine percent of the male population, compared to less than three percent of the female population (Clement, 1990: 472).

Despite its small size, the capitalist class controls almost all the country's financial and productive wealth. This is the source of its economic control over resources and people, including their opportunity to work. It is also the source of its significant political influence and power. The small size of the capitalist class actually facilitates its economic control. Three other factors that enhance economic control and may enhance political influence and power are the highly concentrated ownership pattern in the Canadian economy, the cohesiveness of the capitalist class, and its political organization.

A key measure of aggregate concentration used by Statistics Canada is the share of corporate assets, revenue, profits, etc. accounted for by ranked groupings of enterprises. An enterprise refers to "a grouping of companies under common control" (Statistics Canada, 1990: 71). By themselves, just the top 25 enterprises in Canada controlled almost half (46 percent) of all corporate assets in 1993, an increase from 41 percent in 1987 (see Grabb, Chapter 1 in this volume). Such aggregate measures of concentration have their counterpart in oligopoly situations within particular sectors. When four or fewer firms supply 50 percent or more of a particular market, the situation is characterized as oligopoly or shared monopoly (Veltmeyer, 1987:24). In Canada this measure "reveals the existence of shared monopolies in the major productive sectors of the economy and in 70 key manufacturing industries," such as the auto industry, the brewing industry, and the cement industry (Veltmeyer, 1987: 24–5). In addition, the level of oligopoly increased between 1970 and 1980. These data are consistent with Carroll's (1988) finding that a relatively small number of densely interlocked conglomerates controls large segments of the Canadian economy.

Concentration of ownership affects not only the product and capital market, but also the labour market. Increased concentration raises the bargaining power of capital compared to labour and government, and thus can further skew the unequal distribution of wealth and income. Concentration of ownership has been recognized as a problem within the Canadian economy for several decades (Report of the Royal Commission on Corporate Concentration, 1978; Royal Commission on the Economic Union and Development Prospects for Canada, 1986). Despite this recognition, much discussion of the Canadian economy, as of other developed capitalist economies, assumes a free market of independent producers regulated by supply and demand. The level of concentration that characterizes the Canadian economy is not consistent with this assumption.

Like other developed capitalist economies, the Canadian economy is not characterized by a single industrial structure or a single labour market (Krahn and Lowe, 1988:84–93). On the contrary, the structure of developed capitalist economies is divided into at least two sectors: a dominant core, monopoly, or primary sector on the one hand, and a peripheral, competitive, or secondary sector on the other. The core sector is dominated by large enterprises that, to varying degrees, control market forces rather than responding to them. Ownership within this sector is highly concentrated, and the market is often closer to pure monopoly (one supplier in the market) than to pure competition. In contrast, the peripheral sector of the economy is characterized by intense competition by relatively small firms.

Concentration of ownership is not an inevitable consequence of economic development. The economic climate, the laws relating to competition and merger activity, and the taxation structure may facilitate or inhibit concentration. Canadian laws regarding competition and mergers are relatively weak, and the tax system, through its rate structure, actually encourages corporate concentration (Wolfson, 1987).

Contrary to conventional wisdom, the Canadian capitalist class is relatively cohesive in comparative terms. Michael Ornstein's analysis of the largest 256 Canadian corporations has demonstrated that the Canadian inter-corporate network is not particularly fragmented when compared to the networks in nine Western European countries and the United States; furthermore, there are no marked divisions between industrial and financial capital, nor between foreign and domestic capital (Ornstein, 1989). Cohesiveness obviously facilitates not only concerted economic decision-making, but also political organization and lobbying. The advantage of capital cohesiveness is enhanced in terms of power relations because of the relatively fragmented Canadian labour movement.

Several sectoral organizations represent the Canadian capitalist class (Coleman, 1986). Nationally, the Canadian Manufacturers Association, the Canadian Chamber of Commerce, and the Business Council on National Issues (BCNI) fulfil this role for large capitalists, while the Canadian Federation of Independent Business (CFIB) and the Canadian Organization of Small Business represent small businesses. Coleman (1986: 272) argues that the system of business organizations in Canada is underdeveloped. However, Languile's analysis of the BCNI challenges this interpretation (Languile, 1987). This organization, founded in 1976, identifies itself as the foremost business representative organization (McQuaig, 1987). It "is composed of the chief executive officers of 150 leading 'Canadian' corporations. These corporations administer in excess of $700 billion in assets, which annually produce more than $250 billion in revenues" (Languile, 1987:42). Languile argues that the BCNI was founded in response to increasing conflict between business and the state in the 1970s, and has the central objective of creating "a policy framework sensitive to the needs of business" (Languile 1987: 77), in particular, the multinational sector. Further, he argues that it has been eminently successful in this project, as reflected in its success in relation to competition policy, fiscal and tax policy, energy policy, and the US-Canada free trade agreement.

Such organizations are one mechanism used by the business community to pursue economic and political interests. Direct participation in political parties and funding of political parties are other key avenues of political influence and power. Comparative research clearly indicates that the mobilization of power resources by social classes influences social and economic policy choices (Castles, 1982; Korpi, 1989; O'Connor and Brym, 1988). However, one key implication of the dual structure of contemporary capitalist societies—the coexistence of a capitalist economic system and a democratic political system—is that, while economic power may be limited through the exercise of political power, political power may be constrained or reinforced by the exercise of economic power.

In summary, ownership of productive resources in the Canadian economy is highly concentrated. The Canadian capitalist class is small and relatively cohesive, exercises considerable economic power, and has the potential to exercise political influence and power directly through business-representative groups and indirectly through political parties. This distribution of economic and political power has major consequences for the policy options chosen to cope with social inequality. I now consider some of the options chosen in three crucial areas: employment, social transfer expenditure, and taxation.

Policy Options and Choices

Employment and Unemployment as Political Choices

Canada's pattern of unemployment since World War II demonstrates a clear upward trend: the average annual percentage of the labour force unemployed was approximately 3 percent in 1945–59, 4.8 percent in 1960–67, 5.4 percent in 1968–73, 7.2 percent in 1974–79, and 9.3 percent in 1980–89. In 1991 unemployment was over 10 percent, although by early 1998 it had declined somewhat, to less than 9 percent. Thus, even in periods of economic prosperity, Canada's unemployment rate has been relatively high. Many Canadian analyses tend to explain unemployment as an inevitable consequence of economic conditions: openness of the Canadian economy, the growth and changing composition of the labour force, and so on. In contrast, comparative studies indicate that the key determinant of unemployment is the policy configuration adopted to cope with economic conditions. Most of these studies conclude that unemployment is amenable to government action, and that high unemployment is not inevitable but is a political and strategic choice (Schmidt, 1984; Scharph, 1984; Therborn, 1986). Of course, external factors, such as Canada's position in the international economic order and its high level of foreign ownership, do constrain the policy options and outlook for the achievement of economic and social goals (Martin, 1986). However, low unemployment is achievable through various policies and within a variety of conditions relating to the size of deficits, economic growth, labour-force supply, labour costs, social expenditure, and the age of industrial structures. What has distinguished low unemployment countries, such as Sweden, Norway, Japan, Switzerland, and Austria, from high-unemployment countries, such as Canada and the United Kingdom, is the extent to which full-employment policies have been consistently pursued and institutionalized over the long term (Therborn, 1986: 23). An institutionalization of the commitment to full employment involves four aspects:

> a) an explicit commitment to maintaining/achieving full employment; b) the existence and use of countercyclical mechanisms and policies; c) the existence and use of specific mechanisms to

> adjust supply and demand in the labour market to the goal of full employment; d) a conscious decision not to use high unemployment as a means to secure other policy objectives (Therborn, 1986:23).

There has been no commitment to full employment in the post-World War II period in Canada, although public policy documents have affirmed the desirability of a *high and stable* level of employment. In general, reducing the level of inflation has been pursued at the expense of high unemployment. This policy has been explicit in the statements of federal finance ministers and the Governor of the Bank of Canada throughout the late 1980s and early 1990s. It is noteworthy that the definition of the "full employment" unemployment rate has been adjusted upwards each decade since the 1950s (Muszynski, 1985). In other words, what is politically acceptable has been adjusted to match the prevailing rate of unemployment.

The one period when there was a relatively active labour-market policy, as reflected in an emphasis on training and job creation, was in the late 1960s and early 1970s. This was a period of relatively widespread progressive social legislation (O'Connor, 1989). It was also a period when the relative power of capitalists and workers was somewhat more evenly balanced than is usually the case (Doern, 1985; Muszynski, 1985: 299). In most other periods, business lobbying has been influential in public-policy formation, with government policies consistently sensitive to its needs (Muszynski, 1985; Mendes, 1990). Changes during the 1980s in employment and training policies are consistent with this interpretation (Prince and Rice, 1989; Mahon, 1990). While these changes reflect a more active approach to labour-market problems, their emphasis is on efficiency rather than equity. Specifically, the focus is on meeting skill shortages and up-grading of skills, and this is to be funded out of the Employment Insurance Fund; the money is to be made available through more stringent conditions of access to employment insurance and a reduction in the duration of benefits. This will disproportionately affect those in the secondary sector of the labour market, in which jobs are low-skilled and insecure and, consequently, the dependence on employment insurance is greatest. The federal government has also withdrawn its partial funding of the Employment Insurance Fund, making employment insurance totally contributory, as in the United States. The major implication of all these changes is that increased costs associated with training have to be met through employment insurance premiums.

In summary, Canada's average annual unemployment rate, until recently, has been consistently rising since the 1960s. This pattern reflects a lack of political commitment to full employment. The recent emphasis on a more active labour-market policy has been achieved at the cost of lessening the protection afforded by the employment insurance system.

Redistribution: Social Transfer Expenditure

In Canada in 1996 the primary distribution of income—that is, the distribution before the payment of taxes and the receipt of social transfer payments—yielded only 0.8 percent of total income to the lowest quintile of families and unattached individuals, and 49.5 percent to the top quintile; in other words, the share of the richest 20 percent was more than 60 times that of the poorest 20 percent (see Urmetzer and Guppy, Chapter 5 in this volume). Social transfer payments and taxation are mechanisms that can be used to correct these gross disparities. Social transfer payments refer to expenditure on programs such as pensions, unemployment insurance, family allowances, and social assistance. Canada's social transfer expenditure, at 11.8 percent of gross domestic product (GDP) in 1989, is relatively low. Amongst 18 Organization for Economic Cooperation and Development (OECD) countries at a broadly similar level of economic development, Canada ranked 13th throughout most of the 1980s. Standardizing Canada's expenditure for need, as reflected in the size of the pension-age population, the dependent-child population, and the labour-force unemployed, does not improve its relative position.

In Canada, as in other economically developed capitalist countries, the social transfer system is more redistributive than the taxation system. In 1996, social transfer payments increased the share of money income of the lowest 20 percent of families and unattached individuals by almost three percentage points, from 0.8 percent to 4.7 percent, while the tax system increased it by just one percentage point more, to 5.7 percent. Even after paying income tax, the richest 20 percent of families and unattached individuals still received 41.1 percent of the total, or more than seven times the share of the poorest 20 percent (Urmetzer and Guppy, Chapter 5 in this volume).

In a review of Canadian social transfer programmes, Keith Banting (1987) identified a pattern of benefit-level erosion or stagnation and increased emphasis on income-tested access from the late 1970s to mid-1980s. The pattern varied by program, with pensions being the most favoured and employment insurance and the Canada Assistance Plan being the least favoured. This pattern continued throughout the rest of the 1980s, and has intensified in the early 1990s. The 1989 budget introduced a clawback on old age security and family allowances of 15 cents on each dollar of individual or family income in excess of $50 000 in the 1989 tax year. Since this threshold is only partially indexed for inflation, it is estimated that, by the end of this decade, the clawback will apply to incomes equal to $37 400 in 1990 (Ross, 1991:14). The effect of this change was to impose a special tax on old age security and family allowances, and to end the universality of these programs. This follows a pattern established in 1985, when child benefit programs were partially de-indexed for inflation. Unless inflation was zero, this meant an effective decrease in benefits of up to 3 percent annually, since payments were increased only by the amount of inflation over 3 percent. The 1992 budget went further in this direction with the elimination of universal family allowances. In effect from January 1993, these will be replaced by targeted programs to those with lower incomes, with further targeting of the working poor.

The 1990 federal budget put a limit of 5 percent on the Canada Assistance Plan payments to British Columbia, Ontario, and Alberta. This was extended for a further three years in the 1991 budget. In 1989, welfare payments for a couple with two children were equivalent to 61 percent of the poverty line in Ontario, 53 percent in British Columbia, and 58 percent in Alberta (National Council of Welfare, 1990: Table 3). In addition to these low levels before the cutbacks, need is increasing rapidly because of restrictions in access to, and on the duration of, employment insurance, and the exhaustion of benefits due to high levels of long-term unemployment. These cutbacks are part of a broader pattern that also includes cutbacks in social housing expenditures and the freezing of Established Programme Payments—that is, payments for health and post-secondary education—to the provinces.

How can this general pattern of cutbacks be explained? Social programs were increasingly under attack while the federal deficit was increasing. In addition, although the process of retrenchment was initiated before they came into office, the ideology and agenda of the former Conservative government of Brian Mulroney was directly linked to the intensification of the process. This ideology is premised on the primacy of the market and a reduced role for government. It is consistent with the opposition by business groups to government action that would limit private market activity. For example, there has been pressure from business groups to move towards the harmonization with the United States of at least some Canadian social programs, especially employment insurance. In addition, these groups have pressed for the targeting of other programs, such as pensions and family allowances, to those perceived to be most in need. This process has now been initiated.

Increased targeting of programs, through income testing or clawbacks, may have the short-term desirable impact of contributing to a lessening of poverty amongst the targeted groups, such as elderly poor people and low-income families, but only if benefit levels are substantially increased. This has not happened. The possible increase in redistribution associated with targeting is achieved at the expense of the universality that ensures a political constituency for the defense of programs in the long term. The objective of increased redistribution could be achieved on a more cost-effective basis through a progressive income tax and the maintenance of universality.

The changes in the social transfer payment system over the past decade did not take place without opposition. Both opposition parties at the time were opposed to these changes, as were the trade union movement, women's organizations, and social policy groups. Moscovitch (1990) has documented the emergence of social sector coalitions throughout the 1980s. Despite the fact that these groups and the broader opposition have scored victories, such as the reversal of the 1985 proposal to de-index old-age pensions, these victories have been short-term, and the long-term trend, as outlined above, reflects an erosion of their view of the social policy framework.

Redistribution: Taxation

The primary function of the tax system is to raise revenue to finance public expenditure. Taxation policies are also mechanisms for achieving social-policy goals, such as lessening social inequality through the redistribution of income and wealth. The Canadian tax system is relatively ineffective as a mechanism for the redistribution of income and it makes no pretense of redistributing wealth.

Redistribution of income through the tax system is dependent on progressive taxes. Taxes are progressive when those with higher incomes pay a higher proportion of their incomes in taxes. In contrast, regressive taxes impose a heavier burden on those with lower incomes. Income taxes have the potential to be progressive, while consumption taxes, since they do not recognize ability to pay, are generally regressive. Changes in the tax system, specifically the introduction of the Goods and Services Tax (GST), tend to increase the yield from consumption taxes.

Tax revenue in Canada, which was approximately 33 percent of GDP annually in the late 1980s, is at the lower end of the OECD range; it is higher than the United States, Japan, and Australia, and less than all western European countries, with the exceptions of Switzerland and Ireland (OECD, 1990). The major revenue generators are income taxes and taxes on consumption, which yielded respectively 46 and 30 percent of tax revenue in 1988. Over time, the percentage of tax revenue accounted for by personal income tax has increased consistently, while that accounted for by corporate income tax has decreased consistently. In 1965, personal income taxation accounted for 23 percent of total tax revenue, while corporate income taxation accounted for 15 percent; in 1988, personal income tax accounted for almost 37 percent of tax revenue, while the contribution of corporate income tax was less than 9 percent (OECD, 1990).

Income Taxation

The progressive potential of the income tax system can be severely limited by the use of tax shelters and tax-avoidance mechanisms, such as tax exemptions, tax allowances, or tax credits. All of these mechanisms result in revenue losses, and are now recognized as invisible government expenditures made through the tax system (Doern, 1989). While objectives, such as the encouragement of saving and investment, may be quite legitimate, tax expenditures may not be the most equitable and/or efficient way of achieving them.

Tax expenditures are generally regressive, providing their greatest benefit to higher-income earners. While all personal income-tax payers benefit from such tax expenditures as the basic personal tax credit and those for the Canada or Quebec pension plans, most tax expenditures exclusively benefit higher-income earners and wealth-holders. An example is the deduction for contributions to registered pension and retirement saving plans. In addition, the corporate tax system includes a wide range of tax expenditures; for example, the deduction of the cost of interest on borrowing for investment and the dividend income-tax credit. In contrast to social programs in general, and such programs as employment insurance and social assistance in particular, tax expenditures rarely come under scrutiny in Parliament or the media. Furthermore, the exact cost of tax expenditures is not known, because they are not officially regarded as government expenditure. The Auditor General of Canada estimated that these expenditures cost the federal tax system $35 to $50 billion in the mid-1980s (Muszynski, 1988:21).

Wealth Non-Taxation

Despite the fact that statistics on the distribution of wealth are less complete than those relating to income, there is clear evidence that the distribution of wealth is substantially more unequal than the distribution of income. While the top 10 percent of families receive 26 percent of income before tax, it is estimated that the top 10 percent of families and unattached individuals hold 53 percent of aggregate household net worth (Davies, 1991:284). Canada is one of the few countries in the OECD that has neither an annual net wealth nor a wealth transfer tax. The federal and provincial governments abolished all inheritance and gift taxes in the late 1960s and early 1970s (Banting, 1991). Canada does have municipal property taxes, and they accounted for over 9 percent of tax revenue in 1988; these may be considered a form of wealth tax, but they are really payments for municipal services, and are neither equitable nor efficient as a mechanism for taxing wealth. Significantly, they are not based on ability to pay nor on net assets; for example, the cost of mortgages is not taken into account.

Taxation of wealth brings strongly into focus the issue of equity or fairness and also the strongly political nature of taxation. Wealth taxes can be instruments of horizontal equity by equalizing the tax burden between wealth-holders and income-earners. They can also be instruments of vertical equity if used to reduce inequality in wealth holdings between different social classes. They rarely achieve this second objective. Wealth taxes do not produce large revenues, due to the combination of high thresholds and exemptions. These thresholds and exemptions reflect problems with the definition of assets, but they also reflect the ability of wealth-holders to resist wealth taxation entirely, or to prevent anything more than a symbolic taxation of their net wealth (Banting, 1991).

Tax Reform

There have been three major attempts to change the Canadian tax system since the 1960s. In 1967, the Royal Commission on Taxation (the Carter Commission) recommended fundamental reforms of the system, with the objective of achieving greater equity. It recommended that all forms of income be considered taxable, including capital gains, that several tax loopholes that benefited high-income earners be closed off, and that reliance on sales taxes be lessened. Due to a very strong and effective campaign by certain sectors of the business community, especially the mineral-extraction sector and associated interests, the recommendations were either watered down or ignored when the tax system was modified in 1971.

The second major attempt to reform the system was made in the 1981 budget. The primary objective was deficit reduction through increasing revenue, but the reforms would have moved the system in the direction of increased equity. Several of the proposals were aimed at lessening the number of tax shelters that had been put in place throughout the 1970s, most of which benefited higher-income individuals and corporations. These changes were, for the most part, successfully opposed by the interests affected, and the changes eventually brought in, such as the lowering of the marginal tax rates, benefited those in the highest income brackets.

The success of the opposition to reform in both these instances reflects the fact that those who benefited from the status quo were "small in number, easily organized, and had a large financial stake in the outcome" (Maslove, 1989: 10). In contrast, while the population likely to gain was large, individual gains were small, and the constituency was dispersed and without an institutional structure around which it could organize.

The changes proposed in the 1987 White Paper on Taxation related primarily to the efficiency of the system rather than to equity. The overall package was designed to complement the government's domestic agenda of lessening public expenditure and public participation in the private market. The timing and nature of the changes were influenced by changes in the United States and were directed towards bringing the system into line with the U.S. system (Maslove, 1989). It is generally agreed that, in contrast to the earlier attempts at reform, the 1988 changes were successful in the sense that there was no organized opposition to them. A number of reasons for this success have been identified. The changes proposed were relatively modest in terms of their possible offense to vested interests. While the use of tax expenditures was decreased, several were maintained for both individuals and corporations, and tax rates for corporations were lowered. There were some moves towards progressivity in the 1988 tax reform, for example, the conversion of personal exemptions and deductions to tax credits, but these were offset by a lessening of the number of tax bands from ten to three and a lowering of the marginal tax rate; that is, a lessening of progressivity. While the lowest 20 percent of the income range gained through tax reform, the top 1 percent of family units received the largest benefits (Maslove, 1989:2). It is noteworthy that the second and controversial element of tax reform—the introduction of the GST—was separated from the first, and was postponed until after the 1988 election. As a general consumption tax, the GST is regressive and was widely opposed by consumers, labour unions, the NDP, the Liberal party, and small-business groups.

This widespread opposition proved ineffective, again illustrating the ineffectiveness of diffuse interests.

In summary, tax policy is a product of political bargaining between contending social forces. However, not all of these groups have equal resources to mount effective opposition. In Canada the pattern is clear: business groups are effective opponents of change that would lessen the benefits they enjoy under the status quo.

DISCUSSION AND CONCLUSIONS

The foregoing review of policy choices in three areas relating to distribution and redistribution of resources in Canada illustrates well the dual structure of liberal democratic societies; that is, a democratic political system and a capitalist economic system. Modifications in the redistribution of societal resources have been made through the political system, but basic economic and social inequalities are pervasive, and the possibilities for the modification of these inequalities are constrained by the unequal distribution of economic resources and power. In addition, the exercise of power at the political level is enhanced for some classes and constrained for others by the exercise of economic power.

The recognition of the role of business-representative organizations in this paper is not meant to imply that state officials act merely as the instruments of the capitalist class, or that the structure of the system automatically results in the pursuit of capitalist class interests. Rather, it is a recognition that, while the mobilization of political power and influence is significant for all social classes, mobilization takes place within an unequal structure of economic power, and this has consequences for policy development and change. The impact of the unequal structure of power is clearly evident when changes in labour market policy, social transfer payments, and taxation over the past decade are considered.

Banting concluded that, by the mid-1980s, "policy changes had not significantly altered the overall impact of the tax-transfer system," in terms of its ability to combat the increasing inequality in market incomes that characterized the recession of the early 1980s (Banting, 1987: 309). The changes throughout the rest of the 1980s and, in particular, the early 1990s, have shifted the balance in social policy towards class and away from citizenship. Increasingly, the demonstration of need, rather than membership in society, is the criterion for access to services. The impact of this shift has been particularly marked because of the increase in unemployment, especially long-term unemployment, and the stagnation, and in some provinces decrease in real terms, in the minimum wage. In addition, the changes in the tax system are likely to lessen opposition to cutbacks in social programmes. Specifically, the increasing burden of taxation on personal income relative to corporate income, and the increase in consumption taxes, are likely to increase the resistance of middle-income voters to maintenance, at more than a minimal level, of social programs from which they do not benefit due to targeting (Bakker, 1991). While on their own, none of the changes outlined above reflects a fundamental threat to the traditional Canadian social policy framework, the persistent trend and scope of incremental changes do reflect a fundamental restructuring of the tax-transfer framework. This signals a consolidation of the liberal nature of the Canadian welfare state.

The liberal welfare state is characterized by state intervention "designed to compensate for market imperfections while remaining compatible with the basic principles of market organization" (Ruggie, 1984: 13). It is characterized by a relatively strong emphasis on income-tested programmes and, while there may be a commitment to universalism, it is universalism with an equal-opportunity focus, as reflected in equality of access to education. This contrasts with the social-democratic welfare state, as exemplified by Norway and Sweden, which is unique in its emphasis on universal citizenship rights, its strong role for the state, its integration of social and economic policy, and its emphasis on the primacy of full employment as a public-policy objective (Korpi, 1983; Ruggie, 1984; Esping-Andersen, 1989).

There is now considerable evidence, based on cross-national analysis, that these contrasting welfare-state regimes reflect the outcome of struggles between social forces at the political and economic levels over long periods of time. The pattern of social-policy development in Canada is consistent with its relatively low level of working-class mobilization and the weak organizational strength of the labour movement. Despite this, there is considerable evidence that working-class mobilization, or fear of it, played a part in the development of all the major social programs in Canada (Guest, 1985; Swartz, 1977; Struthers, 1983). However, the balance of class forces is reflected in the type of welfare state that Canada has; that is, a liberal welfare state as outlined above. Developments over the past decade have enhanced this characterization. In particular, the increased emphasis on targeting of social programs and privatization has shifted the balance towards an emphasis on class and away from rights based on citizenship.

REFERENCES

Bakker, I. 1991 "Canada's social wage in an open economy, 1970–83." pp. 270–87 in D. Drache and M.S. Gertler, (eds.) *The New Era of Global Competition* Montreal: McGill-Queen's University Press.

Banting, K.G. 1991 "The politics of wealth taxes." *Canadian Public Policy* XVII no. 3:351–67.

Banting, K.G. 1987 "The welfare state and inequality in the 1980's." *Canadian Review of Sociology and Anthropology* 24(3):311–38.

Black, D. and J. Myles 1986 "Dependent industrialization and the Canadian class structure: a comparative analysis of Canada, the United States and Sweden." *Canadian Review of Sociology and Anthropology* 23(2):157–81.

Canada 1966 *Report of the Royal Commission on Taxation* Ottawa: Queen's Printer and Controller of Stationery.

Canada 1978 *Report of the Royal Commission on Corporate Concentration* Ottawa: Minister of Supply and Services.

Canada 1985 *Report: Royal Commission on the Economic Union and Development Prospects for Canada* Ottawa: Minister of Supply and Services.

Carroll, W.K. 1988 "Class and corporate power." pp. 53–68 in J. Curtis, E. Grabb, N. Guppy, and S. Gilbert. (eds.) *Social Inequality in Canada: Patterns, Problems, and Policies* Scarborough: Prentice Hall Canada.

Castles, F.G., (ed.) 1982 *The Impact of Parties* London: Sage.

Clement, W. 1990 "Comparative class analysis: locating Canada in a North American and Nordic context." *Canadian Review of Sociology and Anthropology* 27(4): 462–86.

Coleman, W.D. 1986 "Canadian business and the state." pp. 243–90 in K. Banting, (ed.) *The State and Economic Interests* Toronto: University of Toronto Press.

Davies, J.B. 1991 "The distributive effects of wealth taxes." *Canadian Public Policy* XVII no. 3: 279–308.

Doern, G.B. 1985 "The politics of Canadian economic policy: an overview" pp. 1–95 in

G.B. Doern, (ed.) *The Politics of Economic Policy* Toronto: University of Toronto Press.

Doern, G.B. 1989 "Tax Expenditures and Tory Times: More or Less Policy Discretion?" pp. 75–105 in K.A. Graham, (ed.) *How Ottawa Spends 1990–91* Ottawa: Carleton University Press.

Esping-Andersen, G. 1989 "The three political economies of the welfare state." *Canadian Review of Sociology and Anthropology* 26(l): 10–36.

Field, F. 1983 "Introduction: the politics of wealth." pp. 1–8 in F. Field, (ed.) *The Wealth Report 2* London: Routledge and Kegan Paul.

Guest, D. 1985 *The Emergence of Social Security in Canada* Vancouver: University of British Columbia Press.

Korpi, W. 1983 *The Democratic Class Struggle* London: Routledge and Kegan Paul.

Korpi, W. 1989 "Power, politics and state autonomy in the development of social citizenship: social rights during sickness in eighteen OECD countries since 1930." *American Sociological Review* 54: 309–28.

Krahn, H.J. and G.S. Lowe 1988 *Work, Industry and Canadian Society* Scarborough: Nelson Canada.

Languile, D. 1987 "The Business Council on national issues and the Canadian state." *Studies in Political Economy* 27: 41–85.

Mahon, R. 1990 "Adjusting to win? The new Tory training initiative." pp. 73–112 in K.A. Graham, (ed.) *How Ottawa Spends 1990–91* Ottawa: Carleton University Press.

Martin, A. 1986 "The politics of employment and welfare: national policies and international interdependence." pp. 157–241 in K. Banting, (ed.) *The State and Economic Interests* Toronto: University of Toronto Press.

Maslove, A.M. 1989 *Tax Reform in Canada: The Process and Impact* Halifax: Institute for Research in Public Policy.

McQuaig L. 1987 *Behind Closed Doors* Toronto: Viking.

Mendes, S.P. 1990 *The Politics of Unemployment in Sweden and Canada* Stockholm: International Graduate School, Stockholm University.

Moscovitch, A. 1990 "Slowing the steamroller: the federal Conservatives, the social sector and child benefits reform." pp. 171–217 in K.A. Graham, (ed.) *How Ottawa Spends 1990–91* Ottawa: Carleton University Press.

Muszynski, L. 1985 "The politics of labour market policy." pp. 251–304 in G. B. Doern, (ed.) *The Politics of Economic Policy* Toronto: University of Toronto Press.

Muszynski, L. 1988 *Is It Fair? What Tax Reform Will Do to You* Ottawa: Canadian Centre for Policy Alternatives.

National Council of Welfare 1988 *Poverty Profile 1988* Ottawa: Minister of Supply and Services.

National Council of Welfare 1990–91 *Poverty Profile 1989* Ottawa: Minister of Supply and Services.

O'Connor, J.S. 1989 "Welfare expenditure and policy orientation in Canada in comparative perspective." *Canadian Review of Sociology and Anthropology* 26(l): 127–50.

O'Connor, J.S. and R.J. Brym 1988 "Public welfare expenditure in OECD Countries: towards a reconciliation of inconsistent findings." *British Journal of Sociology* XXXIX (1): 47–68.

OECD 1990 *Revenue Statistics of OECD Member Countries 1965–89* Paris: OECD.

Ornstein, M. 1989 "The social organization of the Canadian capitalist class in comparative perspective." *Canadian Review of Sociolgy and Anthropology* 26(l): 151–177.

Prince, M.J. and J.J. Rice 1989 "The Canadian jobs strategy: supply side social policy." pp. 247–88 in K.A. Graham, (ed.) *How Ottawa Spends 1989–90* Ottawa: Carleton University Press.

Ross, D.P. 1991 "The facts on income security,1990." *Perception* 15(2):B–14.

Ruggie, M. 1984 *The State and Working Women: A Comparative Study of Britain and Sweden* Princeton: Princeton University Press.

Schmidt, M.G. 1984 "Labour market performance and inflation in OECD nations—a political institutionalist view." pp. 35–66 in K. Gerlach, W. Peters, and W. Sengelberger, (eds.) *Public Policies to Combat Unemployment in a Period of Economic Stagnation* New York: Campus Verlag.

Struthers, J. 1983 *No Fault of Their Own: Unemployment and the Canadian Welfare State 1914–41* Toronto: University of Toronto Press.

Swartz, D. 1977 "The politics of reform: conflict and accommodation in Canadian health policy." pp. 311–42 in L. Panitch, (ed.) *The Canadian State: Political Economy and Political Power* Toronto: University of Toronto Press.

Therborn, G. 1986 *Why Some Peoples Are More Unemployed Than Others* London: Verso.

Veltmeyer, H. 1987 *Canadian Corporate Power* Toronto: Garamond Press.

Wolfson, M.C. 1987 "Notes on corporate concentration and Canada's income tax." No. 8, Social and Economic Studies Division, Statistics Canada.

FOR FURTHER REFERENCE: POWER AND CLASS

Allahar, Anton and James Cote 1998 *Richer and Poorer: The Structure of Inequality in Canada* Toronto: James Lorimer. The authors use a framework that centres on the role of dominant ideology to examine social inequality in Canada, with a special focus on issues of class, gender, age, and race/ethnicity. A key claim in this analysis is that Canadians are in a state of denial about the existence of major inequalities in their society.

Baer, Douglas (ed.) 1998 *Political Sociology: An Introduction* Toronto: Oxford University Press. This collection includes a number of papers that deal with issues of political power and inequality, the role of the state in contemporary Canadian society, and related questions.

Carroll, William 1992 *Contemporary Social Movements* Toronto: Garamond. This book considers the significance of contemporary social movements in Canada, including the women's movement, the Native Indian movement, and others that focus on important problems of social inequality.

Dunk, Thomas 1991 *It's a Working Man's Town: Male Working-Class Culture in Northwestern Ontario* Montreal and Kingston: McGill-Queen's University Press. Based on a detailed description of male working-class life, this book links a rich account of working-class culture with a sophisticated treatment of theoretical debates on class consciousness.

Bryan Evans and John Shields 1998 *Reinventing the State: Public Administration Reform in Canada* Halifax: Fernwood. This book looks at the trend toward a shrinking role for government in Canadian society in the 1990s, and links this trend to such contemporary developments as globalization and the state economic crisis. The authors suggest alternatives to this reduced role of government in the lives of Canadians.

Forcese, Dennis 1997 *The Canadian Class Structure* (4th ed.) Toronto: McGraw-Hill Ryerson. This text focuses on class-based inequalities in Canada, but also touches on other topics in social inequality, including gender, age, ethnicity, and race.

Laxer, Gordon 1989 *Open for Business* Toronto: Oxford University Press. In this monograph, Laxer employs a comparative perspective to examine the historical pattern of foreign ownership in the Canada economy.

Laxer, Gordon 1991 *Perspectives on Canadian Economic Development: Class, Staples, Gender, and Elites* Toronto: Oxford University Press. This is an edited collection of classic writings in the genre of political economy. It is particularly useful as a source for some of the earlier and best writings from this critical perspective.

Section 2

SOCIO-ECONOMIC BASES OF SOCIAL INEQUALITY

In the previous section we saw that the private ownership of productive economic property contributes to a fundamental social division in Canadian society. For a very small number of Canadians, variously defined as an elite or as a ruling, upper, or capitalist class, ownership provides power and privilege. However, beyond ownership there are many other dimensions of social inequality, three of which are explored in this section. These include inequalities that are tied to *income, wealth, and poverty*; *occupation*; and *education*.

These three bases of inequality are closely interrelated. A causal connection tends to run from education through occupation to income, in that schooling typically affects job prospects, and a person's job largely determines income in most cases. Furthermore, income has consequences beyond an individual's own lifetime, influencing, for example, the educational opportunities of one's children, and thus their jobs and incomes too. Several issues involved in this complex interrelationship should be emphasized.

First, in the study of these forms of inequality, it is necessary to clarify whether the focus is on individuals or families. When seeking to explain the occupations or incomes of people, sociologists normally study individuals. However, when looking at intergenerational job mobility or the inheritance of wealth, the focus is mainly on families. Thus, the unit of observation (individuals or families) should be made clear.

Second, discussions about inequality often involve the idea of transmission across generations. To what degree is social inequality *reproduced* over time? Research of this type investigates how family origin or family background influences the attainment or inheritance of education, occupation, or income levels. Questions of the openness or rigidity of opportunities in society are central here, as is the awareness that inequalities have a history that often endures through multiple generations.

Third, the relations between the three dimensions—income or wealth, occupation, and education—are not fixed and, although they are intertwined, the associations among them are not perfect. That is, even though these forms of inequality are closely tied in Canada, some people with little education do earn large incomes, for example. Such individuals are relatively rare, however, as are people who live in poverty or lack jobs, despite having high levels of education. In other words, the connections linking these three types of inequality are not deterministic, but *probabilistic* (although often quite strong).

Fourth, while social inequality is a feature of all societies, the *degree of inequality is variable*. At different times and in different societies the amount of inequality varies. Sociologists studying inequality in Canada, therefore, have been concerned with how inequality here compares to that in other countries, and also with how levels of inequality may be changing over time.

Explanations for the levels of social inequality in Canada often vary. While this section of the book stresses facts about inequality, issues of interpretation are equally important. Contrary to popular wisdom, facts do not speak for themselves. For example, how are we to understand or explain the consistent finding that women on average earn less money than men? As the selections in Section 3 indicate (see, e.g., the Saunders and Creese and Beagan chapters) there are several competing and even conflicting reasons that sociologists have put forward to explain such examples of gender inequality.

Throughout this book, you will encounter certain ideas that are consistent touchstones for interpreting social inequality. Two of these basic perspectives are raised here, so that you will recognize, compare, and assess them when you think about the reasons behind social inequality in Canada.

One way people try to explain inequality is by pointing to its positive consequences for societal well-being. This line of reasoning holds that people will only be motivated to acquire useful skills and to work at responsible jobs if they receive high rewards for doing so. In this way, people with drive, talent, and ability will be encouraged to use these attributes for the benefit of both themselves and the society in general. From this perspective, tangible incentives, including high incomes, prestige, and influence, must go to those occupying key positions in society. The *achievement* principle is central to this explanation for differences in income, prestige, or rank (see Davis and Moore, 1945, for more detail).

A very different line of argument is taken by those who emphasize that certain groups in society benefit more than others from the way in which social structures are organized. Tensions and disputes over aspects of inequality are seen to stem from the opposing interests of different groups, as one group attempts to control profit or privilege at the expense of another group. For some researchers, these interest groups are class-based, while for others they are defined by non-class factors such as gender or ethnicity. In all of these instances, however, the interpretation is that conflict or struggle is the key to understanding social inequality. The struggle for control over economic resources, power, and privilege is understood as the key motor of social change (see, e.g., Wright, 1985, for a class-based account of this perspective).

The tension between these two perspectives underlies much of the writing on inequality, although there are several variants of each approach. In general, though, those who stress achievement tend to focus on equality of opportunity. They also emphasize the freedom of individuals to pursue their own goals, interests, and destiny. However, an emphasis on equality of condition or outcome, for all people, usually comes from those who argue that the control and accumulation of power and profit by one group gives them (and their children) an unfair advantage in society. These competing ideas continue to inform much of the discussion about the causes of social inequality in the present day.

INCOME, WEALTH, AND POVERTY

We begin this section by exploring the distribution of money. At the extremes of the income distribution are affluence and poverty, the rich and the poor. The readings in this section examine how economic rewards are distributed in Canadian society, how that distribution has changed over time, what the government has and has not done in attempting to influence the distribution, and what arguments are made for and against income redistribution.

The first reading, by Peter Urmetzer and Neil Guppy, explains that while the economic pie has grown bigger in the post-World War II era, the sizes of the slices apportioned to various income groups have remained remarkably stable. What makes this surprising is that these decades since World War II have often been described in terms of a growing welfare state. Whatever else the state may have done during this period, it is not true that the government played Robin Hood, taking from the rich and giving to the poor. The state looked after everyone's welfare equally, such that very little, if any, redistribution of income occurred. More recently, that is in the 1980s and 1990s, the size of the economic pie has not grown, for wages and salaries have been stubbornly stable. For many people this has meant working harder and longer just to keep pace with inflation. One consequence is the resistance of Canadians to any tax increases.

Many believe that the government uses the tax system to collect from the rich to give to the poor. As Urmetzer and Guppy describe, the poor do receive some transfer income, but so too do the rich. The result is that little income redistribution occurs. To understand this it is important to realize that we pay tax in many forms—sales tax, income tax, gasoline tax, excise tax, and so forth. Some of these are progressive taxes, where the size of the tax bite increases with your income, while others are regressive, in that the tax bite is bigger for those with less income. People with large incomes are also able to use tax shelters (and to hire well-paid tax accountants to find such shelters). The net result is that the overall rate of tax paid by all Canadians varies surprisingly little over the entire income scale.

Income, however, is only one part of the material resources Canadians possess. For some, the super-rich, income is far less important than are assets. Wealth is accumulated and stored in land, buildings, stock, precious metals, art, and so on. As James Davies demonstrates in his paper on the distribution of wealth in Canada, there are some extremely rich families in this country. In fact, comparisons with the U.S. show that there are more rich families per capita in Canada. Furthermore, the distribution of wealth is far more unequal than is the distribution of income, with inheritance of wealth being the major cause of this pattern.

At the other extreme of the distribution of economic resources is poverty. The National Council of Welfare monitors poverty in Canada and publishes many informative papers on issues faced by the poor in this country. The paper we reproduce here begins with a description of how Statistics Canada calculated their "low-income lines" (a phrasing which avoids the word poverty!). Details are also provided on how poverty lines compare to the expectations of Canadians about how much money is absolutely necessary to support a family. Poverty lines are also contrasted with average incomes, showing just how far the poverty line falls below the typical earnings of Canadians.

Juxtaposing poverty and wealth raises the issue of the actual distribution of economic benefits. In the final paper in this section, Morley Gunderson discusses the pros and cons of income redistribution. What would be the advantages and disadvantages of taking money from the rich and giving it to the poor? As you read his paper, keeping Urmetzer and Guppy's results in mind is important. Very little redistribution of income occurs in Canada. As a policy concern, the question is whether or not redistribution should occur, and if it should, how it should be done.

OCCUPATION

People's occupations are of fundamental importance, because working is what many of us do with most of our waking lives. Our jobs or careers are often at the core of our personal identities, frequently defining who we are in our own minds and in the eyes of others. And, of course, our occupations generate the incomes on which most of us make a living. Occupations also provide at least an approximate measure of where we stand on a wide variety of other inequality dimensions. These include income, education, skill level, degree of responsibility in the workplace, amount of authority over other workers, prestige ranking, and so on.

Perhaps for these reasons, occupation has been viewed by some researchers as the best overall indictor of a person's general social-class location or socio-economic rank. The relevance of occupation to the field of social inequality is revealed in the range of problems involving work or occupation that researchers in this field have addressed. These include, for example, the changing composition of the labour force, the extent to which occupational status depends on the attainment of educational credentials, the degree to which the occupational backgrounds of parents influence the occupational attainments of their children, and the problems posed by the changing nature of work in technologically-advanced societies.

Such issues form the focus of the three papers chosen for our section on occupational inequality. In the first article, Douglas Baer looks at the increasingly important role that higher education plays in determining occupational attainment in Canada. This paper shows, in particular, that having a post-secondary education, though not a guarantee of occupational success, has recently become even more important as a necessary pre-condition for getting the "good" jobs in management and professional-technical fields. Those who lack advanced education, on the other hand, are more likely to be relegated to the "bad" or routine jobs in the clerical, blue-collar, and lower-level service sectors. These latter types of job are typically lower-paying, less secure, and less likely to lead to a higher career position in the future than jobs that require post-secondary education.

In the second chapter, Andrew Heisz provides evidence on changes in job tenure in the Canadian work force. He finds that, between the early 1980s and mid-1990s, there was a polarization of new jobs in Canada into more short-term and more long-term employment, with a decline in medium-term jobs (those lasting between one and five years). Heisz also considers whether this pattern varies by gender, age, region of residence, industry type, and education.

In the final chapter on occupation, Graham Lowe provides a detailed analysis of Canada's occupational structure, with special concern for the nature of present-day labour markets and the future of work. Among the major issues considered are the movement to a service-based economy in recent decades, the trend toward more "non-standard" work, including temporary and part-time employment, and the prospects for a growing gap between "good" and "bad" jobs. This selection also addresses the question of gender segregation and gender inequality in the Canadian labour force, including the gap in earnings between male and female workers. Throughout the chapter, the author considers the possible implications of several of these issues for policy-makers in business and government.

EDUCATION

How much education a person attains is arguably the most important of the three inequality dimensions under discussion in this section—income, occupation, and education. The argument would be that education is the most important because educational credentials are among the best predictors of attainment of the other two rewards. Studies of social mobility show this to be the case (Creese, Guppy, and Meissner, 1991). Education is very often the sole avenue to the best jobs and the highest salaries.

It is little wonder, then, that academic researchers, educational practitioners, and politicians have devoted substantial attention to the question of providing equality in the opportunity to acquire education. The first selection by Elaine Fournier, George Butlin, and Philip Giles asks how a child's educational attainment is affected by how much education his or her mother and father possessed. If there were complete equality of educational opportunity in Canada, this effect would be minimal, so that schooling attainment would depend upon your own effort and ability and not be strongly influenced by your parents' education. Conversely, if the level of education of your parents affects your own educational attainment, this suggests that equality of educational opportunity is not strong in Canada. Fournier, Butlin, and Giles find that people's chances of proceeding to higher levels of schooling are linked to their parents' level of education. Furthermore, there is evidence that this link between parental schooling and children's schooling is the most powerful predictor of educational attainment (e.g., Guppy and Davies, 1998).

Scott Davies picks up the theme of explaining how these inequalities in educational attainment come about. Why, he asks, does family socio-economic status have such an important impact on schooling destinies? He examines a host of explanations, from purely economic to cultural. If money, for example, were the key, then we would expect to see the link between parents' education and their offspring's education greatly reduced, if not eliminated, in countries where post-secondary schooling was free. There is no evidence to support this, which suggests that money is not the key factor. Another explanation could depend on the expectations of working- versus middle-class parents. Perhaps, Davies suggests, it is the social organization of family life that is the major explanatory factor. Working-class parents undervalue education as compared to middle-class parents. Perhaps, Davies suggests, it is the social organization of family life that is the major explanatory factor. Working-class families have more rigid working lives, buffeted by shift work, tiring commuting schedules, moonlighting, and so forth, all of which make it harder for them to contribute to school-related activities than for middle-class parents. As Davies concludes, explaining the link between family origin and educational destination has proven to be a very difficult issue. His paper makes a significant contribution to such explanations, however, by showing us some promising lines of argument.

The final selection by Neil Guppy, Scott Davies, and Alison Ludditt shifts the focus. They look at an idea for reforming the way we organize schooling. In many countries the idea of charter schooling has taken hold. This would give local neighbourhood schools the ability to specify particular strengths and foci that they would like to develop. Parents and students would be encouraged to select schools that they felt were the best for their children. All schools would need to teach the basic curriculum, but some schools might choose to emphasize one or more qualities, such as computing, drama, athletics, music, outdoor education, or science. This could effectively shift more power to local school educators and to parents who participated in school decision-making. What would the consequences be for students from different backgrounds? It is this latter issue that is one focus of their paper. In this discussion they also highlight another aspect of social inequality. How should resources be allocated in a society? How much influence should markets have in comparison to governments? This is a second issue that the paper addresses.

REFERENCES

Creese, Gillian, Neil Guppy, and Martin Meissner 1991 *Ups and Downs on the Ladder of Success: Social Mobility in Canada* Ottawa: Statistics Canada.

Guppy, Neil and Scott Davies 1998 *The Schooled Society: Changes and Challenges in Canadian Education* Ottawa: Statistics Canada and Nelson Publishing.

INCOME, WEALTH AND POVERTY

Chapter 5

CHANGING INCOME INEQUALITY IN CANADA

Peter Urmetzer and Neil Guppy

(An original chapter written for this volume.)

INTRODUCTION

Misconceptions about income inequalities are widespread. Frequently, information is tainted by personal impressions and media accounts. Thus, while the homeless have become a common and very visible feature of the urban landscape, they comprise only a small portion of Canada's population. The same is true for sports stars and executives earning the seven figure salaries reported in the media: Only a small number of Canadians fall into this million dollar club. These impressions, although powerful in influencing our perceptions about inequality, are unrepresentative. Most Canadians fall outside the extremes of excessive poverty and wealth. The majority of people in this country have such typical incomes that they remain inconspicuous to both the average observer and the sensationalist eye of the media.

Such "typicality," however, does not mean that inequalities do not exist beyond these extremes. Canada's economy has historically followed a cycle of bust and boom, and not all Canadians are affected equally by these cycles (see the following on poverty). For example, a recession is directly mirrored by a slowdown in housing starts, causing lay-offs in the construction industry, while universities and colleges may benefit from the same downturn as more people upgrade their skills, translating into more jobs for teachers. Examples such as these illustrate that we need a more comprehensive way of looking at inequality, an approach that does more than focus narrowly on the rich and the poor. In other words, we want to move beyond personal and journalistic accounts which tend to gravitate towards the unusual and to apply a more rigorous, less biased method, inclusive of all Canadians. How this is done and what the resulting data are will be the focus of this chapter.

INCOME

Some people may question the relevance of asking questions about income inequality, especially in a wealthy country such as Canada. From a social science perspective, patterns of economic inequality are important because they reveal the consequences of various social processes and political decisions. Although seldom acknowledged, many political debates directly address issues of distribution since economic policies have consequences benefiting some while disadvantaging others. The point is that we need some way of assessing these outcomes. Claims about the superiority of market forces over government intervention are precisely that, claims. Evidence of how these policies affect income distribution becomes an indispensable tool in evaluating these claims. Invariably, a cut in social programs, a change in tax structure or interest policy makes some people richer and some people poorer, and we want to know who. The abolition of minimum wage legislation, resulting in higher profits for employers and lower pay for workers, does not affect everyone equally. The increased cost of borrowing suggests that a policy of high interest rates also has diverse consequences, as the borrower's larger interest payments end up as increased profits in the pockets of investors. One person's loss is another person's gain. This holds true for the majority of economic policy decisions we have grappled with as a country over the past decade—the struggle over the welfare state, free trade, the deficit, and 'globalization.' Rarely are the consequences of these decisions neutral.

Statistics on income distribution serve to illuminate, at least indirectly, the outcome of these policies. As we shall see, careful examination of trends in income distribution reveal interesting patterns about the organization of Canadian society. It is this question, then, that provides the primary focus of this chapter: how has income inequality changed in Canada in recent decades? We begin by tracing changes in income.

Subsequent to the poverty and hardship of the Depression years in the 1930s, Canadians have experienced relative affluence. From the 1950s right through to the late 1970s, Canadians, whether as individuals or in families, enjoyed rising incomes and general economic prosperity. This is true even after inflation is taken into consideration.[1] Figure 5-1 charts the average real income of Canadian families from 1951 through to 1996, showing two distinct periods: i) rising real incomes year upon year from 1951 to 1979, and ii) income stagnation from 1980 through to 1996.

The growth of real incomes in the 1950s through the 1970s reflects a period of sustained and unprecedented expansion in the Canadian economy. Throughout this period, levels of productivity rose, largely based on an increase in technology and a more highly skilled labour force. Organized labour succeeded in tying wages to productivity and, consequently, earnings grew. However, beginning in the early 1980s, family earnings began to stagnate. This occurred despite the increasing number of married women entering the workforce (from 50 percent in 1980 to about 65 percent in 1995). Figure 5-1 shows that although average earnings fluctuated somewhat, family purchasing power remained essentially flat from 1980 to 1996.[2] But averages suffer from a major shortcoming: they only measure central tendency and are silent about dispersion or variation around that central point. In order to gain a better understanding of these variations we need an easy method of examining the *distribution* of earned income.

FIGURE 5-1 Average income for families and unattached individuals, Canada 1951–1996 (in constant 1995 dollars)

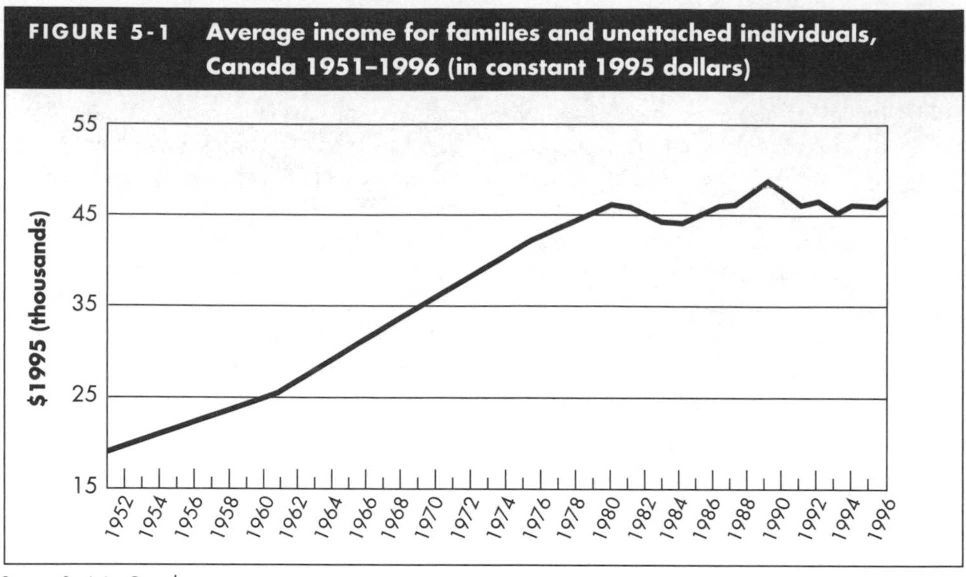

Source: Statistics Canada.

Distribution of Income: Quintiles

A common way to measure income distribution is to divide the population into a small number of equal-size groups, usually fifths, and then examine each group's relative share of the total income. An intuitively appealing way of doing this is to imagine a queue that contains all the families in Canada. At the head of this line is the family that earns the highest income; at the tail, the family that earns the least. This line is then divided into five equal-size groups called fifths or quintiles. Next, the sum of the income of each of the five groups is calculated. The resulting sum for each group is then presented as a portion of the total income of all five quintiles (or the total income of all families in Canada). As Table 5-1 shows, for the top quintile this turns out to be 44.5 percent in 1996. So, of all the money earned in Canada in 1996, 44.5 percent of it was earned by the wealthiest 20 percent of families. Such disproportion means that only 55.5 was left for the remaining 80 percent. The lowest income earners, the 20 percent of people at the end of the line, shared a meagre 4.6 percent of all income.

If income were distributed perfectly equally in Canada, every group would be allotted an identical share of income (i.e., 20 percent). But in reality this is not so. As the table shows, the highest quintile is successful in acquiring more than double its 20 percent share, while the lowest quintile receives less than a quarter of its fifth. Another way to compare these figures is to contrast the highest and lowest quintiles, a calculation which reveals that the former receives almost 10 times the income of the latter.

Table 5-1 also tracks how income shares have changed between the years 1951 and 1996. At first glance, there appears to have been little change in the proportion of income that each quintile receives. Closer examination, however, shows a shift of approximately three percent from the second and middle quintiles to the two highest quintiles. Surprisingly, perhaps, it is not the lowest of

TABLE 5-1 Percentage of total before-tax income going to families and unattached individuals by quintile, 1951–1996

Income quintile	1951	1961	1971	1981	1991	1995	1996
Lowest quintile	4.4	4.2	3.6	4.6	4.7	4.7	4.6
Second quintile	11.2	11.9	10.6	10.9	10.3	10.2	10.0
Middle quintile	18.3	18.3	17.6	17.6	16.6	16.4	16.3
Fourth quintile	23.3	24.3	24.9	25.1	24.7	24.5	24.7
Highest quintile	42.8	41.4	43.3	41.7	43.8	44.1	44.5

Source: Statistics Canada, Cat. 13-207-XPB.

the quintiles, the point of focus of most poverty studies, where the majority of losses have occurred, but in the second and middle quintiles. The top quintile, which arguably needs it the least, has also experienced the biggest increase since 1951, an increase of 1.7 percent. Between 1981 and 1996 this increase is especially evident, a total of 2.8 percentage points.

As a matter of fact, between 1981 and 1996, the top quintile is the only one that can claim an increase in its share of the national income, with all of the three middle quintiles losing ground. Meanwhile, the share for the bottom quintile has remained essentially constant. This confirms what many middle income Canadians are feeling—that it is increasingly difficult to make a living in the nineties. A 2.8 percentage point gain for the top quintile may appear to be a trivial amount, but given that the total income generated in Canada surpasses half a trillion dollars a year, this increase translates into more than 14 billion dollars—enough to eliminate poverty in Canada (Osberg 1992: 42).

Transfers and Taxes

The figures in Table 5-1 reflect all forms of income. For example, for those families in the top quintile, earnings from stock market dividends, real estate holdings, pension plans, and professional salaries would be included. By comparison, earnings in the bottom quintile primarily consist of income from employment insurance, pension plans, wages, and government assistance (often informally referred to as 'welfare'). The crucial difference to note here is between *market* income and government *transfers*. That is, income is either *market* based (wages, return on investment, etc.) or collected in the form of *transfers* (payments designed to help people who are out of work or retired, including social assistance, employment insurance payments, and government pensions). Once we acknowledge this important distinction, the distribution of income changes dramatically. As shown in Table 5-2, when only market income is considered, the lowest quintile receives less than 1 percent of all income (0.8 percent), while the highest quintile earns nearly half (49.5 percent). Unlike 'total income,' the distribution of market income has not remained static over time, but intensified. Evidence indicates that since the early 1970s high income families have consistently acquired a larger share of the national income, with lower income earners increasingly having to depend on transfers.[3] In summary, pretransfer incomes (shown in Table 5-2), when considered in the context of the distribution shown in Table 5-1, suggest that the transfer system via government is quite effective in redistributing income.

Beyond the transfer system, the tax system can also be used to aid redistribution.

TABLE 5-2 Percentage of different income concepts going to families and unattached individuals by quintile, 1995

Income quintile	Income before transfers	Total money income	Income after taxes
Lowest quintile	0.8	4.7	5.7
Second quintile	7.5	10.2	11.5
Middle quintile	16.1	16.4	17.2
Fourth quintile	26.2	24.5	24.5
Highest quintile	49.5	44.1	41.1

Source: Statistics Canada, Cat. 13-210-XPB.

Income tax, at least in theory, is a progressive tax in that high income earners are taxed at a higher rate than low income earners.[4] The government then takes these revenues and redistributes them in favour of poorer families. In other words, what high income earners pay in the form of proportionally higher taxes goes into the pockets of poorer families as proportionally higher transfers. The end result is a more equitable distribution of income.

For 1995, the most recent data available, the redistributing effect of income taxation is apparent, albeit only minimally so (see Table 5-2). Only the highest quintile experienced a decrease in its share (3 percentage points), with all other quintiles either staying the same (the fourth) or gaining (the first, second, and third). The second quintile experienced the largest increase (1.3 percentage points). Comparing the 'income before transfers' and 'income after taxes' columns shows the effect income tax has on national income, and the redistributive characteristic of the welfare state becomes obvious. Here is good evidence of the state acting as the legendary Robin Hood, taking from the rich and giving to the poor.

But this is not the full picture. At this point, we have only examined income taxes, and the bulk of government revenues comes from consumption (e.g., sales taxes, excise taxes) and property taxes. In theory, consumption taxes are flat, as everyone pays exactly the same rate, regardless of income. However, many economists and sociologists have argued that in practice consumption taxes are effectively regressive; that is, low income earners end up paying a higher proportion of their income in consumption taxes than do high income earners. This conclusion is based on two related arguments.

One line of argument points out that the consumption tax on any one item constitutes a higher proportion of the income of a poor family than a rich one. This is best illustrated by an example. Compare two families, the Browns and the Greens, similar in many respects, with the exception of income. After income tax, the Greens earn half ($30 000) of what the Browns do ($60 000). Now, both families purchase a car costing $10 000. The sales tax on this purchase, including the Goods and Services Tax (GST) and Provincial Sales Tax (PST), would amount to around $1 500 in most of Canada's provinces. Given the differences in their income, the net result is that the Greens spend 60 percent of their monthly (or 0.5 percent of their annual) income on the consumption tax on this item, and the Browns only 30 percent of their monthly (or 0.25 percent or their annual) income (see for example Pass and Lowes 1993).

The argument can be made, though, that the wealthier family is likely to spend more on a car, say $20 000, and thus end up paying the equivalent proportion of consumption tax. And this is a major shortcoming of this argument: it rests on hypothetical examples which can easily be countered using other hypothetical examples. The argument that consumption taxes are regressive, however, gathers steam once spending patterns are taken into consideration. This second criticism focuses less on hypothetical examples and more on outcomes. The fact is that families in lower income brackets are forced to spend most of their income and therefore contribute a higher proportion of it to taxes. For example, a family earning $30 000 a year is likely to spend all of its income on food, shelter, clothing, and other basics. By contrast, a family earning $300 000 a year can afford to save or invest a considerable portion of its income in mutual funds or real estate holdings. Money saved is not subject to consumption taxes. Moreover, not all products and services are taxed equally. For example, the purchase of a home is not subject to provincial sales tax (PST), and post-secondary tuition fees are taxed by neither the provincial nor federal government. We know that high income earners are more likely to be homeowners or send their kids to university, thus benefiting from these exemptions. Low income earners, on the other hand, have less opportunity to take advantage of these tax breaks and therefore end up paying proportionally more of their income in taxes. Thus, with a consumption tax the proportion of tax paid increases as earnings decrease, the direct opposite to the relationship found with income tax. As we saw above, income tax is structured in such a way that high income earners pay a higher proportion of tax than do low income earners, a structure that is considered progressive. Applying similar reasoning reveals consumption tax to be regressive.

Once both income and consumption taxes are taken into consideration, the overall redistributing effect of the Canadian taxation system becomes less apparent. As Hunter (1993: 104) explains, "what taxes on income give, ... taxes on spending take away." In other words, income taxes help to redistribute, but consumption taxes erode much of this redistributive effect. The final outcome is that after different taxes (and tax breaks) are considered, very little Robin Hood remains in the welfare state.

Income Distribution in Other Countries

How fair is the distribution of income in Canada? In the abstract, this is a difficult question, and a response depends on all kinds of philosophical assumptions about merit and property ownership. On a more practical level, though, we can answer this question by comparing Canada's income distribution to that found in other countries. Table 5-3 shows that Canada shares its income more equally than the United States, Australia, or the United Kingdom, countries that share cultural ties and economic philosophies that date back to the colonial days of the British Empire (with the exception of Quebec, of course). Canada also has the wealthiest middle quintiles of all the countries in the table. Canada, however, does less well when it comes to the lower quintiles. This is true in comparison to Western European countries in general and Scandinavian countries in particular. Not surprisingly, Sweden, often heralded as the exemplar of the welfare state, also has the most equitable distribution of income found in the West. What *is* surprising is that Japan, a country which cannot even boast a welfare state (but has very low unemployment), has the most generous distribution toward the lowest quintile. (Interestingly, it is also more generous toward the highest quintile than is Sweden).

Table 5-3 demonstrates that income can be distributed in a variety of ways and follows no overall or consistent pattern. Income

TABLE 5-3 Income distribution according to quintiles in various countries (various years)

	Lowest Quintile	Second Quintile	Middle Quintile	Fourth Quintile	Highest Quintile
Canada*	5.7	11.8	17.7	24.6	40.2
USA	4.7	11.0	17.4	25.0	41.9
UK	4.6	10.0	16.8	24.3	44.3
Sweden	8.0	13.2	17.4	24.5	36.9
Germany	7.0	11.8	17.1	23.9	40.3
Australia	4.4	11.1	17.5	24.8	42.2
Singapore	5.1	9.9	14.6	21.4	48.9
Hong Kong	5.4	10.8	15.2	21.6	47.0
Philippines	6.5	10.1	14.4	21.2	47.8
Thailand	5.6	8.7	13.0	20.0	52.7
Korea (Rep)	7.4	12.3	16.3	21.8	42.2
Malaysia	4.6	8.3	13.0	20.4	53.7
Japan	8.7	13.2	17.5	23.1	37.5
Russia	3.7	8.5	13.5	20.4	53.8
Mexico	4.1	7.8	12.5	20.2	55.3
Brazil	2.1	4.9	8.9	16.8	67.5
South Africa	3.3	5.8	9.8	17.7	63.3

*Figures for Canada vary slightly from those presented in Table 5-1 because of different working definitions.
Source: World Bank Development Report, 1995, 1996, 1997..

is least equally distributed in Russia, South Africa, Mexico, and particularly Brazil, where the highest quintile receives over two-thirds of the national income. In these countries, a wealthy top quintile occurs at the expense of an impoverished bottom quintile. This, however, does not necessarily have to be the case, as a wealthy top quintile can also mean less affluent middle classes, as occurs in many South East Asian countries. In Hong Kong, Singapore, and Philippines, for example, the high incomes of the top quintile are offset by relatively poor middle (second, middle, and fourth) quintiles.

In comparison to countries in South America or Asia, Canada's distribution is more equitable. But this could change, especially as the assault on government social programs continues. The elimination or reduction of social programs would dramatically alter the distribution of income in this country, no doubt most directly affecting those in the lower quintiles. The contagion of cuts that has swept Canada in recent decades has raised concerns about the "Brazilianization" of our economy, a term that is meant to reflect the stark inequities that plague Brazil, a country completely lacking a welfare state (Therborn 1986). The fear is that by investing too much faith in markets, some governments, including ours from time to time, have turned their backs on social programs and ignored the poor. But the stability of income shares in this country suggests that this view may be overly pessimistic. This stability, however, does not mean income shares are immutable. Why they have stayed so consistent is therefore worthy of closer examination.

STABILITY

Given the dramatic changes that Canadian society has undergone since the Second World War, it is remarkable how obdurately stable the distribution of income has remained. In addition to an increase in the participation of women in the labour force and a decline in industrial jobs, these changes include a marked increase in government expenditures on social programs. The fact that income distribution has remained more or less constant alongside the increase in government involvement has led some commentators to question the efficacy of the welfare state as a mechanism for the redistribution of income (e.g., Teeple 1995). An often referred to study conducted by Hewitt (1977) argues that the redistributive effect of the welfare state is minimal at best. Hewitt's study also shows that the Canadian welfare state lags behind in its redistributive effectiveness, particularly when compared to Western European countries. Given the monumental and pervasive presence of the welfare state in Canadian society—in the form of employment insurance, pensions, education, health services, and other services too numerous to mention—most Canadians would, no doubt, find such a conclusion surprising.

On the face of it, it seems almost inconceivable that Canadian society would be identical in the absence of the welfare state. Yet the quintile approach shows precisely that: between the early 1950s and the mid-1990s, a period which saw an explosion of welfare state services, income shares changed very little. Does this mean that the seemingly interminable political wrangling over social programs in Canada is essentially about nothing? The answer to this is a resounding no. Those who claim that welfare is ineffective must take note that the quintile approach itself does not reveal important changes in Canada's income composition. As we saw, the most common way to present quintiles is total income; i.e., market and transfer income combined. This approach ignores how the composition of income has changed over the years, specifically the ratio of market income to government transfers. Were it not for these transfers, the poorest group would be allotted less than one percent of the national wealth, less even than in Brazil.

Another change that quintiles ignore is that Canada's most costly social programs, such as health and education, are not included in income statistics, because they are received in kind (i.e., as a service) rather than as monies. Nonetheless, this has an effect on income distribution, in that *not* having to pay for health care or education translates into a decrease in expenditure. This saving rises proportionally as income declines. For example, $1 000 for an operation represents a bigger portion of income saved for someone in the bottom quintile (average income for individuals and families, $10 760 for 1995) than the top quintile ($99 976 same categories, same year) and therefore can be considered as contributing toward equality.

These observations are not consistent with views that perceive little utility in the welfare state. The reason income shares have stayed so consistent over the years is precisely because of social programs (transfers) that have steadily kept pace with a decline in market income. In short, income distribution has remained relatively uniform because of the welfare state, not despite it.

CONCLUSION

Because this chapter is an introduction to the subject, we have just scratched the surface of the various ways one can study income inequality. We have examined only how income varies among the different quintile groups and neglected the effects on income attainment of important sociological variables such as sex, ethnicity, and region.

Another intriguing question asks who occupies the different quintiles? Individuals may occupy the lowest quintile, but do so only on a temporary basis (e.g., retired individuals drawing a small pension [counted as income], but relying on extensive savings accumulated over a lifetime [not counted as income]). Most people occupy the lowest quintile at some point in their lives—as students, when learning a trade, when retired or unemployed —without suffering from the consequences normally associated with poverty, such as inadequate diet or shelter. This dynamism is not reflected in the figures. Conversely, some individuals are permanent occupants of the lower quintiles. This includes the homeless, who have increased their presence in most Canadian cities, yet are not included in this type of study, primarily because they are notoriously difficult to track in income surveys.

This chapter is more descriptive than theoretical, and we do not dwell on why income inequality has changed (e.g., in market versus transfer aspects). Even a cursory inventory shows that theories abound: the advent of neoconservatism, changes in the labour market, a change in income tax structure, globalization, and so on. Whatever the issue, it is worthwhile to adopt a critical stance and ask who is likely to benefit, or lose.

And who benefits is not beyond empirical verification. In this chapter we have learned that although income has risen substantially since the early fifties, income distribution has stayed relatively stable. Closer inspection, however, showed that, as no doubt many middle class Canadians can attest, the second and middle quintiles have been less successful at holding onto their share. Much of this income has escaped upward to the fourth and the highest quintile.

We also saw that the primary statistic used to compare incomes, income quintiles, is not without its problems. Its primary shortcoming is that it obscures how the composition of income has changed over the past few decades (market income versus transfer income). One reason for the stability of incomes is that social programs have done a remarkable job of subsidizing the incomes of those in the lower quintiles, thus preventing their fall into absolute poverty.

Canada has a fairly typical distribution of income for an industrial economy. As study after study shows, Canada is a wealthy country, and how to divide that wealth continues to stimulate much political debate. In the end, definitive answers about what is fair continue to elude us, and we are no closer to an answer today than when Marx, Smith, and Ricardo debated this issue over a century and a half ago. The lack of a conclusive answer, however, should not deter us from asking this question. Once we fail to do so, someone else's version of "what's fair" is sure to win out.

NOTES

1. Inflation refers to rising prices. To remove the effect of inflation, a common procedure applied to historical comparisons of this sort, we use "real" or "constant" dollars. This method better reflects the purchasing power of money than using non-adjusted or "current" dollars. A bottle of coke that cost ten cents in the 1950s costs a dollar or more now. The purchasing power of our money has decreased in that what once cost a dime now costs a loonie. But then, our incomes have also increased, so the question becomes "Is a coke more affordable now than in the fifties?" In Canada we use the Consumer Price Index (CPI) as a method of evaluating price changes (and inflation). By purchasing a similar basket of goods and services (e.g., milk, haircuts) month after month, we can calculate how much prices are increasing because of inflation. Incomes can then be adjusted so that we subtract or remove the effect of inflation, and examine real purchasing power.
2. When Statistics Canada presents its findings on income it provides both average (total

earnings divided by the number of cases) and median incomes (the amount earned by the family located mid way between the highest and lowest income). Statistics Canada tracks both types of income because averages can be unduly inflated by even a small number of very high incomes. For example, the average of a bank president earning $1 000 000 a year and 100 bank clerks earning $12 000 a year would be close to $22 000, vastly overstating the salary of the average bank employee. For that reason, some argue, median income is a better indicator of what the "typical" family or individual earns (which, by the way, would be $12 000 for the bank in our example).

3. Between 1973 and 1991 (in constant 1991 dollars), market income for low income families dropped from $3400 to $2600, while transfers increased from $1900 to $4600 respectively (Myles and Picot 1995). For evidence of the growing proportion of market income flowing to the highest quintile see any of the recent issues of *Income Distributions by Size in Canada*, Statistics Canada Catalogue 13-207XPB, especially the 1996 data.
4. The precise amount of income tax people pay depends upon a complex array of factors, including the amount of money earned and the methods by which the money was earned (e.g., wages, interest, capital gains). The following information includes federal tax only, and each province also collects its share of income tax. At present, all Canadians pay no federal income tax on the first $6 456 they receive. After that, any additional earnings below $29 590 are taxed at a rate of 17 percent. Between $29 590 and below $59 180, income is taxed at a rate of 26 percent. Earnings starting at $59 180 and above are taxed at 29 percent. In effect, as your income rises, you pay higher rates of income tax. This is progressive taxation.

REFERENCES

Hewitt, Christopher 1977 "The effect of political democracy and social democracy on equality in industrial societies: a cross national comparison." In *American Sociological Review* 42: 450–64.

Hunter, Alfred 1993 "The changing distribution of income." In *Social Inequality in Canada* (3rd ed.) Curtis, Grabb, and Guppy (eds.) Scarborough: Prentice Hall.

Osberg, Lars 1992 "Canada's economic performance: inequality, poverty and growth." pp 39–52 in *False Promises, the Failure of Conservative Economics* Allen and Rosenbluth (eds.) Vancouver: New Star Books.

Pass, Christopher and Bryan Lowes 1993 *Dictionary of Economics* (2nd ed.) Glasgow: Collins Publishers.

Picot, Garnett and John Myles 1995 *Social Transfers, Changing Family Structure, and Low Income Among Children* Research Paper No. 82 Ottawa: Statistics Canada.

Statistics Canada 1995 *Income after Tax, Distributions by Size in Canada* (13-210XPB) Ottawa.

Statistics Canada various years *Income Distributions by Size in Canada* (cat. 13-207-XPB) Ottawa.

Teeple, Gary 1995 *Globalization and the Decline of Social Reform* Toronto: Garamond Press.

Therborn, Göran 1986 *Why Some Peoples are More Unemployed than Others* London: Verso Books.

World Bank various years *The World Development Report* Washington D.C.

Chapter 6

THE DISTRIBUTION OF WEALTH AND ECONOMIC INEQUALITY

James B. Davies

(Revised from the previous edition of this volume.)

INTRODUCTION

This paper addresses a series of questions about the distribution of wealth and economic inequality in Canada. First, what is wealth and how is it distributed among families in Canada? Second, what determines how wealth is distributed? Third, why should we care? Finally, how does wealth mobility affect our views about wealth inequality?

WHAT IS WEALTH?

A person's wealth equals the value of all their assets minus debts at a moment in time. This concept is also referred to as "net worth". The assets that must be included cover a wide range. They include cash, bank deposits, owner-occupied housing, guaranteed investment certificates (GICs), registered saving plans (RSPs), stocks, bonds, mutual funds, consumer durables, real estate, and machines and equipment used in unincorporated businesses. There is also a wide variety of debts—mortgages, credit card balances, personal loans, small business loans, and so forth.

Table 6-1 indicates the relative importance of the different forms of wealth at the end of 1993. Note first that 37.6 % of the total value of assets is made up of real estate, the most important form of which is residential housing. There is about an even split between non-financial and financial assets. Of the latter, stocks and bonds (excluding Canada Savings Bonds—"CSBs") make up only 13.5 % of total assets. More widely distributed assets like cash, bank accounts, CSBs, life insurance, and pensions make up the bulk of the total.

Some urge the use of a broader definition of wealth—one that would include, for example, the value of pension rights, both private and public. Although such wealth is non-liquid, people with pension rights are better off than others. The amounts involved are also substantial. This is reflected to some extent in Table 6-1 on the pensions and insurance line. However, the value of rights

TABLE 6-1 Year-end national balance sheets—persons and unincorporated business, Canada, 1993

	Assets (in millions)	% of Assets
I. Non-Financial Assets		
Residential Structures	$599 871m	22.2%
Non-Residential Structures	34 198	1.3
Land	388 014	14.3
Consumer Durables	256 157	9.5
Machinery, Equipment & Inventories	26 861	1.0
Total	1 305 101	48.3
II. Financial Assets		
Cash and Deposits	476 686	17.6
Canada Savings Bonds	32 623	1.2
Other Canadian Bonds	31 159	1.2
Life Insurance and Pensions	424 353	15.7
Stock	332 079	12.3
Miscellaneous	102 429	3.8
Total	1 399 329	51.7
Total Assets	2 704 430	100.0
III. Debt		
Mortgages	328 891	12.2
Other Debt	154 318	5.7
Total	483 209	17.9
Net Worth	2 221 221	82.1

Source: Calculated from Statistics Canada (1995, Table 4, p. 13).

to old age pension (both OAS and GIS) and CPP/QPP benefits should also be included. Estimates of such "social security wealth" in the United States vary from about 40% to 200% of conventional net worth.[1]

Finally, it is often argued that the present value of future labour earnings, or "human wealth," should be included. As for social security wealth, data availability is a barrier. Estimating human wealth requires projecting future earnings. A wide range of estimates of aggregate human wealth are available. (See the appendix to Davies and Whalley, 1990.) A best guess estimate is that the total value of human wealth equals about three times that of non-human or "physical" wealth.

HOW IS WEALTH DISTRIBUTED IN CANADA?

The best answer to the question, "how is wealth distributed in Canada?" may be "we don't know." In Canada the major source of information on the distributions of income and wealth among families has been Statistics Canada's Survey of Consumer Finance (SCF).[2] This survey provides estimates of income distribution every year, and also covered wealth in 1970, 1977, and 1984. Like all surveys, it is subject to sampling and non-sampling error. These errors are especially important in wealth surveys.

Sampling error is the difference between the *sample* value of a statistic, for example, average wealth, and its true *population* value. The larger the sample, the smaller this error is likely to be. For characteristics like national means, the error is generally small, since the sample sizes used by Statistics Canada are very large. In estimating the shape of the overall *distribution* of a highly skewed variable like wealth, however, sampling error can be significant.[3] Most samples will select too few rich households, and a few will have too many. This problem can be addressed by oversampling in the upper tail. However, such an approach has only been used on one occasion in Canada (the 1977 SCF).[4]

Non-sampling error is an especially serious problem in wealth surveys. It takes two forms. First, some people refuse to be interviewed. Studies indicate that the likelihood of this non-response varies with age, region, and income. These differences can be corrected through weighting families according to their likelihood of being in the sample. Differential response across age groups, for example, can be almost entirely corrected. However, it is only if differential response according to wealth is highly correlated with the differential according to observable characteristics (age, region, size of urban area, etc.) that it can be adequately corrected by weighting. Since the correlation is far from perfect, differential response remains a problem.

Another form of non-sampling error—misreporting—occurs because people sometimes refuse to report certain items, or make mistakes. In cases in which people report that they own an asset but do not report its value, an imputed value can be assigned. However, no correction is possible if the interviewers do not know that the family owns an asset. U.S. studies indicate that, on average, assets like bank accounts are under-reported by 40% to 50%. Other assets are more accurately reported. The value of owner-occupied houses, for example, is, on average, reported with surprising accuracy. (See Davies, 1979b.)

Some of the results of these combined errors are well known for the SCF *income* distribution. While wages and salaries are, on average, reported fairly accurately, SCF estimates of average transfer payments are about 20% less than the true figures, and the shortfall is about 50% for investment income. The situation is worse for wealth surveys. The Spring 1984 SCF estimates of stock ownership, for example, were only about 14% of the year-end 1983 national balance sheet totals. Estimates for other assets are not so bad, and some, such as housing, are fairly accurately represented.

Keeping all these reservations in mind, let us look at Table 6-2, which shows 1984 SCF estimates of both income and wealth distributions in Canada. Note first that there is more dispersion in the distribution of wealth than in income. In 1984, for example, the share of the top 10% of families (according to wealth) was 51.3%. The corresponding income share (when the families are sorted by income) was 26.3%. The same contrast is observed in other countries.

Also note from Table 6-2 that mean wealth equals about three times mean income.[5] This allows us to guess how much wealth would have been found per family if the SCF wealth survey had been repeated more recently. For 1995, for example, mean income was $45 329. If the wealth-income ratio were 3:1, then mean wealth would have been about $136 000. Median wealth, which gives a better idea of the wealth of the "typical" family,[6] would have been only about $59 500 in 1995, according to a similar calculation.

It is also interesting to note some of the characteristics of the top 1% of wealth-hold-

TABLE 6-2 Distribution of income and wealth, families and unattached individuals, Canada, 1984 SCF

	Income	Wealth
Decile Shares:		
1	1.4%	-0.4%
2	2.9	0.1
3	4.4	0.6
4	5.9	1.8
5	7.7	3.6
6	9.4	5.7
7	11.4	8.2
8	13.7	11.6
9	16.9	17.6
10	26.3	51.2
Mean:	$29 113	$85 344
Median:	24 894	39 876

Source: Decile shares-Davies and Shorrocks (1989, Tables 2 and 4, pp. 105 and 107). Means and medians-Statistics Canada (1986, Tables 1 and 2, pp. 26 and 29).

ing families. There were approximately 100 000 families in this category, and their average wealth was $1 434 000. Only about half of those in the top 1% were millionaires. Thus, the "top 1%" and the "super rich" are not the same thing. The latter are a small minority of the top 1%.

For the reasons discussed above, the figures shown in Table 6-2 are affected by important sources of error. When attempting to get an accurate picture of a highly skewed distribution, it is inevitable that less accuracy will be achieved in the "tails" of the distribution. The Canadian SCF wealth distribution estimates miss much of the upper tail. The richest family in 1984, for example, had a net worth of only about $6 million, whereas it is well known that Canada has several billionaire families.

The limitations of the SCF sample survey mean that we must turn to alternative sources. Davies (1993) has examined a number of these. They include both journalistic accounts and studies by private firms.

From time-to-time *Forbes* magazine publishes a list of the world's super-rich. In 1997 they listed four Canadian billionaire families (*Forbes*, July 28, 1997, pp. 174–175).

This number fluctuates from year to year, but it is clear that some Canadians figure among the world's super-rich and need to be taken into account. There are even indications that there may be more Canadian billionaires than counted by *Forbes*. *Fortune* magazine counted eight billionaire families with at least partial Canadian residence in 1989, while Francis (1986) listed six.

Other journalistic evidence provides more information on the sub-billionaries. Newman (1975) attempted to provide a complete list of all Canadian families with wealth over $20 million. There were 160 families on his list. The list of the corporate wealthy provided by Francis (1986) indicated 32 families with wealth over $100 million. Using this evidence, Davies (1993) "guess-timates" that the share of the top 1%

in the Canadian wealth distribution in the 1970s and 80s was probably around 25%. This implies considerably more concentration than suggested by the SCF wealth distribution.

There are two other pieces of information. As reported in *Maclean's* magazine (November 5, 1990, p. 49), a Toronto management consulting company surveyed 1350 Canadians over 50 in 1989, and found that, on average, families with at least one person over 50 "had nearly $350 000 in assets." Is this number consistent with the 1984 SCF? If wealth/income ratios and the age profile of relative wealth in 1989 were the same as in the 1984 survey, the over-50s would average $170 000 in net worth. Thus, the consultants' study suggests again that the SCF survey underestimates wealth-holding in Canada.

The last piece of evidence comes from a study done by the accounting firm of Ernst and Young ("Millionaires: They're Not So Rare Any More," *London Free Press*, Dec. 15, 1990, p. A2). This study used the 1984 SCF as a starting point for estimating current patterns of wealth-holding by income group in Canada. This involved updating the 1984 numbers, and making various imputations and adjustments. Details are not publicly available. The information that was publicly released included an estimate of average Canadian household net worth at the end of 1989 equal to $260 000, with 425 000 households having net worth over $1 million. Again this suggests that Canadians are, on average, wealthier than suggested by the SCF. The estimated number of millionaires reinforces the expectation built up from other evidence that the upper tail of the wealth distribution is a long one.

It is interesting to try to put the Canadian wealth distribution in international perspective. Both the United Kingdom and the United States have "estate multiplier" evidence on the distribution of wealth among *individuals*, and the United States in addition has considerable survey evidence for families. The estate multiplier evidence indicates consistently falling wealth inequality in the U.K. in the 20th century, and a somewhat more complicated pattern for the U.S. (falling up to 1970, but increasing somewhat thereafter). As of 1980 both countries' estimates showed the share of the top 1% of families at about 20%. This is above the levels indicated by the Canadian SCF survey, but below my alternative estimate.

Several sample surveys of wealth-holding are available for the U.S. over the last two or three decades. These generally indicated greater wealth concentration than the estate multiplier estimates. For example, the 1963 Survey of Financial Characteristics of Consumers (SFCC) estimated a share of the top 1% of families at 31.8%. And, after all adjustments (including the imputation of an upper tail for wealth-holders with more than $60 million), the 1983 Survey of Consumer Finance (SCF) indicated the share of the top 1% at about 37% (Avery et al., 1988, pp. 356–361)! These figures are higher than both the estate multiplier estimates in the U.S. and all the estimates discussed above for Canada.

The gap between survey and estate multiplier estimates in the U.S. reminds us how uncertain our knowledge of the distribution of wealth is. In terms of levels, all that we know for sure is that wealth is much more concentrated than is income. We may be a little more confident about changes over time: as long as we use consistent techniques, we may get a reasonably accurate idea of the direction and magnitude of *changes* in concentration.

The fact that survey estimates indicate more wealth concentration in the U.S. than in Canada likely reflects a real difference between these countries. Such a difference is not surprising. The U.S. is the most important international centre of corporate wealth. It has "more than its share" of millionaires. In contrast, about 35% of Canadian business is foreign-owned. Thus, Canada has a large number of "missing millionaires."

WHAT DETERMINES HOW WEALTH IS DISTRIBUTED?

Wealth is the result of past accumulation, coming from two main sources: labour income ("earnings"), or gifts and inheritances. Both provide resources which can be either saved or consumed. Resources which are saved can accumulate at different rates. Wise or lucky investors earn high rates of return; others, lower rates. Finally, given the lifetime path of earnings, savings, etc., up to retirement, the older the consumer, the greater tends to be his/her wealth. Thus, current wealth depends on past earnings, inheritances (including gifts), saving rates out of earnings and inheritances, rates of return, and age.

It is sometimes suggested that a large part of wealth differences might simply be explained by age. To show this, examples of societies which, although egalitarian, would display considerable wealth concentration, are sometimes devised. For instance, consider a society with zero population growth and a zero rate of interest, in which everyone worked for 40 years, and then retired for 10 years. Assume that, while earning a constant amount during their working years, people save at a constant rate, and then *dissave* at a constant rate during retirement, ending life with zero wealth. The wealthiest people would be those just before and after the retirement age. In this world the share of the top 10% of wealth-holders would be about 19%.

At first glance, the fact that a 19% share for the top 10% could be generated from age differences alone might seem impressive. However, this does not mean that a large part of wealth concentration is explained by age in the real world, for at least two reasons. First, if we look at the top 1% in the example, we find that their wealth share is just 2%. By altering the details of the example, one could get this share to 3 or 4 %, but this would still be far short of the estimated real-world shares. Second, the assumed variation of wealth with age is not realistic. In the real world there is a less extreme pattern. On average, people save for the first few years after retirement, and only dissave slowly beyond that point. (See Burbidge and Robb, 1985.)

In Davies (1979a), I developed a microsimulation model which can be used to *decompose* wealth inequality. (See Davies, 1982, for a summary.) That is, it is possible to see how wealth inequality would be reduced if we eliminated differences in earnings, inheritances, saving rates, rates of return, and age. The most important factor was inheritance, followed by differences in saving rates. Differences in earnings, rates of return, and age were of lesser importance (and similar to each other in impact). (See Davies, 1982, Table I, p. 489.)[7]

There is other evidence of the importance of inheritance. First, Wedgwood (1929) investigated the sources of wealth held by wealthy Britons who died in a twelve-month period during 1924–25. Of 99 persons dying with at least 200 000 pounds (a fortune at the time), about 60% had a predecessor (usually a parent) who had died leaving at least 50 000 pounds, and about 70% had predecessors who left at least 10 000 pounds (Wedgwood, 1929, pp. 138–139). This work was updated by Harbury and Hitchens (1979), who found similar results for the 1950s, 1960s, and 1970s. As reported by Brittain (1978, Ch. 1), studies by *Fortune* magazine in the U.S. on top American wealth-holders concluded that about half were "self made." However, sample surveys of the entire population indicate that a larger fraction—as many as 60%—of those in top wealth groups had received *some* inheritance (Brittain, 1978, p. 18). The implication of these studies is that, in both the U.K. and the U.S., at least half of the genuinely wealthy have benefited to some extent from inheritance.

While the distribution of wealth is more unequal than that of income, the distribution of inherited wealth is much more unequal than that of wealth in general. Sample surveys indicate that the majority of people have never received an inheritance (see, e.g., Brittain, 1978, p. 18), and a majority will likely never receive significant amounts in gift or bequest. On the other hand, a small minority receive truly spectacular amounts. It is this extreme concentration, rather than the total amount being passed on, which makes inheritance an important determinant of wealth inequality.

What makes inherited wealth so concentrated? Ironically, part of the answer lies in the great importance of *human* wealth. The majority of families find that investing in their children's human capital, via upbringing and education, is more effective than providing gifts and bequests. Why are all families not in this position? First, some provide for their heirs by passing along family businesses (including farms). Second, some exhaust the attractive opportunities for investing in their children's education and upbringing before their benevolence has been used up. Third, the lure of bequests may be used to elicit attention from children in a form of exchange. (See Sussman *et al.*, 1970, and Cox, 1987.) The genuinely wealthy would almost all be in one of these three categories, and we therefore expect to see them making good use of bequests.

The extent of concentration in inheritance depends on practices of estate division, fertility, and choice of marital partner. (See Atkinson, 1983, pp. 183–189.) At one extreme, in some societies *primogeniture* is practised. Under this arrangement, the entire estate passes to the eldest son (or daughter in the absence of a son). This keeps large estates intact, and preserves wealth inequality over time. At the opposite extreme, many families practise equal division of estates. Especially when families are large (which was true in North America in the 19th and early 20th centuries), this contributes to the rapid breakdown of wealth concentration. It appears that in North America today equal division of estates is the norm, although departures from this norm are observed.

Differences in fertility according to wealth can also have a sizeable effect. If the wealthy had smaller families than others, their wealth would be broken up relatively slowly by division among heirs, and wealth concentration would tend to be preserved. While this factor may have been important in some societies at some times, in Canada today fertility differences across income and wealth groups are not large, so that it likely has a relatively small effect.

Finally, the extent of assortative mating is important. If wealthy sons marry wealthy daughters, inherited wealth can remain confined to a small minority of families. While there is a positive sorting of mates according to wealth and income, the correlation in mates' backgrounds is far from perfect. Thus, there is a tendency for inequality to be broken down through wealthy children marrying non-wealthy spouses, as well as through the division of estates.

WHY SHOULD WE CARE HOW WEALTH IS DISTRIBUTED?

One reason some people are concerned about the distribution of wealth is that they believe it has much to do with the distribution of power in society. This concern has several facets, since power can take political, social, or economic forms. As an economist, I am not especially qualified to comment on the first two forms of power, but it is important not to exclude them entirely from the discussion.

Some believe that the wealthy exert vastly greater political influence than others. This could be achieved through funding political campaigns, by bribing politicians and civil servants, by control of media, and through funding researchers who obtain congenial findings. Similarly disproportionate *social* power may accrue to the wealthy, for example, through the impact of advertising and media content on values and attitudes.

While not all would agree about the extent of political and social power conferred by wealth in Canada today, there is little doubt that the wealthy can exert considerable influence through the channels mentioned. But what of the *economic* power created by the concentration of wealth? At first blush, it might appear that the concentration of corporate wealth observed in our society must imply great concentration of economic power. However, to the extent that we maintain internationally open and competitive markets, the power of even large corporations is limited by the rigours of the marketplace.

In competitive markets, business initiatives are governed by the logic of profit and loss. In order to survive, firms have to strive to make as much profit as possible. If they do not take advantage of opportunities, someone else will. Factors like technology, consumer preferences, supplies of productive inputs, the regulatory environment, and taxes and subsidies really determine what happens. The preferences of individuals who control even large corporations may ultimately be unimportant.

One should not be complacent about the limitations which competitive and open markets place on individuals' economic power. The wealthy do not like such limitations, and like other groups (such as trade unions), can be expected to use their political power to try to achieve protection from competition. It is important for the electorate to be critical of weak competition policy, subsidies to private firms, special tax breaks, and other preferential treatment for private firms and wealthy individuals. In the long run, such vigilance may be more effective in preventing an unhealthy concentration of power in society, and indeed in preventing undue concentration of wealth itself, than a strategy which attacks wealth concentration directly.

I turn now to a discussion of the second reason why wealth inequality may matter, that is, because of its implications for differences in economic well-being.

What determines the distribution of economic well-being at a moment in time? Often we attempt to summarize this distribution by looking at households' incomes over the calendar year. This is informative, but has its limitations. If two families have equal income, but one has $1 million in non-human capital and the other just $100 000, their well-being is likely to be quite different. This realization has prompted many observers to argue that we should look at wealth as well as income.

Wealth differs from income in that it is a store of purchasing power for the future. While most income is consumed in the year it is received, consumption of wealth usually takes place gradually over the lifetime of the consumer or, possibly, by his/her heirs. Thus, when we turn to wealth, we must change our focus to the long run.

The long-run differences in well-being of a cohort of Canadians of similar age are determined largely by the sum of their human and non-human resources, that is, by "total wealth." We might try to estimate the distribution of this total wealth among people aged 20–24, 25–29, 30–34, and so on up through the age groups. Knowledge of net worth (including the net value of pension rights and social security wealth) would be an important component of this exercise, but so also would be knowledge of the distribution of human wealth.

Since human wealth, on average, dwarfs non-human wealth, one might ask whether there is much point in studying the distribution of non-human wealth by itself. The answer is that while looking at the distribution of wealth alone is a limited exercise, it is an important one. Although there is not a perfect correlation, people with high labour income also tend to have high wealth, so that, overall, wealth differences tend to reinforce differences in earnings. Also, the extremes reached by wealth in the upper tail are not matched by the distribution of human wealth. Thus, at the highest reaches, one can almost say that the distribution of non-human wealth *is* the distribution of total wealth. Looking at the top of the wealth distribution, therefore, tells us about the upper extreme of individual economic resources in our society.

Finally, we may ask a deeper question about whether the observed differences in wealth are really important. To what extent are these differences inequitable; that is, do they represent true *inequality*? There is a wide range of possible answers. Perspectives range from those of libertarians on the right to socialists on the left.

Libertarians believe that as long as wealth has been accumulated honestly, differences in wealth-holding are fair. Nobody has any superior right to that of the individual to enjoy the fruits of his or her past accumulation. Since there is no injustice involved, there is no "inequality." This is a highly individualistic approach.

Socialists have a very different viewpoint. The component of wealth which can be traced to inheritance, first of all, is considered undeserved, and certainly indicative of inequality. Second, some of the differences in past earnings and rates of return, which led to current differences in wealth, are regarded as unfair. In other words, aside from differences due purely to age, saving rates, or to "reasonable" differences in rates of return and labour earnings, all wealth differences would be regarded as unjustifiable by a true socialist.

Between the libertarian and socialist positions there is a large gap. What would a representative or "typical" Canadian think about wealth differences? It would be interesting to answer this question by means of a sample survey. In the absence of such evidence, one can only conjecture. My guess is that the typical Canadian probably believes that differences in inheritance are less justified than those in labour earnings. However, I would also guess that he or she does not believe that differences in inheritance have *no* justification. Parents' rights to pass on to their children the fruits of their labour are considered important by many. Public concern about tax loopholes is also widespread, so that the typical Canadian is likely also not entirely happy with differences in self-accumulated wealth. Thus, the average Canadian probably thinks that there is some true "inequality" involved in wealth differences.

HOW DOES WEALTH MOBILITY AFFECT OUR PERCEPTIONS OF INEQUALITY?

Wealth mobility exists if people change their relative position in the wealth distribution over time. Such mobility can take place both within lifetimes and from generation to generation. Within a lifetime, what is important to look at is a person's wealth relative to others of about the same age. If this changes over time, and the change is not offset by changes in human wealth, then there is meaningful wealth mobility.

In fact, there is considerable wealth mobility both within lifetimes and across generations. (See, e.g., Menchik, 1979.) While the majority of the rich have benefited from inheritance, there are many well-known, true-life "rags to riches" stories. Conversely, there are many wealthy heirs who have squandered their fortunes. And, over successive generations, there is even more mobility. It is sometimes claimed that "shirtsleeves to shirtsleeves in three generations" is typical. While this claim is exaggerated, the work by Wedgwood, Harbury and Hitchens, Menchik, and others does show that there is substantial intergenerational wealth mobility.

It is sometimes asserted that, given any level of wealth concentration, the greater the degree of wealth mobility, the less concern there is about inequality. But this is not obvious. It may depend very much on what kind of mobility we are talking about. For example, while there is widespread respect for those who build up their wealth by working hard and by saving and investing wisely, there can be great resentment toward those who get rich via exploitative, questionable, or illegal activity. And while the public probably doesn't have much sympathy with the downward mobility of spendthrift heirs, it may feel concern for those who have been forced out of business by unexpected technological change, recession, or international trade shocks.

It seems likely that people regard wealth mobility as desirable only when it occurs for good reasons. This brings us back to the earlier discussion. Upward mobility due to moderate inheritance, working and saving hard, and perhaps also bearing risk and having good luck in investments, may be considered healthy and acceptable, just as the wealth differences created by these factors may not be resented. However, people may disapprove of mobility due to what are regarded as excessive inheritances or earnings differences, unequal tax treatment, and so on, just as they disapprove of wealth differences caused by these factors.

Summing up, a reasonable degree of wealth mobility may be *necessary* for the mechanisms determining wealth differences in a society to be regarded as fair. However, it is not *sufficient.* Thus, the fact that there is considerable wealth mobility in Canada and other Western countries means that they are not caste-ridden societies, but it does not imply that no one should be concerned about wealth inequality in these countries.

CONCLUSION

This paper has tried to make clear the concept of wealth, has summarized the available evidence on how it is distributed in Canada, has discussed the determinants of wealth differences, and has asked whether these matter. It has emphasized that, ideally, a comprehensive concept of wealth needs to be used, one which includes pension rights and social security wealth in addition to more narrowly defined net worth. The paper has also stressed that even this broad concept of wealth leaves out the bulk of people's economic resources, which take the form of expected future labour earnings, or human wealth.

We have seen that wealth differences are much greater than income differences, although the precise shape of the wealth distribution is unknown, not only in Canada but also in countries like the United Kingdom and the United States, where much more research has been done. In descending order of importance, concentration in wealth-holding appears to be the result of differences in inheritances, saving rates, and then three roughly equally important variables: labour earnings, rates of return, and age. Inheritance is the strongest influence, because it is responsible, in large degree, for the extreme length of the upper tail of the wealth distribution. This is true despite the fact that the prevailing equality in estate division, even among the wealthy, and imperfect sorting of marital partners according to wealth in our society both tend to reduce differences in inherited wealth.

The paper concluded with a discussion of why wealth differences matter. There are three answers. The first is that great wealth may spell disproportionate power in our society. While public vigilance and participation in democratic political institutions can reduce this power difference, these factors are unlikely to eliminate it fully. A second reason is that, particularly in the upper tail, differences in non-human wealth have an important influence on the distribution of economic well-being. Finally, some wealth differences reflect factors such as age, widely accepted differences in labour income, and voluntary differences in saving rates, and are widely regarded as justifiable, but other differences reflect factors such as inheritance, unequal treatment by the tax system, and extreme differences in labour income, all of which may not win such uniform approval. Such factors may be taken to reflect true wealth "inequality."

NOTES

1. Feldstein (1976) estimated aggregate social security wealth in the U.S. in 1962 at $382 billion. This was 54% of conventional net worth ($711 billion) in his study. Wolff (1987) obtains a range of figures for 1969, when conventional net worth had risen to $2904 billion. The estimates for social security wealth vary from $1194 billion (41% of net worth) to $5649 billion (195% of net worth), depending on assumptions about future growth in earnings, and social security contributions and benefits. See Wolff (1987, Table 9.1, p. 219.)
2. A new Asset and Debt Survey is currently in the planning stages at Statistics Canada. Results from this survey are unlikely to be available before 1999.
3. A variable is skewed if its frequency histogram has one "tail" longer than the other. Distributions of income and wealth are highly positively skewed, meaning that they have very long upper tails. (A negatively skewed distribution has a long lower tail.)
4. The 1977 SCF had 12 734 families in total, 184 of whom were from a special high income sample. This compares with an overall sample of 4103 and a high income sample of 438 in the 1983 U.S. SCF survey. (Avery, 1988) While introducing the high income sample in 1977 increased the income shares of top groups slightly, it had a negligible direct effect on the estimated distribution (Oja, 1981).
5. The ratio is 2.93. A very similar ratio (2.92) was found in the 1977 SCF.
6. The median is the level of wealth such that one half of the families have less and one half more. In sampling from a heavily skewed distribution like that of wealth, it is likely to be much more reliable than the average. Also, it is a better indicator of the wealth of the "typical" family. A family with wealth equal to the average would be at about the 70th percentile. That is, it would be at an "upper middle" wealth level rather than in the "middle."
7. At about the same time that I was developing my simulation model, Michael Wolfson built another model which he used to address similar questions. The Davies and Wolfson models differ in many respects, but they agree in ascribing the most important role in explaining the concentration of wealth in the extreme upper tail to differences in inheritance. See Wolfson (1977, and 1979).

   Interestingly, the conclusions from the Davies and Wolfson studies are consistent with the assessment of the famous University of Chicago economist Frank Knight, who devoted considerable thought to the determinants of personal wealth. Knight wrote in 1923, "The ownership of personal or material productive capacity is based upon a complex mixture of inheritance, luck, and effort, probably in that order of relative importance" (Brittain, 1978, p. 1).

REFERENCES

Atkinson, A.B. 1983 *The Economics of Inequality*, (2nd ed.) Oxford: Clarendon Press

Avery, Robert B., Gregory E. Elliehausen, and Arthur B. Kennickell 1988 "Measuring wealth with survey data: an evaluation of the

1983 survey of consumer finances." *Review of Income and Wealth*, 34 (December): 339–370.

Brittain, John A. 1978 *Inheritance and the Inequality of Material Wealth* Washington: The Brookings Institution.

Burbidge, J.B. and A.L. Robb 1985 "Evidence on wealth-age profiles in Canadian cross-section data." *Canadian Journal of Economics*, XVIII (November): 854–875.

Clement Wallace 1975 *The Canadian Corporate Elite* Carleton Library No. 89 Toronto: McClelland and Stewart.

Cox, Donald 1987 "Motives for private income transfers." *Journal of Political Economy*, 95: 508–546.

Davies, James B. 1979a *Life-Cycle Saving, Inheritance, and the Personal Distribution of Income and Wealth in Canada.* Ph.D. thesis, London School of Economics.

Davies, James B. 1979b "On the size distribution of wealth in Canada." *Review of Income and Wealth*, 25 (September): 237–259.

Davies, James B. 1982 "The relative impact of inheritance and other factors on economic inequality." *Quarterly Journal of Economics*, 47: 471–498.

Davies, James B. 1993 "The distribution of wealth in Canada." In Daniel J. Slottje and Edward N. Wolff (eds.) *Research on Economic Inequality, Vol. 4* JAI Press, Greenwich Connecticut.

Davies, James B. and A.F. Shorrocks 1989 "Optimal grouping of income and wealth data." *Journal of Econometrics*, 42: 97–108.

Davies, James B. and John Whalley 1991 "Taxes and capital formation: how important is human capital?" In D. Bernheim and J. Shoven (eds.) *National Saving and Economic Performance* Chicago: University of Chicago Press.

Feldstein, M. 1976 "Social security and the distribution of wealth." *Journal of the American Statistical Association*, 71: 800–807.

Francis, Diane *1986 Controlling Interest: Who Owns Canada?* Toronto: Macmillan.

Harbury, C.D. and D.M.W.N. Hitchens 1979 *Inheritance and Wealth Inequality in Britain* London: George Allen and Unwin.

Menchik, Paul L. 1979 "Inter-generational transmission of inequality: an empirical study of wealth mobility," *Economica*, 46: 349–362.

Newman, Peter C. 1975 *The Canadian Establishment,* Vol. 1 Toronto: McClelland and Stewart.

Oja, Gail 1986 "The wealth of canadians: a comparison of survey of consumer finances with national balance sheet estimates." Labour and Household Surveys Analysis Division Staff Reports, Statistics Canada.

Shorrocks, A.F. 1987 "UK wealth distribution: current evidence and future prospects." In Edward N. Wolff (ed.) *International Comparisons of the Distribution of Household Wealth* Oxford: Clarendon Press.

Statistics Canada 1986 *The Distribution of Wealth in Canada, 1984* Publication No. 13-580.

Statistics Canada 1995 *National Balance Sheet Accounts, Annual Estimates 1984–1993* Publication No. 13-214.

Statistics Canada 1996 *Income Distributions by Size in Canada*, 1995 Publication No. 13-207.

Sussman, Marvin B., Judith N. Cates, and David T. Smith 1970 *The Family and Inheritance* New York: Russell Sage Foundation.

Wedgwood, Josiah 1929 *The Economics of Inheritance* London: George Routledge & Sons.

Wolff, Edward N. 1987 "The effect of pensions and social security on the distribution of wealth in the U.S." In Edward N. Wolff (ed.) *International Comparisons of the Distribution of Household Wealth* Oxford: Clarendon Press.

Chapter 7

POVERTY IN CANADA

National Council of Welfare

(From: Poverty Profile 1995, A Report by the National Council of Welfare, Spring 1997. Minister of Supply and Services, Canada Cat. No. H67-1/4-1995E Reprinted with permission.)

INTRODUCTION

Every year, Statistics Canada conducts a household survey known as the Survey of Consumer Finances to obtain information on the distribution of income and the nature and extent of poverty in Canada. The survey on which this chapter is based, conducted in April of 1996, sampled 32 785 private households from all parts of the country except the Yukon, the Northwest Territories, Indian reserves, and institutions such as prisons, mental hospitals, and homes for the elderly. The survey looked at incomes for the 1995 calendar year.

Information about poverty is obtained by comparing the survey data with the low income cut-offs of Statistics Canada. The cut-offs represent levels of gross income at which people spend disproportionate amounts of money for food, shelter, and clothing. The Bureau has decided over the years—somewhat arbitrarily—that 20 percentage points is a reasonable measure of the additional burden. The average Canadian family spent 36.2 percent of gross income on food, shelter, and clothing according to 1986 data on spending patterns, so it was assumed that low-income Canadians spent 56.2 percent or more on the necessities of life.

The low income cut-offs vary by the size of the family unit and the population of the area of residence. There are seven categories of family size, from one person to seven or more persons, and five community sizes ranging from rural areas to cities with 500 000 or more residents. The result is a set of 35 cut-offs. The cut-offs are updated annually by Statistics Canada using the Consumer Price Index.

The National Council of Welfare, like many other social policy groups, regards the low income cut-offs as poverty lines and uses the term poor and low-income inter-

TABLE 7-1 Statistics Canada's low income cut-offs (1986 base) for 1995

Family Size	1	2	3	4	5	6	7+
Community Size							
Cities of 500 000+	15 819	21 442	27 256	31 383	34 287	37 219	40 029
100 000-499 999	13 895	18 835	23 941	27 561	30 114	32 686	35 159
30 000-99 999	13 574	18 399	23 387	26 927	29 419	31 932	34 347
Less than 30 000	12 374	16 771	21 318	24 547	26 818	29 109	31 311
Rural Areas	10 769	14 600	18 556	21 364	23 343	25 337	27 252

changeably. Statistics Canada takes pains to avoid references to poverty. It says the cut-offs have no official status, and it does not promote their use as poverty lines.

Regardless of the terminology, the cut-offs are a useful tool for defining and analyzing the significantly large portion of the Canadian population with low incomes. They are not the only measures of poverty used in Canada, but they are the most widely accepted and are roughly comparable to most alternative measures.

Figure 7.1 shows the 1986 base and 1992 base low income cut-offs or LICOs of Statistics Canada along with seven other poverty lines sometimes seen in published reports.[1] Most of the lines fall in a middle range from $29 170 to $32 805 for a family of four living in a large city in 1995. One line is substantially higher than the rest, and three are substantially lower.

Toronto SPC, the description of the first bar of Figure 7.1, refers to the budget guides of the Metropolitan Toronto Social Planning Council updated to the year 1995. CCSD refers to the Canadian Council on Social Development's income guidelines, which are based on one-half of average family income and do not vary from one area of the country to another. The calculation for the bar labelled Croll uses the methodology first proposed in 1971 by a special Senate committee on poverty headed by Senator David Cross. The Gallup bar is an update of responses to a public opinion poll that asked: "what is the minimum weekly amount of income required for a family of four, consisting of two adults and two children?" LIM means the low income measures of Statistics Canada, an alternative measure based on one-half of median family income with no geographic variations. Montreal Diet refers to the income needed for a minimum adequate standard of living for a two-earner couple with a 15-year-old son and a ten-year-old daughter in Montreal as calculated by the Montreal Diet Dispensary. The group also has basic needs guidelines strictly intended for short-term assistance that are somewhat lower. Sarlo/Toronto is the poverty line for Toronto calculated for 1994 by Christopher A. Sarlo and updated to 1995 by the National Council of Welfare. Professor Sarlo also has "social comfort lines" that are twice as high as his poverty lines.

Poverty statistics are often broken down according to families and unattached individuals. The Statistics Canada survey which gathered the data defined a family as a group of individuals sharing a common dwelling unit and related by blood, marriage, or adoption. The definition includes couples living in common-law relationships. Most of the data in this report are expressed in terms of families rather than the number of people in family units. Unattached individuals are defined as people living alone or in households where

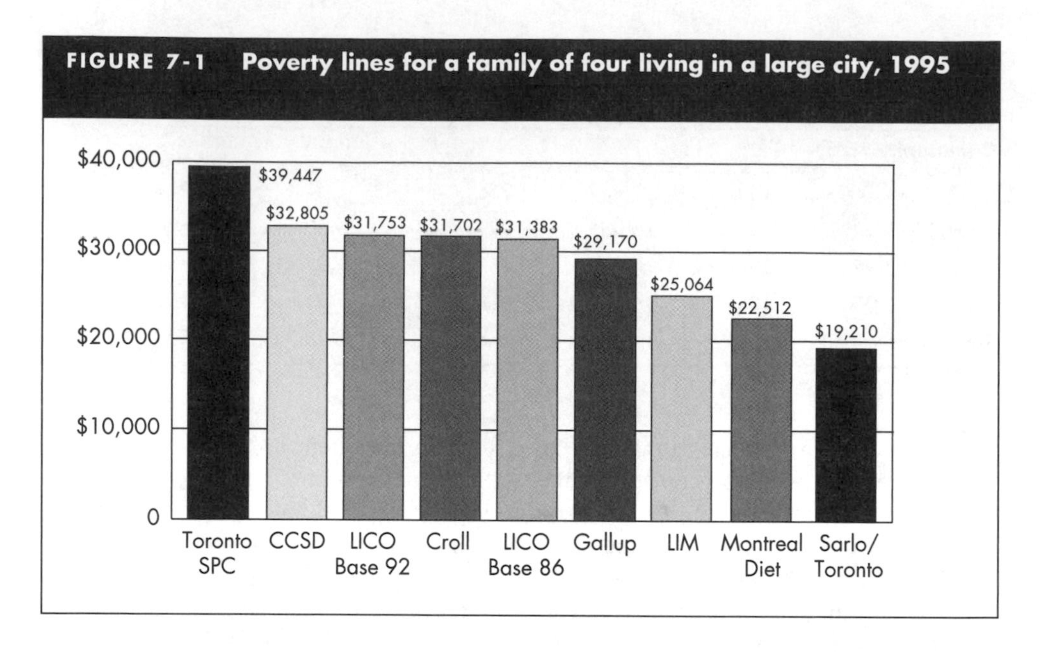

FIGURE 7-1 Poverty lines for a family of four living in a large city, 1995

they are related to other household members.

Poverty rates compare the number of poor persons, families, or unattached individuals in a particular category to all the persons, families, or unattached individuals in the same category. For example, there were an estimated 323 000 poor families with children under 18 headed by a female single parent under age 65 in 1995. The estimated total number of families with children under 18 headed by a female single parent under 65 was 565 000. The poverty rate was 323 000 divided by 565 000 or 57.2 percent.

Sometimes the terms incidence of poverty or risk of poverty are used instead of the poverty rate. The meaning of all three terms is the same.

Income refers to money income reported by all family members 15 years or older and includes gross wages and salaries, net income from self-employment, investment income, government transfer payments (for example, the federal Child Tax Benefit, Old Age Security, and provincial tax credits), pensions, and miscellaneous income (scholarships and child support payments, for example). The definition of income excludes gambling wins or losses, capital gains or losses, receipts from the sale of property or personal belongings, income tax refunds, loans received or repaid, lump sum settlements of insurance policies, and income in kind.

RECENT POVERTY TRENDS

The National Council of Welfare was expecting to see a slight decrease in the overall poverty rate between 1994 and 1995. The Canadian economy continued to grow modestly as the recession of 1990-1991 faded into the past. Unemployment remained relatively high, but dropped slightly from one year to the next. The most draconian of the cuts in federal transfer payments to the provinces and territories were not scheduled to hit until later years. All things considered, it seemed reasonable to assume that 1995 would be a better year than 1994.

The actual 1995 poverty statistics came as a shock. The poverty rate for all persons rose to 17.4 percent. The child poverty rate jumped to 20.5 percent, and the poverty rate for adults 18 to 65 was up to 16.2 percent. Seniors were the main group bucking the trend, as the poverty rate for people 65 and older fell to an all-time low of 16.9 percent.

One type of poverty statistics published by Statistics Canada gives the number of poor people and the poverty rates for people as individuals. In 1980, the number of people living in poverty was just over 3.6 million and the poverty rate was 15.3 percent. Both the number of poor people and the poverty rate rose following the recession of 1981-1982, declined slowly through 1989, and rose again with the recession of 1990-1991. Instead of improving after the recession ended, however, they continued their upward trend.

By 1995, the number of poor people was nearly 5.1 million and the poverty rate was 17.4 percent. Both those figures were well above the figures for the years just prior to the last recession. Bluntly put, the modest economic growth of the last several years was simply not filtering down to the ranks of the poor.

Similar trends were evident in child poverty statistics. Child poverty rates and the number of poor children peaked in 1984 following the recession of 1980-1981 and declined through the rest of the decade. Following the recession of 1990-1991, the trend appeared to be strongly upward. In 1995, the number of poor children was at a 16-year high of more than 1.4 million and the poverty rate was 20.5 percent, the second highest in 16 years.

Children are poor because their parents are poor, and one of the main reasons for poverty among parents is a lack of good jobs. It should come as no surprise that the poverty rates for adults under 65 tend to move up and down in line with changes in the unemployment rate. In 1995, the unemployment rate was 9.5 percent and the poverty rate was 16.2 percent. Since 1980, the poverty rate for people 18 to 65 has normally been three to five percentage points higher than the unemployment rate. The gap in 1995 was 6.7 percentage points, the highest in 16 years.

While the poverty statistics for all persons give a good overview of poverty, it is often more revealing to look at poor people in terms of families or unattached individuals. Throughout most of the period 1980 to 1995, the poverty rates for unattached people were roughly three times higher than the rates for families. In 1995, however, the poverty rate for unattached individuals was 36.1 percent and the rate for families was 14.4 percent for a ratio of 2 1/2 times to one.

One reason that families have poverty rates that are consistently much lower than unattached individuals is they often have a second family member in the labour force. The percentage of younger married couples with both spouses in the work force has grown dramatically during the last generation, and two-earner couples now far outnumber one-earner couples. Many older families are couples in which both spouses had careers outside the home and in which both get pension benefits aside from the federal government's Old Age Security pension.

DEPTH OF POVERTY AND THE POVERTY GAP

It is one thing to measure the risk of poverty and another to measure its severity. Poverty rates show the percentage of the population which is poor each year, but they do not show whether poor people are living in abject poverty or a few dollars below the poverty line. For that, we need measures of the "depth of poverty." Depth of poverty statistics also allow us to calculate the "poverty gap" to show how much additional income would be needed to bring all Canadians out of poverty.

Figure 7-2 shows the average incomes of poor Canadians as a percentage of the poverty line for eight family types. The groups are arranged with the poorest at the left of the graph and the least poor at the right. Unattached men under 65 were the poorest of the eight family types in 1995,

FIGURE 7-2 Depth of poverty by family type, 1995

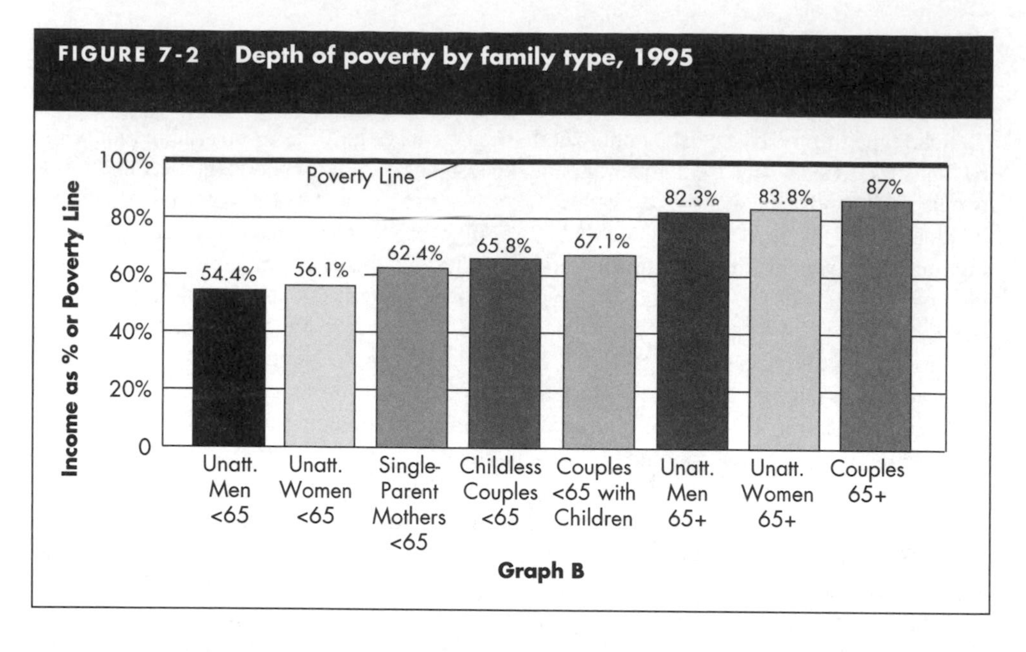

with total incomes that were on average only 54.4 percent of the poverty line. Poor married couples 65 and older were at the other end, with average incomes of 87 percent of the poverty line.

Another measure of the financial plight of poor people is how their incomes compare to average incomes. Table 7-2 gives the average income of poor Canadians by family type in 1995, the average income of *all* Canadians by family type, and the relationship between the two. For example, unattached men under 65 who were poor had a total income of $8 022 on average in 1995. The income of all unattached men under 65, both poor and non-poor, was $27 398 on average. The average income of the poor amounted to 29 percent of the average income of all unattached men under 65.

The differences between the average incomes of the poor and all Canadians are sometimes striking. Poor couples under 65 with children under 18 had an average family income of $19 691 in 1995, for example, while the average income of all couples with children under 18 was $62 116, or three times as large.

The differences were much smaller in the case of unattached seniors and single-parent mothers, because average incomes were much less. The average income of poor single-parent mothers under 65 with children under 18 was $14 696 in 1995, but the average income of all single-parent mothers was only $25 122—much less than average incomes for all husband-wife families.

THE LOW-WAGE POOR

The low-wage poor or "working poor" are poor people who are normally in the labour force. Some researchers reserve the term for poor people who have full-time jobs for virtually the entire year. Others include poor people who have strong ties to the labour market regardless of the number of weeks worked or the normal hours of work each week.[2]

Overall, 24 percent of poor family heads under 65 worked full-time in 1994, 37 percent worked part-time, and the remaining 40 percent did not work at all for wages.[3] Among poor unattached individuals under 65, 16 percent worked full-time, 52 percent

TABLE 7-2 Incomes of the poor compared to average incomes, 1995

Family Type	Averge Income of Poor	Average Income of All	Income of Poor as Percentage of All
Unattached Men under 65	$8 022	$27 398	29%
Unattached Women under 65	$8 271	$23 474	35%
Unattached Men 65 and Older	$12 184	$23 763	51%
Unattached Women 65 and Older	$12 422	$18 741	66%
Childless Couples under 65	$12 828	$55 646	23%
Single-Parent Mothers under 65 with Children under 18	$14 696	$25 122	58%
Couples 65 and Older	$17 905	$38 861	46%
Couples under 65 with Children under 18	$19 691	$62 116	32%

worked part-time, and the other 33 percent did not work at all for wages.

Another way to define the low-wage poor is families and unattached individuals living below the poverty line who get at least half of their total income from employment. This definition puts aside the distinction between full-time and part-time work and focuses on poor people who spend a substantial part of the year in paid jobs. Fifty-four percent of the poor unattached men under 65, 51 percent of the poor unattached women, 45 percent of the poor couples without children, and 56 percent of the poor couples with children were working poor. The exception to the rule was single-parent mothers. Only 20 percent of the poor single-parent mothers under 65 with children under 18 got half or more of their total income from earnings.

NOTES

1. Some of the information for Figure 7-1 comes from Chapter 2 of *The Canadian Fact Book on Poverty - 1994* by David P. Ross, E. Richard Shillington and Clarence Lochhead, published by the Canadian Council on Social Development, and the 1996 edition of *Poverty in Canada* written by Christopher A. Sarlo and published by Fraser Institute. Some of the poverty lines were originally calculated for earlier years and were updated by the CCSD or the National Council of Welfare.
2. For a very strict definition of the term, see *The Canadian Fact Book on Poverty - 1994*, p. 75. For a very loose definition, see the study commissioned by the Canadian Advisory Council on the Status of Women entitled *Women and Labour Market Poverty* by Morley Gunderson and Leon Muszynski with Jennifer Keck, pp. 57–61.
3. Full time means the person worked at least 49 weeks during the year and the normal work week was 30 hours or more. Part time means the person worked less than 49 weeks a year or less than 30 hours a week.

Chapter 8

THE PROS AND CONS OF REDISTRIBUTION POLICIES

Morley Gunderson

(Revised from Morley Gunderson, *Economics of Poverty and Income Distribution* (Toronto: Butterworths, 1983), pp. 13–21. Reprinted with permission.)

INTRODUCTION

Arguments about income redistribution often evoke emotional responses, because the well-being of individuals is involved and because the position of the debaters is often dependent upon where they themselves are on the income distribution scale. Whatever the motives, numerous arguments for and against income redistribution have been advanced.

ARGUMENTS FOR REDISTRIBUTION

In dealing with the arguments in favour of more equitable income distribution, it is useful to distinguish between two interrelated issues. One is the normative issue of why income redistribution should occur; the other is the positive issue of why it does occur. Income redistribution may well occur for reasons other than to satisfy a set of principles upon which society deems it should occur. The following arguments in favour of redistribution are advanced sometimes to explain why redistribution should occur, sometimes to explain why it does occur, and at others times to explain both. The first two arguments—diminishing marginal utility of income and underconsumption—are seldom advanced today; they are discussed because historically they have been advanced as arguments in favour of redistribution.

Diminishing Marginal Utility of Income

Early welfare economists advocated a move toward a more equal distribution of income on the grounds that the marginal utility of income to the rich was less than the marginal utility of income to the poor. Therefore, total utility or welfare could be increased by redistributing from the rich (who valued the income less) to the poor (who valued it more). This intuitively reasonable principle followed from the economic principles of diminishing marginal utility; that is, for a given individual the additional utility generated by an additional unit of consumption decreases as more of the commodity is consumed.

While it may be reasonable to assume that this principle eventually applies to the consumption activities of a given individual, there is no scientific basis upon which to make the comparison across individuals: interpersonal comparisons of utility are not valid.

It may well be reasonable to assume that an extra dollar to a rich person means less than an extra dollar to a poor person, even though one could never formally prove that statement. Decisions often have to be made on the basis of beliefs that cannot be proven; for this reason, the concept of diminishing marginal utility of income may not be a bad rule of thumb.

Underconsumption View

To the extent that the poor consume a greater portion of their incomes than do the rich, redistribution from the rich to the poor could increase consumption—and hence aggregate demand—in the economy. This view has taken on particular appeal in periods of depression: redistributing from the rich who save to the poor who consume would help the economy spend its way out of the depression. The argument is in contrast to the one often advanced today that tax cuts to the rich would encourage them to invest (thereby improving the ability of the economy to produce without inflationary pressures), and this spending would eventually trickle down to the poor in the form of job opportunities and lower product prices.

While the underconsumptionist view has some intuitive appeal, there are a number of problems with the argument. First, it is not always clear that aggregate demand should be increased; in inflationary times the opposite forces may be needed. Constantly changing the income distribution so as to achieve macroeconomic objectives of having just the right amount of aggregate demand could clearly be dangerous. Second, if the objective is to change aggregate demand, then there are other well-known policy instruments, such as monetary and fiscal policies, to achieve the objective; there is no need to tinker with the income distribution. Third and most important, it is not clear what redistribution would do to aggregate consumption in the economy. Redistribution involves *changes* in income and, while the poor may well consume a larger portion of their *level* of income, it is not clear that they would consume a larger portion of small changes in that income.

It is hazardous to support redistribution on the grounds that it will have a desirable effect on aggregate demand in the economy; numerous hidden assumptions are involved for it to have such an impact. In recent years this rationale has also lost much of its effect because higher aggregate demand has not always been desirable owing to its inflationary impact. For these reasons the underconsumption view or the diminishing marginal utility of income idea tend not to be advanced today as rationales for redistribution.

Interdependent Utility

An economic efficiency rationale for redistribution can occur if potential donors (e.g., rich persons) care about the welfare of potential recipients (e.g., poor persons); that is, if the utility of the rich is a function not only of their own welfare but also of the welfare of others. Such benevolence or interdependent utility means that the donors can be made better off when the recipients are better off.

Unfortunately, such redistribution will not occur automatically through the marketplace because of the public-goods nature of redistribution. There would be insufficient incentive for an individual who cares about the poor to give to the poor, because the benefits of that redistribution would also go to other individuals who care about the poor but who do not give to the poor. In such circumstances it would make sense for the potential donors to vote for a certain amount of redistribution and to pay for that by taxes upon themselves. In that way they can share the costs of the redistribution they desire. The public-goods nature of redistribution implies that it may have to occur through the public sector under its tax system rather than through the private sector and its marketplace.

Donors may not only care about the welfare of the recipients; they may also care about the things that make up the welfare of the recipients. For example, donors may not value an increase in the leisure of the poor, but they may attach considerable weight to the poor spending on education, shelter, or food for their children. In such circumstances efficient redistribution may involve transfers-in-kind of these items rather than unconditional lump-sum transfers that the poor can use as they want.

Buy Behaviour and Avoid Conflict

Redistribution may also be seen as a device to influence the behaviour of the recipients, usually in the hope of reducing conflict between the rich and the poor. It can be used, for example, to avoid rioting, or in the extreme, revolution. Although the "War on Poverty" in the United States was conceived prior to the rioting in the 1960s, some would regard the substantial social expenditures at that time as attempts to bribe the poor to end the rioting. Marxists often regard redistribution (e.g., from land reform or from social expenditures) as a way of buying off the working classes in an attempt to thwart ultimate revolution. Such is especially the case if the redistribution is to those who pose the main threat, for example, potential leaders.

Buy Insurance

Redistribution to influence the behaviour of the poor can be thought of as insurance against consequences such as rioting or revolution, with taxes on the donors being the insurance premium. Donors may also want redistribution so as to guarantee a certain income floor in case *they themselves* should become poor. In this case they are insuring not against the behaviour of others but rather against a possible calamity that may happen to them. For this reason, donors may support, for example, certain programs like welfare, health care, or employment insurance.

Voting and the Political Process

The importance of voting and the political process has already been alluded to in the discussion of the rationales for income redistribution. Basically, the political process was seen as a device to set up taxes and transfers through the public sector, since the private marketplace would not guarantee the income distribution desired by society—the socially optimal distribution. Individuals were seen as willing to tax themselves so as to provide redistribution transfers because donors simply cared about the recipients, wanted to buy the good behaviour of the recipients, or wanted to buy insurance in case they themselves became poor.

The political process, however, may also be used in a more narrow self-interested fashion for voters to redistribute income in their favour. Downs (1957), for example, argued that individuals form political coalitions so that the state will redistribute income in their favour. Since the average income is inflated by the very high income of a few very rich people, more people will have an income that is below, rather than above, average. In seeking to maximize the probability of being reelected, politicians will try to obtain the support of the mass of voters with below-average incomes by redistributing in their favour.

This process may be offset, in part at least, by other factors. The rich, having the most to lose, will try to control the political process through mechanisms other than the "one-person, one-vote" procedure which gives them little influence. They may use their wealth and influence to support a candidate; they may support policies to restrict the voting franchise to those with property; and they may support amending formulas requiring more than a majority vote. The rich may also try to "bribe" some of the lower-income groups out of a coalition that would involve mass redistribution. The poor themselves may not always support such coalitions because they feel they themselves will be upwardly mobile.

Marxists tend to emphasize that the rich will use the instruments of the state to maintain their position and prevent redistribution through the voting mechanism. Hence, transfers to the poor will be used selectively to co-opt revolution, and public expenditures on such items as the police and military will be used by the rich to protect their privileged position. In such circumstances the political process may be used to redistribute from the rich to the poor; however, in general it will be used to redistribute from the poor to the rich.

Raise Income of Providers of Redistribution

Redistribution may also be supported to raise the income of those whose jobs and livelihood depend upon the redistribution *process* (as opposed to recipients who receive the transfers and donors who pay). In some cases this may be an obvious motive, for example, in the case of rich countries providing conditional aid to poor countries (on the condition that they use it to make purchases in the donor country), or providing transfers-in-kind such as farm produce or military equipment. In such circumstances the objective of the donor is probably a mixed one: to provide aid but to provide it in a form that benefits the donor country.

The motivation may be more subtle, for example, in the case of government employees whose jobs depend upon the redistribution process. (It is probably no accident that voters in Washington, D.C., tended not to support Reagan in the 1980 United States election.) Other groups, such as social workers (and even economists who do research in the area of income redistribution!), may also depend on their livelihood on the redistribution process. That is not to say that they would support income redistribution programs mainly to increase their own incomes; however, it certainly is easier to support redistribution when it is consistent with one's self-interest.

Social Contract Perspective

While theorists of social justice (e.g., Rawls, 1971) are mainly concerned with the issue of developing a set of first principles for determining how income ought to be distributed in society, and often with critically assessing the market as one instrument of income distribution, they can provide a rationale for redistribution within a market perspective. That is, income redistribution may be supported on the grounds that it is part of a social contract. We may simply prefer a society that provides a reasonable degree of equality to one that does not provide any. As Rawls (1971) suggested, if we were risk averse and had no information on where we could be in the income redistribution, we might well agree to a social contract that guaranteed a degree of equality. The fact that some individuals would not currently support such a notion simply reflects that they know where they are in the income distribution, and hence would not support redistribution from themselves to others. If they did not know whether they were going to be rich or poor, however, they might well support a social contract involving redistribution.

In this context the social contract can be thought of as a form of insurance. It is a set of principles that we agree to be bound by, presumably because the existence of the contract makes society better off than it would be without the contract—even though the contract may turn out to make some individuals worse off than they would be without the contract, once their position in society was determined or changed.

ARGUMENTS AGAINST REDISTRIBUTION

Incentive Problem

The main concern with income redistribution probably stems from its possible effect on incentives, and hence on economic growth and the size of the pie to be distributed. The concern is that if public policy taxes the rich to make transfers to the poor, then the work incentives of the rich and poor may be reduced.

The rich may have less incentive to work or invest because their earnings from these activities are being taxed. The poor may also have less incentive to work because they can afford not to, and because they often have to give up some of their transfer payments when they work.

While there may be counterarguments as to why these effects are theoretically or quantitatively not important, or at least overemphasized, the fact remains that they can be important. In the extreme, if redistribution were to guarantee complete equality of income, what would be the incentive to work or invest? While existing redistribution schemes are not designed to achieve complete equality, the fact remains that their redistribution toward equality can have effects on the incentive to work or invest; these effects may reduce economic growth and hence the size of the economic pie available.

For this reason, those who are concerned with the adverse incentive problem tend to emphasize that it is easier to share a growing economic pie than to share one that is dwindling, because redistribution reduces incentives. Their belief is that the best way to raise the income of the poor is not through redistribution but rather through attaining growth through economic efficiency. This belief that the benefits of growth will "trickle down" to the poor is exemplified by the statement of goals in the *First Annual Review* of the Economic Council of Canada (1964:200): "The most effective 'war on poverty' will be effective achievement of potential output ... . Steady economic growth would also make possible significant improvements in standards for low-income groups, and provide rising margins of income and resources over time for further advances toward more comprehensive and adequate services and facilities in the social welfare field."

Encroachment of the State

Concerns are also expressed over the fact that redistribution involves an encroachment of the state in areas where some feel that individuals or the family should be the principal decision-making unit. This can give rise to "state sovereignty" over "consumer sovereignty," and it can lead to the redistribution process being demeaning to the self-respect of recipients. It can give rise to large administrative costs that support public employees administering the redistribution. These costs may be irreversible and not necessarily responsive to the needs of the poor once a bureaucracy becomes entrenched.

Perverse Redistribution

Redistribution may end up benefiting the well-to-do more than the needy; in that sense it becomes perverse. This may occur not only because those who administer the redistribution may depend upon it for their livelihood (and they may be well-to-do professionals), but also because those who need the redistribution least may be better able than those who need it most to appropriate the benefits of redistribution. In addition, some universal programs designed to benefit everyone may in fact go disproportionately to high-income families, if, for example, they live longer to receive pensions, or if they have larger families to receive family allowances.

Some people may be poor because they lack the skills to make themselves eligible for income transfers. On the other hand, those who are skilled at making themselves eligible for transfer payments may be the least in need because they can utilize their skills elsewhere to earn a reasonable income. They are also the ones most likely to be able to obtain information on the availability of transfers and how best to become eligible, and they are probably more skilled at hiding their long-term position of wealth as opposed to their short-term low income.

As a result, there is some concern that income distribution programs beginning with the best intentions may evolve into perverse redistribution, as those least in need are best able to take advantage of the programs. This argument is not so much against the principle of redistribution but rather against what redistribution may evolve into. It becomes an argument against redistribution if such an evolution is inevitable.

REFERENCES

Downs, A. 1957 *An Economic Theory of Democracy* New York: Harper and Row.

Economic Council of Canada 1964 *First Annual Review: Economic Goals for Canada to 1970* Ottawa: Queen's Printer.

Rawls, J. 1971 *A Theory of Justice* Cambridge, MA: Belknap Press.

FOR FURTHER REFERENCE: INCOME, WEALTH, AND POVERTY

Ambert, Anne Marie 1997 *The Web of Poverty: Psychological Perspectives* Binghamton, New York: The Haworth Press. An interesting attempt to link social structure and individual circumstance in the debate about poverty. Focuses upon both Canada and the United States.

Cheal, David J. 1996 *New Poverty: Families in Postmodern Society* Westport, Conn.: Greenwood Press. Reflecting recent currents in postmodernism, this text examines family life and poverty in new ways.

Macklem, R. Tiff 1994 *Wealth, Disposable Income and Consumption: Some Evidence for Canada* Ottawa: Bank of Canada. A technical but rich assessment of issues related to the distribution of income and wealth in Canada.

Rashid, Abdul 1994 *Family Income in Canada* Scarborough, Ont.: Prentice-Hall. An overview of changing patterns of income attainment in Canada.

Robson, William and William Scarth 1997 *Equality and Prosperity: Finding Common Ground* C.D. Howe Institute. An economic assessment of linkages between economic growth and social equality.

Statistics Canada *Annual Income Distributions by Size in Canada* Ottawa: Ministry of Supply and Services. This annual report presents the most recent data on income distributions. The statistics are derived from the annual Survey of Consumer Finances conducted by Statistics Canada.

Statistics Canada Quarterly *Perspectives on Labour and Income* Ottawa: Statistics Canada. Published four times a year, this is an excellent source of up-to-date information on various topics related to the study of inequality.

OCCUPATION

Chapter 9

EDUCATIONAL CREDENTIALS AND THE CHANGING OCCUPATIONAL STRUCTURE

Douglas Baer

(An original chapter written for this volume.)

The Post-Industrial Economy

The Canadian occupational structure has undergone major changes since the early 1970s. As Clement and Myles (1994:3) note, "average wages and earnings have not grown and their distribution has become more unequal, and everywhere workers are faced with the insecurities and dislocations associated with globalization and technological change." This slowing of economic growth and widening of social inequality comes on the heels of late 20th century trends which were witnessed even during periods of sustained economic expansion prior to the 1970s. The most notable of these trends has been the shift in advanced Western economies from an economic system based primarily on the manufacture of physical goods (cars, television sets, refrigerators) to one based on "knowledge goods" (computer software, television and movie entertainment, etc.) and on personal services (restaurant services, for example). This trend signifies what many writers refer to as a **post-industrial** economic order (Bell, 1973; see also Esping-Anderson, 1993; Myles et al. 1993; Clement and Myles, 1994).

For people working in it, the new post-industrial economy has good and bad features compared to the previous world of work, which was dominated by industrial manufacturing. The "new" knowledge-based jobs are said to involve a less hierarchical (or "post-Fordist") structure with less routine and more room for individual initiative. For those painting an optimistic picture of this quickly emerging social future (see Bell, 1973), technology has created a work world of meaningful, more pleasant jobs. At the same time, however, the new economy can also be said to promote unemployment and disruption through de-industrialization (Lovatt, 1984), to create a cadre of low-paid service workers whose jobs hardly partake in the advantages of the new "knowledge" economy (Myles et al., 1988), and to create a massive cultural divide between those with "good jobs" and those with "bad jobs" (Picot et al., 1990).

More Women in the Workforce

During the same period that the economy has moved away from an emphasis on industrial manufacturing, there has also been a rapid increase in the employment of women in the workforce. While there is a substantial literature on the continued occupational segregation of women, both between occupations and within occupations (Charles, 1992; Fox and Fox, 1987; Wright and Jacobs, 1994; Birkelund et al., 1994; Hakim, 1996), it is clear that the proportion of women in the workforce (and the proportion of the workforce which is female) has been increasing in most Western societies over the past twenty years.

Changes in the proportion of the Canadian workforce that is female can be seen in Table 9-1, which provides data from the 1971, 1981 and 1991 Canadian Censuses.[1]

The Canadian workforce steadily increased in size during this period, from 8.97 million in 1971 to 14.62 million in 1991. During the same time period, the female proportion of the workforce rose from 36.5% to 45.7%. Both changes—in the size of the workforce and in the female proportion—were slightly more pronounced in the period between 1971 and 1981 than they were in the period between 1981 and 1991.

Discretionary Versus Routine Jobs

Which types of occupations have become relatively more or less important since 1971? To examine this question, we can employ the occupational coding scheme used by Bernard et al. (1994; see also Bernard et al., 1997). The original version of this scheme divides all jobs into 12 major categories on the basis of job skills and other related occupational attributes. For non-manual occupations, these categories are: higher managers, professionals, middle managers, semi-professionals (mostly teachers), technicians (including nurses), a single category for supervisors, forepersons and artisans, and a category for all clerical workers. To simplify the tables somewhat, these major categories are further collapsed into 1) managers (middle and higher); 2) professionals; 3) technicians and semi-professionals; 4) forepersons, supervisors, and artisans (simply labelled "supervisors") and 5) clerical workers. Manual workers are divided into two categories: 1) service workers[2] and 2) all other blue-collar workers. The division between "good jobs" and "bad jobs" does not correspond exactly to the division between manual and non-manual work. As Rinehart (1996) notes, many white-collar jobs share with blue-collar jobs a number of negative attributes. These include low pay, a high likelihood of layoff associated with swings in the economy and with seasonal factors, routine work, an absence of job autonomy or job authority, and relatively low

TABLE 9-1 Gender composition of work 1971–1991

Year	Female	Male	Total	Number
1971	36.5%	63.5%	100.0%	8 972 135
1981	42.0%	58.0%	100.0%	12 619 015
1991	45.7%	54.3%	100.0%	14 617 220

skill levels. In the end, only the degree of physical labour and some technical aspects of production (for example, the presence of assembly lines) differentiate blue-collar and white-collar jobs. A more important distinction, then, is probably the division between what might be called "discretionary" jobs—jobs with skill requirements, interaction with people, and some degree of job autonomy and authority—and jobs that might be labelled "routine" jobs. This latter category would include both clerical workers and service workers.

Table 9-2 provides a picture of changes in the relative importance of the seven major job categories over the twenty-year period between 1971 and 1991. From 1971 to 1991, the number of routine jobs rose from 6.16 million to 9.19 million—an increase of 49%. At the same time, the number of discretionary jobs went from 2.81 million to 5.42 million —an increase of 92.8%. In both 1971 and 1991, there were more routine jobs than there were discretionary jobs, but the gap narrowed during the twenty-year time period. Of the seven major occupational categories in Table 9-2, the categories with the least absolute growth (exhibiting a *decline* in relative terms) were supervisors and blue-collar workers. Many of the occupations listed under "supervisor" were forepersons and supervisors in factory settings, although white-collar supervisory jobs are also included in this category. In general, there has been a reduction in the proportion of workers involved in "lower management," signifying that jobs have tended to become less hierarchically ordered at the lower levels, or that there has been a decline in those job areas (industrial manufacturing, for example)

TABLE 9-2 Distribution of discretionary vs. routine jobs, 1971 & 1991

		Female	Male	N
1971	Managers	3.0%	8.3%	571 240
	Professional	0.8%	3.9%	250 000
	Semi-professional, technical	14.9%	8.3%	961 825
	Supervisors	4.6%	15.4%	1 029 520
	Total Discretionary	23.2%	36.0%	2 812 585
	Clerks	28.8%	6.0%	1 285 275
	Service	22.8%	11.7%	1 411 025
	Blue collar	25.3%	46.3%	3 463 250
	Total Routine	76.8%	64.0%	6 159 550
1991	Managers	8.5%	12.0%	1 522 415
	Professional	2.1%	5.4%	567 745
	Semi-professional, technical	17.5%	10.5%	2 003 630
	Supervisors	6.3%	11.4%	1 329 310
	Total Discretionary	34.5%	39.3%	5 423 100
	Clerks	29.1%	7.6%	2 543 110
	Service	18.1%	10.5%	2 039 945
	Blue collar	18.4%	42.6%	4 611 065
	Total Routine	65.5%	60.7%	9 194 120

in which multiple-level hierarchies extend down to the shop floor. Management jobs, however, are not disappearing: of the seven occupational categories shown in Table 9-2, the category with the largest percentage increase was that of managers. The size of this group rose from 571 thousand in 1971 to 1.522 million in 1991. The professional and semi-professional/technician category also saw growth rates of over 100% in the twenty-year time period. Only in the "supervisor, foreperson, and artisan" category has the expansion of discretionary jobs been relatively modest.

The percentages shown in Table 9-2 are column percentages, indicating what percentage of men and what percentage of women find themselves in a particular occupation. For example, the table shows that 3% of all women in the workforce in 1971 were employed as managers; the equivalent percentage in 1991 was 8.5%. The percentages in this table indicate that, for both males and females, the overall percentage of the workforce involved in discretionary employment has increased from 1971 to 1991. The increase has been more dramatic in the case of females; in 1971, only 23% of women in the workforce had discretionary jobs, whereas by 1991 this figure had risen to 34.5%. The comparable male percentage increased only slightly during the same time period, from 36.0% to 39.3%. For women, the major shifts were away from manual labour (down from 25% to 18%) and service work (down from 23% to 18%) and into discretionary job categories. The decline in the importance of blue-collar work was slightly less pronounced for males (dropping from 46.3% to 42.6%), but there has been an overall decline in this sort of work. The proportion of individuals in management increased in the case of males, from 8% to 12%. This increase is substantial, though not quite as dramatic as the increase observed among females. While women's likelihood of holding a management job improved in the time period from 1971 to 1991, it was still the case that, in 1991, a woman was less likely to hold a job in middle or upper management than a man (8.5% versus 12.0%).

The data presented in Table 9-2 do not show a massive expansion of jobs in the service sector—the so-called "McJobs" associated with waiting on tables and flipping hamburgers at fast food outlets. Instead, the category of routine jobs that experienced a small amount of growth was the "clerical" category, which included receptionists, bookkeepers, secretaries, salespersons, and related occupations. Like jobs labelled "service," these jobs typically involve a moderate to high level of interaction with people, fairly low levels of formal skill requirements (for example, formal education qualifications required for the job), and relatively low earnings.

Overall, the numbers presented in Table 9-2 demonstrate the increasing importance of jobs with formal skill requirements in the newly emerging post-industrial economy. While traditional manual labour remains a significant facet of the occupational structure for males, its relative importance is declining. Many of the jobs in the expanding "discretionary" job categories have formal educational requirements in addition to specific skill requirements. All of them involve modest to high levels of generic "people skills," such as managing and coordinating the work of others, or interacting with the public.

Age Cohorts: Is Getting a Good Job a Matter of Being Born at the Right Time?

The distinction between discretionary and routine jobs points to the importance of education in the process by which individuals end up with either good or bad jobs.

Educational requirements are not the only factor influencing whether individuals will find themselves in one of the discretionary job categories. A body of mobility research points to the continued importance of parental social status on occupational outcomes (Erikson and Goldthorpe, 1992; Biblarz et al., 1997; Teachman, 1997; Westergaard, 1990; Slomczysnki and Krauze, 1987). For many discretionary jobs, occupational attainment may also be related to the sheer availability of positions, as members of one age cohort either block the mobility chances of successive generations by filling all available positions, or create new opportunities by retiring and leaving room for younger workers to enter vacant positions. While the demand for discretionary workers has clearly increased, it does not necessarily follow that the availability of these "good jobs" extends equally to all age groups. Some managerial jobs, for example, entail at least a nominal requirement of prior experience in the sector in question; thus, we might expect individuals who are under, say, age 30 or 35, to be fairly unlikely to obtain these jobs even if the demand increases. At the extreme, some professions may even be locked out to younger individuals who are better qualified than the older individuals already occupying jobs in that profession, as many graduates of teachers' college programs in the early 1990s can attest.

Table 9-3 provides some indication of whether individuals in one particular age cohort did better than those in other age cohorts. It is clear from this table that individuals under the age of 25 were largely pegged into routine occupations in both 1971 and 1991. What changed, though, was that the proportion of individuals in this age group still in the education system went up. For employed individuals under the age of 25, the jobs they held were probably "transitional" jobs—either low-wage part-time or temporary jobs held at the same time as they went to school or between periods of schooling, or temporary jobs held just after graduation, from which they hoped to move eventually into more secure discretionary-sector jobs. It is common, when assessing the question of what happens to individuals at different levels of schooling or different levels of parental background, to focus on those who have completed their education, and to treat separately individuals under the age of university graduation (see, for example, Wanner, 1996).

In Table 9-3, we follow this procedure by distinguishing those in the 15–24 age

TABLE 9-3 Discretionary vs. routine jobs by age, 1971–1991

Year	Job Type	15–24	25–34	35–49	50–65	Over 65	Overall/ Total
1971	Discretionary	16.2%	36.8%	36.8%	36.2%	39.4%	31.3%
	Routine	83.8%	63.2%	63.2%	63.8%	60.6%	68.7%
	N	2 353 215	2 026 445	2 599 910	1 699 890	292 675	8 972 135
1981	Discretionary	14.5%	39.1%	42.4%	38.5%	44.7%	33.6%
	Routine	85.5%	60.9%	57.6%	61.5%	55.3%	66.4%
	N	3 285 620	3 500 955	3 389 660	2 147 840	294 940	12 619 015
1991	Discretionary	15.6%	37.7%	45.3%	41.2%	51.3%	37.1%
	Routine	84.4%	62.3%	54.7%	58.8%	48.7%	62.9%
	N	2 720 190	4 127 365	5 102 740	2 352 530	314 395	14 617 220

group. We also place people over the age of 65 into a separate category. The number of workers in this latter category is relatively small and also did not increase substantially from 1971 to 1991. This is because most individuals have retired at age 65. It is possible that, aside from individuals who are able to set up self-employed circumstances in their post-retirement years, these people consist mostly of high-demand workers or workers in a small number of professions in which mandatory retirement may not apply, such as medicine and law. The big increase in the proportion of people in discretionary jobs in the over-65 age group may simply reflect the increased inability of workers in routine jobs to hold on to a job or to find employment after mandatory retirement at age 65.

Aside from workers under the age of 25 and over the age of 65, there are slight increases in the proportions of people in the 35–49 and again in the 50–65 age group who hold discretionary jobs. In 1971, 36.8% of those in the 35–49 age group held discretionary jobs; by 1991, this percentage was 45.3%. Likewise, 41% of those in the 50–65 age group held discretionary jobs, which represents an increase from 36% in 1971. The shifts seemed to occur throughout the twenty-year period, although the improvement for the 35–49 age group was a bit higher from 1971 to 1981 (37% to 42%) than it was from 1981 to 1991 (42% to 45%). In addition to having a greater likelihood of obtaining a discretionary job, the 35–49 age group doubled in size from 1971 to 1991, a reflection of the passage through these age thresholds of the "baby boom" generation, i.e., individuals born after World War Two and roughly prior to 1960. Did this generation fill up all of the "good job" spaces and leave the subsequent generation disadvantaged? From 1971 to 1991, the percentage of individuals in the 25–34 age group who were able to obtain discretionary jobs hardly changed—from 36.8% to 37.7%—while, in the entire labour force, this percentage increased from 31.3% to 37.1%. More dramatically, the proportion of individuals in the 25–34 age group who obtained discretionary jobs actually declined from 39.1% in 1981 to 37.7% in 1991; at the same time, there was an increase in the proportion of discretionary jobs across the entire workforce. These figures are at least consistent with the idea that earlier generations may have been more advantaged than those who entered the labour market between 1981 and 1991.

The Increasing Importance of Education

The importance of educational credentials in obtaining both stable, high-paying jobs and promotions into better jobs is fairly well known (see Blau, 1967; Ornstein, 1981; Blakely and Harvey, 1988; Hou and Balakrishnan, 1996; Isheda et al., 1997). All other things being equal—including the age cohort one was born into—it can be expected that better-educated individuals will do better in the job market, and will be more likely to obtain discretionary as opposed to routine jobs. The data presented below support this contention. Aside from the question of just how substantial this effect is in Canada, one can also ask about trends over the period from the 1970s. Has the general rise in educational credentials in the population, along with increasing demands on the part of prospective employers for educated individuals, eliminated the possibility that individuals without educational qualifications can still obtain a "good job"?

Table 9-4 provides an overview of the relationship between education and occupation from 1971 to 1991, using the broad categories of "discretionary" and "routine" jobs. Education is grouped into 5 categories: less than grade 12 (essentially, those without a high school diploma), grades 12 or 13 (usually, those with a high school diploma), some post-secondary (including community college graduates and individuals who attended but did not complete university), an undergraduate university degree, and a post-bachelor's university degree or certification (e.g., a Master's degree, a professional degree, or PhD).

It is clear from Table 9-4 that individuals with high school education are fairly unlikely to obtain non-routine or discretionary jobs, and that individuals with university credentials are fairly likely to obtain them. Individuals with some post-secondary education stand somewhere between these extremes. It is also clear that there has been a pronounced rise in the educational background of the Canadian workforce. In 1971, 55.9% of all individuals in the workforce did not have a high school diploma; by 1991, this proportion had dropped to 26.7%. The proportion of individuals with university education (adding the B.A. and post-B.A. columns) rose from 6.9% in 1971 to 14.3% in 1991.

At each level of education, the likelihood of obtaining discretionary work dropped from 1971 through to 1991. The competition for "good jobs" appears to have become stiffer over time, and the likelihood that a university graduate will end up with a routine job in 1991, while still fairly small, is slightly higher than it was in 1971. For individuals with one university degree (bachelor's-level), the likelihood of ending up in the "routine" job sector actually went down from 1971 to 1981, from 21.3% to 19.8%, but rose to 22.4% in 1991. For individuals with post-bachelor's education, there was an increase in the likelihood of ending up with a "routine" job from 1981 to 1991, after virtually no change from 1971 to 1981. Of course, it is also the case that the size of this group of individuals increased fairly substantially from 1981 to 1991.

While the overall working population only increased from 12.6 million to 14.6 million, the number of individuals with post-bachelor's university education increased from 464 thousand to 710 thousand in the

TABLE 9-4 Discretionary vs. routine jobs by level of education, 1971–1991

		<Grade 12	Gr. 12/13	Some Post-sec.	B.A.	Post B.A.	Overall
1971	Discretionary	20.2%	28.3%	45.2%	78.7%	92.1%	31.3%
	Routine	79.8%	71.7%	54.8%	21.3%	7.9%	68.7%
	N	5 016 215	1 390 160	1 954 100	319 450	292 210	8 972 135
1981	Discretionary	18.9%	23.4%	40.2%	80.2%	92.0%	33.6%
	Routine	81.1%	76.6%	59.8%	19.8%	8.0%	66.4%
	N	4 763 850	2 356 020	4 177 210	857 520	464 415	12 619 015
1991	Discretionary	18.6%	25.5%	40.0%	77.6%	90.3%	37.1%
	Routine	81.4%	74.5%	60.0%	22.4%	9.7%	62.9%
	N	3 901 495	3 167 265	5 466 295	1 371 985	710 180	14 617 220
Percentages of workforce in each education category:							
1971		55.9%	15.5%	21.8%	3.6%	3.3%	100.0%
1981		37.8%	18.7%	33.1%	6.8%	3.7%	100.0%
1991		26.7%	21.7%	37.4%	9.4%	4.9%	100.0%

same period. In other words, there was much more competition for any available jobs at this level. An even more dramatic expansion took place in the group with B.A.-level education. While the overall labour force increased in size by 63% from 1971 to 1991, there was an increase of over 300% in the bachelor's category—from 319 thousand in 1971 to 1372 thousand in 1991. Despite this major increase in size, this group came very close to holding on to its relative advantage in the workforce since, as mentioned earlier, the likelihood of obtaining a "discretionary" job only dropped marginally, from 78.7% in 1971 to 77.6% in 1991.

Individuals with low levels of education do not appear to have been shut out of discretionary jobs entirely, even in 1991, since 18.6% of those with less than grade 12 education held such jobs in 1991. This may, in part, be due to older individuals, who obtained their jobs when credential requirements were not nearly so high, and continued to hold down places prior to their retirement and replacement by a new cohort with higher levels of credentials. Or it could simply be that education is not the only determining factor: it might still be possible for individuals in some sectors of the economy to hold management jobs, by establishing their own companies or by rising through the ranks of existing companies without holding educational credentials. The latter possibility is more likely to occur in the case of individuals who entered the job market decades ago, when educational credentials were less important, and can be sorted out to some degree by examining the effects of education within particular age categories.

What Happens to People Who Are New to the Labour Market?

Examining the occupational outcomes for individuals in a cohort in which many are still in the process of completing their education is likely to render a misleading impression of the relationship between education and occupational outcomes. Individuals who are still in the process of completing educational credentials will typically hold part-time or summer jobs which are "routine" jobs. Such jobs hardly represent important elements in an individual's career trajectory, although small numbers of individuals, as suggested in Table 9-4, may find themselves chronically unable to obtain a good job both immediately after graduation and later in life. To obtain a sense of how succeeding generations fare in the job market, we can consider the situation of the 25–34 age group in each of the three census years. This is the youngest age category within which most individuals have completed their education. Certainly, a small number of individuals will still be in the process of completing professional university degrees after age 25, but this is the age at which the vast majority of individuals, even at the higher levels of credentialization, have entered the job market.

Table 9-5 shows that the educational credentials of those in the 25–34 age group have increased substantially over the 20-year period from 1971 to 1991. Especially between 1971 and 1981, there was a big increase in the proportion of individuals, both male and female, with university degrees. By comparison, the proportion of individuals with university degrees remained fairly stable from 1981 to 1991, increasing slightly in the case of women (11.4% to 13.5%) and hardly at all in the case of men (from 11.9% to 12.0%).[3] By 1991, the proportion of the female workforce with university degrees in the 25–34 age group actually exceeded the proportion of men with such credentials.

The picture provided by Table 9-5 is more dramatic than that which is shown in Table 9-4, because this new table concentrates on those in the 25–34 age group, and

TABLE 9-5 Workforce education level, individuals age 25–34 in workforce by gender, 1971–1991

		Education Level: <Grade 12	Gr. 12/13	Some Post-sec.	B.A.	Post B.A.	Overall
1971	Females	309 615	125 425	225 305	35 680	21 085	717 110
	%	43.2	17.5	31.4	5.0	2.9	100.0
	Males	648 050	177 520	316 555	80 210	87 000	1 309 335
	%	49.5	13.6	24.2	6.1	6.6	100.0
1981	Females	348 805	322 090	604 670	172 885	62 010	1 510 460
	%	23.1	21.3	40.0	11.4	4.1	100.0
	Males	539 555	329 190	777 320	237 320	107 110	1 990 495
	%	27.1	16.5	39.1	11.9	5.4	100.0
1991	Females	270 070	463 030	859 880	261 895	82 790	1 937 665
	%	13.9	23.9	44.4	13.5	4.3	100.0
	Males	446 420	494 825	891 400	263 065	93 990	2 189 700
	%	20.4	22.6	40.7	12.0	4.3	100.0

does not include older workers who entered the workforce 30, 40, and even 50 years earlier. In 1971, 49.5% of the working males and 43.2% of the working females in the 25–34 age range had less than a grade 12 education. By 1991, these proportions had dropped to 20.4% in the case of males and only 13.9% in the case of females.

By 1991, individuals with less than high school education were the exception, not the norm. The most pronounced decline in the relative size of this group took place between 1971 and 1981 (from 50% down to 27% in the case of males, and from 43% down to 23% in the case of females).

Table 9-6 shows how individuals aged 25–34 with differing levels of education fared in each of the three census years. This table is also divided by gender, so that outcomes are examined separately for males and females. To simplify the table, only the percentage of individuals with discretionary jobs is displayed; in each cell, the percentage of individuals with routine jobs will simply be 100% minus the reported discretionary percentage. Thus, for example, 91.0% of the females with less than a grade 12 education in 1971 held routine jobs (100% minus 9.0%).

In addition to showing the clear relationship between having higher education and obtaining a discretionary job, Table 9-6 contains some interesting gender patterns.

In 1971, there was a male-female difference in the likelihood of getting a discretionary job at all levels of education, but this pattern was much more pronounced in the lower education categories. By 1991, this gender difference for individuals with lower levels of education had been reduced considerably. This result occurred because the likelihood that women with low education would obtain discretionary jobs actually went up between 1971 and 1991. For men, the reverse was true: the likelihood that less-educated males would obtain discretionary jobs went down from 21% to 15% among those with less than grade 12, and from 46% to 25% among of those with grade 12 or grade 13 education. It should

TABLE 9-6 Type of job by education by gender, 1971–1991
Individuals in the workforce age 25–34

		Education Level: <Grade 12	Gr. 12/13	Some Post-sec.	B.A.	Post B.A.	Overall
1971	Female % Discretionary	9.0%	17.7%	53.2%	83.0%	88.3%	30.4%
	Male % Discretionary	21.1%	46.0%	50.1%	86.3%	93.1%	40.3%
1981	Female % Discretionary	11.3%	18.0%	39.9%	77.2%	86.8%	34.8%
	Male % Discretionary	18.6%	32.9%	43.7%	83.1%	92.1%	42.4%
1991	Female % Discretionary	13.4%	21.6%	38.4%	75.4%	86.4%	37.9%
	Male % Discretionary	14.6%	24.5%	38.7%	78.3%	88.1%	37.5%

be noted, however, that obtaining a discretionary job with less than some post-secondary education was still fairly unlikely for both men and women.

From 1971 to 1991, there was a drop in the proportion of discretionary jobs among individuals age 25–34 with some post-secondary education but without a university degree. This drop occurred for both males and females. In 1991, 38% of both males and females held a discretionary job, a proportion twice as large as that for people with high school education. Even so, this 38% figure is lower than the 53% (female) and 50% (male) proportions observed in 1971.

Among those who were university-educated, there was a slight erosion from 1971 to 1991 in the odds of getting a discretionary job, but this was not as severe as it was in the case of those with only some post-secondary education. For individuals with one university degree, there was a drop of roughly 8% for both males and females. For individuals with post-bachelor's credentials, the drop was roughly 2% for females and 5% for males. Here, unlike the case of individuals with some post-secondary education, the erosion was more or less continuous from 1971 through to 1991, except for males with post-bachelor's degree credentials, in which case the majority of the decline took place between 1981 and 1991.

Table 9-7 provides a detailed breakdown of occupational outcomes for the 25–34 age group, using the seven major occupational categories noted earlier, rather than the simple distinction between routine and discretionary jobs. To simplify this table, gender divisions and the intermediate 1981 year are omitted. Table 9-7 is organized so that columns add up to 100%. Each percentage represents the proportion of individuals in each education category who end up in the listed occupation. For example, 10.3% of all those individuals age 25–34 with less than grade 12 education ended up in a supervisory job in 1971. This figure fell to 6.5% by 1991.

Where do individuals with varying levels of education end up in the job market? Those with less than a grade 12 education are most likely to end up with blue-collar work; if anything, this likelihood is stronger in 1991 (59.3%) than it was in 1971

TABLE 9-7 Occupational placement of individuals age 25–34 by education level, 1971 and 1991

	Education Level: <Grade 12	Gr. 12/13	Some Post-sec.	B.A.	Post B.A.	Overall	N
Occupation							
1971							
Managers	3.9%	7.6%	6.2%	11.4%	8.4%	5.8%	116 900
Professional	0.3%	1.1%	2.2%	13.7%	43.6%	4.0%	81 110
Semi-professional, technical	2.7%	11.6%	32.9%	53.0%	36.1%	16.7%	339 005
Supervisors	10.3%	14.0%	10.1%	7.2%	4.1%	10.3%	208 415
Clerks	11.8%	24.2%	13.5%	6.2%	3.7%	13.4%	270 700
Service	16.2%	16.3%	11.2%	4.2%	1.8%	13.4%	271 800
Blue collar	54.8%	25.2%	23.9%	4.3%	2.3%	36.4%	738 515
	100.0%	100.0%	100.0%	100.0%	100.0%	100.0%	
Number:	957 665	302 945	541 860	115 890	108 085	2 026 445	
1991							
Managers	5.0%	8.8%	9.8%	15.1%	12.3%	9.5%	392 615
Professional	0.4%	0.7%	2.2%	13.8%	33.8%	4.4%	179 745
Semi-professional, technical	2.3%	5.2%	17.1%	39.5%	36.4%	15.5%	637 765
Supervisors	6.5%	8.4%	9.5%	8.4%	4.9%	8.4%	345 890
Clerks	11.5%	21.5%	18.4%	10.4%	5.7%	16.4%	675 940
Service	15.0%	16.8%	13.6%	6.7%	3.4%	13.3%	547 515
Blue collar	59.3%	38.7%	29.4%	5.9%	3.6%	32.7%	1 347 895
	100.0%	100.0%	100.0%	100.0%	100.0%	100.0%	
Number:	716 490	957 855	1 751 280	524 960	176 780	4 127 365	

(54.8%). People in this education category are fairly unlikely to get jobs as managers, professionals, or semi-professionals. As mentioned in the example above, the likelihood that they will get jobs as supervisors dropped somewhat from 1971 to 1991, although this decline was balanced partially by a slight increase in the likelihood of obtaining managerial jobs, from 3.9% to 5.0%.

In 1971, individuals who had completed high school grades 12 or 13 had only a 25% probability of holding a blue-collar job; they were as likely to work in clerical occupations, which in this scheme includes retail sales jobs, and were also found working in job classifications such as semi-professionals/technicians and supervisors. By 1991, this picture had changed substantially. Individuals with only grade 12 or 13 education were much more likely to end up with blue-collar jobs (38.7%), and much less likely to obtain jobs as semi-professionals or as supervisors. There was also a slight decline in the probability that they would obtain jobs in clerical occupations.

For university-educated individuals, jobs as managers, professionals, or semi-professionals represented the norm in 1971, and the odds of working in either the service sector or in blue-collar jobs were fairly low. The likelihood that an individual would hold a managerial job increased for everyone from 1971 to 1991, but was a bit more pronounced for individuals with university education, whose chances of obtaining such a job remained higher than those with less educational qualifications. There was a drop, from 43.6% to 33.8%, in the percentage of individuals with post-bachelor's qualifications holding jobs as professionals, balanced by concomitant increases in all other job categories. The one exception is semi-professionals, which remained more or less stable at 36%. This may be a reflection of a tougher job market or an indication of an expansion between 1971 and 1991 in the number of graduates with non-professional post-graduate degrees (e.g., individuals with M.A. degrees in English and the Social Sciences) relative to graduates with professional degrees. For this group, there was an increase in the proportion of individuals ending up in blue-collar (2.3% to 3.6%), service (1.8% to 3.4%), or clerical (3.7% to 5.7%) work, but the proportions were rather small and consistently lower than those for individuals with less education.

For individuals with some post-secondary education but without a university degree, there was a slight increase in the likelihood of obtaining employment in routine jobs—the blue-collar, clerical, or service occupations. Whereas individuals with this level of education previously had a fairly high probability of obtaining jobs in the semi-professional/technician category, by 1991 they were considerably less likely to find themselves in this occupational grouping in relation to their counterparts with university degrees. These two changes suggest that this "boundary" group between routine and discretionary work encountered a dramatic shift in job prospects over the 20-year period being studied. This is especially significant because this group was, in 1991, the category that included the largest number of individuals. With 1.75 million people, it was over twice the size of the university-educated groups (at 525 thousand and 177 thousand). In contrast, the modal education level in 1971 was less than grade 12. In 1971, then, individuals entering the job market with some post-secondary education represented a privileged group. They were in the top quarter of the working population with respect to educational credentials, and had a fairly good chance of obtaining a discretionary job, although significant numbers still ended up with routine work (about 49%). By 1991, there was nothing special about this level of educational qualification. It represented the population average. While pockets of individuals with this level of certification obtained "good jobs"—as semi-professionals or supervisors—and were able to do so with a greater likelihood than those with less education, the times had passed many of them by, as the new economy's demand for educated workers and an increasingly competitive labour market reduced their likelihood of finding discretionary jobs to about 39%.

This is not to suggest that individuals with community college diplomas were universally disadvantaged. Had data discriminating between those with community college diplomas and those with merely some exposure to post-secondary education (dropouts from university or community college) been available from the 1971 Census, a more fine-grained picture might have been produced. Undoubtedly, in some key skill areas in which industry-specific demands couple well with community college programs, graduates of these programs do very well.[4] The overall picture, however, is one in which university education has increasingly become a requirement in an ever-more competitive market for "good jobs."

Conclusions

A series of profound changes in the structure of the Canadian labour force seems to have originated in the period between 1971 and 1981, and continued through to 1991. These changes involved the mostly male, fairly uneducated, and largely blue-collar workforce that held down relatively secure employment being replaced by a better-educated, mixed-gender workforce that was split between those holding "good jobs" with secure employment and generous conditions and those holding less well-paying jobs with higher risks of unemployment. Education has been crucial to the changes that have been observed, both from the standpoint of analysts looking at the occupational structure as a whole and from the standpoint of individuals faced with the need to live their lives in the work world that has been created. At one level, the skill requirements of the typical job have been increased; the jobs identified here as "discretionary" require, as part of their everyday function, knowledge levels and skills that were not present in the "routine" jobs which were more predominant 20 and 30 years ago.

While there has been an expansion of jobs with skill requirements congruent with those holding university credentials, it may also be the case that there has been a degree of "credential inflation" within jobs that 20 years ago were performed quite adequately by individuals with less education. A hint of the possibility of this process lies in the evidence that some university-educated individuals find employment in areas such as clerical occupations, and that the proportion of university-educated individuals doing so has increased over 20 years, although it still remains small. The evidence would be more conclusive if it could be demonstrated that those university-educated individuals who had difficulty finding a professional, semi-professional, or managerial job were nevertheless more successful at obtaining particular clerical jobs than those individuals without university credentials. Unfortunately, this question cannot be tested with census data.

The data presented here do not necessarily point to the disappearance of work in traditional manufacturing enterprises in Canada, although it is probably in such enterprises that the replacement of human unskilled or semi-skilled workers by technology is the most pronounced. These data do suggest, though, that males having less than a university or college education can no longer expect a ready supply of jobs that require only physical strength and exertion.

The data presented here do not demonstrate that the occupational opportunity structure is closing for university graduates. Nevertheless, a small but increasing number of university graduates is also failing to secure appropriate employment and has joined the ranks of the under-employed. Post-secondary education has become an admission ticket to the job market, but not a guarantee of placement within it. Without higher education, individuals are truly disadvantaged in the workforce, but these credentials alone, with a few notable exceptions in a very small number of professions, are not sufficient for good, stable employment in a well-paying job. It is still not clear whether the retirement from the workforce of the large baby boom generation will open up enough opportunities to improve the future job picture significantly.

An equally interesting question for the future is whether the social class of one's parents has become increasingly important to a person's occupational outcome. At the very least, the increased difficulty faced by students with working-class or lower-income parents in completing university, in the face of rising tuition costs and decreased summer job opportunities, suggests that class background will be important. Without parental support, completing post-secondary education is difficult, in a way that completing high school, the "admission ticket" in a previous generation, was not.

NOTES

1. Data for these tables were taken from aggregate data tables made available by Statistics Canada and discussed in Bernard et al. (1997).
2. Are service workers correctly classified as "manual" workers? Within this group, which includes taxi drivers, babysitters, waiters, hotel clerks, and service station attendants, there can be an argument either way. Treating such jobs as a separate category renders this question unimportant for purposes of this discussion. What these jobs have in common is fairly low skill/job requirement levels, but, at the same time, a fairly high level of interaction with the public. The use of the term "service" here is quite at odds with the use of the term by English sociologists describing a "service class of professionals, capitalists, and financiers" (see Savage, 1994), but consistent with its usage by a wide variety of other researchers (see Blossfeld, 1993). It is important when reading the literature to determine which use of the term is applicable to the discussion at hand.
3. These results may overstate the case slightly, since people without jobs are excluded from all the tables. It should be noted, though, that to be excluded an individual had to have been without any employment over the past year. The tables include individuals who were not currently working at the time of the census but who had worked in the previous year.
4. But see Bernard et al. (1997) for an examination of 1981 and 1991 census data including a better measure of community college education (separate from those with "some" post-secondary education), which suggests findings similar to those found in Table 9-7. Bernard et al. were not, however, able to distinguish between individuals with trade school certificates and those with community college diplomas (though most of the people in this combined category were probably community college grads).

REFERENCES

Bell, D. 1973 *The Coming of Post-Industrial Society* New York: Basic Books.

Bernard, P., D. Baer, J. Boisjoly, J. Curtis, and M. Webber 1994 *A New Typology for Work Roles for Canadian Data* Paper presented to the Annual Meeting of the Canadian Sociology and Anthropology Association, Calgary, June 7–11, 1994.

Bernard, P., J. Boisjoly, D. Baer, J. Curtis, M. Webber 1996 *Work in Canada, 1971–1991: The Redistribution of Labour Across Workroles* Paper presented at the Canadian Population Society Annual Meeting, St. Catharines Ontario.

Bernard, P., J. Boisjoly, D. Baer, J. Curtis, M Webber 1997 *How Canadians Work: Changes in the Makeup of the Labour Force in the 1970s and 1980s* Ottawa: Statistics Canada.

Birkelund, G. E., L. Goodman, et al. 1996 "The latent structure of job characteristics of men and women." *American Journal of Sociology* **102(1)**: 80–113.

Blakely, J. and E. Harvey 1988 "Market and non-market effects on male and female occupational status attainment." *Canadian Review of Sociology and Anthropology* 25(1): 23–40.

Blossfeld, H.-P., G. Giannelli, et al. 1993 Is there a new service proletariat? The tertiary sector and inequality in Germany. *Changing Classes* G. Esping-Anderson. Newbury Park: Sage: 109–135.

Charles, M. 1992 "Cross-National Variation in Occupational Sex Segregation." *American Sociological Review* 57(4): 483–502.

Clement, W. and J. Myles 1994 *Relations of Ruling: Class and Gender in Postindustrial*

Societies Montreal: McGill-Queen's University Press.

Crewe, I. 1991 "Labor force changes, working class decline and the labor vote." *Labor Parties in Postindustrial Societies* F. F. Piven Cambridge: Polity Press: 20–46.

Erikson, R. and J. Goldthorpe 1992 *The Constant Flux: A Study of Class Mobility in Industrial Societies* Oxford: Clarendon Press.

Esping-Anderson, G. 1991 "Postindustrial cleavage structures: a comparison of evolving patterns of social stratification in Germany, Sweden and the United States." *Labour Parties in Postindustrial Societies* F. F. Piven Cambridge: Polity Press: 147–168.

Esping-Anderson, G. 1993 Post industrial class structures: an analytical framework. *Changing Classes: Stratification and Mobility in Post-Industrial Societies* G. Esping-Anderson Newbury Park, CA: Sage: 7–31.

Fox, B. and J. Fox 1987 "Occupational gender segregation in the Canadian labour force, 1931–1981." *Canadian Review of Sociology and Anthropology* 24(3): 374–397.

1996 "The sexual division of labour and women's heterogeneity." *British Journal of Sociology* 47(1): 178–188.

Ishida, H., S. Spilerman, et al. 1997 "Education and promotion changes in the United States and Japan." *American Sociological Review* 62(6): 866–882.

Myles, J. 1988 "The expanding middle: some Canadian evidence on the deskilling debate." *Canadian Review of Sociology and Anthropology* 25(3): 335–364.

Myles, J., G. Picot, et al. 1993 Does post-industrialism matter? The Canadian Experience. *Changing Classes* G. Esping-Anderson. Newbury Park, CA: Sage: 171–194.

Myles, J., G. Picot, et al. 1988 "Wages and Jobs in the 1980s: Changing Youth Wages and the Declining Middle." Ottawa, Social and Economic Studies Division, Statistics Canada.

Picot, G., J. Myles, et al. 1990 "Good Jobs/Bad Jobs and the Declining Middle: 1967–1986." Ottawa, Business and Labour Market Analysis Group, Analytical Studies Branch, Statistics Canada.

Rinehart, J. 1996 *The Tyranny of Work* Toronto: Harcourt Brace Canada.

Savage, M. 1994 "Social mobility and class analysis: a new agenda for social history?" *Social History* 19(1): 69–79.

Slomczynski, K. and T. Krauze 1987 "Cross-national similarity in social mobility patterns: a direct test of the Featherman-Jones-Hauser hypothesis." *American Sociological Review* 52(5): 598–611.

Wanner, R. 1996 *Trends in Occupational Opportunity in Canada in the Twentieth Century* Paper presented at the Canadian Sociology and Anthropology Association Annual Meeting, St. Catharines, Ontario.

Westergaard, J. 1990 "Social mobility in Britain." *John Goldthorpe: Consensus and Controversy.* J. Clark, C. Modgil, and S. Modgil London: Falmer Press: 277–288.

Wright, R. and J. Jacobs 1994 "Male flight from computer work: a new look at occupational resegregation and ghettoization." *American Sociological Review* 59(4): 511–536.

Chapter 10

CHANGES IN JOB TENURE

Andrew Heisz

Revised from Andrew Heisz, "Changes in job tenure." In Statistics Canada's (*Perspectives on Labour and Income*, Catalogue No. 75-001, Winter 1996, Vol. 8, No. 4, pp. 31–35. Reprinted with permission.)

INTRODUCTION

It is widely thought that the tradition of steady, long-term employment is becoming less of a reality for Canadian workers. Many labour analysts believe that employers are tailoring job spells to respond to fluctuations in demand, with the result that offers of long-term employment are on the decline. They argue that firms are increasingly using a core of full-time, skilled employees, and hiring temporary workers when the need arises.

There are other reasons to believe that job instability may be increasing. These include the rise in non-standard work arrangements like part-time, temporary, and contract work, and the recently documented rise in earnings inequality. To the extent that these changes are related to job stability, changes in job length would also be expected. Examining job tenure is important because workers employed for the long term have more chance to build up skills, earn a high wage, and gain access to career advancement opportunities. Workers employed for the short term are exposed to more spells of unemployment, have more difficulty accumulating a pension, and have more need for mid-career retraining.

Is job instability on the rise? Are short-term jobs becoming more common? Are long-term or "life-time" jobs becoming less common? If so, for whom? This study addresses these questions by presenting estimates of the average length of a new job started over the period 1981 to 1994, using Statistics Canada's monthly Labour Force Survey.

The sample used for this study includes all employed full- and part-time paid workers, but excludes the self-employed, students and unpaid family workers. It represents about 85% of the employed labour force in 1994.

CHANGES IN JOB STABILITY

The average duration of a job started over this period was 3.7 years. Although the average job length follows a cyclical pattern, varying from a low of 3.0 years in 1991 to a high of 4.9 years in 1994, it has shown no significant trend (Figure 10-1). The average new job lasted 3.8 years between 1981 and 1985, 3.4 years between 1986 and 1990, and 3.8 years between 1991 and 1994.

Important changes in the distribution of completed job lengths over this period are masked by the stability in the average job length. There was a substantial shift from jobs that lasted between one and five years to those that lasted one year or less. Between the 1981–85 and 1991–94 periods, the proportion of jobs that lasted between one and five years dropped from 21% to 16%. At the same time, the figure for jobs lasting 12 months or less increased from 59% to 64%. The fraction of jobs that lasted between 5 and 20 years (14%) and more than 20 years (6%) remained relatively unchanged between the periods. This increase in the proportion of short-term jobs combined with an unchanging proportion of long-term jobs represents a polarization of jobs.

How is it that the proportion of long-term jobs remained stable even though the proportion of short-term jobs increased? The answer is that once a job passed the 12-month milestone, it had a better chance of becoming a long-term job at the end of the period than it did at the beginning.

FIGURE 10-1 The average new job has lasted less than four years

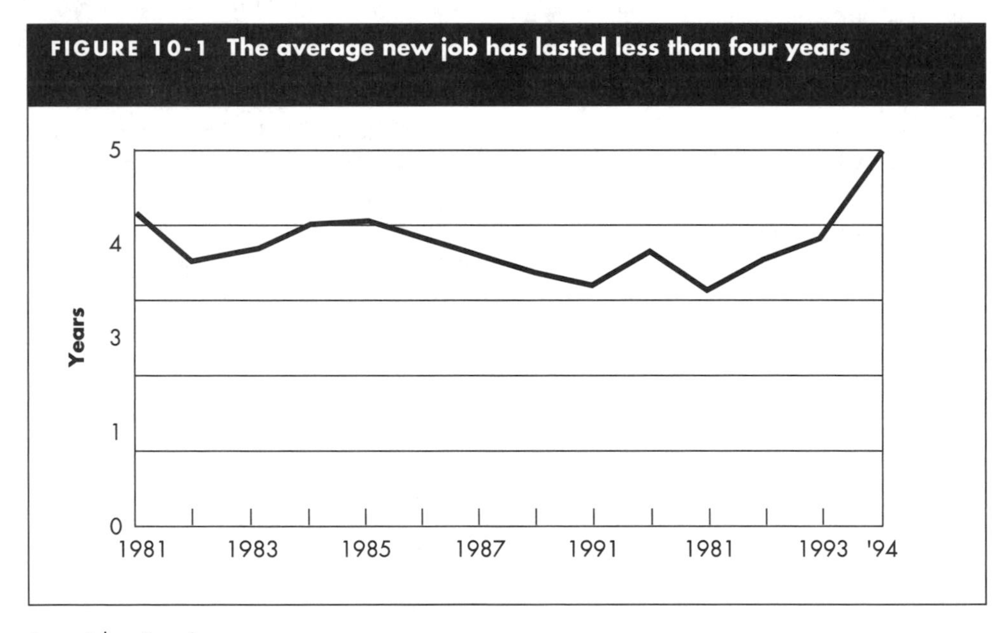

Source: Labour Force Survey

While the proportion of new jobs that lasted more than one year declined over the period, the proportion of year-old jobs that lasted longer than five years increased from an average of 48% between 1981 and 1985 to an average of 54% between 1991 and 1994. The combined result is that workers with more than one year of job seniority have been enjoying increasing security, while others have found it more difficult to join their ranks.

THE POLARIZATION OF JOBS: A CLOSER LOOK

This section investigates this polarization further to see whether the pattern occurs for different groups in the economy. Polarization of job tenures could occur if some demographic groups were enjoying lengthening tenures while others were not. Alternatively, polarization could occur within all groups, suggesting that an economy-wide change is taking place.

Investigation reveals a pattern of polarization that persisted among all demographic sub-groups studied (Table 10-1). The proportion of new jobs lasting longer than one year declined for virtually all groups. It dropped most for the following: workers who were aged 45 and over when their jobs began, workers in Atlantic Canada and Quebec, and workers in the community services and manufacturing industries. At the same time, the proportion of one-year-old jobs that lasted more than five years rose for all groups. It increased most for the oldest and youngest age groups, for workers in Quebec and Western Canada, and for workers in the community services and manufacturing industries. This pattern of change suggests that it is not particular groups that have been responsible for the aggregate changes in job lengths; rather, the changes have been happening within each group.

Despite these changes in the distribution of job tenure, the average job duration for most groups remained steady, with some notable exceptions. First, workers aged 45 to 54 and 55 to 64 when they started their jobs experienced significantly shorter job tenures at the end of the period than at the beginning. For both of these groups, the average job length fell by 0.8 years, or 9.5 months, between 1981 and 1994. Second, workers in the Atlantic provinces experienced a decline in the average job length of 0.5 years. Third, workers in the business and personal services industry held on to their jobs longer at the end of the period than at the beginning (an increase of 0.7 years).

The decline in average job tenure among older people starting in a new job raises the concern that these workers have experienced particular difficulty finding stable employment. One reason for this may be that older displaced workers have been left with skills not in demand and with few employment prospects. Another is that they have been retiring earlier. The proportion of job starters who achieve stable employment has been declining at a much faster rate for older workers than it has for younger workers. Between 1981 and 1985, 41% of jobs started by workers aged 45 to 54 and 37% by workers aged 55 to 64 lasted more than 12 months. These percentages dropped by 10 and 16 percentage points, respectively, for the 1991-94 period. It is these large changes in the proportion of new jobs lasting more than 12 months that account for much of the decline in average job length for older workers. The corresponding drops for other age groups were much more muted, with the result that stability for job starters dropped as the age at which the worker began the job increased.

Similar trends underlie the decline in job lengths in Atlantic Canada. In this region workers with more seniority have not been at higher risk of having their job come to an end. In fact, the proportion of five-year-old jobs that went on to last more than 20 years rose slightly from 30% to 33% over the period. The declining average job length has been caused by a large drop in the proportion of jobs that last longer than one year. This proportion fell from 30% between 1981 and 1985 to 21% between 1991 and 1994.

FOCUS ON LONG-TERM JOBS

An often-heard argument is that because of structural changes in the economy, older workers and workers in declining industries are more at risk of losing their jobs. This study sheds some light on this question by asking what proportion of jobs that have lasted 10 to 15 years are expected to continue for at least 5 more years (Table 10-2). Changes in these proportions over time reveal to what extent the stability of long-term jobs has changed. These changes may not have been observed up to this point in the analysis because only a minority of new jobs reach 10 or 15 years in length.

This study shows that for each age group, the probability that a 10-year-old job would last an additional 5 years was relatively steady over the period. For example, for both the 1981–85 and 1991–94 periods, 73% of 10-year-old jobs started by workers when they were between the ages of 25 and 34 lasted an additional 5 years. The probability that a job that had lasted for 15 years would continue for at least 5 more declined significantly only for workers who started their jobs when they were aged 35 to 44. Jobs for these workers had a 62% probability of lasting another five years between 1981 and 1985 and a 51% chance of lasting five more years between 1991 and 1994. Long-term jobs for these workers have become less stable, but some of this change may be explained by an increased prevalence of early retirement.

Long-term jobs held by workers in certain industries have also become less stable, but this is offset by the situation in other industries. For example, the probability that a 10-year-old job in the manufacturing or trade industries would reach 15 years declined by 4 and 10 percentage points, respectively. At the same time, the probability that a 10-year-old job in the community services or business and personal services industries would last another 5 years rose by 3 and 9 percentage points, respectively.

CONCLUSION

From 1981 to 1994, new jobs became more polarized into short- and long-term jobs. Although the average complete duration of jobs showed no significant trend over the period, the distribution of complete job lengths shifted from medium- to short-term jobs. This means that new job holders experienced more instability at the end of the period than at the beginning. However, once the 12-month tenure milestone was passed, workers enjoyed greater job stability, with the result that the proportion of long-term jobs remained unchanged. This result persisted across all sub-groups, except for older workers and workers in Atlantic Canada, where the shift to short-term jobs caused shorter average job lengths.

The degree and persistence of job polarization into long- and short-term jobs point to a significant trend. The presence of this change within all demographic and industrial groups suggests that it has not been driven by changes particular to any group or sector of the economy. Rather, an economy-wide explanation may be required. Increasingly, firms seem to be using a core of long-term employees, leaving more Canadians with less stable jobs.

TABLE 10-1 Job tenure by sex, age, region, industry, and education

	Complete job length		The proportion of new jobs lasting longer than...					
	Average	Change*	12 months		5 years, given they have lasted longer than one year		20 years, given they have lasted longer than 5 years**	
	1981–94	1981–94**	1981–85	1991–94	1981–85	1991–94	1981–85	1991–94
	years		%					
Total	**3.7**	**-**	**41.0**	**36.2**	**48.3**	**54.2**	**30.7**	**32.1**
Men	3.6	0.1	38.2	34.2	49.6	54.5	31.1	32.4
Women	3.8	–0.1	44.6	38.6	47.2	54.0	28.8	31.1
Age when job began:								
15–24	3.7	0.4	39.4	37.2	44.1	51.8	41.7	39.1
25–34	4.3	–0.2	43.2	38.6	49.4	53.4	39.1	41.2
35–44	4.0	–0.3	43.5	38.3	55.4	57.6	25.9	22.3
45–54	3.2	–0.8	40.9	31.3	56.6	59.6	4.2	5.1
55–64	1.9	–0.8	36.8	21.0	38.5	45.6	1.1	2.1
Atlantic Canada	2.6	–0.5	29.8	21.2	49.2	53.3	30.0	32.9
Quebec	3.6	–	38.4	31.8	50.4	58.2	29.9	31.7
Ontario	4.5	0.2	46.9	45.0	52.0	54.3	32.4	32.3
Western Canada	3.4	0.2	40.6	36.8	42.8	51.6	28.6	32.7
Manufacturing	4.0	0.1	43.8	36.3	48.6	60.1	29.9	24.3
Trade	3.8	–0.4	49.6	45.7	44.0	47.2	23.8	17.6
Community services	5.4	–0.7	49.7	39.1	57.1	69.7	39.8	47.3
Business and personal services	2.7	0.7	38.7	38.6	35.1	41.4	16.1	24.8
No post-secondary	2.9†	...	35.8	23.3	44.6	45.5	...	...
Some post-secondary	5.7†	...	52.9	41.3	54.8	56.3	...	...

Note: Estimates for individual provinces and industries are not available because of small sample size.

* Change implied from results of regression of 168 monthly average job length values on the unemployment rate, monthly dummy variables and a time trend.

** A change in LFS definitions in 1990 prohibits calculation of these statistics by educational attainment.

† 1981-1989 only.

Source: Labour Force Survey

TABLE 10-2 Proportion of jobs lasting an additional 5 years, by selected age and industry

	Current length of job			
	10 years		15 years	
	1981–1985	1991–1994	1981–1985	1991–1994
	%			
Total	**66.0**	**66.2**	**76.2**	**76.5**
Age when job began:				
15–24	71.9	70.1	91.1	91.0
25–34	72.9	73.0	84.0	82.1
35–44	67.4	62.8	61.8	51.4
45–54	42.4	42.3	–	–
Manufacturing	65.4	61.3	74.3	70.6
Trade	61.4	51.3	70.2	63.6
Community services	74.8	77.6	75.6	80.5
Business and personal services	47.7	56.8	76.3	78.4

Source: Labour Force Survey

LABOUR MARKETS, INEQUALITY, AND THE FUTURE OF WORK

Chapter 11

Graham S. Lowe

(An original chapter written for this volume.)

INTRODUCTION

Debate and controversy surround the present and future of work. The 1990s have witnessed profound changes in Canadians' working lives, accentuating trends already under way in the 1980s. Futurists have seized upon these trends, offering conflicting images of where work is headed. Compare, for example, Jeremy Rifkin's (1995) bleak picture of a "workerless world," as new technologies replace humans, to William Bridges' (1994) rosy image of a "de-jobbed world," where work becomes more flexible, rewarding, and entrepreneurial.

Sociologists also are concerned about the changing work world and the implications of these trends for society. However, they reject futuristic predictions in favour of a careful consideration of evidence, explanations, and public policy options. A sociological analysis of work is rooted in a firm understanding of labour markets. This chapter examines what labour markets are and how they operate. It also considers major Canadian labour market trends and the implications of these trends for social inequality.[1]

A labour market can be defined as the processes and institutions through which workers are allocated to paid jobs. Because jobs provide income and other rewards—such as pensions, paid vacations, opportunities for career advancement, and personal development and fulfillment—they have a direct bearing on an individual's living standard and quality of life. Sociologists also use information about a person's job or occupation to locate her or him in the class structure. Thus, labour markets are central to understanding broader issues of the ways inequality is structured in a society (Van den Berg and Smucker, 1997).

A POST-INDUSTRIAL SOCIETY?

We will begin by examining changes in jobs in the context of debates about an emerging post-industrial society. The post-World War II expansion of white-collar occupations and service industries, along with increasing living standards, gave rise in the 1970s to a theory of "post-industrial society." Daniel Bell (1973) argued that the industrial phase of capitalism was over, replaced by a post-industrial society that was based on knowledge rather than goods production. While industrialization had brought increased productivity and living standards, post-industrial society would usher in reduced class conflict and less concentration of power. Bell underscored the importance of knowledge, suggesting that it was the new basis of power. Knowledge workers, such as technicians, scientists, and other professionals, would become the new elite.

An alternative, critical view is provided by neo-Marxist scholars (Braverman, 1974; Rinehart, 1996). Examining changes in the "labour process"—how work is actually performed—these researchers suggest that work under corporate capitalism has become more alienating and that class divisions are widening. The growing numbers of non-managerial white-collar workers in offices, shops, or the public sector form, in this view, a new working class. More sophisticated managerial control techniques and computer technology extended the degradation of working conditions from the factory into offices and other white-collar settings.

However, a close inspection of labour market trends reveals a far more complex and contradictory picture than portrayed by either the post-industrial or the labour process perspective. In the United States, Robert Reich (1991) points out that the real winners in the high-tech, global economy are the symbolic analysts—Bell's knowledge workers. However, Reich argues that their rise to power and wealth has created even greater inequality. In Canada, John Myles (1988) has found some support for both theoretical positions. Myles shows that shifts in employment patterns across industries, coupled with changing skill requirements within industries, have created jobs at the top and the bottom of the occupational ladder, and a decline in middle-level blue-collar jobs in the manufacturing sector. In sum, the shift to a service-based economy has been accompanied by growing signs of polarization in the labour market.

EXPLAINING LABOUR MARKETS

The debates about post-industrialism draw our attention to how and why certain individuals or groups occupy particular locations in the labour market. Who gets to be a corporate executive, a computer technician, or a parking-lot attendant? Are these jobs allocated on the basis of ability, other personal characteristics (such as age, gender, ethnicity, or social class), luck, or some combination? These are key sociological questions, given that one's job determines one's "life chances." Furthermore, an understanding of how the labour market operates is essential for designing public policies that can shape the future of work, thereby addressing concerns about a lack of good jobs.

There are two major theoretical perspectives on labour markets. Human capital theory comes from economics, while labour market segmentation theory is more sociological. Both recognize that some jobs are better than others, in terms of pay and benefits, career opportunities, personal rewards, and social status. Beyond this similarity, these two perspectives offer alternative views of how labour markets are organized and operate.

Human Capital Theory

Human capital theory draws on neo-classical economics (Becker, 1975). It assumes that the labour market is one large, open arena in which everyone with similar qualifications competes on the same basis for available jobs. The market rewards those individuals who have the greatest "human capital" as measured by education, training, experience, and ability. A job's rewards are based on its economic contribution to society. By focusing on the supply of labour, in terms of workers' characteristics, this theory does not address the influence of employers' hiring practices or the organization of work on inequality. The theory simply assumes that employers make rational hiring and promotion decisions based on ability.

This view of the labour market is similar to the functionalist theories that were popular in sociology several decades ago. These theories also saw people's socio-economic position as a product of the functional importance of their jobs in society. Human capital theory presents a consensus view of society; issues of class and power are ignored. However, the theory does accurately predict the returns for education. There is solid evidence that, on average, individuals with university degrees have higher incomes, greater life-time earnings, a lower risk of unemployment, and a generally higher probability of being in a "good" job, in comparison to individuals who have lower levels of education. This has been starkly clear in the 1990s, when the vast majority of new full-time jobs have gone to university graduates.

However, human capital theory can't explain why some groups get better jobs than others, regardless of ability or education (Blau and Ferber, 1986). For example, many young people from poor families don't even get the opportunity to apply to a university and are at risk of dropping out of high school. In 1996, the 100 highest-paid corporate executives in Canada earned over $700 000 (Saunders, 1997). Yet, equally able and educated individuals in socially useful occupations—say, primary school teachers or coordinators of recycling programs—earn far less. And members of recent immigrant groups often end up working in low-status jobs, such as taxi drivers or airport security guards, even though they may be highly educated and experienced.

Labour Market Segmentation Theory

Such inequalities among different jobs provide the starting point for labour market segmentation theory (Clairmont et al., 1983; Rubery, 1988; Kalleberg and Berg; 1987, Gordon et al., 1982). This perspective rejects human capital theory's assumption of a homogenous labour market, in which everyone competes on the basis of education and other human capital. Instead, it depicts the labour market as composed of unequal segments, where movement to a better or "primary" market from a worse or "secondary" market is often difficult. The segmentation perspective examines the barriers that many qualified individuals face in trying to enter the primary labour market.

There are different versions of this basic labour market segmentation perspective. A dual economy model highlights the uneven development of economic sectors in industrial capitalist societies (Hodson and Kaufman, 1982). This model distinguishes between core and periphery industries, with the majority of better jobs being found in organizations located in core sectors, mainly large corporations and government. The Japanese economy is organized along these lines, with corporations such as Toyota providing good careers and benefits to its workers, while subcontracting for parts and services to an extensive network of small firms, in which wages and working conditions are poor. In Canada, General Motors and the Royal Bank are core firms; peripheral firms would include small family-run motels or restaurants.

Small firms tend to have lower profit margins, invest less in new technologies, require less skilled workers, and be more labour-intensive than large organizations. Hence, there is greater pressure to keep down wage costs, and workers are considered to be easily replaceable. Unions and professional associations also influence labour market outcomes. The majority of public sector workers in Canada belong to unions, and unionization is much higher in large than in small firms. The concentration of professionals in the primary labour market creates shelters that limit access only to individuals with recognized credentials, increasing the bargaining power of professional associations (Krahn and Lowe, 1998: chapters 3, 7).

The size, profitability, and market dominance of core firms (those in primary labour markets or in the central work world) enable them to use stable employment conditions to gain the cooperation of workers. This employment system is known as an internal labour market (Althauser, 1989). These firms are pyramid-shaped bureaucracies that recruit at specified entry-level positions and then provide security, career paths, and training to workers once they are inside, as long as they meet management's expectations for hard work and commitment to corporate values. Most job openings, therefore, are filled internally, essentially creating a sheltered organization-based labour market.

Until recently, the internal labour market has been a hallmark of core sector organizations. However, in the last decade, widespread "downsizing" has shaken internal labour markets. Staff cuts, a "de-layering" process whereby the bureaucratic hierarchy is flattened, and a shift to contracting out and temporary workers have all reduced internal career mobility and shaken the employee commitment that these organizations once cultivated. Even in Japan, where major corporations have developed elaborate internal labour markets based on the concept of "life-long employment," a corporate career is no longer guaranteed in return for loyalty and hard work.

Nevertheless, the dualistic thinking of labour market segmentation theory, involving primary versus secondary or core versus periphery jobs, tends to over-simplify current employment realities. A growing number of large corporations are moving to flexible staffing, using lower-paid, part-time or temporary workers in place of full-time employees. This is evident in the retail sector, where large grocery chains and department stores rely on a "just-in-time" workforce. Another example is the fast-food industry, in which multi-national chains such as McDonald's and Burger King recruit their staff from secondary labour markets populated by students, women, and recent immigrants (Reiter, 1991).

WORK IN A SERVICE ECONOMY

The post-industrialists and their critics would agree that Canada is a service-based economy. From the perspective of human capital theory, the rise of a service economy poses questions about possible changes in the relationship between education and jobs, and the relative "pay-offs" of investing in education. For labour market segmentation theory, the recent restructuring of industries and labour markets raises questions about which groups have benefited (or not) from these changes.

Changing Industrial Patterns of Employment

To understand these changes, we need to look at industrial patterns of employment over time. Industry classifications focus on the type of economic activity occurring within the workplace. We can distinguish three major sectors: primary (agriculture, mining, forestry and other resource extraction industries); secondary (manufacturing and construction); and tertiary (which creates services rather than products). The service sector includes a wide range of industries, from finance and retail trade to education, government, and health and social services.

Much of Canada's industrialization has entailed a drop in primary-sector employment and a growth in manufacturing jobs. Service industries also have expanded, accounting for almost half of all jobs by 1951 (Picot, 1987: 11). Since then, the proportion of the workforce in the primary and secondary sectors has declined steeply, although through technological change and new production methods these sectors still contribute significantly to national economic output. As Figure 11-1 shows, between 1961 and 1995, agricultural employment fell from 11 to 3 percent of the total and manufacturing jobs fell from 24 to 15 percent of the total. The service sector now employs close to three-quarters of the labour force.

Given the size and diversity of the service sector, it is useful to divide it into an upper tier (distributive services, business services, education, health and welfare, and public administration) and a lower tier (retail trade and other consumer services) (Krahn and Lowe, 1998, chapter 2; also see Economic Council of Canada, 1991). Figure 11-2 documents that, in 1996, just over one-quarter of employed Canadians were working in the goods-producing sector, while almost one-half of the employed were located in the upper-tier services, and approximately one-quarter had jobs in the lower-tier service industries. This distinction between upper- and lower-tier service industries is especially relevant to our later discussion of "good" and "bad" jobs.

Occupational Changes

We also can examine employment by looking at occupations, or the kind of work that

FIGURE 11-1 Distribution of employment by industry, Canada, 1961 & 1995

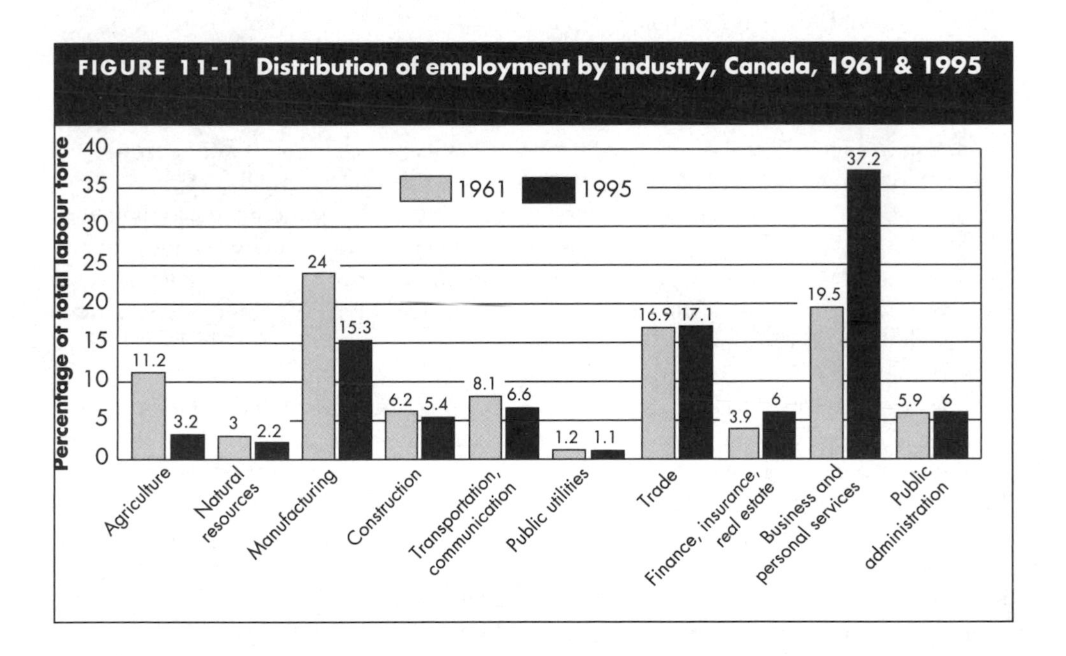

FIGURE 11-2 Share of total employment by industry, Canada, 1996

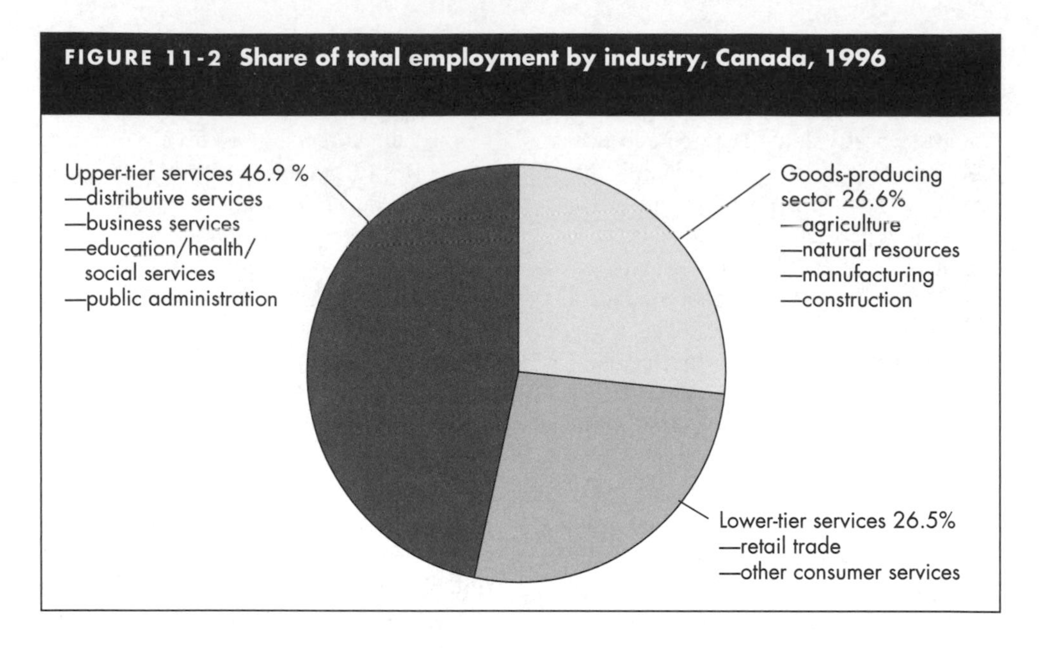

individuals perform in their jobs. Most of the workers in primary and secondary industries would be classified as blue-collar (or manual) workers, while the growth of service industries is directly related to the expansion of white-collar occupations. Historically, white-collar occupations tended to be viewed as having higher status. However, as service industries grew and diversified, the white-collar occupational category came to include well over half of the labour force, some performing less desirable jobs. Because many of the new white-collar positions—especially clerical, sales, and personal service jobs—have been filled by women, the term, "pink-collar," has been applied to these occupations.

Another related change in the labour force is the rising educational level of workers. Canadians are becoming increasingly well-educated. The proportion of the workforce with a university degree increased from 7 percent to 17 percent between 1975 and 1995. Furthermore, occupational projections suggest that about 40 percent of the new jobs created in the next several years will require post-secondary education (Betcherman and Lowe, 1997: 24). Rising educational levels raise the problem of "underemployment," however, and make some people wonder whether well-educated workers, especially recent graduates, will be able to find jobs that adequately reward their investment in education (Kelly et al., 1997).

NON-STANDARD WORK

Despite public concerns about declining job security, the majority of employed Canadians still have a full-time, year-round, permanent job. Public insecurity is fuelled by the recent wave of downsizing, but perhaps more so by the spread of alternatives to the standard type of employment, a trend visible throughout the industrialized economies (International Labour Organization, 1997). Non-standard work takes four forms: part-time, multiple job-holding, own-account self-employment, and temporary work (Krahn, 1995). Figure 11-3 documents that these four types of non-standard work accounted for 28 per cent of all employed Canadians (ages 15 to 64 years) in 1989, rising to one-third by 1994.

The non-standard work trend is double-edged. It has advantages, to the extent that it

FIGURE 11-3 Poverty lines for a family of four living in a large city, 1995

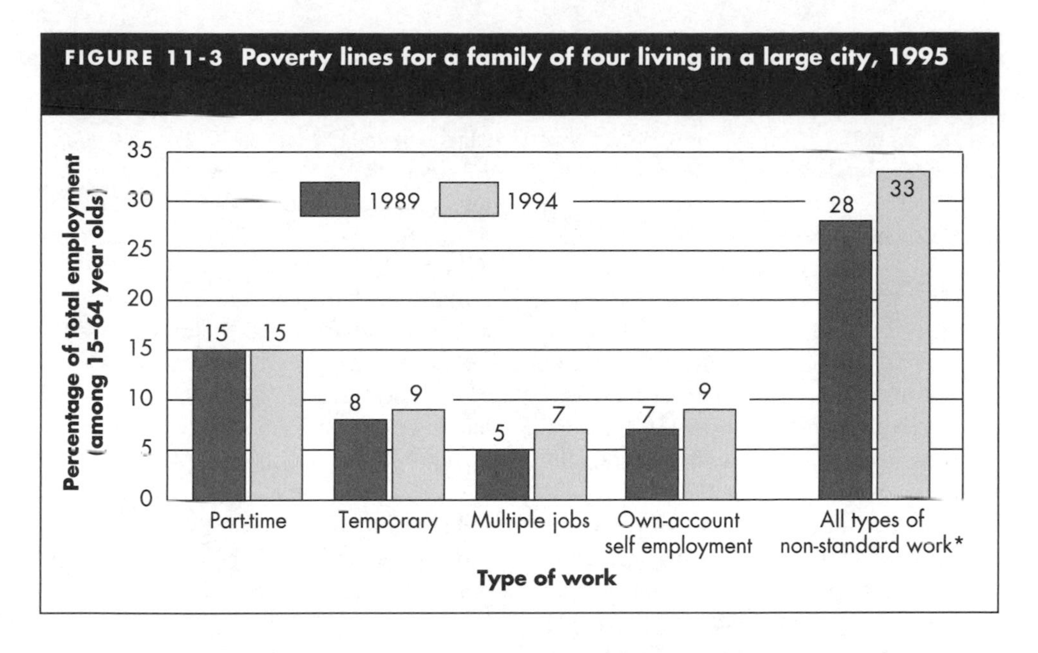

provides some individuals with greater choice and flexibility in the way they organize their work life. For example, parents (especially mothers) with young children, university students, older workers wanting to ease out of a full-time career, or highly skilled professionals seeking the continual challenge of new projects may seek out part-time or contract work. Given women's generally greater family responsibilities, it is perhaps not surprising that 40 percent of female workers in 1994 were in non-standard jobs, compared to 27 percent of men (Krahn, 1995: 40; Duffy and Pupo, 1992). Often, though, this choice involves significant trade-offs. The main disadvantage of non-standard work is that it tends to offer lower wages and fewer benefits than full-time jobs, because employers use non-standard work as a "flexible" strategy for reducing labour costs.

Part-time work is normally defined as working less than 30 hours per week in one's main job. Part-time work is the most common type of non-standard employment, accounting for 18.9 percent of all employment in 1996 (note that Figure 11-3 uses a slightly different definition that results in a lower figure). This percentage represents a modest increase from 1977, when part-time employment was 13 percent of the total. About three-quarters of part-timers are women, and youth of both genders are also concentrated in these jobs. However, what has increased much more quickly in the past two decades is involuntary part-time employment (having to accept a part-time job because a suitable full-time job is not available). In 1995, 31 percent of all part-time workers were "involuntary," up from 11 percent in 1975. This change reflects the fact that most of the new jobs created since the 1981–82 recession have been part-time (Krahn and Lowe, 1998: chapter 2).

HOURS OF WORK

We can gain a more complete picture of how labour market restructuring affects employment opportunities by examining trends in work hours. In Canada a 40-hour work week was established as the standard in the late 1950s. Despite expectations of more leisure time due to the productivity gains of computers and other new technologies, by 1996 the average length of the work week was not much shorter than in the 1950s, at just under 38 hours. At the same time, a substantial polarization in work hours has occurred, as both part-time jobs and jobs with long hours tended to increase.

By 1993, 61 percent of paid workers put in 35 to 40 hours weekly, down from 71 percent in 1976 (Sunter and Morissette, 1994:9). Young workers (ages 15–24) experienced the largest drop in work hours, resulting in a sharp decline in real earnings (i.e., adjusted for inflation) since the 1980s (Betcherman and Leckie, 1997). Over the same period, many adult workers, especially males, have put in longer hours. This is mainly due to organizational downsizing, which tends to increase the workloads (usually without more pay) for remaining employees. There has also been a rise in multiple job-holding. Thus, by 1995, almost a quarter of male workers (and 9 percent of females) reported work weeks longer than 40 hours (Sunter and Diversy 1996: C-12).

The fact that some people don't have enough work and others have too much is a reflection of a more polarized labour market (Duffy et al., 1997). In this context, it is not surprising that a growing number of policy analysts and interest groups are calling for a reduced work week. Shortening the work week to 35 or 30 hours is seen as a way of redistributing work. This policy would redistribute income, because those with no job or with too few hours would see increased incomes, while groups of full-time workers would have small cuts in both income and hours (Human Resources Development Canada, 1994). Work redistribution has attracted interest because of persistently high unemployment and the absence of effective job creation policies. During 1996, an average of 1.5 million Canadians were unemployed (that is, out of a job but actively seeking one). Since the end of World War II, unemployment rates have increased, from an average of 4 percent in the 1950s to around 10 percent in the 1990s.

Some public policy analysts urge governments to adopt more active job creation measures (Betcherman and Lowe, 1997; MacLean and Osberg, 1996; *Policy Options,* July-August 1996). However, creating new jobs is a more difficult challenge than redistributing existing work time. Even Jeremy Rifkin (1995), who argues in *The End of Work* that there will be less work to go around in the future, advocates reducing the work week as a partial solution to unemployment. Several European nations are moving in this direction. Unionized German automobile workers have negotiated shorter work hours in order to create more jobs and, in France, there is widespread popular support for a legislated 35-hour work week to help reduce high unemployment.

GOOD JOBS AND BAD JOBS

There is considerable debate about whether the service economy has created more good jobs than bad ones, and how public policy can encourage the creation of better quality jobs in the future (Banting and Beech, 1995; Osberg et al., 1995; Duffy et al., 1997). The language of "good" and "bad" jobs refers to widening disparities on a range of job characteristics: wages, benefits, skill requirements, security, working conditions, and intrinsic rewards such as challenging and satisfying work. The good jobs-bad jobs dichotomy seems to capture the basic difference between standard and non-standard jobs. In the 1980s, 44 percent of all employment growth was in non-standard jobs (Economic Council of Canada, 1991:81), a trend that continues in the 1990s. However, not all of these non-standard jobs are what critics call "McJobs." There is a minority that are well-paid and require high levels of professional and technical skills; business consultants and project engineers would be good examples.

Income is an obvious criterion for identifying jobs that may be more or less desirable. Looking at incomes of paid employees (i.e., excluding the self-employed), individuals in the service sector earn about 20 percent less than in the goods-producing industries. However, there is wide variation in income within the service sector, with workers in the upper-tier industries earning much more than those in the lower-tier industries. For example, in 1994, paid employees in engineering, architectural, and computer-related services earned an average of about $800 per week, almost four times as much as those in food and beverage services (Grenon, 1996).

There also are substantial occupational differences in earnings. In 1995, all managers reported average annual earnings of $41 352 (Statistics Canada; 1997). In contrast, clerical workers earned an average of $21 825 and waitresses, hairdressers, security guards, and people in other service jobs earned an average of $17 160. Some of these earnings differences are due to a higher percentage of part-time and part-year workers in service occupations and in the lower-tier service industries. Higher earnings in some goods-producing industries and upper-tier services, and in managerial and professional occupations, result partly from the influence of unions and professional associations. And the higher earnings of managers and professionals also reflect their higher educational attainment.

Employment benefits are another measure of job quality. Benefits such as Employment Insurance, the Canada/Quebec Pension Plan, and Workers' Compensation are part of the "social safety net." While mandatory, these benefits only provide a minimum level of support. Employer-provided benefits, therefore, give some workers better security and living standards. In 1995, almost three-quarters of paid employees in Canada received some vacation pay and between 50 and 60 percent had an employer-sponsored pension plan, health plan, dental plan, and paid sick leave (Akyeampong, 1997: 52). Only about one in five received work-related training paid for by their employer (Human Resources Development Canada, 1997). Especially in the 1990s, training is viewed by workers as a personal "safety net" that increases their employability in a volatile labour market.

Benefits are unequally distributed, again supporting the distinction between good and bad jobs. Fewer than one in five part-timers are provided a pension plan, health coverage, dental coverage, or paid sick leave by their employer, compared to at least three in five full-timers. We find a similar pattern if we compare temporary and permanent employees (Akyeampong, 1997: 52). Generally, workers in the lower-tier services receive few benefits. Benefits are more common in large organizations and in unionized workplaces (which tend to be larger). Furthermore, workers who receive employer-sponsored training already have labour market advantages, to the extent that they are better-educated, work in large firms, or have full-time positions.

LABOUR MARKET GENDER INEQUALITIES

One of the most profound changes in Canadian society over the last three decades has been the sharp rise in female employment. In 1970, 38 percent of all adult women in Canada worked outside the home for pay; by 1996, this figure had jumped to 58 percent. Deeply-rooted barriers to female employment have been eroding. Many factors underlie this change, particularly feminism's critique of traditional female stereotypes, women's rising educational levels, and economic pressures for women to support themselves or their families.

Most wives in the 1950s and 1960s left the labour force to raise families. By the 1980s, a growing proportion of mothers with young children were also employed, greatly increasing the female labour force participation rate (Logan and Belliveau, 1995). Dual-earner families now account for 3 out of every 5 families, and 15 percent of all mothers in the workforce are single parents. Sociologists use terms like the double day, or the second shift, to refer to how most married women spend their days in paying jobs, yet still assume most of the responsibilities of child care and domestic chores when they get home (Hochschild, 1989). Most workplaces have not adapted to this social change by becoming more flexible and family-friendly.

Gender-Segregated Employment

The concept of occupational gender segregation describes the concentration of men and women in different occupations. Gender-role socialization and education reinforce this pattern. Consequently, many women end up in occupations that are predominantly female, such as clerical work or nursing. The concept of a female job ghetto emphasizes the unequal rewards and opportunities built into the labour market on the basis of a worker's gender. Women in job ghettos lack easy access to the more challenging and lucrative occupations dominated by men. These male segments of the labour market (e.g., senior management and some professions, such as engineering), set up success criteria that are male-biased (Kanter, 1977; Powell 1993, Canadian Committee on Women in Engineering, 1992).

Figures 11-4 and 11-5 describe two major trends associated with occupational gender segregation. Figure 11-4 identifies the percentage of employees in each occupation who are women. Women now make up 45 percent of the total labour force. Clerical jobs and medicine and health-related occupations have the highest concentrations of women (80 percent). Teaching, social sciences, and traditional service occupations (e.g., jobs in restaurants, bars, hotels, tourism, hairdressing, child-care facilities, domestics, and building cleaners) are between 57 and 65 percent female. All of these categories could be labelled job "ghettos," in the sense that the majority of employees are women, although pay and other

FIGURE 11-4 Women's employment by occupational group, Canada, 1996

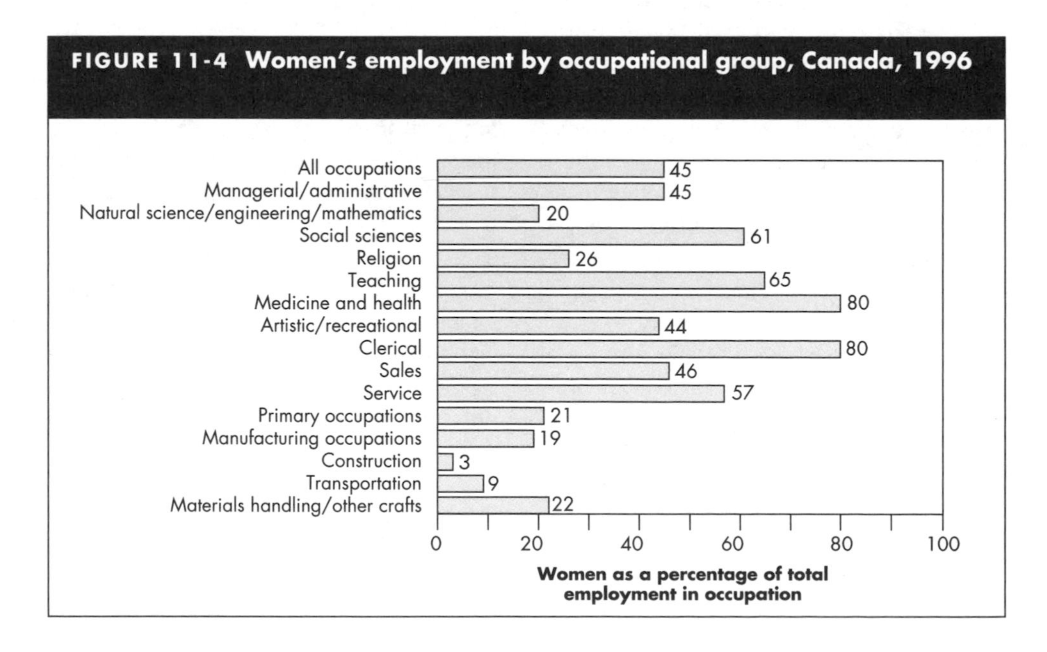

FIGURE 11-5 Occupational distribution of employed women, Canada, 1996

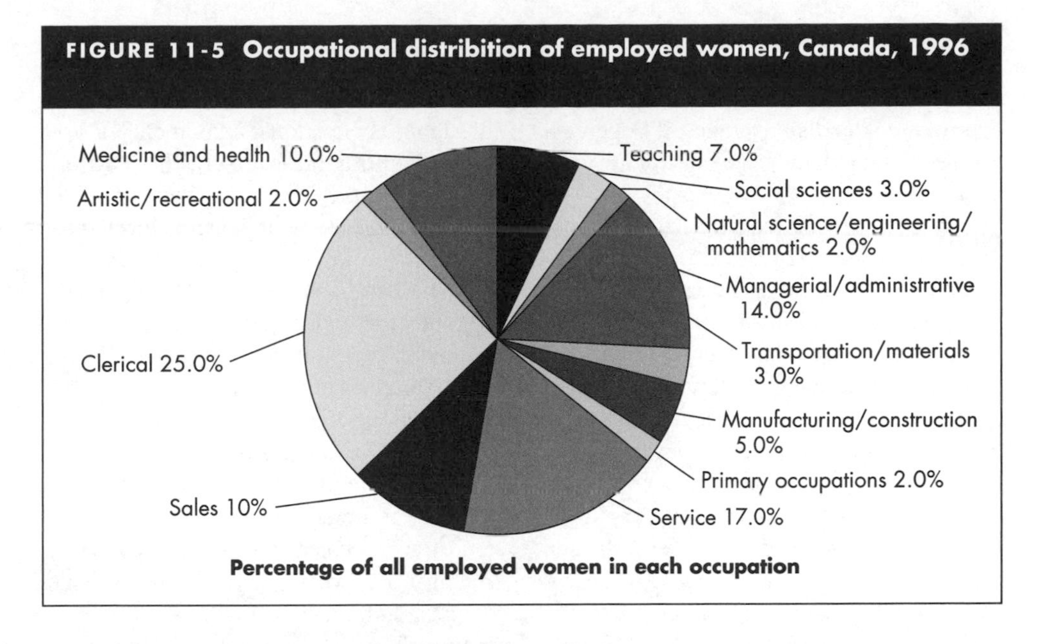

working conditions in some (particularly nursing and teaching) are relatively good. By contrast, no more than one in five workers in natural sciences, engineering and mathematics occupations, manufacturing, transportation, and construction are women.

Figure 11-5 shows the distribution of the female labour force across all occupations. Clerical occupations employed one in four women workers in 1996 (down from one in three in 1991). Over half of the female labour force is in service, sales, and clerical jobs. This figure demonstrates women's continued presence in lower-status occupations, or what we have referred to as job ghettos. Only one in ten female workers is in traditional male areas of work, such as primary, manufacturing, and other manual occupations.

Occupational gender segregation is slowly being reduced as women move into a broader range of occupations. Over the past 20 years, women have made strides into non-traditional jobs (in which men historically predominate), especially management and some professions (Hughes 1995). Note in Figure 11-5 that 14 percent of employed women are in management and administrative jobs. This is a rapidly growing area of female employment. Still, women continue to encounter a "glass ceiling." This concept refers to the often-invisible barriers to women's advancement that persist despite formal policies, such as employment equity, that are designed to eradicate such obstacles.

The Gender Wage Gap

Male-female wage differences reveal that gender is a major source of labour market inequality. For example, female managers reported average annual earnings in 1995 of $32 306, two-thirds of the earnings of their male counterparts ($48 753) (Statistics Canada, 1997). Similar differences are observed in all major occupations. The average 1995 earnings of all employed women in Canada ($20 219) represented only 65 percent of the average earnings of all employed men ($31 053). Examining only full-time, full-year workers (perhaps a better comparison, given women's higher level of part-time employment), male average earnings increase to $40 610, compared to $29 700 for females. Expressed as a female-to-male earnings ratio, or gender wage gap, in 1995 women received an average of 73 percent of the average male wage, up from 60 percent in 1970.

Women's rising incomes can only partly be explained by their rising educational attainment and access to better-paying jobs. Another factor is that, since 1975, real earnings for men have fallen slightly (Krahn and Lowe, 1998: chapter 3). During this period, women were moving into intermediate-level professions and junior and middle-level management. At the same time, males were losing ground in well-paying (often unionized) manual jobs, some professions, and management positions, because of downsizing and industrial restructuring. While different factors affected male and female employment, the overall result was rising wages for some women and falling wages for some men.

Women can face two kinds of labour market discrimination. Employers could pay a women less than a man for performing the same job, a form of wage discrimination rare in Canada today. More common is indirect discrimination resulting from the gender-segregated structure of the labour market, and gender-based stratification within organizations, whereby men have greater access to jobs with the highest rewards. Thus, when male-female differences in education, training, work experience, occupation, industry of employment, and geographic location are taken into account (using statistical models), the wage gap shrinks. Applying this analysis to men and women employed in the same jobs within a single establishment, the earnings ratio narrows even further, to between 90 and 95 percent (Gunderson, 1994; Coverman, 1988).

Given that more women than ever before are graduating from university, how has their higher educational attainment affected their labour market success? Overall, a university education is a good predictor of higher occupational attainment for both women and men. Even so, the National Graduate Survey did find a wage gap of 92 percent at the bachelor's degree level, when it followed up 1990 graduates in 1992 (Wannell and Caron, 1994). However, gender and other individual characteristics tend to have far less impact on graduates' earnings than does program of study (Davies et al., 1996). In other words, gendered enrollment patterns in post-secondary institutions—for example, women choosing nursing and men choosing engineering—are directly linked to occupational gender segregation. Overall, there are positive signs suggesting that women will have increased employment opportunities in the future, although the path towards gender equality has not always been smooth.

Another important point of note is that most of the reduction in occupational gender segregation in Canada has resulted from women moving into male-dominated jobs, and not from men moving into female-dominated jobs. Public policy has been a catalyst for many of these changes. Since the mid-1980s, the federal government, some provincial governments, and a number of large employers have implemented employment equity and pay equity policies. The goal of employment equity policies is the elimination of barriers to the recruitment or advancement of four social groups that historically have been disadvantaged in the Canadian labour market: women, visible minorities, aboriginal peoples, and persons with disabilities. Pay equity promotes the principle of equal pay for work of equal value. It uses job evaluation systems to compare predominantly female jobs with predominantly male jobs within the same organization, and thereby attempts to redress the undervaluing of women's work.

Both policies are good examples of the way in which public policy can positively influence employer practices by promoting gender equality in the labour market. Of course, employment equity policies address more than gender-based inequities in the labour market. While our focus in this chapter has been on gender, it is important to apply the same kind of labour market analysis to other groups. Such analyses can be found in other chapters in this volume.

CONCLUSION

Many of the concerns Canadians have about the future of work are, in fact, concerns about present labour market trends (Betcherman and Lowe, 1997). Widespread feelings of economic insecurity among Canadians are a reaction to high unemployment and underemployment, the spread of non-standard work, declining real incomes, and a more polarized labour market with clear winners and losers. A paradox in today's labour market is that some workers—the unemployed and involuntary part-timers—don't have enough work, while a growing number of full-time workers are putting in longer hours than they consider ideal. These changes have a direct impact on society, as more of the risks associated with economic change are transferred to individuals, families, and communities, and as the divide between "haves" and "have-nots" widens. The study of labour markets can inform public policies to address these problems.

This chapter has focused on paid work in the formal economy. Such an emphasis makes sense if we consider that the livelihoods of the vast majority of Canadians depend, either directly or indirectly, on earned income from employment. Still, it is important to recognize that a fully comprehensive discussion of work would have to include unpaid work performed in households and in volunteer-based community organizations, and paid work in the "informal" economy outside government regulation (e.g., the backyard mechanic who fixes your car for cash). So, while the labour market has a huge impact on social inequality because it is based on paid work, it does not account for all the work performed by Canadians. Looking to the future, it is interesting to speculate about changes in how Canadians value and participate in all forms of work.

NOTES

1. This chapter relies extensively on data and analysis from Statistics Canada. Useful sources in this regard are two quarterly publications, *Perspectives on Labour and Income* and *Canadian Social Trends*, as well as *The Labour Force* (monthly) and the *Labour Force Annual Averages* (annual). Students also are encouraged to visit Statistics Canada's website (www.statscan.ca) for daily updates and extensive background information on labour market, demographic, economic, and social trends.

REFERENCES

Akyeampong, Ernest B. 1997 "Work arrangements: 1995 overview." *Perspectives on Labour and Income* (Spring): 48–52.

Althauser, Robert P. 1989 "Internal labor markets." *Annual Review of Sociology* 15: 143–61.

Banting, Keith G. and Charles M. Beach, (eds.) 1995 *Labour Market Polarization and Social Policy Reform* Kingston, ON: School of Policy Studies, Queen's University.

Becker, Gary S. 1975 *Human Capital: A Theoretical and Empirical Analysis with Special Reference to Education* (2nd ed.) Chicago: University of Chicago Press.

Bell, Daniel 1973 *The Coming of Post-Industrial Society* New York: Basic Books.

Betcherman, Gordon and Graham Lowe 1997 *The Future of Work in Canada: A Synthesis Report* Ottawa: Canadian Policy Research Networks Inc.

Betcherman, Gordon and Norm Leckie 1997 *Youth Employment and Education Trends in the 1980s and 1990s* Ottawa: Canadian Policy Research Networks Inc., Working Paper no. W03.

Blau, Francine D., and Marianne A. Ferber 1986 *The Economics of Women, Men and Work* Englewood Cliffs, NJ: Prentice-Hall.

Braverman, Harry 1974 *Labor and Monopoly Capital: The Degradation of Work in the Twentieth Century* New York: Monthly Review Press.

Bridges, William 1994 *JobShift: How to Prosper in a Workplace Without Jobs* Don Mills, ON.: Addison-Wesley.

Canadian Committee on Women in Engineering 1992 *More than Just Numbers: Report of the Canadian Committee on Women in Engineering* Fredericton: Faculty of Engineering, University of New Brunswick.

Clairmont, Donald, R. Apostle, and R. Kreckel 1983 "The segmentation perspective as a middle-range conceptualization in sociology." *Canadian Journal of Sociology* 8: 245–71.

Coverman, Shelley 1988 "Sociological explanations of the male-female wage gap: individual and structuralist theories." In Ann Helton Stromberg and Shirley Harkess (eds.) *Women Working: Theories and Facts in Perspective* (2nd ed.) Mountain View, CA: Mayfield.

Davies, Scott, Clayton Mosher, and Bill O'Grady 1996 "Educating women: gender inequalities among Canadian university graduates." *Canadian Review of Sociology and Anthropology* 33:125–42.

Duffy, Ann, and Norene Pupo 1992 *Part-time Paradox: Connecting Gender, Work and Family* Toronto: McClelland & Stewart.

Duffy, Ann, Daniel Glenday, and Norene Pupo (eds.) 1997 *Good Jobs, Bad Jobs, No Jobs: The Transformation of Work in the 21st Century* Toronto: Harcourt Brace Canada.

Economic Council of Canada 1991 *Employment in the Service Economy* Ottawa: Supply and Services Canada.

Gordon, David. M., R. Edwards, and M. Reich 1982 *Segmented Work, Divided Workers: The Historical Transformation of Labor in the United States* New York: Cambridge University Press.

Grenon, Lee 1996 "Are service jobs low-paying?" *Perspectives on Labour and Income* (Spring): 29–34.

Gunderson, Morley 1994 *Comparable Worth and Gender Discrimination: An International Perspective* Geneva: Organization for Economic Cooperation and Development.

Hochschild, Arlie 1989 *The Second Shift: Working Parents and the Revolution at Home* New York: Viking Penguin.

Hodson, Randy, and Robert L. Kaufman 1982 "Economic dualism: a critical review." *American Sociological Review* 47: 727–39.

Hughes, Karen D. 1995 "Women in non-traditional occupations." *Perspectives on Labour and Income* (Autumn):14–19.

Human Resource Development Canada 1994 *Report of the Advisory Committee on Working Time and the Distribution of Work* Ottawa: Supply and Services Canada.

Human Resources Development Canada (and Statistics Canada) 1997 *Adult Education and Training in Canada: Report of the 1994 Adult Education and Training Survey* Ottawa: Supply and Services Canada.

International Labour Organization 1997 *World Labour Report 1997–1998: Industrial Relations, Democracy and Social Stability* Geneva: ILO.

Kalleberg, Arne, and Ivar Berg 1987 *Work and Industry: Structures, Markets and Processes* New York: Plenum.

Kanter, Rosabeth M. 1977 *Men and Women of the Corporation* New York: Basic Books.

Kelly, Karen, Linda Howatson-Leo, and Warren Clark I feel overqualified for my job...'" *Canadian Social Trends* (Winter):11–16.

Krahn, Harvey 1995 "Non-standard work on the rise." *Perspectives on Labour and Income* (Winter): 35–42.

Krahn, Harvey and Graham S. Lowe 1998 *Work, Industry and Canadian Society* (3rd ed.) Scarborough: ITP Nelson, 1998.

Logan, Ron and Jo-Anne Belliveau 1995 "Working mothers." *Canadian Social Trends* (Spring):24–28.

MacLean, Brian K. and Lars Osberg (eds.) 1996 *The Unemployment Crisis: All for Nought?* Toronto: University of Toronto Press.

Myles, John 1988 "The expanding middle: some Canadian evidence on the deskilling debate." *Canadian Review of Sociology and Anthropology* 25: 335–64.

Osberg, Lars, Fred Wien and Jan Grude 1995 *Vanishing Jobs: Canada's Changing Workplace* Toronto: Lorimer.

Picot, W. Garrett 1987 "The changing industrial mix of employment, 1951–1985." *Canadian Social Trends* (Spring): 8–11.

Policy Options 1996 *Special Issue on Unemployment* 17(6).

Powell, Gary N. 1993 *Women & Men in Management* (2nd ed.) Newbury Park, CA: Sage.

Reich, Robert B. 1991 *The Work of Nations: Preparing Ourselves for 21st-Century Capitalism* New York: Alfred A. Knopf.

Reiter, Ester 1991 *Making Fast Food: From the Frying Pan Into the Fryer* Montreal and Kingston: McGill-Queen's University Press.

Rifkin, Jeremy 1995 *The End of Work: The Decline of the Global Labor Force and the Dawn of the Post-Market Era* New York: Putnam.

Rinehart, James 1996 *The Tyranny of Work: Alienation and the Labour Process* (3rd ed.) Toronto: Harcourt Brace Canada.

Rubery, Jill 1988 "Employers and the labour market." In Duncan Gallie (ed.) *Employment in Britain* Oxford: Basil Blackwell.

Saunders, John 1997 "Dollars and sense." *Globe and Mail* (12 April, p. B1) .

Statistics Canada 1997 *Earnings of Men and Women 1995* Catalogue no.13-217.

Statistics Canada *Labour Force Annual Averages* Catalogue no. 71-220-XPB.

Statistics Canada *The Labour Force* Catalogue no. 71-001 monthly.

Statistics Canada *Perspectives on Labour and Income*

Statistics Canada *Canadian Social Trends*

Sunter, Deborah and Rene Morissette 1994 "The hours people work." *Perspectives on Labour and Income* 6:8–13.

Sheridan, Mike, Deborah Sunter, and Brent Diverty 1996 "The changing work week: trends in weekly hours of work in Canada, 1976–1995." *The Labour Force Survey* (June) Ottawa: Statistics Canada. Catalogue no. 71–001.

Van den Berg, Axel, and Joseph Smucker, (eds.) 1997 *The Sociology of Labour Markets: Efficiency, Equity, Security.* Scarborough: Prentice Hall Allyn and Bacon Canada.

Wannell, Ted and Nathalie Caron 1994 *The Gender Earnings Gap Among Recent Post-secondary Graduates, 1984-92* Analytic Studies Branch, Research Paper Series, No.64. Ottawa: Statistics Canada.

FOR FURTHER REFERENCE: OCCUPATION

Betcherman, Gordon, and Graham Lowe 1997 *The Future of Work in Canada. A Synthesis Report* Ottawa: Canadian Policy Research Networks Inc.

Drache, Daniel, and Harry Glasbeek 1992 *The Changing Workplace. Reshaping Canada's Industrial Relations System* Toronto: Lorimer. This book considers major changes in the nature of work in Canada, especially those tied to such developments as the growing power of global transnational companies, the push toward newer workplace technologies, and the declining role of government as both an employer and a regulator of private business.

Krahn, Harvey, and Graham Lowe 1998 *Work, Industry, and Canadian Society* (3rd ed.) Scarborough: ITP Nelson. This text provides a comprehensive review of employment, labour market, and workplace trends in Canada, and helps students to interpret these trends using different theoretical perspectives.

Statistics Canada *Perspectives on Labour and Income and Canadian Social Trends* These two quarterly publications are invaluable sources of information on Canadian labour market and employment trends and issues.

Van den Berg, Axel, and Joseph Smucker (eds.) 1997 *The Sociology of Labour Markets: Efficiency, Equity, Security* Scarborough: Prentice Hall Allyn and Bacon Canada. This collection of essays covers the major theoretical perspectives on labour markets and presents research findings from various studies of how labour markets operate.

Rinehart, James 1996 *The Tyranny of Work* (3rd ed.) Toronto: Harcourt Brace and Company Canada. This monograph explores the nature of work in Canada from a critical perspective, with a particular emphasis on the labour process and the alienating nature of work under capitalism.

EDUCATION

Chapter 12

INTER-GENERATIONAL CHANGE IN THE EDUCATION OF CANADIANS

Élaine Fournier, George Butlin, Philip Giles

(Abridged from the authors' "Intergenerational change in the education of Canadians," in Statistic Canada's *Education Quarterly Review*, Catalogue No. 81-003, 1995, 2, 2, pp. 22–23. Reprinted with permission.)

INTRODUCTION

How does a person's socio-economic status compare with his or her parents'? Using data collected in January 1993 as part of the 'Survey of Labour and Income Dynamics' (SLID's) preliminary interview, this article examines the relationship between a person's educational attainment and that of his or her parents by comparing the academic achievements and mobility of different generations.

Educational attainment is a strong predictor of occupational success and income level. For example, in 1993, average income for persons with a university degree was $40 247, compared with $23 644 for those with a high school diploma (Statistics Canada, 1994).

THE NATURE OF EDUCATIONAL ATTAINMENT

As Grabb (1992) has noted, some sociologists have argued that academic success or failure is based mainly on individual talent and motivation rather than on factors related to social background (for example, sex, ethnicity, religion, and family social class). Put in terms of social mobility, a society may be characterized either by a weak linkage between social origin (in this article, parents' education) and personal position (educational attainment), allowing considerable intergenerational movement, or by a strong connection entailing less movement.

Readers should be mindful of structural mobility; that is, mobility arising from changes in the population as a whole. With the expansion in the Canadian educational system that started in the 1950s, there has been a general upgrading of educational levels between generations. Persons born during or after the 1950s are likely to be better educated than their parents' generation, particularly at the postsecondary levels (Pomfret, 1992).

Against the backdrop of structural mobility, this article looks at circulation mobility (Creese, Guppy and Meissner, 1991), which is movement attributable to factors such as an individual's talent and motivation.

Measuring Level of Education

Our educational level variable has five categories: university degree; college or university (with or without a certificate or diploma); high school diploma; some secondary schooling; and some elementary schooling or completion.

The following groups have been excluded from the analysis: respondents who did not have a university degree and are still attending school; those who did not report a level of education; and those whose parents' level of education was not reported. People who are still studying but have already reached the highest level of education (that is, university degree) have been included in the analysis; those who have not achieved a university degree and are still studying have been excluded because they may eventually reach a higher level. Respondents without a reported parents' educational level are more likely to be older. Their exclusion from the analysis will slightly bias the measures of mobility upwards since, in general, older respondents have less upward mobility.

CANADIANS' EDUCATIONAL ATTAINMENT HAS RISEN

Canadians have traditionally attained a higher educational level than the previous

TABLE 12-1 Educational attainment of Canadians and their parents, by sex, 1993

	Daughters*	Sons*	Mothers*	Fathers*
Education				
Total**	100.0	100.0	100.0	100.0
University degree	12.3	15.4	3.2	7.1
College or university (with or without a certificate or diploma)	39.4	39.0	8.6	7.0
High school diploma	18.9	15.7	18.3	14.9
Some secondary schooling	15.1	15.9	20.1	18.8
Some elementary schooling or completion	14.3	14.0	49.9	52.1

* "Sons" and "daughters" correspond to the Canadian population, so these columns could also be labelled "males" and "females." On the other hand, "mothers" and "fathers" refer to the parents of those aged 15 and over in the Canadian population; some of these people are also part of the Canadian population, some were members of the Canadian population but have since died or moved out of the country, and some were never part of the Canadian population.

** Total may not sum to 100.0 due to rounding.

Source: Survey of Labour and Income Dynamics preliminary interview (January 1993).

generation. In 1993, just over half the population had attended a postsecondary institution, compared with a little over 10% of their parents' (Table 12-1). Moreover, while 70% of the parents had not graduated from high school, only 30% of their children had failed to do so.

Educational attainment varies considerably by age. Two out of three baby boomers (aged 25 to 44) had some postsecondary education, compared with two out of five persons born before the baby boom (aged 45 and over). Compared with baby boomers, proportionately fewer young (aged 15 to 24) people (one in two) had some postsecondary education, but since one-quarter of them did not have a high school diploma, they may have left school temporarily (dropping out is widespread). Age, therefore, has a significant effect on educational level.

Mobility Tables[1]

The analysis of intergenerational mobility starts with a cross-classification of a respondent's educational level with that of one parent (see below—*Measuring Mobility*); for example, a daughter's educational level and her mother's (Table 12-2). The cells above the diagonal describe *downward mobility* (for example, a mother with a university degree and a daughter with a high school diploma). Each segment to the right of the shaded diagonal represents one step of *downward mobility*. Similarly, the cells below the diagonal contain cases of *upward mobility*, and each segment to the left represents one step upward. For example, four steps of upward mobility are captured by daughters with a university degree whose mothers had elementary schooling.

The cell values in a mobility table can be aggregated to show the degree of mobility. Table 12-3 contains these distributions for the four possible parent/child combinations.

Measuring Mobility

The measure of mobility depends largely on the number of categories used. The higher the number, the lower the likelihood that a person will not move. (In the extreme case, with only one category, there would be no mobility.) In defining the categories, SLID has ranked the educational levels and, by doing so, has made a value judgment.

In this article, a person with a university degree is judged to have attained a higher educational level than someone with college or university (but no degree), even though this is not always the case. For example, a person can be certified as an electrician after taking courses and working several years, while another person can obtain a university degree after only three years of university. Moreover, SLID does not take into account "equivalences" in education. For example, a person now requires a university degree to teach at all levels of education, which was not the case previously.

Two Out of Three Canadians Exceeded Their Parents' Educational Level...

Individuals who exceeded their parents' academic achievement very often gained up to three steps. In most cases, the parent had attended elementary school and the child had college or university (no degree). Of those who moved up two steps, slightly less than half had college or university education, while their parents had not graduated from high school. An equivalent proportion received a high school diploma, whereas their parents had only an elementary school education.

... and Fewer Than One in Ten Achieved a Lower Level

Only about 7% of Canadians acquired less education than their parents and most of

TABLE 12-2 Mother's and daughter's educational attainment, 1993 daughter's education

Daughter's Education:	University degree	College or university (with or without a certificate or diploma)	High school diploma	Some secondary schooling	Some elementary schooling completion	Total %
Mother's education:						
Total*	**100.0**	**12.2**	**39.3**	**19.0**	**15.2**	**14.3**
University degree	3.1	1.5	1.1	–	–	–
College or university (with or without a certificate or diploma)	8.7	2.4	4.5	1.2	0.5	–
High school diploma	18.0	3.4	9.1	3.6	1.5	0.3**
Some secondary schooling	19.8	2.2	8.8	5.2	3.0	0.6
Some elementary schooling or completion	50.3	2.6	15.9	8.5	10.0	13.2

* Total may not equal sum of parts due to rounding.

** High sampling variance (coefficient of variation between 16.5% and 25 %); use with caution.

Note: The shaded diagonal from top left to bottom right refers to cases with no mobility (that is, the educational level of daughter and mother are the same.)

Source: Survey of Labour and Income Dynamics preliminary interview (January 1993).

them were just one level lower. Individuals who achieved a lower level in comparison with their fathers most often had attended but not completed college or university, while their fathers had obtained a university degree. In contrast, those with less schooling than their mothers had some high school education, while their mothers had graduated from high school.

Since the fathers are often slightly more educated than the mothers, the proportion of children with lower academic achievement than their fathers is a little higher. Logically, children of parents with the highest educational attainment cannot move up but have to settle for achieving the same level or moving down one or more steps.

Sex of Child or Parent Does Not Affect Mobility

Traditionally, research into social mobility has focused on the impact of the father's occupation on the son's. If the mother was not in the labour market, she was excluded from the analysis. Yet this study has shown that the mother's education is no less important an influence than the father's on the educational attainment of the child. Intergenerational mobility is similar regardless of the sex of parent or child (Figure 12-1).

As gender is not a significant variable in the analysis of educational mobility, a person's educational attainment was compared

FIGURE 12-1 In 1993, most children exceeded their parents' educational level

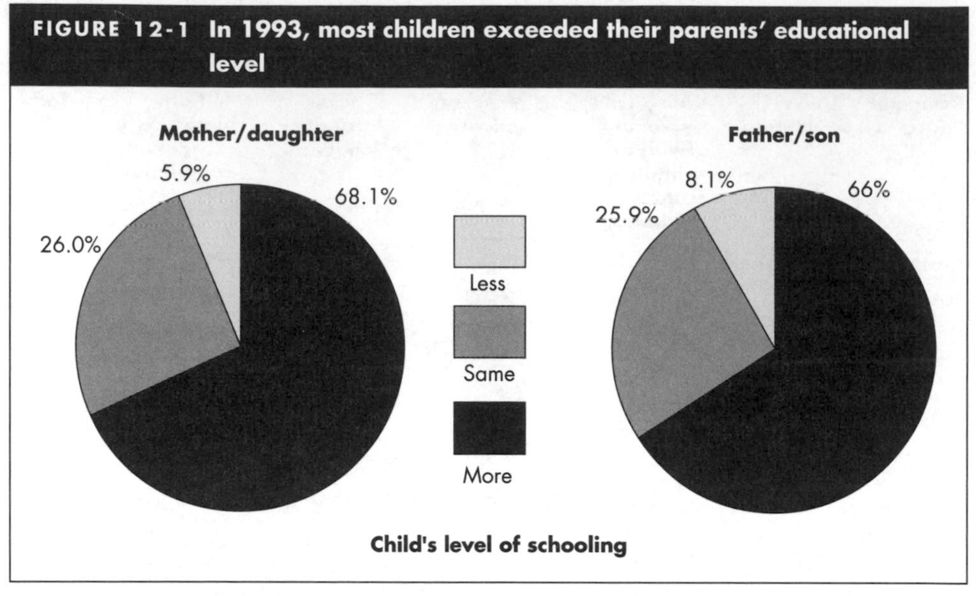

Source: Survey of Labour and Income Dynamics preliminary interview (January 1993).

with the highest level reached by either the mother or father, rather than looking at each separately. This simplifies the analysis because only one comparison is made. However, it has the effect of lowering the apparent achievement of each individual because only the parent with the higher level is considered.

Overall Upgrading Does Not Account For All Educational Achievement

For the 7 out of 10 Canadians whose education differed from their parents', SLID has sought to determine what proportion of the change was attributable to overall upgrading of educational levels (structural mobility), and what proportion was due to individual abilities and merit (circulation mobility). For example, in an environment in which the distribution of educational levels was identical from one generation to the next, circulation mobility would explain any changes in the child's educational attainment compared with the parents'. Cases of upward mobility and downward mobility would balance each other.

The General Social Survey (GSS) also measured the changes attributable to overall upgrading and to individual abilities and merit, using their 1986 data (see box entitled *Structural Mobility and Circulation Mobility*). By comparing an individual's educational attainment with that of the parent who reached the higher level, SLID found that structural mobility was 33% and circulation mobility was 37%; 30% of the population remained at the level of the previous generation. If persons who did not move were excluded, structural mobility accounted for just under half the increase in educational attainment, and circulation mobility accounted for the remainder. These results suggest that the improved educational attainment of persons from disadvantaged backgrounds need not be linked solely to the general increase in educational attainment.

TABLE 12-3 Steps of intergenerational educational mobility, 1993

Mobility steps	Mother/daughter	Mother/son	Father/daughter	Father/son
			%	
Total	**100.0**	**100.0**	**100.0**	**100.0**
Upward mobility				
4 steps up	2.6	3.6	2.6	3.8
3 steps up	18.1	20.1	19.3	20.3
2 steps up	20.8	19.6	20.4	18.3
1 step up	26.7	24.3	23.6	23.5
No mobility	**26.0**	**25.3**	**26.6**	**25.9**
Downward mobility				
1 step down	4.5	5.3	5.7	6.1
2 steps down	1.2	1.2	1.3	1.4
3 and 4 steps down	0.2**	0.5	0.5	0.5

* Total may not sum to 100.0 due to rounding.

** High sampling variance (coefficient of variation between 16.5% and 25%); use with caution.

Source: Survey of Labour and Income Dynamics preliminary interview (January 1993).

A calculation of mobility for each parent/child combination in this study yielded results comparable to the GSS. For the mother/son combination, however, the results were different, with much greater structural mobility observed by SLID than by the GSS. The latter calculated mobility using six educational levels, while SLID used only five. This likely affects the results, because the higher the number of categories, the greater the chances of movement.

Parents' Postsecondary Education Makes a Difference

The figures for postsecondary attainment range from just over 40% for children whose parents did not complete secondary school, to 65% for children of high school graduates, to almost 80% for those whose parents had a postsecondary education (Figure 12-2).

Structural Mobility and Circulation Mobility

Structural mobility refers to changes linked to the general increase in the educational level of the population, whereas circulation mobility results from individual effort. To calculate these two types of mobility, the Survey of Labour and Income Dynamics (SLID) used the same definitions as the 1986 General Social Survey (GSS). To measure the effect of structural mobility, an index of dissimilarity was calculated. This index, expressed as a percentage, reflects the difference between two distributions; in this case, the educational level of daughters and their mothers (Table 12-2). Structural mobility is one half of the absolute difference between the percentages in the two univariate distributions for each educational level (Creese, Guppy and Meissner, 1991). An index of

FIGURE 12-2 The likelihood of studying at the postsecondary level is greater if one parent has a postsecondary education

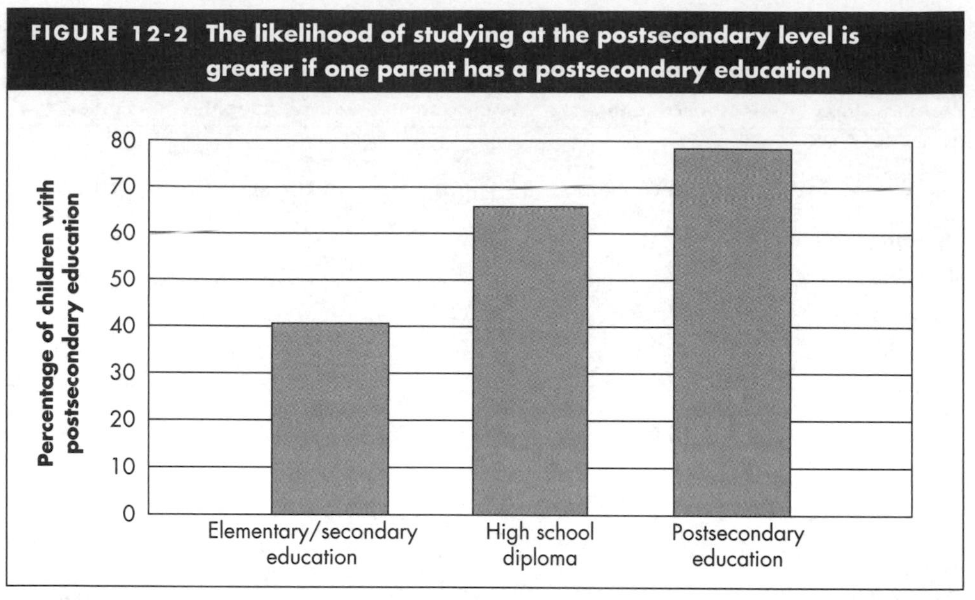

Source: Survey of Labour and Income Dynamics preliminary interview (January 1993).

0% would mean that the two univariate distributions are identical, whereas an index of 100% would mean that they are extremely different. In this case, structural mobility is 41%. If the proportion of cases with no mobility (the sum of the shaded cells in Table 12-2, i.e., 26%) and the proportion of structural mobility (expressed by the index) are subtracted from 100%, a proportion of 33% for circulation mobility is obtained. This figure corresponds to all other movements in the table.

Individuals Under Age 40 Achieved a Lower Level Than Other Canadians

It was relatively easy for most Canadians to attain if not exceed their parents' educational level, since 62% of all parents did not graduate from high school. However, for individuals under age 40, it was more difficult to surpass their parents' level, which was higher than that of parents of individuals aged 65 or over. In fact, the proportion of parents with postsecondary education ranges from 11% for parents of individuals aged 65 and over to more than 25% for parents of individuals under 40.

Moreover, almost 70% of the parents of Canadians aged 65 and over had only an elementary education, so it was difficult for their children to achieve a lower level by comparison. Thus, 44% of individuals aged 65 and over attained the same educational level as their parents (elementary in 80% of cases). Still, 46% achieved a higher level than their parents. A large proportion of these persons are in the "secondary" category, one step above their parents' elementary level, and an almost equally large proportion are in the "college or university" category, three steps above their parents' elementary education. Most individuals in the 40-to-64 age group are also in the latter category (Table 12-4).

CONCLUSION

The increase in Canadians' educational level is not merely the result of structural changes in the education system, but also depends

TABLE 12-4 Educational attainment of Canadians in comparision with their parents, by age, 1993

	Total	Higher	Same	Lower
Age				
15–39	100.0	60.1	26.2	13.7
40–64	100.0	63.9	27.3	8.8
65 and over	100.0	46.1	44.1	9.8

Source: Survey of Labour and Income Dynamics preliminary interview (January 1993).

on each individual's abilities and merit. However, there is a link between the parents' educational level and that of their children. Children have a much greater chance of studying at the postsecondary level if one parent has a postsecondary education. While some may believe that the father's educational level has a greater impact on the children's education, this study reveals that the mother's educational attainment is probably equally important.

NOTE

1. This section applies methods drawn from Creese, Guppy, and Meissner, 1991.

REFERENCES

Creese, G., N. Guppy, and M. Meissner 1991 *Ups and Downs on the Ladder of Success: Social Mobility in Canada* General Social Survey Analysis Series, Catalogue 11–612E no. 5. Ottawa: Statistics Canada.

Grabb, E. 1992 "Social stratification." In *Introduction to Sociology: A Canadian Focus*, (4th ed.) James J. Teevan (ed.) Scarborough: Prentice–Hall Canada, pp. 195–235.

Pomfret, A. 1992 "Education." In *Introduction to Sociology: A Canadian Focus*, (4th ed.) James J. Teevan (ed.) Scarborough: Prentice–Hall Canada, pp. 369–402.

Statistics Canada 1994 *Income Distributions by Size in Canada, 1993*. Catalogue 13–207. Ottawa.

STUBBORN DISPARITIES: EXPLAINING CLASS INEQUALITIES IN SCHOOLING

Chapter 13

Scott Davies

(An original chapter written for this volume.)

INTRODUCTION

Canada has been transformed over this century from a predominantly rural, agricultural society to an urban, post-industrial nation. Whereas one hundred years ago most people were self-employed in family-owned farms and small businesses, today the vast majority earn their livelihood by competing in the labour market. Coinciding with these changes, the school system has expanded enormously, greatly increasing the educational attainments of Canadians. Most Canadians, regardless of social origin, earn more school credentials than did their ancestors. Indeed, Canada has more citizens attending school at its various levels—elementary, secondary, and post-secondary—than almost any other country (see Guppy and Davies, forthcoming).

Schooling has become an increasingly important determinant of one's chances of securing a good job and a stable income, and by extension, education has become a prime arena for social competition. Schools sift and sort people into highly stratified career paths.

This raises a key question: have all Canadians benefited equally from the expansion of the school system? Recent studies have examined trends in educational outcomes by race, gender, and social class.[1] As for race, most visible minorities, whether immigrant or Canadian-born, fare better in school than Whites, except for Aboriginal Canadians (Geschwender and Guppy, 1995; Davies and Guppy, 1998). Non-aboriginal minorities, taken as a group, are less likely to drop out of high school, and are more likely to attend university. With the exception of Aboriginals, race or ethnic heritage is not a strong predictor of Canadians' educational attainment.

In terms of gender, Canadian educational trends resemble those of most other nations: an overall movement toward male-female parity (Bradley and Ramirez, 1996). Whereas males still earn more advanced degrees (masters, doctorates), and continue to dominate lucrative fields of study such as computer science and engineering, females are catching up in these and other areas. Females now attend and graduate from university at higher rates than males, and are less likely to drop out of high school. Despite some lingering female disadvantages, the main trend in Canadian education, as elsewhere, is toward gender equality.

However, a very different story emerges for social class. Whether measured by high school dropout rates, standardized test scores, or university attendance rates, youth from working class and underclass backgrounds do not fare as well as their middle and upper class peers. Students' class origin markedly influences their school success regardless of their race, gender, or ethnicity. Certainly, the relation between class and educational outcomes is not a perfect fit. Within every socioeconomic (SES) category a wide range of outcomes exists and some working class students are very successful in school. Nevertheless, SES is the strongest and most enduring social determinant of educational attainment. Indeed, in Canada, as in most nations, socioeconomic disparities in educational attainment have persisted despite decades of educational expansion and reform (see Shavit and Blossfeld, 1993, but also Deng and Treiman, 1997).

This chapter presents and evaluates sociological explanations for the persistence of these SES inequalities. While acknowledging the variation in education achievements within any SES category, I dwell on explanations of the unequal average attainments of working class versus middle class youth. I focus on Canada, though draw heavily on American and British research, since socioeconomic patterns of educational inequality in Canada and the United States are remarkably similar, and because much British research on the topic has influenced Canadian sociologists.[2]

HOW INEQUALITIES EMERGE: SELECTION AND CUMULATIVE DISADVANTAGE

Educational inequality is best understood as a series of dissimilar transition and survival rates between groups (see Mare, 1993 for an elaboration). Schooling is laddered, with student pools becoming smaller and smaller with successive transitions. For instance, most students now finish elementary schooling and enter high school. But since approximately 20% of Canadians who enter high school fail to graduate by age twenty-four (Frank, 1996), the pool of high school graduates is selective relative to the entering high school cohort. Since SES is an important predictor of dropping out (Gilbert *et al.*, 1993), high school graduates have a smaller proportion of working class students than high school entrants. In turn, another selection takes place when only some high school graduates pursue postsecondary schooling. The "survivors" of this transition are again relatively select, as the proportion of students from lower SES origins again shrinks (for Canada, see Guppy and Davies, forthcoming, for other countries, see Shavit and Blossfeld, 1993). And there is still more. In the US, lower SES students are less likely to attend prestigious universities, even controlling for academic ability (Davies and Guppy, 1997). What causes these class disparities in educational attainment?

ECONOMIC ARGUMENTS: MONEY MATTERS

Perhaps the most elemental explanation for working class underachievement in school focuses on how working class families face economic constraints that impede their educational progress. Although publicly funded, school attendance and performance requires money to pay for optional field trips, learning materials, and private tutors (e.g., piano, reading). Research shows that class background affects students' decisions about attending university, even controlling for their academic ability. This is usually interpreted as an effect of the increasingly prohibitive costs of tuition (Porter, 1979, Gambetta, 1996, Steelman and Powell, 1991). Private schools, which send the vast majority of their graduates to universities, are largely unaffordable to lower income families. Wealthier parents are more likely to pay for additional private tutoring outside school hours (though lower income parents would hire tutors "if they had the time and/or money" [Environics, 1997]). Another economic factor is the quality of public schooling. Public schools in more affluent neighborhoods enjoy superior resources and attract better teachers.[3] Though resource level itself does not directly produce better educational outcomes, better-funded schools produce an environment that is more conducive to educational success.

Nevertheless, economic resources—whether used for tuition, transportation, private tutors, or to avoid the need for part-time work—are not the sole factor that affects school outcomes. Countries that largely eliminated university tuition fees, such as Great Britain, France, and Australia, have class inequalities in university attendance similar to those in Canada and the U.S. This suggests that pure economic factors, while palpable, are not all-determining. There is an explanatory gap, something unexplained by economic factors. To complement economic explanations, sociologists have turned to the realm of culture.

CLASS AND FRAMES OF REFERENCE

People's economic conditions affect their sense of life options. SES origins influence their perceptions of the kinds of jobs they are likely to obtain, and the lives they are likely to lead. Judgments about school are thus influenced by these surrounding economic conditions. In particular, this context shapes the various "push" factors providing disincentives for remaining in school, and the "pull" factors providing incentives to leave school. Working class students confront two obvious push factors: economic constraints (as elaborated above), and their underachievement relative to middle class children (as elaborated below). Other factors give push and pull forces extra strength and efficacy.

When explaining socioeconomic disparities in education, the key factor is the gap between people's abstract values and their concrete aspirations and expectations (see Mickelson, 1990). Everyone "values" education in an abstract sense. Whether through surveys, interviews, or policy statements, virtually all Canadians stress the importance they place on education. Our consumer-driven, success-striving society encourages people to pursue the "North American Dream" of a prestigious, well-paying job. As a result, the number of young people wanting professional careers greatly exceeds the number of such positions that exist. Hopes for professional jobs are unrealistically high (Jacobs, Karen, McClelland, 1991).

Expressing an appreciation for education is one thing, but converting desires into reality is another. Part of this gap between expressed values and reality can be traced to factors beyond the economic realm.

"Frames of reference" refer to people's sense of desirable yet possible life options, their mental horizons that influence what they expect they can realistically attain. Immediate family and friends influence these frames greatly. We develop expectations by comparing ourselves to similar people, aligning our aspirations and efforts accordingly. These frames of reference shape our ideas of what kind of jobs and lifestyle we want, and the role school plays in our desires.

Social class strongly influences peoples' frames of reference. Middle class students have higher expectations for jobs and education than do working class students, even controlling for differences in measured academic ability. Their higher aspirations can be attributed largely to the influence of their family and friends (Sewell and Hauser, 1980; McClelland, 1990).[4] These differences in frames of reference explain part of the socioeconomic gap in educational success (Sewell and Hauser, 1980; Jacobs, Karen, McClelland, 1991).

How does class shape these frames? In some instances, people's past experience and current social position cause them to "come to terms" with their circumstances and adjust their expectations to what is "realistic." When asked what they would like to be when they grow up, very young children often reply "police officer," "nanny," or "teacher." As they grow older, learning about the jobs of their parents' friends, these choices change. The choices change again as young people hear others encouraging or remaining mute about their occupational dreams. When confronting barriers, economic or otherwise, they often lower their original goals. Additionally, "pull factors" disproportionately entice working class youth out of school. Especially for youth not faring well in school, domestic and employment roles act as school-leaving incentives. Relatively secure blue collar jobs requiring few educational credentials appear as viable alternatives to schooling (Brown, 1987), as do marriage plans. Even among the previously ambitious, and among the talented, early marriage reduces aspirations (Jacobs et al., 1991).

PUSH FACTORS: THE STRUCTURE OF SCHOOLING

Working class students in most countries, including Canada, are more likely than their middle class counterparts to be streamed into less challenging, terminal programs in high school (Davies, 1992; Curtis, Livingstone, and Smaller, 1992). The very existence of these streaming systems, critics contend, disadvantages working class students. These youth would fare better in a non-streamed high school environment that offered them the same curricula and expectations as other students. Being stuck in lower tracks offers these students less challenging work, and lowers their expectations and aspirations for the future. Once in different tracks, fatalistic frames of reference are reinforced, as opportunities to rise in school and learn are limited. The incentives of available jobs and/or impending domestic roles, when combined with streaming, lead these youth to perceive school as irrelevant to their future. School becomes a pointless dress rehearsal that is irrelevant to their upcoming roles.

American Catholic schools place far fewer students in lower streams, and as a result greater proportions of working class students in these schools score well on standardized tests, graduate from high school, and attend post secondary institutions (Lee, Bryk, and Smith, 1993). Such research findings encourage the "de-streaming" movement, which seeks to abolish differential grouping and to mix students of all abilities. In the early 1990s, Ontario removed streams in grade nine, and planned eventually to phase out all streaming. However, for a variety of reasons—but largely due to teacher complaints about the practical difficulties imposed by heterogeneous ability groups—the government ended the experiment. Nevertheless, American research suggests that de-streaming could be a valid tool for easing class disparities in schooling if practical problems associated with student heterogeneity can be overcome.

Another factor shaping frames of reference, and their relation to class, is knowledge about education. Even when students from humble origins have lofty aspirations, and are academically gifted, other factors mitigate against their success. The daunting variety of choices available in modern postsecondary education, such as the distinctions between community colleges and universities, different types of degrees, the informal ranking of institutions, and the wide variety of programs available within any institution, creates an elaborate system of selection with many ports of entry. To make wise choices and maximize one's benefit, one must understand how the system operates; for example, what are the efficacious strategies for success or the informal rankings of programs and institutions? Such navigational savvy is held disproportionately by students from middle-class origins. These youth have superior information about the academic marketplace, they are more likely to know which fields offer lucrative rewards, and how to find competitive advantages. As a result, students from disadvantaged origins have a lower probabilty of survival in advanced stages of the education system (Davies and Guppy, 1997).

MORE PUSH FACTORS: THE CULTURE OF SCHOOLING

A notable characteristic of class inequality in education is that disparities in skills such as the ability to read, write, and reason, can be detected from the earliest days in school (Alexander, Entwisle, and Horsey, 1997). Why does this occur? As has been well documented, some parents can pass to their children non-material resources that facilitate school success. Because parental education attainment better predicts student success than parental income or class position, many sociologists have looked to the role of non-material resources in facilitating class differences in educational attainment.

More educated parents pass on to their children "human capital"—basic reading, writing, and vocabulary skills, disciplined work habits—giving their children a distinct advantage in school. More highly educated parents spend more time helping their children with school-related activities (Environics, 1997), a finding which is likely a consequence of their more flexible work schedules, and greater familiarity with academic matters (Lareau, 1989).

Another cultural approach places less emphasis on particular skills and focuses instead on cultural tastes and aesthetics. "Cultural capital," the signature concept of French sociologist Pierre Bourdieu (Bourdieu and Passeron, 1990) refers to the advantage enjoyed by students who possess sophisticated (as opposed to merely competent) conversational abilities and who have acquired a taste for literature and the arts.

In addition to the culture of the home, the culture of the classroom is also important. Many sociologists focus less on working class culture and more on possible school cultures in order to understand class disparities. For instance, Bourdieu contends that since schools reward children who possess a certain type of cultural sophistication that is less likely to be found among the working class, schools in essence are rewarding middle class culture. The way school is conducted—expected styles of speech, dress, and the content of the curriculum—are deemed to be largely foreign to working class youth.

For instance, Basil Bernstein's (1973) research in East London (England) led him to postulate that middle class children and working class children come to school speaking different "codes," that is, different styles of language with different grammatical rules and themes that lead to different ways of communicating. Schooling, Bernstein argued, is conducted in the more elaborate code of the middle class, putting working class students at a distinct linguistic disadvantage. Other cultural idioms used in schools also may be class-biased. For instance, critics of standardized testing have long contended that such tests are more tests of "culture" than of cognitive ability, in that success in these tests is dependent upon having a certain cultural exposure (Contenta, 1993).

Another longstanding charge of systematic bias in North American schools is that teachers, themselves middle class, hold higher expectations for middle class students than for working class students (see Wineburg, 1987). Teachers are said to generalize, perhaps unconsciously, from the physical and social attributes of students (e.g., dress, demeanor, and speech style) to their abilities. According to this argument, teachers subtly expect well-dressed, presentable, and articulate children to be good students, and expect those with the opposite traits to be poorer students. This typecasting is also said to create a self-fulfilling prophecy. Whether via body language or the attention they give to students, teachers are said to express their expectations by treating students differently, and students are said to internalize these subtle messages. Thus, students for whom teachers have low expectations are said to eventually develop poor self images which in turn lead to poor academic performance.

Creating bold theories of working class underachievement is one thing; providing convincing empirical evidence to support such theories is another. How have these theories fared over decades of sociological research?

Results are mixed, offering only qualified support. Beginning with cultural capital theory, sociologists have tested whether school outcomes are statistically correlated with various indicators of cultural capital, such as whether students have attended art galleries or museums, or whether their household provides reading material such as newspapers, magazines, and books. Findings suggest that students who regularly visit art galleries and museums achieve superior test scores (DiMaggio, 1982). High school students exposed to household reading material are more likely to complete high school, attend selective universities, and enter lucrative postsecondary programs (Davies and Guppy, 1997; Tanner, Davies, and O'Grady, 1997). However, the link between cultural capital and class background is not exactly as Bourdieu imagines. Class background affects school success independently of cultural capital, and conversely, students with cultural capital enjoy advantages in school, independently of SES (Aschaffenburg and Maas, 1997). Not all middle class youth participate in high status culture—far from it—and not all lower SES children are excluded from this culture.

Bernstein's theory of language codes is less successful. His theory, while popular in the 1970s, lacks any large-scale empirical confirmation, and many researchers are highly skeptical as to whether it is applicable beyond the setting of East London in the 1960s and 1970s. Similarly, sweeping claims that working class students are culturally alienated in schools appear to be based more on assertion than argument and detailed evidence. Examples of successful "working class schools," where such students thrive in a culturally proletarian environment, would aid the case for these theories, but, to my knowledge, no such schools exist. In fact, research suggests that working class student performance is raised in schools that have a more middle class composition.

As with studies of cultural capital, research on teacher biases offers mixed findings. Proof for the famous "self-fulfilling prophecy" thesis was originally said to be provided by the famous "Pygmalion in the Classroom" experiment (Rosenthal and Jacobson, 1968). Rosenthal and Jacobson tested whether labelling a group of elementary students as "gifted" (when in reality they were chosen at random) would cause those children to markedly improve not only their grades but their IQ scores as well. Any improvement, the researchers reasoned, would be strong evidence of the self-fulfilling prophecy. One year later, the researchers claimed they had evidence of a strong labelling effect. The study quickly became famous, and remains one of the best-known in the history of educational research. Other studies quickly followed which argued that teacher typecasting was a root cause of working class and minority under-achievement in schools.

But is there clear evidence to support this claim? Few observers at the time noticed that the actual Pygmalion results were weak and uneven, and that the conclusions drawn from the data far overshot the content of the actual study, which did not directly test whether teachers negatively stereotyped working class students. Subsequent attempts at replication have produced mixed results. Teacher expectations do not appear to consistently influence student ability.

Other types of research on teacher expectations find nuanced effects. While some conclude that teacher expectations are largely the consequence of the academic actions of students, and not vice versa (see Weinburg, 1987, Entwisle, Farkas et al, 1990, Hurn, 1993:170-6), some suggest working class students do endure biased treatment. Teachers from high status origins appear to have lower expectations and give lower grades to low SES students (Alexander, Entwisle, and Thompson, 1987). These students, even controlling for academic ability, are less likely to be assigned to upper tracks (Hurn, 1993:165-170). Thus, while sweeping claims that schools are culturally biased and directly "push out" able working class students may be overstated, evidence suggests that those youth encounter some unequal treatment in schools.

SOCIAL CAPITAL AND ACTIVE CAPITAL

What might account for the complex and somewhat inconsistent effects found in research on resources and school biases? Research frequently underplays agency. The concept of cultural capital points to a potential. Parental endowments in human capital and cultural capital aid educational success, but their influence is contingent upon whether those resources are acted upon in those families. Families with impressive resources "on paper" may not spend time helping their children. Exposure to music, art galleries, and world travel may offer advantages, but only if this potential is actualized through strategic action.

Family advantages can be reinforced in different ways. Having a sizable income, for instance, can boost one's cultural capital in the form of tutoring services, attending cultural events, or travelling to exotic locales. Money allows one to take advantage of one's knowledge of the school system. Knowledge that a high LSAT score is crucial to one's chances of acceptance into Law School, for example, is especially helpful if one can afford the books and study courses that can improve such scores. Conversely, families that lack advantages in some areas can compensate by excelling in other areas. For instance, many Asian immigrant parents possess little of the dominant cultural capital, few English skills, and have relatively little direct contact with teachers, yet compensate by enrolling their children in private tutoring and monitoring their children's homework at higher-than-average rates (Schneider and Coleman, 1993).

"Active capital" (Looker, 1994) refers to the conversion of potential resources, economic or cultural, into real educational advantage. Research shows that academic advantages are enjoyed by children whose parents more actively monitor their children's homework, spend more time with their children, and intervene positively if their children run into difficulties at school (Schneider and Coleman, 1993; Lareau, 1989).

What activates capital? At one level, motivation is an individual, idiosyncratic matter. Yet, sociologists know that individual effort does not occur in a social vacuum, but is embedded in broader social contexts. Relationships among students, parents, neighbouring communities, and educators can influence and channel an individual's actions. In conceptualizing these broader social effects, Coleman has referred to "social capital" as the set of collective expectations within a community that affects the goal-seeking behaviour of its members (see Coleman, 1988). Communities create social capital by forging reciprocal norms of obligation among parents, youth, and schools. Such norms breed strong bonds of trust, cooperation, and mutual respect, and can channel motivation and effort. Conversely, communities with weak obligations and expectations may be less committed to their educational goals.

Differences in social capital can reinforce socioeconomic disparities. Studies show that parents from lower SES categories are less active in their children's schooling (Schneider and Coleman, 1993). Working class parents are disadvantaged vis-à-vis middle class parents by their relatively inflexible work schedules, less detailed knowledge of the school system, lesser familiarity with the social culture of teaching, and by schools that do not actively encourage parental participation (Lareau, 1989; Epstein, 1995).

However, these effects can be counteracted. Working class students appear better motivated in more academically-oriented schools. Researchers have found that schools with strong expectations of success raise the attainment of all children, particularly lower SES students (Willms, 1986; Shouse, 1996). Schools of mixed socioeconomic composition benefit working class children by exposing them to an enriched academic environment, high status role models, and peers with high aspirations (see Hurn, 1993:168).

THEORIES OF DEEP CULTURAL DIVISIONS: DEPRIVATION AND RESISTANCE

Notions of frames of reference and forms of capital, described above, portray middle class versus working class families as having different outlooks and unequal resources regarding school. These cultural differences are not seen to be "deep," in the sense of reflecting profoundly dissimilar values or norms, but rather stem from their adjustments to their respective socioeconomic conditions. Yet, some sociologists see much deeper cultural differences. A controversial idea that has haunted sociologists for over 40 years is that working class children are outperformed by their middle class counterparts because of a fundamental mismatch between the cultural orientations required for school success and the culture of lower socioeconomic groups. There are two versions of this thesis.

The first version, called "cultural deprivation" or "cultural deficit" theory, was popular in the 1950s and 1960s (see Hyman, 1953). In this view, modern schools, as part of the societal contest for economic status and social climbing, require of the populace a set of "middle class" orientations aimed at achievement, competition, and aspiration for upward social mobility. Families from lower socioeconomic strata, these theorists reasoned, desire the same material goals of income and wealth as their middle class counterparts, but fail to embrace the attitudes or orientations needed to reach those goals. Working class families were seen to be behind the times, mired in a pre-modern value set.

Cultural deficit theory met a barrage of criticism in the late 1960s and early 1970s. Much of this criticism consisted of moralistic charges of elitism and "blaming the victim," but there were substantive sociological criticisms as well. Perhaps the most powerful was a challenge to the claim of deep cultural divisions rooted in class. Writers like William Ryan (1970), drawing on notions of frames of reference, passionately argued that virtually everyone in North America shares common aspirations for material wealth, but the working class adjust their expectations in response to their lower objective chances of realizing their aspirations.

The idea of deep cultural division did not vanish, however, but resurfaced in a new guise. Many sociologists in the 1970s and 1980s, influenced by Marxism, offered a novel account of deep cultural differences to explain why working class students under–performed. In what became known as *Resistance theory* (see Davies, 1995 for a review), Marxists such as Paul Willis (1977) argued that class disparities in school stem less from a working class inability to compete, but more from their *unwillingness* to compete. This unwillingness, they argued, is rooted in a profound culture clash. Rather than sharing an orientation of status striving, Willis and his followers argued, the working class has its own defiant mores which it forged through historic struggles with its capitalist employers. These values are said to include a preference for solidarity over competitiveness, pride in manual labour, and an antagonism to institutional authority.

Resistance theorists make two crucial inferential leaps. First they argue that many, if not most, working class youth are generally indifferent to school, exert little effort in classes, and participate in school deviance. Second, they argue that these anti-school subcultures have a proletarian character that, in essence, is a youthful version of factory culture. The solidarity of the shopfloor is said to be mimicked by close peer relationships among teens. The pride in heavy, manual labour is said to be expressed by their disparaging of the "pencil-pushing" that pervades school work, and a resentment toward the second-class status that is accorded to manual labour in schools. The antagonism to authority, as visibly expressed in workers' conflicts with factory supervisors and bosses, is transferred to student-teacher relations.

These subcultural values, in this account, lead these youth to reject school and eagerly anticipate the 'real world' of employment. Simply put, working class kids get working class jobs by developing rebellious subcultures, thereby condemning themselves to educational failure. While acknowledging that not all working class students engage in deviance, resistance theorists view working class resistance to school as a prime cause of their educational underachievement.

Resistance theory has had a huge impact in sociology, but has sparked much criticism. Willis and his followers stand accused of greatly exaggerating the extent to which working class students actually oppose school, and of offering overly romantic interpretations of school deviance. Indeed, most concrete instances of "resistance"—often amounting to little more than expressions of boredom—are simply unconvincing as evidence of a deep and ideologically-charged cultural division.

CONCLUSION: CHANGING SOCIETY, PERSISTING INEQUALITIES?

Class disparities in education stem from a variety of factors—unequal economic constraints, different frames of reference and endowments in various forms of capital, and some forms of bias in school. Each of these interacting factors have multiple levels of influence, from the individual, to the family, to the surrounding community, to the school. Documenting class inequalities is relatively easy, but the complexity of how class affects schooling makes convincing explanations backed by solid evidence much harder to find. Part of this difficulty stems from the fact that society and its educational institutions are constantly changing.

Schools have changed. One possible reason why recent research on school bias finds such uneven effects is that teachers and their methods have been continually altered over recent decades. While the notion of the self-fulfilling prophecy perhaps had a stronger reality thirty years ago, educators today are generally far more sensitive and alert to issues of equity and bias. Teacher colleges focus much of their training on issues of "diversity." Curricula and tests have been modified constantly in an effort to better suit a diverse student body.

Cultural configurations are shifting as well. Sociologists, more than before, doubt that social class is a primary source of cultural division in our society. Before the mid 1980s, many commonly referred to a "working class culture" as a recognizable and coherent entity. These ideas led Resistance theorists, like the Functionalists before them, to depict a deep culture clash between working class youth and schools. But this notion of such a distinct culture, in semi-opposition to the middle class, seems less and less plausible in North America. Most sociologists now stress instead race, ethnicity, religion, or region as more potent sources of social attachments, self-conceptions, group loyalties, and cultural conflict. Class may continue to shape frames of reference and senses of people's life options, but it is not a source of deep cultural attachment. An essential irony is that while working class culture may have faded, class remains the key objective barrier to school success.

These culture shifts can be linked to changing economic conditions. De-industrialization is transforming the job structure that helped forge class-differentiated frames of reference. Until the mid 1980s, blue collar jobs in resources and manufacturing that required few educational credentials attracted many working class youth, particularly males, out of school. But the stock of such jobs is now smaller. More school leavers now encounter service sector jobs (often requiring educational credentials, even if not high levels of skill) or the spectre of unemployment. Further, on average, women are marrying and bearing children at later ages, and perhaps as a result, female educational attainments among all classes have shot upwards. Thus, two viable alternatives that previously attracted many working class students out of school have been recently undercut.

What impact will this change have on frames of reference and aspirations? One might expect that the weakening of these pull factors will strengthen most youth's attachments to schooling. As our society transforms itself into a "knowledge economy," lifetime learning is being hailed as the next source of educational expansion. People of all descriptions, so the argument goes, will return to school numerous times over their employment lifetimes to upgrade their skills. Will this alter the frames of reference of those who would not otherwise consider postsecondary schooling? It might, but we need to remember that educational inequality is a relational concept, not an absolute measure of attainment. Often overlooked is the fact that over the past four decades, working class families have substantially boosted their attainments, but inequalities have remained largely stable because the middle class has boosted equally its attainments. An understanding of inequality requires not only recognition of the barriers faced by working class youth, but the advantages and strategies of middle class youth. Even if working class frames of reference change, and school biases are removed—which would render working class students more competitive—middle class families will likely develop new strategies to keep ahead. The sharp increases in recent years in the number of families seeking private schooling and private tutoring is an likely indication of a new middle class strategy aimed at maintaining a competitive edge in education.

NOTES

1. Although the terms "class" and "socioeconomic status" (SES) have different theoretical and empirical meanings in sociology, I use them interchangeably to refer to one's relative economic standing. Canadian trends are taken from data cited in Guppy and Davies (forthcoming).
2. Two very important and related topics—group differences in "equity," that is, the power to shape and influence the content and form of education, and the question of how class interacts with region, race, ethnicity, or gender—cannot be pursued here for reasons of space.
3. This tends to be a much starker phenomenon in the US than in Canada. In fact, schools in neighborhoods populated by racial minorities in urban areas like Toronto and Vancouver receive greater funds than the average.
4. The relation between frames of reference and class, like the relation between educational outcomes and class, is far from a perfect fit. Research needs to be further developed to understand why there is wide range within any class. One possibility is that low-income communities that are *less* tight-knit and bonded, allow their members to develop expectations that are atypical of those communities (see Portes and Sensenbrenner, 1993). Some low-income communities may have resources that can compensate for their class position (see Kao, Tienda and Schneider, 1996).

REFERENCES

Alexander, Karl L., Doris R. Entwisle, and Maxine S. Thompson 1987 "School performance, status relations, and the structure of sentiment: bringing the teacher back in." *American Sociological Review* 52(5): 665–682.

Alexander, Karl. L, Doris R. Entwisle, and Carrie S. Horsey 1997 "From first grade forward: early foundations of high school dropout." *Sociology of Education* 70(2): 87–107.

Aschaffenburg, Karen and Ineke Maas 1997 "Cultural and educational careers: the dynamics of social reproduction." *American Sociological Review* 62(4): 573–587.

Blossfeld, Hans-Peter and Yossi Shavit 1993 "Persisting barriers: changes in educational opportunities in thirteen countries." pp.–24. In Shavit, Yossi, and Hans- Peter Blossfeld (ed.) *Persistent Inequality: Changing Educational Attainment in Thirteen Countries* Boulder, CO: Westview Press.

Bourdieu, Pierre and Jean-Claude Passeron 1990 *Reproduction in Education, Society and Culture* (2nd ed.) London: Sage.

Bradley, Karen and Francisco O. Ramirez 1996 "World polity and gender parity: women's share of higher education, 1965–1985." *Research in Sociology of Education and Socialization* 11:63–92.

Brown, P. 1987 *Schooling Ordinary Kids: Inequality, Unemployment, and the New Vocationalism* London: Tavistock.

Coleman, James S. 1988 "Social capital in the creation of human capital." *American Journal of Sociology* 94: s95-s120.

Contenta, Sandro 1993 *Rituals of Failure: What Schools Really Teach* Toronto: Between the Lines.

Curtis, Bruce, David W. Livingstone, and Harry Smaller 1992 *Stacking the Deck: The Streaming of Working Class Kids in Ontario Schools* Toronto: Our Schools / Our Selves.

Davies, Scott 1992 "In search of the culture clash: evaluating a sociological theory of social class inequalities in education." Doctoral Dissertation, Department of Sociology, University of Toronto.

Davies, Scott 1995 "Reproduction and resistance in Canadian high schools. An empirical examination of the Willis thesis." *British Journal of Sociology* 46(4): 662–87.

Davies, Scott and Neil Guppy 1997 "Fields of study, college selectivity, and student inequalities in higher education." *Social Forces* 75(4): 1417–38.

Davies, Scott and Neil Guppy 1998 "Race and Canadian education" In Vic Satzewich (ed.) *The Racist Imagination: The Sociology of Racism in Canada* Toronto: Thompson Educational Publishing.

Deng, Zhong and Donald J. Treiman 1997 "The impact of the cultural revolution on trends in educational attainment in the People's Republic of China." *American Journal of Sociology* 103(2): 391–428.

DiMaggio, Paul 1982 "Cultural capital and school success: the impact of status culture participation on the grades of U.S. high school students." *American Sociological Review* 47(2): 189–201.

Environics 1997 *Focus Canada Report 1997–2* Toronto: Environics.

Epstein, Joyce L. 1995 "School/family/community partnerships." *Phi Delta Kappan* 72(5): 701–712.

Farkas, George, P. Grobe, D. Sheehan, and Y. Shuan 1990 "Cultural resources and school success: gender, ethnicity and poverty groups within an urban school eistrict." *American Sociological Review* 55(1): 127–42.

Frank, Jeffrey 1996 *After High School: The First Report of the School Leavers Following-up Survey, 1995* Ottawa: Minister of Public Works and Government Services Canada.

Gambetta, Diego 1996 *Were They Pushed or Did They Jump? Individual Decision Mechanisms in Education* Boulder, CO: Westview Press.

Geschwender, Jim and Neil Guppy 1995 "Ethnicity, educational attainment, and earned income among Canadian-born men and women." *Canadian Ethnic Studies*, 1995, Vol. XXVII (1), 67–84.

Gilbert, Sid, Lynn Barr, Warren Clark, Matthew Blue, and Deborah Sunter 1993 *Leaving School: Results from a national survey comparing school leavers and high school graduates 18 to 20 years of age* Ottawa: Statistics Canada.

Guppy, Neil and Scott Davies (forthcoming) *Education in Canada: Recent Trends and Future Challenges* Ottawa: Statistics Canada and Nelson Canada.

Hurn, Christopher J. 1993 *The Limits and Possibilities of Schooling* (3rd ed.) Boston: Allyn and Bacon.

Hyman, Herbert H. 1953 "The value systems of different classes: a social psychological contribution to the analysis of stratification." pp. 426–442 in Reinhard Bendix and Seymour Martin Lipset (eds.) *Class, Status and Power: A Reader in Social Stratification* Glencoe, Illinois: Free Press.

Jacobs, Jerry A., David Karen, and Katherine McClelland 1991 "The dynamics of young men's career aspirations." *Sociological Forum* 6(4): 609–639.

Kao, Grace, Marta Tienda, and Barbara Schneider 1996 "Racial and ethnic variation in academic performance." *Research in Sociology of Education and Socialization* 11:263– 297.

Lareau, Annette 1989 *Home Advantage: Social Class and Parental Intervention in Elementary Education* London: Falmer.

Lee, Valerie E., Anthony S. Bryk, and J.B. Smith 1993 "The organization of effective secondary schools." *Review of Research in Education* 19.

Looker, E. Dianne 1994 "Active capital: the impact of parents on youths' educational performance and plans." *Sociology of Education in Canada: Critical Perspectives on Theory, Research and Practice* Toronto: Copp Clark Longman.

Mare, Robert D. 1993 "Educational stratification on observed and unobserved components of family background." pp. 351–376 in Y. Shavit and H.P. Blossfeld (eds.) *Persistent Inequality: Changing Educational Attainment in Thirteen Countries* Boulder, CO: Westview Press.

McClelland, Katherine 1990 "Cumulative disadvantage among the highly ambitious." *Sociology of Education* 63(2): 102–121.

Mickelson, Rosalyn A. 1990 "The attitude-achievement paradox among black adolescents." *Sociology of Education* 63: 44–61.

Porter, Marion, John Porter, and Bernard Blishen 1979 *Does Money Matter*? Downsview, Ontario: Institute for Behavioural Research.

Portes, Alejandro and Julia Sensenbrenner 1993 "Embeddedness and immigration: notes on the social determinants of economic action." *American Journal of Sociology* 98(6): 1320–50.

Ryan, William 1971 *Blaming the Victim* New York: Vintage.

Schneider, Barbara and James S. Coleman 1993 *Parents, Their Children, and Schools* Boulder:Westview Press.

Sewell, William and Robert Hauser 1980 "The Wisconsin longitudinal study of social and psychological factors in aspirations and achievements." *Research in Sociology of Education and Socialization* 1:59–99.

Shavit, Yossi and Hans-Peter Blossfeld (eds.) 1993 *Persistent Inequality: Changing Educational Attainment in Thirteen Countries* Westview Press. Boulder, CO.

Shouse, Roger C. 1996 "Academic press and sense of community: conflict and congruence in American high schools." *Research in Sociology of Education and Socialization* 11: 173– 202.

Steelman, Lala Carr and Brian Powell 1991 "Sponsoring the next generation: parental willingness to pay for higher education." *American Journal of Sociology* 96(6): 1505–29.

Tanner, Julian, Scott Davies, and Bill O'Grady 1997 "Whatever happened to yesterday's rebels? Longitudinal effects of teenage delinquency on educational and occupational attainment." Unpublished manuscript, University of Toronto.

Teachman, Jay D. 1987 "Family background, educational resources, and educational attainment." *American Sociological Review* 52:548–557.

Willis, P. 1977 *Learning to Labour* Farnborough: Saxon House, Teakfield.

Willms, J. Douglas 1986 "Social class segregation and its relationship to pupils' examination results in Scotland." *American Sociological Review* 51(2): 224–41.

Wineburg, Samuel S. 1987 "The self-fulfilment of the self-fulfilling prophecy: a critical appraisal." *Educational Researcher* 16(9): 28–37.

A NEW TWIST IN EDUCATION REFORM: BRINGING THE MARKET TO SCHOOLS[1]

Chapter 14

Neil Guppy, Scott Davies, and Alison Ludditt

(An original chapter written for this volume.)

INTRODUCTION

Allocating resources is a problem faced by all societies. Whether the issue is health care, clean water, or educational programs, decisions must be made about how to distribute—and therefore who can access—such national resources. In recent decades in Canada, these services have been equally available to everyone. Canadians may opt to buy bottled water or purchase additional educational services (e.g., piano lessons, private tutors), but basic access to water, to schooling, and to health care is publicly available to all.

The operative principle of allocation for basic societal resources has been one of equal opportunity. These essential services are deemed so critical that everyone has been guaranteed access. Market principles are commonly used to decide allocation in capitalist societies and government regulation of access is restricted to essential services (raising the question of what constitutes an essential service). Supply and demand, not the power of centralized government, is the "invisible hand" of allocation.

Governments have granted many of Canada's essential services monopoly status—health care, electrical utilities, municipal transit systems, the postal service. And many of these monopolies are increasingly the target of critics. The primary criticism of these institutions is that as monopolies they are too powerful, are less and less responsive to the specific needs of the public, and increasingly resist external demands for change.

Why are monopolies so rigid, so unaccountable? The answer, say the critics, is that facing no competitive pressures, these organizations become complacent. Post office managers or Hydro executives, lacking the competition of the marketplace, allow inefficiencies to fester rather than face the necessary realities of tough decision-making. Introducing market principles is thus seen as a way of reforming these institutions. We should, the critics of monopolies argue, allow consumer choice (supply and demand) in an open market to dictate the kinds of services that should be available.

This is a debate about the use of power. Whose voice should be heard? Who should decide on the distribution of essential services? Should power rest with the consumers' sovereignty in the marketplace or should governments have a direct say in both the provision of and access to core services? Markets are frequently the choice of those who have the disposable income to purchase what they want, but are viewed less favourably by those with meagre economic resources.

In the realm of education, "market reform" entails introducing major changes to the current system of assigning children to schools. At present, families have limited options regarding the schools in which they enroll their children. In elementary grades, residential location largely determines the public school a child attends. Parents can exercise choice by moving to neighbourhoods with preferable schools or by enrolling their children in private or alternative schools. These options, however, belong mainly to families whose financial situations afford them the choice. Special public education programs offer some alternatives in the form of charter and home schooling, language immersion (Mandarin, French), alternative education streams (such as Montessori and Fine Arts) and downtown-based "storefront schools" for at-risk students. In practice, however, these options are open only to a small subset of children. The vast majority of students attend neighbourhood public schools simply because funding does not allow for many alternative schools. About 6 percent of Canadian children attend private schools, mainly religious schools or schools for students with special needs.

The linkage between neighbourhood schools and neighbourhood children has recently changed in both the United Kingdom and the United States, where school choice movements have begun to radically alter the politics of schooling. School choice is seen as a solution to the inefficiencies and rigidities of the public system. Rather than allowing geography to regulate attendance, the choice movement supports introducing market principles to school selection.

How does this actually work? One method is for governments to fund schools directly, rather than funding school boards, who then allocate money to neighbourhood schools. Individually-funded schools receive money based on the number of students they enroll. Schools are free to spend this money as they see fit, so long as they insure that the basic curriculum is taught. School budgets are thus enrollment-based, and schools actively compete for the patronage of parents and students. Families, in turn, "shop around" for the school that best meets their requirements. Greater accountability results, the argument continues, since schools failing to attract students get the smallest revenues. The key premise is that competition enhances school quality by devolving power to families to make choices, eroding the centralized power of education ministries and top-down school boards.

MARKET SUPPORTERS

Choice advocates see the school system as possessing the rigidities endemic to any bureaucracy having a service monopoly (e.g., Freedman, 1996, Raham, 1996). Direct control of education now resides with district school boards, district administrators, provincial ministries of education, and other arms of government. Parents, teachers, and principals lack the discretionary power to use their expertise and knowledge to introduce effective change. The result is that bureaucracy subverts school success by restricting incentives for the major stakeholders in the system (see also Lawton, 1996).

Under the current structure, bureaucracies maximize budgets, determine clientele, and press for maximum uniformity among schools. Choice advocates argue that parents are eager to participate more fully in their children's education, but are rarely given a genuine opportunity. They see this as a consequence of an unaccountable, top-down structure: parents lack incentives for constructive participation since they hold little effective power, and educators lack the flexibility to integrate this input. This is especially so for poor and/or minority parents who are the most unfamiliar with the public school system and may be intimidated by it. The result is a "one-size-fits-all" system, in which students are assigned to schools with little regard to their needs or preferences.

Market enthusiasts are discontented with such system-level standardization, arguing instead for mechanisms to empower consumers and provide producer incentives. Under market conditions, consumers search for the optimal way to use their purchasing power. With school choice, parents and students will opt for those schools offering what are for them the best programs. Parents are seen as the best decision-makers for their offspring because of their knowledge of, sensitivity to, and partiality to their children. Furthermore, since families make all other major decisions affecting their children's welfare, why should they be denied the same liberty with schooling?

In all markets, producers seek newer products, better products, or cheaper production methods. How would schools compete with each other? They would try to offer attractive packages to educational shoppers. Lacking guaranteed funding, schools would seek patrons by stressing a combination of excellence, standards, novel programs, state-of-the-art facilities, specialized instruction, and so forth. The competition would lie not only in attracting good students, but also in keeping them. As well, since parents and children will themselves be competing to remain in the best schools, students would be motivated to improve their performance.

School choice reduces the power of centralized administrators, redistributing it at the local community level. Power would shift from the school officialdom and teachers' unions to the immediate participants—educators, parents, students, principals. A new system of incentives would result with parents, now able to wield direct influence, being motivated to better inform themselves about effective teaching. Devolved authority would liberate teachers and principals from standardized bureaucratic regulation, allowing more latitude regarding pedagogical style and content as well as greater opportunities for innovative and personalized approaches. This would promote educational diversity, said to be essential in a truly multicultural Canada. As product demand diverges, schools will respond by offering a variety of curricula and techniques.[2]

Globalization rhetoric also fuels the arguments of choice advocates. Through increased international trade, emphasis is placed on the skill sets of labour forces, the productivity of enterprises, and the proficiency of scientific and technical workers. This economic competition in turn affects education. Those calling for choice declare that schools must adapt to the increasingly important role that knowledge plays in production. Low-skill jobs will become scarce; education systems must be tailored and relevant enough to guarantee that students will be equipped for this new job market. Parents can choose the type of schooling that they see as best preparing their children for the "real world."

One particular, but controversial, strategy for implementing the school choice option could be the introduction of educational vouchers (Wilkinson, 1994). Each child would be entitled to a voucher or scholarship, the value of which would depend upon the educational needs of the pupil (e.g., higher values for at-risk children or children with special learning needs). Schools would receive cash equivalents for each voucher a student cashes with them. Since programs designed for special needs children are more costly, the higher voucher values these children receive would compensate for their more expensive requirements, making them as attractive to schools as children without special needs.

Advocates claim that vouchers would promote equity. Youth from prosperous backgrounds presently receive superior educations, it is argued, because they are already engaged in a market situation within the private school sector. Vouchers would level this playing field by providing appropriate subsidies for all, thus extending choice to poorer families.

In essence, market advocates wish to replace top-heavy administration with what they consider a more efficient structure, in which resources are given directly to the school to administer. A more diverse, meritocratic, and accountable education system results with power devolved to the local level.

MARKET SKEPTICS

Critics of school choice often dismiss market schemes as a superficial play on populist sentiment (see Ball, Bowe, and Gewirtz, 1995; Barlow and Robertson, 1994). They see the actual implementation of choice as complex, costly, and logistically cumbersome at minimum (travel costs could be enormous, planning difficult due to volatility). Skeptics fear that "choice" policies invite ambitious privatization agendas, bringing market philosophies to allocation decisions that would undermine the common good (Calvert with Kuehn, 1993).

Perhaps the sharpest criticism of choice plans strikes at the heart of market principles, the drive to maximize profit. Schools are not profit-making, so what exactly would they maximize? Schools in demand, those with a high market share, will drive up the "price" by inflating entrance requirements. Rather than seeking to expand and diversify their clientele, they will become increasingly selective. This will result in a multi-tiered system: elite schools, mediocre schools, and residual schools.

In a competitive education market, where school size cannot grow indefinitely, survival will depend upon methods of selection and exclusion. Which students will be considered the most desirable? Will they be those with good academic records, who are well behaved, who have a mastery of French or English, and who possess no special learning problems? Schools, choice critics worry, will focus their attention on students with the highest ability and/or the most vocal and influential parents. What some parents want for their children is exclusivity and distinction. The sort of school they value is one that is difficult to enter. Indeed, existing private schools with privileged clientele may refuse to enter a voucher-based choice system, thereby obstructing the creation of a true "open market."

However, there will still be "low-quality" schools, since "unappealing" students will need somewhere to attend school. The most appealing students (and parents) will be "creamed off" from the schools unable to competitively recruit high achievers. Thus, poorer public schools will be drained of these resources, promoting low morale among their "second rate" constituents. This will have a ghettoizing effect which, in theory, a school can escape, but in practice may find difficult to reform.

Skeptics also worry about the criteria that parents will use, and schools will trumpet, when exercising choice. Glossy advertising, not useful information, is the likely means by which schools would compete for students. Advertising might increasingly consume school budgets, and is not only costly, but distorts both real information and the true mission of schools. Schools will be "packaged" and marketed to promote enrollments. This will distract resources, shifting funds away from educational innovation and substance. The promoters of markets counter, of course, that parents are not so gullible as to succumb to flashy advertising, especially when it concerns the future of their children. Nevertheless, any assessment of our consumer culture, with its heavy emphasis on promotional advertising, suggests that the skeptics have a point.

For instance, what performance indicators will be available? Parents will probably be urged to compare schools on the raw scores students earn on achievement tests—'enroll in School X', the advertisement will read, 'because our students achieved the highest scores on standardized test Y.' This procedure, while intuitively appealing, is plagued with selection problems. Schools with the highest scores are not necessarily those that enhance student learning the most. Schools might add very little by way of educating students, but be very good at attracting and retaining pupils who excel in the mastery of the material the tests measure.

To work around the selective information campaigns of schools, informal networks and "knowing the system" will become a major basis for entrance to the best schools. Consumers vary in their abilities as active and strategic choosers, be it in their skill at decoding key information, deciphering promotional material, or making positive impressions on gatekeepers. This will perpetuate a "home advantage" for upper-middle class youth with knowledgeable, well-connected parents.

Market critics also fear increased segregation along religious, ethnic, and class lines. Students or parents may choose schools matching their social backgrounds, and social groups will be increasingly isolated from one another. Such a process will perpetuate societal division and separation.[3] Thus, the potential separation of education streams threatens the process of building mutual tolerance. Can Canada, already a fragmented nation lacking a cohesive common culture, afford this?

There are additional worries about whether or not the interest of families and society are complementary. What are the social purposes of public schooling? While schools should be responsive to the needs of their clientele, it does not necessarily follow that what is in the interests of particular students and parents is equally beneficial for the local community or for Canada as a whole. Proponents of a common education system often cite the social benefits of exposing children to a common value system and to an ethic of consideration and sensitivity to others, by which competitive self-interest is minimized.

Along this same line, market skeptics express concern about "parent power." A group of parents can be a very effective organizational force, as can be seen in such bodies as minor league sporting councils. However, parents can be less than objective and fair when it comes to issues concerning their children. Personal politics and narrow agendas often skew the greater vision of the group. As well, parents who are so intimately involved with and partial to their children tend to overlook other value systems and points of view, some ultimately refusing compromise.

CANADA IN COMPARISON

Public and academic discussion on educational choice, in its broadest form, is relatively new to Canada. It is more developed in the U.S. and the U.K. where concrete experiments with choice have been initiated (Davies and Guppy, 1997). Still, the debate has been long on advocacy and short on analysis. The politicization of school choice has made existing research findings hotly contested and difficult to generalize.

Nonetheless, this research has some relevance for Canadians. For example, while American surveys repeatedly reveal that most parents support educational choice (Elam and Rose, 1995), they also consistently find that school propinquity is the best indicator of choice. That is, evidence from both the U.S. and Scotland shows that most families prefer to have their children educated in their local schools. Most Canadians would probably feel the same way.

U.S. surveys also report that African Americans and Hispanics particularly favour choice reform. Historically, these groups have had access only to the lowest-quality public schools, and a deep-rooted suspicion of public schooling may make choice a palatable alternative (see Wells, 1996). Especially appealing for U.S. minorities has been the idea of including more of their cultural experiences and histories in the school curriculum.

Religious and ethnic groups exert strong political influence in Canadian educational matters, so it should not be surprising if pressures for choice come from these quarters. Especially in Quebec and Ontario, issues of religious schooling and language education have sparked much of the interest in choice options.

Given these realities, what would school choice look like in Canada? Further moves to broader, more inclusive choice programs probably will be gradual and piecemeal because union contracts stipulate maximum classroom sizes. In an era of ever-tightening budgets, every classroom must be filled to capacity. However, effective choice means pupil movement between classrooms, an organizational planning nightmare when little slack exists in the system. Furthermore, movement requires transportation, a luxury that students living in poverty cannot afford, and a nightmare for choice options in rural areas. Either choices are curtailed or free transportation must be organized to allow movement.

Under these conditions, if a public education market were to evolve, it would surely be a "regulated market." That is, in such a system of "controlled choice," governments would impose various regulations and minimal standards delimiting the range of acceptable choice. Equity measures probably would be imposed to ensure that schools receiving public funds are open to a variety of socioeconomic strata, ethnic minorities, and so on. The automatic assignment of pupils to the closest school would be abolished, but local students would be given preference in their neighbourhood schools. Parents would obtain information about all options, but assignments would be made according to preferences so far as they were consistent with locally available capacities and policies.

DISCUSSION AND CONCLUSION

Today there is great controversy in educational circles over the meaning of the terms "accountability" and "responsiveness," and over the mechanisms that have been proposed to create more accountability within the system. There are two such proposals: market-styled reforms, as we have discussed, and local democracy intiatives. The latter, often supported also by market enthusiasts, aims to reform the school system through a gradual democratization of decision-making. Community input would arise through the formation and strengthening of local political bodies, such as school councils, that would hold direct power over neighbourhood schools. In some versions, however, schools would respond not to market forces, but to local political pressure. If parents wanted more diversity, for instance, they could affect change, not by removing their children from neighbourhood schools and sending them elsewhere, but by making local schools more responsive to community wishes.

The controversy stems from the fact that many educators feel that both of these movements—market reforms or the promotion of local democracy—threaten teacher autonomy, and may potentially give too much power to small groups of self-interested parents. As a result, while many of Canada's monopolies face the same pressures for accountability and responsiveness, debate continues over whether or not education in Canadian society should be reformed by introducing market and/or political principles. In comparison to other nations, Canada has favoured greater government control over public resources. Any future movement toward choice, if it is to occur, will likely be a compromised version of "controlled choice."

Although markets have not come to Canadian education yet, there has been some response to greater calls for choice. Alberta has adopted Charter legislation, the first of its kind it Canada, allowing for alternative schools to be publicly funded. As well, the Surrey Traditional School in B.C. and Flowervale in Ontario are alternative schools designed to attract families who value consistency, discipline, and more traditional teaching methods. But, as these examples reveal, the choice option is limited in Canada. Although Canadians' confidence in public education, and in most public institutions, has fallen (Guppy and Davies, 1997), the choice option has not experienced the same growth that it has in other Anglo-American democracies. Nevertheless, this is an educational policy innovation which may yet be more influential in Canada as the government's strategy for allocating resources continues to evolve. If this policy is adopted, the implications for inequality will depend upon exactly how the theory is put into practice, and in particular how conscious choice implementors will be of issues of equality of opportunity and common core experiences for all children.

NOTES

1. This paper is a major revision of "The Market Comes to School: Debates on School Choice" by Scott Davies and Neil Guppy in *Policy Options*, 14(9), 24–27, 1993.
2. In any system a common core curriculum would likely still be required if public money were to flow to any school. This core would constitute perhaps fifty percent of the overall curriculum with sufficient flexibility to allow for different ways of teaching it, different forms of integration, and different ancillary education initiatives.
3. The power of this point is diluted by recalling that many of our neighbourhood schools already have limited diversity along religious, ethnicity, or class lines because our neighbourhoods are segregated (e.g., working class neighbourhoods, Indo-Canadian communities).

REFERENCES

Ball, Stephen, Richard Bowe, and Sharon Gewirtz 1995 "Circuits of schooling: a sociological exploration of parental choice of school in social class contexts." *The Sociological Review*, Vol. 43, pp. 52–78.

Barlow, Maude and Heather-Jane Robertson 1994 *Class Warfare: The Assault on Canada's Schools* Toronto: Key Porter Books

Calvert, John with Larry Kuehn 1993 *Pandora's Box: Corporate Power, Free Trade, and Canadian Education* Toronto: Our Schools, Our Selves.

Davies, Scott and Neil Guppy 1997 "Globalization and educational reforms in Anglo-American democracies." *Comparative Education Review*, Vol. 41(4), pp. 435–59.

Elam, S.M. and L.C. Rose 1995 "The twenty-seventh annual Phi Delta Kappa gallup poll of the public's attitudes toward the public schools." *Phi Delta Kappa*, Vol. 77, pp. 41–56.

Freedman, Joe 1996 *Charter Schools in Ontario: An Idea Whose Time has Come* Unionville: Ontario Coalition for Education Reform.

Guppy, Neil and Scott Davies 1997 "Understanding the declining confidence of Canadians in public education." Paper presented at the American Sociological Association Meetings, Toronto.

Lawton, Stephen 1995 *Busting Bureaucracy to Reclaim our Schools* Montreal: Institute for Research on Public Policy.

Raham, Helen 1996 "Revitalizing public education in Canada: the potential of choice and charter schools." *Fraser Forum*, Special Issue, Vancouver.

Wells, Amy Stuart 1996 "African-American students' view of school choice" In B. Fuller, R. Elmore, and G. Orfield (eds.) *Who Chooses? Who Loses? Culture, Institutions, and the Unequal Effects of School Choice* Teachers College Press.

Wilkinson, Bruce 1994 *Educational Choice: Necessary but not Sufficient* Montreal: Institute for Research on Public Policy.

FOR FURTHER REFERENCE: EDUCATION

Anisef, Paul and Paul Axelrod (eds.) 1993 *Schooling and Employment in Canada* Toronto: Thompson Publishing. A collection of papers addressing an array of education issues as they relate to the transition between schooling and employment.

Barlow, Maude and Heather-Jane Robertson 1994 *Class Warfare : The Assault on Canada's Schools* Toronto : Key Porter Books. A powerful statement, from a left leaning perspective, on power struggles in Canadian education.

Bercuson, David, Robert Bothwell, and J.L. Granatstein 1997 *Petrified Campus: The Crisis in Canada's Universities* Toronto : Random House of Canada. A look from the political right at changes influencing Canadian universities.

Binda, K.P. 1997 *Aboriginal Education* Mississauga, Ont.: Canadian Educators' Press. An overview of issues related to education and First Nations peoples.

Canadian Education Statistics Council 1996 *A Statistical Portrait of Elementary and Secondary Education in Canada* (3rd ed.) Ottawa, Ont.: Statistics Canada. A technical report on the state of education in Canada. Good for statistical information.

Gaskell, Jane 1992 *Gender Matters from School to Work* Milton-Keyne: Open University Press. An examination of how gender influences schooling, and in particular, the ways in which women and men shift from the classroom to the labour force.

Guppy, Neil and Scott Davies 1998 *The Schooled Society: Changes and Challenges in Canadian Education* Ottawa: Statistics Canada and Nelson Publishing. An assessment of Canadian education, from Confederation to the present, using materials from the Canadian Census. More recent decades are stressed.

Schweitzer, Thomas T., Robert Crocker, and Geraldine Gilliss 1995 *The State of Education in Canada* Montreal : Institute for Research on Public Policy. An examination of education in Canada, relying heavily on outcomes (e.g., standardized tests). Asks whether Canadians are receiving their money's worth from schooling.

Section 3

ASCRIPTION AND SOCIAL INEQUALITY

An historic moment was signalled by the signing in 1948 of the Universal Declaration of Human Rights (a United Nations initiative) proclaiming the rights of all citizens. In the next decade, inspired principally by Martin Luther King, the U.S. civil rights movement riveted attention on the plight of Blacks in North America. Throughout this era, the promotion of equality in human rights spread to include other ethnic, linguistic, and religious groups. Based also on equal rights for groups defined by sex, nationality, region, and physical ability, powerful social movements arose in the aftermath of the Second World War, transforming politics, economics, and culture the world over.

Many grievances of these disadvantaged groups were long-standing, with, for example, the struggles of women and aboriginal peoples having had a tortuously long history. But in the late 1940s and early 1950s, following a world war in which millions had died battling Hitler's racism, a new surge of human energy focused on promoting and advancing the opportunities of oppressed people. The racial bigotry of fascism had been crushed at immense cost, and a world sensitized to the brutality of human hatred was more accommodating to the idea of equal opportunity.

Perceiving a maturing of industrial capitalism in the post-war era, some social thinkers came to believe that the political fault lines of society, in the past often based on territory, religion, race, and ethnicity, would dissolve as democratic freedoms and economic opportunities flourished. With economic prosperity would come political modernization. An era of equal opportunity would follow, in which merit and effort would determine the distribution of social resources. Traditional social cleavages would pale in the face of a growing meritocracy, in which competence, achievement, and motivation would determine individual life chances.

In sharp contrast to this modernization view, other social thinkers foresaw growing conflict along class lines. Rather than a maturing of competitive capitalism, these theorists saw a period of monopoly capitalism, in which a class of wealthy owners prospered at the expense of others. The gap between the rich and the poor would widen, they believed. As consciousness of class interests grew, the eclipse of traditional cleavages would result, and class antagonism would obliterate old hostilities. The significant fault line of modern society now would be based on class interests grounded in the differential ownership of private property. Traditional conflicts among religious, racial, or regional groupings would be forgotten.

Neither of these two perspectives has served us particularly well in understanding the most recent social movements dominating the Canadian political scene. Neither view fits closely with the facts. The women's movement, the quest for Native self-government, the rise of Quebec nationalism — these are all phenomena whose emergence, and magnitude, theorists of class antagonism or political modernization did not anticipate. People from a diversity of class backgrounds expressed group rights with vigour and dedication in a variety of "modern" countries.

At the core of any of these particular movements is a collective membership based on birthright. The women's movement or the Black civil rights movement focuses upon social groups defined by birth. Sex, for example, is not attained or achieved; it is determined at conception, and individuals have no say in the matter. However, as an ascribed attribute, sex is important sociologically only to the extent that people use it as a significant marker. Others react to us, make judgments about us, and generally orient themselves to us based on a variety of ascribed features, including our sex, race, age, ethnicity, and region.

Although distinctions involving sexes, races, or age-groups are based on birthright, notice that it is the socially constructed distinctions around these birthrights that are significant for sociologists. The concept of "race" perhaps best illustrates this point. In apartheid South Africa "race" was established by committee (under the Population Registration Act). This occurred because no group was "pure-blooded," no genetic differentiation could separate "white," "mixed," and "black" South Africans — such was the history of sexual mixing.

This is true more widely, in that all human groups are genetically mixed populations. The distinctions we make are based on those observable physical characteristics that we collectively choose to use as group markers. Race is not a biological construct, but a socially created system of classification. No "pure" racial groups exist.

Not only a process of social differentiation is at work here, but also invariably a hierarchical structuring, a stratification of dominant and subordinate groupings, occurs. Races were not only separated (differentiated) in South Africa, they were also ranked (stratified). The degree and the strength of this hierarchy varies across societies, but inequality based on ascription is a common feature of all societies. Ascriptive attributes are correlated with different scarce rewards: income, power, prestige. This is the context — the "vertical mosaic," as John Porter (1965) labelled the phenomenon of ascriptive inequality in Canada — within which various social groups have rallied to press for increased human rights.

In Canada these social movements have found expression in an array of formal agencies and organizations, including the Assembly of First Nations, the National

Action Committee on the Status of Women, the Canadian Human Rights Commission, and the National Advisory Council on Aging. Government policy initiatives in such areas as multiculturalism, bilingualism and biculturalism, non-traditional job training for women, and regional development have reinforced these movements.

GENDER

Social scientists distinguish between sex and gender. Sex is a biological concept referring to physiological differences between women and men (e.g., reproductive functions, hormonal variation). Gender is a social concept referring to socially constructed differences between women and men (e.g., femininity and masculinity).

In modern Canada, masculine traits entail being adventurous, forceful, and stern, whereas more feminine attributes include being gentle, sensitive, and warm. What it means to act or to think in a feminine, as opposed to a masculine, way depends on social expectations that vary both in time and space (see, e.g., Mackie, 1991: 1-7). As you will know from your own experience, although gender roles are social creations that we learn, there are powerful social expectations that allow relatively little deviation (which is why we treat gender here as ascribed).

The importance of this distinction for us is to underscore the idea that many differences between women and men are more the result of gender roles than of biological destiny. In modern Canada, women occupy a disadvantaged position on a variety of inequality dimensions, but this ought not to be regarded as some immutable, unchangeable fact of human nature. Although women who work full-time, full-year earn only about 70 percent of what men do and typically find themselves in jobs with relatively little power and responsibility, this does not mean that such inequalities are unalterable. Instead, as we noted in our preface, it means that the economic, political, and ideological control of privileged groups play a formidable role in structuring and maintaining inequality.

How best to understand and confront those forces has been a central debate in feminist sociology. We begin the subsection on Gender with an excellent overview, written by Eileen Saunders, of various theoretical approaches to the study of women. After providing succinct discussions of three traditional perspectives—conservatism, early feminism, and Marxism—she sketches in the outline of an emerging theoretical alternative, socialist feminism.

In their chapter on who does the housework in Canadian households, Kevin McQuillan and Marilyn Belle look at recent Canadian evidence that confirms the well-established tendency for women to do consistently more housework than men. They show also that domestic labour still tends to be divided along conventional gender lines, with women performing most of the traditional "female-typed" tasks, such as cooking, inside cleaning, and laundry work, and men doing more of the traditional "male-typed" jobs, such as yard work and household maintenance. There is some tendency for men to do more domestic labour today than in the past. However, the gender differences remain clear, and are not fundamentally altered even after considering which member of the couple has greater economic power (e.g., which person generates a higher income), or which member of the couple has more free time available. The authors offer a number of suggestions as to why women continue to do more of the domestic labour than men, including the possibility that because of continuing gender differences in socialization, women still give the idea of a "clean house" greater symbolic value than do men, as well as the likelihood that the division of household labour is really an everyday reflection and reproduction of the patriarchal nature of contemporary Canadian society.

Gillian Creese and Brenda Beagan, in the final chapter in the Gender subsection, review trends in women's employment opportunities between 1930 and 1995, pointing to specific policy changes of particular significance to women. Their empirical evidence considers employment rates, earnings ratios, and occupational segregation, and they especially highlight policies dealing with both pay and employment equity.

ETHNICITY, RACE, AND ANCESTRY

What are the implications for inequality of the ways in which ethnicity, race, and ancestry are socially constructed? The selection by Feng Hou and T.R. Balakrishnan starts to address this question, at the beginning of the section on Ethnicity and Race. The analyses of recent census data in this article demonstrate that educational attainment and income vary considerably across ethnic groups. The data show particularly that some "visible minorities" have lower levels of income than other ethnic groups, and have lower incomes than would be expected from their education levels. Further, some "non-visible minorities"— i.e., certain European-origin groups—have attained income parity with the majority "charter groups," the British and French. This has occurred despite the fact that these European-origin groups have somewhat lower educational attainment levels than the average for the total population. Most visible minorities have higher educational attainment but lower incomes than the average for the population.

Hou and Balakrishnan go on to speculate about the causes of these patterns. They hypothesize that some groups may do better than their educational credentials suggest they should because of "economic mobilization within the ethnic community." The ethnic community provides social support by providing employment and business opportunities for ethnic group members. Further, the authors believe that the earnings disadvantages of some visible minorities are likely related, at least in part, to employment discrimination. Programs intended to compensate for discriminatory practices against ethnic and racial group members have helped to lessen income inequality, but the effects of discrimination have not been completely erased (cf., e.g., Agocs and Boyd, 1993).

Frances Henry and Effie Ginzberg's work appears next in the Ethnicity and Race section. This research shows that there were explicit and undeniable processes of discrimination in hiring practices among samples of job interviewers. The results held across two samples of interviewers studied a few years apart. Using an experimental design in which job applications were made in person, these researchers measured the extent of preferential hiring of Whites relative to Blacks. Not content with this single procedure, they altered the research design to incorporate job searches by telephone as well, and examined the success rates of different "audible" minorities. Based on these two types of evidence, Henry and Ginzberg arrived at a "discrimination ratio" of 3:1, showing that racial minorities suffered substantial obstacles compared with the dominant White majority group in their ability to find employment.

The researchers also did a follow-up study a few years later which showed the same pattern of results as the original study, once a variation in the procedure from the first to the second study was taken into account. In this second study, conducted in a time of expansive hiring, when the Black applicants approached employers first, they were as likely to get jobs as the White applicants applying later. If the White applicants applied first, they were more likely to get a job offer than the Black applicants applying after them.

Henry and Ginzberg's work dramatically demonstrates one of the very direct forms which discrimination still takes in Canadian society. Other, more subtle forms of discrimination also occur in the labour market. Word-of-mouth hiring procedures, the use of irrelevant job qualifications, biased screening techniques, and systematic misinformation are all examples of more disguised forms of preferential treatment in employment. Such discrimination practices are likely implicated in some differences in earnings between visible minorities and other groups shown in the earlier selection by Hou and Balakrishnan.

We should mention, too, that Reitz (1988) has built upon the Henry and Ginzberg results by making Canada-British comparisons. Reitz noted that a study very similar to Henry and Ginzberg's had been undertaken in Britain as well. Comparisons across the Canadian and British studies do *not* suggest that there is less employment discrimination by race in Canada, as popular understanding might hold. (People tend to think that Canadians are comparatively high in tolerance and acceptance of racial and ethnic minorities.) Reitz argues that there are, however, *other* important Canadian-British differences around race and ethnicity. He makes the case that there is less *racial conflict*, rather than less racial discrimination, in Canada. He attributes the national difference to various factors that differ across the countries, including (1) the better average socio-economic status of visible minorities in Canada than in Britain (because of immigration policies concerning who is accepted for admission to the country); (2) the greater stability of immigration policy in Canada, with less debate over the appropriateness of immigration to the country; and (3) Canada's policies of multiculturalism and bilingualism which give legitimation to minority ethnic and racial communities, which have no counterparts in Britain.

Historical evidence reveals, of course, a litany of discriminatory acts around ethnicity and race in Canada. We need think only of Black slavery, Chinese head taxes, and Japanese internment to know that there have been many serious instances of discrimination in Canada. Another example is the treatment of aboriginal peoples by the majority groups over the centuries. As Judge Rosalie Abella (1984:33) reported in her Royal Commission on inequality of opportunity in Canada, "it is not new that their [aboriginal peoples'] economic conditions are poor. Study after study has documented the facts." What is less often realized, Abella continues, is that

> their economic plight has taken its inevitable toll on social conditions. Native people are angry over the disproportionate numbers of native people who drop out of school, who are in prison, who suffer ill health, who die young, who commit suicide. They are saddened by the personal, communal, and cultural dislocation of their people.

In the next selection, Charles Menzies examines the relations of aboriginal peoples with the rest of Canadians, showing that none of this is outdated. Ancestry matters, and it matters as much now for First Nations people as it did at the time of first European contact. He enumerates forms of disadvantage in socio-economic attainment and important life chances experienced by aboriginal peoples in Canada. He traces some of the history of dislocation that has beset the aboriginal peoples of Canada, pointing out that this dislocation has its origins in the imperialist encroachment of European nations in pursuit of riches from

North America's resources. For several centuries aboriginal people have been placed in an increasingly dependent position, with their protests over land claim settlements or their calls for greater self-determination going unheeded. More recently, while these old demands remained unresolved, a new Canadian constitution was signed which contains no statements on the aboriginal rights of the indigenous population. These rights, including self-government, have remained a basic demand of the aboriginal peoples. Menzies describes how some progress toward self-determination has been made in recent years. However, he cautions us that this process will be particularly helpful for Aboriginals only if it is built on a sound economic base.

AGE

Gender and ethnicity/race/ancestry are but two ascribed attributes that have served to unite people around social issues. Age is a third. Consider this: is it reasonable to have a minimum wage policy specifying that people under a certain age, often 16, 17 or 18, should be paid a lower wage rate than people a few weeks or months older? Should people be forced out of the labour force once they reach age 65, even if they are willing and able to continue working? Especially in the last decade, age discrimination has become a rallying point for social protest. One particularly dramatic incident occurred in 1985, when Canadian pensioners successfully organized to oppose legislation proposed by the federal government to reduce pension benefits for seniors. Using the concepts of age-grading and dependency, Guppy, Curtis, and Grabb show how age relates to a variety of dimensions of social inequality.

The relation between age and inequality has also been explored in the context of the welfare state and the aging population. Put succinctly, can we afford the old-age security system now in place in Canada, once a greater percentage of our population is over the age of 65? If the answer to this question is no, then given the link between poverty and old age (especially among older women), the consequences could be catastrophic. John Myles takes on this debate in the next selection, investigating in particular various ways of understanding the "crisis" in old-age security. He contrasts a demographic perspective, focusing on the number of elderly people, with a social conflict perspective, featuring the class interests of capital versus labour, as explanations for the crisis in old-age security.

REGION

The last subsection on ascription shifts our attention from individual attributes to the community and regional contexts in which Canadians live. At first glance, it might seem odd to include region in a section on ascription. After all, people can choose to move from region to region. Thus, region of residence could be viewed as an achieved or attained status, because it can be changed by individual choice in a way that ascribed statuses like gender or race are not.

Nevertheless, there clearly are ascribed aspects to the region variable. Region of birth, for example, is not a matter of personal choice and, moreover, it is a good predictor of a person's ultimate place of residence. That is, people who are born in a particular region often stay in the same locality during their adult lives, because of strong community allegiances, regional identities, and social ties that arise in early life and that constrain people to stay where they are, in spite of pressures or opportunities to go elsewhere. This may be especially true in a region such as Quebec, where the French language is another strong bond, keeping a large proportion of the population in that part of the country. However, the holding power of regional ties is apparent throughout the entire country—in the Atlantic provinces, the West, and elsewhere.

Region can also have lasting effects on people's stratification position and life chances for at least two reasons. First, some Canadians have developed stereotypes about regional cultures and personality traits—"rednecks" from the West, "laid-back" Vancouverites, or "unsophisticated" Newfoundlanders, for example. Certain expectations are then formed and judgments made on the basis of what are typically misleading perceptions or impressions. Second, and equally important, inequalities of reward and opportunity are also structured by the communities and regions in which Canadians live. The regional disparities of the country reinforce many of the structural inequalities that arise within the larger population, including the differences in corporate economic power, wealth, income, occupation, and education, that were discussed in Sections 1 and 2 of this book.

We begin our consideration of regional differences with Fred Wien's analysis of regional socioeconomic differences. Wien's chapter also reviews key explanations for regional inequalities and discusses some of the policies that governments have implemented to alleviate problems of regional disparity.

The second paper, by Kenneth Stewart, examines the position of Quebec in Canada's regional make-up, and the possible role of the federal government's economic policies in defining this position. Stewart makes the somewhat provocative and controversial argument that Ottawa's long-standing policy of transferring wealth from the richer provinces to poorer areas, especially to Quebec and the Atlantic region, has made these areas increasingly dependent economically. At the same time, in Stewart's view, these policies have actually encouraged the cause of Quebec independence.

The central concern of this section is the degree to which social inequalities are related to ascriptive factors. Despite those optimistic social commentators who predicted the eclipse of ascriptive influences on inequality, either through modernization or through revolution, life chances continue to be affected greatly by race and ethnicity, sex and gender, age, and region. We are still a long way from the elimination of ascriptive inequalities.

REFERENCES

Abella, Judge Rosalie Silberman 1984 *Equality in Employment: A Royal Commission Report* Ottawa: Minister of Supplies and Services.

Agocs, Carol And Monica Boyd 1993 "The Canadian ethnic mosaic recast for the 1990." pp. 331–352 in J. Curtis, E. Grabb, and N. Guppy (eds.), *Social Inequality in Canada: Patterns, Problems, Policies* Scarborough, Ont. Prentice-Hall, (2nd ed.).

Mackie, Marlene 1991 *Gender Relations in Canada* Toronto: Butterworths.

Porter, John 1965 *The Vertical Mosaic* Toronto: The University of Toronto Press.

Reitz, Jeffrey G. 1988 "Less racial discrimination in Canada, or simply less racial conflict?: Implications of comparisons with Britain." *Canadian Public Policy*, 14, 4, pp. 424–441.

GENDER

Chapter 15

THEORETICAL APPROACHES TO THE STUDY OF WOMEN

Eileen Saunders

(Revised and expanded from Eileen Saunders, "Theoretical Approaches to the Study of Women," in Dennis Forcese and Stephen Richer, eds., *Social Issues: Sociological Views of Canada* (Scarborough: Prentice-Hall Canada, 1982) pp. 218-35. Reprinted with permission.)

INTRODUCTION

Theoretical Analysis of Gender: Classic and Contemporary

At first glance, the profusion of analytical work on gender might seem confusing or bewildering. However, in spite of this apparent diversity, it is possible to classify the attempts of social scientists to make sense of the social situation of women into three classic approaches. By that, I mean there are underpinning theoretical positions which represent the "foundational" work in social science theoretical inquiry about gender. Contemporary theoretical writing can then be understood as either extensions of these classic approaches, reformulations of earlier positions or, in some cases, attempts to realign early theoretical divisions in a manner that incorporates insights from different approaches. My classification of these classic approaches is based on the different ways each defines the problem to be analyzed and then explains the problem in question.

The *conservative approach* focuses on sex differentiations and argues that differentiated sex roles can be explained by the contribution this differentiation makes to the maintenance of social order. The *feminist approach* argues that sex differentiations also result in inequality in the relations between the sexes, and argues that this situation is largely a consequence of cultural values and ideologies. The *Marxist approach* agrees with the feminist that differentiation and inequality go hand-in-hand, but locates the explanation for this relationship at the level of class analysis.

These classic approaches were well established and entrenched within social science inquiry by the 1970s; during the later years of that decade and throughout the 1980s, these models underwent renewed scrutiny within the feminist academic community. The result was the development of a body of contemporary theoretical work which in some cases reproduces earlier theoretical arguments, and in other cases substantially redirects theoretical inquiry.

It is important, then, to appreciate how each of the classic approaches defines and explains the emergence and persistence of the patterns of social relations between men and women. Moreover, it is necessary to determine the implications for social change in these theoretical models. Only then will we be able to understand contemporary theorizing about gender, and evaluate its capacity to make sense of the position of women in Canadian society.

CLASSIC APPROACHES

Conservatism

The thrust of the *conservative* approach is the *imperative* nature of sex differentiation. There are three variants of conservatism: the biological, the psychobiological, and the sociological. Their common link, in spite of their different conceptions of the nature of the imperative in question, is the retention of a static conception of the relation between the individual and society, and an evolutionary or gradualist approach to social change. While we will focus particularly on the sociological approach, a brief discussion of the other two views serves as a useful backdrop.

The *biological* and *psychobiological* arguments are deterministic views which posit a *natural* basis for sex inequality. The thrust of research in the biological tradition has been the anatomical, genetic, and hormonal differences between males and females. The psychobiological stream has focused on psychological differences in such areas as skill, aptitude, attitude, temperament, and other characteristics that are viewed as related to biological differences. Both positions have come under a great deal of criticism in recent years for their tendency to *assume* a direct link between biology and behaviour.

The critiques levelled against the *biological argument* can be classified into three general categories. First, there is the failure of the various assumed relationships between biology and behaviour to "stand up" in cross-cultural comparisons. We know, for example, that the assumed correlation between hormonal levels at certain periods in the female menstrual cycle and emotional states such as tension, anxiety, or irritability does not exist in many other cultures (see Bardwick, 1971:27-33). This indicates that emotional fluctuations during hormonal cycles are, to a large extent, *learned* rather than innate behaviour.

A second problem is the tendency to ignore or downplay the impact of cultural patterns on a particular sex difference. Margaret Mead, for example, found that in Arapesh culture, the lack of emphasis on strenuous work for *either* sex decreased the differences in somatotype—particularly muscular build (Mead, 1935). In other words, there is some social capacity to affect sex differences through cultural practices.

Finally, a taxonomy of particular biological sex differences in no way serves as an explanation for the differential social *evaluation* of these differences. To argue that women, for biological reasons, perform tasks associated with the family sphere cannot in itself lead to an understanding of how differential rewards and values are attached to the different tasks.

Very similar objections are raised against the psychobiological approach to sex inequality. To illustrate this, we can point to the classic position in the psychobiological tradition: the work of Sigmund Freud. Infamous for his view that "anatomy is destiny," Freud attempted to tie the unequal social treatment of the sexes to sex differences in personality patterns, which emerge as a response to physiological differences. The cornerstone of his argument is the assumption that "penis envy" in the female child necessarily persists into adulthood, in the form of feelings of inferiority, passivity, and an unhealthy "superego." The implication is that the psychological inferiority of women is translated into inferior social status.

The major problem with this Freudian position is that it cannot be tested. The assumption, for example, of an innate faulty female superego is not open to question, given that Freud sees the latter as part of the unconscious aspect of personality. Moreover, even those assumptions that are testable have been shown to lack empirical support; e.g., the role of phallic gratification in personality development (see Nielsen, 1979:106).

A related problem, and one shared by the biological variant of conservatism, is Freud's attempt to use an invariant to explain a variant. Anthropological research has shown that female role behaviour *has* varied from one culture to another. (For a review of this literature, see Quinn, 1977; Friedl, 1975; Reiter, 1975.) Therefore, the attempt to reduce the origin of female behaviour to an invariant or universal psychobiological makeup simply is inadequate. It just is not able to explain the cross-cultural fact of diversity. It is largely for this reason that sociologists have attempted to locate the explanation for sex differences in terms of social factors.

The *sociological* variant of conservatism shifts the explanation of sex differentiation from a *natural* imperative to a *social* imperative. The classic illustration of this position is the *functionalist* framework of analysis.

The basic theme in functional analyses is that society is an integrated and relatively stable system, composed of interdependent parts or elements. Social order exists when the different parts of a society are integrated, or in equilibrium. However, because these parts are interdependent, a change in any one will have consequences for the system as a whole. Social change, in this context, becomes the adaptive adjustment process whereby the equilibrium of the system is reconstituted. The major concern of the functionalists is thus to discover the *function* or contribution that each social element makes to the needs of the system, to social integration, and to societal equilibrium.

Functionalist analysis begins with the assumption that the origin and the persistence of differential sex roles can both be explained by reference to the contribution these differences make to the maintenance of social stability. In other words, functionalists attempt to explain sex-role patterns by reference to the *invariant social needs* that necessitate a particular form of sex-role arrangement. This analysis of *functional necessity* is assumed to hold true for both preindustrial and industrial societies, although specific features of the sex-role pattern may vary.

Functionalists have argued that, in early hunting and gathering societies, sex-role differentiation was a consequence of two basic survival requisites: reproduction and subsistence. They argued that the mobility of the female was restricted, due to the lengthy period of dependence of her children for nursing, care, and protection. Because of the lack of cultural or technological alternatives (e.g., bottle-feeding, prepared foods, etc.) the female was unable to share in the major subsistence activities with males. This is particularly the case with hunting, which required long periods of absence from the community. The sexual division of tasks and labour which emerged was thus a *complementary* division of interdependent roles along sex lines, rather than a stratification or ranking by sex. Moreover, it was a division of labour which met basic survival requisites and thus ensured the stability and persistence of the society.

A similar analysis is employed by functionalists who examine the persistence of a sexual differentiation in modern industrial societies. Two key assumptions are retained:

1. the complementarity of sex roles and positions; and
2. the functional necessity of sex-role differentiation.

An important example of this type of analysis is the work of Talcott Parsons. Parsonian functionalism, while sharing the basic principles of general functionalist analysis, also served as a benchmark in the orientation of sociological research toward sex roles. It attempts to understand the position and role of women in industrial society in terms of their relationship to the *family institution*.

Parsons begins with an attempt to discern the relationship between the kinship structure and the occupational structure of modern societies. Social status is assumed to stem from both structures: one is *ascribed* (given) a status through membership in a particular family unit, and one *achieves* (earns) a status through differential participation in a hierarchical occupational system. The essential element in the nuclear family form is the emotional bond between both husband and wife, and parent and child. The defining element in the occupational structure, on the other hand, is the competition ethic between participants for the unequal rewards attached to differentially evaluated positions. The dilemma in modern society, argued Parsons, is the possibility of destabilizing the nuclear family through the presence of a competition structure external to the family. In other words, if husband and wife engage in occupational competition external to the family, the solidarity of the family structure would be threatened. The resolution of the dilemma for Parsons is the evolution of an internal structure for the nuclear family, which is adapted to the functional imperatives of the occupational system. Sex-role differentiation is essential to that structure, if kinship competition is to be avoided.

The internal structure, sustained by cultural norms prescribing family relationships, is based on a division between *instrumental roles* and *expressive roles*. Instrumental roles are those defined as achievement- and task-oriented and related largely to occupational behaviour outside the family. Expressive roles are those defined as emotionally-oriented and related largely to integrative behaviour within the family. Parsons argues that women are logically more suitable for the latter, given their biological tie to childbirth and nursing, roles which already include expressive components. Instrumental roles are therefore best suited to males, who do not have a "pre-established" relationship to the familial role.

Parsons argues that the effect of the sex-role segregation is to contribute to the stability of the family institution directly, and thus to the welfare of the entire social system indirectly. The positive aspects of this structure are highlighted by Parsons:

> There are perhaps two primary functional aspects of this situation. In the first place ... it eliminates any competition for status, especially as between husband and wife ... . Second, it aids in clarity ... by making the status of the family in the community relatively definite and unequivocal. (Parsons, 1954:192).

It is important to point out that Parsons does not consider the fact of sex-role differentiation as evidence for the presence of sex-role inequality. Quite the opposite: Parsons posits an egalitarian relationship between males and females for several reasons:

1. Marriage, he argues, is necessarily an egalitarian relationship, given the fact that the social status of the wife is identical to her husband's, through status ascription to the family unit.
2. The housewife has *functional equivalents* to compensate for her segregation from occupational achievement. He argues that such equivalents exist in the form of the "glamorous" female, the "humanistic" volunteer, or the "good companion" roles.
3. For females who reject the expressive role, there exists an equal-opportunity structure in the occupational system. Thus, those women who are unequal in this context are assumed to be the products of *individual* failure to seize opportunity.

In keeping with the overall functionalist focus on order and stability, Parsons defines non-traditional sex roles as dysfunctional or threatening to the total system. It is in this context that he introduces the functional necessity of the nuclear family form. The family is more than a mere agency for reproduction in his scheme; it is the principal agency for assuring the continuation of social norms and values, and patterned relationships, via its role in the primary socialization of children. In addition, it serves an important role as a "cooling-out" agency, an arena in which tension derived in the occupational sphere may be diffused. Thus the functional significance of the nuclear family is ultimately found in its performance as an integrating agency, as an institution that reaffirms and recreates the cultural order in each succeeding generation.

Social change in Parsonian functionalism occurs as an adaptive response to an alteration in the relationship between elements in the total system. In his later work, there emerges an assumption that certain changes in the industrial structure of modern societies would bring about a gradual equalization in sex-role behaviour. Essentially the argument is that sex-role segregation will ultimately become increasingly *dysfunctional*, given changes in the occupational system that result in a demand for increased female participation. In a context of role equalization, persisting sex inequality would be seen as a consequence of the individual failure of particular women to seize educational, economic, legal, and political opportunities.

In summary, functionalism is a framework which argues that differentiation by sex is functionally related to the needs of the system at a particular stage of evolution. Segregation of males in the labour process and females in the family in modern society serves a stabilizing function, while equality of opportunity in the labour process serves as a protective mechanism against the possibility of inequality. Because change is an evolutionary process, there is little need for an interventionist politics to redress sex-role differences.

Evaluation

There are several arguments one can raise against the sociological variant of the conservative paradigm. First, the major impact of Parsonian functionalism is to direct the focus of sociological research on women to the relationship of women to the family. Because functionalism assumes that the primary position and role of women is within the family unit, it generally ignores the role women play in the paid labour force. Moreover, a functionalist discussion of the female role in the family is usually couched in normative terms. In other words, the "effective" role of the housewife and mother is conceptualized largely as a socializing role, having little utilitarian value in an economic sense. Second, equality of opportunity is too often assumed rather than demonstrated. Parsons, and functionalists who followed in his wake, often choose to ignore various forms of opportunity restriction, such as discrimination in employment, channelling of career aspirations, and the differential socialization of the sexes in the family. There are institutionalized forms of sex discrimination which functionalist theory does not and cannot address.

Third, Parson's assumption of an egalitarian structure within the family seems to be based more on a North American conception of romantic love than a realistic appraisal of status differences between husband and wife. One cannot ignore the possibility that the instrumental, or income-earning, role of the male may place him in a position of greater control within the family. Functionalist theory is not able to account for the possibility of a hierarchy of power in the family unit. This is also true of the functionalist conception of "alternative roles" for women, which are deemed to be *functional equivalents* to the male occupational role. Given that social status in Western industrial societies derives from occupational achievement, it is difficult to discern how being a "good companion" to one's husband is equivalent in terms of derived social and interpersonal reward.

Fourth, the functionalist focus on sex differentiation rather than sex inequality ignores the fact that social rewards, and the power to control those rewards, attach to the differentiated positions in a critically different manner. Thus, the social structuring of the roles men and women play goes beyond mere specialization in tasks. There is also a differentiation in reward and status which is necessarily involved.

Fifth, the functionalists fail to pursue the question of whether there is a link between the female role in the family and the female role in the labour force. Instead, they argue that the family serves as an "allocating agency" for placing women in the occupational hierarchy. It is her family status, not her gender, which is seen as the determinate factor in the process (see, for example, Parkin, 1971:14–16). This is a questionable argument, one that is open to empirical test. We will return to this issue in the following sections.

Finally, one must question the functionalist assumption that sex-role differentiation is an *integrative* mechanism ensuring social stability. Functionalist theory in general is an *order-oriented* analytical framework seeking to demonstrate the functional contribution of each societal element to social order. Thus, in order to "prove" the functionality of sex-role differentiation, it is necessary to posit an ideology of equality of opportunity and an egalitarian family structure. Such a position leads functionalism into the dilemma of ignoring or explaining away the inequalities that do, in fact, exist between the sexes. As a result, integration remains an assumption in functionalist theory and serves to mask the issue of whether sex-role differentiation may, in fact, translate into sex-role inequality.

Early Feminism

Feminism is an analytical framework which emerged as a counterpoint to the conservative position. While different feminists disagree on the type of intervention necessary to effect change, they all focus on the exclusion of and discrimination against women in the distribution of socially valued resources, such as marketable skills, wealth, prestige, and power. The issue, then, for feminism is more than sex differentiation; it is sex inequality. The explanatory thrust of the feminist argument focuses on *ideological factors* in the culture of a society, factors which serve to justify the exclusion and subordination of women.

A key concept in feminist analysis is *patriarchy*, a term which first received popular exposure in the work of K. Millet (1969). Though often used loosely in the literature, patriarchy essentially refers to a hierarchical system of power, in which males possess greater economic and social privilege than females. This differential power is reflected in differential sex roles. Explicit in a feminist position is the insistence that patriarchy is a universal feature of all known societies.

Sex inequality is located in the relationships between males and females; these relationships are thought by feminists to be the manifestation of a cultural system that defines women as inferior to men. In other words, once patriarchy emerges, it is maintained and reproduced through an ideological system that justifies inequality. The *original basis* for the emergence of patriarchy lies in the importance of biological differences in size, strength, and relation to reproduction between the sexes in early preindustrial societies. The male's biological "advantage" allows him to take control of the important resources in society, such as food, land, weapons, and implements of production. More importantly though, according to feminist theory, the economic and social rewards that this control allows are maintained through the cultural definition of appropriate sex roles. Thus, the persistence of male privilege, or patriarchy, is ensured through the emergence of a culture that defines men as superior. As a result, while biological differences are now no longer as important in a technological industrial society, the preservation of male privilege continues because of the persistence of a "patriarchal ideology." This is not to suggest that sex inequality is apparent only in the realm of ideas, attitudes, and values. Rather, feminist theory argues that the exclusion of women from access to economic or social power can only be understood by reference to the role of ideology. They argue that ideology has replaced biology as the determinant in the reproduction of sexism.

Early feminist work focused on two areas of inquiry: the role of the family as a mechanism in transmitting patriarchal ideology, and the role of various socio-economic institutional practices in excluding women from equal opportunities with men.

Essentially, feminists share with functionalists a conception of the nuclear family as a socializing agency. Where they differ is in their conception of the content and consequence of such socialization. Functionalists argue that family socialization allows for the integration of the individual into a stable, consensual culture. Feminists, on the other hand, claim that the role of family socialization is to reaffirm and justify the pattern of segregated, unequal role differentiation. It does this largely through the creation of what Millet calls a *psychic structure* for women which is very different from that of men. The psychic structure for women is predicated on an image of the female as passively related to her social world. De Beauvoir conceptualizes this relation as a dichotomy between male as subject of action and female as object of action (De Beauvoir, 1952). The consequences of the differential psychic structure are felt on several levels: women develop a different temperament than men, they have inferior self-images, and channel their motivational aspirations toward different role behaviour. Essentially the argument is a restatement of the "self-fulfilling prophecy" notion that is so popular in socialization research. In other words, if a culture defines men and women differently, and organizes its socialization practices on that assumption, then the consequence is the objective difference in the status of men and women. But the primary level of explanation is the realm of cultural attitudes and expectations, which both sexes are socialized into accepting. Because the institution of the family is the first and most important source of cultural ideas, its role in transmitting and reproducing patriarchy is crucial.

As indicated earlier, another body of feminist research focuses on institutional practices that reinforce a patriarchal system. Again, these practices are assumed to be manifestations of cultural beliefs about women. The unity of this approach lies in the attempt to demonstrate how the consistent ideology of women as being different from men in temperament, skill, and attitude is translated into practices that exclude women from access to institutional positions. For example, Reuther (1974) has argued that the ideological association of the male image of divinity figures in various religions has supported the official exclusion of women from participation in certain levels of the religious hierarchies. Therefore, the fact of male control of theological decision-making is maintained through ideological support that defines theology as a male preserve.

The feminist consensus regarding a definition of the problem is unfortunately not reflected in feminists' approach to a solution to the problem. The classical feminist framework polarized at the level of intervention strategy between views that can be loosely called liberal feminism and radical feminism.

Liberal feminism is predicated on the assumption that the social system is "reformable," that patriarchy can be eliminated within the parameters of society as it now exists. This approach retains a classic conception of liberal democracy as a *meritocracy*, a system providing equal opportunity to achieve unequal rewards. In this view, the problem is to "restore" the meritocracy, so that women can compete equally with men. Given equal opportunity, all individuals can rise or fall to their own level of merit, rather than have their mobility predetermined by their gender. Thus, intervention for liberal feminists is directed largely toward the occupational sphere, and involves the removal of cultural attitudes about gender that impede equal opportunity. In positing equal opportunity as their goal, they focus their attack on both the socialization process that transmits patriarchal beliefs and the legislative process that permits particular discriminatory institutional practices. Thus liberal feminists would argue, for example, in favour of content regulation of educational texts or the broadcast media, in order to control sexist images. At the same time, they would lobby for the enforcement of equal-pay legislation to prevent wage discrimination at work. Actually, the two levels of intervention are interrelated, in that it is assumed that if one can expose myths about working women through re-education (e.g., the assumption that women only work for "pin money"), the justification for unfair employer practices is necessarily removed. Liberal feminism, then, does not question the premise of hierarchical positions and rewards in society; what it questions is the distribution of those positions and rewards on the basis of gender.

Early radical feminism shares with liberal feminism a belief that effective change must involved an alteration in cultural ideology. However, it disagrees on the nature of intervention. Radical feminism does not place particular emphasis on the occupational discrimination of women; that is dealt with as merely one manifestation of a deeper problem. In radical feminist strategy, the psychic structure formed in family socialization is defined as the key target of attack. Consequently, the family institution is defined as the major agent in the reproduction of inequality; the implication for strategy then involves an attempt to restructure the family institution, in order to strip it of its patriarchal form. There are some radical feminists who suggest this be accomplished on an individual basis, primarily using the technique of "consciousness-raising." This is conceived as a process whereby individual women, through dialogue with others, come to see the patriarchal form and roots of their own "psychic structures," and come to translate that newfound awareness into attempts to regain control over their own development. It is essentially an individual, voluntaristic model for change.

There are other radical feminists, however, who question the very existence of heterosexual marriage and the family institution. They argue that the contemporary form of the family is premised on a dependency relationship between the male and the female, a dependency that is personified even at the level of sexuality: hence, they believe the elimination of sex inequality requires the abolition of monogamous marriage and the nuclear family. Once the family institution is destroyed, patriarchy as a power system will collapse.

What emerges in the latter version of radical feminism is a conception of a fundamental alteration in society as we know it, rather than a reform in certain elements of society as liberal feminism suggests. Moreover, the model of change moves from an individual to a collective level and questions the very basis of hierarchical privilege. As Firestone argues, a hierarchial society breeds a "power psychology" (1970:12) which is at the root of all forms of oppression against women, children, ethnic groups, etc. Thus a challenge of power psychology in its sexist form implies a challenge to its basis: hierarchical society. Radical feminism of this type has not yet clarified its image of an alternative form of society to modern capitalism, other than to suggest socialism is not the solution. Moreover, as a political strategy, it shies away from violent confrontation, arguing that a revolutionary is in reality a teacher who will use the power of ideas to provoke radical change.

Evaluation

In summary, the classic feminist framework assumes the universality of patriarchy, and attempts to explain it by reference to ideological factors. There are several problems inherent in this approach, at the level both of explanation and of intervention. First, there is a tendency toward biological determinism in the explanation of the origin of patriarchy. It is assumed that biological differences universally hindered the female in her access to participation in, or control over production in early societies. However, anthropological studies indicate that the productive role of women in many hunting and gathering societies equalled and sometimes surpassed that of men.

A second, and more serious, problem is the characterization of patriarchy as a universal system of power. On the one hand, this analysis fails to specify how patriarchy changes in form from one historical period to another; for instance, sexism in feudal societies cannot be equated simply with sexism in modern capitalist societies (Mitchell, 1971). Thus, to treat patriarchy as an ahistorical, autonomous system of male power ignores its specific features in particular periods. On the other hand, the feminist conception of patriarchy as a system of male power over females ignores the differential relationship particular groups of men and women have to patriarchy. In other words, not all men benefit equally from patriarchy as feminist theory would suggest: often, a particular class of men benefits more than others (e.g., male employers of cheap female workers). In the same vein, not all women suffer equally under patriarchy. Particular groups of women may have more access to status and reward than others (e.g., middle- and upper-class women). To simply portray the contradiction as lying between men as a group and women as a group is to mask the actual contradictions in status that exist *within* each sex group. This "glossing" of the problem is reflected in particular strategies for intervention. For example, legislation directed at equal opportunity to compete ignores the fact that different strata of women, depending on their class background, bring different resources to the labour market. In addition, consciousness-raising may be more of a middle-class luxury. For many women, it is the lack of basic life necessities that is their most immediate concern.

A third and related problem is the primacy of ideology in feminist analysis. To argue that patriarchal ideas create particular structural conditions for women ignores the possibility that patriarchal ideas may emerge as a consequence of, and support to particular material conditions. In other words, the belief that women are not as "valuable" workers as men in the labour market may be the result of the necessity to maintain a relatively cheap labour pool. We shall see in the following discussion how Marxists make this argument in reversing the causal sequence of sex inequality.

Finally, feminism fails to analyze the specific links *between* the female role in the family and the female role in the labour market. They are treated as two separate dimensions of inquiry, other than to suggest patriarchal ideology shapes females status in each sphere. It is necessary to inquire whether the structure of the family institution at a given point in history is related to the structure of the labour market. In this way, one could investigate whether female entrance into the occupational sphere is shaped by factors in women's familial position. The failure to tie these two spheres of female participation analytically is reflected in the polarization of feminist theory strategically. On the one hand you have liberal feminists fighting for reform of institutions on a piecemeal basis, through legislative lobbying, educational content regulation, rights within unions, political representation, and other such changes. On the other hand you have radical feminists focusing on inequality in the family, through improved birth control rights, contractual marriage, or ultimately abolition of marriage. The fatal flaw is their failure to analyze and deal with the interdependence between these various manifestations of sex inequality.

Marxism

Marxism is a theoretical framework that focuses on the relation between the way a society organizes production and the ideologies that develop to protect the class interests of those who control production. In this context, Marxism argues that the position of women reflects the class relations that emerge within a capitalist form of production. For Marxists, these relations *exploit* the female, as a worker in the labour force and *oppress* her as a form of property in the family institution. Her exploitation, according to Marxism, has no specific features outside of the general mechanisms that exploit all workers, and her oppression or powerlessness in the family is determined by factors in capitalist society that are external to the family institution. Thus, Marxist analysis sees the female as simply one more victim of capitalism, and the material conditions that are perceived to underlie her "victimization" are seen as identical to those that underlie exploitation in general.

Because Karl Marx himself wrote very little on the *origin* of sex inequality, it is necessary to go to the work of his friend and theoretical collaborator Friedrich Engels for the classic Marxist position on the emergence of women as a subordinate group. Engels' argument, presented in *The Origin of the Family, Private Property and the State*, is essentially that the original subordination of women is historically tied to the emergence of *private property* in agricultural and herding societies (allowed for in the transition from a subsistence to a surplus form of society). The monogamous family and the isolation of women to guarantee sexual exclusivity evolved as means to ensure "legitimate" heirs. Thus the notion of *patriarchy* came to be defined as a relationship reflecting a property relation between husband and wife in the context of the family. In other words, it refers to the fact that the husband controlled the existence and disposal of property in the family.

The important point in Engels' analysis is his claim that earlier forms of society—such as hunting and gathering—were sexually egalitarian, and that it was only the emergence of private property that led to a subsequent subordination of the female role. The existence of a sexual division of labour or specialization in tasks in early societies was never questioned by Engels. Instead, he argued that while men and women performed different types of subsistence labour, the absence of production-for-exchange precluded an unequal relationship between them. The crucial step, for Engels, was the development of resources for production that allowed *production-for-exchange* in addition to *production-for-use*. Male tasks tended to be located in the sphere where production resources expanded—e.g., irrigation of land: hence, their labour became part of production-for-exchange. Female tasks, on the other hand, tended to be located in the sphere where production resources were stabilized—e.g., preparation of food for consumption: hence their labour remained part of production-for-use. In Marxist terms, they did not receive an *exchange value* (e.g., a wage) for their work. What Engels was attempting to describe was the emergence of a break between two types of labour spheres and the segregation of sexes in different spheres. Moreover, he claims that this break created the condition necessary for the subordinate role of women: their exclusion from participation in "valued" production.

In the industrial transition to early factory capitalism, this break was retained and solidified as a break between a *public sphere* of production and a *private sphere* of the family. This is because the production process was removed entirely from the household locus, and the family (and any labour performed within its boundaries) became a secondary institution, which merely reflects the economic relations of production. For Marxists, the family is now *epiphenomenal*; its form is a reflection of the material conditions of capitalism. In other words, it is part of the super-structure of society. It performs an essential role for capitalism by being the institution for the appropriation and transmission of private property. Moreover, the female role in the family is argued to be a consequence of women's lack of access to participation in public production, and thus lack of control over property. This is important in informing Marx's conception of patriarchy in capitalism. When Marx made reference to patriarchy, he defined it as a particular relationship of household production, whereby the household head owned or controlled the resources of production and organized the labour power of its members (McDonough and Harrison, 1978). For Marxists, patriarchy as a power relationship involving subordination of women to men has no meaning or existence, apart from its base in the family institution. More importantly, it is possible, in Marx and Engels' terms, to postulate the disappearance of patriarchal relations *within* a capitalist society. As proof, they refer to the absence of patriarchy among working class or "proletarian" families. They argued that the development of capitalism had led to the increased entry of working class women (and children) into the labour force. Consequently, their role in the family altered to reflect their role in social production; equal exploitation in production supposedly provoked non-oppressive relations in the family. Thus, the patriarchal treatment of women as property is characteristic of the "bourgeois" family, not the proletarian.

> The proletarian is without property; his relation to his wife and children has no longer anything in common with the bourgeois family relations. (Marx and Engels, 1970:25)

The specific Marxist "map" for *intervention* aimed at changing sex inequality is tied to a larger conception of the kind of social change necessary in capitalist society. Since capitalist relations, not men, are defined as the "enemy," consequently capitalist society must be the target of intervention. The model of change suggested by Marxist theory is one of revolutionary alteration in the basic structures of society. Specifically, it calls for a transformation at the level of organization of production, whereby class ownership of the means of production is abolished and replaced by a socialist or collective organization of production. The thesis is that the seizure of economic control, at the level of production, by a previously subordinate proletariat class will lead to a transformation in all other social spheres, including the political, the judicial, and the ideological. Marxists posit three specific strategic factors as being necessary to "equalize" the position of women. First, there must be a large-scale entrance of women into the social production labour force. Second, the labour now performed by the housewife in the sphere of the family (caring for children, provision of meals, maintenance tasks such as laundering, etc.) must be transferred to the sphere of social production. Third, the capitalist *form* of the family must be abolished through the elimination of its *raison d'être*: private property. To repeat, in Marxist theory these interventionist policies are linked to the overall program of a transition from capitalist to socialist society.

Evaluation

In summary, Marxist analysis redirects our focus to several major issues defined as crucial to the subordinate role of women. To begin, Marxism directs attention to the historical link between *variability* in female status and changes in the form of production in a society. Second, Marxism focuses on patriarchy as a *specific* power relation vested in the family structure. Finally, the Marxist conception of household, or domestic labour (i.e., production-for-use, performed usually by the wife in the context of the family institution) involves a recognition of the "alienating" nature of such work, particularly when the woman is also engaged in wage labour in the public sphere. Thus their argument that:

> The emancipation of women will only be possible when women can take part in production on a large social scale and domestic work no longer claims anything but an insignificant amount of her time. (Engels, 1951:11)

What needs to be questioned is whether the analytical framework of Marxism can fully account for an understanding of sexual inequality. There have been several critiques raised against this position.[1]

One of the more serious flaws in the Marxist argument is its assumption that increased female entrance into public production would bring about an objective equalization in sex status. As we will see more clearly in the following section, one fact that is clear from recent research is the persistence of objective difference in social reward along sex lines, *despite* the increased labour force participation of women. What seems to be more important than the entrance of women into the labour force is the *context of entrance*. In other words, it is essential to investigate whether women go into different sectors of the labour market and, if so, what the economic characteristics associated with those sectors actually are. The failure of Marxism to deal with this area of inquiry stems from the absence of any theory regarding *sexual division of labour*. In Marxism, the sex division exists between the public and private spheres of labour: there is no conception of its existing both *between* and *within* the two spheres. As a result, one cannot use Marxist theory to account for the fact that men and women do different and differentially evaluated tasks both in the family and in the public labour force. Moreover, it does not permit one to question whether there is a *link* between female labour in the private sphere and the public sphere.

This relates to a second problem in Marxist analysis. The family sphere is analytically divorced from the economic sphere; there is no theory of the family, other than a conception of it as a product of relations in the production process. Labour performed in the family is defined as unproductive, in that it creates no value for the capitalist class. The family's main role is characterized as a property institution. This approach conceals, on the one hand, an inquiry into the link between household labour and capitalism and, on the other hand, an analysis of the ideological function of the family. There is recent analytical work that suggests that the labour of housewives *does* provide essential services for capitalism, and not just the family unit. Housewives not only provide a new generation of workers through biological reproduction; they also supply capitalism with a continued source of daily labour power through their care and maintenance of the male worker (see Benston, 1969). In other words, the domestic work of women in the home frees the male to devote his energy to creating profit for the capitalist in his public labour.

The ideological role of the family is important in considering whether a particular cultural definition of the family serves certain class interests. For example, if women are defined as dependent on males economically and psychologically in the family, could this provide the labour force with an individual who, when she does seek work, is easier to manipulate (i.e., less militant or more likely to accept low wages)? These are important questions, and require investigation in a variety of areas. The problem is that Marxist theory does not offer the analytical tools for even formulating the questions.

Finally, there are aspects of the Marxist definition of patriarchy that require consideration. It is a definition based on property relations; one that assumes that the basis for patriarchy will erode as more women enter the work force. Moreover, patriarchy is conceptualized as residing solely in the family institution. The problem with this approach is its failure to address the role of particular conditions and ideologies outside the family that specifically oppress women as a group. This critique relates back to the problem of a sexually segmented labour force. In other words, if women enter the labour force along the lines of a sexual division of labour (whereby males' jobs are economically and ideologically "superior"), then the basis for her lack of control in the family will *not* be eroded. Recognition of this *dual* nature of female inferiority—lack of control both in the family and outside it—could point to a reworking of the definition of patriarchy.

Thus, Marxism essentially reduces the female problem to women's inability to work or have access to property resources. Consequently, Marxism sets up an "*A priori* symmetry" between feminism and socialism as political movements, without ever demonstrating a real basis for the unity (Mitchell, 1971).

CONTEMPORARY THEORY: CONTINUITY AND CHANGE

Several developments in the theoretical literature on gender took place in the late 1970s and the 1980s, developments that both expressed a frustration with the inadequacies of the classic approaches, and served to further fragment the women's movement in Canada as well as abroad. Obviously, I cannot provide a full account of these developments here, but I do think it is possible to point to three key shifts in the literature. First, there emerged an attempt to rework the frameworks of feminism and Marxism in a manner that drew from each, and yet went beyond their limitations. Second, a strand of North American radical feminism came to the fore, which was predicated on the assumption of an essential "female nature," one that could be counterpoised to an essential "male nature." Finally, the work of particular feminists in Europe (often referred to in the literature as French feminism) had a significant impact in redirecting theoretical work on gender.

The first key shift in the theoretical terrain was the emergence of socialist feminism. Socialist feminism (or feminist materialism) is not simply a synthesis of Marxism and feminism. Rather, with its analytical foundation in these two traditions, it sought to avoid the inadequacies of each and to develop new insights into the phenomenon of sex subordination.[2] The theoretical mandate for this work is to establish the interrelationship of a capitalist mode of production and structures of sex inequality (see, for example, Kuhn and Wolpe, 1978).

The thrust of their work is twofold, and focuses on:

1. the relationship of patriarchal relations to historical modes of production; and
2. the relationship of the organization of the household to the organization of production.

The analytical roots of socialist feminism lie within both feminist and Marxist traditions. Their links with feminist analysis are reflected in the attempt to explain patriarchy as a system of sexual power that cuts across the family sphere and the public sphere. However, while socialist feminists recognize the importance of patriarchal ideologies in sustaining power, they reject the ahistorical primacy this concept occupies in feminist analysis. The analytical links with Marxism are found in the focus on the *material base* of inequality and on the *historical variability* of status. Moreover, there is a recognition of the importance of domestic, or household, labour as a form of production, as is suggested by contemporary Marxist arguments. The points of departure from Marxist analysis are found in a reworking of the concept of patriarchy and a reanalysis of the interaction of the family institution and social production.

The ideological support for the particular expression of the sex division of labour is found in the "social construction of gender" (Young, 1978:125). In other words, it involves the socializing process through which symbolic structures frame the acquisition and internalization of the attitudes and behavioural expectations embedded in sex roles.

The conceptualization of the sex division of labour as the systematic allocation within, or exclusion from, production processes is sufficiently broad to allow for the consideration of both the family and the productive spheres. In other words, socialist feminists would ask whether women are allocated solely to production-for-use in particular periods; whether they are excluded from particular types of production-for-exchange in other periods; and, finally, how sex criteria are used in varying periods as a basis for allocation and exclusion.

The argument is not that sex subordination is a necessary constant consequence of a sex division of labour. Rather, the primary question is how the *particular* operation of this division, in conjunction with other relationships (e.g., capitalist relations of production), can intensify or restrict power differentials between men and women. A related question is how economic conditions in various historical periods can intensify or restrict the operation and emphasis of a sex division of labour. This is precisely where socialist feminist analysis goes beyond previous explanatory frameworks; it offers a basis for investigating the *interplay* of political economy and patriarchy.

Socialist feminists reconceptualize patriarchy as a set of historically situated relations of sex subordination within the overall organization of production and symbolic structures. As a force in history, patriarchy interacts with other sets of relationships within varying modes of production. Socialist feminist analysis is not as concerned with the penultimate issue of the *origin* of subordination in early societal forms: rather it deals with the question of the *expression* and *maintenance* of sex subordination in various periods. This is because dominance and subordination are historically specific concepts: they make sense only in the context of the prevailing social arrangements.

Thus, in order to investigate the expression and maintenance of patriarchy, one must look at both its material and ideological forms. Socialist feminism argues that the material expression of patriarchy is the *sex division of labour*, and that it is supported ideologically by particular *cultural values and beliefs* regarding sex roles. The sex division of labour has two levels of appearance (Young, 1978:125).

1. It is a systematic *allocation* of individuals to positions in the process of production on the basis of sex criteria.
2. It is a systematic *exclusion* of individuals from positions in the production process and social relations at large on the basis of sex criteria.

In the same period that socialist feminist work was shifting attention to new areas of theoretical investigation, radical feminist theory was engaged in its own internal re-examination. As Hester Eisenstein notes, the key defining characteristics of this phase in radical feminist work have been: a strong hostility to leftist political theory, a focus on psychological processes over socioeconomic processes, and an assumption of universalism or "sisterhood" among women, which transcends class, race, and other relations of power (see Eisenstein, 1983:125-134). In that sense, it very much represented a clear extension of early radical feminist arguments, but with new emphases and a concomitant redirection for political intervention.

The work of influential American radical feminist Mary Daly, for example, takes as its focus the inherently patriarchal nature of culture, and more specifically, language (see Daly, 1978 and 1984). Her argument rests on her assumption that language and all forms of symbolization are necessarily patriarchal because they have originated with, and are controlled by, men. Her political project for social change is consequently a project organized around the "dismantling" of conventional language and the "recovery" and building of a language, and hence culture, that reflects a female perspective on reality. In her book *Gyn/Ecology: The Metaethics of Radical Feminism*, Daly attempts to both expose, in sometimes very shocking terms, the misogynist nature of culture and various cultural practices and rituals throughout history, and suggest a mechanism for social change. In regards to the latter, she argues that we must move beyond exposing "false realities" as they have been constructed by men over and against women, and toward reclaiming the unique, essential female spirit within all women. This consciousness-raising "journey" of discovery for Daly was predicated on both recognizing one's oppression and reorganizing language to allow for a women-centred meaning system.

The work of Daly, and others such as Dale Spencer in Britain, has usefully served to reveal a range of patriarchal underpinnings that organize our symbolic realities. But it promises more than this; Daly essentially argues that reality is created through language; hence to create a new language is to recreate reality itself. Consequently, she has been criticized by socialist feminists for her idealist, ahistorical stance. Lynn Segal, for example, has argued that Daly's extension of radical feminism defined a new political path, because it "promotes as its solution to male-domination an individual and psychic voyage, on which only women can embark" (Segal, 1987:18). In a similar context, Hester Eisenstein argues that the development of radical feminism through the work of Mary Daly, and others who share her assumptions, meant a redirection of radical feminism away from the early work of Kate Millett and from political engagement. As she notes: "the radical feminist voyage became a metaphysical or spiritual journey, rather than a political one" (Eisenstein, 1983:13). It posited the existence of a women-centred culture in opposition to a male-centred one and offered the promise of female "empowerment" through control of language. But in its blindness to class and race differences between women, and its reduction of social reality to questions of language, Daly's radical feminism lapses into an essentialist, idealist argument, which ultimately returns feminism full circle to the determinism that was earlier challenged in its conservative form.

Finally, the third key shift in feminist theory in recent years has been the turn, in a different strand of radical feminism, toward incorporating questions of female subjectivity and cultural representation. Unlike the strand of radical feminism elaborated above, wherein there is assumed to be an essential universal female self or "female subject," this theoretical shift draws together feminists concerned with the origins of consciousness and nature of subjectivity, and feminists concerned with the relation between gender and language. It has meant the merger of reinterpretations of Freudian psychoanalysis (through the French feminist work in particular) and Marxian post-structuralist work on language and discourse.

While there is not sufficient space to elaborate here the full theoretical complexity of their arguments, the shift has been toward a renewed focus on questions of "sexual difference" and the "constructed" nature of subjectivity. In reinterpreting Freud, recent feminist literature argues that the real value of psychoanalysis to feminist theory lies in its emphasis on the role of unconscious psychic processes and on the significance of sexual difference for sexual identity. In rejecting the biological determinism implicit in Freud's approach, they have turned to the reformulations of Freud advanced by the French psychoanalytic school of Jacques Lacan. Unlike Freud, who located the roots of female subjectivity and identity in the existence and subsequent recognition of biological difference, Lacan shifted attention to the cultural realm, wherein sexual difference is "represented" symbolically in language. His argument is that the infant enters a world that is constructed symbolically in difference; i.e., the infant first apprehends the social world through symbolic practices such as language, practices that are organized around and reproduce sexual difference. French feminism, as exemplified in the work of writers such as Julia Kristeva and Luce Irigary, have used Lacan's work to argue for the importance of sexual difference in constructing identity, and to insist that all symbolic structures are necessarily patriarchal.

What this has meant for a politics of intervention is remarkably similar to the politics of Daly's radical feminism outlined above. The alignment of radical feminism with psychoanalysis and poststructuralist theories of language has meant a shift of political emphasis to the cultural realm, to the realm of symbolic practices. As with Daly, it has led to a search for a female "voice" and for radical signifying practices, which are assumed to serve as the basis upon which social structures will then change. The agenda for social change is largely reduced to a question of "smashing" patriarchal structures of language and replacing them with feminist structures. As I have argued elsewhere (see Saunders, 1985), the problem of identifying feminist cultural interventions is not easily dismissed. What is the relation between *feminine* and *feminist* in cultural practice? Too often in this strand of radical feminism, they are simply assumed to be synonymous. As a result, patriarchal ideology is divorced from an analysis of material structures, and feminist practice is unconnected to socioeconomic processes of subordination. We are left with an ahistorical conception of ideology as necessarily patriarchal and a reductionist view of the social world as determined by symbolic structure.

CONCLUSION

We are left with the question of where do we go from here? While space limitations prevent me from providing a fully developed answer to this question, I can at least establish the directions in which we might move. I have argued in this discussion that the traditional frameworks are inadequate as they stand, and I have attempted to show the paths in which some feminist work has moved in the past decade, and the consequences of those shifts. It should be clear from my comments that I do not see either cultural feminism, as exemplified by Mary Daly, or poststructuralist feminism of the French feminist school as the routes that are analytically or politically valuable. It is my argument that socialist feminism holds the most promise for theory and for social change. That said, socialist feminism is not without its own internal problems. It is important to identify those areas that socialist feminism has either failed to address or given insufficient attention.

One crucial area of silence in socialist feminist work has been the question of female subjectivity and identity. While I argued above that particular radical feminist attempts to deal with this area are inadequate, I nevertheless believe that it is important to problematize this area for analysis. What is needed is an understanding of the *socially-constructed* nature of gender identity, which does not fall victim to ahistorical arguments rooted in transcendental psychic processes. We need to examine how femininity and masculinity are historically and culturally situated; we need to understand how class and race intersect in the construction of subjectivity; and we need to analyze the specificity of cultural representations of sexual difference. We need, in other words, a materially grounded understanding of human identity and human agency.

Another area in which socialist feminist work would benefit from further inquiry is the role of the state in the reproduction of subordination. Early socialist feminist work tended to assume the necessary class character to the capitalist state, and hence saw the state as simply reflecting class interests. Recent work in the area of state theory and political discourse has much to offer socialist feminism; it suggests that the state, in order to secure its legitimacy, must actively grapple with the challenge posed by feminist movements.

Finally, any feminist theory that remains unconnected to the real experience of women is doomed to fail on both the level of explanatory analysis and of social change. Certainly the 1980s was a decade of increasing factionalism within the women's movement at large, a factionalism partially fuelled by the seeming abstracted theoreticism of much feminist analysis. This was true for socialist feminism as well. As Segal notes "the voice of socialist feminism is now remarkably silent in popular feminist debate" (1987:44). What is needed is a form of theorizing that C.W. Mills first described in *The Sociological Imagination*; we must be able to link questions of social structure and history in a way that makes sense of the biological experience of women.

NOTES

1. It should be noted that, while there is some support for his general account, there is considerable disagreement among anthropologists as to the evolutionary sequence Engels posits.
2. It is generally agreed that J. Mitchell's book *Woman's Estate* (1971) was the first serious attempt to rework Marxist theory on women through a redefinition of the materialist basis of sex inequality. The most intense period of theoretical work, however, has been since 1975.

REFERENCES

Bardwick, J. 1971 *The Psychology of Women* New York: Harper & Row.

Benston, M. 1969 "The political economy of women's liberation." *Monthly Review*, 21. no. 4:13–27.

Daly, Mary 1978 *Gyn/Ecology: The Metaethics of Radical Feminism* Boston: Beacon Press.

Daly, Mary 1984 *Pure Lust* London: The Women's Press.

Eisenstein, Hester 1983 *Contemporary Feminist Thought* Boston: G.K. Hall & Co.

Engels, Frederick 1951 *The Woman Question* New York: International Publishers.

Engels, Frederick 1972 *The Origin of the Family: Private Property and the State* (ed.) E. Leacock New York: International Publishers.

Firestone, S. 1970 *The Dialectic of Sex* New York: Bantam Books.

Freud, Sigmund 1933 "Essay on femininity." *New Introductory Lectures of Psychoanalysis* New York: W.W. Norton & Co.

Marx, Karl and Friedrich Engels 1970 *The Communist Manifesto* New York: Pathfinders Press edition.

McDonough, R. and R. Harrison 1978 "Patriarchy and relations of production." In *Feminism and Materialism* A. Kuhn and A. Wolpe (eds.) Boston: Routeledge and Kegan Paul.

Mead, Margaret 1935 *Sex and Temperament* New York: Mentor.

Millet, K. 1969 *Sexual Politics* New York: Avon Books.

Mitchell, J. 1971 *Woman's Estate* New York: Pantheon.

Nielson, J. 1979 *Sex in Society: Perspectives on Stratification* Belmont, California: Wadsworth.

Parkin, F. 1971 *Class Inequality and Political Order* St. Albans, England: Paladin.

Parsons, Talcott 1954 *Essays in Sociological Theory* New York: Free Press.

Reuther, R. 1974 *Religion and Sexism* New York: Simon and Schuster.

Segal, Lynne 1987 *Is The Future Female: Troubled Thoughts on Contemporary Feminism* London: Virago Press.

Saunders, Eileen 1985 "Teaching media and gender." *Canadian Journal of Communication*, Vol. 11:1, pp. 35–50.

WHO DOES WHAT? GENDER AND THE DIVISION OF LABOUR IN CANADIAN HOUSEHOLDS

Chapter 16

Kevin McQuillan

Marilyn Belle

(An original chapter written for this volume.)

INTRODUCTION

Although the study of housework was once seen as a marginal topic in sociology, the classic work by Friedan (1963) and Oakley (1974) forced sociologists to take the issue seriously and to explore the ways in which sociological theory can help us to understand the factors that determine the performance of household work. In recent years, the study of housework has become the focus of a growing body of sophisticated research. Work in this area has not yet produced a consensus, but certain findings do appear consistently in the literature. The most well-documented finding is that women perform a greater share of the domestic chores than men (Shelton and John, 1996). The relative shares performed by men and women vary according to the characteristics of the individuals and the circumstances of the households in which they live, but women almost invariably perform the larger share of the domestic duties (Shelton, 1992). Yet, there is also evidence that the situation has been changing (Ferree, 1991). Sociologists are now struggling to understand the role of men in the household and to identify the factors that may lead some couples to a more balanced sharing of housework.

This paper has three goals. It briefly reviews the findings of recent research on housework, noting areas that have seen significant change. Second, it examines some of the most important attempts at explaining the findings in this area. And, finally, it presents some recent Canadian data on the topic, looking at how much housework is done and by whom in households in which a heterosexual couple resides.

RECENT RESEARCH ON HOUSEWORK

The tone for modern research on the problem of housework was set by Betty Friedan's (1963) classic study of American women, *The Feminine Mystique*. Discussing what she termed "the problem that has no name," Friedan explored the sense of dissatisfaction felt by many American women in the post-World War II era who felt trapped in the household, their lives entirely taken up by the care of their husband, their children, and their home. Friedan and later observers (Cowan, 1983) noted that the emergence of modern technology—washing machines, vacuum cleaners, dishwashers—had not lessened the demands on women in the household. On the contrary, Friedan entitled a chapter in her book, "Housewifery expands to fill the time available," and went on to describe how the introduction of labour-saving gadgets simply led to an increase in the standards demanded of housekeepers. Higher standards of cleanliness, decoration, and childcare, which, with the growth of suburbia, included the chauffeuring of children to numerous activities, made the performance of housework a daunting task. What Friedan and others also emphasized, of course, was that meeting these rising standards of care was a woman's responsibility—husbands and children might offer occasional "help," but it was women who were ultimately responsible and who would face the condemnation of relatives and friends if the household failed to meet expectations.

Whether the situation Friedan described was a new one that emerged in the prosperity that followed World War II, or the modern incarnation of a long-standing pattern, is a subject of much dispute. There is considerable agreement among historians that women have long been almost exclusively responsible for such traditional household tasks as cooking, laundry, and the care of young children (Tilly and Scott, 1978; Segalen, 1980; Sabean, 1990). Nevertheless, many would also argue that the growth of wage labour and the increasing separation between domestic labour and paid work performed outside the home fundamentally changed our perception of housework (Coontz, 1992; Fox, 1993). When men worked in closer proximity to their families, indeed, when they worked side-by-side with their wives and children on the family farm or at a trade, all forms of work were seen as contributing to the economic well-being of the family. But as men began to work in ever larger numbers in factories and offices while the majority of married women remained in the home, a more rigid division of labour emerged and housework, increasingly the responsibility of wives and mothers, became an isolating and devalued form of labour (Young and Willmott, 1973).

In recent decades, of course, we have seen yet another transformation of the working world, one that has brought ever-greater numbers of women into the labour market. The proportion of married women employed outside the home has risen dramatically from less than 27% in 1966 to 61% in 1992 (Labour Canada, 1978; Vanier Institute of the Family, 1994). In light of such changes, researchers have sought to determine whether a more egalitarian sharing of household tasks is beginning to emerge, or whether women continue to carry the major load when it comes to doing housework. The question is difficult to answer, because good evidence on the changing distribution of household labour has not been readily available. The evocative work of Friedan (1963), Oakley (1974), and Luxton (1980) suggested a rather rigid division of family duties, but only in the 1970s did data on housework from large samples of households become available. Some of the early work using these data (Meissner et al., 1975) confirmed that women performed the lion's share of household tasks. It also pointed to a clear division of labour by task, with women taking almost sole responsibility for chores such as cooking, cleaning, washing dishes, and doing laundry, while men's contributions were limited to outdoor work and certain elements of childcare.

More recent studies from both Canada and the United States suggest that women continue to perform the majority of domestic chores, even when employed in the labour force. However, these studies also suggest that some movement towards a more egalitarian division of labour has been occurring (Shelton and John, 1996). Studies based on the Canadian General Social Survey (Marshall, 1993), as well as studies of specific communities (Bernier et al., 1996), have found that men are doing more housework than in the past, though still not as much as their wives. Similarly, a series of American studies found that men in dual-earner couples nearly doubled their contribution to indoor work between the early 1970s and mid-1980s. At the same time, women, who are now increasingly in the paid labour force, reduced the amount of time they spent on housework. Still, the net results suggest that men contributed only about one-quarter of the time spent on indoor domestic tasks (Coltrane, 1995).

It is not only the amount of time spent that differs between men and women, but also the nature of the work performed (Blair and Lichter, 1991). Men's contributions tend to be limited to certain types of tasks. They perform the majority of maintenance, repairs, and yardwork. They also make significant contributions to child care, shopping, and cooking (Berk, 1985; Lupri, 1991; Ferree, 1991). Such tasks as laundry and vacuuming still seem to be largely handled by women, however (Coltrane, 1996:65). Men are also less likely to take on the "managerial" side of housekeeping. They may, for example, go grocery shopping, but will usually rely on a list of required items drawn up by their wives. Women often express considerable frustration with having to plan and supervise the chores that their husbands agree to do (Luxton, 1983).

Overall, then, the evidence indicates that women continue to do significantly more than their partners, although the gap seems to be closing somewhat in recent years. It is also true, of course, that the amount of work men and women do varies greatly between households. An enormous amount of research has been undertaken on this problem, and we will do no more in this paper than summarize some of the major findings. One thing that does seem clear is that higher-status women—those with higher education and better-paying jobs, for example—normally do less housework than other women (Coverman, 1985; Brines, 1993; Marshall, 1993; Shelton and John, 1996). The result is a more equitable distribution between the partners, even though men do not always increase the amount of work they perform. It appears that the higher income in such families may simply allow couples to purchase services they might otherwise perform themselves. In other words, such families may be more likely to hire a cleaning service or eat out at restaurants rather than cooking for themselves.

It is clear that the arrival of children has a significant effect on the work patterns of family members. Not surprisingly, young children place additional demands on adults in the household. Most, though not all, studies indicate that a larger number of children in a family increases the amount of housework mothers perform, while the effects for men are far less (Berk, 1985; South and Spitze, 1994). Fathers may, of course, do a significant amount of childcare, but their wives often end up using this time to do other household tasks. As the children age, they are able to take on some of the housework burden. Yet, some researchers suggest that children today are doing far less in the home, choosing to spend their time on schoolwork and extracurricular activities rather than on household chores (Goldscheider and Waite, 1991). Moreover, when they do contribute, sons and daughters are likely to follow traditional patterns, with girls doing more around the house and boys taking on outdoor tasks like mowing the lawn (Blair, 1992).

One of the more interesting lines of recent research has focused on the effects of people's attitudes on the sharing of housework. We might expect that men who hold more egalitarian ideas about gender roles will be significantly more involved in doing housework. To some extent, this is true. Most studies do find a more equitable distribution among couples holding egalitarian values (Goldscheider and Waite, 1991; Shelton and John, 1996). Still, good intentions on the part of husbands are not enough. Some analysts argue that a more equal distribution of housework is only likely to come about when women feel this to be important and are ready to insist on it (Presser, 1994:94; Coltrane, 1995:265).

The impact of many variables, such as education, income, and gender role attitudes, are also mediated by external factors. One innovative line of research has emphasized the importance of work schedules that are usually imposed by employers. Presser (1986; 1994) has noted that men, even those who do not hold especially progressive attitudes, are more likely to play an important role in housework when husbands and wives work different shifts. Whether they like it or not, men who find themselves at home with the children while their wives are off at work are pressed into performing various household chores by sheer necessity (Brayfield, 1995). Oddly, then, changing work patterns over which individuals have little control may sometimes lead to greater change in the household than a transformation of people's ideas about what is fair.

EXPLAINING GENDER DIFFERENCES

Most of the recent attempts to account for patterns of housework have built on one of three theoretical approaches: models of time availability, resource-power theories, and gender theories of domestic labour. Because excellent reviews of these approaches are already available (Berk, 1985; Shelton and John, 1996), this section highlights only the literature that is most salient for the analysis undertaken in this paper.

First, time availability models, which have their roots in neoclassical economic theory (Becker, 1981; Coverman, 1985), emphasize competing demands on the time of household members. The amount of housework that needs to be done is a function of the characteristics of the household and its members. The number of dependent children in the household, for example, increases the absolute amount of work that must be done. How household members respond to these demands is influenced by the other commitments they have made. Most important among these other commitments is their involvement in the paid labour force. As their hours of paid labour increase, their availability to fulfill household roles diminishes, and the hours of housework performed decline. It has been suggested that households may benefit from a degree of role specialization. If some members are better positioned to find paid employment, or are able to attract higher wages than are other household members, it will be in the household's interest to allocate a greater share of the household work to the members with more limited opportunities in the paid labour market. In practice, this has usually meant that women assume a greater share of household labour.

A second perspective is contained in resource-power theories. These theories adopt a more sociological view of the operations of the household, one that emphasizes the role of power differentials in the allocation of household tasks (Blood and Wolfe, 1960; Greenstein, 1996). The disproportionate share of housework performed by women reflects not their greater availability to do domestic labour, but the lower level of resources they bring into the household. Because they are more likely to work in part-time jobs or to have lower incomes when they work full-time, women typically earn less than their partners. This puts them at a relative disadvantage in bargaining over the distribution of housework (Nakhaie, 1995). In addition to income, other valued traits, such as higher education or occupational prestige, may strengthen the position of one partner in the bargaining process. The result is that, on average, women do a larger share of the housework. By the same logic, however, it can be argued that, in households in which wives hold greater resources than their partners, a more equitable distribution of household tasks will occur.

The resource-power and time-availability approaches are, of course, more sophisticated than these brief summaries suggest. Research using these frameworks has drawn attention to important factors that influence the division of household labour. Yet, empirical research on housework in a variety of settings indicates that the variables these theories identify account for only a modest proportion of the variance in either the absolute amount or relative share of housework performed by men and women. Moreover, analyses that include such factors still show large differences between males and females. These findings suggest that the greater share of work undertaken by women does not simply reflect differences in human capital attributes between women and their partners.

A third approach builds on gender theories of social behaviour. These theories have tried to remedy the shortcomings in the first two approaches by directing explicit attention to the influence of gender on the distribution of household work. The earliest work in this tradition emphasized the different perceptions of household work that women and men held. Friedan (1963) underlined the sense of obligation women felt to insure proper order in the household. Oakley's (1974) path-breaking study, based on detailed interviews with British housewives, vividly depicted the different views and expectations of men and women concerning what chores needed to be done and how they should be done. More recently, Ferree (1991) has redirected attention to differences between men and women in what might be called the symbolic significance of household labour. Performing household tasks is more likely to be viewed by women as something more than accomplishing necessary work. Doing housework and doing it well may be an expression of love and commitment (Luxton, 1983). It may also indicate successful performance of one's role and hence be a mark of social status.

A second stream of thought, popular among current writers, emphasizes the relational element of gender (Hartmann, 1981; Berk, 1985; West and Zimmerman, 1987). Proponents of this view accept the fact that males and females experience socialization differently, and that this shapes their values and behaviour. However, these theorists argue that gender is not simply a characteristic of individuals or even a learned role, but takes on its full sociological significance when viewed as an ongoing relation. In this view, the daily actions of men and women are guided by our ideas about appropriate conduct for men and women, and these actions, in turn, serve to reinforce differences between the sexes. Goffman (1977) illustrates this process in his discussion of the choices men and women make about appropriate partners. Women tend to choose men as boyfriends and husbands who are older, taller, and stronger. While it is true that men, on average, are taller and stronger than women, it is perfectly possible to conceive of a situation in which a substantial proportion of couples involved women who were taller and stronger than their husbands. Similarly, in the case of age, there is no necessary reason why the vast majority of husbands should be older than their wives. Goffman argues that in making the choices they do, men and women are guided by their sense of what is appropriate and desirable. At the same time, these choices serve to reinforce the notion that men are more powerful and "naturally" occupy a more dominant role in the marriage. Building on this theme, Berk (1985) and others argue that this image of the male as the dominant partner leads women in couple relationships both to take on a larger share of the workload and to consider such arrangements fair.

PATTERNS OF HOUSEWORK IN CANADA

In this final section of the paper, we will examine some recent evidence on patterns of housework in Canadian households. The analysis is based on a time-use survey of Canadian households that forms part of Statistics Canada's General Social Survey Program (Statistics Canada, 1993). This was a telephone survey conducted throughout 1992, with interviews spread evenly across the twelve calendar months. Basic demographic information was collected on all household members and one member was selected at random to complete the time use survey. Respondents maintained a time-use diary and supplied additional social and demographic information about themselves and the households in which they lived. The survey covered all types of households, but this paper focuses only on those households that contained a married or cohabiting couple, which produces a sample size of 4953.

Respondents who completed the time diary supplied information on their activities over a twenty-four-hour period. They were asked to report on their main activity in each fifteen minute period during the day. The data were weighted to allow for estimates of the amount of time spent per week on various activities. In the analysis presented here, the housework measures are reported in hours per week.

The diary approach allows for great specificity in the reporting of activities. The original survey data provided detailed reports of the activities of respondents. We have reduced these activities to a smaller set of categories that match those commonly used in recent research. The major categories are cleaning, cooking, maintenance and yard work, paying bills, childcare, and shopping. As other authors have noted, a small number of respondents report spending an extremely large number of hours on a particular type of work. Following South and Spitze (1994), we set the maximum number of hours at the 95th percentile and recoded all values above that level equal to this maximum. We then summed the recoded values to give a measure of the total amount of housework done by a respondent.

Data were also available on a wide range of demographic characteristics that allow us to assess the importance of a number of variables identified by the various theoretical perspectives. Time availability models point to the importance of the demands that household members face inside and outside the home. In the empirical analysis, we included four measures that might be expected to influence the amount of labour to be done and the ability of the respondents to carry it out. Included are the number of dependent children, the number of hours of market work, home ownership, and the use of paid help for housework. The time-availability approach would lead us to expect that home ownership and a larger number of dependent children would increase the amount of housework, while longer hours of paid work and the use of hired help would reduce the amount of housework people do.

Resource-power models stress that it is not just the number of hours worked outside the home that counts, but the resources that flow from that work. Thus, higher income and higher status should allow an individual to limit his or her involvement in household work. Past studies have differed in the treatment of these variables. Both absolute and relative measures have been employed. However, given the fact that the income data were collapsed into fairly broad categories, it was impossible to compute a meaningful measure of the proportion of household income earned by the respondent.

Finally, age and gender were included in the analysis. Once again, the age data were grouped into categories by Statistics Canada, a feature that makes the data analysis more difficult. Nevertheless, the data do allow us to examine the relationships between housework and a number of theoretically relevant variables. These data also allow us to see how gender differences in housework change when the effects of such variables are taken into account.

RESULTS

Figure 16-1 presents evidence on the amount of housework performed per week by men and women in couple relationships. These findings confirm what many previous studies have found—women, on average, do significantly more housework. Among couples without children, the woman does about 60% more. The gap is even larger in families with children, in which women spend more than twice as much time on domestic work.

FIGURE 16-1 Mean hours of housework per week by gender and presence of children

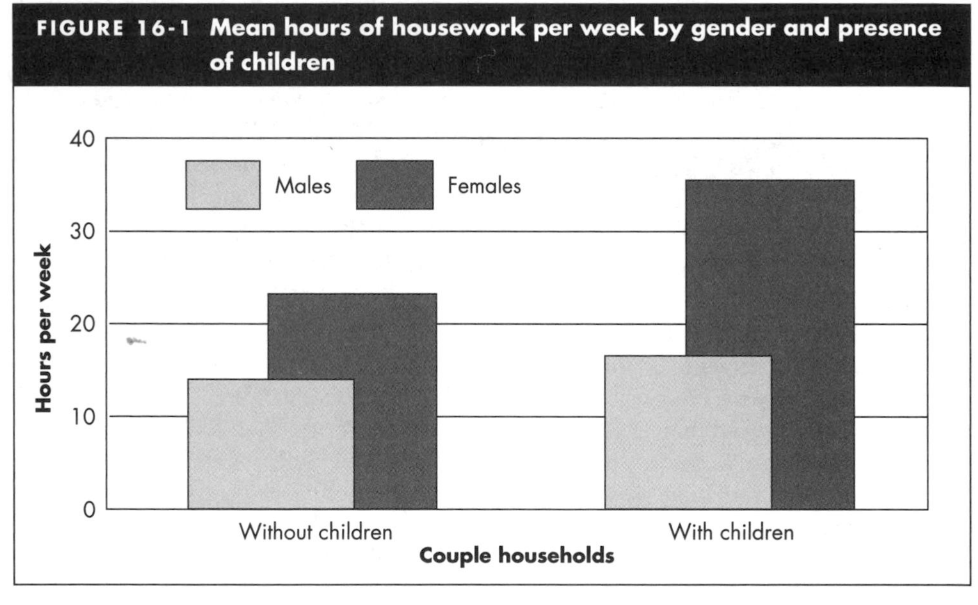

Source: Statistics Canada, GSS 1992

This finding also confirms the conclusions of previous researchers that the presence of children leads to greater differences in domestic work between men and women. Men do spend more time on housework when children are present, but the increase among women is vastly greater and produces a much larger gap between partners. It is important to remember that both dual-earner and single-earner households are included in this section of the analysis.

Figures 16-2 and 16-3 break down the time spent on domestic work by the specific tasks being performed. This breakdown makes it apparent that gender differences also extend to the type of work that people are doing. Women spend more time than men on all types of tasks, except for household maintenance and repairs, a traditionally male type of task. The differences are greatest in the categories of cooking and cleaning. Among couples without children, women spend about three times as many hours on these activities, and the gap is even larger in families with children. Aside from maintenance, men are most likely to contribute to shopping and childcare, although even here women do significantly more.

These very basic findings support the notion that, despite the changes that have occurred in Canadian society in recent years, women still perform the bulk of chores in couple households. To understand the situation better, however, it is important to see how the characteristics of couples influence the distribution of domestic labour. This can be a difficult task, given the great variability among households and the limited information contained in the survey. However, in Table 16-1, we address this problem using multiple regression analysis. This technique allows us to examine the relationship between a number of individual and household characteristics and the amount of housework performed in an average week. Households with children and those without children were analyzed separately.

The first four independent variables listed are factors that have been cited by proponents of time-availability models of

FIGURE 16-2 Mean hours spent on various household tasks by gender (couples without children)

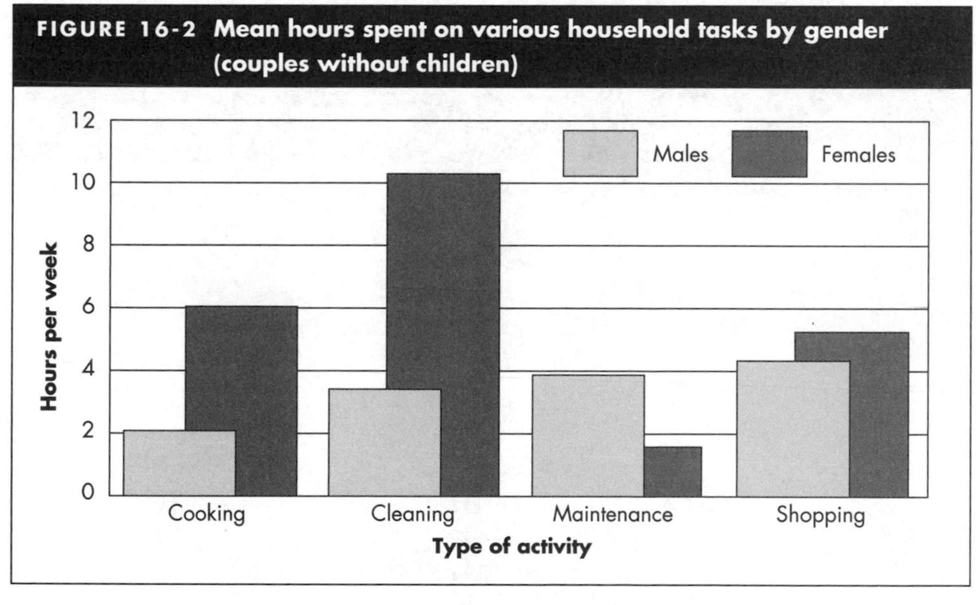

Source: Statistics Canada, GSS 1992

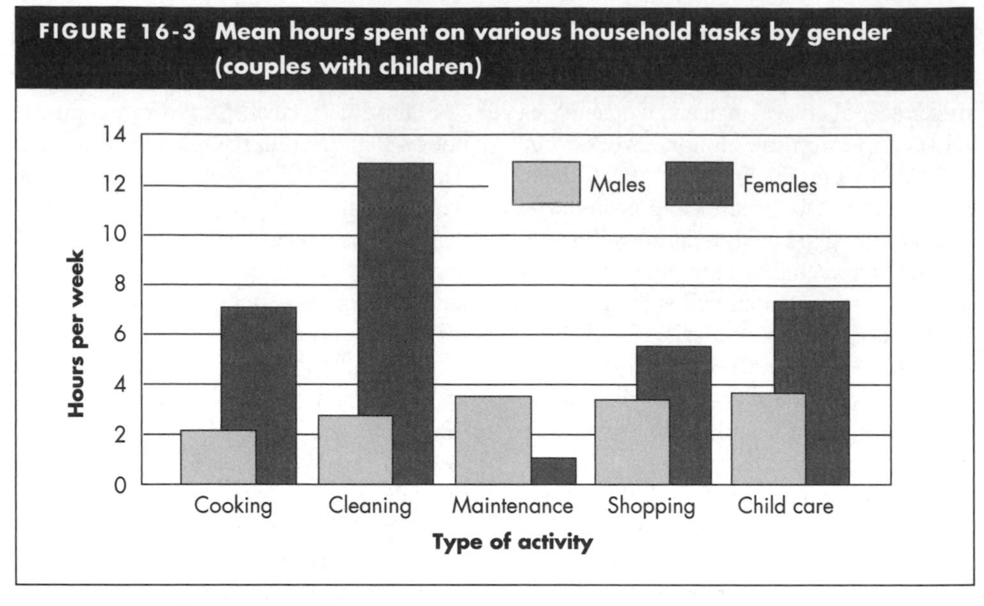

FIGURE 16-3 Mean hours spent on various household tasks by gender (couples with children)

Source: Statistics Canada, GSS 1992

household labour. In general, the results support the predictions of this theory. The coefficients for the hours employed variable are negative and statistically significant, indicating that the more hours persons devoted to a paid job, the less work they did at home. On the other hand, if their dwelling was owned by a member of the household, individuals spent significantly more time on housework. In couple-only households, for example, those who owned their homes spent about two and one-half hours (2.54)

TABLE 16-1 OLS coefficients for regression of hours of housework per week on selected variables, for couples with and without children

Independent Variables	Couples without Children	Couples with Children
Hours Employed	-0.16**	-0.25**
# of Children Under 13	N/A	3.27**
Home Ownership	2.54**	1.77**
Use of Paid help	-1.84	-0.93
Education	0.05	0.33**
Income	-0.18	-0.06
Age	0.37**	-0.55**
Gender	7.69**	13.41**
Constant	14.19**	23.30
R^2	0.19	0.35
Number of Cases	1986	2967

Note: • p <.05 ** p < .01

per week more on housework than did those who rented their place of residence. Among couples with children, the number of children present was associated with considerably more work. For each additional child in the household, respondents reported doing 3.27 more hours of work. Finally, the coefficient for the paid help variable is negative, suggesting that the use of paid help reduced the amount of housework people did for themselves. However, this coefficient was not statistically significant, probably because of the relatively small number of couples who reported using paid help.

Variables associated with the relative-resource theory received less support in the analysis. For couple-only households, neither education nor earned income played a significant role. However, the income and education variables were grouped into categories, which may have affected the ability of these two variables to show significant effects. For couples with children, more education was associated with more hours of work, contrary to the predictions of the theory. It is also important to remember that this analysis shows the relationship between education and hours of housework after controlling for the number of hours worked.

Interestingly, age is positively associated with housework among those without children. This result probably reflects the fact that many of the older couples include persons whose children have grown up and left home. Doing a good deal of housework may have become a "habit"during the years the children were at home. For younger couples, housework may be a lower priority as they seek to establish themselves professionally or enjoy a more active social life. For those with children, the negative effect of age probably reflects the reduced demands on parents' time as their children age and begin to do more for themselves.

Having controlled for a variety of other factors suggested by leading theories, it is striking to see that gender continues to play such an important role. Among couples without children, women do 7.69 hours more per week than men, while, in families with children, women do over thirteen hours more. As yet, neither the changes in the labour market nor the changes in the ideas of men and women about gender roles have created a situation in which men and women share equally the burdens of maintaining the home.

CONCLUSION

The findings of this paper reinforce the conclusions of a number of similar studies while also raising some new issues for research. They demonstrate that women continue to carry the major burden of housework in couple households, despite the wide-ranging changes that have been occurring in Canadian society in recent decades. Men do contribute to the work of the household, but they spend significantly less time than their partners and their efforts are concentrated on a narrow range of tasks.

Obviously, the amount of work done by both men and women varies significantly with a number of characteristics of both individuals and households. Work outside the home leads both men and women to reduce the amount they do at home. This may result in less work being done or it may lead families to use some of the money they earn to hire others to perform necessary chores. With large numbers of women now in the paid labour force, the long-term consequence of this fact may be a change in perceptions regarding women's duties at home. The arrival of children, a joyful event for most families, also brings about greater pressure on mothers and fathers. An increase in housework of more than three hours per week for each additional child suggests that homelife becomes more central to the lives of men and women as their families grow. While the results for such achievement or resource indicators as income and education were weak, it would be premature to dismiss the effects of these factors. Statistics Canada's practice of categorizing this information makes it harder to assess their statistical significance. Certainly, more attention should be devoted to the influence of such factors as education and social class on the division of domestic labour.

One of the great challenges for research in this area is to understand why gender consistently appears as the strongest predictor of hours of housework, even in the presence of a wide range of controls. Many attempts have been made to account for these enduring differences. Some have pointed to the different perceptions and evaluations of housework, or what might be called the symbolic significance of household labour (Spitze, 1988; Ferree, 1991). Both performing the work itself and being able to display the results of that work—a clean, well-decorated house, well-dressed children, etc.—may mean very different things to men and women. Women may be more likely to draw status and self-esteem from doing such tasks and doing them well. Women may also see the performance of these tasks as a way of communicating love and caring for other members of the household. For men, on the other hand, housework may be seen in simpler, more pragmatic ways, and may lead many men to resist increasing their contribution to the household when women increase their hours of paid work. In simple terms, the additional labour may just not seem worth it to men.

It is also true, however, that living as a couple increases the differences between the sexes, and this is particularly true once children enter the picture. This pattern could reflect greater specialization and what economists would term "a rational division of labour." Or, as recent sociological approaches suggest, it may indicate an unconscious process in which the gender relations in the larger society, which involve inequality of power between men and women, are carried over and reproduced within the household. The result of this process is that women are consistently placed in a disadvantaged role. Evaluating the competing claims of these theories is by no means easy, since the empirical evidence can be used to support various interpretations. The sheer tenacity of gender differences underlines the sociological significance of these patterns, however, and should lead researchers to explore more fully the different ways in which men and women adapt to the many demands placed on them inside and outside the home.

REFERENCES

Becker, Gary S. 1981 *A Treatise on the Family* Chicago: University of Chicago Press.

Berk, Sarah Fenstermaker 1985 *The Gender Factory: The Apportionment of Work in American Households* New York: Plenum.

Bernier, Christiane, Simon Laflamme, and Run-Min Zhou 1996 "Le travail domestique: tendances à la désexisation et à la complexification." *Canadian Review of Sociology and Anthropology* 33(1):1–21.

Blair, Sampson Lee and Daniel T. Lichter 1991 "Measuring the division of household labor." *Journal of Family Issues* 12:91–113

Blair, Sampson Lee 1992 The sex-typing of children's household labor: parental influence on daughters' and sons' housework." *Youth and Society* 24(2):178–203

Blood, Robert O. and Donald M. Wolfe 1960 *Husbands and Wives* Glencoe, Il: Free Press

Brayfield, April A. 1992 "Employment resources and housework in Canada." *Journal of Marriage and the Family* 54:19–30.

Brayfield, April A. 1995 "Juggling Jobs and Kids: The Impact of Employment Schedules on Fathers' Caring for Children." *Journal of Marriage and the Family* 57:321–332.

Brines, Julie 1993 "The Exchange Value of Housework." *Rationality and Society* 5:302–340.

Coontz, Stephanie 1992 *The Way We Never Were* New York: Basic.

Coltrane, Scott 1995 "The Future of Fatherhood." In William Marsiglio, (ed.), *Fatherhood: Contemporary Theory, Research, and Social Policy* Thousand Oaks, CA: Sage Publications.

Coltrane, Scott 1996 *Family Man: Fatherhood, Housework, and Gender Equity* New York: Oxford University Press.

Coverman, Shelley 1983 "Gender, domestic labor time, and wage inequality." *American Sociological Review* 48:623– 37

Coverman, Shelley 1985 "Explaining husbands' participation in domestic labor." *The Sociological Quarterly* 26:81– 97

Cowan, Ruth Schwartz 1983 *More Work for Mother* New York: Basic Books.

Ferree, Myra Marx 1991 "The gender division of labor in two-earner marriages." *Journal of Family Issues* 12(2):158–180.

Fox, Bonnie J. 1993 "The rise and fall of the breadwinner-homemaker family." In Bonnie J. Fox, (ed.), *Family Patterns, Gender Relations* Toronto: Oxford University Press.

Friedan, Betty 1963 *The Feminine Mystique* New York: Dell Publishing.

Goffman, Erving 1977 "The arrangement between the sexes." *Theory and Society* 4:301–331.

Goldscheider, Frances K. and Linda J. Waite 1991 *New Families, No Families? The Transformation of the American Home* Berkeley, CA: University of California.

Greenstein, Theodore N. 1996 "Husbands' participation in domestic labor: interactive effects of wives' and husbands' gender ideologies." *Journal of Marriage and the Family* 58:585–595.

Hartmann, Heidi I. 1981 "The family as the locus of gender, class, and political struggle: the example of housework." *Signs* 6:367–394.

Labour Canada 1978 *Women in the Labour Force: Facts and Figures* Ottawa: Minister of Supply and Services.

Lupri, Eugen 1991 "Fathers in transition: the case of dual-earner families in Canada." In Jean E. Veevers, (ed.), *Continuity and Change in Marriage and Family* Toronto: Holt, Rinehart and Winston.

Luxton, Meg 1980 *More Than a Labour of Love: Three Generations of Women's Work in the Home* Toronto: Women's Press.

Luxton, Meg 1983 "Two hands for the clock: changing patterns in the domestic division of labour." *Studies in Political Economy* 12:27–44.

Marshall, Katherine 1993 "Employed parents and the division of labour." *Perspectives on Labour and Income* 5(3):23–30

Meissner, Martin, Elizabeth W. Humphreys, Scott M. Meiss, and William J. Scheu 1975 "No exit for wives: sexual division of labour and the cumulation of household demands." *Canadian Review of Sociology and Anthropology* 12:424–439

Nakhaie, M.R. 1995 "Housework in Canada: the national picture." *Journal of Comparative Family Studies* 26(3):409–425

Oakley, Ann 1974 *The Sociology of Housework* New York: Pantheon.

Presser, Harriet B. 1986 "Shift work among American women and child care." *Journal of Marriage and the Family* 48:551–563.

Presser, Harriet B. 1994 "Employment schedules among dual-earner spouses and the division of household labor by gender." *American Sociological Review* 59:348–64.

Sabean, David Warren 1990 *Property, Production, and Family in Neckarhausen, 1700–1870* Cambridge: Cambridge University Press.

Segalen, Martine 1980 *Mari et Femme dans la Société Paysanne* Paris: Flammarion.

Shelton, Beth Anne 1992 *Women, Men, and Time: Gender Differences in Paid Work, Housework, and Leisure* Westport, CT: Greenwood

Shelton, Beth Anne and Daphne John 1996 "The division of household labor." *Annual Review of Sociology* 22:299–322.

South, Scott J., and Glenna Spitze 1994 "Housework in marital and nonmarital households." *American Sociological Review* 59:327– 47

Spitze, Glenna 1988 "Women's employment and family relations: a review." *Journal of Marriage and the Family* 50:595–618.

Statistics Canada 1993 *The 1992 General Social Survey—Cycle 7: Time Use* Ottawa: Statistics Canada.

Tilly, Louise and Joan Scott 1978 *Women, Work and Family* New York: Holt, Rinehart and Winston.

Vanier Institute of the Family 1994 *Profiling Canada's Families.* Ottawa: Vanier Institute of the Family.

West, Candace and Don Zimmerman 1987 "Doing gender." *Gender and Society* 1:125–151.

GENDER AT WORK: SEEKING SOLUTIONS FOR WOMEN'S EQUALITY

Chapter 17

Gillian Creese
Brenda Beagan

(An original chapter written for this volume.)

INTRODUCTION

Women employed in the labour market are often referred to as 'working women.' In reality, paid employment is only part of the work most women do. In 1992 alone, Canadians spent 25 billion hours on unpaid work in the home; two-thirds of these hours were performed by women. On average, each Canadian woman performed 1 482 hours of unpaid domestic work in 1992 (Jackson, 1996: 26-27)! The gendered division of labour is bound up in market-based notions of value and, until recently, unpaid domestic work was not considered to be work at all, though it has always been work that has to be done. Just thirty years ago the majority of women did not combine unpaid work with participation in the paid labour force.[1] Today most women are also engaged in paid employment, but they do not enjoy equal opportunity in the workplace. This chapter explores trends in women's paid work and identifies strategies to increase gender equality in the workplace.

TRENDS IN WOMEN'S LABOUR FORCE PARTICIPATION: THE NEW MAJORITY

The number of women in the labour force has increased steadily since the Second World War, increasing from one in four (24%) in 1951, to one in two (52%) in 1981, and nearly three in five (57%) in 1996 (Table 17-1). In the 1950s young women were most likely to be in the labour force prior to marriage and child-bearing, perhaps returning once their children had grown up and left home. By the 1990s this was no longer so. The employment rate of women in peak child bearing years, between 25 and 44 years of age, was 70% in 1994, including a majority of women (55.7%) with children under the age of 3 (Statistics Canada, 1995:72). At the same time that women have increased their participation in wage labour, the participation rate of men has dropped from 84 to 74 percent[2] (Table 17-1). As a

TABLE 17-1 Labour force participation rates in Canada, by gender, 1951–1996

Year	Women	Men
1951	24%	84%
1961	29	81
1971	39	78
1981	52	79
1991	59	75
1996	57	74

Source: Liviana Calzavara, "Trends and Policy in Employment Opportunities for Women", in *Social Inequality in Canada* Second Edition, ed. James Curtis et al. (1993):312. The figures for 1996 are from Ernest Akyeampong, "The Labour market: year-end review", *Perspectives on Labour Income* (1997):16.

result of these twin trends the participation rates of women and men are now more similar than different. The majority of women and men are employed (or seeking employment) throughout most of their adult lives.[3] One key difference that remains, however, is the likelihood of part-time versus full-time employment. In 1994 more than one quarter of women (26.1%) were employed part-time, compared to less than one in ten men (9.4%) (Statistics Canada, 1995:73).

It is worth noting some key variations in employment trends among different groups of women (Table 17-2). Canadian-born and immigrant women have similar rates of employment, unemployment, and

TABLE 17-2 Employment, unemployment, and employment income among selected groups of women in Canada, 1991

	Percent Employed (Ages 15–64)	Percent Unemployed (Ages 15–64)	1990 Average Employment Earnings, Full-Year, Full-Time
Canadian Born	62.9	10.1	26 478
Immigrant	62.0	10.8	26 601
Immigrant Women arriving after 1986	49.0*	18.4*	—
Visible Minority	60.0	13.4	24 712
Non-Visible Minority	62.9	9.9	26 160
Aboriginal	47.1*	17.7*	23 773*
Non-Aboriginal	54.0*	9.9*	25 908*
With Disabilities,** living in household	40.7	16.0	—
Without Disabilities	66.1	9.9	—

*15 years and over

** Women with disabilities living in a household excludes those in institutional settings.

Source: *Women in Canada: A Statistical Report,* Third Edition, Statistics Canada, 1995: 121, 123, 129, 130, 132, 143, 145, 160, 161, 174.

earnings, except those immigrants most recently arrived who experience much higher unemployment. Visible minority women have slightly lower employment rates (3%), higher unemployment rates (3.5%), and lower annual earnings ($1 448 less). More significant differences are observed for Aboriginal women, who have lower rates of employment (7%), higher rates of unemployment (8%), and nearly 10% lower annual earnings ($2 135 less). The greatest differences, however, are found between women with and without disabilities; only 40% of women with disabilities are employed. Notwithstanding this great diversity among women, the gender gap between women and men is even more significant and continues to form a central feature of the Canadian labour market.

OCCUPATIONAL SEGREGATION AND THE INCOME GAP

Not only are more women employed today, but women are employed in a much broader range of occupations than at any time in the

TABLE 17-3 Distribution of employment in Canada, by occupation and gender, 1996

Occupation	Women	Men	Women as a Percentage of Employment
Managerial/ administrative	12.7	14.0	44.9
Natural Sciences/ engineering/ mathematics	.8	5.8	20.2
Social Sciences/ religion	.2	2.0	57.5
Teaching	6.6	3.0	64.6
Doctors/dentists	0.5	0.9	32.1
Nursing/other health related	9.1	1.2	86.1
Artistic/literary/ recreational	2.3	2.4	44.4
Clerical	25.0	5.3	79.7
Sales	10.2	9.9	46.1
Service	17.5	10.9	57.1
Primary industries	2.2	6.5	21.5
Manufacturing	5.1	18.0	19.0
Construction	0.3	8.9	2.6
Transportation	0.8	6.3	9.3
Material handling/ other crafts	1.7	5.1	22.0
Total	100%	100%	5.3%

Source: *The Labour Force: Annual Averages*, Statistics Canada, 1996: B-39.

past. In little more than two decades women have made considerable inroads into such prestigious, traditionally 'male' professions as medicine, dentistry, law, and corporate management. In spite of these success stories, occupational segregation on the basis of gender is still firmly entrenched in the Canadian labour market. Compared to men, women work in a narrower range of occupations, and remain concentrated in those with lower pay and less social prestige. Two-thirds of all women are employed in just four occupational sectors: clerical (25.0%), service (17.5%), sales (10.2%), and nursing (9.1%) (Table 17-3). As Table 17-3 shows, most occupational sectors are either dominated by men or, less often, are dominated by women: natural sciences, medicine/dentistry, primary industries, manufacturing, construction, transportation, and material handling are disproportionately male, while teaching, nursing, and clerical work are mostly female occupations. Although some women have made considerable occupational gains over the last two decades, most women continue to work in the 'pink collar' occupations.

Gendered occupational segregation might not be so noteworthy were it not for the economic consequences for most women. As Table 17-4 shows, women earned less than men within each occupa-

TABLE 17-4 Average annual earnings, by occupation and gender, full-time full-year workers, 1995

Occupation	Women	Men	Women's Earnings as a Percentage of Men's
Managerial/ administrative	36 583	52 561	69.6
Natural Sciences	41 253	49 259	90.0
Social Sciences/ religion	37 622	60 904	61.8
Teaching	40 568	49 817	81.0
Medicine/health	36 671	61 375	59.7
Artistic/ recreational	27 151	35 200	77.1
Clerical	26 414	33 641	78.5
Sales	25 600	38 033	67.3
Service	19 734	31 539	62.6
Agriculture	13 800	22 181	62.2
Processing	24 272	37 769	64.3
Product assembly/ fabrication/repair	24 324	37 274	65.3
Transport equipment operation	28 209	35 884	78.6
Material handling	21 857	33 378	65.5
Total	29 700	40 610	73.1

Source: *Earnings of Men and Women in 1995,* Statistics Canada, 1996, Tables 1 & 5.Source: *The Labour Force: Annual Averages,* Statistics Canada, 1996: B-39.

TABLE 17-5 Average annual earnings, by education and gender, full-time full-year workers, 1995

Educational Attainment	Women	Men	Women's Earnings as a Percentage of Men's
Less than grade 9	20 637	29 634	69.6
Some secondary school	21 971	33 735	65.1
Secondary school graduate	25 760	35 650	72.3
Some postsecondary	27 399	37 859	72.4
Postsecondary certificate/diploma	28 840	39 710	72.6
University degree	42 584	55 976	76.1
Total	29 700	41 610	73.1

Source: *Earnings of Men and Women in 1995*, Statistics Canada, 1996, Table 3

tional sector, even those in which women predominate. Overall, women employed full-time, full-year in 1993 earned 73.1 cents for every dollar men earned ($29 700 compared to $40 610). Even in clerical jobs, among the most 'feminine' of occupations, women earned over $7 000 less per year than men!

Moreover, as Table 17-5 illustrates, the gendered wage gap appears across all educational levels, ranging from just over 60% of equivalent men's wages for women with some secondary schooling, to 76.1% for those with a university degree. A woman with a university degree earns an average annual income of $42 584, considerably more than most female workers, but $13 392 less than the average man with a university degree (Table 17-5). One reason for this is that occupational segregation cuts across educational levels. Most often, women and men with similar levels of education are trained in different fields and are not employed in the same jobs. While women are a majority of university students enrolled in bachelor's degrees in health professions (67.7%), education (66.8%), fine arts (62.8%), and humanities (61.2%), women are a minority in the fields of science (29.9%) and engineering (18.5%) (Statistics Canada, 1995:60). Even within identical occupations requiring specialized educational qualifications, however, a gendered wage gap remains: female judges earn 72.5%, doctors 65.7%, lawyers 58.1%, senior managers 54.6%, and university professors 74.6% of what their male counterparts earn in the same occupations (Armstrong and Armstrong, 1994:46). Educational streaming alone does not explain these pronounced gender differences in occupations and wages.

GENDERING AND RE-SEGREGATION: 'DOING GENDER' AT WORK

Gender is not just a product of historical trends, it is an ongoing process in the workplace. As Cynthia Cockburn points outs, "people have a gender and their gender rubs off on the jobs they mainly do" (1985:169). Thus, eliminating gender segregation is not just a matter of getting more women to enter 'men's jobs' and vice versa. In fact, as workers of one gender enter into an occupation previously dominated by the other gender, one of two processes usually happens: the occupation becomes re-gendered, or vertical or horizontal subdivisions develop within the occupation. It is rarely the case that an occupation becomes truly integrated by gender (Miller-Loessi, 1992).

When an occupation re-genders, it is usually in the direction of feminization; what was 'men's work' becomes redefined as 'women's work' (Reskin and Padavic, 1994). Traditionally female jobs pay less and are less desirable than traditionally male jobs. Men are unlikely to flock to them in large numbers. In contrast, traditionally male jobs tend to be a step up for most women, in pay as well as status (Padavic, 1991).

There are two key reasons a job may re-gender: employers' preference for workers shifts, or the job loses its appeal for some workers. Employers who have traditionally defined an occupation as male, and have preferentially hired male workers, may cease to do so: when an occupation expands quickly and outstrips the supply of qualified workers; when the content of the work changes, usually through technology;[4] if those who do the hiring change over time and do not share their predecessors' hiring preferences; when the cost of excluding women increases through legislation; or when the cost of including women decreases if a predominantly male workforce reduces its level of resistance to women co-workers (Reskin and Roos, 1990). Male workers often resist women's entry into previously male enclaves through practices as varied as engaging in sexual harrassment to refusing to pass on job related knowledge and skills (Cockburn, 1985, 1991). Men are less likely to oppose the entry of women when the job is losing its appeal to men due to changes in the content or nature of the work, decline in job security, occupational prestige, opportunities for mobility, or declining earnings (Reskin and Roos, 1990). The decline in wages and prestige in a feminizing occupation is usually a circular process: women are less able to enter the field unless men are losing interest; once women enter, the occupation declines and men lose interest more rapidly (Padavic, 1991).

When an occupation begins to incorporate more women but does not result in outright feminization, horizontal or vertical segregation within the occupation usually occurs. In most occupations which appear gender-balanced in numbers, men and women actually do different jobs; they are in different subspecialties, in different sectors of the occupation, or work for different clients (Roos and Reskin, 1992). This is horizontal segregation. For example, in medicine, one of the more elite occupations, while roughly 50% of medical school graduates are female, women disproportionately enter family practice, pediatrics, and psychiatry while some of the most highly-paid medical specialties have 90% to 97% male residents.[5]

Horizontal segregation may be accompanied by vertical segregation, according to which men hold higher-ranking, higher-paid positions, and women fill lower-status positions, often in less desirable settings. Another elite profession, law, illustrates both horizontal and vertical segregation. Though law schools graduate approximately equal numbers of men and women, once in practice women and men tend to congregate in different areas of law. At the same time, women are more likely than men to be in the lowest positions in the legal hierarchy, and are less likely to be promoted to partners in their law firms even when all other factors are equal (Hagan and Kay, 1995). Female lawyers hit a 'glass ceiling,' a point above which women are unlikely to advance.

There are emotional costs borne by individuals as an occupation is undergoing transition. When women enter a traditionally male workplace they often face highly gendered workplace cultures as men and women 'do gender' in their personal interactions at work. Part of 'doing gender' may involve 'boundary heightening,' exaggerating gender differences to exclude women by increasing the sexual banter, or more overt sexual hostility (Reskin and Padavic, 1994). Sexual harassment is a common experience for women in non-traditional trades, and a central part of male workers' resistance to the re-gendering of their occupations (Cockburn, 1991). Women who find ways to cope and stick it out to do work equal with the men are often seen as 'not real women' (Cockburn, 1985).

When men work in a field that has traditionally been defined as 'women's work' they too may feel like outsiders, excluded by conversations about families, babies, weddings, and so on. Such men also face assumptions that they are 'not real men.' In fact stereotypes about homosexuality are a major reason men hesitate to enter fields such as nursing (Williams, 1989). Men in predominantly female occupations seem to want to be set apart, however, emphasizing their distinctness from their women co-workers. In contrast, women in predominantly male occupations appear torn between equality and difference, unable to both claim to be able to do men's jobs and insist that they have distinct workplace needs. For women, the price demanded for acceptance into a predominantly male occupation is assimilation, becoming just 'one of the guys' (Cockburn, 1991). Assimilation leaves little room for the realities of women's lives: the fact that most women get pregnant, are primary caregivers for children and elderly family members, and do the majority of housework, shopping, and other domestic tasks.

With regard to the overall trends toward de-segregating the labour market, then, the results are disappointing. Women have entered formerly-male occupations, but most are either in new female subspecialties or occupations that become almost entirely feminized. Women in such previously male occupations are economically advantaged relative to other women, but not relative to men. This ongoing process of gendering remains a central factor perpetuating the income gap between women and men in spite of the occupational gains some women have made since the 1970s.

ACHIEVING EQUALITY: SEEKING SOLUTIONS

There are a number of strategies designed to achieve greater gender equality in the labour market. These include measures to get more women into higher paying jobs traditionally held by men (employment equity), attempts to raise the value of work traditionally performed by women (pay equity), organizing a larger segment of the low wage workforce (unionization), and accommodating and redistributing domestic responsibilities in the household (domestic labour). Each of these initiatives promises some improvement in the situation of women workers, but each also has limitations.

Employment Equity

Given the depth of gendered occupational segregation, one of the most important policy initiatives is to equalize employment opportunities. In Canada this has been attempted through employment equity programs. The 1986 Employment Equity Act[6] was passed by the Federal government requiring federally regulated employers, Crown corporations, and federal contractors with 100 or more workers to implement programs to ensure equitable representation of four groups who fair poorly in the labour market: women, Aboriginal peoples, people with disabilities, and visible minorities.

There is mixed opinion about whether employment equity is achieving its goals. A recent review of the program shows that employers tend to think the Employment Equity Act is working well, while members of the four designated groups generally see room for improvement (Canada, Employment and Immigration, 1991). Some small increases in rates of hiring and promotion of these four groups have been recorded, but these are almost entirely in service and clerical positions. Improvements are least impressive for Aboriginal women, visible minority women, and women with disabilities, those who are the most disadvantaged (Canadian Advisory Council on the Status of Women, 1992).

Several limitations of employment equity legislation that restrict its impact in equalizing job opportunities among women have been identified. First, it only covers a fraction of the workforce, restricted to businesses with 100 or more employees that fall under federal labour regulations.[7] Second, equality is defined as a proportion of women in a business relative to the proportion of women found in that position in the 'external workforce.' This fails to address systemic gender segregation which, as we have seen, results in very small proportions of women in some occupations.[8] Third, employment equity is still essentially voluntary. Noncompliance with filing a report can be penalized, but there is no penalty for failing to reach employment equity targets. Fourth, employment equity focuses too narrowly on occupational segregation at the expense of other concerns such as the under-valuation of the work that women now perform (Canada, Employment and Immigration, 1991: 47). Employment equity could be made more effective by legislative changes broadening its scope and enforcement, but it is unlikely to have much impact on processes of gendering and the value assigned to different types of work.

Pay Equity

While employment equity policies seek to equalize women's representation in male-dominated occupations, pay equity policies seek to address the consistent underpaying of 'women's work' relative to comparable 'men's jobs.' As early as the 1950s legislation was passed in most provinces requiring equal pay for equal work, but occupational segregation meant that women and men seldom did the same work (Wilson, 1996: 129). The move to require equal pay for 'comparable work' was a direct response to this situation, and beginning in the late 1970's the federal government and several provinces introduced pay equity legislation that requires 'equal pay for work of equal value'.[9] Equal value means jobs are comparable in terms of skill, effort, working conditions and responsibility, usually assessed through complex systems of job evaluation. This process allows very different job categories to be compared across segregated occupations (for example, comparing male janitors and female receptionists working at a university, or female nurses and male lab technicians working at a hospital).

The outcome of pay equity depends on processes of implementation and legislative directions. Though pay equity has led to significant pay settlements for some groups of women, (Wilson, 1996) it also has limitations. One key limitation is that it only addresses gender-based wage gaps, ignoring gaps based on race or disability. It hinges on evaluations of skill, which are complex, subjective, and political. Pay equity is usually limited to comparisons within an individual workplace, so if women predominant as employees there may be no appropriate male comparison group. Moreover, major portions of the workforce are not covered by pay equity legislation. Finally, pay equity focuses on technical solutions that can actually entrench 'male work' as the standard so that women who most closely emulate men are rewarded while others lose out (Fudge and McDermott, 1991; Hallock, 1991). On the other hand, pay equity has helped to demystify the gendered assumptions buried in definitions of skill and the value of work.

Unionization

Another possible solution is increased unionization of low-wage sectors that employ women. On average, unionized workers enjoy higher wages and better benefits than their non-union counterparts, and the gap is greatest for part-time workers, most of whom are women. The average wage for unionized part-time workers is $16.68 an hour compared to $9.77 for non-union part-timers; full-time unionized workers earn $18.87 an hour compared to $15.32 for non-union full-timers (MacQueen & Beauchesne, 1997). Historically, unions have been strongest in blue collar industries such as manufacturing, construction, logging, and mining; all areas in which men predominate. Since the 1970s, however, large numbers of public sector workers have formed unions bringing civil servants, nurses, teachers, and postal workers into the labour movement. As a result of public sector unionization, and also due to job reductions in blue collar industries with high rates of male unionization, forty percent of all union members today are women (White, 1993a:56). Most areas in which women work have low levels of unionization, however, including clerical work in the private sector, sales and service occupations, and work that is part-time, temporary, and/or in small companies (White, 1993b).

Unionization clearly has the potential to increase women's wages. It is less clear whether unionization will substantially decrease the wage gap between men and women which persists, in part, because unions have not decreased gender segregation in the workplace. Moreover, unions have historically been male-dominated institutions and women remain under-represented in positions of leadership. Issues of gender equity are often not seen as union priorities. Women unionists have identified a number of strategies that would make unions more sensitive to gender equity and could make unionization an important vehicle for reducing the wage gap. These include targeting union organizing among part-time and low wage workers, pursuing "solidarity" bargaining so that the gap between higher and lower paid workers becomes narrower,[10] and promoting stronger bargaining for 'women's issues' such as day care, pay equity, employment equity, and policies on sexual harassment (Briskin and McDermott, 1993; Hallock, 1991).

Domestic Labour

One of the most important dimensions of the gendered division of labour, as we have seen, is the uneven distribution of domestic labour in the household. Even when women work full-time in the labour force, most retain primary responsibility for child care, elder care, housework, shopping, and food preparation (Armstrong and Armstrong, 1994; Jackson, 1996; Wilson, 1996). These family responsibilities often require women to find someone else to care for sick children or attend dentist appointments in order to avoid taking time off the job. Domestic responsibilities may limit women's ability to compete for jobs or promotions that demand long hours, to relocate for employment purposes, or to pursue further education to upgrade skills. The uneven division of labour in the household disadvantages women in the workplace, making it difficult to compete with male colleagues who have a wife to shoulder the greater burden of domestic responsibilities. In fact, workplaces have been structured around the experience of men who have someone else to care for home and hearth; as such, most workplaces allow little flexibility for employees to perform domestic tasks (Hessing, 1992).

In order to level the playing field for women and men in the workplace, therefore, the division of unpaid domestic work must also be reconsidered and better accommodated in the workplace. Important initiatives include government supported low-cost daycare and better maternity and paternity leave provisions as well as 'family friendly' programs offered by employers, such as on-site day care, flex-time, family-leave, and the promoting of a work-culture that does not demand excessive overtime or frequent relocation. These measures would improve the situation of all parents, especially single parents, the majority of whom are women. In the long run, however, men must begin to take on a much larger share of domestic responsibilities. Men are doing more domestic work today than in the past, but the division of labour is still far from equal: "women, on average, spent 78% more time in 1992 on unpaid work than men did" (Jackson, 1996:26). Without significant change on the domestic front, gender segregation in low paying jobs will likely remain the reality for most women. Women who do pursue high-powered careers, for example in areas like law, are still more likely to be single and/or childless (Hagan & Kay, 1995; Reskin & Padavic, 1994). Men do not have to make a choice between children and a successful career, and women should not have to make that choice either. Redefining the domestic division of labour may also help to erode the sharp gendered distinctions and associated definitions of value attached to 'men's work' and 'women's work.' We might just begin to 'do gender' differently at work if we also do it differently, and more equitably, at home.

CONCLUSIONS

Since the Second World War the labour force participation rates of women and men have become more similar, yet major differences remain in the gender segregation of occupations, in the wages earned by women and men, and in the uneven distribution of unpaid work in the household. Gender segregation and a significant income gap are not easy to overcome, as demonstrated by the ongoing processes of gendering and re-segregation that occur as women enter formerly 'male' occupations. The most important measures proposed to provide women with access to more and higher paying jobs in the labour market include employment equity, pay equity, unionization, and various initiatives related to accommodating and equalizing responsibilities for domestic labour. Although none of these proposals alone provides a solution to existing forms of gender inequality, in combination these strategies promise to improve substantially the situation of women in the workplace.

NOTES

1. Lower labour force participation rates for women in the early part of this century were not only the result of heavy domestic responsibilities that tied women to the household. Other factors pushed women out of the labour force, including government legislation, male trade unions, and employer preferences. In addition, much of the income-generating work women performed (such as taking in lodgers, childcare, laundry, sewing, and growing and preserving food for sale) remained part of the hidden economy that was not counted in official statistics.
2. Some of the main reasons for the decline in men's labour force participation rates include the development of universal old age pensions, income security programs for ill and injured workers, and economic restructuring and job loss.
3. The unemployment rates for women and men have fluctuated during the last two decades but are currently almost identical. In 1996 the unemployment rate for adult women was 8.4%, and for men 8.5% (Akyeampong, 1997:16).
4. It may be that changes in the content of work are not so much reasons for employers to alter their hiring practices as justifications for decisions made on other grounds. Robin Leidner (1991) makes a strong argument that virtually all work contains both stereotypically masculine and feminine elements, and

which stereotypes get invoked depends on the will of employers and workers, rather than on anything inherent in the job. Two types of 'interactive service jobs' she studied, serving fast food and selling insurance, are very similar in terms of the skills workers draw upon, yet fast food servers were mostly women, while insurance was sold exclusively by men and was identified as work for which women were completely unsuited.

5. Of all medical residents in Canada in 1994-95, the specialties with the lowest proportions of women were urology (2.4%), cardiovascular/thoracic surgery (3.8%), and orthopaedic surgery (9.5%) (Association of Canadian Medical Colleges, 1995:82-83). Cardiovascular/thoracic surgery and orthopedic surgery are two of the top three specialties in earnings as well as public prestige (Gellman, 1992; Rosoff and Leone, 1991).
6. In the United States affirmative action legislation has a longer history, requires employers to meet numerical quotas for hiring and promotion, and is backed by stronger legislative force (though in some jurisdictions, such as California, legislation outlawing affirmative action in many cases has recently been passed). In Canada, employment equity legislation requires employers to set targets or goals rather than quotas, with much weaker enforcement.
7. Most labour law in Canada is under provincial jurisdiction. Federal labour law covers those who work directly (civil service) or indirectly (crown corporations) for the federal government, industries regulated by the federal government (including transportation, fisheries, and communications), and, for the purposes of employment equity legislation, federal contractors. Thus, most employers are not subject to this legislation.
8. A broader comparison would be with the pool of all those qualified for a position, or indeed, qualified to be trained for a position. This would necessitate more non-traditional on-the-job training for women.
9. While federal and most provincial provisions require individuals or groups to initiate complaints, some provinces have proactive legislation requiring employers to take positive steps to assess and reduce wage gaps (for example, Manitoba and Ontario). In contrast, other provinces have no pay equity legislation at all (for example, British Columbia).
10. Traditionally, unions negotiate for percentage wage increases that, over time, increase the gap between higher and lower wage workers. Solidarity wage bargaining requires a commitment to raise the wages of workers at the bottom end of the pay scales (usually women) more than those at the top (usually men) to narrow the wage gap over time. This is a common practice in some countries, for example in the Swedish labour movement, but uncommon in Canada.

REFERENCES

Akyeampong, Ernest 1997 "The labour market: year-end review." *Perspectives on Labour and Income*, Statistics Canada, Volume 9, Number 1, Spring 9-17.

Armstrong, Pat and Hugh Armstrong 1994 *The Double Ghetto: Canadian Women and Their Segregated Work* (3rd ed.) Toronto: McClelland & Stewart.

The Association of Canadian Medical Colleges 1995 Canadian Medical Education Statistics, Vol 17.

Briskin, Linda and Patricia McDermott, (eds.) 1993 *Women Challenging Unions* Toronto: University of Toronto Press.

Calzavara, Liviana 1993 "Trends and policy in employment opportunities for women." In *Social Inequality in Canada* (2nd ed.) James Curtis, Edward Grabb, and Neil Guppy, (eds.) Toronto: Prentice Hall Canada, 311-326.

Canada, Employment and Immigration 1991 *Consultations in Preparation for the Review of the Employment Equity Act* Ottawa: Minister of Supply and Services, 1991.

Canadian Advisory Council on the Status of Women 1992 *Re-evaluating Employment Equity: A Brief to the Special House of Commons Committee on the Review of the*

Employment Act Publication Number 92-E-184, Ottawa.

Cockburn, Cynthia 1985 *Machinery of Dominance: Women, Men and Technical Know-How* London: Pluto Press.

Cockburn, Cynthia 1991 *In The Way of Women: Men's Resistance to Sex Equality in Organizations* London: Macmillan.

Fudge, Judy and Patricia McDermott (eds.) 1991 *Just Wages: A Feminist Assessment of Pay Equity* Toronto: University of Toronto Press.

Gellman, Derek D. 1992 "Growing medical income disparities threaten fee-for-service medicine." *Canadian Medical Association Journal*, Volume 147: 1682–1686.

Hagan, John and Fiona Kay 1995 *Gender in Practice: a Study of Lawyers' Lives* New York: Oxford University Press.

Hallock, Margaret 1991 "Unions and the gender wage gap: an analysis of pay equity and other strategies." Eugene: Labour Education Research Center, University of Oregon, Working Paper No. 8.

Hessing, Melody 1992 "Talking on the job: office conversations and women's dual labour" In *British Columbia Reconsidered: Essays on Women*, Gillian Creese and Veronica Strong-Boag (eds.) Vancouver: Press Gang Publishers, 391–415.

Jackson, Chris 1996 "Measuring and valuing households' unpaid work." *Canadian Social Trends*, Statistics Canada, Number 42, Autumn 25–29.

Leidner, Robin 1991 "Serving hamburgers and selling insurance: gender, work, and identity in interactive service jobs." *Gender and Society*, Vol. 5, No. 2, 154-177.

MacQueen, Ken and Eric Beauchesne 1997 "Labor peace is disturbed by mounting piles of garbage." *The Vancouver Sun*, A1, A17.

Miller-Loessi, Karen 1992 "Toward gender integration in the workplace: issues at multiple levels." *Sociological Perspectives*, Volume 35, Number 1, 1–15.

Padavic, Irene 1991 "Attractions of male blue-collar jobs for Black and White women: economic need, exposure, and attitudes." *Social Science Quarterly*, Volume 72, Number 1, 33–49.

Reskin, Barbara and Irene Padavic 1994 *Women and Men at Work* Thousand Oaks, California: Pine Forge Press, 1994.

Reskin, Barbara and Patricia Roos 1990 *Job Queues, Gender Queues: Explaining Women's Inroads Into Male Occupations* Philadelphia: Temple University Press.

Roos, Patricia and Barbara Reskin 1992 Occupational desegregation in the 1970's: integration and economic equity?" *Sociological Perspectives*, Vol. 35, No. 1, 69–91.

Rosoff, Stephen M. and Matthew C. Leone 1991 "The public prestige of medical specialties: overviews and undercurrents." *Social Science and Medicine*, Vol. 32, 1991: 321–326.

Statistics Canada 1995 *Women in Canada: A Statistical Report* (3rd ed.) Ministry of Industry.

White, Julie 1993a *Sisters and Solidarity: Women and Unions in Canada* Toronto: Thompson Educational Publishing.

White, Julie 1993b "Patterns of unionization." In *Women Challenging Unions*, Linda Briskin and Patricia McDermott (eds.) Toronto: University of Toronto Press, 191–206.

Williams, Christine 1989 *Gender Differences at Work: Women and Men in Nontraditional Occupations* Berkeley: University of California Press.

Wilson, S.J. 1996 *Women, Families and Work* (4th ed.) Toronto: McGraw-Hill Ryerson.

FOR FURTHER REFERENCE: GENDER

Ng, Roxana, Joyce Scane, and Pat Stanton 1995 *Anti-racism, Feminism, and Critical Approaches to Education* Westport, Conn.: Bergin & Garvey. Studying racism and feminism in the context of class analysis has been a frequent approach to central issues of inequality. This book uses that trilogy to examine issues in education.

Agnew, Vijay 1996 *Resisting Discrimination: Women in Asia, Africa, and the Caribbean and the Women's Movement in Canada* Toronto: University of Toronto Press. An examination of issues of visible minority women in the Canadian women's movement.

Brodie, M. Janine 1995 *Politics on the Margins: Restructuring and the Canadian Women's Movement* Halifax, N.S.: Fernwood, 1995. An examination of how the women's movement responds to economic changes in Canadian society.

Brodie, M. Janine 1996 *Women and Canadian Public Policy* Toronto: Harcourt Brace. A very good collection of papers on issues of public policy related to women and gender.

Cossman, Brenda 1997 *Bad Attitudes on Trial: Pornography, Feminism, and the Butler Decision* Toronto: University of Toronto Press. Legal battles over what is and what is not pornography are the focus of this collection. It raises key issues related to inequality and the legal system.

Wintemute, Robert 1996 *Sexual Orientation and Human Rights: the United States Constitution, the European Convention, and the Canadian Charter* New York: Clarendon Press. How do lesbian and gay rights intersect with discussions of human rights more generally, and how are these rights articulated in the context of national constitutions? This work brings a comparative perspective to the key questions.

Ross, Becki 1995 *The House that Jill Built: A Lesbian Nation in Formation* Toronto: University of Toronto Press. A historical account of the rise of the lesbian movement in Canada.

ETHNICITY, RACE, AND ANCESTRY

THE ECONOMIC INTEGRATION OF VISIBLE MINORITIES IN CONTEMPORARY CANADIAN SOCIETY

chapter 18

Feng Hou
T.R. Balakrishnan

(Abridged from the authors' "The integration of visible minorities in contemporary society." *Canadian Journal of Sociology*, 21, 3, 1996, pp. 307–26. Reprinted with permission.)

INTRODUCTION

Two hypotheses have been advanced to explain ethnic stratification in Canada. The first is the "ethnically blocked mobility" thesis, introduced first in Porter's *The Vertical Mosaic* (1965), which considers ethnicity to be an important factor in Canadian class structure. In this view, the socioeconomic achievement of members in an ethnic group is related to their entrance status when they immigrated to Canada. An entrance status inferior to that of the charter groups may be intensified by the ethnic affiliation of the members. Ethnic affiliation may restrain the status aspirations and achievement motivations of the members of the ethnic group. As a consequence, they may have limited educational qualifications and may find themselves in a segmented labour market (Blishen 1970; Porter 1975). This view has come under attack in the past two decades following some empirical studies. On the basis of the finding that ethnic occupational dissimilarity decreased over 1931–1971, Darroch (1979) questioned the assumption that the entrance status of an immigrant group may lead to permanent stratification linked to ethnicity. Some studies also indicate that any privileged position the charter groups may have had historically in the occupational structure was being effectively challenged by other European ethnic groups (Pineo and Porter 1985; Tepperman 1975: 149–152). Furthermore, some authors have suggested that simplistic claims of ethnic identity as a hindrance to social mobility must be rejected because the causal relationship between ethnic identity and social mobility is minimal or non-existent (Isajiw, Sever, and Driedger 1993).

The second hypothesis, the discrimination thesis, attributes the inferior position of some ethnic minority groups to the socioeconomic structure of the society. In this view, unequal relations arise that systematically discourage and exclude some minorities from fully participating in mainstream society. For example, visible minorities may be put into an inescapable socioeconomic trap because of racial prejudice and discrimination such that access to the full range of job opportunities and other socioeconomic resources of the country may be limited for them. Often they are forced to stay at the periphery of the civic, political, and economic centres of society (Driedger 1989; Wiley 1967). Although passage of human rights legislation and official promotion of multiculturalism are aimed at eliminating structural discrimination in Canadian society, it is believed that discrimination persists in institutional settings and interpersonal relations. Some institutions or individuals may limit rights or access to resources for certain ethnic groups by deliberately or otherwise imposing sets of unfair entry restrictions (Elliott and Fleras 1992). Although it can manifest itself in many ways, discrimination is often identified in income disparity among ethnic and racial groups (Li 1988; Satzewich and Li 1987; Reitz 1990).

The objective of this paper is to examine the differences in social mobility among various ethnic groups in contemporary Canadian society. In particular, we will compare the entrance status and mobility experiences of the two strata of Porter's (1965) ethnic hierarchy of socioeconomic status, namely, those of Southern and Eastern European groups such as the Italians, Poles, Greeks, and Portuguese, who immigrated mostly between 1950–1970, and some visible minorities such as Blacks, Chinese, and South Asians who immigrated mostly after 1970. We hope to discover whether ethnicity and/or visibility remains an important determinant of social stratification in Canadian society. Furthermore, we investigate variations in the integration processes between and within the two strata.

THE ROLE OF EDUCATION

Virtually all ethnic groups in Canada have experienced overall improvement in education attainment over the past several decades. Hence the relative differences among ethnic groups have attenuated (Herberg 1990; Shamai 1992). As a group, Asians have experienced the greatest improvement. This fact may imply that there is a place in the vertical mosaic for the upward mobility of some ethnic groups (Shamai 1992). However, some studies attribute the apparent success of Asians to the immigration point system and an increase in the number of Asian immigrants over the last two decades (Beaujot, Basavarajappa, and Verma 1988: 32–35). It has also been suggested that new immigration regulations may have been more stringently applied in the selection of non-European than traditional European immigrants, thereby increasing their entry levels of human capital (Kalbach and Richard 1988). Therefore, it is important to control for immigration status when comparing educational levels among ethnic groups. Meanwhile, the educational attainment of immigrants is a good indicator of entrance status. Hence a comparison of the educational attainments of adult immigrants and those of the Canadian born, and those of individuals who immigrated as children, may partially reflect the extent of blocked mobility.

EXPLAINING INCOME DIFFERENCES

Influences of confounding factors on income differences are complicated. Without careful controls, ethnic differences in income may be either exaggerated or underestimated. For instance, it has been found that foreign-born visible minority members are at a disadvantage in the wage labour force, yet visible minorities who are native-born and self-employed do substantially better than the general self-employed Canadian-born population (Maxim 1992). Based on simple comparison of total income, certain visible minority groups have higher incomes than some white ethnic groups. However, this may simply be due to group differences in education and occupational structure. Therefore, multivariate analysis is essential in adjusting the effects of other influential factors, such as schooling, age, sex, nativity, language, occupation, and labour force activity (Boyd 1992).

Education, income, and occupational status are highly related, but they also reflect different dimensions of social stratification. Education is usually achieved early in life, and in contemporary society it depends primarily on personal motivation, as well as the economic and cultural background of one's family. Occupational attainment and income come later in an individual's life cycle and are more likely to be influenced by socioeconomic conditions. They are also the major factors in establishing quality of lifestyle and social prestige. Hence, to detect discrimination, it is necessary to examine the causal links between education, occupation, and income (Herberg 1990). Some minority groups may have high educational attainments, due either to the selectivity of immigration or to high aspirations and individual efforts. However, they might have low occupational returns from this education and consequently lower income. Similarly, the same type of occupations may yield different incomes for different ethnic groups.

Using 1981 census data, Herberg (1990) analyzed the differentiation among Canadian ethno-racial groups in education and compared these patterns to those for occupation and income. He found that Chinese, East Indians, Japanese, Blacks, and Filipinos had educational or both educational and occupational attainments that were higher than the income positions which they held in relation to the charter groups of British and French, or to other European groups such as the Portuguese and the Greeks. He concluded that different rates of returns from personal qualifications may reflect the effect of institutional and individual discrimination, which persist in spite of federal and provincial human rights legislation (Herberg 1990).

However, Herberg's conclusions about the degree of consonance of occupational standing with a group's educational attainment, and a group's income level relative to its educational and occupational foundations, were based only on a comparison of rankings over educational, occupational, and income statuses. Thus it is not clear whether ethnicity and/or race was the sole factor contributing to group differences in occupation or income. Using the 1981 census data, Li (1988: 117–119) controlled for the effects of education, age, gender, occupation, and industry on ethnic differences in income, and found that Chinese and Blacks were the most disadvantaged in terms of income. However, adequate attention was not given by Li to the effects of age at immigration, period of immigration, and official language proficiency.

Using 1986 census data, Balakrishnan (1988) found that minority groups who immigrated mostly since 1970 had higher educational attainment but lower incomes than the national average, even after controlling for age, year of immigration, education, and official language. However, Balakrishnan did not take occupation into account, nor did he study South Asians (Balakrishnan 1988). Similar findings of relatively lower income of recent immigrants after controlling for factors such as age, education, and language are reported by Beaujot and Rappak, although they did not do the analysis for separate ethnic groups (Beaujot and Rappak 1988). Based on 1971, 1981, and 1986 census data, Kalbach and Richard (1988) also found that groups with non-European origin were relatively high or above average with respect to levels of educational attainment, primarily due to stringent selectivity of immigration, but lower than expected in terms of economic rewards. In explaining the inconsistencies, however, they confined their analysis to the role of religious orientation on acculturation and socioeconomic status achievement for post-war ethnic minority groups (Kalbach and Richard 1988).

Ethnic stratification needs to be analyzed dynamically. An increase or decline in relative socioeconomic status over time indicates the extent of integration of minorities into the mainstream Canadian society. Simple comparisons over time are one way to examine the change of relative position among ethnic groups. However, the continuous flow of new immigrants makes comparisons of the socioeconomic status of recent immigrant groups such as visible minorities with other European groups difficult without proper control for selectivity at entry and duration of stay. An ideal approach is to compare the trends of change between immigrant parents and their children, but this cannot be done without specific survey data. An approximation to this approach is to compare first generation immigrants with those whose parents were foreign born, or with those whose grandparents were foreign born, as was done in a study in the United States (Neidert and Farley 1985). Unfortunately, this information is not available in the Canadian census data. In this study, members of specific ethnic groups are identified by their immigration status, age, and year of immigration.

From the above theoretical considerations, we hypothesize that visibility and social distance will manifest themselves in the degree and speed of integration. Therefore, we predict that European groups such as Italians, Portuguese, Greeks, and Poles will find it easier to integrate than Blacks, Chincsc, South Asians, and other visible minorities. We view equality in income as the final measure of integration. When education and occupation are controlled for, we would expect the visible minorities to have lower incomes only if visibility is a negative factor. Similarly, while incomes of visible minorities will increase with duration of stay in Canada, such an increase will still be small compared to those of European minority groups.

DATA AND METHOD

The data for this paper are from 1991 three percent individual files of Canadian Census Public Use Sample. The ethnic groups specified in this study include the two charter groups—British and French—and four European groups—Italians, Greeks, Poles, and Portuguese. For visible minorities, four groups are specified: Blacks, Chinese, South Asians, and other visible minorities (Arabs and West Asians, Filipinos, Vietnamese, Other East/South East Asians, Latin/Central/South Americans). Only those 30–60 years of age were selected, based on the consideration that most people within this age range have completed their formal education. The resultant sample size for the selected ethnic groups ranges from 2086 to 81 401 (see Table 18-1).

RESULTS

Educational Attainment

Table 18-1 shows differentials in educational attainment among the selected ethnic groups. For each ethnic group, a proportional distribution of three educational levels is calculated respectively for the whole

TABLE 18-1 Sample size and percentage distribution of educational levels by ethnicity and immigration status for population aged 30–60 years, 1991

	British	French	Polish	Greek	Italian	Portuguese	Black	Chinese	South Asian	Other Visible	Total Population
1) Sample size											
Total	81 401	78 096	3643	2086	10 190	3113	3783	7503	5294	8748	304 652
Canadian-born	69 803	76 975	1626	242	3076	114	495	717	412	1346	235 029
Age at immigration											
<10	2098	142	237	110	1490	244	53	126	59	75	8374
10–19	1892	189	227	532	2377	607	438	827	543	541	12 525
20–29	5145	512	595	917	2595	1222	1562	2565	2215	3068	28 276
≥30	2463	278	958	285	652	926	1234	3268	2065	3718	20 448
2) Percentage distribution											
Total											
University & +	21.4	16.7	27.0	9.5	12.8	4.3	17.7	31.8	33.4	39.3	21.3
Some postsec.	34.9	28.9	34.7	19.3	25.0	16.0	41.3	26.1	26.0	26.1	32.9
≤Grade 13	43.7	54.3	38.3	71.2	62.2	79.7	41.0	42.1	40.6	34.6	45.8
Canadian-born											
University & +	20.8	16.4	23.2	28.9	24.9	17.5	13.9	42.5	25.5	38.9	20.2
Some postsec.	33.7	28.9	31.9	32.6	35.0	27.2	34.3	30.3	27.7	30.6	33.0
≤Grade 13	45.5	54.7	44.9	38.4	40.1	55.3	51.7	27.2	46.8	30.5	46.8
Age at immigration											
<10											
University & +	27.4	38.0	31.6	20.0	20.5	12.3	41.5	48.4	54.2	42.7	27.2
Some postsec.	38.5	33.1	33.3	33.6	34.2	36.1	35.8	32.5	27.1	36.0	36.9
≤Grade 13	34.1	28.9	35.0	46.4	45.3	51.6	22.6	19.0	18.6	21.3	35.9
10–19											
University & +	21.0	32.3	18.9	6.6	4.4	4.4	20.8	34.3	25.6	33.3	17.8
Some postsec.	39.5	33.9	35.2	15.8	21.0	18.6	45.9	28.3	33.9	28.5	32.1
≤Grade 13	39.5	33.9	45.8	77.6	74.6	77.0	33.3	37.4	40.5	38.3	50.1
20–29											
University & +	26.0	41.4	26.6	5.5	3.4	3.2	19.3	34.4	39.2	41.2	25.6
Some postsec.	44.6	35.0	39.8	17.0	15.0	13.7	45.4	25.6	27.7	27.0	34.1
≤Grade 13	29.3	23.6	33.6	77.5	81.6	83.1	35.3	40.0	33.1	31.8	40.3
≥30											
University & +	24.0	36.0	34.2	7.7	6.3	1.9	15.1	26.2	30.3	38.6	28.1
Some postsec.	43.3	30.5	36.5	16.1	12.1	10.6	37.5	24.7	21.6	23.2	28.8
≤Grade 13	32.7	33.5	29.2	76.1	81.6	87.5	47.4	49.1	48.0	38.2	43.1

Source: The 1991 Census Public Use Sample.

Notes: 1) Other Visible minorities here include Arab and West Asians, Filipino, Vietnamese, other East/South East Asian, Latin/Central/South American. 2) Education: university & + with university certifi-

group, Canadian born, and immigrants by age at immigration.

Considerable heterogeneity exists both among the selected groups of European origin and among visible minorities. We will discuss each ethnic group first, and then try to identify some common patterns.

Among the four groups of European origin, the Polish group is distinguished from the others, in that the Poles have the highest educational attainment, higher than British and total population. Clearly, this is due to the fact that Polish immigrants at all entry ages had higher education levels. The overall education levels of the other three European groups—Italians, Portuguese, and Greeks—are the lowest among all the selected groups. This can be explained by the very low levels of education among those immigrants who came to Canada after the age of 10. For these three groups, the Canadian born and immigrants who came as small children have much higher education levels than the older immigrants. This may suggest that in spite of the low entrance status of immigrants, their children do achieve education levels similar to those of the population average.

Among visible minorities, the Chinese, South Asians, and "other" visible minorities have much higher education levels than the British and the total population among both the Canadian born and the foreign born segments. The average education level of Blacks, on the other hand, is lower than that of the British and that of the average for the total population. Among the Canadian-born, Blacks have the smallest proportion with university education. An exception are those Blacks who immigrated before age 19. In this group, there was a larger proportion with university education. However, they account for only a small portion of the Blacks (about 13%).

With the exception of Blacks, the blocked mobility thesis does not appear applicable to visible minorities, at least with regard to education. Education has long been regarded as the prerequisite for gaining access to high paying and prestigious jobs in Canada and in other societies. The ambition to integrate into, and get ahead in society may encourage members of ethnic minorities to acquire necessary educational credentials. This is clear from the fact that the Canadian born and those who immigrated before the age of 10 among most minorities have education levels similar to or higher than the British and total population. Even the low socioeconomic status of some minority groups at entrance did not limit their children's mobility achievements. The belief that education can eventually equalize social and economic opportunities may be the underlying reason for the "over-achievement" in education of children of immigrants.

Income

Equality of opportunity in a society implies that an individual's accomplishments are basically determined by personal attributes and efforts. Earnings are the rewards for an individual's investment in human capital. Therefore, income differentials among individuals should simply reflect their differences in education, occupation, age, and other achieved social and economic characteristics. The ascribed status of individuals, such as ethnicity and race, should not enter into the equation. In this sense, any ethnic differences in income may be an important indicator of discrimination.

Table 18-2 presents the results of Multiple Classification Analysis (MCA), which is a modified form of analysis of variance. Wage income of employed workers aged 30–60 is the dependent variable. Control variables include immigration status, schooling, occupation, home language, gender, province of residence, and age. The continuous variable age is introduced in the models as a covariate. Thus its effects are

TABLE 18-2 Multiple classification analysis showing wage income differences among ethnic groups, for employed workers aged 30–60 (in dollars, grand mean = $26 521), Canada, 1990

Variable & categories	# of cases	unadjusted Deviation	Models (1)	(2)	(3)	(4)	(5)
			Deviation from grand mean				
Ethnic Group		(.09)	(.05*)	(.04*)	(.05*)	(.06*)	(.04*)
British	71 357	2297	823	816	977	1083	798
French	63 694	−1555	−61	−525	−276	284	−22
Polish	3144	−1458	−389	1462	445	−26	781
Greek	1707	−5474	−1577	−4382	−2748	−5168	−3195
Italian	8489	808	2453	534	1177	173	1203
Portuguese	2572	−3034	2829	136	1458	2	1812
Black	3340	−4150	−3526	−3607	−3687	−2226	−3039
Chinese	6399	−3551	−1153	342	635	−2340	−245
South Asian	4600	−3254	−2457	−1036	−2163	−3112	−1956
Other visible	7298	−6131	−4359	−1918	−3600	−4897	−3402
Others	88 964	520	−189	20	−204	−174	−246
Immigration		(.09)		(.06*)	(.07*)	(.08*)	(.06*)
Canadian-born	201 832	216		−135	52	234	33
Im.<1960	13 686	2818		1421	1401	1216	1268
61–70	15 476	2424		2673	2101	1718	2094
71–80,<20	2815	−2758		527	599	−72	508
71–80,≥20	14 450	−139		1829	993	222	1057
81–91	13 305	−8262		−4617	−5893	−7024	−5494
Schooling		(.25)	(.18*)		(.25*)	(.18*)	(.18*)
uni. & +	60 900	9221	6551		9316	6645	6590
some postsec.	90 577	132	100		−97	122	76
≤grade 13	110 087	−5210	−3707		−5073	−3777	−3708
Occupation		(.31)	(.21*)	(.28*)		(.21*)	(.21*)
manager.	39 052	13 198	10 088	11420		10 129	10 046
profess.	51 025	4200	2194	5500		2220	2159
c.s.s.	94 752	−6215	−2326	−3166		−2261	−2291
other	76 735	−1834	−3719	−5559		−3839	−3720
Home Language		(.10)	(.07*)	(.07*)	(.07*)		(.06*)
English/French	237 261	678	515	484	519		417
other	24 303	−6620	−5029	−4726	−5072		−4075
Gender		(.30)	(.30*)	(.32*)	(.29*)	(.30*)	(.30*)
male	141 439	6153	6102	6469	6019	6134	6115
female	120 125	−7246	−7184	−7617	−7088	−7223	−7200
Province		(.08)	(.08*)	(.08*)	(.09*)	(.08*)	(.08*)
Ontario	107 931	2199	2100	2012	2257	2116	2102
Quebec	71 339	−1882	−1890	−1709	−1661	−1958	−1870
Others	82 294	−1253	−1116	−1158	−1520	−1077	−1136
R Squared			.214	.193	.178	.215	.217

Notes: 1) Deviation—deviation from grand mean; the numbers in brackets for unadjusted means are eta values which measure the variation across the categories of each factor, the square of eta indicates the proportions of variance explained by all categories of the factor. 2) the numbers in brackets for MCA models are beta values that are equivalent to the standardized partial regression coefficient. 3) * significant at p< .01.

controlled statistically, which means that each group would have the same age distribution as the average of total population. The effect of each category in each factor is indicated as the deviation of the category mean income from the grand mean. The first column of the table lists the sample distribution across the categories for each variable. The second column lists the income deviation from grand mean for the categories of each variable. Model 5 controls for all the selected variables. Compared with Model 5, Models 1 to 4 identify the various effects of immigration status, schooling, occupation, and language on the income levels of various ethnic groups. Model 1 controls for all the selected variables except immigration status. In Model 2, schooling is not controlled, in Model 3, occupation is not controlled, and in Model 4 the effect of home language is not controlled.

All the selected ethnic groups have a lower "average unadjusted income" than the British. Compared with the total population, only Italians have a higher average unadjusted income than the British. When adjusted for the effects of all the selected control variables, the income variation across ethnic groups decreases (Model 5). However, the remaining ethnic differentials are still statistically significant. All the visible minorities have average incomes lower than the grand mean and especially lower than that of the British. On the other hand, among the four selected minority groups of European origin, only the Greeks still have an average income lower than the grand mean, while the other three groups have average incomes close to or higher than the British. Assuming that similar educational and occupational attainment should yield similar incomes, there does not appear to exist systematic income inequality among European groups. Nevertheless, ethnic differentials in income still exist, and visible minorities are generally at a disadvantage in this regard. However, ethnic inequality in income is not exclusively along the colour line, since some non-visible minorities, for example, the Greeks, suffer as much as certain visible minorities.

Besides the income variations due to possible discrimination as implicitly suggested in Model 5, various factors also strongly influence the income differentials among ethnic groups. The difference between Model 1 and Model 5 reflects the effect of immigration status. Among the four European minorities, only the Polish group is in a disadvantaged position due to its composition in age at and period of immigration, as indicated by the fact that its income level increases after controlling for this variable (from –389 to +781). Meanwhile, immigration status is detrimental to the income level of all the visible minorities, with recency of immigration depressing their earnings. The effect of schooling is revealed by comparing Model 2 with Model 5. Poles, Chinese, South Asian, and other visible minorities have higher than expected income levels before controlling for education. This suggests that these minority groups would obtain incomes even lower than their present overall income levels if they had the same education levels as the total population. The effect of occupation is shown by the differences between Model 3 and Model 5. It seems that only the Greeks and the Chinese among the minority groups have benefited from their occupational structure, because they have higher income levels before controlling for occupation. All the selected minorities except Blacks would likely improve their incomes if they had higher proficiency in the official languages (Model 4 vs. Model 5). We assume that when the home language is neither English nor French, proficiency in these languages is likely to be low and hence, detrimental in the labour market as far as earning potential is concerned. Overall, there are evident variations within non-visible minority groups and within visible minorities in terms of the effects of various factors on their income levels. Improvement in education and official language proficiency would benefit the income levels of the Greek, Italian, and Portuguese groups. Large proportions of new immigrants and difficulties with the official languages are the major problems for the Polish and Chinese groups. Immigration status, schooling, and occupational structure are all unfavourable to Blacks. Immigration status, occupational structure, and difficulties with official languages are the drawbacks to South Asians and "other" visible minorities.

If we treat the income differentials among ethnic groups in Model 5 as an indicator of inequality after controlling for qualifications, the discrepancy between unadjusted income deviation and the income deviation in Model 5 should show how much the observed unadjusted income deviation is due to discrimination and how much is due to group differences in qualifications. In this sense, the low level of unadjusted income for the Portuguese is totally related to their corresponding qualifications. Immigration status and language can mostly explain the low level of unadjusted income for Poles and Chinese. For Greeks, Blacks, South Asians, and "other" visible minorities, however, a large portion of their low unadjusted income cannot be explained by controlling for qualifications.

CONCLUSION

This study arrives at two basic conclusions. First, the integration processes for non-visible minorities and visible minorities are different and distinct. In explaining the success of Italians and Poles in the United States since 1920, Greeley (1976: 25) suggests that their social mobility has "come first in income, then in education, and finally in occupation," because most immigrant groups must acquire some kind of basic financial success before they can exploit the opportunities of educational and occupational mobility. He further suggests that income parity comes before educational and occupational parity in the case of ethnics, although education is a more general institution for facilitating upward mobility in American society. Based on the 1981 census data, and survey data in Toronto, Reitz (1990) suggests that the above pattern may still exist for the immigrants of some European groups. However, he believes that the relative success in income of those immigrants with low entrance status may not mean income parity coming before education and occupation, but rather that it has more to do with "the priority needs of immigrants from impoverished backgrounds" (Reitz 1990: 189). His tentative explanation is that income mobility for ethnic minorities often depends on minority businesses based on resources within the ethnic community (Reitz 1990). Our analysis suggests that Italian and Portuguese groups obtain much higher income levels relative to their educational and occupational achievements. The relative positions of the Polish group in occupation and income are similar to those of the Italian and Portuguese. According to the mobility model suggested by Greeley, we may say that the Polish group has reached the second step in the mobility process, that is, improvement in education. Before and around the early 1980s, the Polish group had a lower educational level than the average of total population (Herberg 1990; Shamai 1992). The 1991 data show that Poles have achieved a higher educational attainment than either the British or total population due to the selectivity of immigration and the upward mobility of their Canadian-born segment in education (Table 18-1). It is possible that other European minority groups will experience a similar process. In fact, Canadian-born and young immigrants among them have achieved an educational level and occupational status close to or even higher than the British or the average of total population.

On the other hand, visible minority groups generally have higher educational attainment than the average of the total population and the charter groups. The selectivity of immigration only contributes partly to the achievement of visible minorities in education. Their Canadian-born and young immigrant segments have also attained much higher levels of education than the charter groups and the average of total population, with the exception of Blacks. On the other hand, the percentages of visible minority groups working in managerial and professional occupations are generally smaller than for the British and the French. For the Chinese, difficulties with the official languages may be the major factor influencing their occupational status. However, Blacks, South Asians, and other visible minorities have lower occupational status than the British and French, even adjusting for educational qualifications. In spite of their remarkable accomplishments in education and occupational attainment, visible minorities are generally disadvantaged in income. In this sense, we can say that visible minorities follow a different path of integration into Canadian society.

The second conclusion, which is closely related to the first, is that ethnic differences in socioeconomic status still exist in contemporary Canadian society. However, racial/ethnic minority groups are not necessarily disadvantaged in all the dimensions of socioeconomic stratification. Social inequality is primarily manifested in income inequalities. Italians and Portuguese have lower levels of educational and occupational achievements than the average of total population, yet they have relatively higher incomes than other groups. The average incomes of all the visible minorities remain significantly lower than for the British and average population. Compared with their relative position in educational attainment, the income achievements of the Chinese, South Asians, and other visible minorities are lower than would be expected. The income differences would be even larger if these three visible minorities had not attained higher educational levels than the average of total population.

In Canada, income differentials exist among many ethnic groups, with some of these differentials explained by variations in educational and occupational distributions. After adjusting for these factors, some ethnic groups, such as Italians, Poles, and Portuguese, are no longer in inferior positions. In contrast, most visible minorities receive less income return from educational and occupational achievements. The important question that remains to be answered is why some European groups gain relatively high incomes while visible minority groups do not. The collective capacity for economic mobilization within an ethnic community may be able to explain the success of Italians in Toronto, as suggested by Reitz (1990). However, that may not be the reason for more recent and smaller groups like Poles and Portuguese. For the majority of ethnic minorities, average incomes will depend on the conditions in the broader labour market. Therefore, income inequality on the basis of qualifications is most probably related to discrimination. All the visible minorities experience a certain amount of income inequality. This suggests that visibility has an additional effect on income inequality in Canadian society. In a sense, the disparate integration processes of non-visible and visible minorities are not only determined by group differences in some demographic factors such as immigration status and language, and by motivations as manifested in the improvement of education, but also probably by social inequality. It has been suggested that ethnic disparities have decreased continuously first in education, then in occupation over the last several decades in Canada. The existing ethnic income disparity, as a remaining "vestige of the elitist sponsorship that once drove the Canadian society in all socioeconomic elements," is believed to be similar to those in education and occupation two or three decades ago, and may decline over time (Herberg 1990: 218). However, our analyses show that while income equality has materialized in spite of educational differences for some European groups, it has not for visible minorities. Whether the increasing proportion of visible minorities and their longer stay in Canada will reduce income inequalities in the future is an important issue, and will continue to have implications for policy interventions.

REFERENCES

Balakrishnan, T.R. 1988 "Immigration and the changing ethnic mosaic of Canadian cities." Report for The Review of Demography and Its Implications for Economic and Social Policy. Ottawa: Health and Welfare Canada.

Beaujot, Roderic, K.G. Basavarajappa, and Ravi B.P. Verma 1988 *Income of Immigrants in Canada* Ottawa: Minister of Supply and Services Canada.

Beaujot, R. and Peter J. Rappak 1988 "The role of immigration in changing socioeconomic structures." Report for The Review of Demography and Its Implications for Economic and Social Policy. Ottawa: Health and Welfare Canada.

Blishen, Bernard R. 1970 "Social class and opportunity in Canada." *Canadian Review of Sociology and Anthropology* 7: 110–127.

Boyd, Monica 1992 "Gender, visible minority, and immigrant earnings inequality: reassessing an employment equity premise." In Victor Satzewich (ed.) *Deconstructing a Nation: Immigration, Multiculturalism and Racism in '90s Canada* Halifax: Fernwood.

Darroch, Gordon A. 1979 "Another look at ethnicity, stratification and social mobility in Canada." *Canadian Journal of Sociology* 4: 1–25.

Driedger, Leo 1989 *The Ethnic Factor: Identity in Diversity* McGraw Hill–Ryerson.

Elliott, Jean L. and Augie Fleras 1992 *Unequal Relations: An Introduction to Race and Ethnic Dynamics in Canada* Toronto: Prentice–Hall.

Greeley, Andrew M. 1976 "The ethnic miracle." *The Public Interest* 45: 20–36.

Herberg, Edward N. 1990 "The ethno–racial socioeconomic hierarchy in Canada: theory and analysis of the new vertical mosaic." *International Journal of Comparative Sociology* 31: 206–221.

Isajiw, Wsevolod W., Aysan Sever, and Leo Driedger 1993 "Ethnic identity and social mobility: a test of the 'drawback model.'" *Canadian Journal of Sociology* 18: 177–196.

Kalbach, Warren E. and Madeline A. Richard 1988 "Ethnic–religious identity, acculturation, and social and economic achievement of Canada's post–war minority populations." Report for The Review of Demography and Its Implications for Economic and Social Policy. Toronto: University of Toronto Population Research Laboratory.

Li, Peter S. 1988 *Ethnic Inequality on a Class Society* Toronto: Thompson.

Maxim, Paul 1992 "Immigrants, visible minorities, and Self–employment." *Demography* 29: 181–198.

Neidert, Lisa J. and Reynolds Farley 1985 "Assimilation in the United States: an analysis of ethnic and generation differences in status and achievement." *American Sociological Review* 50: 840–850.

Pineo, Peter C. and John Porter 1985 "Ethnic origin and occupational attainment." In Monica Boyd, John Goyder, and Frank E. Jones (eds.) *Ascription and Achievement: Studies in Mobility and Status Attainment in Canada* Ottawa: Carleton University Press.

Porter, John 1965 *The Vertical Mosaic* Toronto: University of Toronto Press.

Porter, John 1975 "Ethnic pluralism in Canadian perspective." In Nathan Glazer and Daniel Moynihan (eds.) *Ethnicity: Theory and Experience* Cambridge, MA: Harvard University Press.

Reitz, Jeffrey 1990 "Ethnic concentrations in labour markets and their implications for ethnic inequality." In Raymond Breton, Wsevolod Isajiw, Warren Kalbach, and Jeffrey Reitz, *Ethnic Identity and Equality* Toronto: University of Toronto Press.

Satzewich, Victor and Peter S. Li. 1987 "Immigrant labour in Canada: the cost and benefit of ethnic origin in the job market." *Canadian Journal of Sociology* 12:229–241.

Shamia, Shmuel 1992 "Ethnicity and educational achievement in Canada 1941–1981." *Canadian Ethnic Studies* 24: 43–51.

Tepperman, Lorne 1975 *Social Mobility in Canada* Toronto: University of Toronto Press.

Wiley, Norbert F. 1967 "The ethnic mobility trap and stratification theory." *Social Problems* 15: 147–69.

Chapter 19

TWO STUDIES OF RACIAL DISCRIMINATION IN EMPLOYMENT

Frances Henry

(Revised from the previous edition of this volume.)

INTRODUCTION

Until the publication of our report *Who Gets the Work?* (Henry and Ginzberg, 1985), efforts to demonstrate that there is racial discrimination in the Canadian employment arena have been limited to census data analysis, personal reports of victims of discrimination, and attitude studies. Each of these three types of research is limited in its capacity to prove that discrimination based on race is actually the cause of discrepancies in income and access to employment. Critics, skeptics, and racists have easily been able to doubt the presence of racial discrimination in view of weaknesses inherent in these indirect measures of discrimination. *Who Gets the Work?* sought to test directly for the presence or absence of discrimination in the Toronto labour market through the process of field testing—a quasi-experimental research technique.

For the first time in Canada, a study tested racial discrimination in employment by actually sending individuals, White and Black, to apply to advertised positions in order to find out if employers discriminate by preferring White to non-White employees. We believe we were successful in proving definitively that racial discrimination in Canada affected the employment opportunities of non-White Canadians. Whites had greater access to jobs than do equally qualified non-Whites.

Our study was guided by two questions. One, is there a difference in the number of job offers that White and Black applicants of similar experience and qualifications receive when they apply to the same jobs? And two, are there differences in the ways in which White and Black job applicants are treated when they apply for work? Both questions were tested by two procedures: *in-person testing and telephone testing.*

DEFINING DISCRIMINATION

Discrimination can take place at any point in the employment process. It may exist in such areas as recruitment, screening, selection, promotion, and termination. At the level of employee selection, for example, discrimination against non-Whites can take place when job applicants are called to the initial interview. To the extent that the employer's staff or the other employees themselves practise discrimination, either as a result of racial attitudes of the interviewer or because of instructions to screen out non-Whites as a matter of company policy, non-Whites will not get beyond the initial screening of job applicants. Similarly, in terms of promotion policies, non-Whites may be hired at lower levels, but their promotion to the upper ranks is effectively stopped by discriminatory barriers to mobility. For example, the employer may believe that the other employees will not accept a non-White as their supervisor.

Discrimination in employment can be intentional as well as inadvertent. Employers may not realize that their practices and policies have the effect of excluding non-Whites. The use of standard tests of personality or intelligence to select employees places certain minority groups at a disadvantage since they come from cultures other than the one for which the tests were designed. Recruiting through in-house, word-of-mouth techniques often excludes minority applicants since they do not hear about available positions. Requiring Canadian experience and education can effectively eliminate non-Whites, many of whom are immigrants, from job opportunities even though such experience is not necessary to successful job performance.

Thus, there are numerous types of discrimination and numerous ways in which discrimination can be carried out. Our study concentrated essentially on the entry point and/or the selection procedure. In this study, the dynamics of discrimination are studied as discriminatory practices occur, that is, when a job seeker either makes an inquiry on the phone or comes in person to be interviewed. It is at this point that the applicant can run into a prejudiced employer or "gatekeeper" who either presumes that non-Whites are not desired, or merely acts according to company policy. The telephone inquiry is particularly crucial at this stage since it is often the first approach made by the job applicant. An individual can be screened out; that is, told quickly and efficiently either that the job has already been filled or that the applicant's qualifications are not suitable. In all likelihood, the applicant will not know that he or she has been the victim of discrimination.

For the purposes of this study, we defined discrimination in employment as those practices or attitudes, willful or unintentional, that have the effect of limiting an individual's or a group's right to economic opportunities on the basis of irrelevant traits such as skin colour rather than on an evaluation of true abilities or potential.

IN-PERSON TESTING

In the in-person testing, two job applicants, matched with respect to age, sex, education, experience, physical appearance (dress), and personality, were sent to apply for the same advertised job. The only major difference between our applicants was their race—*one was White and the other Black*. We created four such teams: one junior male, one junior female, one senior male, and one senior female. The youngest teams applied for semiskilled and unskilled jobs such as gas station attendant, bus boy, waitress, and clerk and sales help in youth-oriented stores. The senior teams applied for positions in retail management, sales positions in prestigious stores, and waiting and hosting positions in expensive restaurants. The senior team members were, in fact, professional actors. Applying for middle-class type jobs meant that they would be required not only to present a sophisticated image but also to participate in a fairly demanding job interview. Professional actors, we believed, would be more convincing in playing the many roles required for this project. The résumés of the team members were carefully constructed to be as alike as possible. In order to further control possible biases, the staff of testers was changed several times so that no individual personality could account for the results.

The younger teams were composed of high-school and university students who would normally be applying for the same types of jobs that they applied for in the testing situation. Since we were not testing for sex discrimination and did not want this type of discrimination to account for any of our results, the male teams were sent to traditionally male jobs and the women went to jobs traditionally associated with women's work. In some types of jobs, for example waiter/waitress, both men and women were acceptable. Men and women were sent to such jobs but never to the same job. Each tester had a different résumé for the various types of positions that he or she was applying for, so each member of the senior female team, for example, carried several résumés, one for a secretary, another for a retail sales assistant, a third for a dental technician, etc. Each résumé contained the names of references supplied by business people and friends who had agreed to support our research. Our applicants could thus be checked out by a potential employer who could obtain a reference for the applicant. In actuality, only two employers ever called for references.

Each evening, a listing of jobs would be selected for the next day from among the classified advertisements. Some types of jobs were excluded such as those involving driving, for which licences could be checked. Jobs which required highly technical skills were also excluded.

The testers were instructed either to go to a certain address or to phone for an appointment. They used standard Canadian accents when phoning sincc we did not want them to be screened out over the phone. The testers arrived within approximately one half-hour of each other so that there would be little chance that a job had been legitimately filled. In most cases the Black applicant went first. After their interviews the testers completed a summary data sheet especially designed for this project in which they wrote down the details of their treatment and the kinds of information they had been given. Their résumés listed telephone numbers which were in actuality lines connected to the research office. Call-backs for second interviews or with offers of employment were received and recorded by the researchers. On-the-spot offers to the field testers were accepted by them. In the case of call-backs and on-the-spot offers, employers were phoned back, usually within an hour, and informed that another position had been accepted, in order to make sure that the employer could fill the vacancy as soon as possible

RESEARCH RESULTS: THE IN-PERSON TEST

In three-and-one-half months of field testing, the testers were able to apply for 201 jobs for a total of 402 individual applications.

For our purposes, racial discrimination in employment was tested in two ways. First, was an offer of employment made to one of the applicants, both applicants, or neither applicant? Second, during the interview, were there any differences in the treatment of the two applicants? The following tables present the numerical results.

Blacks received fewer job offers than Whites. Of a total of 37 valid job offers, 27 went to Whites, 9 to Blacks, and in one case

TABLE 19-1 Offer of a job versus no offer

	Number	%
Both offered job	10	5.0
White offered job; Black not	27	13.4
Black offered job; White not	9	4.5
No offer to either	155	77.1
Total	201	100.0

TABLE 19-2 Treatment of applicants

	Number of Cases
Treated the same	165
Treated differently	36

both were offered the job. There were an additional 10 cases in which both were offered jobs, but these were for commission sales which involved no cost to the employer. Our overall results therefore show that *offers to Whites outnumber offers to Blacks by a ratio of 3 to 1.*

We had thought that the nature of the job might influence whether Blacks or White would be hired. Only Whites received offers for managerial positions or jobs as waiters or waitresses or hosts and hostesses in the restaurant trade. A Black was offered a job in the kitchen when he had applied for a waiter's job!

As noted above, the second measure of discrimination was whether differential treatment had occurred during the interview. Table 19-2 presents the results.

Blacks and Whites were treated differently 36 times, and in all cases but one, the White applicant was preferred to the Black. The ways in which differential treatment took place provide a great deal of insight into the nature of discrimination and its subtleties.

Differences in treatment were sometimes very blatant, as the following examples show.

1. Mary, the young Black tester, applied for a sales position in a retail clothing store and was told that the job had already been taken. Sylvia, our White tester, arrived a half-hour later and was given an application form to fill in and told that she would be contacted if they were interested in her.
2. In a coffee shop, Mary was told that the job of cashier was taken. Sylvia walked in five minutes later and was offered the job on the spot.

   This pattern occurred five times. Another form of differential treatment was as follows: the Black was treated rudely or with hostility, whereas the White was treated politely. This occurred 15 times.
3. Paul, our White tester, applied for a job as a waiter. He was given an application form to fill out and an interview. He was told that he might be contacted in a week or so. Larry, the Black tester, was also given an application form and an interview. But as the Manager looked over Larry's résumé, he asked Larry if he "wouldn't rather work in the kitchen."

4. Applying for a gas station job, the White tester was told that there were no jobs at present, but that he could leave a résumé. The Black tester was told that there were no jobs, but when he asked if he could leave a résumé, he was sworn at: "Shit, I said no didn't I?"

Another form of differential treatment occurred when the wage offers to Blacks and Whites were different. There were two occasions in which the Black tester was offered less money than the White tester for the same job. On a few occasions, derogatory comments were made about Blacks in the presence of our White testers. The Blacks being referred to were our testers!

These results indicate that Black job seekers face not only discrimination in the sense of receiving fewer job offers than Whites, but also a considerable amount of negative and abusive treatment while job hunting. The psychological effects of such experiences became evident in the feelings expressed by the research staff. The Black staff felt rejected, and some doubted their own ability: "I was beginning to wonder what was wrong with me and why Jean [the White tester] was so much better than me."

In sum, the findings of the in-person test reveal that in 48 job contacts, or 23.8 percent of the cases, some form of discrimination against Blacks took place. These findings indicate that Blacks and Whites do not have the same access to employment. *Racial discrimination in employment, either in the form of clearly favouring a White over a Black, even though their résumés were equivalent, or in the form of treating a White applicant better than a Black, took place in almost one-quarter of all job contacts tested in this study.* When we examine the results of telephone testing, we see that this pattern of discrimination occurs again and, if anything, more clearly and strongly.

RESEARCH RESULTS: THE TELEPHONE TEST

We have all had the experience of calling for a job and being told that the job has been filled. We experienced a twinge of disappointment, but we rarely felt the need to ask ourselves seriously if we had been told the truth. Members of minority groups have good reason to question whether they have indeed been told the truth. Our study tested this by having callers' phone numbers listed in the classified employment section of the newspaper to present themselves as job applicants.

In total, 237 job numbers were phoned. Each job was called four times, once by someone with no discernible accent (apparently a White-majority Canadian), once by someone who had a Slavic or Italian accent, once by a Jamaican-accented caller and finally by a person with a Pakistani accent. Many different jobs were called, ranging from unskilled labour, secretarial, and service, to skilled trade, to managerial. To exclude sex discrimination, callers did not cross traditional sex-role categories. Men were of the same age, education, number of years of job experience, and so on for each type of job. Callers were "older" for jobs requiring more experience and maturity. A profile was provided for each of the callers for each type of job so that they had a secretarial profile, a managerial one, one for waitressing, and so on. Jobs to be called were selected from among those that had not appeared in the newspaper the previous day; they were all new jobs. Callers within each sex were given identical lists of jobs to call on the next day and were instructed to begin their calls from the top of the list and proceed in order down the list. All callers were to begin the calling at the same time so that the time span between callers would be minimized. All callers were instructed to use standard

English, full sentences, and correct grammar so that the lack of language would not be a discriminating factor against them.

In the telephone testing, discrimination was said to occur when one caller was told that the job had been filled while another caller was told that the job was still available. Discrimination was also said to take place when one caller-applicant with a certain set of qualifications was screened out and told that he or she did not qualify, although other callers with the same qualifications were told that they did qualify and were invited to apply. Another form of discrimination was identified as occurring when callers were treated differently from one another in that some and not others were screened to see if they had the experience the employer sought. It has been argued that screening some applicants and not others is not necessarily discriminatory. However, if there is no systematic discrimination present, then we would expect all racial or immigrant groups to be subject to the same proportion of screening.

Results of this procedure were that in 52 percent of all jobs called there was some form of discrimination present. Either one of our testers was told that the job was filled when another tester was told that the job was open, or one of our testers was treated differently in that he or she was screened while another was not.

There were nine instances in which our accented callers were told that they did not qualify for the job even though they presented the same experience and qualifications as the White-majority callers. Needless to say, the White callers were told by these same nine employers that they qualified and were invited to apply. In addition, the employers did not perceive the need to screen all of the four minority-accented callers to the same degree. Employers who treated callers differently, that is, the 123 employers who discriminated in some way, never screened non-accented callers. Italian- or Slavic-accented callers were screened 5 percent of the time and the two non-White minority callers received three times as much screening as the Whites, on between 15 percent and 20 percent of all their calls.

Minority-accented callers did not receive the same information about the status of the job as did Whites. Forty-eight percent of the jobs were closed to Blacks and 62 percent were closed to Pakistanis in that the employers told them that the job was filled when the non-accented caller was told that the job was available. Statistical analysis revealed that there were significant differences in the treatment and the type of information that Whites and non-Whites received about work. The Toronto employers discriminated against immigrants in general, but to a significantly greater degree against non-White immigrants.

The results of our telephone testing demonstrate that to secure 10 potential job interviews a White Canadian had to make about 11 to 12 calls. White immigrants had to make about 13 calls. Racial minorities had to work harder and longer since they had to make 18 calls to get 10 potential job interviews. Clearly there were differences in what Whites and non-Whites were being told over the phone about the availability of work. And, as noted in the in-person testing, discrimination did not end when a job interview was obtained.

A RATIO OF DISCRIMINATION

An Index of Discrimination was developed by combining the results of the in-person test and the telephone testing to demonstrate the degree of discrimination experienced by equally qualified persons prior to actual employment. On the phone, Blacks were told that the job was closed to them 20 percent of the time, whereas the job was closed to Whites only 5.5 percent of the time. In the in-person test, Blacks experienced discrimination in some form in 18.3 percent of their job contacts. If these figures are translated into the actual chances of having success in the job search, they become even more revealing. Blacks have a 64 percent chance of getting through a telephone screening, which means that they can secure 13 interviews out of 20 calls. But their chances of actually getting a job *after* an interview are only about 1 in 20. White applicants, on the other hand, are able to pass through screening very successfully, 87 percent of the time. They can achieve an interview in 17 out of 20 calls. Out of these 17 interviews they manage to receive three offers of employment. *The overall Index of Discrimination is therefore 3 to 1.* Whites have three job prospects to every one that Blacks have.

AFTERMATH OF THE STUDY

Who Gets the Work? was one of those relatively rare social science studies which actually had a significant impact on public policy initiatives. It also generated considerable controversy while at the same time providing communities of colour and other disadvantaged groups with the empirical data needed to validate their grievances. Over the dozen or so years since its publication, it has remained one of the most often cited studies in the literature on racism, ethnicity, multiculturalism, and pluralism in Canadian society. Its citations have not, however, been limited to academic materials, since it has also been frequently referred to by politicians in the federal as well as several provincial parliaments. In its first few years, it was cited at least half a dozen times in the federal parliament alone, and I have since lost count of its continuing usefulness in these political arenas.

Why did this one study generate so much interest, and why does it still continue to resonate? The answer lies in the fact that it was the first, and is still among only a small handful of studies, which actually document empirically what many people of colour, community organizations, anti-racist groups, human rights advocates, and individual grievers to human rights commissions and others have complained about for years—racial discrimination in employment. Access to employment is a fundamental right in democratic societies, but one which is at times constrained or influenced by irrelevant social factors such as racism, sexism, and the many other factors which severely limit the life chances of people in complex societies. While complaints of racial discrimination by individuals and ethno-racial groups could easily be dismissed because they provide merely "anecdotal" evidence, *Who Gets the Work?*, using a quasi-experimental methodology was able to provide the all-important "numbers" which, for the first time, could be used to validate the day-to-day experiences of people of colour.

Moreover, it provided useful information not only for individual grievers but also for community groups and especially for lobby groups, such as the many employment equity organizations and committees which were created in the public and private sectors throughout the eighties and early nineties in all parts of Canada.

Perhaps its most important contribution to policy, however, lies in its impact on legislation. It was published shortly after Abella's (1984) federally commissioned report on Employment Equity was released. One of that report's key recommendations was employment equity legislation, and a committee of the Federal Parliament was in the process of preparing that legislation when the results of *Who Gets the Work?* were published. The disadvantaged groups covered by the employment equity legislation were to be women, Aboriginals, and people with disabilities. While the Abella report had also included people of colour as a target group, most politicians at the time believed that their relatively small numbers did not warrant inclusion in the legislation. It was when *Who Gets the Work?* hit the news media and was very widely disseminated throughout the country that the decision to include "visible minorities" in the Federal Employment Equity legislation was made.[1]

A RESTUDY

Further evidence of the important of *Who Gets the Work?* in the policy arena is provided by the fact that a restudy was commissioned. In the late eighties, the Federal governments asked the Economic Council of Canada to prepare a report on the benefits and disadvantages of its immigrant policies.[2] Specifically, it wanted to find out if the numerical levels from the initial study needed adjustment; it was particularly interested in the question of the social integration of immigrants, and especially immigrants of colour. Data on these issues were, and still are, hard to come by in Canada. Accordingly, the Council contracted me to conduct a restudy (see Economic Council, 1991, p. 30ff).

The restudy followed the same research procedure as in the earlier study, except that the employers contacted were, of course, different. The same kinds of jobs were used in the study. A different set of students and actors was employed as job seekers, but they were subjected to exactly the same training and preparation as those who participated in the original study.

What was allegedly distinctive about the restudy were the results of the in-person test; 20 Blacks were offered jobs as compared to 18 Whites. The telephone survey results were almost exactly similar to those of the earlier study.

The Economic Council reported on the results of the restudy as follows: "a dramatic change in that no discrimination was discernable in the in-person job offers—an outcome that cannot be accounted for by the tight labour market conditions in 1989 since the employers had the option of hiring Whites." (Economic Council, 1991, p. 30). While acknowledging that racism had not vanished from the job market, the report further stated that "our results do point to a decreasing level of prejudice in Toronto as the visible minority population grows. This reinforces the Council's broad finding that the tolerance of Canadians for immigration generally and for visible minorities in particular is, in fact, increasing" (Economic Council, 1991, p. 31).

I took great exception to the Council's interpretation of the restudy's results since the original report submitted to them provided evidence that the labour market in the late eighties had markedly tightened, and that employers seeking qualified employees were more likely to overlook the factor of race when presented with a competent applicant. Although the Council wanted to publish the report as a research monograph, I refused permission since I felt that they had misinterpreted the results in their monograph.[3]

Subsequently, Reitz and Breton (1994, p. 84) conducted a further analysis of the results in order to counter the Council's interpretation. The research procedure clearly specified that the Black job seekers were to apply for all the jobs before the White applicants. In half the cases in which the Black was given an offer, it was made "on the spot," that is, before the White even had a chance to apply. When Reitz and Breton removed those cases from the total sample "the results show that more job offers were made to Whites than to Blacks" (1994, p. 84). They conclude that the research procedure may have given the Black applicant an advantage in a tight labour market, thereby offsetting employer bias. Thus, the results of the restudy are basically the same as those of the earlier study, and cannot be taken as evidence of a decrease in racial prejudice or an increase in the tolerance for ethno-racial minorities.

INTERNATIONAL COMPARISONS

My colleagues and I did not invent this quasi-experimental technique of testing for racial discrimination in employment. It had already been successfully used in a study in England conducted in the late seventies that had produced results similar to those obtained in Canada (Smith, 1977; see also Reitz, 1988). As well, studies were conducted in the U.S. using the same methodology in the early nineties to counteract the mythical belief that the U.S. is "well on the way to becoming a color-blind society" (Reitz and Breton, 1994, p. 85). In the studies conducted by Turner, Fix and Struyk (1991) in both Washington and Chicago in the 1990s, it was found that Whites also received three times as many job offers as Blacks and they were also three times as likely to be invited for a job interview.

CONCLUSION

The results of our studies clearly indicate that there is very substantial racial discrimination affecting the ability of members of racial minorities to find employment, even when they are well qualified and eager to find work. The studies examined discrimination only at the very early stages, or entry level, of the employment process. Once an applicant is employed, discrimination can still affect opportunities for advancement, job retention, and level of earnings, to say nothing of the quality of work and relationships with co-workers.

The findings also support the results of other types of studies done in Canada. We know that indirect measures of discrimination, such as those which reveal income disparities between Whites and others, all come to similar conclusions: people of colour in this country are discriminated against.

Our studies suggest that discrimination is more widespread than has been thought. Employment discrimination appears not to be the result of a few bigoted employers; there seems to be systematic bias against hiring people of colour. The systemic nature of the discrimination implies that attempting to change the behaviour or the attitudes of individual discriminators will not address the problem. What is required is redress at the system level in order to remove the barriers to the employment of people of colour so that all Canadians, regardless of colour, can achieve to their full potential.

The methodology used in our studies is very useful in providing the quantitative data on racial discrimination which appear to be required for policy decision-making. Thus, studies like *Who Gets the Work?* should be systematically replicated every few years both in the employment area and other areas (such as housing) where discrimination may occur. This would allow us to monitor changing public attitudes toward people of colour.

NOTES

1. They were also subsequently included in the employment equity legislation enacted in the province of Ontario and since rescinded by the present government.
2. The Council has since been disbanded.

3. The complete restudy has therefore never been published.

REFERENCES

Abella, Judge Rosalie Silberman 1984 *Equity in Employment: A Royal Commission Report* Ottawa: Minister of Supply and Services.

Economic Council of Canada 1991 *New Faces in the Crowd: Economic and Social Impacts of Immigration* Ottawa: Ministry of Supply and Services.

Henry, Frances and Effie Ginzberg 1985 *Who Gets the Work? A Test of Racial Discrimination in Employment* Toronto: Urban Alliance on Race Relations and the Social Planning Council of Toronto.

Reitz, Jeffrey G. 1988 "Less racial discrimination in Canada, or simply less racial conflict? Implications of comparisons with Britain." *Canadian Public Policy*, 14, 4, 424–41.

Reitz, Jeffrey G. and Raymond Breton 1994 *The Illusion of Difference: Realities of Ethnicity in Canada and the United States* Toronto: C.D. Howe Institute.

Smith, David J. 1977 *Racial Discrimination in Britain: The PEP Report* Hammondsworth: Penguin Books.

Turner, Margery Austin, Michael Fox and Raymond J. Struyk 1991 *Opportunities Denied, Opportunities Diminished: Discrimination in Hiring* Washington: Urban Renewal Project.

Chapter 20

FIRST NATIONS, INEQUALITY, AND THE LEGACY OF COLONIALISM

Charles R. Menzies

(An original chapter written for this volume.)

INTRODUCTION

> ... it would not be accurate to assume that even pre-contact existence in the territory was in the least bit idyllic. The plaintiffs' ancestors had no written language, no horses or wheeled vehicles, slavery and starvation was not uncommon, wars with neighbouring peoples were common, and there is no doubt, to quote Hobbes, that Aboriginal life in the territory was, at best, "nasty, brutish and short."
>
> Chief Justice, BC Supreme Court Allan McEachern, Delgamuukw: Reasons for Judgment (1991)

> Racism is racism, and racism stings. All the good intentions in the world do not take away the sting and do not take away the pain.
>
> Patricia Monture-Angus, Thunder in My Soul (1995)

First Nations' response to Justice Allan McEachern's decision (quoted above) was angry and tearful. For the First Nations people living in the Gitksan and Wet'suwet'en Territories, the four-year-long court case was about the right to live as they and their ancestors had for millennium upon millennium. From the point of view of the governments of British Columbia and Canada, a large tract of land full of crucial economic resources was at stake and had to be defended. The Gitksan and Wet'suwet'en people, elders, and chiefs had placed their trust in an institution they saw as foreign and had opened their box of stories and experience to a court they saw as a foreign institution. In return, they felt that they had been repaid with insult and disdain. While McEachern's decision stands out from recent court rulings and was to a certain extent overturned in appeal,[1] his basic interpretations of First Nations people as having existed without 'real' social organization or culture until the arrival of Europeans in the Americas is itself a product of the colonial encounter.

Canada is built upon a colonial system in which Aboriginal lands have been expropriated, Aboriginal institutions banned, and Aboriginal peoples relegated to marginal sectors of the mainstream economy. Put simply:

> Colonialism involves a relationship which leaves one side dependent on the other to define the world. At the individual level, colonialism involves a situation in which one individual is forced to relate to another on terms unilaterally defined by the other (McCaskill, 1983:289).

Five hundred years of European settlement in the Americas is painfully and tragically represented in standard indices of social pathologies such as high rates of suicide, un- and under-employment, and substance abuse. This is not to deny impressive and important examples of successful First Nations people. Rather, it is important to underline the fact that the structure of social inequality experienced by First Nations people is directly linked to the processes of colonialism and government policies directed at undermining Aboriginal institutions and social organization. In this chapter I describe the contemporary structure of inequality, outline the general process of colonialization and expropriation of First Peoples in Canada, and suggest strategies for improving the current situation.

STORIES TO CRY OVER

Social inequality cannot simply be captured in a set of cold, apparently objective numbers (although you will see some below). Think of the everyday stories we tell among friends, in school, or at work. These stories form the basis of our regular communication. They are important sources of knowledge and cultural codes. For the social scientist, these stories are also important places to search out experiences and expressions of inequality. Who is telling the story? Where is it being told? Who is excluded from the audience? We recognize that some stories are not public, that they are in some sense restricted to special places or social settings.

An important part of my writing details the semi-private stories of Euro-Canadian men and the role their storytelling plays in the maintenance of colonial structures.[2] These are emotionally wrenching stories. While one may wish to deny or ignore them, it is more important to listen to these stories. How does it feel to be the target, the butt of the joke, the object of ridicule? A cousin told me how, some years after I had given her a copy of Stories From Home (Menzies, 1994), that the stories of hate I recounted made her cry.

"I know these men, or men just like them. My husband has worked alongside of them. We raised our children in the same community as them. To hear how they talk about us [First Nations people] in your paper still makes me cry," she said. The telling of these stories is important to my cousin, even though they are painful to hear. They reveal more than any graph the everyday experience of racism and inequality. Here is a version of a story I first heard while sitting on the deck of a fishing boat one summer afternoon in a northern BC port.

A small gathering of men were relaxing in the quiet time between the end of work and heading up town or home for the night. Ed, a crewmember from an adjacent boat, joined our circle and began to talk about his exploits of the previous evening. He had spent most of his time participating in a 20th year high school reunion—by all accounts it had been a smashing success.

Ed is a respected member of the local fishing community,[3] an accomplished storyteller, and an effective public speaker (the public here being a group of predominantly Euro-Canadian fishermen). I began to tune out—I've heard this story before, at least versions of it—drink, party, and drink ... . I had almost decided to leave when Ed's story took an unexpected turn.

"Jim had all this paint up at his place, so we loaded it into my car and drove back downtown. Parked off third, took a look for the cops and then went to it."

"Doing what?" I asked.

"Hey? What do you think we were doing?"

"Painting the town red," somebody said to a chorus of laughs.

"No," said Ed, "we were painting the town white. Yeah, we painted a bloody white cross-walk from the Belmont [Hotel] right into the Empress. Help all those drunken Indians make it across the street."

"I wonder'd who did that when I came down to the boat this morning," I said. "But why is it so jagged? It's crooked."

"That's the beauty of it," said Ed. "It's designed just right. Your Indian stumbles out of the bar, into the street. 'Hey look, he says, 'a cross walk.' And he's right over into the other bar. First class."

The irony of Ed's own drunkenness seemed to have escaped him. He plays up popular explanations of the so-called "Indian Problem." Yet his story is only one example in a multitude of narratives of colonialism in which the disparate threads of racial superiority and intolerance are wound. Ed's story is part of the day-to-day experience of social inequality felt by people of Aboriginal descent.

THE CONTEMPORARY STRUCTURE OF INEQUALITY

Social scientists typically measure inequality using social indicators such as income level, rate of participation in employment and education, and quality of life measures such as health and housing. To demonstrate inequality objectively, it is necessary to show that significant differences between groups of people do in fact exist. In this section, statistics concerning income, health, and justice are presented. You will notice that although there are some very successful First Nations' individuals (in business, entertainment, politics), many are relatively impoverished when compared with mainstream Canadian society.

Income

Data reported by Statistics Canada (1995) show significant discrepancies between income levels of First Nations' people and those of other Canadians. In 1991, for example, the average income for First Nations' people was 70% of that for other Canadians. In terms of average family income, First Nations' families earned about half the national average ($21 800 versus $38 000). Fully two-thirds of First Nations' people earned less than $20 000 per year compared with about 50% of all other Canadians. On the upper end of the income scale, just under 20% of First Nations people earned more than $30 000 compared with one-third of other Canadians. The discrepancy widens further as income levels increase.

In examining income data one must consider more than just how much people earn. The source of income also provides important information about the structure of inequality. For the majority of Canadians over the age of 15 (Aboriginal and non-Aboriginal), earned income is the major source of income. However, Aboriginal people (especially those living on-reserve) receive a higher portion of their income in the form of government transfers. Seventy-eight percent of all Canadians derive their income from employment. However, only 11% of non-Aboriginal Canadians receive the bulk of their income in the form of government transfers compared to 18% of Aboriginal people. For on-reserve populations, the figures show 60% of income coming from employment and 38% from government transfers.

Health

Although the basic health of First Nations people has improved over the last several decades, significant differences remain between the health of Aboriginal people and members of mainstream Canadian society (Statistics Canada, 1995). Illnesses resulting from poverty, overcrowding, and poor housing have led to chronic and acute respiratory diseases, which take a heavy toll among Aboriginal people. The standardized death rate for the Aboriginal population is more than double that of the general population (15.9 versus 6.6 deaths per 1000 population). The average age of death is more than 20 years below that of the average for non-Aboriginal Canadians. The rate of infant mortality among First Nations, though improved, is still more than twice the Canadian average (17.5 versus 7.9 per 1000). More than 33% of all Aboriginal deaths are related to violence (compared with 8% in mainstream society). These statistics highlight a significant discrepancy between non-Aboriginal and Aboriginal Canadians.

The Law

The interaction between First Nations people and Canadian law occurs at a collective and individual level. Collectively, particular social institutions have been banned or restricted (such as the feast or potlatch system on the Northwest Coast). The right to vote in federal elections was denied to all status Indians until 1960. Between 1927 and 1951 activity related to land claims (e.g., protesting) was illegal (Tennant 1990, Cole and Chaikin 1990). And, many Aboriginal children were forcibly removed from their home communities and placed in residential schools (Haig-Brown 1988). The impact of these assimilationist policies on First Nations' individuals is clearly seen in the overrepresentation of First Nations' people in the criminal justice system.

As of 1996, Aboriginal people accounted for slightly less than 3% of the total Canadian population. However, they accounted for 12% of federal and 20% of provincial admissions to prison. In western Canada, the percentage of new admissions to prison who are Aboriginal, ranged between 16 and 69% (Ponting and Kiely 1997:154-155). The ratio of Aboriginal people incarcerated in Canadian jails has been steadily increasing over the course of the 20th century. In Saskatchewan, for example, the percentage of the prison population of Aboriginal descent has gone from 5 percent in the 1920s to over 55% in the 1990s (Monture-Angus, 1996:341). In Manitoba, the percentage of Aboriginal prisoners has doubled between 1965 and 1989 (from 22 percent to 40% of the prison population).

Patricia Monture-Angus highlights an important difficulty with this statistical picture: "The overrepresentation of Aboriginal people in the system of Canadian criminal justice is all too often seen as an Aboriginal problem (that is, a problem with Aboriginal people (1996:335)." In a careful examination of all aspects of the Canadian criminal justice system, Ponting and Kiely conclude that "each stage of the judicial process is punctuated with a disproportionate number of Aboriginal people. [Their data] suggest that Aboriginal people are victims of a discriminatory criminal justice system" (1997:155).

EXPLAINING INEQUALITIES: COLONIALISM'S LEGACY

The socio-economic context of First Nations' people is one that is clearly disadvantaged in comparison to mainstream society. Popular explanations of this imbalance of power and resources typically blame the victim. Such explanations fail to take into account the rich, vibrant way of life which pre-existed European arrival in the Americas, or the many examples of individual and community success (more on this below). By focusing on individuals, popular explanations deny the overpowering dominance of European traditions and economic processes that were forced upon Aboriginal peoples. An important and powerful set of explanations roots social inequality in the historical and cultural phenomena of colonialism, the expropriation of First Nations' land and resources, and government policies designed to undermine Aboriginal social institutions.

Colonial History: A Northwest Coast Illustration

On the northwest coast of British Columbia, people of European and First Nations descent have come together and separated over the years as the result of the historical movement of capital. Initial contact revolved around the exchange of commodities such as fur, iron, beads, or other trade goods. As European settlement extended into First Nations' territories, marriages between Euro-Canadian businessmen and First Nations' women became increasingly common. According to several commentators, these early marriages followed customary First Nations' practices and were ostensibly designed to facilitate trade and cooperation between groups (Fisher 1977).

The extension of industrial capitalism into this region fundamentally altered the basis for alliance. No longer valued as trading partners, First Nations were slotted into the developing resource economy as a subordinate part of the growing industrial labour force in which workers were segregated by race and gender. Union organizers and social activists have attempted, with little success, to overcome these structural divisions.

In British Columbia, a maritime-based fur trade structured the early contacts between Europeans and First Nations (1774-1858). In this period a European-based mercantile capitalism interacted with an indigenous kin-ordered mode of production,[4] in which the control over labour power and the production of trade goods remained under the control of the native American traders who were for the most part "chiefs." They "mobilized their followers and personal contacts to deliver ... otter skins, and [their] power grew concomitantly with the development of the trade" (Wolf 1982:185). The merging of these two modes of production—one based on the family and one based on European capitalism—produced new wealth and intense inflation for both First Nations and Europeans (Fisher 1977:18-20, Codere 1961:443-467, Wolf 1982:186-192). However, as Europeans prospered from this fur trade and developed industrial enterprises, First Nations' people lost control over trade and were displaced by a settler-based industrial capitalism.

Vancouver Island, and British Columbia more generally, began the change from colonies in which Europeans exploited indigenous labour power to colonies of settlement in the 1850s following the discovery of gold in the interior of the province. With the exception of the fishing industry, First Nations' labour power "was only of marginal significance in the economic concerns of the Europeans" (Fisher 1977:96, 109). Mining, forestry, and fishing supplanted the fur trade and became the backbone of British Columbia's economy.

By the mid-1880s indigenous control of commercially valuable land and resources was almost completely destroyed through a variety of legal (and extra-legal) measures introduced by Canada and the provinces (McDonald 1994). One of the most insidious changes was the creation of the legal category of "food fishing" in the 1880s which prohibited Aboriginal fishers from catching fish without a permit from the federal government (Newell 1993). At the same time First Nations' people were integrated "into virtually every major resource industry in [British Columbia] as workers and owner-operators" (Knight 1996:10).

Alliances between First Nations and non-Aboriginal resource workers have played a major role in shaping British Columbia's union movement, especially in the fishing industry. Although union organizers have attempted to include them in pan-racial organizations, First Nations' workers ultimately found themselves in conflict with many of their Euro-Canadian co-workers. The major point of contention between non-Aboriginal and First Nations' resource workers has been the issue of land claims. Despite their common confrontation with capital as workers, non-Aboriginal workers' associations have not been able to develop a united policy on redressing the expropriation of First Nations' territories or Euro-centric attacks against First Nations' social institutions. While unions have been successful in addressing some aspects of First Nations' experiences as workers, they seemed incapable of effectively confronting and overcoming the racism and segregation of 20th century industrial society.

Assimilation and Government Policies

Colonialism is not simply an economic process. It also involves social policy and regulation. In Canada, the underlying premise of most 20th century social policies directed at Aboriginal people has been assimilation, and the central instrument of assimilationist policy was the residential school. "By taking children away from the old ways and 'civilizing' them into European ways, so the argument ran, 'the Indian problem' would be solved" (Barman, 1996:273). However, residential schools did not fulfill their stated goals. Instead, they "served as vehicles for marginalizing generations of young men and women from the Canadian mainstream and from home environments" (Barmen, 1996:273).

In the early 1900s, attempts were also made to assimilate mobile Aboriginal people by settling them into agricultural communities. From the government point of view, forcing nomadic First Nations' people into settlements would allow other instruments of assimilation, such as local government, church, and school, to be more easily brought into effect. Settlement also freed up large tracts of land which could then be developed by non-Aboriginal people.

SUCCESS STORIES

The story of First Nations is not all social pathology and economic disadvantage. First Nations' people have maintained a strong sense of their social identity and their place within their traditional territories. On the northwest coast of Canada, for example, First Nations' cultural institutions have been maintained despite concerted attacks from missionaries, government offices, and economic interests to dislodge them. The Nisga'a, Tsimshian, Gitksan, and Haida in north-coastal British Columbia have persisted in asserting their Aboriginal rights and title from the moment Europeans first arrived to occupy their land.

Examples of political organization are not restricted to British Columbia. The James Bay Cree, for example, won an important battle against the government of Quebec which guaranteed them their homeland. The Native Women's Association of Canada fought for a redress of sexual discrimination under the Indian Act and played an important role in the passage of Bill C-31 which reinstated status to First Nations' women (and their children) who had married non-Aboriginals (Frideres 1998).

The Calder case, named after Frank Calder (an important Nisga'a leader and former member of the BC legislature for the New Democratic Party), began the legal process in British Columbia which led the way to the important 1995 Agreement in Principle between the Nisga'a, Canada, and British Columbia. Throughout the 1980s, the Gitksan and Wet'suwet'en people waged a strategic struggle for the recognition of their aboriginal rights, a struggle which included tactical blockades, legal actions, and economic restraints. Taken together, the concerted political action of First Nations' people has forced Canada and non-Aboriginal Canadians to take notice (as witnessed, for example, by the apology to First Peoples in January 1998 by the federal government of Canada).

STRATEGIES FOR THE FUTURE

In *What is the Indian Problem?*, Noel Dyck cogently argues that "the only way to rectify the ravages that Indian bands have suffered is to stop looking for 'experts' and 'masterplans' and to refuse to accept the presumption that Indians do not know what is in their best interests" (1991:162). Mainstream Canadian society has to accept its collective responsibility for the legacy of colonialism. An important first step is to accelerate the process of treaty negotiations and finally to dismantle the colonial apparatus of the Canadian state.

Self-determination is not a panacea for all the past wrongs. It is, however, an important place to start. But, for self-determination to have any meaningful remedial effect on the experience of First Nations' social inequality, it must be built upon a solid economic and resource base.

The 1997 Supreme Court of Canada ruling on the Delgamuukw case (see opening quote) lays the basis for a fundamental change in Canadian law that could vastly improve the economic situation of First Nations. The court found that Aboriginal people have a right to fair compensation for lands expropriated by the Canadian state, that they have a right to use their traditional lands as they see fit, and that their oral traditions should be accorded the same evidentiary weight as written sources in cases concerning aboriginal rights and title. This decision may well usher in a new era of economic and political cooperation between First Nations and the non-Aboriginal peoples of Canada. At the very least, it can be read as the beginning of a process of national reconciliation in which mainstream Canada finally accepts its complicity in the process of colonialism.

NOTES

1. In 1997, the Supreme Court of Canada decided that aboriginal rights have not been extinguished and that McEachern's decision was flawed because he did not accept the Gitksan and Wet'suwet'en adaawk (oral history).
2. See for example: Menzies 1994, 1997.
3. The physical location of this fishing community is not specifically relevant to the main issue of this chapter. Nor does this one man's storytelling necessarily reflect widespread opinion within the larger community.
4. The kin-ordered mode of production is one in which access to and control of labour power is mediated by relations of kinship. For an elaboration of this concept see Wolf (1982:88-96).

REFERENCES

Barman, Jean 1996 "Aboriginal education at the crossroads: the legacy of residential schools and the way ahead." In David Alan Long and Olive Patricia Dickason (eds.) *Visions of the Heart: Canadian Aboriginal Issues* Toronto: Harcourt Brace and Company, pp. 271–303.

Codere, Helen 1961 *Fighting with Property: A Study of Kwakuitl Potlatching and Warfare 1729–1930* American Ethnological Society Monograph #18, New York: J.J. Augustin.

Cole, Douglas and Ira Chaikin 1990 *An Iron Hand Upon the People* Vancouver: Douglas & McIntyre Ltd.

Dyck, Noel 1991 *What is the Indian Problem? Tutelage and Resistance in Canadian Indian Administration* St. John's, NFLD: ISER, Memorial University of NFLD

Fisher, Robin 1977 *Contact and Conflict: Indian-European Relations in British Columbia, 1774–1890* Vancouver: University of British Columbia Press.

Frideres, James S. 1998 *Aboriginal Peoples in Canada: Contemporary Conflicts* (5th ed.) Scarborough, Ontario: Prentice Hall Allyn and Bacon Canada.

Knight, Rolf 1996 *Indians at Work* (2nd ed.) Vancouver: New Star Books.

McCaskill, D. 1983 "The Urbanization of Indians in Winnipeg, Toronto, Edmonton, and Vancouver: a comparative analysis." *Culture*, 1:82–89.

McDonald, James A 1994 "Social change and the creation of underdevelopment: a northwest coast case." *American Ethnologist* Vol. 21(1):152–175.

McEachern, Justice Allen 1991 *Delgamuukw: Reasons for Judgment* B.C. Supreme Court.

Menzies, Charles R. 1994 "Stories from home: First Nations, land claims, and Euro-Canadians." *American Ethnologist* Vol. 21(4):776–791.

Menzies, Charles R. 1997 "Indian or White? racial identities in the British Columbian fishing industry." In Anthony Marcus (ed.) *Anthropology for a Small Planet: Culture and Community in a Global Environment* St. James, New York: Brandywine Press, pp: 110–123.

Monture-Angus, Patricia 1995 *Thunder in My Soul: A Mohawk Woman Speaks* Halifax: Fernwood Publishing.

Monture-Angus, Patricia 1996 "Lessons in decolonization: Aboriginal overrepresentation in Canadian criminal justice." In David Alan Long and Olive Patricia Dickason (eds.) *Visions of the Heart: Canadian Aboriginal Issues* Toronto: Harcourt Brace and Company, pp. 335–354.

Newell, Diane 1993 *Tangled Webs of History: Indians and the Law in Canada's Pacific Coast Fisheries* Toronto: University of Toronto Press

Ponting, J. Rick and Jerilynn Kiely 1997 "Disempowerment: 'justice', racism, and public opinion." In J. Rick Ponting (ed.) *First Nations in Canada: Perspectives on Opportunity, Empowerment, and Self-Determination* Toronto: McGraw-Hill Ryerson Ltd., pp. 152–192.

Statistics Canada 1995 *Profile of Canada's Aboriginal Populations* Ottawa: Statistics Canada.

Tennant, Paul 1990 *Aboriginal Peoples and Politics: The Indian Land Question in British Columbia, 1849–1989* Vancouver: UBC Press.

Wolf, Eric R. 1997 *Europe and the People Without History* (2nd ed.) Berkeley: University of California Press.

FOR FURTHER REFERENCE: ETHNICITY, RACE, AND ANCESTRY

Anderson, Kay J. 1991 *Vancouver's Chinatown* Montreal and Kingston: McGill-Queen's University Press. A case study, including analyses of public documents and official records from three levels of government, on racial discourse in Vancouver's Chinese quarters, 1975-1980.

Breton, Raymond, Wserolod W. Isajiw, Warren E. Kalbach, and Jeffrey G. Reitz 1990 *Ethnic Identity and Equality: Varieties of Experiences in a Canadian City* Toronto: University of Toronto Press. Studies of ethnic inequality and the persistence of ethnic culture in Toronto. Special attention is given to the topics of ethnic identity retention, residential segregation, occupational and labour market concentrations, and political organization.

Driedger, Leo (ed.) 1987 *Ethnic Canada: Identities and Inequalities* Toronto: Copp Clark Pitman. This collection of 21 articles presents a good overview of issues of ethnic inequality, including: the social standing of ethnic and racial groupings, ethnicity and collective rights, ethnic stereotypes, discrimination, and affirmative action.

Elliott, Jean Leonard and Augie Fleras 1996 *Unequal Relations* Scarborough, Ontario: Prentice Hall Canada. An introduction to patterns of racial and ethnic group inequalities and racial/ethnic group relations in Canada.

Fleras, Augie and Jean Leonard Elliott 1992 *The Nations Within* Toronto: Oxford University Press. This volume compares the patterns of "aboriginal-state relations" in Canada, the United States, and New Zealand.

Henry, Frances, Carol Tatom, Winston Mattis, and Tim Rees 1995 *The Colour of Democracy: Racism in Canadian Society* Toronto: Harcourt Brace. An overview of racist ideology and practice in Canada, including specific chapters related to separate institutional spheres (e.g., education, law).

Li, Peter S. 1988 *Ethnic Inequality in a Class Society* Toronto: Wall and Thompson. An introductory-level analysis of ethnic-group differences in attainment of education and income in Canada.

Pal, Leslie A. 1993 *Interests of State: The Politics of Language, Multiculturalism and Feminism in Canada* Montreal: McGill-Queen's University Press. This book covers the history, since 1900, of various groups, mostly funded by the Department of Secretary of State, that have been active in the areas of language, multiculturalism, and gender relations. An analysis of public policy initiatives by these groups and their power struggles with various organizations is included.

Ponting, Rick, (ed.) 1997 *First Nations in Canada: Perspectives on Opportunity, Empowerment, and Self-Determination* Toronto: McGraw-Hill Ryerson. An overview of many of the First Nations' issues confronting all Canadians. Contributors bring a variety of perspectives to the issues.

Reitz, Jeffrey and Raymond Breton 1994 *The Illusion of Difference: Realities of Ethnicity in Canada and the United States* Toronto: C.D. Howe Institute. A comparative assessment of ethnicity as understood in both Canada and the United States.

Warry, Wayne 1998 *Unfinished Dreams: Community Healing and the Reality of Aboriginal Self Government* Toronto: University of Toronto Press. Drawing on research among Anishnanbe communities and material from the Royal Commission on Aboriginal Peoples, this volume explores the political and social processes required for a successful move to self-government.

AGE

Chapter 21

AGE-BASED INEQUALITIES IN CANADIAN SOCIETY

Neil Guppy, Jim Curtis, and Ed Grabb

(An original paper revised from an earlier edition of this volume. Our thanks to Valerie Bednarski and Martha Foschi for their constructive comments on an earlier version of this article.)

INTRODUCTION

Age defines many of the rights and privileges people experience. For instance, obtaining a driver's licence before age sixteen is impossible, and most car rental firms will not lease a vehicle to anyone under twenty-one. As another example, children cannot begin formal public schooling before age five, but once enrolled in school, attendance is mandatory until age sixteen.

Age also shapes certain aspects of people's working lives. Provincial wage laws often contain special clauses allowing employers to pay lower *minimum* wages to young workers than to adults. At age sixty-five, many employees are required to retire. Both minimum wage provisions and mandatory retirement may seem unfair, if we consider that one or two years of age makes little difference to how effectively most people can perform at work. However, just as with the right to drive or go to school, age is used as an automatic trigger affecting both the wages we receive and our date of retirement.

In these examples age is used as an inflexible criterion for making decisions about what we can or cannot do. This process, often called "age-grading," can seem very unfair. Determining access to rights and privileges solely based on age, despite individual merit or ability, runs strongly against the premise of equal opportunity and merit-based decision making. It is a huge assumption to use chronological age to fix a date in our lives at which point we can (or cannot) be counted on to act reliably or responsibly. This presumption applies to a host of formal rights, ranging from voting or running for public office, through to serving in the armed forces or drinking alcoholic beverages.

Sometimes age can be a barrier to rights and privileges, not so much by law but through social custom. In the workplace, for example, mere seniority often takes precedence over performance or merit in determining pay, layoffs, or promotions. Less formally, such activities as leaving home, having children, or investing in retirement savings plans may be constrained by age. This constraint occurs because people come to believe that these and other behaviours typically *should* take place at certain stages in the life course, but not at others.

Whether resulting from legal regulation or social norms, such age-based delineations of human behaviour are primarily social creations. In other words, while aging can be partly understood as a physiological process, it is also a social process. Age, in this latter sense, is used as a socially constructed criterion for classifying and ranking people, a process with significant implications for generating and sustaining patterns of inequality.

AGE, PUBLIC POLICY, AND HUMAN RIGHTS

The Canadian Charter of Rights and Freedoms was designed, in part, to ensure that all Canadians enjoy equal access to fundamental opportunities and rewards. Equal rights for people of all ages is a key Charter principle:

> Every individual is equal before and under the law and has the right to the equal protection and equal benefit of the law without discrimination and, in particular, without discrimination based on race, national or ethnic origin, colour, religion, sex, age or mental or physical disability [Section 15.1].

The wording of Section 15.1 suggests that using age to decide the rights and privileges of individual Canadians is discriminatory. How, then, can age be used as an automatic trigger effectively barring someone from obtaining a driving license at age 14 or voting in provincial elections at age 15? Similarly, if someone were not hired for a job simply because she/he were too young or too old, this would clearly seem to contravene the Charter, as would forcing people to quit their job at age sixty-five. However, this latter policy of mandatory retirement at age sixty-five is still widely applied, because it is believed that under certain conditions age restrictions are justifiable.

Typically, when age-grading determines rights and privileges, the argument is that these practices place *reasonable limits* on people's activity. In obtaining a driver's licence or renting a car, for example, age-grading is justified as a reasonable criterion to invoke by citing the higher accident rates of younger drivers. Age restrictions on buying alcohol are similarly justified. Alcohol consumption impairs judgment, and so restricting access to alcohol for young people is viewed as reasonable. Unequal access is thought to be justified in these circumstances because the infringement of individual rights and privileges is beneficial for the whole of society. In special circumstances, the rights of the individual are given lower priority than the rights of the community, and this too is reflected in the Canadian Charter, which

> guarantees the rights and freedoms set out [herein] subject only to such *reasonable limits* prescribed by law as can be *demonstrably justified* in a free and democratic society [Section 1—emphasis added].

For example, although mandatory retirement contravenes the individual wishes of some older workers wanting to work beyond age sixty-five, in 1991 the Supreme Court ruled that mandatory retirement at sixty-five is reasonable since it can be justified by the jobs it opens for young workers (see also Guppy, 1989; Lowe, 1991).

Notice that of all the categories listed in Section 15.1 of the Charter (e.g., sex, race), age is fundamentally different. Age is a universal attribute. Aging happens to everyone and, therefore, any age restrictions eventually apply to us all. None of the other attributes listed in Section 15.1 is universal. Unless they die a premature death, all Canadians experience every age category, whereas in our lifetime normally we occupy only one category of sex, race, and so on.

Despite this difference between age and the other attributes listed in Section 15.1 of the Charter, age is, like most of the others, an *ascribed* characteristic. Ascribed characteristics are determined at birth, rather than being chosen or achieved (as is religion or education, for example). Our age is something we cannot change. To the extent that other people use ascribed attributes to make judgments about us, our opportunities and rewards may be diminished (e.g., we are too old or too young to be doing something) or enhanced (e.g., our age is taken to signal maturity or judgment).

AGE AND DEPENDENCY

Age-grading is also related to dependency (Turner, 1988). The judgments others hold of us, or the entitlements others grant to us, depend upon whether we are believed to be responsible citizens, capable of making rational decisions about the welfare of ourselves and others. Ariès (1962) has argued that childhood, as a recognizable feature of the life course, began to emerge in European societies through the late 1600s. Children came to be seen as a group with special needs, especially susceptible to poverty, vagrancy, and social and moral corruption. Various child protection laws were thus enacted to safeguard children.

In contemporary Canada, the debate continues over children's rights. In the Canadian justice system, for example, policy makers have attempted to grant special rights to young offenders (aged 12 to 17), while also requiring young persons to be accountable for their actions (see e.g., Caputo, 1987 for a discussion of the *Young Offenders Act*).

The elderly, as a group, are also frequently defined as dependent. Partially this is a consequence of degenerative diseases, such as Alzheimer's, that erode an individual's ability to function independently (see Burke, *et al.*, 1997). However, the social arrangements of work and family are also consequential for relations of dependency, or independence. As discussed below, retirement and pension arrangements make it difficult for many Canadians, especially women, to support themselves economically in their later years. Many elderly people also find their traditional support systems (i.e., children, relatives) no longer live in close enough proximity to provide substantial care.

DIMENSIONS OF ECONOMIC INEQUALITY OVER THE LIFE COURSE

Dependency is common at both ends of the age spectrum. As we mature we gradually acquire more and more individual autonomy until in our later years dependency increases again. This ebb and flow in dependency is illustrated by examining how aging relates to various dimensions of inequality.

Figure 21-1 shows the average individual incomes, from all sources, that women and men receive at different periods in their

FIGURE 21-1 Average individual income by age and sex

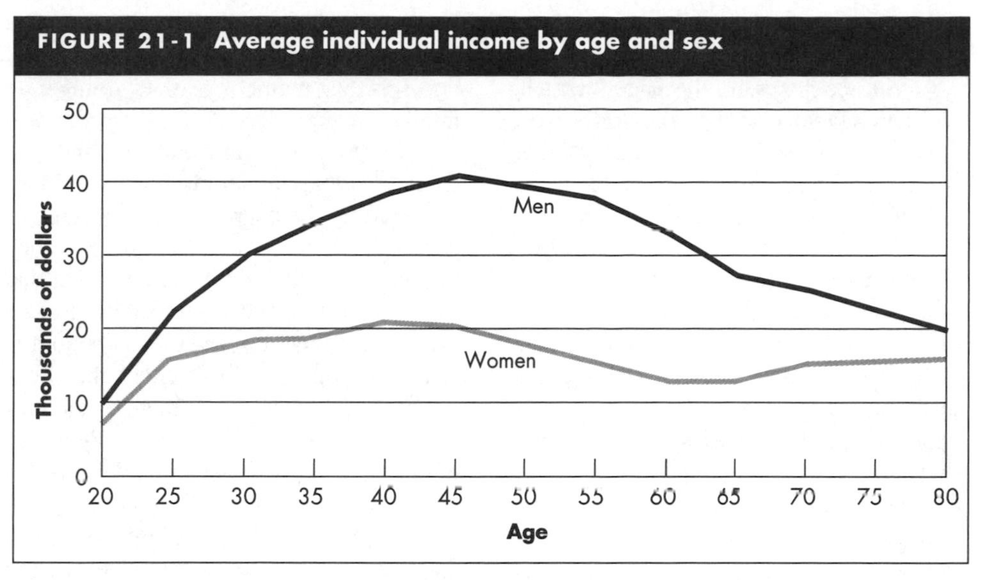

Source: Calculated from1991 Canadian Census, Total Individual Income reported for 1990.

lives. Average incomes increase for men to a peak at age 45, declining throughout later life. Women's average incomes are always lower, rising only moderately to about age 40, declining to a low plateau between 60 and 65, before rising moderately through their senior years (an increase attributable, in part, to the inheritance of their spouses' assets). The contrasting nature of the two curves for women and men reflects the greater continuity of occupational careers for men and the greater variability of

FIGURE 21-2 Living in a family owned home by age and sex

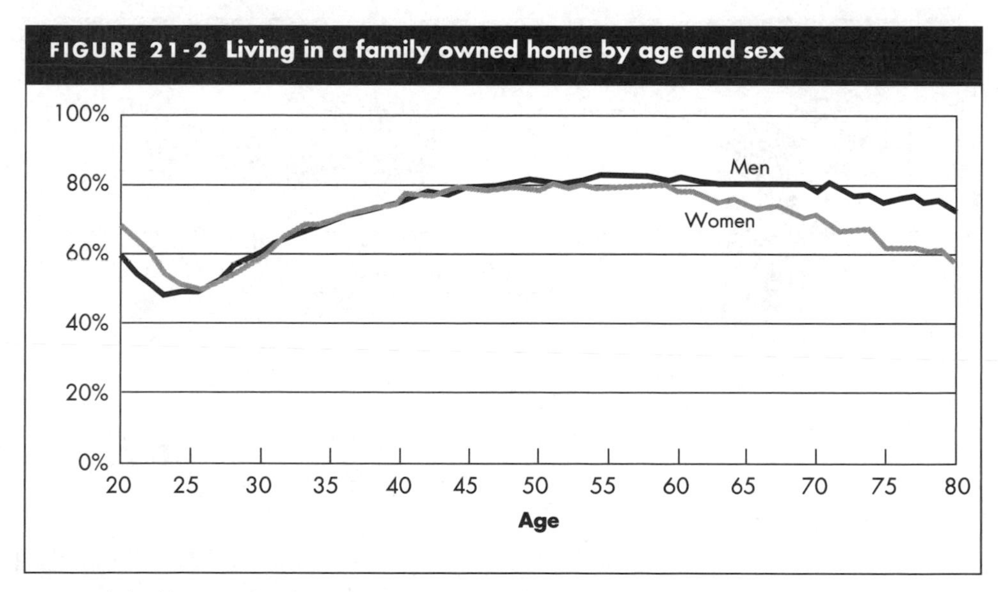

Source: Calculated from1991 Canadian Census.

women's attachment to the labour force (Jones, Marsden, and Tepperman, 1990).

Evidence shows that the wages of young workers have declined substantially since the late 1970s. An increased polarization in wage income between high and low earners has been, in part, a consequence of a 15% reduction between 1975 and 1993 in average earnings (adjusted for inflation) of young full-time, full-year workers (Picot and Myles, 1996).[1] Furthermore, Betcherman and Morrissette (1994) show that the earnings of young workers have declined across all occupational and industrial sectors and for individuals within all levels of schooling. A consequence of this wage depression for young workers has been a greater dependence among young people on the welfare state (e.g., on transfer income from welfare and child tax credits).

Annual income is a good indicator of cash flow, but it says little about an individual's net worth or asset holdings. Home ownership is a good measure of the latter since this is the principal source of wealth for most Canadians. Figure 21-2 shows the likelihood of living in a home owned by yourself or a member of your immediate family.

In their early twenties, women and men are still leaving the family home, a pattern reflected by the decreasing percentage of people reporting living in a home that they or their immediate relatives own (see also Boyd and Norris, 1995). Women leave home earlier than men, however. This pattern is caused by young women facing tighter family restrictions than young men, restrictions women seek to avoid by leaving home earlier in search of freedom and independence (Mitchell, 1992). Starting at about age 25, the curve reverses direction for both women and men, peaking over the 45 to 65 age range, when approximately 80% of women and men live in a family-owned home.

For women, the likelihood of remaining in a family-owned home starts to decline around age 55, and drops to below 60 percent for elderly women. In contrast, both the timing and the decline in living in a fam-

FIGURE 21-3 Living arrangements of elderly (75+) women and men, 1991

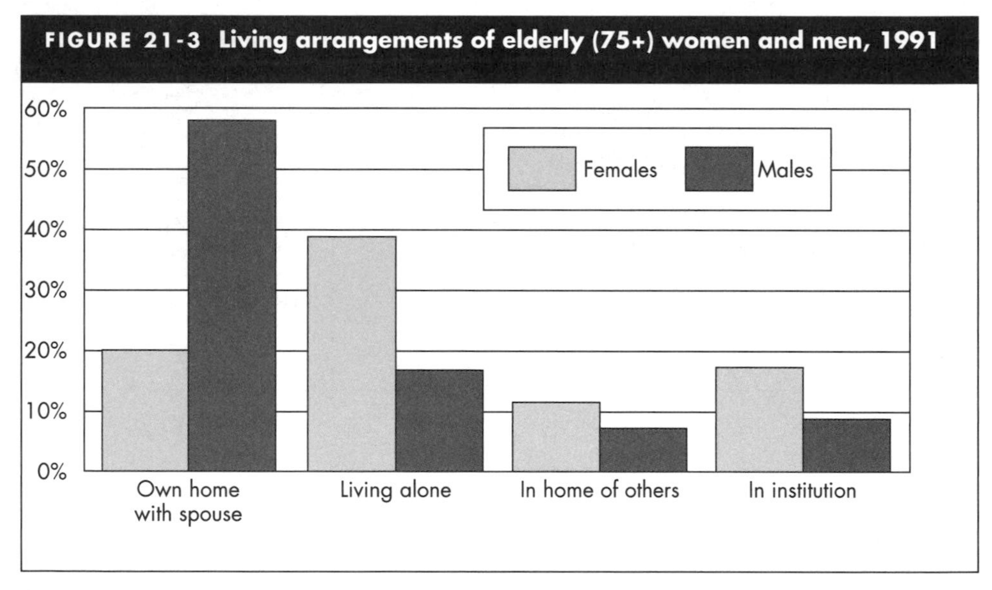

Source: Priest, 1993.

ily-owned home differs for men. About 80 percent of men continue living in a family-owned home past age 65 and, even as this rate declines among elderly men, the percentage remains substantially higher than for women.

The significantly different living arrangements of male and female elderly Canadians are captured more directly in Figure 21-3. Women and men over the age of 75 in 1991 are compared across four different living arrangements: living with a spouse in their own home; living on their own; living in other people's homes (e.g., children's or relative's); and living in an institution (e.g., hospitals, seniors' homes). One important fact to keep in mind here is that there are many more women than men over age 75, because women outlive men by about 6.5 years, on average.

Most elderly men (58%) live with a spouse, whereas most elderly women live either alone (39%) or in an institution (18%). Furthermore, these different arrangements are drifting further apart. In 1971 just over 50% of men lived with their wives, while 40% of elderly women lived alone or in an institution.

As a consequence of these different arrangements, women are much more likely than men to live their final years in relative isolation from family members, a pattern likely to intensify in the future (Priest, 1993). This means that "when men get older and frailer, most of them have built-in housekeepers and nurses—their wives. Women are not so fortunate" (National Council of Welfare, 1990).

The risk of living in poverty is also high among the elderly. In 1995 an estimated 386 000 elderly women—half of all unattached women 65 or older—lived below the poverty line (see Table 21-1). Not only do many elderly women live alone or in an institution, but they also do so in poverty. For elderly, unattached men the picture is still bleak, although proportionately not quite so desperate. Just under one-third (28.7%) of these men live below the poverty line.

For the elderly living in family situations, the poverty rates are lower, although still substantial. In families headed by a woman 65 or over, the poverty rate is 14%. About 7% of families with a male head 65 or over live in poverty.

Although the number of people living in poverty remains high, the trend over the past two decades has been one of improvement (Oja and Love, 1988; Rashid, 1990). Figures 21-4 and 21-5 reveal that among

TABLE 21-1 Percentage of families and unattached individuals with low-income by age and sex, 1995 (1992 Base)

	65+ Poverty Rate	<65 Poverty Rate
Families		
Female Head	14.0	43.9
Male Head	7.0	11.3
Individuals		
Female	50.6	40.4
Male	28.7	34.8

Source: Statistics Canada, *Income Distributions by Size in Canada* 1996, p. 176.

FIGURE 21-4 Trends in poverty rates among elderly families

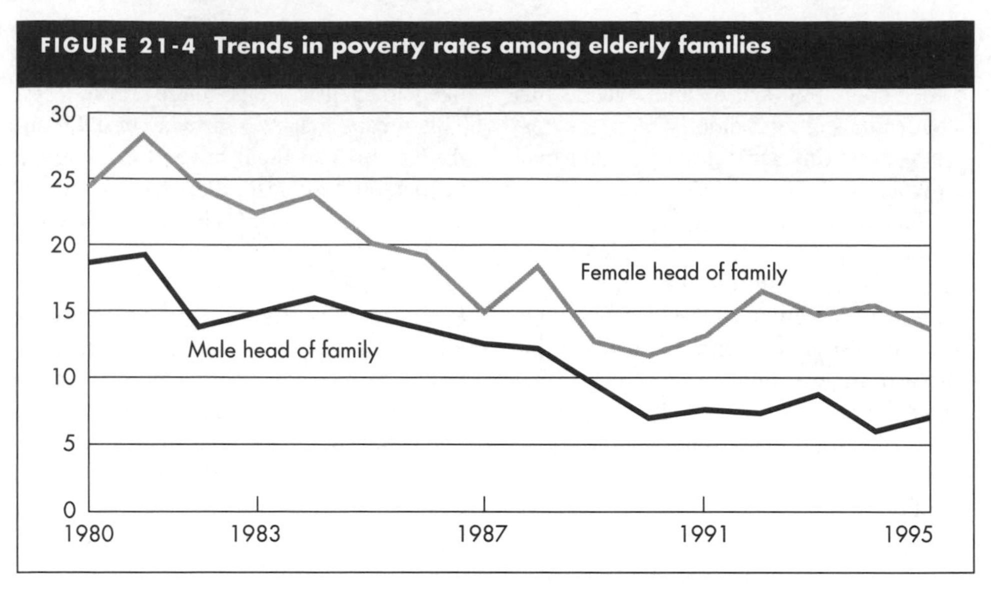

Source: Statistics Canada,1996 (Cat. 13-207); 1992 base.

both families and unattached individuals poverty rates for elderly Canadians declined in the 1980s and early 1990s.[2] Again, however, the feminization of poverty is evident in the increasing gap between women and men over time. In other words, the improvements in living standards for elderly men were greater than for elderly women.

FIGURE 21-5 Trends in poverty rates among elderly individuals

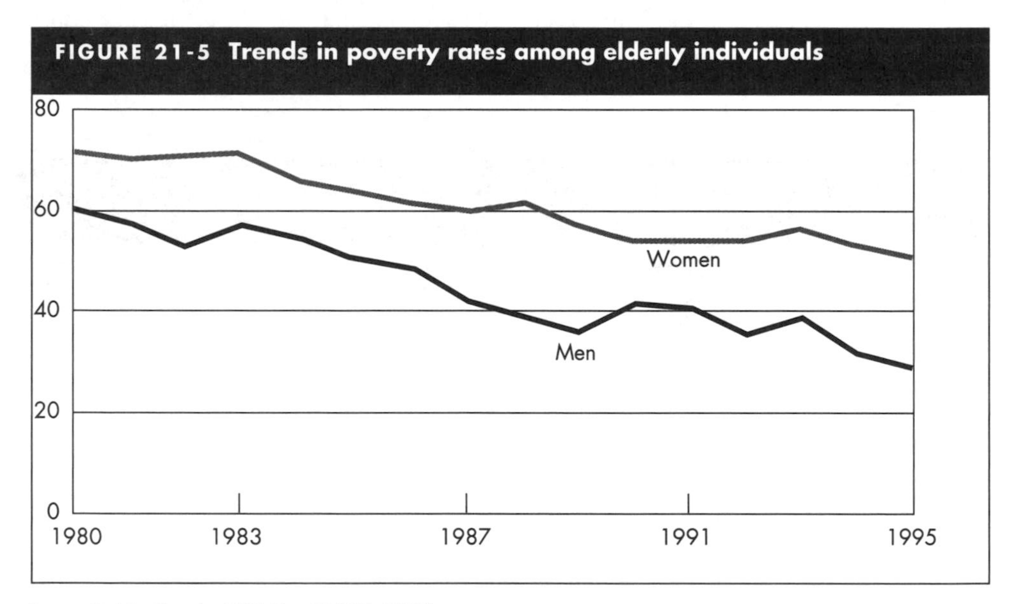

Source: Statistics Canada; 1996 (Cat. 13-207); 1992 base.

INCOME AND THE OLD AGE SECURITY SYSTEM

Why are so many older Canadians, and especially elderly women, living in poverty? In large part poverty among the elderly results from the lack of an adequate income security system in this country, a problem that is especially acute for women (Galarneau, 1991).

The basic retirement income system for elderly Canadians works as follows (see also National Council of Welfare, 1996; Oderkirk, 1996). Virtually all Canadians 65 and over receive taxable Old Age Security (OAS) payments (the maximum annual benefit was about $4775 per person in 1996). As well, just under four out of every ten elderly Canadians receive the Guaranteed Income Supplement (GIS), an income-tested[3] benefit designed to help the elderly poor (in the spring of 1996 the maximum monthly benefit for a single pensioner was $470.07 per month). As well, most provinces provide additional income supplements and special tax breaks for the elderly. However, despite these support programs, the monies provided are not enough to keep many elderly Canadians out of poverty (see Table 21-1).

In addition to these age-related pension packages, there are two important employment-related components of the elderly income security system. One employment-related component is the Canada and Quebec Pension Plan (CPP/QPP), while the other is the private occupational pension plans to which some Canadians subscribe.

Since 1966 all Canadians who have been members of the paid labour force, either as employees or self-employed, have been required by law to contribute to the CPP/QPP. Upon retirement a pension equal to 25% of a person's average "pensionable earnings" is paid,[4] to a maximum ceiling of about $8,724.96 annually (1996). In 1993, 28% of all unattached senior women did not receive any CPP/QPP benefits compared to 16% of unattached senior men.

CPP/QPP pension income is low for everyone. It is, however, especially low for people who only held labour force jobs intermittently (many women) and for people who earned low incomes even when they did work (again many women, as well as many members of the Native Indian community and the disabled population). And, of course, CPP/QPP income is zero for those who never held a labour force job.

Private occupation-based pension plans are also available and some Canadians, especially those in secure management jobs or union members, benefit from these funds as well. However, most employed Canadians are not enrolled in occupational pension plans, and the percentage enrolled has been declining for men but increasing for women. In 1978, 37% of employed women were covered by occupational pension plans, a percentage that had risen to 42% by 1993. For men the comparable figures were 54% in 1978 and 47% in 1993.

Although many elderly Canadians continue to live in poverty, as noted above there has been recent improvement in the overall picture. This improvement is due in large part to a strengthening of the income security system in the past two decades. Pensions now cover more Canadians and, since 1971, age-related pension increments have generally kept pace with or bettered inflation.

The significance of this trend is that government transfer income now represents a crucial portion of the income that the elderly receive. In fact, in 1989, 54% of the income for unattached elderly people and 37% of the income for elderly families came as government transfer payments (Chawla, 1991a: 59). Furthermore, without transfers from the income security system, Chawla estimates that 76% of the unattached elderly and 56% of elderly families would be living in poverty.

However, as the proportion of Canadians over the age of 65 continues to grow, there is now concern that the income security system for the elderly probably cannot withstand this growth. The Head of Statistics Canada has asked "can we afford an aging society?" (Fellegi, 1988), and has answered affirmatively. Nevertheless, opinions are divided, especially because some projections show that, among industrialized countries, Canada will have one of the highest dependency ratios by the year 2030 (Chawla, 1991b).

If these projections about the size of the dependent population in Canada are correct, severe pressure will be brought to bear on social benefits. Some argue that "Canadians will most likely have to choose between increasing tax rates and social security contributions or lower levels of social benefits" (Burke, 1991: 8). However, this too is contested hotly. Myles (1989) argues that the root of the crisis in old-age security lies not in the numbers of elderly (what he calls the "demographic imperative"), but in the political alignments between capital and labour in the welfare state. Myles outlines this argument in our next chapter.

AGE-BASED CONFLICT AND STRAIN

Age is correlated with the *distribution* of inequality (e.g., the elderly are more often poor than the non-elderly). In addition, though, the privileges and rewards of different age groups are also *relational* in nature. Age-group relations entail issues of inter-generational equity or justice. Mandatory retirement illustrates this relational tension between generations. The 1991 Supreme Court decision ruled that forced retirement was justifiable because of the opportunities it creates for a younger generation, even though the decision infringes on the rights of some older workers. Tension between generations occurs when the rights and privileges favouring one age group impinge on the opportunities or fortunes of another age group.

Generational disputes can have lasting consequences. The 1960s is one historic period when inter-generational conflict led to significant social change, from policies on the Vietnam War to procedures for student involvement on many college and university committees. More recently, with the growth in the number of elderly Canadians, concern has been focused on another intergenerational trade-off. Can we continue to provide adequate funding for childhood education in the face of escalating medical costs for the care of the elderly (Foot, 1996)?

Population aging also induces strain within institutions. For example, institutional strain due to aging occurs in health care. The medical system is oriented more towards treating acute illness (e.g., kidney transplants) than towards coping with chronic ailments. However, medical patients increasingly are elderly Canadians who are much more likely to suffer from chronic ailments (e.g., arthritis) that the system is least able to handle (Myles and Boyd, 1988: 195-6). Social strain due to age composition also occurs in the workplace when organizations must reduce their size. Tindale (1987) has documented the age-based conflicts among younger and older teachers in Ontario that resulted from the Government's decision to reduce the number of teachers in the school system. Seniority, not ability, was used as the criterion to dismiss individuals, and this led to intense struggles across age groups as teachers fought to save jobs.

However, the extent of age-based conflict must not be exaggerated. Conflict between generations has never been as prominent as tensions between religious or ethnic groups, for example (see Davis and van den Oever, 1981). While there is no denying the existence of intergenerational conflicts within families, allegiances to kin temper these disputes, thereby dampening antagonism, as do rules of inheritance and support.[5] Also, the universal nature of age mentioned earlier means that one cannot maintain a life-long identification with a specific age group. Being a member of an "adolescent gang" all of one's life is impossible. Furthermore, even though teenage "rebellion" frequently occurs, such rebellion only rarely leads to a long-term disintegration of family solidarity. Age-based conflict of a relational nature is thus not as significant a force in Canadian society as are other conflicts based on different ascriptive factors.

CONCLUSION

Age-grading practices affect our access to rights and opportunities. Age is often an automatic trigger overriding merit or ability in determining the citizenship rights a person can, or cannot, enjoy. Several dimensions of inequality, especially income and home ownership, vary significantly across the age spectrum. The distribution of inequality, we have argued, is related to dependency. This dependency is illustrated most graphically by the number of elderly Canadians who live in poverty.

Although the income security system in Canada has improved the economic circumstances of elderly Canadians, substantial numbers of people over the age of sixty-five still live in poverty. The risk of living in poverty is especially acute for elderly women. Exacerbating the economic misfortunes of many women is the likelihood that they will live alone or in an institution during their final years of life. Even when living in poverty, older men are much more likely to have at least the comfort of a spouse to share the burden of later life.

The ability of taxpayers to support the swelling ranks of the aged has also been noted. Especially if immigration levels are kept low, the proportion of Canadians over the age of sixty-five will rise substantially in the next few decades. This trend will in turn add pressure to the old-age pension system. The ability of the welfare state to manage this pressure will depend, in part, upon accommodations reached between labour and business (Myles, 1989).

We have also briefly noted other issues of inter-generational tension and have reviewed how changes in the age composition of the population can cause strains for the social system. John Myles discusses these latter themes in the next reading when he examines the dynamics of citizenship rights and income security. He explores, in particular, the crisis in old-age security.

NOTES

1. Average inflation-adjusted earnings of higher paid workers have been relatively stable between 1975 and 1993.
2. Statistics Canada uses a relative definition to calculate low-income lines. As a consequence of this relative definition, changes must be made regularly in the baseline calculations to reflect changes in the standard of living. A 1992 base is used in Figures 21-4 and 21-5 as well as in Table 21-1.
3. Whether or not a person receives GIS income depends upon the total amount of income an individual receives. As total income rises, GIS income declines. The GIS was instituted to help the elderly poor. It is significant that over half of all seniors receive the GIS, with many still remaining below the poverty line!
4. Numerous technical details influence exact CPP/QPP payments (see National Council of Welfare, 1996 for a useful primer). CPP/QPP income is indexed to average lifetime earnings, which means that low wage earners in the labour force also will be low pension recipients in retirement.

5. Families can be violent places but frequently such violence is not age-related.

REFERENCES

Ariès, P. 1960 1962 *Centuries of Childhood: A Social History of Family Life* Penguin.

Betcherman, Gordon and Rene Morrissette 1994 "Recent youth labour market experiences in Canada." Ottawa: Statistics Canada, Analytic Studies Branch, Research paper #63.

Boyd, Monica and Doug Norris 1995 "Leaving the nest? The impact of family structure." *Canadian Social Trends*, No. 38, Autumn, 14-17.

Burke, Mary Anne 1991 "Implications of an aging society." *Canadian Social Trends* Spring, 6-8.

Burke, Mary Anne, Joan Lindsay, Ian McDowell, and Gerry Hill 1997 "Dementia among seniors." *Canadian Social Trends*, No. 45, Summer, 24-27.

Caputo, Tullio 1987 "The Young Offender's Act: children's rights, children's wrongs." *Canadian Public Policy* Vol. 13 (2), 125-143.

Chawla, Raj 1991a "Dependence on government transfer payments, 1971-1989." *Perspectives on Labour and Income* Summer, 51-67.

Chawla, Raj 1991b "Dependency ratios." *Canadian Social Trends* Spring, 3-5.

Davis, Kingsley and P. van den Oever 1981 "Age relations and public policy in advanced industrial societies." *Population and Development Review* Vol. 7 (1), 1-18.

Fellegi, Ivan 1988 "Can we afford an aging society?" *Canadian Economic Observer* October, 4.1-4.34.

Foot, David 1996 *Boom, Bust, and Echo* Toronto: Macfarlane, Walter, and Ross.

Galarneau, Diane 1991 "Women approaching retirement." *Perspectives on Labour and Income* Vol. 3 (3), 28- 39.

Guppy, Neil 1989 "The magic of 65: issues and evidence in the mandatory retirement debate." *Canadian Journal on Aging* Vol. 8 (2), 173-186.

Jones, Charles, Lorna Marsden, and Lorne Tepperman 1990 *Lives of Their Own: The Individualization of Women's Lives* Toronto: Oxford University Press.

Lowe, Graham 1991 "Retirement attitudes, plans and behaviour." *Perspectives on Labour and Income* Vol. 3 (3), 8-17.

Mitchell, Barbara 1992 "The role of family structure and social capital on the timing and reasons for homeleaving among young adults." Unpublished paper, Anthropology & Sociology, University of British Columbia, Vancouver, B.C.

Myles, John 1989 *Old Age in the Welfare State: The Political Economy of Public Pensions* University Press of Kansas.

Myles, John and Monica Boyd 1988 "Population aging and the elderly." In D. Forcese and S. Richer (eds.) *Social Issues: Sociological Views of Canada* Toronto: Prentice-Hall, pp. 186-204.

National Council of Welfare 1990 *Women and Poverty Revisited* Ottawa: Minister of Supply and Services

National Council of Welfare 1996 *A Pension Primer* Ottawa: Minister of Supply and Services

Oderkirk, Jillian 1996 "Government sponsored income security programs for seniors: old age security." *Canadian Social Trends,* No. 40, Spring, 3-7.

Oja, Gail and Richard Love 1988 *Pensions and Incomes of the Elderly in Canada, 1971-1985* Statistics Canada, Catalogue 13-588, No. 2, Ottawa.

Priest, Gordon 1993 "Seniors 75+: living arrangements." *Canadian Social Trends* No. 30, Autumn, 24-25.

Picot, Garnett and John Myles 1996 "Children in low-income families." *Canadian Social Trends* No. 42, Autumn, 15-19.

Rashid, Abdul 1990 *The Changing Profile of Canadian Families with Low Incomes, 1970-1985* Statistics Canada, Catalogue 13-588, No. 2, Ottawa.

Statistics Canada 1996 *Income Distributions by Size in Canada* Catalogue No. 13-207.

Tindale, Joseph 1987 "Age, seniority and Class patterns of job strain." In V. Marshall (ed.) *Aging in Canada: Social Perspectives* Toronto: Fitzhenry and Whiteside, pp. 176-92.

Turner, Bryan 1988 "Ageing, status politics and sociological theory." *British Journal of Sociology* Vol. 40 (4), 588-606.

Chapter 22

DEMOGRAPHY OR DEMOCRACY? THE "CRISIS" OF OLD-AGE SECURITY

John Myles

(From *Old Age in the Welfare State: The Political Economy of Public Pensions*, 1989, University of Kansas Press. Reprinted with permission.)

INTRODUCTION

During the decades following World War II, the rapid growth in old-age security entitlements in all capitalist democracies was widely hailed as a necessary, indeed inevitable, consequence of industrialization and economic growth. Industrialization, it was thought, had simultaneously rendered the labour of older workers redundant and provided the wealth to make their labour unnecessary. A retirement wage sufficient to permit or induce withdrawal from the labour force in advance of physiological decline could, and should, be made available to all.

In the mid-seventies, however, a contrary view began to take form. According to this revised view, a combination of rising entitlements and an increase in the number of retirees was creating a long-term process bound to self-destruct. In the long run, the old-age security systems that were the pride of the postwar state were doomed to collapse under the weight of changing demographic and fiscal realities. The "crisis' of old-age security had been discovered (see Myles, 1981).

The roots of this crisis are usually attributed to demography: the system of old-age security entitlements currently in place in the capitalist democracies simply cannot withstand the projected rise in the number of old people. Wilensky (1975) argued that changing demographic realities gave rise to the modern welfare state; it is now claimed that demography will bring about its demise.

But what is the nature of this demographic imperative? In the pages that follow, I shall propose that the usual formulation of the demographic argument is, at best, highly misleading. This is not to say that demography is irrelevant to our understanding of the current situation. The size and composition of populations represent real constraints on any national political effort, whether for warfare or for welfare. What is required, however, is identification of the forms of social organization and institutional arrangements that make a particular demographic formation into a "problem." I suggest that to understand the current situation we must situate it within the broader context of the postwar welfare state and the political and economic foundations upon which it was constructed. The current conflict over the future of old-age security is a symptom of a larger conflict over the proper role of the democratic state in a market economy. This postwar Keynesian consensus upon which the welfare state was constructed has broken down, with the result that the various social institutions it spawned (including retirement wages for the elderly) have now become the focus of renewed debate and political confrontation. The implication is that the long-term future of old-age security—and hence of old age as we now know it—depends less on innovative fiscal management practices than on the eventual political realignments of a post-Keynesian political economy.

POPULATION AGING AND THE CRISIS IN OLD-AGE SECURITY

The conventional explanation of the crisis in old-age security is a rather straightforward exercise in demographic accounting: the current generation of adults is simply not producing enough children to support it in its old age (Keyfitz, 1980). Because of declining fertility, the size of the elderly population will grow to a point where the economic burden on the young will become intolerable. Eventually the demographic bubble will burst, old-age security programs will go broke, and an intergenerational "class struggle" will ensue (Davis and van den Oever, 1981). To avoid this eventuality, it is argued, people must begin to show restraint now (Clark and Barker, 1981). Promises that future generations will be unwilling or unable to keep should not be made to the current generation of workers (Laffer and Ranson, 1977). In this scenario, we have a social responsibility to dismantle the welfare state for the sake of our children and grandchildren, who must support us in the future.

Several core assumptions underlie this argument. In this view, old-age pensions are not the product of a wage-setting process mediated by the state, but the product of an implicit social contract made between sequential age cohorts (Friedman, 1978). Each cohort agrees to support the preceding cohort, under the assumption that it will receive similar treatment from the cohort that follows. But since age cohorts vary in size, the contract is inherently unstable. Although it is relatively easy to provide generous benefits to a small retired population, providing the same benefits to a very large cohort of retirees may become an intolerable burden (Keyfitz, 1980). The result is a conflict between cohorts, leading to dissolution of the contract. It is argued that North Americans can expect such a dissolution when the baby-boom generation retires.

The notion of a social contract between age cohorts is a metaphor intended to enable us to understand and to predict changes in popular support for old-age entitlement programs. The question to be answered is whether the empirical evidence gives any indication that the metaphor is appropriate. Where the conditions specified by the model have been met, it would seem reasonable to expect some evidence of the intergenerational conflict and the resistance to public spending on the elderly that it predicts.

Several Western nations are already quite "old" by demographic standards. The elderly constitute more than 16 percent of the populations of West Germany, Austria, and Sweden—a figure that is not far from the 18 percent at which the North American population is expected to peak in the next century. As Heinz and Chiles (1981: iii) observe:

> Western European social security systems have already experienced the impact of population aging for some time now. The Federal Republic of Germany, for example, currently has a ratio of social security contributors to beneficiaries of less than 2 : 1, which is the level not projected to be reached in the United States until the year 2030, when the postwar baby boom generation reaches old age.

Moreover, the tax burden necessary to finance old-age security in these countries has already reached levels that exceed those projected for North America in the next century. Prior to the amendments of 1983 that reduced the projected costs of the program, the tax rate for U.S. Social Security was projected to peak at 20.1 percent in the year 2035 (Leimer, 1979). But by 1978, the effective tax rate to support old-age security was already 18 percent in Germany, 20 percent in Sweden, 23 percent in Italy, and 25 percent in the Netherlands (Torrey and Thompson, 1980: 43). The experience of these nations, however, provides little evidence of the growing backlash and intergenerational hostility anticipated by the proponents of the conventional view.

Although several countries experienced a "welfare backlash" in the late seventies, Wilensky (1981) has shown that this pattern was unrelated either to the size of the elderly population or to levels of public spending and taxation. Indeed, according to Wilensky's estimates, the very "oldest" of the capitalist democracies (Germany, Austria, Sweden) were among the countries that experienced the least amount of popular resistance to rising welfare expenditures. And informed observers (Ross, 1979; Tomasson, 1982) generally agree that, despite *official* concern over rising costs, *public support* of old-age security systems remains high in these countries.

Moreover, where there has been popular reaction against the growth of public spending, support for the elderly appears to occupy a special place. In 1981, only 11 percent of Americans under the age of 65 agreed that Social Security benefits should be reduced in the future. And the majority of those under the age of 65 were prepared to accept further tax increases to keep Social Security viable (Employee Benefit Research Institute, 1981). Coughlin's (1979) comparative review of public opinion poll data indicates that support for old-age security programs is uniformly high and shows little variation from country to country, despite wide differences in the size of elderly populations and in the quality of pension entitlements.

There are some obvious reasons for such widespread support for old-age security, even in the face of rising costs. First, familial bonds provide a strong basis for solidarity between generations. In the absence of suitable public provision for the elderly, adults of working age would be required to provide for their aging parents directly. For these individuals a generous old-age security system is not a burden but relief from a burden. Second, those of working age are generally capable of recognizing that they will require similar support in the future. In the long run, they will suffer if the terms of the "contract" are not met.

Less obvious but perhaps more important is the fact that the key claim of the demographic model—that population aging increases the burden of dependency on the working force population—is incorrect. As Table 22-1 demonstrates, population aging has generally been associated with a decline in both total and age-based dependency, because of a decline in the size of the very young population and an increase in female

TABLE 22-1 Age dependency and total economic dependency, 1959–1979

	Youth dependency[a] (ages 0–14)		Old-age dependency[a] (ages 65+)		Total age dependency[a]		Total economic dependency[b]	
	1959	1979	1959	1979	1959	1979	1959	1979
Australia	30.1	25.7	8.5	9.4	38.6	35.1	n.a	55.0
Austria	21.8	21.1	12.1	15.5	33.9	36.6	51.8	58.5
Belgium	23.3	20.5	11.9	14.3	35.2	34.8	60.2	58.0
Canada	30.3	23.5	7.8	9.3	38.1	32.8	63.6	52.3
Denmark	25.7	21.3	10.4	14.2	36.1	35.5	54.3	47.9
Finland	30.7	20.6	7.1	11.8	37.8	32.4	52.1	51.6
France	26.1	22.6	11.6	14.0	37.7	36.6	56.3	56.9
Germany	21.0	18.9	10.7	15.5	31.7	34.4	52.0	56.9
The Netherlands	30.0	22.9	8.9	11.4	38.9	34.3	63.2	64.8
Norway	26.1	22.6	10.7	14.6	36.8	37.2	59.2	53.1
Sweden	22.8	20.0	11.6	16.1	34.4	36.1	51.4	48.5
Switzerland	24.0	20.1	10.1	13.7	34.1	33.8	54.0	54.9
United Kingdom	23.2	21.5	11.6	14.7	34.8	36.2	52.5	54.9
United States	30.8	22.8	9.1	11.2	39.9	34.0	60.1	52.4

[a] Defined as a percentage of the total population.
[b] Total non-working population as a percentage of the total population.

Source: Organization for Economic Cooperation and Development *Labour Forces Statistics, 1959-70* (Paris: OECD, 1972); *Labour Force Statistics, 1968-79* (Paris: OECD, 1981).

labour-force participation. Canadian and U.S. projections indicate a similar trend for the future. Although the size of the elderly population will continue to grow, total age-dependency ratios will first decline and then slowly rise again to current levels (see Table 22-2). At no point are they projected to reach the levels achieved during the early sixties, the peak of the baby-boom period.

The issue for the future, then, is not the *size* of the dependent population but rather its changing *composition*—fewer children and more retirees. The usual strategy in evaluating this change is to compare public expenditures on the old with public expenditures on the young. Since public expenditures on the old amount to approximately three times public expenditures on the young, it is clear that total *public* expenditures on the non-working population must increase as the population ages. But to assess the true economic impact on the working population, we must evaluate total expenditures on the young and on the old, not just that portion passing through the public purse. Information on this subject is at best incomplete. Based on the analyses of French demographer Alfred Sauvy (1948), Clark and Spender (1980: 38) conclude that total expenditures on the old exceed those on the young. In contrast, if we accept Wander's (1978) finding that the total cost of raising a child to the age of 20 is one-fourth to one-third *higher* than the total cost of supporting an elderly person from age 60 to death, we can expect that total intergenerational transfers (public plus private) will decline as the population ages.

The empirical foundations for the conventional view, then, appear to be rather

TABLE 22-2 Projected age-dependency ratios for Canada and the United States

	Dependency ratios[a]		
	Ages 0-17	**Age 65+**	**Total**
Canada			
1976	53.5	14.6	68.1
1986	41.9	16.1	58.0
2001	36.7	18.5	55.2
2031	33.3	33.7	67.0
United States			
1976	51.3	18.0	69.3
1985	43.5	19.0	62.5
2000	43.2	19.9	63.1
2025	42.0	29.5	71.5

[a] Dependency is defined as a proportion of the working-age population (population aged 18-64).

Source: Canada: Health and Welfare Canada, *Retirement Age.* (Ottawa: Ministry of National Health and Welfare, 1978), p. 17. Reproduced by permission of the Ministry of Supply and Services Canada. U.S.: U.S. Bureau of Census, *Current Population Reports*, "Projections of the Population of the United States: 1977-2050" (Washington, D.C.: U.S. Government Printing Office), Series P-25, No. 704.

shaky. Whatever its consequences, population aging does not seem to be a source of rising economic dependency, intergenerational conflict, or popular backlash against welfare-state spending. This does not mean that the so-called crisis of old-age security is all sound and fury—only that we must look elsewhere to understand its nature and origins.

At the most general level, the current controversy over the future of old-age security is rooted in the broader economic crisis that has beset the capitalist democracies since the early 1970s. A protracted economic slump (characterized by declining output, rising unemployment, and inflation) brought about a radical reassessment of the postwar welfare state. Rather than a means of reinvigorating capitalism, the welfare state (including the welfare state for the elderly) is now broadly seen by both the left and the right as a fetter on capital accumulation (Gough, 1979; Geiger and Geiger, 1978). The crisis in old-age security is a symptom of this larger crisis of the welfare state.

THE ANATOMY OF THE CRISIS

As Geiger and Geiger (1978: 16) observe, the critical issue raised by the growth of the welfare state is whether or not the market retains enough of its own output to satisfy its requirements. From the viewpoint of the marketplace, the portion of the national product that is administered by the state is "out of control"; that amount is no longer directly available to provide incentives to labour (in the form of wages) or to capital (in the form of profits), nor is it directly available in the form of savings to be used for reinvestment. Access to these resources is mediated by the state. As a result, their distribution is subject to the logic of the political process rather than the logic of the market. The expansion of the public economy increasingly politicizes economic affairs and, by so doing, reverses the great achievement of the bourgeois revolutions of the seventeenth and eighteenth centuries—the removal of the state from the realm of economic decision making (Piven and Cloward, 1982: 42).

Under current arrangements for the distribution of income, population aging exacerbates this process. Because increased public expenditures on the elderly are not offset by a corresponding reduction in public expenditures on the young, population aging increases the size of the public economy and reduces the share of national income directly subject to market forces. Thus, although population aging is unlikely to "break the national bank," it *will* alter the bank's structure of ownership and control. McDonald and Carty (1979), for example, estimate that public intergenerational transfers to the old and young in Canada will rise from 12.8 percent of GNP in 1976 to 17.8 percent of GNP in the year 2031.

But for whom does the expansion of public control over the distribution of income pose a problem? Any major social transformation is likely to generate conflict between those who stand to lose and those who stand to gain from such change. The trick is to identify the probable winners and losers. It is instructive to ask, then, who stands to benefit and who stands to lose as the result of yet further expansion of the public economy in general, and of the old-age security budget in particular. If this question can be answered correctly, we will be in a good position to predict the direction of any conflict that might ensue. More importantly, we will be better able to appreciate the logic of the current controversies and struggles over the future of old-age security.

In the past there have been three quite different answers to the question of who benefits from public control over income distribution. Neo-Marxists have argued that the benefits of the welfare state have gone primarily to the owners and managers of capital; "conservatives" (that is, the proponents of classical liberalism) have argued that the welfare state undermines the power of capital; and the postwar liberals have generally claimed that the welfare state benefits both labour and capital. As Piven and Cloward (1982: 31) point out, however, there is a growing recognition among analysts of all political persuasions that the conservatives were right—the major consequence of the expansion of the public economy has been to alter the structure of power between capital and labour in favour of the latter. Evidence of this shift is found in the market for labour and in the market for capital.

In the labour market, the citizen's wage enhances the bargaining power of labour both individually and collectively. The effects at the individual level have been recognized for some time in the life-cycle model of earnings and labour supply. According to this model, individual workers make employment and wage decisions (whether to work and at what wage) according to the anticipated impact of such decisions on total lifetime earnings. Universal income entitlements, such as those typically contained in old-age security provisions, mean that some portion of each individual's total lifetime earnings is fixed by law. Thus, current decisions to work and at what wage can be made in light of the fact that some amount of future income is assured. This assurance reduces dependency on the labour market and enhances the worker's bargaining position with respect to would-be employers. When good jobs at good wages are not available, individuals may simply choose to withdraw, partially or completely, from the labour force. The "work disincentives" that result from the availability of unemployment, sickness, and old-age entitlements reduce the labour supply and drive up wage levels.

To understand the effects of the citizen's wage at the collective level, we must consider the relationship between unemployment and the bargaining power of labour (Piven and Cloward, 1982: 19). Under normal conditions, a rise in unemployment leads to a reduction in wages by increasing the supply of unemployed workers and the subsequent competition for available jobs. The citizen's wage increasingly insulates the working class from the reserve army of the unemployed. By absorbing the unemployed, the welfare state also absorbs much of the downward pressure on market wages that an increase in unemployment would otherwise create. Thus, wage levels tend to be higher and profit levels lower than they would otherwise be (see Block, 1981: 15-17). Old-age security provisions are very much part of this process. Among the first to be absorbed in periods of rising unemployment are older workers, who join the ranks of the elderly by moving into early retirement (Clark and Barber, 1981).

From the point of view of employers, this problem is compounded by the fact that the social-wage bill and the market-wage bill are interactive. Unemployment lowers the market-wage bill but simultaneously triggers an increase in the social-wage bill for unemployment, welfare, and retirement benefits. Regardless of how they are financed, public benefits must ultimately be paid for by current production. Thus, both market wages and social wages must be construed as a cost of doing business. The problem for employers, then, is that the wage bill as a whole (market wages plus social wages) becomes increasingly rigid and insensitive to market forces.

The problems of employers go beyond the obstacles in the labour market. The effects of the public economy also loom large in the capital market. When the owners and managers of capital attempt to borrow finds to invest in new facilities and equipment or to meet temporary cash-flow problems, they find themselves faced with a very powerful competitor for the supply of available savings—namely, the state. Moreover, state borrowing to finance the public economy tends to increase when individual firms can least afford the resulting rise in interest rates. Downturns in the economy produce rising unemployment, a declining tax base, and an increased level of social spending, thereby increasing government deficits and the need for state borrowing. Increased state borrowing, in turn, produces the rising interest rates that many firms in recent years have found prohibitive. In the competition for the available pool of capital, governments hold a decided advantage: the state can afford to pay the higher interest rates because of its powers of taxation, which are unavailable to private firms.

The public economy also affects the amount of capital available for investment purposes. Most national pension schemes are funded on a pay-as-you-go basis—that is, current expenditures (benefits) are paid for out of current revenues (contributions). Such a system is a form of pseudo-savings: wage-earners make contributions, but no pool of capital is created. Since these contributions generate income entitlements that can be claimed on retirement, the need for other forms of saving (such as a private pension plan) is reduced. But a shift in pension financing from a pay-as-you-go to a funded basis (as practised in Sweden and Canada) simply compounds the problems of the business community.

As has long been recognized, financing a public pension system on a funded basis results in a significant shift of economic power from the private sector to the state, because the capital pool created from contributions is in the hands of government. In Canada, the funds of the Canada Pension Plan have become the major source of provincial debt financing. The funds of the parallel Quebec Pension Plan have also been used to finance a state-directed program of private-sector investment. In the latter part of the seventies, recognition of this situation among the Canadian business class resulted in what came to be called the "great pension debate."

Faced with the obvious inadequacies of Canada's old-age security system, Canadian labour proposed, in 1975, to rectify the situation by significantly expanding the Canada Pension Plan. Objections to this proposal had little to do with the need for improvement; and the superiority of the public system over its private-sector counterparts was never seriously questioned. Rather, the principal objection was that such a change would bring about an increase in government control over capital formation. The editors of the Toronto *Globe and Mail* (October 12, 1977) argued: "Government is already too deep into pension plans—and the savings they represent—for the good of Canada's economic future. We need more savings ... but the savings should be in a variety of hands and not subject to the political vagaries of government." As Murphy (1982) has shown, the reasons for this concern are not difficult to identify. During the decade following the Canada Pension Plan legislation of 1965, corporate savings as a means of amassing new investment capital were in decline, and corporations had to turn increasingly to external sources of financing. During the same period, private pension funds grew to become the single largest source of private equity capital in Canada and the major source of corporate borrowing. Expanding the public system further would transfer a significant portion of these savings to the state and, in the words of the *Globe and Mail*, would subject them to the "political vagaries of government." In this way, democratization of the savings and investment process serves to further undermine the power of private capital. Canadian business has made abundantly clear (Business Committee of Pension Policy, 1982) its view that the defence of this power must take precedence over the income requirements of the elderly.

CONCLUSION

The real crisis in old-age security, then, is an outcome of the adverse effects of the citizen's wage on the power of capital. State intervention to meet social needs created by or not satisfied by the market tends to transform the market itself. When workers, in their capacity as citizens, can claim a social wage that is independent of the sale of their labour power, capitalist social relations are changed. The "mixed economy" that emerges from this transformation is not a happy marriage between complementary principles of social organization but a unity of opposites, a system of tolerated contradictions. Democratic control over wage and capital formation is the antithesis of capitalist control over wage and capital formation; when the one expands, the other must contract. The principal losers are the owners and managers of capital. The result is not an intergenerational class struggle but simply an expression of the traditional struggle between labour and capital. The problem is not one of state control per se but, rather, one of *democratic* control of the state. State policies that assign resources on the basis of need and social equality undermine a system of assignment based on property entitlements and market value. The future of old-age security, then, is a problem of democracy, not of demography.

REFERENCES

Block, Fred 1981 "The fiscal crisis of the capitalist state." In R. Turner and J. Short (eds.) *Annual Review of Sociology* 7, pp. 1–27. Palo Alto, Calif.: Annual Reviews.

Clark, Robert and David Barker 1981 *Reversing the Trend Toward Early Retirement* Washington, D.C.: American Enterprise Institute.

Clark, Robert and Joseph Spengler 1980 *The Economics of Individual and Population Aging* Cambridge: Cambridge University Press.

Coughlin, Richard 1979 "Social policy and ideology: public opinion in eight rich nations." *Comparative Social Research* 2, pp. 1–40.

Davis, Kingsley and Pietronella van den Oever 1981 "Age relations and public policy in advanced industrial societies." *Population and Development Review* 7 (March), pp. 1–18.

Employment Benefit Research Institute 1981 *Louis Harris Survey on the Aged* Washington, D.C.: Employee Benefit Research Institute.

Friedman, Milton 1978 "Payroll taxes no; general revenues yes." In Colin Campbell (ed.), *Financing Social Security*, pp. 25–30. San Francisco: Institute for Contemporary Studies.

Geiger, Theodore and Frances M. Geiger 1978 *Welfare and Efficiency. Their Interactions in Western Europe and Implications for International Economic Relations* London: MacMillan.

Gough, Ian 1979 *The Political Economy of Welfare State* London: MacMillan.

Heinz, John and Lawton Chiles (eds.) 1981 "Preface in United States Senate Committee on Aging." *Social Security in Europe: The Impact of an Aging Population*, pp. iii–iv. Washington, D.C.: U.S. Government Printing Office.

Keyfitz, Nathan 1980 "Why social security is in trouble." *The Public Interest* 58, pp. 102–119.

Laffer, Arthur and David Ranson 1977 "A proposal for reforming social security." In G.S. Tolley and Richard v. Burkhauser (eds.), *Income Support for the Aged*, pp. 133–150. Cambridge, Mass.: Ballinger.

Leimer, Dean 1979 "Projected rates of return to future social security retirees under alternative benefit structures." In *Social Security Administration Policy Analysis with Social Security Files*, Research Report No. 52, pp. 235–257. Washington, D.C.: U.S. Government Printing Office.

McDonald, Linda and E. Bower Carty 1979 "Effect of projected population change on expenditures of government." Appendix 16 in *Canadian Government Task Force on Retirement Policy* Hull, Quebec: Canadian Government Publishing Centre.

Myles, John F. 1981 "The trillion dollar misunderstanding: social security's real crisis." *Working Papers Magazine* 8(4), pp. 22–31.

Piven, Frances F. and Richard A. Cloward 1982 *The New Class War* New York: Pantheon Books.

Ross, Standford G. 1979 "Social security: a world-wide issue." *Social Security Bulletin* 4-2(8), pp. 3–1.

Sauvy, Alfred 1948 "Social and economic consequences of the aging of western european populations." *Population Studies* 2(1), pp. 115–124.

Tomasson, Richard F. 1982 "Government old age pensions under affluence and austerity: West Germany, Sweden, the Netherlands, and the United States." Paper presented at the meetings of the Tenth World Congress of the International Sociological Association, August, 1982, Mexico City.

Torrey, Barbara and Carole Thompson 1980 *An International Comparison of Pension Systems* Washington, D.C.: President's Commission on Pension Policy.

Wander, Hilde. 1978. "ZPG now: the lesson from Europe." In Thomas Espenshade and William Serow (eds.), *The Economic Consequences of Slowing Population Growth*, pp. 41–69. New York: Academic Press.

Wilensky, Harold 1975 *The Welfare State and Equality* Berkeley: University of California Press.

Wilensky, Harold 1981 "Leftism, Catholicism and democratic corporation: the role of political parties in recent welfare state development." In Peter Flora and Arnold Heidenheimer (eds.), *The Development of Welfare States in Europe and America*, pp. 345–382. New Brunswick, N.J.: Transaction Books.

FOR FURTHER REFERENCE: AGE

Côté, James E., and Anton L. Allahar 1994 *Generation on Hold: Coming of Age in the Late Twentieth Century* Don Mills: Stoddart Publishing. The authors ask what the consequences are of being born to a generation that follows the baby boomers through the life cycle.

Galaway, Burt, and Joe Hudson 1996 *Youth in Transition: Perspectives on Research and Policy* Toronto: Thompson Educational Publishers. A collection of papers focusing on the transitions of youths from family to school to work, and the many stops and starts in between.

Moore, Eric G. and Mark W. Rosenberg 1997 *Growing Old in Canada: Demographic and Geographic Perspectives* Ottawa: Statistics Canada. Using Census data as their main body of evidence, the authors trace out some of the current trends and future challenges related to our aging society.

Novak, Mark W. 1997 *Aging and Society: A Canadian Perspective* Toronto: ITP Nelson. A recent state-of-the-art treatment of aging in Canadian society.

REGION

Chapter 23

REGIONAL INEQUALITY: EXPLANATIONS AND POLICY ISSUES

Fred Wien

(Revised and abridged from Fred Wien, "Canada's Regions," in James Curtis and Lorne Tepperman (eds.), *Understanding Canadian Society* (Toronto: McGraw-Hill Ryerson, 1988).)

INTRODUCTION

One distinctive feature of being Canadian and living so close to the elephant next door is the continuing puzzle of what makes Canada different from the United States. The significance and severity of regional *inequalities* is part of the answer. A leading student of regional development planning in North America, Benjamin Higgins, says "... there is probably no advanced country where regional disparities play so great a role, economically, socially, and politically, as they do in Canada." He adds "regional disparities are a pressing problem in Canada; the proportion of the populations of lagging regions living in genuine *poverty* is higher and the regions designated as retarded much larger than those of the United States" (Higgins, 1986: 132,160).

This is perhaps not surprising. Canada is vast; there are significant natural and social barriers separating one *region* from another, and considerable differences in population, resources, and industrial structure as one goes from east to west and north to south. In addition, the overwhelming importance of our links to the United States through trade and investment ties has different implications for different regions.

While regional disparities are important, they do not always occupy a central place in Canada's political concerns. In times of economic expansion, when all regions are registering economic growth, one is likely to hear less about the problem, and this is also the case when important national issues dominate the political agenda. Since the 1960s, governments have sought to alleviate the hardship faced by the unemployed and the poor, and to create conditions of *socioeconomic development* on a regionally equitable basis. Optimists hoped these long-standing problems could be resolved by government intervention.

The climate of the 1990s is considerably more subdued. After extensive efforts to reduce regional disparities in Canada, the stubborn problem is still not easily amenable to policy solution. Much has been learned, especially about what not to do and how ineffective many policy options have been. Those interested in regional development are undertaking a sober assessment of what has been accomplished and are searching for new solutions. New issues, such as the conclusion of free trade negotiations with the United States and Mexico, the rapid movement to a technology-based, post-industrial society, and the changing patterns of the ownership and investment of capital in the world economy, pose new challenges whose implications for regional inequalities are not yet clear.

In this chapter, we review the debate on regional inequality in Canada, with appropriate comparisons to the United States. In particular, we will examine: what is the extent of regional inequality in Canada? How do social science theorists explain it? What have governments, especially national ones, tried to do about the problem? How successful have these measures been? And what lessons can be drawn from this experience as we look ahead to new issues in this perplexing field?

The Dimensions of Regional Inequality

While there is agreement on the importance of regionalism and regional inequality in Canada (Matthews, 1980), the definition of a region remains an important problem. It is an issue for measuring inequality and changes over time—what unit of analysis should be used—and for implementing policy. Successive governments have, in the last few decades, taken quite different interpretations of what constitutes a disadvantaged region for purposes of targeting various policy initiatives; they make their decisions as much on political grounds as on the basis of a rational analysis of pertinent social and economic characteristics.

The issue is this. The larger the area encompassed by the term "region," the more likely it is that it will include significant internal variations or disparities. For example, the Western region (Manitoba, Saskatchewan, Alberta, and British Columbia) has some characteristics in common, but also enormous diversities. Similarly, the Atlantic provinces are often lumped together, but the provinces differ considerably in their potential for the development of agriculture, forestry, manufacturing, or energy, for example. On the other hand, if a small, localized area is targeted (for example, a census district or a disadvantaged area within a province), policy solutions may be handicapped because the underlying conditions contributing to the problem may require consideration of a broader geographic area. Can the problems of Cape Breton be resolved in isolation from the mainland of Nova Scotia? Can the stagnation of Eastern Ontario be considered outside of the context of the developments centred around Toronto, Ottawa, or Montreal?

In practice, the province is most often used as the unit defining a region because data are most readily available at the provincial level, and less so for municipalities and other units. This is also occasioned by Canada's federal nature and the political and legal/constitutional significance of provincial governments.

What are some indicators of regional inequality in Canada, using provincial-level data? Typically, economic measures are used and, among these, per capita income and unemployment rates are most prevalent. Other economic measures often cited reveal the productive capacity of the province (e.g., provincial gross domestic product per person, which measures the value of goods and services produced) and rates of poverty. Other social indicators describe the educational level of the labour force, the health of the population (e.g., infant mortality rates), or living standards (e.g., a crowding index with respect to housing). Some contemporary data measuring regional inequality are found in Table 23-1.

The figures from Table 23-1 show substantial inequalities on all the measures. Per capita income in Newfoundland is only 76 percent of what it is in Ontario. The unemployment rate and the likelihood of having families or unattached individuals in poverty also vary sharply among the provinces.

From these figures, it is obvious that social and economic outcomes of individual and family well-being differ significantly by region. Just as it makes a difference into what family one is born, so it makes a difference where the family is located by region.

EXPLANATIONS OF REGIONAL INEQUALITY

There are some reasonably clear theoretical interpretations of regional inequality available, and we examine three below. Each explains why inequalities exist and each suggests what policies might remedy the situation. The difficulty is that competing explanations suggest strategies that are incompatible with one another, and there is no agreement on which framework is the most appropriate. Many analysts feel none gives a complete explanation, and they pragmatically suggest some wisdom is found in most, if not all, the alternatives. They may also argue some explanations are better at explaining the origin of disparities in previous decades, while others are better under contemporary conditions.

TABLE 23-1 Measures of regional inequality in Canada, by province, recent years

Province	Personal Income per capita 1996	Unemployment Rate 1996	Poverty Rate 1995
Newfoundland	17 958	19.5	20.6
Prince Edward Island	18 708	14.7	12.0
Nova Scotia	19 097	12.6	17.8
New Brunswick	18 802	11.7	17.2
Quebec	21 493	11.8	20.6
Ontario	23 910	9.0	15.3
Manitoba	21 409	7.5	17.6
Saskatchewan	20 889	6.6	16.3
Alberta	23 511	7.1	17.4
British Columbia	23 857	8.9	16.9
Canada	22 681	9.7	17.4
Disparity Ratio (highest/lowest)	1.34	2.96	1.72

Sources: Columns 1 & 2: Statistics Canada, Catalogue 13-213, Provincial Economic Accounts Annual Estimates, 1996.
Column 3: National Council of Welfare, Poverty Profile 1995 Poverty by Province (All Persons).

The Staples Approach

Staples are "raw or semi-processed materials extracted or grown primarily for export markets and dominating the regional or national economies" (Marchak, 1985: 674). In view of Canada's historic reliance on staple production and export, it is not surprising that Canadian social scientists emphasize this factor when explaining regional inequality and national development. The roots of a staples approach trace back to the writings of Mackintosh (1923), Innis (1930;1940;1956), and others who examined successive staples, such as furs, cod, square timbers, and wheat, their social, political, and economic impact, and the factors that shaped their development. More contemporary interpretations that attempt to specify the theory more clearly and to delimit its applicability are found in Watkins (1977) and Scott (1978). Watkins, in particular, suggests staple theory as elaborated in the earlier writings only has explanatory value if applied to "new" countries such as Australia, New Zealand, or Canada. These countries historically have had few people in relation to their land and other resources, and few inhibiting traditions.

In this context, it is argued, a region's prosperity depends on the availability and marketability of its natural resources, and the region's success in using the production or extraction of the staple (and the proceeds derived from this) in developing the rest of its economy. In other words, a region will prosper if it has a valued resource that can be profitably marketed abroad, and if it can extend appropriate linkages to other economic sectors (manufacturing, services, etc.) so that they receive a stimulus from the export sector.

There are many conditions under which a given staple can become the engine of economic growth. Simply discovering a valued resource may be the key; change in technology or transportation may make it economical to produce a staple that has already been discovered, but not exploited. Alternatively, the demand (and price) for a resource may increase, depending on levels of need in importing countries and its availability from other suppliers. In any case, if the conditions are favourable, capital and labour will likely flow into the region to develop and export the staple.

As noted above, whether the exploitation of the staple will lead to significant spread effects to benefit the economy of the region as a whole depends on the linkages established. For example, if a lot of equipment is required to extract or produce the staple, and if that equipment can be locally manufactured, then the manufacturing sector will be stimulated. If the natural resource can be processed locally rather than being exported in a raw state, then the regional economy will gain jobs and income. If labour is attracted to the export sector and receives high wages, then a local demand for consumer goods will be created. The region's long term economic development, therefore, depends on the extent to which the stimulus provided by the exploitation of the staple can be generalized to diversify the economy.

Unfortunately, it is in the nature of staple production that the demand for a given staple, and therefore its price, may eventually decline. Consumer preferences may change, new synthetic alternatives may be found, the resources may be exhausted, production costs may increase, or other regions or countries may take over an established market. If the region has diversified its economy, the decline in the staple exporting sector is less of a problem. Labour and capital freed up in the declining sector can be redeployed to other productive uses. Some migration outside the region can also be expected, depending on factors such as government policy and opportunities elsewhere. It is more likely, however, that dependence on the staple product will continue and that there will be a reluctance to adjust to the situation. Attempts may be made to subsidize and protect the declining industry, rather than encouraging a search for alternative sources of economic growth. Governments may also seek to retain their population base, rather than encouraging migration from the region. Unless a new staple can be found and developed, the region may stagnate and decline.

There are perhaps two additional, important features of staple theory as it has been developed by Canadian political economists. First, the importance of staple production for a region or country is not restricted to its narrowly economic implications. Each staple, including the way its production is organized, leaves its imprint politically, socially, and culturally on the region. The transition in Alberta from an economy dominated by farming, for example, to one dominated by energy production and export sped up the urbanization trend in the province, encouraged the development of a large managerial/entrepreneurial class, and replaced a populist-agrarian political regime with one responsive to the new urban elite (Mansell, 1986). Second, writers, such as Innis and, more recently, Watkins (1977), Drache (1976), and a host of others, have emphasized the negative implications of a staple economy—notably, the dependence on a foreign industrial centre through market and trade relations that are exploitative and constraining, the periodic crisis and boom/bust periods, and the distortions induced in the economy and society by an area that lacks a diversified, self-reliant, and self-regulated economic base. We will return to this theme when we discuss *dependency* theory in a later section.

Critics of a staples approach often suggest the perspective provided important insights historically, when regional economies centred around the fur trade, the cod fishery, or wheat growing. They suggest, however, that staple production has receded in importance over time; Buckley (1958), in fact, dates the decline of the utility of the approach as early as 1820. The Economic Council of Canada (1977:8) concludes "... the maturing Canadian economy has reached the point where resources and transportation are no longer, as in the past, the only important determinants of regional variations in the well-being of Canadians, and we now have productive processes that are more complex and utilize natural resources somewhat differently."

Others disagree, and continue to use the staples approach when analyzing the impact that staple development has on economies such as Alberta's (Mansell, 1986), British Columbia's (Marchak, 1983), Newfoundland's (Royal Commission, 1986), or Canada's North (Berger, 1977).

Perspectives Emphasizing Regional Deficiencies

Students studying the *underdevelopment* of Third World countries in the 1950s and 1960s became acquainted with the modernization, or development, model. It suggested important characteristics of the traditional sector in a given country needed to be overcome if development were to proceed. The source of change, and the model for development, was the modern, urban, industrial sector of the country. Characterized by technologies based on machine production in large factories, the modernization approach suggested the relationships, culture, political institutions, and social structures appropriate to modern industrial society would spread from the (modern) centre to the (traditional) periphery. This spread was to be effected primarily by the competition mechanism of the free market, which would destroy or transform the backward enterprises and the traditional characteristics of the groups working in them. Increased mobility of individuals between country and city, mass communications and transportation, formal education and the development of a modern state, would all serve to disseminate rational, income-maximizing behaviours that would eventually be common to all members of the society.

The development perspective was also applied to explain regional underdevelopment in advanced industrial societies. It was not transferred without modification, however. While it is difficult to speak of development in Latin American countries without dealing with the overwhelming significance of the agriculture sector and the need for land reform, such is not the case in Canada. The debate in Canada also does not dwell particularly on differences in progressive or traditional attitudes, values, and social structures between one part of the country and another.

It is argued, however, that some regions of Canada are underdeveloped because their deficiencies stand in the way of their improving their situation in employment and income terms relative to other regions. Several factors have been identified: location in relation to markets and therefore the burden of transportation costs; lower rates of capital investment; shortcomings in infrastructure, such as roads, railways, harbours, sewers, schools, and hospitals; lower levels of investment in education and training of the work force (human capital); inferior managerial quality; and lower levels of investment in new productive technology. Most of these factors contribute to the productivity of industry and thus to income and employment levels in the region.

Analysts proceeding from different theoretical perspectives identify other deficiencies. Keynesian economists, for example, suggest the demand for goods and services in a region may be too low and should be stimulated by government policy. Regional scientists look at the distribution of people in areas. They argue, for example, that growth in income and employment has occurred more rapidly in urban areas than in small town or rural areas; hence, some regions may be too sparsely populated. Growth centres or development poles need to be encouraged so industries can be located next to each other in an industrial complex and take advantage of complementarities and of a large urban market for goods and services.

Running through much of the mainstream, orthodox approach to regional disparities is a faith in the operation of the free market, characteristic of neoclassical economic perspectives. Here, the deficiencies highlighted are the rigidities and other forms of interference with the market which maintain and exacerbate regional inequalities. As Courchene puts it, regional disparities are to some extent a problem of economic adjustment, a problem of interference with the natural adjustment mechanisms of the economy.

If one were focusing on interregional differences in incomes, the neoclassic approach would assume that, under free market conditions, workers would move from a low income to a high income area of the country as they seek to improve their economic condition. Again, however, artificial impediments prevent this "natural" equalization from occurring. If in the poorer region minimum wage rates are higher than they should be, or if unemployment insurance payments are more generous in the amount paid and their duration, then the incentive to leave the region is correspondingly reduced. The same result occurs if the actions of unions, governments, or corporations keep wages higher than they should be. As these examples illustrate, the deficiency identified by neoclassical economists is not limited to the disadvantaged area, but is also built into the policies and practices of national governments, unions, or corporations in interaction with the poorer region.

Courchene concludes that because the natural adjustment mechanisms of the market are not free to work as they should, provincial governments increasingly depend on federal transfers to sustain themselves, which exacerbates the problem. He suggests the various problems interact—if wages are prevented from moving downward in a poor province, then unemployment remains high. This triggers an influx of federal funds (e.g., for unemployment insurance). But the more money that flows in, the less incentive there is for the province or region to worry about the adequacy of wage adjustment and factor (labour, capital) mobility. "This is a vicious circle, and it is imperative that it is broken" (Courchene, 1986:35).

Perspectives Emphasizing Exploitation and Dependence

Dependency theory first appeared in the late 1960s, and generated considerable intellectual excitement because it directly challenged the main tenets of modernization theory (Frank, 1972). Articulated primarily by Latin American intellectuals, the approach contains three main arguments.

First, dependency theory suggests underdevelopment is caused by exploitation by capitalist metropolitan centres. Far from being models of modernity to be emulated, the "developed" areas prosper at the expense of the "traditional" societies. Further, the exploitative relationship between, for example, the United States and Latin America is reproduced within both developed and underdeveloped countries—thus accounting for regional inequality. One early application of the dependency perspective to Canada by A.K. Davis (1971) divided the country into metropolitan (e.g., the urban industrial core) and hinterland (e.g., the North, the West, and Atlantic Canada) areas. Davis argued the metropolis continuously dominates and exploits the hinterland, but the hinterland groups and interests tend to fight back against their metropolitan exploiters.

Second, underdevelopment occurs when resources are drained from peripheral to central areas. The latter control the terms of trade for products. Thus, raw materials are exported from hinterland or satellite regions at prices below their true value, and manufactured goods from the central area are sold at exorbitant prices. Banks headquartered in metropolitan or core areas drain the regions of their savings and invest them outside these areas, and labour is attracted to the core when needed, but sent back to the periphery when not. Often, the multinational corporation is regarded as the chief agent of exploitation, and the relationship between core and periphery is seen as uniformly negative. In other versions, multinationals located in a peripheral area and producing goods for a local market can be acknowledged as a source of growth and dynamism, since they need to create some internal prosperity in order to sell their consumer goods. However, while some local wealth is generated, substantial losses of capital resources from the area occur through profit remittances, interest payments, and royalties. If the result is not uniform underdevelopment in the peripheral region, it is at best uneven development or dependent development (Cardoso, 1972).

Numerous Canadian studies in the dependency tradition emphasize this theme—for example, examinations of the de-industrialization of the Maritimes from 1890 to 1920 and its continuing underdevelopment in the interim (Archibald, 1971; Acheson, 1977; Forbes, 1977; Matthews, 1977; House 1981; Bickerton, 1990). A similar perspective has been used in studies of agriculture and oil development on the prairies (Fowke, 1957, 1968; Pratt, 1976; Knuttilia and McCrorie, 1980) and in examinations of Native-White interactions in the context of resource development in the Canadian North (Watkins, 1977; Kellough, 1980; Elias, 1975).

If development is externally controlled and exploitative, economic and social distortions will arise in the dependent area. In economic terms, development usually focuses on extracting raw materials according to a timetable dictated by the external interests. The development of an integrated, balanced economy, in which local resources are harnessed by local entrepreneurs to meet local needs, is hampered by external decision-making and the co-optation of social resources. Here, the dependency theory argument is similar to the more pessimistic version of staples theory, which suggests that the backward, forward, and final demand linkages that would stimulate the development of a balanced economy do not, in fact, materialize. In social terms, dependency theory focuses on the class structure of the metropolitan and satellite areas. While different analysts of particular regions or countries will identify various kinds of social class constellations, all analyses identify dominant elites and subordinate labourers in both centre and periphery. Parts of the dominant periphery elite are linked to the centre elite and serve as its agent in the satellite area (Matthews, 1980; Dos Santos, 1971; Stavenhagen, 1974). In the Canadian context, for example, Clement argues that a portion of the economic elite of Canada's peripheral regions has been bought out by central Canadian and American business interests, and serves those interests in the region (Clement, 1983).

Dependency theory as an explanation for regional inequality in Canada has numerous critics. Some question the applicability of a model articulated initially to explain underdevelopment in the Third World to the Canadian context, where neither low returns for labour (i.e., low wages), nor low returns for the exported resource product, nor a large traditional population sector have obtained (Marchak, 1985). Others have questioned whether the theory has much to add to what has already been articulated, perhaps more appropriately for Canada, by staple theorists such as Innis and Watkins. In many ways, the debate has moved on to larger questions and broader perspectives due to dissatisfaction with the rather simplistic dyadic relationships of dependency theory (Friedman and Wayne, 1977). Indeed, in the 1970s and 1980s, a good deal of attention was devoted to encapsulating dependency theory (and also staples theory) within the broader Marxist paradigm. (See Veltmeyer, 1979; Naylor, 1975; Clement, 1975, 1977; Niosi, 1978, 1981; Brym and Sacouman, 1979.)

PUBLIC POLICY MEASURES

While regional issues are of ongoing importance in Canada, perhaps the earliest policies explicitly directed to alleviating regional disparities were the measures undertaken to counter the drought and depression experienced by Canada's regions in the 1930s. World War II intervened and shifted attention to the need for mobilization in support of the war effort and to national reconstruction when the war ended. Economic prosperity lasting until the mid-1950s kept regional inequalities off the national agenda.

In the last few decades, however, and until recently, regional disparities have been a more important consideration in government policy. This results, in part, from less favourable economic circumstances, and also because of a more interventionist approach by governments in resolving social and economic problems. Perceptions of the issue also changed with the growing recognition that the relative gap between regions was the important consideration, not their absolute level of poverty or well-being, nor their current rates of economic growth or stagnation.

In examining the policies pursued, one is struck by the variety of measures implemented and by the frequent changes in approach. There is a myriad of policies designed to promote regional development or reduce disparities, and all three levels of government are active in the field. And, although some policies are clearly and explicitly directed at the problem, others have only indirect implications, while still others are not directed to the problem at all, and end up frustrating the intent and effect of the more explicit approaches.

There is considerable and frequent change in policies, in part because regional development policies are important for voter support. Thus, each successive government wants to put its stamp on regional development efforts. The approaches change, as well, because conditions change—policies appropriate during a period of economic growth may be inappropriate in a period of decline.

What is the source of regional development policy? One source is the theoretical perspectives outlined in the previous section, each suggesting certain policies consistent with the analysis presented. Political concerns also influence regional policy. A good example is the 1970s shift in resources and attention designed to counteract separatist sentiment in Quebec.

The major kinds of initiatives that have been undertaken by the federal government—sometimes in co-operation with the provinces and sometimes unilaterally—are:

1. Investments in infrastructure such as roads, harbours, schools, hospitals, wharves, and railroads.
2. Human capital investments and personal adjustment. Here the emphasis is on providing education, training, and mobility grants for the unemployed who wish to change careers or move to an area that offers better opportunities.
3. Policies of industrial assistance. These have included tax exemptions, tax credits, loan guarantees, or cash grants to individual firms to encourage them to locate in a depressed area. The same measures have been used to help new firms get started or existing ones to expand, diversify, or export more of their products. Much debate has taken place about the effectiveness of industrial assistance policies. They have been criticized for supporting capital-intensive (rather than employment-intensive) establishments, and for attracting "footloose" industries to a region—that is, firms with few backward and forward linkages and with little commitment to their new location.
4. Policies directed to resource and sectoral development. The federal government, under its Department of Regional Economic Expansion in the late 1970s and more recently under other auspices, has signed general development agreements with the provinces. The agreements have provided federal financial support for the development of forestry, agriculture, or tourism. In the early 1980s, attention was given to stimulating the economy through investments in energy-sector mega-projects such as the extraction of coal in British Columbia and oil in Alberta. In the late 1990s, major new oil and natural gas developments off the east coast have also attracted government support.
5. Compensatory and transfer policies. By far the greatest amount of federal money in support of the provinces and their residents is spent not for explicit development policies, but as cash transfers to the provinces and to individual citizens or families. Equalization grants, funds

for hospitals, medicare, and post-secondary education, payments for unemployment insurance, family allowances, and similar grants make up the bulk of these transfers. They greatly overshadow the budgets of the explicit regional development programs mentioned above (Lithwick, 1986). The grants to the provinces have made the provincial governments of the poorer regions very dependent on federal transfers for their total spending budget. The dependence of individuals on personal transfer income is also substantial in the poorer provinces and is growing over time.

The policies designed to stimulate regional development have been pursued within several organizational frameworks. In the late 1950s and for much of the 1960s, discrete policies, such as the Federal Fund for Rural Economic Development, were administered by a variety of departments. The Trudeau administration, beginning in 1969, tried to consolidate all relevant programs under the newly created Department of Regional Economic Expansion. DREE was disbanded in 1982, however, in favour of an approach that provides for a federal coordinator's office in each region and the consideration of regional implications by Cabinet for all economic policies, not just those explicitly directed to regional development. Many DREE programs were allocated to other departments in the 1982 reorganization. Subsequently, the Mulroney government established regional development agencies in Atlantic Canada and the West.

Different target areas have also been used—whole provinces, disadvantaged areas within and/or across provinces, focused growth poles and their hinterlands, and so forth.

As noted above, however, regional development policy is only one aspect of federal policy. Other policies, whether intended or not, also have regional consequences. In fact, one theoretical approach to the explanation of regional inequalities focuses on broader policy areas such as those governing tariffs, trade, transportation costs, and fiscal and monetary policy. Building on the work of Fowke (Fowke, 1952), writers in this tradition advance the argument that a given set of national policies is successful for only a limited period of time. Then international conditions change, internal political pressures build up, and the search is on for a new set of national policies, one that will set the economy on a new path of development (Brodie, 1997).

In this view, the political economy of Canada has been characterized by three sets of national policies—the first lasting from 1867 to the 1940s, the second from the Second World War to the 1970s, and the third in the past three decades. While the intent of such policies is to find a new formula for promoting national economic growth, in fact they have uneven impacts on the regions. In the present time, for example, when the emphasis is on free trade agreements, market-driven development, and a reduced role for the state, there is less room to sustain regional development and equalization policies of the kind described above. Success in the new economy is likely to be linked to how well different regions can integrate into the continental and global market. Some regions, such as British Columbia, with its access to the Pacific Rim, are likely to be more successful in this venture than others as long as the Asian economies remain healthy (Brodie, 1997).

THE PERSISTENCE OF REGIONAL DISPARITIES

There is widespread agreement among experts in regional development on the main conclusions to be drawn.

First, in per capita income, one of the main measures usually employed to measure regional inequality, the gap between the richest and the poorest provinces has decreased over time. Table 23-2 shows the poorest provinces improved their relative per capita incomes from approximately 60 percent of the national average in 1961 to just over 80 percent in 1996. The richer provinces, Ontario, Alberta, and British Columbia, have also moved closer to the national average over time. Overall, there has been considerable improvement in relative per capita incomes over the period when policy intervention has been most intense (Economic Council, 1977).

Second, Table 23-2 shows almost all the improvement can be attributed to transfer payments, such as employment insurance, family allowances, old age security, payments under the Canada Assistance plan, and so forth. If these kinds of compensatory transfers to individuals and families are excluded from per capita income, as they are in Table 23-3, the improvement in relative per capita incomes has been rather small. Put another way, the attack on regional inequality has resulted in greater equity in the country as a result of transfers from the richer provinces to the poorer ones (via the federal treasury), but it has not significantly improved the productive capacity of the poorer regions, enabling them to generate higher earned incomes relative to the national average on the basis of their own productive resources.

Similarly discouraging data are provided in Table 23-4, which gives the results for unemployment rates, another common measure of regional disparity. We see improvement in the disparity between 1971 and 1981, reduced disparity in the subsequent decade, and then again increased inequality between 1991 and 1996 as the extremes moved further apart.

We began this chapter by suggesting regional inequality was a substantial and persisting problem in Canada, which made it unique among advanced industrial (or post-industrial societies). We are, perhaps, in a

TABLE 23-2 Personal income per capita, by province, 1961–1996 (Relation to the national average, Canada = 100)

Province	1961	1971	1980	1990	1996
Newfoundland	58.2	63.6	64.0	71.4	79.2
Prince Edward Island	58.8	63.7	71.0	73.6	82.5
Nova Scotia	77.5	77.4	79.1	81.8	84.2
New Brunswick	67.8	72.2	71.1	76.9	82.9
Quebec	90.1	88.8	94.5	92.7	94.8
Ontario	118.3	117.0	107.0	113.4	105.4
Manitoba	94.3	94.0	89.5	86.8	94.4
Saskatchewan	70.8	80.3	91.0	80.2	92.1
Alberta	100.0	98.9	111.6	99.0	103.7
British Columbia	114.9	109.0	111.3	101.0	105.2
Canada	100.0	100.0	100.0	100.0	100.0
Disparity Ratio (highest/lowest)	2.03	1.84	1.74	1.59	1.34

Source: Adapted from Polese (1987) with 1990 data from Statistics Canada, Catalogue 13-201, Annual System of National Accounts, 1991. 1996 data from Statistics Canada, Catalogue 13-213, Provincial Economic Accounts, 1996.

TABLE 23-3 Earned income per capita, by province, 1966–1990 (Relation to the national average, Canada = 100)

Province	1966	1971	1976	1981	1986	1990
Newfoundland	52.6	54.8	56.1	53.4	57.2	58.9
Prince Edward Island	53.6	57.0	60.2	59.0	66.1	65.4
Nova Scotia	71.5	74.2	74.2	73.4	79.3	77.5
New Brunswick	65.1	68.1	69.0	64.9	70.1	70.5
Quebec	89.2	87.8	90.4	89.9	90.4	90.2
Ontario	118.3	119.2	112.5	110.6	114.3	117.2
Manitoba	91.0	93.7	93.9	92.9	89.6	84.5
Saskatchewan	92.3	78.7	99.5	98.9	86.5	76.6
Alberta	99.0	98.6	105.0	114.4	106.3	100.9
British Columbia	111.0	109.5	109.5	109.7	99.4	101.5
Canada	100.0	100.0	100.0	100.0	100.0	100.0
Disparity Ratio (highest/lowest)	2.25	2.17	2.00	2.14	2.00	1.98

Source: Statistics Canada, Provincial Economic Accounts

TABLE 23-4 Provincial unemployment rate, 1966–1996, by province (Relation to the national average, Canada = 100)

Province	1966	1971	1976	1981	1986	1991	1996
Newfoundland	171	135	189	186	208	178	201.0
Prince Edward Island	—	—	135	150	140	163	151.6
Nova Scotia	138	113	134	134	140	116	129.9
New Brunswick	156	98	155	154	150	123	120.6
Quebec	121	118	123	137	115	115	121.7
Ontario	76	87	87	87	73	93	92.8
Manitoba	82	92	66	79	80	85	77.3
Saskatchewan	44	56	55	61	80	71	68.1
Alberta	74	92	56	50	102	79	73.2
British Columbia	135	116	121	88	131	96	91.8
Canada	100.0	100.0	100.0	100.0	100.0	100.0	100.0
Disparity Ratio (highest/lowest)	3.88	2.41	3.43	3.72	2.85	2.50	2.96

Source: Statistics Canada, The Labour Force. 1996 data from Statistics Canada, Catalogue 13-213, Provincial Economic Accounts Annual Estimates, 1996.

somewhat better position now to look at the United States' experience, so as to gain a comparative perspective on the problem.

Geography's influence is important. While Canada has significant natural resources, the United States has the added advantage of a wide dispersion of good agricultural land, mineral resources, and forests. Its people are also more evenly distributed and its urban centres are more balanced in size and location at various points along the coast and in the interior. By contrast, much of the Canadian population is concentrated in the Toronto–Montreal area, as is the preponderance of its manufacturing capacity and financial institutions. The greater concentration in Canada is explained not only by the advantages of a central location to serve the more peripheral areas of the country, but also because most foreign (i.e., American) investment is located in southern Ontario, close to the major U.S. markets and to American head offices. Thus, the overwhelming importance of the United States in trade and investment exerts its influence on the regional distribution of productive resources and population in Canada (Semple, 1987). The United States has no similar relationship to a foreign power. Many different centres relate to a number of international contexts—Boston/New York on the Atlantic relating to Europe, Miami in the south oriented to Latin America, Los Angeles and San Francisco on the Pacific, and so forth. In addition, regional centres in the interior provide urban focal points for their surrounding areas—St. Louis, Minneapolis-St. Paul, and Chicago, to name a few.

Canada is also much more dependent on resource exports and is therefore more subject than the United States to the distortions, uncertainties, and pitfalls that this kind of economic development brings, as the staple and dependency theorists have described.

Another significant difference between Canada and the United States is the cultural make-up and distribution of the two populations. In Canada, the large concentration of the French-speaking population in Quebec and adjacent areas overlaps with regional disparities. In the United States, the significant ethnic and racial minorities are not concentrated in one area. Higgins (1986) argues that the United States has had an extraordinary mobility of labour and capital, and that this has helped to even out regional disparities. The attachment of Canadians to their cultural communities is said to have reduced mobility.

As a result of these factors, regional disparities are less significant in the United States, and less entrenched. Significant reductions in regional disparities have taken place over the long term, and in the short run some regions have declined (as New England did in the 1970s), while others have grown rapidly (as did the so-called Sunbelt in the same period). The intractable problems of localized underdevelopment seem more associated with problems of the decay, neglect, and exploitation of core areas within large urban centres than with large geographic regions. In the urban context, however, racial/ethnic divisions often overlap with areas of underdevelopment.

CONCLUSION

The stability of regional inequality patterns in Canada is impressive, perhaps more so than the changes caused by thirty years of concerted effort (Polese, 1987). This is not to say that the policy measures undertaken have failed, since there is improvement on some measures and since the situation could have worsened without these measures.

Also, much has been learned in the process. For example, it is now clear that transferring funds to provincial governments and to families and individuals reduces inequalities in regional per capita incomes, and is defensible on equity grounds. The debate about whether such transfers have a negative effect on the economic development of the region, by interfering with the adaptive processes, as Courchene (1986) maintains, continues.

The key issue is clearer now than it was before: how to bring about self-sustaining, indigenous economic development in the disadvantaged regions. How should or can a region overcome locational disadvantages, resource shortages, or external dependencies? A good deal of searching and experimenting is taking place. In the Atlantic region, for example, there is considerable interest in community-based economic development—setting up non-profit community development agencies that rely on local initiative and external support to promote economic and social development (MacLeod, 1986). Consistent with this thrust, there is concern that regional development policy has been too narrowly focused on economic measures and has neglected necessary and complementary community development initiatives (MacNeil, 1997). Provincial governments are charting plans for the economic development of their provinces: in Nova Scotia through a policy of "building competitiveness," in Newfoundland through "building on our strengths" (Report of the Royal Commission on Employment and Unemployment, 1986). And significant changes are taking place in the private sector as the trend toward the consolidation of ownership in the hands of a few local families continues in provinces such as New Brunswick.

In addition, the federal government has retreated from regional development issues—in budget terms because of federal deficits, in ideological terms as renewed faith is placed in the workings of the market, and in priority terms as national issues such as free trade dominate the agenda.

Thus, the future of Canada's disadvantaged regions will also be shaped by events and trends impinging on the regions from outside, as well as by internal dynamics. The Canada-U.S. Free Trade Agreement is a case in point. While there is agreement that the disadvantaged regions will gain as consumers (in that prices are likely to be lower as trade barriers with the United States are reduced), it is not clear what the differential impact of free trade will be on the productive capacity of the regions (Watson, 1987; Pinchin, 1986). The shift to an information-based economy, signalled by the continued growth of the service sector and the increased significance of knowledge-based industries, also holds out opportunities and problems. The trend is potentially positive for disadvantaged regions in that the new technology could overcome some locational and natural resource disadvantages (Macrae, 1986). There are questions, however, about the speed of adoption of new technology in disadvantaged regions, and about limitations in the size of markets and urban centres, among other considerations (Lesser, 1987; Osberg, Wien, and Grude, 1995).

The study of regional inequality is therefore at a turning point in that the perspectives and policies prevalent for many years are increasingly being questioned, especially with respect to their results and usefulness in dealing with present and future issues. In this time of reassessment, it is comforting to know that those of us who live in Canada's disadvantaged areas have a fall-back position to rely on. As the chairman of the 1957 Royal Commission on Canada's Economic Prospects once suggested, the poorer regions of the country could always be converted into national parks!

REFERENCES

Acheson, T.W. 1977 "The Maritimes and 'Empire Canada.'" In D.J. Bercuson (ed.) *Canada and The Burden of Unity* Toronto: Macmillan.

Archibald, Bruce 1971 "Atlantic regional underdevelopment and socialism." In L.

LaPierre et al. (eds.) *Essays on the Left* Toronto: McClelland and Stewart.

Berger, Justice Thomas R. 1977 *Northern Frontier, Northern Homeland: The Report of the Mackenzie Valley Pipeline Inquiry* Ottawa: Supply and Services Canada.

Boudeville, J.R. 1968 *Problems of Regional Economic Planning* Edinburgh: Edinburgh University Press.

Brodie, Janine 1997 "The new political economy of regions." In Wallace Clement (ed.) *Understanding Canada: Building on the New Canadian Political Economy* Montreal and Kingston: McGill-Queen's University Press.

Brym, Robert and James Sacouman (eds.) 1979 *Underdevelopment and Social Movements in Atlantic Canada* Toronto: New Hogtown Press.

Buckley, Kenneth 1958 "The role of staple industries in Canada's economic development." *Journal of Economic History,* 18 (December): 439–50.

Cardoso, Fernando 1972 "Dependency and development in Latin America." *New Left Review*, 74 (14) (July–August): 83–95.

Clement, Wallace 1975 *The Canadian Corporate Elite* Toronto: McClelland and Stewart.

Clement, Wallace 1983 *Class, Power and Poverty: Essays on Canadian Society* Toronto: Methuen.

Courchene, Thomas 1986 "Avenues of adjustment: the transfer system and regional disparities." In Roger Savoie (ed.) *The Canadian Economy: A Regional Perspective* Toronto: Methuen.

Davis, A.K. 1971 "Canadian society and history as hinterland versus metropolis." In R.J. Ossenberg (ed.) *Canadian Society: Pluralism, Change and Conflict* Scarborough, Ontario: Prentice Hall.

Department Of Development 1984 *Building Competitiveness: The White Paper on Economic Development in Nova Scotia* Halifax: Government of Nova Scotia.

Dos Santos, Theotonio 1971 "The structure of dependence." In K.T. Fann and D.C. Hodges (eds.) *Readings in U.S. Imperialism* Boston: Porter Sargent.

Drache, Daniel 1976 "Rediscovering Canadian political economy." *Journal of Canadian Studies*, 11 (3) (August):3–18.

Economic Council Of Canada 1977 *Living Together: A Study of Regional Disparities* Ottawa: Supply and Services Canada.

Elias, Peter 1975 *Metropolis and Hinterland in Northern Manitoba* Winnipeg: The Manitoba Museum of Man and Nature.

Forbes, Ernest 1977 "Misguided symmetry: the destruction of regional transportation policy for the maritimes." In D.J. Bercusson (ed.) *Canada and the Burden of Unity* Toronto: Macmillan.

Fowke, Vernon 1952 "The national policy — old and new." *Canadian Journal of Economics and Political Science*, 18 (3) (August): 271–86.

Fowke, Vernon 1957 *The National Policy and the Wheat Economy* Toronto: University of Toronto Press.

Fowke, Vernon 1968 "Political economy and the Canadian wheat grower." In Norman Ward and Duff Spafford (eds.) *Politics in Saskatchewan* Toronto: Longmans Canada.

Frank, Andre Gunder 1972 " Sociology of development and underdevelopment of Sociology." In James Cockcroft et al. (eds.) *Dependence and Underdevelopment: Latin America's Political Economy* New York: Doubleday.

Friedman, Harriet and Jack Wayne 1977 "Dependency theory: a critique." *Canadian Journal of Sociology*, 2(4) (Winter): 399–416.

Higgins, Benjamin 1959 *Economic Development: Principles, Problems, and Policies* New York: W.W. Norton.

Higgins, Benjamin 1986 "Regional development planning: the state of the art in North America." In Donald Savoie (ed.) *The Canadian Economy: A Regional Perspective* Toronto: Methuen.

House, Douglas 1981 "Big oil and small communities in coastal Labrador: the local dynamics of dependency." *Canadian Review of Sociology and Anthropology*, 18 (4) (November): 433–52.

Innis, Harold 1930 *The Fur Trade in Canada* Toronto: University of Toronto Press.

Innis, Harold 1940 *The Cod Fisheries* Toronto: University of Toronto Press.

Innis, Harold 1956 *Essays in Canadian Economic History* Mary Q. Innis (ed.) Toronto: University of Toronto Press.

Isard, Walter 1975 *Introduction to Regional Science* Englewood Cliffs, New Jersey: Prentice Hall.

Kellough, Gail 1980 "From colonialism to economic imperialism." In J. Harp and J. Hofley (eds.) *Structured Inequality in Canada* Scarborough, Ontario: Prentice Hall.

Knuttila, K.M., and J.N. Mccrorie 1980 "National policy and prairie agrarian development: a reassessment." *Canadian Review of Sociology and Anthropology*, 17 (3) (August): 263–72.

Lesser, Barry 1987 "Regional development: some thoughts arising from a review of research sponsored by the Institute for Research on Public Policy." In William Coffey and Mario Polese (eds.) *Still Living Together: Recent Trends and Future Directions in Canadian Regional Development* Montreal: The Institute for Research on Public Policy.

Lithwick, Harvey (ed.) 1978 *Regional Economic Policy: The Canadian Experience* Toronto: McGraw-Hill Ryerson.

Lithwick, Harvey 1986 "Regional policy: the embodiment of contradictions." In Donald Savoie (ed.) *The Canadian Economy: A Regional Perspective* Toronto: Methuen.

Mackintosh, W.A. 1923 "Economic factors in Canadian history." *Canadian Historical Review,* IV (1) (March): 12–25.

Macleod, Greg 1986 *New Age Business: Community Corporations That Work* Ottawa: The Canadian Council on Social Development.

Macrae, Norman 1986 "A forecast of what the knowledge-based society will bring." Presentation to the Symposium on the Revolution in Knowledge: Atlantic Canada's Future in the Information Economy. Halifax: Dalhousie University.

Mansell, Robert 1986 "Energy policy, prices and rents: implications for regional growth and development." In William Coffey and Mario Polese (eds.) *Still Living Together: Recent Trends and Future Directions in Canadian Regional Development.* Montreal: The Institute for Research on Public Policy.

Marchak, Patricia 1983 *Green Gold: The Forest Industry in British Columbia* Vancouver: The University of British Columbia Press.

Marchak, Patricia 1985 "Canadian political economy." *Canadian Review of Sociology and Anthropology,* 22 (5) (December) : 673–709.

Matthews, Ralph 1977 "Canadian regional development strategy: a dependency theory perspective." *Plan Canada*, 17 (2): 131–43.

Matthews, Ralph 1980 "The significance and explanation of regional differences in canada: towards a canadian sociology." *Journal of Canadian Studies*, 15(2): 43–61.

Meire, Gerald M. 1984 *Leading Issues in Economic Development* (4th ed.) New York: Oxford University Press.

Naylor, Tom 1975 *The History of Canadian Business* (2 volumes) Toronto: Lorimer.

Niosi, Jorge 1978 *The Economy of Canada* Montreal: Black Rose Books.

Niosi, Jorge 1981 *Canadian Capitalism* (Trans. By Robert Chodos) Toronto: Lorimer.

Osberg, L., F. Wien, And J. Grude 1995 *Vanishing Jobs: Canada's Changing Workplaces* Toronto: James Lorimer and Co.

Pinchin, Hugh 1986 "A framework for assessing the impact of free trade in North America." In W. Shipman (ed.) *Trade and Investment Across the Northeast Boundary: Quebec, the Atlantic Provinces, and New England* Montreal: Institute for Research on Public Policy.

Polese, Mario 1987 "Patterns of regional economic development in Canada: long term trends and issues." In William Coffey and Mario Polese (eds.) *Still Living Together: Recent Trends and Future Directions in Canadian Regional Development* Montreal: The Institute for Research on Public Policy.

Pratt, Larry 1976 *The Tar Sands* Edmonton: Hurtig Publishers.

Ross, David, and Peter Usher 1986 *From the Roots Up: Economic Development as if Community Mattered* Croton-on-Hudson, New York: Bootstrap Press.

Royal Commission On Employment And Unemployment 1986 *Building on Our Strengths* St. John's: Queen's Printer.

Savoie, Donald 1986a "Introduction: regional development in Canada." In *The Canadian Economy: A Regional Perspective* Toronto: Methuen.

Savoie, Donald 1986b "Defining regional disparities." In *The Canadian Economy: A Regional Perspective* Toronto: Methuen.

Savoie, Donald 1986c *Regional economic development: Canada's Search for Solutions* Toronto: University of Toronto Press.

Scott, A.D. 1978 "Policy for declining regions: a theoretical approach." In H. Lithwick (ed.) *Regional Economic Policy: The Canadian Experience* Toronto: McGraw-Hill Ryerson.

Semple, R. Keith 1987 "Regional analysis of corporate decision making within the Canadian economy." In William Coffey and Mario Polese (eds.) *Still Living Together: Recent Trends and Future Directions in Canadian Regional Development* Montreal: The Institute for Research on Public Policy.

Stavenhagen, Rodolfo 1974 "The future of Latin America: between underdevelopment and revolution." *Latin American Perspectives*, 9(1) (Spring): 124–48.

Velmeyer, Henry 1979 "The capitalist underdevelopment of Atlantic Canada." In R.J. Brym and R.J. Sacouman (eds.) *Underdevelopment and Social Movements in Atlantic Canada* Toronto: New Hogtown Press.

Watkins, Mel 1963 "A staple theory of economic growth." *Canadian Journal of Economics and Political Science*, 29(May):141–58.

Watkins, Mel 1977a "The staple theory tevisited." *Journal of Canadian Studies*, 12 (Winter): 83–95.

Watkins, Mel 1977b *Dene Nation—The Colony Within* Toronto: University of Toronto Press.

Watson, William 1987 "The regional consequences of free(r) trade with the United States." In William Coffey and Mario Polese (eds.) *Still Living Together: Recent Trends and Future Directions in Canadian Regional Development* Montreal: The Institute for Research on Public Policy.

Chapter 24

FISCAL FEDERALISM AND QUEBEC SEPARATISM

Kenneth G. Stewart

(Revised from Kenneth G. Stewart, "Fiscal Federalism and Quebec Separatism." *Policy Options* June 1997, pp. 30–33. Reprinted with permission.)

INTRODUCTION

To the English Canadian mind Quebec is an enigma, the reasons for Quebec's dissatisfaction with the country a bewildering puzzle. Is it not the case that existing constitutional and legislative arrangements provide the province with virtually complete autonomy in the areas of language and culture, and with great independence in many other areas as well, including immigration? Should it be necessary to effectively bribe the province to remain within confederation, the bribes taking the form of federal largesse in a multiplicity of programs ranging from dairy quotas to equalization payments? In their longstanding rejection of any option involving outright separation of the province, do not Quebecers themselves recognize the historical symbiotic unity of the nation and the essential role that Quebec plays in creating a uniquely Canadian culture? How does one reconcile this with widespread support for political leaders committed to separation, to a point that includes the election of openly separatist governments in 1976, 1981 and 1994, the election to 53 of 75 federal seats members advocating separation in some form, and a 49.6 percent vote in the last referendum in favour of pursuing a separatist agenda?

FISCAL FEDERALISM

The thesis of this essay is that the emergence of separatism in the last three decades is related to Canada's system of fiscal federalism. Prior to 1957 the fiscal responsibilities of Canada and the provinces were divided along lines such that, to a very large extent, those who were taxed were in turn the beneficiaries of that taxation. In 1957 the government of Louis St. Laurent introduced a system of equalization payments from well-off provinces to poorer provinces having the laudable objective of equalizing the public services available to all Canadians. This was followed, in the 1960s and early 1970s, by the establishment and expansion of a variety of cost-shared and other social programs. These fall into essentially two categories: federal transfers to individuals, and transfers from the federal government to the provincial governments. The most important examples of the former are employment insurance and pensions; the latter consist primarily of transfers associated with the financing of health, education, and welfare.

These programs were created in a historically unique spirit of generosity and social progress of which Canadians have rightly been proud. At the same time they have had two noteworthy consequences which were not anticipated. The first is that the financing of these programs has given rise to one of the highest debt levels in the industrialized west, second only to Italy among the G-7 countries, and a comparatively high tax burden.

The second noteworthy consequence is that this system of fiscal federalism has led to vast cross-subsidies between individuals and regions that have served to undermine the economic and political foundations of the country in a way that is only now coming to be fully appreciated.

The erosion of the economic foundations of the country, particularly in the areas of government expenditure and finance, is now well-documented. As just one example, Unemployment Insurance (UI), now Employment Insurance (EI), generates cross-subsidies not only between individuals and regions but also across industries. By subsidizing seasonal industries at the expense of nonseasonal ones, workers have been attracted to low-skill seasonal employment. In addition to resulting in a self-propagating expansion of UI/EI payments, there has been an artificial inducement for excessive numbers of workers to enter low-skill industries which cannot, ultimately, support them. When the natural resource base upon which the industry depends is exhausted, as has happened in the east coast fishery and may be close to occurring in the west, large numbers of low-skill workers are left to demand compensation. By this process the coastal communities of Atlantic Canada have been reduced in a generation from proud self-reliance to embittering and pitiable dependence on handouts from the rest of the country.

The many problems with UI/EI specifically, and with Canada's patchwork quilt of income security programs generally, have been well-known for many years. The 1986 report of the Newfoundland *Royal Commission on Employment and Unemployment* noted that "[t]he income security system as a whole, in Canada and in Newfoundland as a province of Canada, was never designed rationally to serve a set of well-defined goals ..." and further found that the UI system "... undermines the intrinsic value of work ..., undermines good working habits and discipline ..., undermines the importance of education ..., is a disincentive to work ..., undermines personal and community initiatives ..., discourages self-employment and small-scale enterprise ..., encourages political patronage ..., distorts the efforts of local development groups ...," and "... has become a bureaucratic nightmare."

These are the reasons the 1986 report of the federal *Commission of Inquiry on Unemployment Insurance* concluded that "... a fundamental transformation of the design of the program and of the structure of the organization was essential." Yet a decade later the essentials of the system remain much as originally conceived. Instead of being willing to use the experience of the past 30 years to recognize the weaknesses in Canada's social programs and revise them accordingly, there is a tendency to view the original 1960s conception of these programs as a sacred trust to be defended at all costs.

Less well-understood is the erosion of the nation's political foundations that has

TABLE 24-1 Net federal-provincial transfers, fiscal year 1991–92

Province	Total ($ millions)	Per Capita ($)
Newfoundland	881	1 536
Prince Edward Island	189	1 446
Nova Scotia	698	775
New Brunswick	907	1 249
Quebec	2 984	436
Ontario	–5 015	–506
Manitoba	762	697
Saskatchewan	388	390
Alberta	–809	–321
British Columbia	–986	–306

Source: T. Courchene, *Social Canada in the Millenium* (Toronto: C.D. Howe Institute, 1994). Table 17.

taken place during this time as a result of Canada's system of cross-subsidies. Direct transfers of funds from the federal to the provincial governments are associated primarily with three program categories: "Established Programs Financing" of health care and post-secondary education; the Canada Assistance Plan for the financing of welfare; and the equalization payments referred to earlier. Professor Thomas Courchene of Queen's University has computed the net transfers arising from these programs; his figures are reproduced in Table 24-1. They indicate that, as intended, these payments have the effect of transferring income from the "have" provinces of Ontario, Alberta, and British Columbia, to the remaining seven provinces. In per capita terms by far the greatest beneficiaries are the four Atlantic provinces; however, their populations are small—in total no more than one-third that of either Quebec or Ontario. In contrast, although its net per capita transfers are relatively modest, due to its population, by far the single greatest beneficiary of Canada's system of fiscal federalism is Quebec.

In regions that are beneficiaries of the system two effects are notable. The first is a natural tendency to resent the system. Dependency breeds contempt for those upon whom one is dependent. Sometimes this resentment takes the form of denial that one is a net receiver of transfers; at other times it takes the form of claiming that the subsidies are entitlements having some objective historical basis. The other side is the resentment of the system by those who pay the bills, a resentment that has developed rapidly in recent years as the inequities and perverse incentives of the system become more apparent.

Paradoxically, the second notable effect on the receiving provinces is to attempt, where possible, to negotiate an expansion of the system and an increase in the payment flows. The Atlantic provinces, Manitoba, and Saskatchewan, because their populations are relatively small, are limited in their ability to do this. There is only one province that both benefits from the system and has a large enough population to give it the political clout to negotiate in earnest for an increase in the benefits it receives: that province is Quebec.

Negotiations, of course, can take a variety of forms, and often it is in one's interest to negotiate in a way that does not reveal ultimate objectives. In addition to negotiating within a given set of rules, one may seek to change the rules so as to improve one's negotiating power. In doing this, it is unwise to motivate the proposed rule changes in these terms; instead it is preferable to cite other pretexts, such as historical, cultural, or linguistic grievances, real or invented. At times good negotiation may take the form of engaging in brinkmanship and aggressive rhetoric which cites injustices of the past, of which there are always some to be found.

It is important that these observations not obscure the objectives of the current Quebec leadership, which undeniably seeks separation. Why would such a leadership be elected to power by a populace that, for the most part, does not share that goal? For the same reason that I might elect firebrand Marxists to the executive of my union local even if I believe that Marxism is nonsense; I may simply believe that they will be the best negotiators.

Canada's system of equalization and transfer payments, and federal sponsorship of other social programs such as employment insurance, were originally conceived in part as a unifying influence. Instead, by creating vast cross-subsidization between regions which decouples the benefits of expenditure from the costs of taxation, they have had exactly the opposite effect of balkanizing east and west and serving as a propellant to separatism. Just as employment insurance and welfare sometimes have an economic effect on individuals contrary to that which was originally intended, so too has fiscal federalism had unanticipated political consequences.

The parallel I have drawn between these political and economic effects extends in another disturbing direction. In the same way that Canada seems stuck in a '60s time warp in trying to deal with the economic consequences of fiscal federalism, a similar myopia seems to pervade its political consequences. Instead of seeing the system as an incentive which incites Quebec to ever higher levels of political brinkmanship, modifications to the constitutional rules governing its negotiation that favour the province are proposed as a solution. The history of the past three decades shows just what to expect of all attempts to buy off Quebec in this way; in any system of cross-subsidies the political action will always come to revolve around the nature and magnitude of the subsidies, and regardless of what specifics are negotiated there will always be demands for increased subsidies.

CONCLUSION

The solution to Canada's political and economic problems requires a fundamental rethinking of fiscal federalism in a way that resurrects the principle that, at least at the margin, those who benefit from public programs should also bear their cost. This will not, of course, end separatism among some elements of Quebec society: that will always be present in some form. But it would reduce the incentive of the Quebec populace to elect leaders who are then in a position to advance their own separatist agenda. Canadians must ask themselves what kind of country it will ultimately be easier for Quebec to leave: a financially sound Canada, or a dissipated one?

FOR FURTHER REFERENCE: REGION

Britton, John H. (ed.) 1996 *Canada and the Global Economy* Montreal and Kingston: McGill-Queen's University Press. This book is composed of numerous papers on the economic geography of Canada and its location in the larger international economy. Some articles provide evidence dealing with important issues in regional or geographic inequality, including the concentration of major corporations in core urban centres and the patterns of direct investment, both within Canada by foreign interests and in foreign settings by Canadian investors.

Brodie, Janine 1991 *The Political Economy of Canadian Regionalism* Toronto: Harcourt, Brace, Jovanovich. This book begins by developing a theoretical approach to issues of space and location, and then uses this model to examine the politics of regionalism in Canada.

Coffey, William, and Mario Polese 1987 *Still Living Together* Montreal: Institute for Research on Public Policy. This book considers recent trends and future directions in regional development in Canada. Regional differences in income distribution, economic development, technological change, state policy, and various other issues of relevance to regional inequality are addressed.

De Benedetti, George, and Rodolphe LaMarche (eds.) 1994 *Shock Waves: The Maritime Urban System in the New Economy* Moncton: Canadian Institute for Research on Regional Development. This analysis considers the important role of urban centres in the regional development of the Maritime region.

Savoie, Donald 1997 *Rethinking Canada's Regional Development Policy: An Atlantic Perspective* Moncton: Canadian Institute for Research on Regional Development. In this short monograph, the author reflects on where regional development policy has been and where it is going.

Savoie, Donald, and Benjamin Higgins 1995 *Regional Development Theories and Their Application* New Brunswick, New Jersey: Transaction Publishers. This book outlines the major theoretical frameworks that have been used to explain regional development and underdevelopment, as well as the policy implications that follow logically from each perspective.

Section 4

SOME CONSEQUENCES OF SOCIAL INEQUALITY

The preceding three sections have described this country's main patterns of social inequality with respect to social class, income/occupation/education, and social ascription. Also, various interpretations have been offered for the *causes* of the patterns of inequality. Further, one of the *effects* or *consequences* of social inequality received considerable attention: the ways in which the struggles between classes and between elites have resulted in certain social trends. For example, all of the selections in Section 1, and particularly Grabb's and Laxer's, suggest how the economic structure of this country has changed as a result of both the interplay between capitalists and the state elite and the struggle between classes. The same is true of several selections in other sections—e.g., Urmetzer and Guppy's and Gunderson's papers on income, Armstrong and Armstrong's and Creese and Beagan's pieces on gender relations, and so on. It is difficult to describe Canada's unequal class and elite relations for very long without spelling out how aspects of history have been determined by them.

There is a second important type of consequence of social inequality, though, which was not featured in Sections 1, 2, or 3. This concerns the *consequences for the experiences of individuals* that flow from different forms of social inequality. Here the focus is on how the day-to-day living of Canadians is affected, as opposed to how the society is changing or not changing with time. In this instance, *consequences* refer to any aspects of the experiences of individuals that are influenced by differences in social inequality, including people's life chances, beliefs, and patterns of behaviour.

Our purpose in Section 4 is to portray this second type of consequence. There is a vast number of such consequences, because social inequality touches so many aspects of people's lives. Thus, we cannot pretend to give, in the six selections in this section, the last word on the consequences of social inequality, but we will provide some enlightening examples. To suggest how broad the range of consequences of social inequality for individuals can be, we can recall the thoughts of Hans Gerth and C. Wright Mills, who wrote that they "include everything from the chance to stay alive during the first year after birth, to the chance to view fine arts, the chance to remain healthy and grow tall, and if sick to get well again quickly, the chance to avoid becoming a juvenile delinquent ... and ... the chance to complete an intermediary or higher educational grade"(1953:313). These observations are no less true for Canadian society now than they were for the U.S. years ago when they were made.

There are many reasons behind the various consequences of social inequality for individuals in any society, but two are particularly important for capitalist societies. First, the existence of social inequality in the form of economic advantage means that some can "buy" more or "afford" more of the valued aspects of social life, the "life chances" of the society. Some can easily afford to take time off work when they believe their children might benefit from a doctor's examination; others cannot readily afford this. Some can afford to live in the best neighbourhoods, with the best in leisure and educational facilities for their children; others cannot. There are many such differences in life chances between "haves" and "have-nots."

Second, because differences in economic advantage involve differences in economic interest, we can expect that, often, awareness of these interests will develop, and the haves and have-nots will vie with each other for their interests. If such pursuit of interests becomes at all pronounced, this can be expected to lead to differences between the haves and the have-nots in the areas of political beliefs, behaviour, and life chances. For the same reason, social barriers between the haves and the have-nots may develop, and these, in turn, may lead to still other differences in beliefs, behaviour, and opportunities. In other words, *sub-cultures of different ways of thinking and acting* can easily develop out of the differing interests that surround separate social classes and status groups.

There is no easy way of predicting the full details of these subcultures in advance, no way of saying precisely how they will differ in beliefs, behaviour, and opportunity. For an understanding of the prevalence and character of inequality-based subcultures in any society for any particular time period, a careful large-scale research effort is required. The selections in this section will suggest what a very large task this is, and will give examples of appropriate research topics and research approaches.

The selections here are limited to *three categories* of consequences of social inequality: (1) people's differences in *life chances;* (2) their differences in *ways of thinking* concerning social inequality; and (3) their differences in *orientation to social interaction.*

We shall first deal with the issue of differences in life chances. We will start with an aspect of life chances that involves the toughest of definitions—that of life expectancy. This is "toughest" in the sense that life is one of the prized possessions in Canadian society, and undoubtedly *the* most prized possession for many Canadians. This being the case, using the criterion of life expectancy puts our society's patterns of inequality to a strong test. It would clearly cast doubt on the idea that ours is a society of vast equality if we found good evidence that differences in economic circumstances create differences in how long people live.

Precisely this pattern has been shown to be true of other countries. One of the most complete international studies of this topic was conducted some years ago in the United States by Kitagawa and Hauser (1968). They matched 340 000 death certificates (for deaths occurring during a four month period) with census records. Using educational attainment level as an indicator of socio-economic status, they found a strong inverse relationship between death rates and status. For example, among White men between the ages of 25 and 64, the death rate for those with less than eight years of schooling was 48 percent higher than the rate for the college-educated men.

A research review by the National Council of Welfare (1990) has dramatically shown that social inequality also has a significant impact on life expectancy in Canada. This monograph indicates, for example, that when researchers studied data on income levels and death rates for various census tracts in Canadian cities in 1971 and 1986 they found, at both times, that there were markedly better life expectancy figures for areas with higher average income levels. Among the results was the sobering finding for 1986 that males in the highest income areas had a life expectancy fully 5.7 years greater on average than males in the lowest income areas. This discrepancy was down only slightly from a gap of 6.2 years in 1971.

The first selection in Section 4, which is excerpted from a Health Canada document, gives still further evidence on the relationship between socio-economic status and health and mortality in Canada. Several measures of life chances are reported on—poor vs. good health, limits upon activity, premature deaths of adults, neo-natal deaths, and post-natal deaths. The report concludes that income and socio-economic status are among key factors in health and age at death. The higher people's incomes and socio-economic statuses, the healthier they are and the longer they live. Moreover, various other important factors in health and longevity—including social support networks, education, employment and working conditions, safe and clean physical environments, and coping skills—are also related to income and socio-economic status. The selection ends with policy recommendations designed to address inequalities in health and longevity.

The next selection in this section asks us to consider another very serious problem of life chances. The paper by Eugen Lupri, Elaine Grandin, and Merlin Brinkerhoff deals with information on violence against women in Canadian households. Using women's reports on both physical and psychological abuse, the researchers estimate the extent of violence against women, and they study some of the correlates of the rates of violence. In particular, the authors test a common understanding among the general public and some social researchers that male violence against women is related to socio-economic status; they test the idea that such violence is largely a problem in the lower social classes and is much less frequent in the higher social classes.

The evidence of Lupri and colleagues suggests that socio-economic status is *not* a predictor of violence against women in the home. However, little satisfaction can be taken from this because the rates of violence, for both psychological and physical abuse, are higher than one might expect. Further, these rates are widespread, in the sense of being common to all social class levels. The researchers go on to show how another social status factor—age level—is a considerably better predictor of violence against women in the home, along with marital strife. Violence is considerably more prominent among younger adults. Of course, the phenomenon of violence in the home is gendered too; the rates of violent behaviour, and victim status, vary by gender.

The second type of consequence of social inequality addressed in this section has to do with differences in *ways of thinking*. Here we could start by recalling Karl Marx's famous observation that it is not the consciousness of men that determines their being, but rather their social being, primarily their location in the class structure, that determines their consciousness. We can ask to what extent this view is correct for Canada today. Are the different social classes, and social status groups, aware of their differences? Do individuals try to safeguard or promote their class or group interests? Going further, we can ask whether the different classes and status groups develop still other differences in beliefs and behaviour.

Questions of this type, designed to probe the degree and extent of class and status consciousness, or common thinking by classes and strata, raise problems of obvious significance for understanding the dynamic aspect of Canada's structure of social inequality. For example, class consciousness of common interests has existed at many times and places, and has at times led to organized class actions and class struggles that changed the whole structure of societies (see, e.g., the discussions in Laxer's, Conley's and O'Connor's selections in Section 1). However, class consciousness does not follow automatically from objective class differences. People may have a class position that differs markedly from that of others without being particularly aware of this difference. Thinking and conduct are not determined merely by objective position in the economic or social order, but depend in part upon the way in which people perceive and interpret their social circumstances. For example, socialization through the educational system and the media probably will have some effect upon people's thinking about their class or status position and its meaning. It is likely that these influences, widespread across classes and status groups as they are, will tend to lead people of differing classes and statuses to have a *common assessment* of social inequality. Some scholars believe that much of what is taught in the educational system and through the media is supportive of, or justifies, existing patterns of social inequality. Such ideas have been labelled "dominant ideology" because they generally aid in the domination of the have-nots by the haves (e.g., Parkin, 1972; cf. Abercrombie et al., 1980).

Also, Canadians "carry with them" various achieved and ascribed backgrounds and related sets of experiences at any given point in their lives. A person has, simultaneously, the experiences of a class position, a level of education achieved, an occupation, a certain level of income, an ethnic status, a race, a gender, and an age group. It is, therefore, difficult to know which of these sets of experiences will influence most the person's perceptions of social inequality. We cannot assume the presence of common class or status thinking, but must investigate how Canadians evaluate and respond to their differing circumstances.

Fortunately, over the past few years there have been some well-developed national sample surveys of adult Canadians' beliefs about social inequality, which have helped us to understand this issue better. For example, Johnston and Ornstein (1982) have explored the relationship between social class, defined in the Marxist sense, and three sets of ideological beliefs—beliefs having to do with support for redistribution of income, social welfare expenditures, and support for the labour movement. As would be expected from the class interests involved for each class, the bourgeoisie have a more right-wing position on these issues, and the working class have a left-wing position. The bourgeoisie were less likely to favour pursuing equality through income redistribution and greater social welfare, and they were less supportive of the labour movement. The difference in beliefs between the classes, however, was far from complete. Many members of one class shared in the majority beliefs of the other class, and vice versa. Johnston and Ornstein went on to show how the attitudes of the working class were affected by education, family background, and a number of aspects of working conditions, but the latter were more important. Rates of pay, the manual work versus non-manual work distinction, and whether the job was unionized or not were related to the beliefs about social inequality.

The third selection in Section 4 presents other relevant information. It reports on Canadians' beliefs about the causes of social inequality and how these beliefs are related to people's social statuses. The analyses show that there is widespread support for two sets of beliefs: (1) that it is an individual's personal characteristics (ambition, hard work, and natural ability) and educational attainment that determine how he or she gets ahead, and (2) that social background factors (social class of parents, race, gender, and region) have comparatively little to do with success or the lack of it. These beliefs are sometimes differentially distibuted across social statuses, as the analyses show, but this is not the case for all dimensions of social status. Further, there is remarkably high support for each set of views among people, regardless of their achieved and ascribed statuses. Social status is not highly predictive of these beliefs. The authors argue that these beliefs are part of a "dominant ideology" that simultaneously "describes," and reinforces, the system of social inequality in this society.

Patrick Burman's study, described in the next selection in Section 4, looks at people's views concerning *themselves*. The principal source of the self-esteem of many people, the foremost aspect of their self-identity, is their occupation. One reason for this is that so much of each week's activity is given over to work. Another is that an individual's income, lifestyle, and social status are based on his or her job. For these reasons and more, long periods of unemployment can be expected to cause unemployed people great consternation, stress, and "second guessing" about themselves.

Burman's study explores the reactions of the unemployed, based on intensive interviews with "job losers" who had been off work for varying lengths of time. The author focuses on differences between people in what he calls the "initial stage," who had lost their jobs recently, and those in the "later stages," who had been unemployed for many months. The interviews show major changes in thinking after long periods of unemployment. Just after losing his or her job, a person is shocked and immobilized. Then stress increases over a protracted period. As the stress subsides, the person begins to redefine him-or herself as a non-worker. Eventually, many people develop an entrenched adjustment to unemployment and begin to think that they may never again have much full-time work. Those who weathered the unemployment experience comparatively well, or rose above it, had one of four important resources: non-stigmatized financial backing, social support, higher education, or collectivist ideology.

The excerpt from Burman's study presents a rich selection of quotes. Reading them, we get a good glimpse at the magnitude of social psychological stress the respondents are experiencing, and the wrenching adjustments demanded of those who are unemployed for any length of time. Of course, it is one thing to read about it and quite another to experience it.

The third category of consequences of social inequality explored in this section has to do with *effects upon social interaction*. Archibald (1976) is among researchers who have looked at this issue in detail. He presented a Marxian-oriented theory of how interaction between higher-class and lower-class individuals takes place. The theory presumably also applied to interaction between higher-status and lower-status people, and interaction between those with much power and those with less power. Using a sweeping review of results from many studies already conducted by others, Archibald arrived at the generalization that interactions between unequals will necessarily involve some interpersonal threat and exploitation by the more powerful. The interactions will involve some conflict and coercion, however subtle these may be at times. The literature contains alternative theories based on the idea that there is largely consensus, cooperation, and exchange in interaction between unequals. Archibald acknowledged that these processes may occur, but insisted that they are not the most common forms of interaction between unequals; interactions based on conflict and cohesion are believed to be more common.

The selection in this section by Jeffrey Reitz and Raymond Breton looks at one type of interaction between unequals in Canada, that between the majority group and minority ethnic and racial groups. The authors explore the results of various Canadian and American studies of discrimination and prejudice on the part of the majority toward various minority racial and ethnic groups. Reitz and Breton find that levels of discrimination and prejudice depend upon the minority outgroup involved, and the type of response to the outgroup that is in question. Yet, the levels of negative responses tend to be low in an absolute sense for most measures and most outgroups, suggesting reasonably high levels of tolerance of minority groups. Returning to the consideration raised by Archibald's work—whether interaction between high and low status groups is characterized by coercion and conflict or consensus and cooperation—we would have to conclude that there must be considerable consensus and cooperation in ethnic/race relations in the two countries. Of course, Henry and Ginzberg's studies of employment discrimination and Hou and Balakrishnan's study of differences in income across ethnic groups in Section 3 of this volume are also relevant to the issues discussed by Reitz and Breton.

Reitz and Breton argue that Canada and the United States are more or less the same in levels of discrimination and prejudice. This will come as a surprise to those who think, following the popular view (in this country) that Canada is the nation of tolerance par excellence. The authors believe that there is simply an "illusion of difference" in the perceptions of Canada versus the United States among Canadians (Reitz and Breton, 1994).

In the final selection in this section, Curtis, Grabb, and Chui ask whether Canadians who are higher in regard to various social statuses—majority versus minority ethnic group members, immigrants versus non-immigrants, middle aged versus the young and old, men versus women, those with high education versus those low in education, those with higher incomes, and so on—are higher in involvement in political behaviour. The measures of involvement in politics ranged across several forms of "mass" activity that are generally felt to be open to all Canadians—voting, following politics in the media, interest in politics, attending political meetings, participating in other forms of voluntary associations, public protest activities, and support for social movements. Contrary to the view that there is full openness of political participation, people's social statuses were sometimes found to be related to forms of political involvement. The "haves" were sometimes more involved than others, but this was not always the case; and the patterns often were not strong. The authors emphasize that socio-economic status and ascriptive social statuses are stronger predictors of other more intensive forms of political activity, such as running for and achieving political office. That is, while the "mass" political activities are structured in only a modest way by social status, there is evidence of a more marked degree of inequality for the achievement of higher levels of political power.

It is interesting, though, that the data showed that *public protest* activities— signing a petition, boycotting, engaging in strikes and demonstrations, and occupying facilities—were more common for higher status individuals than lower status individuals. To the extent that these activities arise out of dissatisfaction with life's circumstances, one would think that lower status people would have more reason to protest. This is likely the case *for levels of dissatisfaction.* However, lower status people do not protest more; they protest less. The answer to this apparent inconsistency likely involves two issues. First, higher status people have greater time and resources for protest than those lower in social status. Further, higher status people have *interests* (if not high levels of dissatisfaction) to pursue through protest actions and other forms of mass political involvement.

REFERENCES

Abercrombie, Nicholas, Stephen Hill, and Bryan S. Turner 1980 *The Dominant Ideology Thesis* London: George Allen and Unwin.

Archibald, W. Peter 1976 "Class and social interaction." *American Sociological Review*, 41, 5: 819–37.

Gerth, Hans and C. Wright Mills 1953 *Character and Social Structure: The Social Psychology of Social Institutions* New York: Harcourt Brace and World.

Johnston, William and Michael Ornstein 1982 "Class, work and politics." *Canadian Review of Sociology and Anthropology*, 19, 2:196–214.

Kitawaga, Evelyn M. and Philip M. Hauser 1968 "Education differentials in mortality by cause of death: United States, 1960." *Demography*, 5:318–53.

National Council Of Welfare 1990 *Health, Health Care, and Medicare* Ottawa: National Council of Welfare.

Parkin, Frank 1972 *Class, Inequality and Political Order* London: Paladin.

Reitz, Jeffrey and Raymond Breton 1994 *The Illusion of Difference: Realities of Ethnicity in Canada and the United States* Toronto: C D Howe Institute.

Chapter 25

SOCIAL INEQUALITY IN THE HEALTH OF CANADIANS

Health Canada

(Abridged from pages 10–30, 41–42 of *Strategies for Population Health: Investing in the Health of Canadians*. Ottawa: Health Canada, 1994. Report prepared by the Federal, Provincial and Territorial Advisory Committee on Population Health for the Meetings of the Ministers of Health, Halifax, September, 1994. Reprinted with permission.)

INTRODUCTION

Investing in population health offers benefits in three main areas: increased prosperity, reduced expenditures on health and social problems, and overall social stability and well-being for Canadians.

The prosperity of a nation and the health of its citizens are inextricably linked. Many studies have shown the most powerful indicator of population health is the prosperity of the society within which people live, with an equitable distribution of wealth. At the same time, a healthy population is a major contributor to a vibrant economy. An effective population health strategy will therefore make a significant contribution to Canada's agenda for economic prosperity.

The more prosperous and healthy our population, the less need there will be for illness oriented health care services and the social safety net we are committed to maintaining. These are important social initiatives and will probably always be required to some degree. However, they currently consume a large part of our national resources. An effective strategy to foster population health and well-being should make some of these resources available for other more productive purposes.

Canada prides itself on having a society that values and offers its residents good health and quality of life. For example, social stability, economic well-being, safety, and meaningful and satisfying work are assets Canadians value and expect. These are the same factors that an effective population health approach would emphasize, the very factors that contribute most to good health for individuals, groups, and the entire population. So a population health approach is a natural and logical strategy for governments to adopt as part of their obligation to citizens.

Although some of the benefits of a population health approach will accrue primarily in the longer term, there are also more immediate benefits to be realized. For example, there is increasing evidence that initiatives to promote health in the workplace and improve the quality of work life increase employee satisfaction and productivity almost immediately. And those effects tend to be sustained, so long as the positive working conditions are maintained. At the same time, such initiatives have long term beneficial effects on the health status of employees, effects that seem to result from reductions in stress and an increased sense of control, both of which are key determinants of health discussed later in this paper.

THE DETERMINANTS OF HEALTH: WHAT MAKES PEOPLE HEALTHY?

There is a growing body of evidence about what makes people healthy. The Lalonde Report set the stage in 1974, by establishing a framework for the key factors that seemed to determine health status: lifestyle, environment, human biology, and health services. Since then, much has been learned that supports, and at the same time refines and expands this basic framework. In particular, there is mounting evidence that the contribution of medicine and health care is quite limited, and that spending more on health care will not result in further improvements in population health. On the other hand, there are strong and growing indications that other factors such as living and working conditions are crucially important for a healthy population.

The evidence indicates that the key factors which influence population health are income and social status, social support networks, education, employment and working conditions, safe and clean physical environments, biology and genetic makeup, personal health practices and coping skills, childhood development, and health services. Each of these factors is important in its own right. At the same time, the factors are interrelated.

The rest of this section gives an overview of what we know about the ways in which these factors influence health.

Income and Social Status

There is strong and growing evidence that higher socio-economic status is associated with better health. In fact, these two factors—income and social status—seem to be the most important determinants of health. People's perception of how healthy they are is linked to their income level, as shown in Figure 25-1.

There is extensive research that demonstrates the links between income and health status. One Canadian study found that men in the top 20% income bracket live on average six years longer than those in the bottom 20%, and can expect 14 more years of life free of activity restrictions. Women in the top 20% can expect three more years of life than those in the bottom 20%, and eight more years free of activity restrictions (Wilkins and Adams, 1978). Studies in provinces and cities in all parts of Canada consistently show that people at each step on the income scale are healthier than those on the step below. Figure 25.2 illustrates this with data from Winnipeg, where the rate of premature death (before age 65) decreases at each step of the income scale, from the bottom to the top 20%.

A recent World Bank report (1993) concludes that "Economic policies conducive to sustained growth are among the most important measures governments can take to improve their citizens' health." As well, many studies demonstrate that the more equitable the distribution of wealth, the healthier the population. Japan provides a good example. Over a 30 year period, Japan has moved from being a country with high infant mortality rates and low life expectancy, to

FIGURE 25-1 Percentage of Canadians reporting excellent or very good health by income

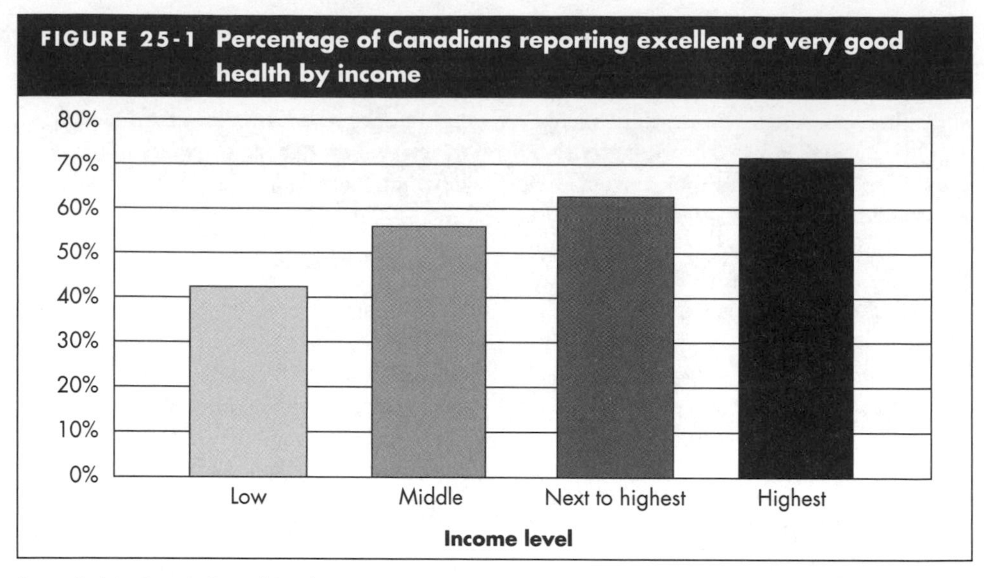

Source: Statistics Canada General Social Survey, 1991.

one having some of the best health status indicators in the world. During the same period, the Japanese economy soared, and incomes increased significantly. As well, Japan now has a very equitable distribution of wealth, with the smallest relative difference in income between the top and bottom 20% of any OECD country. Interestingly, Japan spends only 6.8% of its GDP on health care, compared to about 10% in Canada.

Social status is also linked to health. A major British study (Marmot et al., 1987) of civil service employees found that, for most major categories of disease (cancer, coronary heart disease, stroke, etc.), health increased with job rank. This was true even when risk factors such as smoking, which are known to vary with social class, were taken into account. All the people in the study worked in desk jobs, and all had a good standard of living and job security, so this was not an effect that could be explained by physical risk, poverty, or material deprivation. Health increased at each step up the job hierarchy. For example, those one step down from the top (doctors, lawyers, etc.) had heart disease rates four times higher than those at the top (those at levels comparable to deputy ministers). So we must conclude that something related to higher income, social position, and hierarchy provides a buffer or defence against disease, or that something about lower income and status undermines defences.

A very important aspect of the evidence about income, social status, and health is that the relationship persists, even though the causes of illness and death may change. The relationship holds for different diseases, for men and women, for people in different parts of the country, and different parts of the world. Lower socio-economic status seems to underlie the prevalence of "something wrong" in a very general way, no matter what the specific health problem is.

Why are higher income and social status associated with better health? If it were just a matter of the poorest and lowest status groups having poor health, the explanation could be factors such as poor living condi-

FIGURE 25-2 Premature deaths per 1000 Winnipeg residents by relative affluence of their neighbourhoods

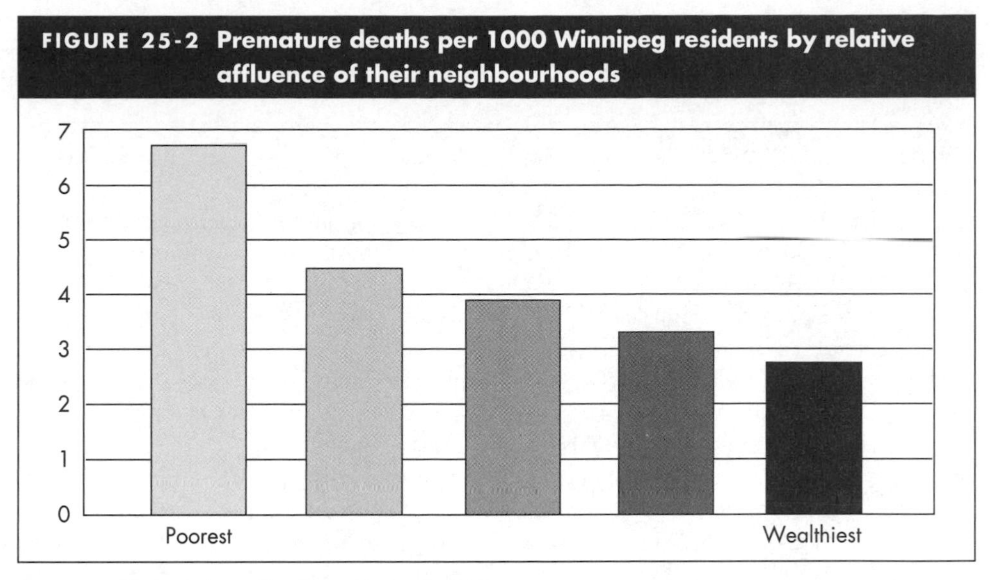

Source: Manitoba Centre for Health Policy and Evaluation, 1994.

tions. But the effect occurs all across the socio-economic spectrum. Considerable research indicates that the degree of control people have over life circumstances, especially stressful situations, and their discretion to act are the key influences. Higher income and status generally result in more control and discretion. And the biological pathways explaining how this could happen are becoming better understood. A number of recent studies show that limited options and poor coping skills for dealing with stress increase vulnerability to a range of diseases through pathways that involve the immune and hormonal systems.

There is still much to be learned, but we now have sufficient knowledge to begin developing and testing interventions to improve population health by focusing on socio-economic status and related factors. Because women on average have lower incomes than men and are concentrated in lower status occupations, particular attention should be given to improving women's health through action targeted at the social and economic environment. Improving people's economic circumstances is one important type of intervention, and the involvement of the economic sector is clearly crucial. But economic development is not the only option. Changes that improve opportunities, for example through education and job training; and interventions that reduce stress and give people a greater sense of mastery and control over their lives at work, at home, and in their communities will also be very important. To accomplish these changes, actions in the economic, education, employment, social services, and other sectors will be needed. Because such changes are likely to have a positive effect across the entire spectrum of the socio-economic scale, even modest success has the potential for significant results in terms of improved overall population health status.

Social Support Networks

Support from families, friends, and communities is associated with better health. An extensive study in California (Berkman and Syme, 1979) found that, for men and women, the more social contacts people have, the lower their premature death rate. Other research supports these results. For example, another U.S. study found that low availability of emotional support and low social participation were associated with all-cause mortality (Hanson, 1986). And the risk of angina pectoris decreased with increasing levels of emotional support in a study of male Israeli civil servants (Groen et al., 1968). As well, it has long been known that married people live longer than unmarried people, and that widowhood is associated with increased illness and death (Rees and Lutkins, 1967). Some experts in the field have concluded that the health effect of social relationships may be as important as established risk factors such as smoking, physical activity, obesity, and high blood pressure (Mustard and Frank, 1991).

Why do social support networks seem to improve health? The importance of effective responses to stress and good personal coping skills discussed above likely come into play here. Support from family, friends, and acquaintances could be very important in helping people solve problems and deal with adversity, as well as in maintaining a sense of mastery and control over life circumstances. As well, family and friends help provide basic support such as food and housing, look after one another when one is ill, and support one another in making lifestyle changes. The caring and respect that occur in social relationships, and the resulting sense of satisfaction and well-being, seem to act as a buffer against health problems.

Population health interventions to strengthen social supports could include initiatives such as programs to maintain strong families; community development focused on making communities good places for social interaction; and initiatives that reduce discrimination and promote social tolerance.

Education

Health status increases with level of education. For example, the 1990 Canada Health

FIGURE 25-3 Percentage of Canadians 15+ years reporting fair or poor health status and activity limitations, by educational level

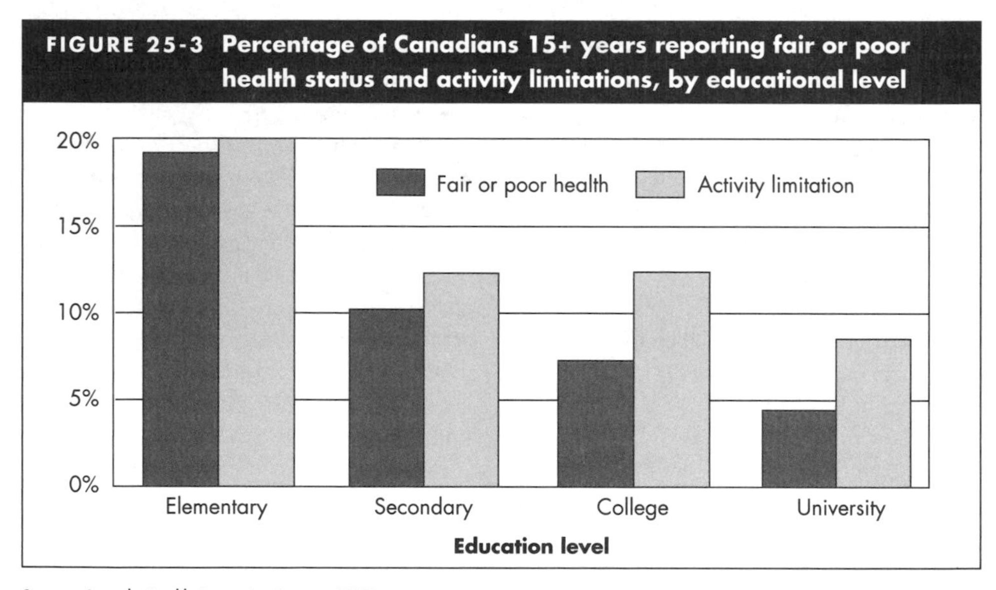

Source: Canada Health Promotion Survey, 1990.

Promotion Survey found that as education increases, self rated health status improves, and activity limitation decreases. This is shown in Figure 25.3. The same survey found the number of lost workdays decreases with increasing education. People with elementary schooling lose about seven work days per year due to illness, injury, or disability, while those with university education lose fewer than four days per year.

Education is closely tied to socio-economic status, and effective education for children and lifelong learning for adults are key contributors to health and prosperity for individuals, and for the country. Education contributes to health and prosperity by equipping people with knowledge and skills for problem solving, and helps provide a sense of control and mastery over life circumstances. It increases opportunities for job and income security, and job satisfaction. And it improves people's ability to access and understand information to help keep them healthy.

Because initiatives to ensure access to effective education for children and youth and opportunities for life long learning must be part of an effective population health strategy, the involvement of the education sector is essential.

Employment and Working Conditions

The above discussion about the effect of job rank on health shows the importance of status in the workplace, and that those with more control over their work circumstances are healthier. But other factors are also important. Workplace social support, measured by the number and quality of interactions with co-workers, is associated with health. The more connections people have, the better their health. Health is also affected by stress-related demands of the job such as the pace of work, the frequency of deadlines, and reporting requirements. A recent study in Sweden (Johnson et al., 1988) found that cardiovascular disease occurred most often among those with high job demands, low levels of control over their work, and low levels of social support at work.

Unemployment is associated with poorer health. One Canadian study found the unemployed have significantly more psychological distress, anxiety, depressive symptoms, disability days, activity limitation, health problems, hospitalization, and physician visits than the employed (D'Arcy, 1986). People with lower incomes reported more anxiety and depressive symptoms, but most health problems seemed to be associated with the stress of unemployment, not with lack of income per se. A major review done for the World Health Organization found that high levels of unemployment and economic instability in a society caused significant mental health problems and adverse effects on the physical health of unemployed individuals, their families, and their communities (Wescott et al. 1985).

Safe workplaces also contribute to population health. Workplace injuries and occupational illnesses exact a large toll on the health of Canada's workers, and most are preventable. Occupational injury rates rose by about one-third in Canada from 1955 to 1987, while rates were declining in most other OECD countries. (OECD, 1989).

Canadian adults spend about one-quarter of their lives at work. Initiatives to make the workplace a safe and healthy setting that promotes, supports, and protects peoples' health will be a key element of an effective population health approach. Model programs that foster health in the workplace, by involving workers in identification of problems and solutions, are increasingly being implemented. The involvement of the employment and business sectors is essential to bring about changes to ensure that the workplace fosters good health.

Physical Environments

Population health is critically dependent on the physical environments in which we live. The workplace as a key physical (and social) environment is discussed above. Other important aspects of the physical environment are our housing, the air we breathe, the water we drink, and the safety of our communities.

Air pollution, including exposure to second hand tobacco smoke, has a significant association with health. A study in southern Ontario found a consistent link between hospital admissions for respiratory illness in the summer months and levels of sulphates and ozone in the air (Bates and Sizto, 1987). However, it now seems that the risks from small particles such as dust and carbon particles that are by-products of burning fuel may be even greater than the risks from pollutants such as ozone (Cotton, 1993). As well, research indicates that lung cancer risks from second hand tobacco smoke are greater than the risks from the hazardous air pollutants from all regulated industrial emissions combined (Repace, 1985).

Safely designed homes, school, roads, and workplaces can help prevent the large number of injuries from motor vehicle accidents and other causes that occur in Canada. Safe and affordable housing is another aspect of the physical environment that contributes to population health. Reducing hazardous wastes that contaminate our ground and water, and more effective waste management, are further avenues for action. Population health strategies to impact the physical environment must address complex and interrelated systems. Actions in the environmental, economic, business, health, and social sectors will be required, including public policy and regulatory action.

Biology and Genetic Endowment

The basic biology and organic make-up of the human body are a fundamental determinant of health. Included are the genetic endowment of the individual, the functioning of various body systems, and the processes of development and aging. As well, there are interactions between human biology and other key determinants of health.

There are complex relationships between individual experience and the development and functioning of key body systems. For example, an earlier section of this paper described how limited options and poor skills for coping with stress increase vulnerability to various diseases, through pathways that involve the immune and hormonal systems. There is also increasing evidence that adult brain structure can be strongly influenced, sometimes in an irreversible way, by experience in early life.

Males and females at all ages and of all socio-economic strata have different life expectancies. The age of onset and the types of diseases, illnesses, and conditions that are the prime causes of morbidity, disability, and mortality are different for women and men. Vulnerability to significant health risks such as physical and sexual violence, STDs, environmental hazards, and inappropriate clinical interventions also varies between men and women. As well, the patterns of correlation between income gradations and health status are different for men and women. These differences are attributable only in part to biological sex. More importantly, they arise from differences in the traits, attitudes, values, behaviours, and roles society ascribes to males and females.

Genetic endowment provides an inherited predisposition to a wide range of individual responses that affect health status. Although socio-economic and environmental factors are important determinants of overall health, in some circumstances genetic endowment appears to predispose certain individuals to particular diseases or health problems. Genetic knowledge therefore has an important place in population health. At the same time, genetic science is developing and changing rapidly, and increasingly may offer solutions for prevention or amelioration of certain genetic predispositions and conditions.

Personal Health Practices and Coping Skills

Personal practices such as smoking, use of alcohol and other drugs, healthy eating, physical activity, and other personal behaviours affect health and well-being. Many of Canada's most common health problems are linked to these practices.

Smoking is the leading cause of lung cancer and a major risk factor for cardiovascular disease. Although the number of Canadians who smoke has been gradually declining, a significant number still do, and the smoking rates are increasing for adolescents. About 30% of Canadians are still regular smokers.

Alcohol is used to some extent by a large proportion of Canadians. Although most people drink responsibly most of the time, alcohol misuse is a leading cause of premature death, injury, and disability. It is primarily associated with injuries and deaths resulting from accidents and violence. Both smoking and alcohol use during pregnancy have been linked to lower birthweights and other negative birth outcomes.

Regular exercise has been shown to reduce the risk of cardiovascular disease, diabetes, obesity, back ailments, and some cancers. It also slows the natural degeneration that accompanies the aging process. In addition, it contributes to positive well-being by reducing tension and anxiety. Many people feel that regular physical activity is a significant contributor to their overall physical and mental health. Research now shows that even very moderate levels of physical activity provide substantial benefits.

Poor nutrition and unhealthy eating habits are associated with diabetes, cardiovascular disease, and cancer. Studies have found that school performance in children is linked to nutrition, body weight, and physical activity. During pregnancy, poor nutrition leads to insufficient weight gain for the mother and a low birthweight for the baby. An appropriate body weight, which is largely determined by diet and exercise, is a significant contributor to people's positive self-concept, which in turn has important effects on their mental health, sense of competence, and control over life circumstances.

Coping skills, which seem to be acquired primarily in the first few years of life, are also important in supporting healthy lifestyles. These are the skills people use to interact effectively with the world around them, to deal with the events, challenges, and stresses they encounter in their day to day lives. Effective coping skills enable people to be self-reliant, solve problems, and make informed choices that enhance health. These skills help people face life's challenges in positive ways, without recourse to risky behaviours such as alcohol or drug abuse. Research tells us that people with a strong sense of their own effectiveness and ability to cope with circumstances in their lives are likely to be most successful in adopting and sustaining healthy behaviours and lifestyles.

People's knowledge, intentions, and coping skills are important in adopting and sustaining healthy behaviours. But their social environments are also extremely important. For example, in the 1990 Health Promotion Survey done by Health and Welfare, 48% of people said the support of friends and family was an important factor in making healthy decisions. Adequate incomes enable people to purchase the food they need for healthy diets for themselves and their children. Public policies also affect health practices—for example, seat belt legislation has significantly increased the number of people who use them.

The values and normative behaviours of peers and social networks are powerful influences on health practices. Social conditioning plays a crucial role in determining and sustaining health behaviours. For example, smoking is strongly linked with socio-economic status. As well, tobacco is an addictive substance, and a propensity to addictive behaviours seems to be established early in life. Therefore, people do not simply "choose" to smoke, or to quit smoking. Population health strategies targeted at personal health practices must therefore focus more on environmental factors and social conditions, and less on individual factors, if they are to be successful.

Healthy Child Development

There is accumulating evidence that the effect of prenatal and early childhood experiences on subsequent health, well-being, and competence is more powerful and long lasting than has previously been understood. Many of the factors affecting childhood development are aspects of other determinants of health. But child development is so important to population health that it is presented here as a separate determinant of health.

A low weight at birth links with problems not just during childhood, but also in adulthood. The negative effects during infancy of low birthweight have long been known. Studies in Montreal found low birthweight babies have a 40 times greater chance of dying during their first four weeks of life. They also have more neurological deficits, congenital abnormalities, and retarded development (Pelchat and Wilkins, 1987). However, there is increasing evidence that the negative effects of low birthweight manifest themselves later in life as well. For example, a study in Britain using longitudinal data on men born between 1911 and 1930 found those with the lowest weights at birth and at one year of age had the highest premature death rates from ischemic heart disease.

Research shows a strong relationship between income level of the mother and the baby's birthweight. This is illustrated in Figure 25-4 with data from Manitoba. The effect occurs not just for the most economically disadvantaged group. Mothers at each

FIGURE 25-4 Mean birthweight, uncomplicated pregnancies with adequate care, by income group (1987–88, Manitoba)

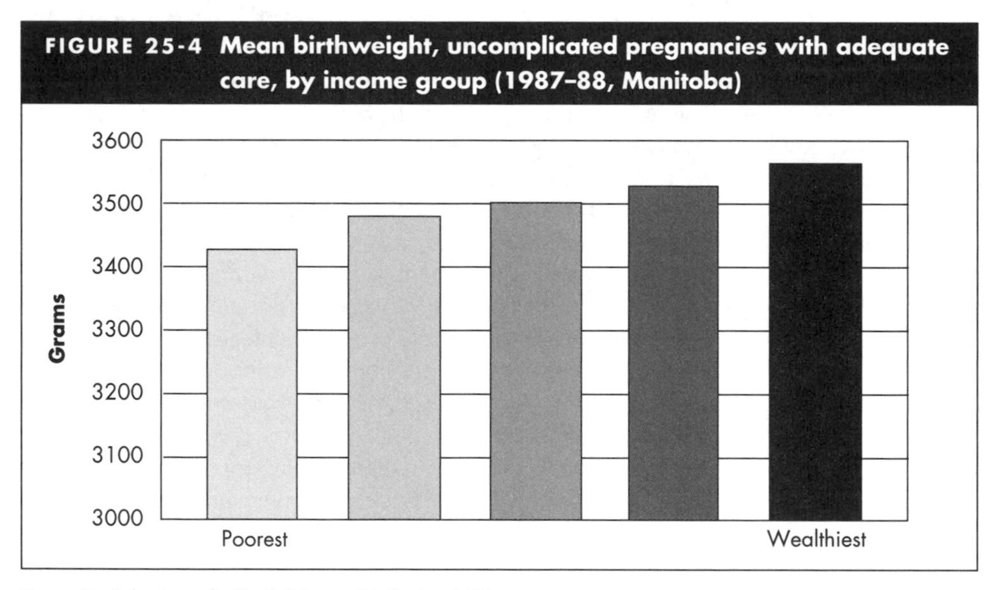

Source: Manitoba Centre for Health Policy and Evaluation, 1993.

step up the income scale have babies with higher birthweights, on average, than those on the step below. This tells us the problems are not just those such as poor maternal nutrition and poor health practices most likely to be associated with disadvantage; although the most serious problems occur in the lowest income group. It seems that factors such as coping skills and sense of control and mastery over life circumstances, with their attendant biological pathways, also come into play.

Increasing evidence shows that the way children are cared for at an early age influences their coping skills and health for the rest of their lives (Johnson and Hall, 1988; Hertzman and Wiens, 1994). A study on the Hawaiian island of Kauai found early childhood development problems caused by severe perinatal stress (problems of pregnancy, labour, and delivery) were successfully counteracted over time in children from high and middle socio-economic status families, but not for those from low socio-economic status families. Something in the care received by children from more affluent families seems not only to protect them from health risks, but also to be able to reverse the impact of problems that already exist (Werner and Smith, 1992). There is also mounting evidence that poor prenatal care and complications at birth are linked to criminal behaviour later in life, and that children involved with the criminal justice system as adults are more likely to have experienced a variety of health and social problems since early childhood (Thompson and Bland, 1993).

Many studies have shown it is possible to reduce early childhood risks such as low birthweight. It is also possible to reduce the later life consequences of early childhood problems. For example, the "graduates" of a preschool enrichment program, provided in Michigan in the 1960s to low income children at significant risk of failing in school, are now 27 years of age. Compared to the control group that received no program, the program group participants had significantly higher earnings, were more likely to own homes, and to have completed more education, were less likely to have used social services, and had significantly fewer arrests. Females in the program had significantly fewer out of wedlock births. The researchers conclude that over the lifetime of the participants, the preschool program returns to the public $7.16 for each dollar invested (Schweinhart et al., 1993).

There is increasing evidence that intervening at critical stages or transitions in the development of children and youth has the greatest potential to positively influence their later health and well-being. Key stages are the period before birth and early infancy, the period when the child begins school, the transition to adolescence, and the transition to adulthood. Focusing our interventions particularly on these periods should provide excellent results in improving child health and overall population health.

Health Services

Health services, particularly those designed to maintain and promote health and prevent disease, contribute to population health. Preventive and primary health care services such as prenatal care, well baby clinics and immunization are very important for maternal and child health. Services that educate children and adults about health risks and healthy choices, and encourage and assist them to adopt healthy living practices, make a contribution. Services to help seniors maintain their health and independence are important as well. And community environmental health services help ensure the safety of our food, water, and living environments.

Health care services designed to treat illness and restore health or functioning also make a contribution to keeping people healthy. However, as noted at the beginning of this paper, these services are not really part of a population health approach, because they focus essentially on individual disease and clinical risk factors.

By ensuring that health services are appropriate and cost-effective, we can ensure that they make the best possible contribution to health. At the same time, efforts to reform the health system should result in more resources being devoted to preventive and primary care services. As well, some resources now spent on inappropriate or ineffective health care should be freed up for other more productive purposes, including investment in the other determinants of health.

Health Status Disparities

Some groups of Canadians have significantly lower health status than others. This is associated primarily with their very low income, socio-economic status, lack of education, and other unfavourable living conditions. As well, women on average tend to have lower incomes and occupational status than men, and face significant stresses in balancing the demands of work and family life. The potential negative effects on women's health of these factors are intensified for women living in disadvantaged circumstances, for example, Aboriginal and immigrant women.

Figure 25-5 shows that different health regions in British Columbia have increasing rates of premature death according to increasing levels of socio-economic disadvantage. Premature death is measured by an index based on potential years of life lost (PYLL) from major diseases, and socio-economic disadvantage is measured by an index constructed from the percentage of the region's population with less than Grade 9 education, the unemployment rate, the percentage of the population on social assistance, and the percentage of lone parent families.

Canada's Aboriginal peoples, as a group, are the most disadvantaged of our citizens, and have the poorest health status. Figure

FIGURE 25-5 Socio-economic indicators and premature deaths for B.C. health regions

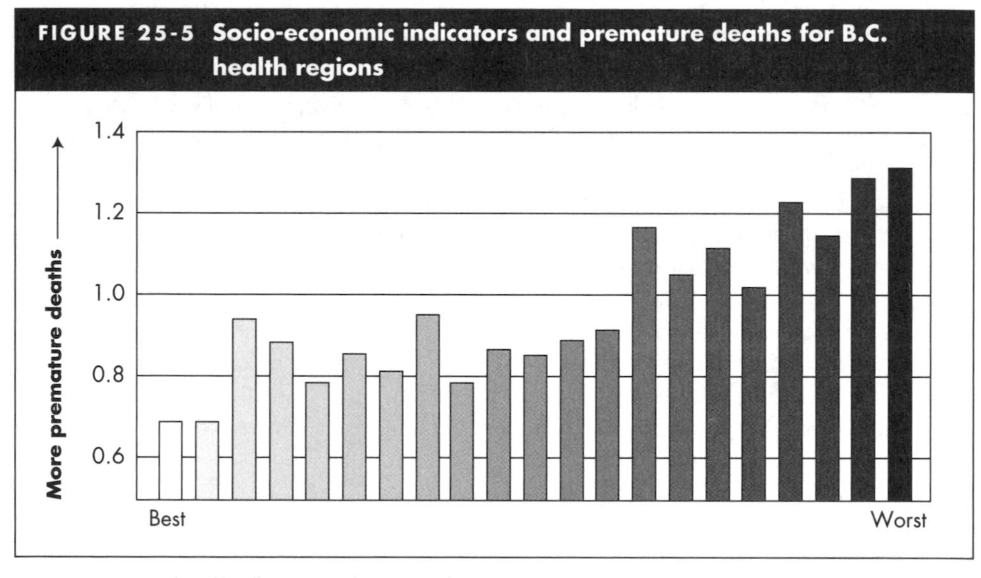

Source: B.C. Provincial Health Officer's Annual Report (Draft), 1993.

25-6 shows the significantly higher infant death rates of registered Indians and Inuit compared to the total Canadian population. Although the gap in infant mortality between Aboriginal peoples and other Canadians has been narrowing, it is still significant.

Tuberculosis rates are about eight times higher for registered Indians than for the total Canadian population. Diabetes rates are two to five times as high, and suicide rates are two to three times higher. There are similar disparities on many other indicators of health status. For example, in Manitoba, hospital morbidity (case rates) for infectious and parasitic diseases; endocrine, nutritional and metabolic diseases and immunity disorders; diseases of the respiratory and digestive systems; complications of pregnancy and childbirth; and injury and poisonings are at least twice as high for registered Indians as for other residents.

The major health problems of disadvantaged groups are a serious issue that must be attended to. However, they should not be the exclusive focus of a population health strategy, because resolving large problems of relatively small groups will not give us the overall results we are looking for in terms of improved health and prosperity of the entire population. But equitable opportunities for health for disadvantaged groups must be a special concern in a caring and democratic society that values the health of all its residents.

CONCLUSION

A Framework for Action on Population Health

It is clear that strategies to influence population health status, if they are to be effective, must address a broad range of health determinants in a comprehensive and interrelated way. The determinants of health discussed in previous sections of this paper in fact establish a framework that could be adopted by the federal, provincial and territorial governments, and other partners as the basis for development of strategies to improve population health.

FIGURE 25-6 Neonatal and postnatal death rates per 1000 live births, 1984–88

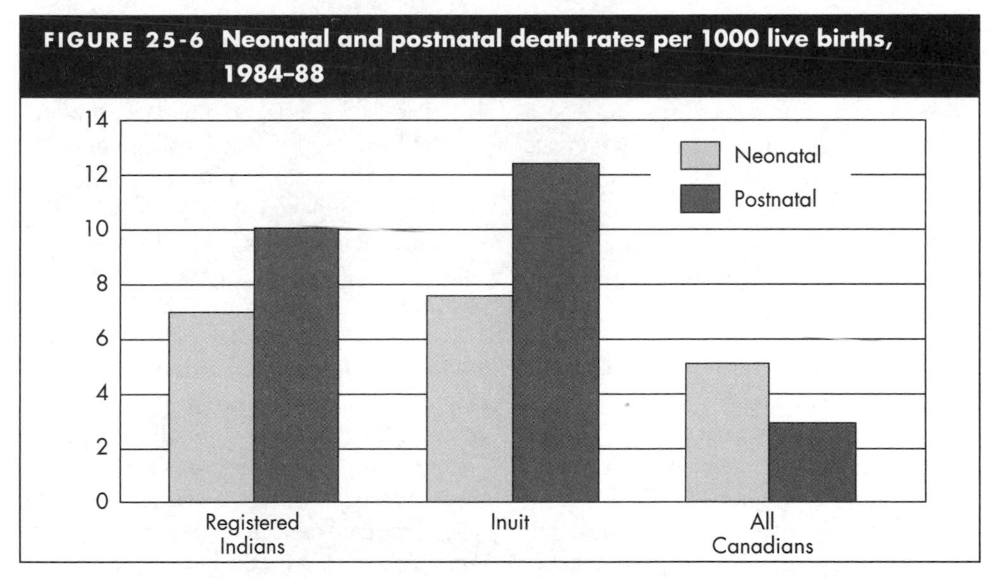

Source: Health Canada Medical Services Branch, 1990.

The framework would consist of the following five categories. A comprehensive population health strategy would include policies and/or interventions to address several or all of these five categories, recognizing their interrelatedness.

Social and Economic Environment: income, employment, social status, social support networks, education, and social factors in the workplace.

Physical Environment: physical factors in the workplace, as well as other aspects of the natural and human-built physical environment.

Personal Health Practices: behaviours that enhance or create risks to health.

Individual Capacity and Coping Skills: psychological characteristics of the person such as personal competence, coping skills, and sense of control and mastery; and genetic and biological characteristics.

Health Services: services to promote, maintain and restore health.

Healthy child development is not included as a separate category of the framework, in spite of its crucial importance as a determinant of health. Rather, each of the categories includes factors known to contribute to healthy child development.

The Role of Information, Research and Public Policy

Effective population health strategies must be built on a foundation of sound evidence about factors that determine health, and information about the potential impact of interventions and programs to address those determinants. Earlier sections of this paper show that we already have considerable evidence and information upon which to base our population health strategies and interventions. But there is still much we do not understand, and much more to be learned.

Support for research, particularly longitudinal research designed to better understand the long term effect of factors such as birthweight and early childhood experiences, will be an essential part of our population health strategies. As well, research to help understand the biological pathways through which the determinants express themselves is important. Because much of our existing research is based on men, there is also a need for gender specific studies about what makes and keeps men and women healthy. Applied research that tests and evaluates new population health approaches is needed, as is information to track the results and outcomes of our interventions on an ongoing basis. Therefore, research and information are key tools for addressing the determinants of health.

Public policy is another very important tool, since it affects almost all aspects of modern life. The influence of public policy on population health is not limited to the health sector. Policies in the economic, education, social services, transportation, housing, recreation, and other public sectors are of crucial importance.

The diagram below illustrates the proposed framework for action, including the foundation of research, information, and public policy. At the top of the pyramid is population health status, the ultimate purpose for our actions. The five categories of health determinants underpin health status. Determinants related essentially to the individual (health practices, capacity, and coping skills) and those related to the "collective" conditions that support population health (supportive environments and services) are shown on two different levels, to convey the idea that the "collective" factors enable or provide the basis for the individual factors.

FIGURE 25-7 Framework for population health

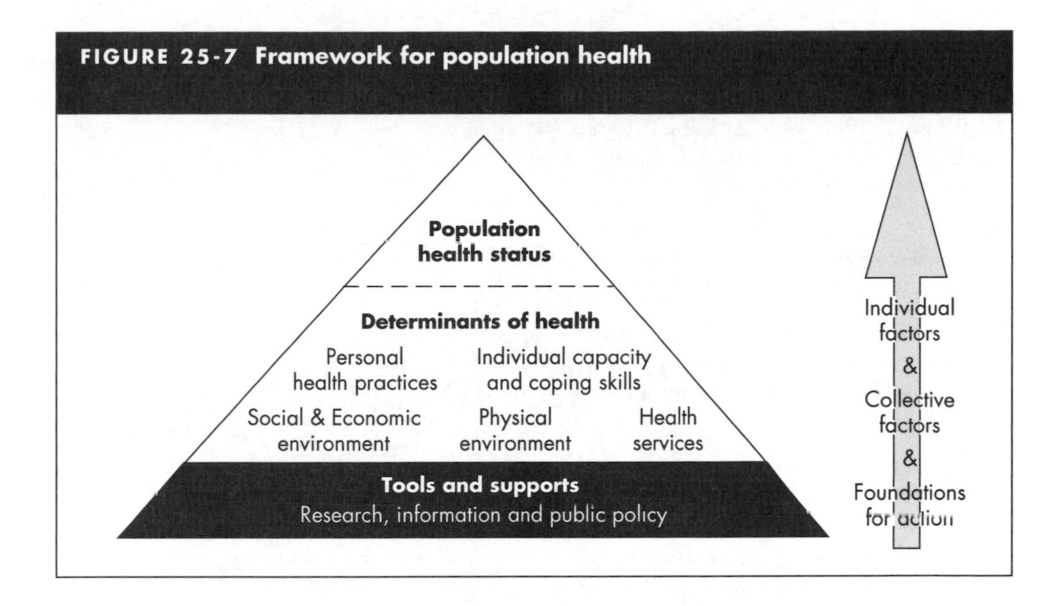

REFERENCES

Bates, David and Sizto, Ronnie 1987 "Air pollution and hospital admissions in southern Ontario: the acid summer haze effect." *Environmental Research*, 43: 317–331.

Berkman, L. and Syme, S.L. 1979 Social networks, "host resistance and mortality: a nine year follow-up study of Alameda County residents." *American Journal of Epidemiology*, 109(2), 186–204.

Cotton, Paul 1993 "Medical news and perspectives: best data yet say air pollution kills below levels currently considered safe." *Journal of the American Medical Association*, 269(24): 3087–3088

D'Arcy, Carl 1986 "Unemployment and health: data and implications." *Canadian Journal of Public Health*, Vol. 77 Supp. 1.

Groen, J.J. et al. 1968 "Epidemiological investigation of hypertension and ischemic heart eisease with a defined segment of the adult male population of Israel." *Israel Journal of Medical Science*, 4(2), 177–194.

Hanson, B. Ostergren 1986 "Social networks, social support and related concepts—towards a model for epidemiological use." In *Social Support in Health and Disease* Isacsson, S.O. (ed.), Almqvist & Wiksel Int., Stockholm.

Hertzman, C. and Wiens, M. 1994 *Child Development and Long-Term Outcomes: A Population Health Perspective and Summary of Successful Interventions* University of British Columbia Department of Health Care and Epidemiology.

Johnson, J.V. and Hall, E.M. 1988 "Job strain, work place social support and cardiovascular disease." *American Journal of Public Health*, 78(10): 1336–1342.

Marmot, M.G., Kogevinas, M.A., and Elston, M. 1987 "Social/economic status and disease." *Annual Review of Public Health*, 8:111–135.

Mustard, Fraser J. and Frank, John 1991 *The Determinants of Health* Canadian Institute for Advanced Research Publication #5, Toronto.

Organization for Economic Development and Cooperation 1989 *The OECD Employment Outlook* Paris.

Pelchat, Yolande and Wilkins, Russell 1987 *Report on Births: Certain Sociodemographic and Health Aspects of Mothers and Newborns in Metropolitan Montreal 1979–1983* Montreal Association of Community Health Departments.

Rees, W.P. and Lutkins, S.G. 1967 "Mortality and bereavement." *British Medical Journal*, 4:13–16.

Repace, J.F. 1985 "A quantitative estimate of nonsmokers lung cancer risk from passive smoking." *Environment International*, 11:3–22.

Schweinhart, L.J., Barnes, H.V., and Weikart, D.P. 1993 *Significant Benefits of the High/Scope Perry Preschool Study Through Age 27* High/Scope Educational Research Foundation Monograph Number 10, High/Scope Press.

The World Bank/International Bank for Reconstruction and Development 1993 *World Development Report 1993: Investing in Health* Oxford University Press.

Thompson, A.H. and Bland, Roger 1993 *System Pathways from Childhood to Adult Crime* Alberta Health.

Werner, E.E. and Smith, R.S. 1985 *Overcoming the Odds: High Risk Children from Birth to Adulthood* Ithaca, N.Y.: Cornell University Press.

Wescott, G. et al. 1985 *Health Policy Implications of Unemployment* World Health Organization, Copenhagen.

Wilkins, Russell and Adams, Owen 1978 *Healthfulness of Life* Institute for Research on Public Policy, Montreal.

SOCIO-ECONOMIC STATUS AND MALE VIOLENCE IN THE CANADIAN HOME

Chapter 26

Eugen Lupri, Elaine Grandin, Merlin B. Brinkerhoff

(Abridged from the authors' "Socioeconomic status and male violence in the Canadian home: a re-examination." *Canadian Journal of Sociology*, 19, 1, 1994, pp. 47–93. Reprinted with permission.)

INTRODUCTION

The relationship between socioeconomic status and wife abuse has been subjected to conflicting interpretations because of underdeveloped theory, imprecise nominal and operational definitions of the dependent variable, measurement problems, discrepant research and sample designs, and varying levels of analysis. Although many family researchers report an inverse relationship between socioeconomic status, particularly when it is measured by income, and the incidence of spousal violence, few studies have investigated this proposition systematically. In this chapter our goal is to address this gap in the literature as well as to examine different styles of violence by focusing on physical and psychological abuse across the life course. In doing so we re-examine previous claims about the inverse relationship and suggest an alternative explanation, which we elaborate later.

Theoretical context

In focusing sharply on the economic structure of Canadian society as an important determinant of women's subordinate status in the home, feminist scholars have demystified the home as a "haven in a heartless world" (Lasch, 1979) and have shown that the "family harmony" model is a myth. Based on the view of patriarchy as an interlocking set of behavioural and ideological traits that lead men to assert dominance over women, an historically grounded theoretical framework has emerged, which links wife abuse to male dominance via the economic and political structure in which men hold the power. Dobash and Dobash write that "violence used by men against women in the family ... attempts to establish or maintain a patriarchal order" (1983: 150). Thus violence against women exists and persists because patriarchy is historically and socially constructed and continues to give men power and control over women, placing women in an inferior, dependent social status in today's society.

In today's marriage, traditional forms of authority still prevent an equal distribution of power between husband and wife (Brinkerhoff and Lupri, 1992). This gender inequity persists because control over important resources is largely determined not by personal factors but by structural conditions and by the overall gender ideology that prevails in a society at any given time. Furthermore, gender inequality in the home translates into gender inequality in the labour market, and vice versa (Armstrong and Armstrong, 1988; Lupri and Mills, 1987; Meissner et al., 1975). Recognizing the political and economic underpinnings of family life does not discount the importance of love, because structured domination and love exist alongside each other and often become entangled, as Simmel (1955; 1958) observed. The dialectic interplay of love and domination, moreover, can create an "arena of struggle" (Hartmann, 1981) between intimate partners.

The family as an institution is inherently contradictory because it is both oppressive and protective, violent and caring, and often is some mixture of the two (Rubin, 1976). Families do not stand apart from society, however; on the contrary, they are tied closely to the political and economic structures of the public world. The view of the public world of work (based on economic relations) and the private world of the family (based on personal relations) as two distinct spheres is rooted in the grand synthesis of Parsonian structural functionalism (Parsons and Bales, 1955), as we noted earlier. Such a perspective ignores the dialectic nature and the reciprocal connection between production and reproduction (O'Brien, 1981; Ursel, 1988), and disregards what Ferguson and Folbre (1981) call "sex-affective production." This conceptual "fallacy of separateness" (Simmel, 1958) also lacks empirical substance, although the "myth of the separate worlds" (Kanter, 1977) lingers on in contemporary family research as well as in the sociology of work. As a major source of power and influence, socioeconomic status provides a crucial link between family and economy. In turn, this power and influence affect life changes and dispositions in many domains, including family life. In fact, socioeconomic attributes tie family members to the public sphere, directly or indirectly, through status ascription and dependency relations.

Empirical issues

Although the research literature on family violence suggests an inverse association between the incidence of wife abuse and factors such as education, occupational prestige, and income, this paper states reasons why research has been equivocal on this larger issue. In their 1975 U.S. national survey, Straus et al. (1980) found that individuals in blue-collar positions showed higher rates of abuse than their white-collar counterparts. This finding is generally supported in the literature by results of other studies, although no uniform method for measuring social class or socioeconomic status has been used. In their systematic assessment of the literature and their subsequent multivariate analysis of data from the 1985 U.S. national study, Hotaling and Sugarman (1990) found a weak negative association between socioeconomic status and *severe* physical abuse, but none for verbal aggression. Similarly, Straus and Sweet (1992) found no association between socioeconomic status and verbal/symbolic aggression in American couples. Canadian data on socioeconomic status also are less clear-cut than those reported on income alone. Although Smith (1990a) reports statistically significant relationships between violence on one hand and education and occupational status on the other for his Toronto sample of female respondents, the data on wives' and husbands' occupational status and violence, as measured by the Blishen Index, are curvilinear, particularly among the wives. Similarly, the correlations between violence and education, occupational status, and SES as reported by Calgary husbands and wives are typically weak, often nonsignificant, and in opposite directions (Brinkerhoff and Lupri, 1988).

The extent to which reporting biases explain some of these inconsistencies is unclear. Walker's (1984) U.S. sample of volunteer respondents revealed higher incidence rates among professional and upper classes than among their nonprofessional and lower-class counterparts; she demonstrates that women with less access to other resources are more likely to use shelters and are less able to hide abuse from public scrutiny. Similarly, Canadian findings based on responses from residents of women's shelters and transition houses (MacLeod, 1987; MacLeod and Cadieux, 1980) are biased because abused women of the lower classes are more likely than their middle- or upper-class counterparts to seek refuge with public agencies. Thus visibility is a problem in establishing an accurate incidence rate, particularly in families with greater resources.

Studies consistently report an inverse relationship between level of income and domestic violence. In his national sample Lupri (1989) found the highest rates of wife abuse among couples in which the husbands' incomes were the smallest; Kennedy and Dutton (1989) showed that in families in Alberta subsisting at or below a household income of $6000 (n=9), the rate of wife abuse was 700 percent higher than among couples who reported annual incomes of $45 000 or above. Similarly, Smith (1990a) found statistically significant differences between low- and high-income Toronto families; abuse rates were highest in families with reported annual family incomes of $28 000 or less, and lowest in families with reported incomes of $70 000 or more. Thus it appears that income is an important risk marker of wife abuse.

Limitations of past research and objectives of this study

Previous research examining the relationship between socioeconomic status and wife abuse suffers from basic shortcomings that are crucial to the present research. Violence often is defined nominally as an "act carried out with the intention or perceived intention of causing physical pain or injury to another person" (see Brinkerhoff, Grandin, and Lupri, 1992; Brinkerhoff and Lupri, 1988; Gelles and Cornell, 1985; Kennedy and Dutton, 1989; Lupri, 1989; Smith, 1987; Steinmetz, 1987; Straus et al., 1980). In their operational definition, these researchers—with the exception of Hotaling and Sugarman (1990)—typically focus on items or scales that are intended to measure *physically* violent acts such as slapping, kicking, beating, hitting, choking, and threatening intimate partners with or using a knife or gun on them. Emotional or psychological violence has been neglected because the consequences are difficult to identify: they do not leave physical scars (Straus and Sweet, 1992). By ignoring psychological violence, however, we fail to recognize that the term violence includes emotional as well as physical mistreatment. Thus we think it important theoretically to incorporate psychological violence into our nominal and operational definitions of violence, both to differentiate it from physical violence and to demonstrate the independent as well as the joint effects of the two.

Such a strategy has important implications for testing the inverse relationship between socioeconomic status and male violence in the home. In following this strategy we are guided by a phenomenology of family violence that places "emotionality and the self at the core of violence" (Denzin, 1984a: 169). The basic meanings of violence include: to treat with force, to abuse, to pursue something with force, or to regain something, often with the use of force. We follow Denzin, who defines violence as "the attempt to regain, through the use of *emotional* or physical force, something that has been lost" (1984a: 169, our emphasis). Clinical studies show that verbal abuse, for example, exacts a fearful toll, especially in younger women: damaged self-esteem, low self-concept, a sense of helplessness, and fear. Emotional violence takes many forms and leaves its own scars, often hidden and undetected. These invisible scars need closer empirical scrutiny and sustained analysis.

METHODS AND DATA SOURCES

Definitional issues

Violence is an ambiguous concept, and difficult to operationalize for research. We define violence nominally as any act carried out with the intention, or perceived as having the intention, to hurt another person physically or emotionally, or both, as suggested earlier. The physical hurt can range from inflicting slight pain, as in a slap, to murder. The emotional hurt can range from cold, stony silence to yelling, sarcasm, and vicious verbal attacks intended to humiliate and degrade the other person (Steinmetz, 1987).

Data collection

The data for this paper were derived from a 1987 national survey conducted in Canada (Lupri, 1989). A probability sample of 1834 women and men over 18 years of age was interviewed. Data on marital conflict and demographic information were derived through the interviews. At the close of the personal interview, self-administered questionnaires with self-addressed stamped envelopes were left behind for completion by respondents who were ever married or cohabiting. A letter accompanied the questionnaire, explaining the purpose of the family life study and encouraging respondents to complete and return the instrument. Usable questionnaires were returned by 652 female and 471 male respondents, or 73.4 percent of the 1530 eligible ever-married or cohabiting respondents. (In this paper we focus on male respondents only, as stated earlier.) To maximize recall accuracy, our analyses excluded men whose separation, divorce, or widowhood occurred before 1985. As in the interviews, the self-administered questionnaire was available in either English or French. Of the six groups of questions, those on interspousal violence were asked last in the questionnaire.

Measures

Wife abuse

The questions on interspousal violence covered a modified version of the Conflict Tactics Scales (CTS) developed by Straus (1979) and associates, and were designed to measure the incidence of physical violence, verbal aggression, and symbolic acts of interspousal conflict. The CTS have been used widely during the past decade and are considered a reliable, valid measure of the incidence of various types of violence.

The scale contained a total of eighteen items. The first ten ranged from efforts at reasoning to acts of verbal aggression and psychological abuse. Of the remaining nine categories, eight were constructed to measure how frequently physical force was used to settle interspousal disagreements. The following eight items describe the use of physical force:

1. Threw object at another
2. Pushed, grabbed, or shoved the other
3. Slapped the other
4. Kicked, bit, or hit the other with a fist
5. Hit or tried to hit the other
6. Beat up the other
7. Threatened the other with a knife or gun
8. Used knife or gun on the other

The items were rated and ordered in the instrument according to severity. Intensity of abuse was measured by asking respondents to state how often they had committed each of the violent acts against their partners during the past year.

The following items were designed to measure *psychological* violence:

1. Yelled at the other
2. Did or said something to spite the other
3. Insulted or swore at the other
4. Sulked or refused to talk
5. Stomped out of the room
6. Smashed, threw, kicked something

These psychological items entail two additional factorially separate variables: verbal abuse (Items 1, 2, and 3) and symbolic abuse (Items 4, 5, and 6). The alpha coefficients of reliability are .76 for verbal aggression and .69 for symbolic aggression, with eigenvalues of 1.58 and 1.28 respectively. The questionnaire required respondents to report on the frequency of occurrence of each act (0 = never; 1 = once; 2 = twice; 3 = 3-5 times; 4 = 6-10 times; and 5 = more than 11 times). Because more than three-fourths of the men studied reported at least one psychologically violent act during the year, we introduced an intensity measure that we call chronicity. Respondents who reported having committed any of the acts 11 times or more during the year preceding the survey were categorized as committing *chronic* psychological violence.

Although our approach is similar to that of Straus and his associates, it differs in two respects. First, in an attempt to reduce response bias, we chose to measure spousal violence by using a self-administered questionnaire rather than an interview, thereby minimizing the impact of a stranger's presence. Second, our study used self-reports of violent acts that male respondents had committed against their intimate partners rather than reports of women's victimization.

Socioeconomic status

To measure socioeconomic status we used three empirical indicators: income, education, and occupation. We also used a SES index that is based on scores combining income, education, and occupation as ranked on the Blishen scale (Blishen and McRoberts, 1976).

Marital conflict

The respondents' perception of the degree to which their marital relations could be described as conflictual was assessed with ten items (e.g., disagreements about money, children's behaviour, housework, in-laws, leisure time).

Life course

In the absence of longitudinal data, we used four age groups to examine the incidence of three types of abuse across the life course. We replicated each analysis by using "length of marriage" as a second measure to assess the incidence of violence across the life course; these two variables were intercorrelated at r=.81 (p≤.001). Because "length of marriage" produced very similar results, we do not report them in the ensuing analysis.

Limitations of the data

The scales contain two basic shortcomings. First, the items deal strictly with acts or incidents. Thus we do not know the context in which physical or psychological abuse occurred or what precipitated the specific acts of violence. Second, because it was too difficult to measure accurately the outcome of the specific violent acts in a self-administered questionnaire, we do not know the severity of the injury, pain, or emotional damage that male respondents inflicted on their females partners.

Yet, despite these defects, the Conflict Tactics Scales provide a fairly reliable measure of the extent to which specific acts of physical and psychological violence take place in the home over the life course. Because these acts are based on self-reports and because men "understate" (Stets and Straus, 1990) how often they inflict violence on their female partners, the rates reported below may well be underestimates. Methodological pitfalls abound in all research, but particularly in studies that attempt to explore the private domain of family interaction, which touches on the respondent's personal experience of love, intimacy, sexuality, power, or abuse of an intimate partner. Thus it is essential to exercise caution and restraint in the ensuing interpretation of these findings on the relationship between socioeconomic status and male violence in the Canadian home.

RESULTS

Multiple forms of wife abuse

Because not all violent intimate relationships are alike and because previous research focused almost exclusively on assault causing physical pain or injury, we constructed scales that identify three mutually exclusive types of intimate violence, which include verbal and symbolic aggression. Thirteen percent of our representative sample of 435 Canadian males admittedly committed physical violence only: throwing objects; shoving, slapping, and beating their intimate partners; threatening with a knife or gun; and actually using these weapons against them. These physically violent acts were not isolated incidents; in 70 percent of the cases they had occurred several times during the year preceding the survey. Steinmetz (1987) refers to these violent males as "silent attackers" because none of them reported engaging in any acts of emotional or psychological violence.

Although physical and psychological violence are correlated moderately (r=.29,p≤.001), we think it theoretically important to distinguish between these two types of violence. Thus, the second type consists of males who frequently committed any of the six psychologically violent acts that we described earlier, but did not engage in any physical violence. These are the "threateners" according to Steinmetz's typology. Because verbal aggression, as we operationalized it, is much more prevalent than physical violence, and reportedly was common in a great majority (76 percent) of Canadian marriages, we introduced the notion of chronicity and agreed with Denzin (1984a) that a victim's self-concept and self-esteem are more likely to be damaged or threatened in an intimate relationship when emotional abuse occurs repeatedly and consistently over a long period. In an attempt to regain through emotional force something that has been lost (e.g., power, ability to control the other), aggressors employ various violent tactics of conflict resolution. These may take the form of *verbal* put-downs such as making nasty, condescending remarks or calling their partners insulting names; *nonverbal*, symbolically humiliating acts such as stony silence, refusing to make love, sulking, smashing something in the presence of the other, or making threatening, degrading gestures; or (typically) both forms of emotional abuse. When intense verbal or symbolic aggression is coupled with unpredictability, such chronic emotional abuse engenders shame, fear, and depression in the victims (Hoff, 1990).

Violent, enacted emotionality is unpredictable in its consequences and is "focused around the interiority and inner meanings of another—a loved family member, most typically" (Denzin, 1984a: 170). Although this type of psychological abuse is often perceived as more harmful than physical violence, our study does not enable us to demonstrate such consequences. Another 13 percent of the males belonged to this category in that they reportedly had committed these emotionally damaging acts eleven times or more during the past year.

The third type consists of male aggressors, 9.9 percent of the sample, who committed both physically and chronic psychologically violent acts. We refer to them as "severe abusers" because it appeared that their use of both physical force and psychological abuse had reached the point where it was an integral part of the intimate relationship. Pointedly, Steinmetz calls them "warriors." We consider this type of violence the most serious of the three, even though we can only surmise the harmful effect of these repeated physical assaults and the severely damaging impact of other forms of violence on the victims' physical, social, and emotional functioning. Thus the sample consists of 155 violent and 280 nonviolent males; the latter are what Steinmetz calls the "pacifists," who reportedly did not commit any type of violence during the year preceding the survey. In sum, the following typology emerged from our 1987 national survey:

Type of violence	**Number of cases**	**Percentage**
Physical-only violence ("silent attackers")	56	13.0
Chronic psychological violence ("threateners")	56	13.0
Severe abusers ("warriors")	43	9.9
Nonviolent males ("pacifists")	280	64.1
Total	435	100.0

The human meaning of these findings can be understood more clearly if we translate the rates into the total number of women affected in 1986. On the basis of approximately 5.9 million couples living in Canada in 1986, the severe abuse rate of 9.9 percent translates into about 585 000 physically and psychologically assaulted women who lived with an intimate, violent male partner during that year. This is a conservative estimate and consistent with MacLeod's (1989) projection that one in ten Canadian women is physically, psychologically, or sexually battered by her husband or live-in partner.

Rates of male violence and their correlates

Table 26-1 displays, for each of the three socioeconomic variables and for the composite index (SES), the incidence rates for each type of violence. To evaluate the plausibility of alternative explanations for the inverse association between socioeconomic status and wife abuse, we also present rates by age of aggressor and level of marital conflict. Zero-order correlations are presented to show the strength of the association between these variables and the three types of violence. Several of the patterns that emerge in Table 26-1 merit brief comment.

Socioeconomic factors

Looking first at the three socioeconomic variables, we find some support, albeit weak, for an inverse relationship between socioeconomic status and the incidence of male violence: low-income males are more likely than high-income males to engage in severe abuse (-.086,≤.05), operationalized as both physical and chronic psychological violence. Indeed, the rate of severe wife abuse among Canadian males with an annual wage of less than $10 000 is more than 350 percent higher than among men who reported incomes of $40 000 or above. This finding corroborates the results of other studies, particularly those of Hotaling and Sugarman (1986): they also found a negative association between income and *severe* physical abuse, but none for verbal aggression. Similarly, our study failed to reveal a significant negative association between income and the incidence of chronic psychological violence (verbal or symbolic aggression). The same holds true for what we call physical-only violence. In fact, the data points in the opposite direction, but in each case the positive relationship lacks statistical significance. The pattern for education is similar: the coefficients for psychological violence and severe abuse are positive, but are not significant; the coefficient for physical-only violence is in the predicted negative direction, but is nonsignificant.

Of theoretical significance are the elevated rates of chronic psychological violence among university graduates, particularly those with graduate degrees, and the relatively low rate of physical-only violence and severe abuse in this group. Is emotional hurt a substitute for physical hurt among these well-educated men? The question is important for three reasons. First, the finding points to the importance of incorporating emotional abuse into our definition of violence. Restricting the definition of violence to physical assault only tends to overrepresent men of lower socioeconomic status and to underrepresent men of higher status, and thus introduces a serious class bias. Second, this finding underscores an argument made earlier: emotional violence is another form of victimization that should not bc ignored. Third, the finding supports the claim that violence is considerably more widespread across the socioeconomic spectrum than was assumed previously by practitioners and researchers alike. (See also the elevated rates of chronic psychological violence among men in the two upper income categories and the rates of those with medium and high SES scores.)

In regard to occupation, we found no overall significant association with any of the three types of violence. Within the occupational categories, farmers reported the highest rates for each type of violence. Blue-collar workers reported the second highest rates for physical-only violence and severe abuse; however, they reported the lowest rates of chronic psychological violence. These findings are consistent with the reasoning of those who believe that these occupations are more stressful than white-collar jobs and that stress is related positively to wife beating (Smith, 1990a; Straus et al., 1980). They also tend to support the "subculture of violence" thesis and its derivative, the "male patriarchal subculture" thesis, as discussed earlier.

The data testing the inverse relationship between the socioeconomic composite (SES) and wife abuse are inconclusive. The coefficients for physical-only violence and severe abuse are in the predicted direction, but are statistically nonsignificant; the association between SES and chronic psychological violence is positive but also nonsignificant.

In summary, the inverse relationship was supported in only one of these 12 comparisons, namely income and severe abuse. Chronic psychological violence was related *positively*, albeit weakly, to all four measures of socioeconomic status. The empirical support for the inversion thesis, according to the findings displayed in Table 26-1, is weak and almost nonexistent.

Age

The data on the potential confounding factors of age and conflict, at the bottom of Table 26-1, present insights into the association between age and wife abuse across the life course and the link between conflict and violence in intimate relationships. The negative association between violence and respondent's age holds for all three types of violence and is monotonic: violence decreases among males of age groups, although the association is nonsignificant for those committing chronic psychological violence only.

Not surprisingly, the sharpest decline over the life course occurred among the severe abusers: the rate of men in the youngest age group (under 30) is ten times that of men in the oldest age group (27.7 and 2.7 respectively). The decline in the use of physical-only violence is less steep, but the rate of the very young "silent attackers" is still 3 1/2 times the rate of that reported by the oldest males. The nonsignificance of the decline across the life course among the "threateners" is an important finding for reasons we suggested earlier, although the reports of the oldest men in that group reflect a fairly significant decrease in psychological violence. Even so, 8 percent of the oldest men committed chronic emotional violence, compared to 5.6 percent who inflicted physical-only violence, and 2.7 percent who engaged in severe abuse against their female partners.

Marital conflict

Conflict in marriage or in the woman-man relationship derives from opposite interests and from power differences; these are inherent in the structure of today's families, as we argued earlier. A tension may exist between the individual's need for maintaining a sense of personal identity and the couple's need for maintaining stability (Lupri, 1990). Sprey (1991: 141) expressed this notion succinctly by stating that there exists in marriage a "perpetual confrontation between the quest for autonomy and jointness." According to Simmel (1958), the more intimate social relations are, the more likely they are to cause conflict and tension. Thus the potential for conflict in marriage is a constant, not an occasional or temporary event.

From the foregoing theoretical argument we would expect marital conflict to precede violence, rather than the reverse, and to be related directly to abuse by the male in the home. Because our data are cross-sectional rather than longitudinal, we cannot test the former empirically, but we can demonstrate the latter. Table 26-1 (bottom) shows that indeed this is the case: the coefficients for all three types of violence reveal a statistically significant positive relationship with conflict. The strength and the consistency of the association between conflict and violence found in this research and in other recent studies have led us to conclude that marital conflict may be another confounding and interacting factor.

DISCUSSION

The findings and their limitations raise interesting questions. In keeping with previous studies conducted in the United States, the results of our national study reveal a consistent decline in male violence across the life course, shown previously in Table 26-1.

Yet, although the incidence of male violence in the Canadian home peaks among younger couples, it also was reported by a fairly large proportion of middle-aged and older males, especially by respondents who committed chronic psychological abuse against their intimate partners. In contrast to severe abuse and physical-only violence,

TABLE 26-1 **Male violence in the home and age, level of conflict, and selected socioeconomic factors: percentage comparisons[1] and coefficients[2], by types of violence[3], Canada, 1987**

Correlates	Physical-only violence			Chronic psychological violence			Severe abuse		
	Percentage	Coefficient (r)	N	Percentage	Coefficient (r)	N	Percentage	Coefficient (r)	N
Income ($)		.020	383		0.61	383		–.086*	383
< 10 000	3.8			14.9			18.2		
10 000 – 14 999	20.5			5.5			10.3		
15 000–24 999	14.3			10.0			10.7		
25,000–39,999	13.9			17.6			10.5		
40 000 or more	14.1			14.0			5.1		
Education		–.015	422		.021	422		.023	422
Elementary	12.1			16.8			1.9		
Some high school	11.3			9.1			13.3		
High school	15.4			13.8			12.3		
Some university	14.9			13.1			12.9		
B.A., B.Sc.	10.8			16.7			4.7		
Graduate degree	7.6			17.4			3.9		
Occupation		.035	427		.011	427		.000	427
Professional & managerial	10.0			11.2			9.6		
Clerical	12.1			17.1			6.8		
Blue collar	16.8			10.5			13.1		
Farmers	31.6			42.4			13.9		
Housewives/students	11.2			11.6			7.4		
SES		–.014	430		.010	430		–.016	430
Low	11.6			12.1			9.0		
Medium	14.7			13.6			11.0		
High	7.7			13.0			5.5		

TABLE 26-1 continued

Correlates	Physical-only violence			Chronic psychological violence			Severe abuse		
	Percentage	Coefficient (r)	N	Percentage	Coefficient (r)	N	Percentage	Coefficient (r)	N
Age		−.139***	430		−.045	430		−.227****	430
18–29	19.5			14.6			27.7		
30–45	16.4			13.3			9.8		
46–64	8.9			13.2			4.8		
65 or older	5.6			8.0			2.7		
Level of partner conflict		.113**	401		.206****	401		.208****	394
Low	6.0			1.9			4.3		
Medium	15.8			18.4			7.5		
High	18.5			19.6			20.3		
All Males (n=435)[4]	13.0			13.0			9.9		

1. Percentages reflect the proportion of each category of men who reported committing any violent act in the past year; i.e., 27.7 percent of all men aged 18–29 reportedly committed severe physically and psychologically abusive acts against their intimate partners in the past year.
2. All coefficients are product–moment correlations and * ≤.05, ** ≤.01, *** ≤.005, and **** ≤.001.
3. *Physical violence is operationalized as committing any of the eight physically violent acts (exclusive of psychologically violent acts)* as discussed earlier (see pp. 54–55); chronic psychological violence is defined as committing any of the six psychologically violent acts (exclusive of physically violent acts). 11 times or more in the past year (see pp. 54–55); severe abuse is operationalized as committing any of the physically as well as any of the psychologically violent acts 11 times or more in the past year.
4. The total sample size of males is 435; however, the number of cases for each variable may vary due to different response rates.

chronic psychological abuse declines less steeply over the life course, and the decline lacks statistical significance. These results confirm the presence and the persistence of several distinct styles of male violence across the life course and show that a "certain proportion of elder abuse is actually spouse abuse grown old" (Lupri, 1993: 232).

The central finding of this study is that our data tend to challenge the inversion thesis because we could not establish support for the negative association between socioeconomic status and wife abuse. Of the three socioeconomic variables, only income emerged as a useful potential predictor of severe abuse, in keeping with previous research (Hotaling and Sugarman, 1986; 1990; Smith, 1990b). However, (in analysis not shown here) when age was controlled the inverse relationship between income and severe abuse became nonsignificant. Previous research failed to control for aggressor's age, which operates as a confounding variable: young men are most likely to be associated simultaneously with high rates of severe abuse (Table 26-1) and with low income. Furthermore, younger couples are more prone to conflict and violence because the early years of marriage or of living together require new levels of commitment and a need to redefine expectations for one another. At this state in the life course, career and family demands often conflict, especially with the arrival of the first child. Thus younger couples have a greater need to examine and fine-tune their mutual expectations of consistency, fairness, and clarity.

Another possible reason why we observe more severe abuse among younger couples is that violent marriages are more likely to end in separation or divorce. About one-third of all couples who filed for divorce in 1987 listed "mental or physical cruelty" as grounds for the breakdown of the marriage. Divorce may reduce the chance that a violent marriage will endure for more than a few years. Yet only a small proportion of victimized women seek to leave a violent marriage; this fact underscores the seriousness of violence in the home. The reasons to leave or to remain in an abusive relationship are manifold and complex, as suggested earlier, but for women economic dependency is one of the most fundamental reasons for remaining (Strube and Barbour, 1990).

In past research, both socioeconomic status and marital conflict were found to be accurate predictors of wife abuse. To be sure, conflicts of interest do not necessarily lead to violence; objective conflict can be negotiated. Conflict resolution is very difficult, however, especially when the partners are at odds over basic values and cannot agree on the rules that govern the relationship. Unresolved marital conflict and discord may accumulate gradually over the life course, may become pervasive and structured, and also may promote the use of physical force when the path toward negotiation is "blocked by inadequate bonds and hidden cross-currents of emotions—that is by unacknowledged alienation and shame" (Scheff and Retziner, 1991: xiv). Because wife abuse occurs in a framework of superordinate and subordinate relationships that tie husbands and wives into the established social order, victimization of females in the home can be viewed as the use of illegitimate force to solve conflicts between two intimate partners, particularly among younger couples (Denzin 1984b; Lupri, 1990; Straus and Gelles, 1990). The high rates of all types of wife abuse in the youngest population are cause for some concern because "this population will constitute the major policy target of health and criminal justice systems in the next decade" (Kennedy and Dutton, 1989: 51). This group also constitutes the major family training ground in violence, which affects thousands of children.

Perhaps the most important finding of this research concerns the relationship between socioeconomic status and chronic psychological abuse. The analyses established consistently nonsignificant associations between this form of victimization and the socioeconomic variables, including SES. In most instances these associations were positive, albeit nonsignificant; thus they suggested that chronic psychological abuse is not related to socioeconomic status, but rather is widespread and broadly based. In addition, we found that its decline across the life course was nonsignificant. We consider these results important because the long-term consequences of chronic psychological violence may be as severe as those of physical violence, and because chronic emotional abuse attacks women's self-esteem (Follingstad et al. 1990). Furthermore, these findings may have implications for the nominal and operational definitions of violence as well as for possible prevention strategies. Thus, the pattern and the sequence of what we currently define as violence need to be reexamined.

All told, the findings of this national study refute the popular myth that violence in the home represents "blue-collar brawls" (Renzetti, 1992: 15). We found little evidence to suggest that violence in the home is related significantly to income. In contrast, the "patriarchal subculture thesis" as an explanation of wife beating is an intriguing hypothesis that appeals to sociologists because it emphasizes structural features. Although we accept the feminist thesis that links wife abuse with adherence to a familial patriarchy, our findings raise questions for those who would attribute such adherence only to the lower classes. It is more likely, we suggest, that such adherence typically occurs in pockets or clusters in all segments of Canadian society, including men in high-income, well-educated, and professional groups. The data from our life course analysis, together with the pervasiveness of chronic psychological abuse across all socioeconomic groups, tend to support such a view. Obviously there is need for further research on the "subculture thesis"; such research must be based firmly on patriarchal beliefs and attitudes reported by the husbands themselves, as suggested by Smith (1990a).

CONCLUSION

In light of the findings of the present national study, we propose what we call the "dispersion" thesis as an alternative to the inverse relationship between socioeconomic status and wife abuse. According to this thesis, wife abuse takes varied forms including physical violence, emotional abuse, and material and psychological deprivation, which are represented in all classes of society. Therefore we suggest that wife abuse is a manifestation of men's power to control women, regardless of their class position. Thus any reduction or elimination of wife abuse must involve a basic restructuring of the power relationship between women and men, inside and outside the household. Prevention programs must take into account multiple forms of victimization and must acknowledge that higher education is no guarantee of nonviolent behaviour, as our study shows. The resolution of conflict through nonviolent strategies is essential for eliminating all forms of violence, including wife abuse.

REFERENCES

Armstrong, Pat and Hugh Armstrong 1988 "Women, family, and the economy." In Nancy Mandell and Ann Duffy, (eds.), *Reconstructing the Canadian Family: Feminist Perspectives* pp. 143–74. Toronto: Butterworth.

Blishen, B. and H.A. McRoberts 1976 "A revised socio–economic index for occupations in Canada." *Canadian Review of Sociology and Anthropology* 12: 71–79.

Breines, Wini and Linda Gordon 1983 "The new scholarship on family violence." *Signs:*

Journal of Women in Culture and Society 8: 490–531.

Brinkerhoff, M.B. and Eugen Lupri 1988 "Interspousal violence." *Canadian Journal of Sociology* 13(4): 407–31.

Brinkerhoff, M.B. and Eugen Lupri 1992 "Power and authority in families." In K. Ishwaran (ed.) *Family and Marriage: Cross–Cultural Perspectives* pp. 213–36. Toronto: Wall & Thompson.

Brinkerhoff, M.B., Elaine Grandin, and Eugen Lupri 1992 "Religious involvement and spousal abuse: the Canadian case." *Journal for the Scientific Study of Religion* 31(1): 15–31.

Denzin, Norman K. 1984a *On Understanding Emotion* San Francisco: Jossey–Bass Publishers.

Denzin, Norman K. 1984b "Toward a phenomenology of domestic, family violence." *American Journal of Sociology* 90(3): 483–513.

Dobash, R. Emerson and Russell P. Dobash 1983 "Patterns of violence in Scotland." In Richard J. Gelles and Claire P. Cornell, (eds.) *International Perspectives on Family Violence*, pp. 120–35. Lexington, Mass.: Lexington Books.

Ferguson, A. and N. Folbre 1981 "The unhappy marriage of patriarchy and capitalism." in L. Sargent (ed.) *Women and Revolution*, pp. 220–45. Boston: South End Press.

Follingstad, D.R., L.L. Rutledge, B.J. Berg, E.S. Hause, and D.S. Polek 1990 "The role of emotional abuse in physically abusive relationships." *Journal of Violence* 5(2): 107–20.

Gelles, Richard J. and C.P. Cornell 1985 *Intimate Violence in Families* Beverly Hills: Sage Publications.

Gelles, Richard and Murray A. Straus 1988 *Intimate Violence* New York: Simon & Schuster.

Hartmann, Heidi I. 1981 "The family as the locus of gender, class, and political struggle: the example of housework." *Signs: Journal of Women in Culture and Society* 6(3): 366–94.

Hoff, Anne Lee 1990 *Battered Women As Survivors* London: Routledge.

Hotaling, G.T. and D.B. Sugarman 1986 "An analysis of risk markers in husband–wife violence: the current state of knowledge." *Violence and Victims* 1: 101–24.

Hotaling, G.T. and D.B. Sugarman 1990 "A risk marker analysis of assaulted wives." *Journal of Family Violence* 5(1): 1–14.

Kanter, Rosabeth Moss 1977 *Work and Family Life in the United State: A Critical Review and Agenda for Research and Policy* New York: Russell Sage Foundation.

Kennedy, L.W. and D.G. Dutton 1989 "The incidence of wife assault in Alberta." *Canadian Journal of Behavioural Science* 21(1): 40–54.

Lasch, Christopher 1979 *Haven in a Heartless World* New York: Basic Books.

Lupri, Eugen 1989 "Male violence in the home." *Canadian Social Trends* 14 (Autumn): 19–31.

Lupri, Eugen 1990 "Harmonie und aggression: über die dialektik ehelicher gewalt." *Kölner Zeitschrift für Soziologie und Sozialpsychologie* 42(3): 474–501.

Lupri, Eugen 1993 "Wife abuse across the life course." *Zeitschrift für Sozlialisationsforschung und Erziehungssoziologie* 13(3): 232–57.

Lupri, Eugen and Donald L. Mills 1987 "The household division of labour." International Review of Sociology New Series (2): 35–54.

MacLeod, Linda 1987 *Battered But Not Beaten: Preventing Wife Battering in Canada* Ottawa: National Council on the Status of Women.

MacLeod, Linda 1989 *Wife Battering and the Web of Hope: Progress, Dilemmas and the Visions of Prevention* Prepared for the Family Violence Prevention Division. Ottawa: Health and Welfare.

MacLeod, Linda and Andrée Cadieux 1980 *Wife Battering in Canada: The Vicious Cycle* Ottawa: Minister of Supply and Services.

Meissner, M., E.W. Humphreys, S.M. Meis, and W.J. Scheu 1975 "No exit for wives: sexual division of labour and the cumulation of household demands." *Canadian Review of Sociology and Anthropology* 12: 424–39.

Pagelow, Mildred D. 1984 *Family Violence* New York: Praeger.

O'Brien, M. 1981 *The Politics of Reproduction* London: Routledge and Kegan Paul.

Parsons, Talcott and Robert Bales 1955 *Family Socialization and Interaction Process* New York: The Free Press.

Renzetti, Claire M. 1992 *Violent Betrayal: Partner Abuse in Lesbian Relationships* London: Sage.

Rubin, Lillian B. 1976 *World of Pain: Men and Women Together* New York: Harper & Row.

Scheff, Thomas J. and Suzanne Retzinger 1991 *Emotions and Violence* Lexington: D.C. Heath.

Simmel, Georg 1955 *Conflict and the Web of Group Affiliations* Translated by Kurt H. Wolff and Reinhard Bendix. Chicago: Free Press.

Simmel, Georg 1958 *Soziologie. Untersuchungen über die Formen der Vergesellschaftung* Berlin: Humblot.

Smith, Michael D. 1987 "The influence and prevalence of women abuse in Toronto." *Violence and Victims* 2: 33–47.

Smith, Michael D. 1990a "Sociodemographic risk factors in wife abuse: results from a survey of Toronto women." *Canadian Journal of Sociology* 15(1): 39–58.

Smith, Michael D. 1990b "Patriarchal ideology and wife beating: a test of a feminist hypothesis." *Violence and Victims* 5(4): 263–73.

Steinmetz, Suzanne K. 1987 "Family violence." In M.B. Sussman and S.K. Stinmetz (eds.) *Handbook of Marriage and the Family* pp. 725–65 New York: Plenum Press.

Sprey, Jetse 1991 "Conflict theory and the study of marriage and the family." In Wesley Burr et al. (eds.) *Contemporary Theories about the Family* pp. 130–59 (2nd ed.), Vol. 2 New York: Free Press.

Stets, Jan E. and Murray A. Straus 1990 "Gender differences in reporting marital violence and its medical and psychological consequences." In M.A. Straus and R.J. Gelles (eds.) *Physical Violence in American Families* pp. 151–65. New Brunswick: Transaction Publishers.

Straus, Murray A. 1979 "Measuring intrafamily conflict and violence: the conflict tactics (CT) scales." *Journal of Marriage and the Family* 41(February): 75–88.

Straus, Murray A. and Stephen Sweet 1992 "Verbal/symbolic aggression in couples: Incidence rates and relationships to personal characteristics." *Journal of Marriage and the Family* 54 (May): 346–57.

Straus, Murray A. and Richard J. Gelles 1990 *Physical Violence in American Families* New York: Transaction Books.

Straus, Murray A., Richard J. Gelles, and Suzanne K. Steinmetz 1980 *Behind Closed Doors: Violence in the American Family* New York: Anchor/Doubleday.

Strube, Michael and Linda S. Barbour 1990 "The decision to leave an abusive relationship: economic dependence and psychological commitment." In C. Carlson (ed.) *Perspectives On The Family: History, Class, and Feminism* pp. 216–29. Belmont, California: Wadsworth.

Ursel, Jane 1988 "The state and the maintenance of patriarchy: A case study of family, labour, and welfare legislation in Canada." In Arlene Tigar McLaren (ed.) *Gender and Society* pp. 108–45. Toronto: Copp Clark Pitman Ltd.

Walker, Lenore E.A. 1984 *The Battered Woman Syndrome* New York: Harper and Row.

SOCIAL STATUS AND BELIEFS ABOUT WHAT'S IMPORTANT FOR GETTING AHEAD

Chapter 27

James Curtis
Edward Grabb

(An original chapter written for this volume.)

THE CONCEPT OF DOMINANT IDEOLOGY

Most social researchers would agree that, in virtually every society, certain guiding principles and basic beliefs arise that are fundamental to how that society comes to be defined or characterized. It is common for sociologists to call this set of essential values or precepts the "dominant ideology" of the society in question.

The concept of *dominant ideology* has been applied in two related but distinct ways by different scholars. First, some use the term in the classical Marxian sense, to indicate the *beliefs that are cherished or promoted by the most powerful group* in society. Marx argued, in particular, that the dominant ideas in nineteenth century capitalist countries were largely the same as the beliefs held by the ruling capitalist class in those nations. These beliefs, moreover, *tend to serve the interests of the dominant group* itself. For example, it is usually emphasized in the belief systems of capitalist societies that all people are relatively free individuals, so that inequalities between the dominant class and the rest of the population mainly occur because members of the ruling class generally work harder or have more talent and ambition than other people (see Marx and Engels 1846: 39–41, 59; 1848: 84–85; also Huber and Form 1973: 2; Lipset 1996: 24–25).

Other sociologists, however, have used the concept of dominant ideology to indicate a second and rather different set of ideas. For these analysts, the dominant ideology or dominant value system refers mainly to the *beliefs that prevail*, not within the ruling elite, but *among the people as a whole* (see, e.g., Williams 1960: 409; Mann 1970). In this case, the ideology is said to be dominant in the sense that its core values are widely believed and accepted by most of the population. Of course, there is usually an overlap between the dominant group's key beliefs and those of the general populace. One likely reason for this overlap is that dominant groups typically play a significant role within the educational, religious, media, and other ideological or "idea" organizations in society, and these organizations greatly influence what viewpoints are fostered and disseminated in the population at large. Nevertheless, as some observers have noted, dominant group values and popular values are not always identical. On the contrary, the elite's beliefs and the people's beliefs are sometimes quite different from one another. In addition, even in those cases in which the values of the dominant group also appear to be widely held by the general population, the latter's commitment to these values may be comparatively less permanent, pervasive, or deeply-felt (see, e.g., Parkin 1973: 81–84, 92–94; Abercrombie et al. 1980, Wright et al. 1992: 44; Grabb 1994: 123; Gregg 1995: 20; Sniderman et al. 1996:11–13, 244–245; Perlin 1997: 106–107).

A related issue that often arises when discussing dominant ideology is whether this set of core values is mainly *descriptive* or *normative* in nature. In other words, do the ideas and principles composing the dominant value system describe what *actually* operates in a particular society, or do they prescribe what *should* operate ideally, at least if the society is faithful to its own self-definition? This is a question that has concerned various researchers studying societal values, and there is no complete agreement on which usage is more appropriate. Whichever meaning of the term is applied, however, evidence suggests that members of ruling or privileged groups are usually more likely than the rest of the population to believe that the normative or ideal version of the dominant value system and the values that actually shape their society are basically the same. This seems to be especially true if the values in question are tied, not to abstract statements of fact or principle, but to the concrete conditions or situations that people face. For example, some studies indicate that most people will agree that equal opportunity is prevalent in their society generally, but these same people may not agree that their own opportunities are equal to those of others (see, e.g., Rodman 1963, Mizruchi 1964, Mann 1970, Huber and Form 1973, Parkin 1973, Kluegel and Smith 1986, Feldman 1988, Bobo and Hutchings 1996). Thus, most disadvantaged individuals may embrace certain dominant values, and may even accept them as accurate depictions of their society in some vague or general sense. Even so, it is advantaged groups that seem most likely to believe that these core values are consistent with the realities of their everyday existence.

INDIVIDUAL OPPORTUNITY AND ACHIEVEMENT AS DOMINANT VALUES

It appears, then, that each society tends to sustain certain key values as part of its dominant ideology, but that not everyone in a society is equally likely to agree that such values are reflected in their own life experience. Another observation that certain researchers have made about the dominant ideology in recent years is that, at least in general terms, many modern countries may also be converging toward a broadly similar group of core values. A few analysts have gone so far as to suggest the possibility that we may eventually arrive at a future set of what Giddens has called "universal values" that are "shared by almost everyone" (Giddens 1994: 20–21). This argument stems partly from the theory that we are experiencing a trend toward more and more "globalization" in modern times, with an increase in economic connections, political affinities, and cultural ties among many of the world's nation-states (see Dogan and Pelassy 1984, Kohn 1989, Giddens 1990, 1994, Inglehart 1990, Nevitte 1996).

Some might see a single global value system as at best a distant possibility. However, the idea that there is a dominant ideology shared by various modern nations may be more plausible if we confine our discussion to the industrialized liberal democracies. Thus, the work of several researchers has led to the conclusion or speculation that there is an increasing similarity in the dominant values of countries such as Canada, the United States, Australia, New Zealand, and the nations of western Europe (e.g., Lipset 1967; Hofstede 1980; Nevitte and Gibbins 1990; for discussion, see also Grabb 1994: 130–131, Baer et al. 1996: 325–326; Inkeles 1997: 381–382).

Of the various core values that are said to be shared in all liberal democratic countries, perhaps the most central are those that emphasize the rights and freedoms of the individual (see, e.g., Marchak 1988, Allahar 1995, Inkeles 1997). It is probably for this reason that a commitment to such ideas as personal liberty and equal rights for all citizens can be found in the formal laws or stated policies of almost every contemporary democracy. Two familiar illustrations of this pattern include Canada's Charter of Rights and Freedoms and the Constitution of the United States (see, e.g., Cairns and Williams 1985, Lipset 1996).

One crucial manifestation of the emphasis on individual rights and freedoms in liberal democracies is the apparently widespread belief in what might be termed "equal opportunity for individual achievement." According to this belief, all citizens of a democracy will not be equal in the material and other rewards they attain in society. Nevertheless, such inequalities in attainment or outcome are considered both appropriate and just, as long as everyone is allowed to succeed or fail on the basis of personal merit, effort, and ability (Pammett 1996: 67). This means that people generally have a more or less equal opportunity to get ahead in life, at least in the sense that any background traits or group affiliations—race, ethnicity, gender, class origin, religion, and so on—will neither help nor hinder the individual in the competition to achieve. Under such a value system, then, *individual* attributes or abilities, as opposed to *group-related* or *structural* factors, will be the main causes for people's success or lack of success.

PREVIOUS STUDIES OF BELIEFS ABOUT OPPORTUNITY AND ACHIEVEMENT

Researchers have been interested in people's beliefs about individual equality of opportunity in a number of countries, but the topic has been of special concern to American social scientists. Although the results from these American studies are somewhat varied, three relatively consistent findings can be noted.

First, a vast majority of American respondents believe in equal opportunity as a normative or ideal circumstance. As an illustration, one recent compilation of opinion poll data reported that 98 percent of Americans believed "everyone should have an equal opportunity to get ahead" (Inkeles 1997: 379; see also Mizruchi 1964, Kluegel and Smith 1986).

Second, a clear majority, often in the range of 75 percent, also appear to believe that equal (or at least considerable) opportunity really does operate in their society. In one early American survey using data from the 1960s, 78 percent of respondents agreed with the statement that there was "plenty of opportunity" in the United States, and that "anyone who works hard can go as far as he wants" (Huber and Form 1973:

90–91). Subsequent research has shown a similarly widespread belief, both in the existence of plenty of opportunity and in the importance of individual causes for success, including hard work, self-reliance, and ability. For example, in one recent survey, 74 percent of Americans believed that most unemployed people "have had the opportunities" but "haven't made use of them." In the same survey, 77 percent of the respondents said that what happens to them personally is "my own doing," while 82 percent attributed any lack of personal success to "not having enough ability" (Inkeles 1997: 379; see also Mizruchi 1964: 82; Mann 1970: 428; Kluegel and Smith 1982: 520; Lipset 1996: 115).

The third consistent finding in most American studies is that a person's own position in the system of social inequality is correlated with whether or not that person believes in the reality of individual equality of opportunity. In particular, members of disadvantaged groups, including racial minorities and those with lower incomes, are usually less likely than people from more advantaged groups to believe that they have a lot of opportunity, especially in comparison to the opportunities of their more privileged counterparts (e.g., Huber and Form 1973: 91–96; see also Robinson and Bell 1978: 125, 138; Kluegel and Bobo 1993; Bobo and Hutchings 1996; Lipset 1996: 126–129). These findings suggest that the less advantaged are more likely to see structural obstacles or group affiliations as playing a significant role in their chances for success.

Although Canadian research on this topic has not been as extensive as the American research, the available evidence suggests broadly similar patterns in both countries. Certainly on the issue of whether the opportunity to get ahead rests mainly on individual or group-related factors, most Canadians appear to agree with their American neighbours that individual factors are more important.

In an early Canadian study from the 1960s, which focused exclusively on people in the 13 to 20 age group, a large majority (over 75 percent) said that individual factors like "hard work" and achieving "good grades in school" were very important for getting ahead in Canada (Johnstone 1969: 8–11). This study also found only a small proportion (under 25 percent) who thought that group or structural factors—having "parents with a lot of money," being "born in Canada," and coming from the "right family" or from the "right religious group"—were very important for success.

A similar image arises from more recent opinion polls. A 1986 Maclean's survey found, for example, that 82 percent of Canadians chose individual "hard work" rather than "luck" or group "privilege" as the factor that matters most for getting ahead in Canada (quoted in Li 1988: 5). A 1997 Maclean's survey showed that 92 percent of Canadians agreed with the opinion that "if you are prepared to work hard, you can still get ahead" in Canada today (Maclean's 1998: 45). Other studies have found similarly high proportions of Canadians favouring such ideas as the value of individual hard work and self-reliance, and the importance of competition to achieve excellence in life (Sniderman et al. 1996: 97–100; Perlin 1997: 114–120). Research by Pammett (1996: 70–73) has shown that the same Canadian belief in individual causes of success is evident in many other countries, as well, including the United States and the nations of western Europe, in particular. This strong Canadian emphasis on the role of individual factors in success is also consistent with findings from a recent study of managers and executives. For example, 96 percent of Canadian managers said that they preferred a job that encouraged individual initiative rather than a more collective or team-based kind of work activity. It is interesting, as well, that this proportion is virtually identical to the 97 percent of

American managers who expressed this view in the same study (Hampden-Turner and Trompenaars 1993; see also Lipset 1996: 294).

Again the evidence is less extensive, but Canadian research also seems to parallel American studies in suggesting that traditionally less privileged groups, such as French Canadians and women, for example, may not be as likely as more privileged groups to believe that equal opportunity exists, or that individual factors are more important than social background factors for achieving success. The study of young people from the 1960s found that only 47 percent of French respondents felt that individual hard work was very important for getting ahead, compared to 94 percent of English respondents. At the same time, French respondents were considerably more likely than the English to believe that group-based factors, such as having parents with a lot of money or being Canadian-born, were very important (Johnstone 1969: 8). Similarly, another study from the 1960s, based on a national representative sample of adults, revealed that French Canadians were significantly less likely than English Canadians to believe that all ethnic groups have equal job opportunities or government influence (Roseborough and Breton 1968: 607).

While it takes a different approach to the analysis of individual factors and success, another study by Baer and Curtis (1993) has found, using national survey data from the 1970s and early 1980s, that French Canadians were more likely than English Canadians to have a high aspiration to personal achievement (see also Baer and Curtis 1984). On each of the following agree-disagree questions, the French were significantly more likely to give the achievement-oriented response: (1) "life is more enjoyable when you are trying to achieve some new goal"; (2) "you should always try to improve your position in life rather than accept what you have now"; (3) "a person ought to set goals for themselves which are difficult to achieve"; (4) "unless one learns how to reduce one's desire, life will be full of disappointment and bitterness"; (5) "those who are always trying to get ahead in life will never be happy"; and (6) "when you come down to it, the best thing is to be content with what you have since you never know what the future will bring." Baer and Curtis interpreted the greater desire to achieve among French Canadians as a response to a more disadvantaged position in income and occupational attainment as compared to English Canadians.

The results of some recent Canadian opinion surveys indicate that there may also be gender differences in people's views on the opportunity structure. A 1995 Maclean's poll found that, while 85 percent of Canadian males believed that women's job opportunities had improved in the previous decade, the comparable proportion among female respondents was only 75 percent (Gregg 1995: 22). The results of a 1996 Conference Board of Canada survey of corporate executives, as reported in a study entitled *Closing the Gap*, reveal a similar pattern. These data showed that 75 percent of male executives, compared to just 56 percent of female executives, felt that women's job opportunities had improved in the previous five years (Williamson 1997).

SOME FURTHER CANADIAN DATA FOR THE 1990S

Some additional data for the 1990s are available that relate to the question of ideological beliefs about individual opportunity in Canada. These are provided by the Canadian component of an international study conducted in 1992–93 by the International Social Survey Program, or ISSP (for more details on the survey see Frizzell 1996). A national sample of Canadian adults was given self-administered interviews about various aspects of social inequality. Most relevant to our present purposes was a set of questions asking about thirteen factors that may affect how people get ahead in life. We present an analysis of these data in this section. Our analysis is limited to responses from people aged 21 and over, although the survey included a small number of respondents aged 18 and over as well. Our reason for selecting only the respondents who were 21 years old or older was that they are more likely than younger people to have had first-hand experience with trying to obtain full-time work and income.

The questionnaire items that deal with possible factors in getting ahead are as follows:

> To begin, we have some questions about opportunities for getting ahead. Please tick one box for each of these to show how important you think it is for getting ahead in life. First, how important is coming from a *wealthy family*? ... *having well-educated parents*? ... having a *good education* yourself? ... having *ambition*? ... a person's *religion*? ... *natural ability*? ... *hard work*? ... *knowing the right people*? ... having *political connections*? ... a person's *race*? ... the *part of the country* a person comes from? ... being *born a man or a woman*? ... a person's *political beliefs*?
>
> [answer options of "essential," "very important," "fairly important," "not very important," "not important at all," and "can't choose/"don't know" were provided]

These items, then, focus on what people think *actually happens* in Canada, and not on what *should occur* in some ideal or normative sense. In addition, because the responses in the survey come from a cross-section of the total adult population, our results profile the views on individual opportunity that are held by Canadians generally, and not just the attitudes of any one group, such as the dominant class. As well, the data include several measures that enable us to assess whether Canadians in more advantaged groups or less advantaged groups are more likely to see particular factors as the key to getting ahead. These social status measures include the respondents' gender, age, region of residence, education level, language group, employment status, income level, and self-identification with a social class.[1]

Following previous research, we would expect most Canadians in the survey to believe that individual factors such as hard work and personal ambition are the key reasons for getting ahead in life, and to believe that social background factors, such as gender or race or having wealthy parents, are less important. We would also expect, based on earlier studies, that people from the traditionally more advantaged or privileged social groupings—men versus women, those with higher incomes versus those with lower incomes, those with more education versus those with less education, English-speakers versus French speakers, etc.—will be more likely than other respondents to emphasize individual factors and less likely to stress social background causes as the reasons why Canadians do or do not get ahead in life. We move now to a description of the responses of the Canadian adult sample.

The Perceived Importance of the Thirteen Factors

Table 27-1 shows the responses of the sample concerning each of the thirteen possible reasons for getting ahead. Of these reasons, there are three that appear to be clearly individual in nature. These are "ambition," "hard work," and "natural ability." Another factor, "having a good education," is also an individual attribute in a sense. However, it is likely to be closely tied to social background influences, such as the wealth and education of parents, as well (see the findings to this effect in the "Education" section of this volume).

The results in Table 27-1 show that the three individual factors, along with having a good education, are the four most frequently mentioned factors people choose for what's important for getting ahead in life. Most frequently mentioned is having a good education (89 percent). Next are the individual factors of ambition and hard work, both of which are chosen as "essential" or "very important" by more than 80 percent of the respondents. The fourth most commonly mentioned factor is the individual characteristic of "natural ability"; 45 percent said this is at least "very important" and another 46 percent thought this factor is "fairly important."

If we attend to the factors that are seen as "not very important" or "not at all important," we find that it is the social background factors that are most likely to be given low degrees of importance. "Religion," in particular, was frequently thought to have little importance; over 85 percent said it is "not very important" or "not at all important." Further, over 60 percent of the respondents assigned little importance to political connections, race, region, gender, and political beliefs. In contrast, only five percent or less thought that ambition, hard work, and education were of such little importance, and less than 10 percent thought natural ability was this unimportant.

Table 27-2 shows the number of individual and social background factors that

TABLE 27-1 Views on the factors that are important in how people get ahead in life: responses from a national sample of (N=871) Canadians ages 21 and older

	Percentage Who Responded			
Factors Asked About[a]	"Essential" or "Very Important"	"Fairly Important"	"Not Very Important"	"Not At All Important"
	%	%	%	%
Wealthy Family	14.1	29.8	34.7	21.5
Well Educated Parents	27.4	49.7	17.6	5.9
Good Education	88.6	15.0	1.2	0.2
Ambition	83.9	13.7	2.3	0.0
Natural Ability	45.0	46.3	7.2	1.4
Hard Work	80.2	16.2	3.1	0.3
Knowing Right People	34.6	48.7	14.7	2.0
Political Connections	12.9	26.5	41.0	19.5
Race	11.1	23.6	34.3	31.1
Religion	4.8	7.0	33.8	54.4
Region	8.0	25.0	31.1	35.9
Gender	14.1	20.7	28.1	37.1
Political Beliefs	7.2	19.4	34.8	33.5

[a] The question asked was: "To begin we have some questions about opportunities for getting ahead. Please tick one box for each of these to show how important you think it is for getting ahead in life." The characteristics were listed in the order in the table above. Excluded are respondents who said they did not know or could not choose. These two responses did not total over four percent for any of the thirteen factors.

TABLE 27-2 Views on the number of individual and social background factors which are important ("essential" or "very important") in how people get ahead in life

Number of Factors Mentioned	Percentage of Respondents Who Said	
	%	(N)
Individual Factors[a]		
None	3.4	(30)
One	18.4	(160)
Two	45.6	(397)
Three	32.6	(284)
Social Background Factors[b]		
None	44.7	(389)
One	23.3	(203)
Two	13.5	(118)
Three	9.0	(78)
Four	3.9	(34)
Five	3.3	(29)
Six to Eight	2.2	(20)

[a] The individual factors were chosen from among: ambition, natural ability, and hard work.
[b] The social background factors were chosen from among: wealthy family, well-educated parents, political connections, race, religion, region, and gender.

people labelled as very important or essential. Here we see that very few respondents (only 3.4 percent) felt that none of the three clearly individual factors is very important, and about one third (32.6 percent) felt that all three are very important. The average number mentioned, from among the three, is 2.07. If we sum the responses concerning the eight social background factors (wealthy family, well-educated parents, knowing the right people, political connections, race, religion, region, and gender) we find that only an average of 1.25 factors, out of a possible total of eight, are mentioned as very important or essential. About 45 percent said *none* of these factors is that important, and another 23 percent of the sample said only one of the eight factors is important. Overall, then, individual factors appear to have much greater significance for Canadians when they are asked what determines who gets ahead in their society.

Social Status and Beliefs About Getting Ahead

In Table 27-3, the proportion of "essential" or "very important" responses on the individual and social background factors is cross-tabulated with seven different social status characteristics of the respondents. Here we find, for all categories of the social status variables, that there is considerable agreement on the great importance of individual factors, and little evidence that social background factors are seen as important. There are some instances in which the respondents' own social statuses are related to how strongly they support individual and social background factors. Specifically, the French,

TABLE 27-3 Social statuses of the respondents and the average number of mentions of individual and social background factors as important in getting ahead in life

Social Statuses of Respondents	(N)[a]	Average Number of Individual Factors Said to be Very Important[b]	Average Number of Background Factors Said to be Very Important[c]
Total Sample	(871)	2.07	1.25
Gender			
Male	(440)	2.06	1.28
Female	(410)	2.09	1.21
		n.s.	n.s.
Age			
21–30	(262)	2.03	1.26
31–40	(246)	2.02	1.21
41–50	(161)	2.11	1.06
51–64	(112)	2.09	1.33
65+	(90)	2.28	1.52
		n.s.	n.s.
Language Group			
French	(258)	1.96	1.14
English and Other	(613)	2.12	1.30
		p<.005	n.s.
Region			
Eastern Provinces	(149)	2.24	1.17
Quebec	(195)	1.80	1.03
Ontario	(208)	2.21	1.41
Prairies	(158)	2.15	1.35
British Columbia	(161)	2.60	1.27
		p<.001	n.s.
Current Employment			
Full-time	(460)	2.03	1.11
Part-time	(94)	2.03	1.30
Occasional	(32)	2.00	1.13
None	(270)	2.18	1.48
		n.s.	p<.05
Personal Income Last Year			
<15 Thousand (K)	(200)	2.04	1.46
15–25 K	(168)	2.08	1.35
25–35 K	(162)	2.11	1.17
34–45 K	(120)	2.06	1.20
45–55 K	(68)	2.00	1.12
55–65 K	(38)	2.221	1.13
65–75 K	(19)	2.00	0.68
75 K	(21)	2.38	0.48
		n.s.	p<.05

TABLE 27-3 continued

Social Statuses of Respondents	(N)[a]	Average Number of Individual Factors Said to be Very Important[b]	Average Number of Background Factors Said to be Very Important[c]
Subjective Social Class			
Lower Class	(23)	1.91	1.35
Working Class	(133)	2.11	1.53
Lower Middle Class	(125)	2.06	1.34
Middle Class	(361)	2.08	1.05
Upper Middle Class	(111)	2.11	1.23
Upper Class	(5)	2.40	0.80
		$p<.05$	$p<.05$
Education Attained			
<High School Grad	(1.22)	2.02	1.82
High School Grad	(175)	2.06	1.02
Some Univ./College	(285)	2.11	1.10
Univ. Grad	(187)	2.10	1.24
Graduate School	(95)	2.03	1.42
		n.s.	$p<.001$

n.s. = not a statistically significant pattern

[a] The first column shows the number of respondents in the sample with the particular social status characteristic.

[b] The second column shows the average number of mentions of the three individual factors (from among ambition, natural ability, and hard work) as "essential" or "very important" for getting ahead.

[c] The third column shows the average number of mentions of the eight social background factors (from among wealthy family, well-educated parents, knowing the right people, political connections, race, religion, region, and gender) as "essential" or "very important" for getting ahead.

when compared to the combined English and "Other" language groups, are less likely to mention individual factors; British Columbians are more likely to mention these factors than those from other regions, with Quebecers least likely to mention them; and people who identified themselves as being in the lower class are less likely than others (particularly compared to those calling themselves "upper class") to mention individual factors as important. These differences are all statistically significant. No significant differences in responses exist across categories of gender, age, employment, income, and education.

The responses dealing with the importance of social background factors show some statistically significant differences across the categories of current employment, income, subjective social class, and education. Those who do not work see social background factors as more important than do people who are employed full-time. Those with lower incomes perceive a greater impact of social background influences on getting ahead than do people making higher levels of income. The patterns by social class identification parallel the findings for income, with the "working class," "lower class," and "lower middle class" respondents citing more social background factors as very important or essential than do the higher classes. Finally, people with lower education (less than high school graduation) and, curiously, those with the most education (those who have gone beyond a first university or college degree) are the most likely to see background factors as important. Despite these differences in responses across social status categories, the large majority of respondents generally do not mention social background factors as important. We see in Table 27-3 that, across the numerous sub-groups of the seven social status variables, there is no category of respondent that averages more than 1.82 mentions of the social background factors, even though as many as eight such factors could have been mentioned. Those with less than high school graduation cited an average of 1.82 factors, the working class identifiers had an average of 1.53 mentions, and older respondents (65 and older) had an average of 1.52. All other social categories had lower averages. On the other hand, although there were only three possible individual factors to choose from, across all seven social status variables the average mention of individual factors is rarely below 2.0.

Other Results

The ISSP survey included questions on three social status variables— gender, education, and region—that also happen to be listed among the thirteen possible factors for getting ahead. In Table 27-4, we assess whether people's own rankings on these three social status variables are correlated with their sense of whether these same three variables are important for getting ahead in life. Given earlier studies, we might expect that the more disadvantaged groups on these three variables (women, the less-educated, and Canadians from poorer regions such as the Atlantic provinces) would be more likely than other respondents to see these three factors as important.

Overall, the results in Table 27-4 provide almost no support for this expectation. As expected, respondents' gender was related to their views on the importance of being born a woman or man, with women seeing this factor as more important than did men; even here, though, only 17 percent of women saw gender as very important, compared to 12 percent of men. Gender of respondents also had no effect on their attitudes about the importance of education and region. In addition, in the case of respondent's education, it was the more highly-educated, not the less highly-educated that were most likely to believe that education was very important or essential; 85 percent or more of those with at least some post- secondary education saw education as very important, compared to 74 percent of those who did not finish high school. Education's effects on the perceived importance of region are somewhat curvilinear, although the least educated are, as expected, the most likely category to mention region as important for getting ahead. Education's relation to the perceived impact of gender is clearly curvilinear, with the most highly-educated and the least highly educated respondents being the most likely to mention gender as important. Finally, region of residence appears to have no connection with Canadians' views on the importance of either region or gender for getting ahead. Region does have some effect on the perceived significance of education, with people from British Columbia and Quebec relatively less likely than other Canadians to believe education is important for getting ahead in life.

In other data not presented in Table 27-4, respondent's education level and region of residence were found to have statistically significant relationships with evaluations of the importance of other factors. The higher the education, the more likely wealthy parents were seen as important ($p<.05$) and the less likely religion was cited as important ($p<.05$). Region was related to perceptions of the importance of wealthy parents ($p<.01$), with Ontarians attaching a high importance and Quebecers a comparatively low importance to this factor. Also, Quebecers see a relatively low importance and Ontarians a relatively high importance for natural abil-

TABLE 27-4 **Percentage who said particular social background factors were important ("essential" or "very important") for getting ahead by the respondents' own statuses with respect to those factors**

Respondents' Social Statuses	Percentage Saying the Factor was Important		
	Gender	**Education**	**Region**
	%	%	%
Gender			
Male	11.7	84.3	9.1
Female	16.9	83.0	7.1
	p<.05	n.s.	n.s.
Education Attained			
<High School Grad	20.0	74.2	15.0
High School Grad	8.5	81.7	4.8
Some Univ./College	10.1	85.9	6.7
Univ. Grad	16.4	85.0	9.1
Graduate School	24.9	91.5	7.4
	p<.001	p<.01	p<.05
Region			
Eastern Provinces	13.8	90.5	6.2
Quebec	8.3	78.0	8.4
Ontario	16.8	90.0	7.2
Prairies	14.7	86.6	9.6
British Columbia	17.2	73.1	8.8
	n.s.	p<.001	n.s.

ity ($p<.05$), while both Quebecers and British Columbians are relatively less convinced than other respondents that hard work matters for getting ahead ($p<.001$). Gender was not significantly related to any of the other factors. Compared to those with lower incomes, people with higher incomes appear more likely to cite the importance of education ($p<.05$), and less likely to cite knowing the right people and political connections ($p<.05$). Respondents with higher social class identifications were much less likely than those saying they were in the lower social class to attach importance to political connections ($p<.01$). Finally, relative to English and "Other" respondents, the French were less likely to attach importance to wealthy parents ($p<.01$), well-educated parents ($p<.01$), education ($p<.05$), or hard work ($p<.001$), and more likely to cite religion as important ($p<.05$).

CONCLUSIONS

Both the results of previous studies and the additional data for the 1990s presented in this chapter indicate that Canadians generally see individual attributes or abilities as very important for achieving success. That is, most Canadians endorse the idea that it is what an individual is or does, based on hard work, ambition, and natural ability, along with the achievement of higher educational credentials, that helps a person get ahead. It is apparent, as well, that relatively few Canadians, especially in the 1990s data, mention social background variables, such as class origin, gender, race, or region, as important impediments or advantages for success. These findings indicate a remarkably high level of agreement among Canadians about these core elements of the dominant ideology.

The findings reported here suggest that these ideological beliefs are *dominant* in both senses of the term noted at the beginning of this paper. That is, not only are these views *widely-held* among the population as a whole, they are also dominant in that they serve *the general interests of dominant groups or elites*. Our results imply that most Canadians would agree with the claim that the people at the top of their society got there, not because of their backgrounds, but because of their own individual efforts and abilities. Such attitudes lend ideological support to maintenance of the status quo—existing arrangements by which the dominant groups should continue to do comparatively well. These beliefs also imply that, in most people's minds, the system works largely as it should, and that there is little reason to want to change it.

As expected, our analysis has revealed that those who occupy higher social statuses tend to be very supportive of dominant ideological principles. What may be somewhat surprising, however, is that large proportions of people with less advantaged social statuses are quite supportive of these ideas as well. In some cases, disadvantaged respondents do appear to discern problems with the dominant ideology, as in the tendency (albeit a modest one) for women to see the background variable of gender as more important for affecting success than do men. In addition, if we consider French Canadians as a disadvantaged category, we have found them to be slightly less likely than the rest of the respondents to mention individual factors as important. In most instances, though, there is little or no evidence of such a pattern. Instead, as with their more advantaged counterparts, only small proportions of the disadvantaged groups either cite background factors as important or reject individual factors as unimportant.

On the other hand, these results may not be all that surprising, if we consider that they are not inconsistent with many of the findings in the American studies reviewed earlier. Recall that these studies usually showed a high degree of acceptance among disadvantaged people that individual factors were crucial for success and that opportunity was good, in general. The less advantaged groups in those studies differed from the advantaged primarily on questions specifically related to whether *they themselves had been held back* by unequal opportunity or discrimination (see, e.g., Huber and Form 1973; Rodman 1963). Because the 1990s Canadian data included no measures of respondents' attitudes about factors affecting their *own personal opportunity experiences*, we cannot be sure that the same pattern would have been found here. However, it is quite possible that the lower status respondents in our 1990s data source share a similar "dual-mindedness," with a clear belief that opportunities are good for Canadians generally but a less certain sense that they themselves have had a completely fair or equal chance at success.

Another possibility is that, like many of the disadvantaged respondents in the American studies, less successful Canadians may largely blame their relatively low position, not on social background impediments, but on their own shortcomings, including a failure to capitalize on existing opportunities, for example. This type of thinking, especially among members of the lower social classes, has been interpreted by some researchers as a so-called "value stretch" (Rodman 1963, Huber and Form 1973), or a form of "passive" or "pragmatic" acceptance (Parkin 1973, Mann 1976). A key common element in these interpretations is the idea that disadvantaged groups come to apply a set of beliefs or values when judging their own situation that is somewhat different from those they apply when assessing the workings of their society as a whole. In this way, subordinate groups may be better able to cope with the sometimes stark discrepancies between what the prevailing value system leads them to believe and what they actually experience in their daily lives. Thus, either self-blaming or pragmatic acceptance may help account for the high level of acceptance, and infrequent questioning, of the dominant ideology among lower status groups.

Yet another possible reason behind the absence of large differences in people's beliefs across most of the social status variables is that some of the groups that were disadvantaged in the past have greatly improved their relative economic position in recent years. The French are a good example. They once were significantly disadvantaged in Canada's stratification system, but, as a number of recent studies have shown (including Hou and Balakrishnan's paper in the present volume), there now is little difference between the English and French on income and other measures of inequality. It is perhaps for this reason that French Canadians in the 1990s data are far less likely to see background factors as the causes of success than they were in earlier studies (compare Johnstone 1969, Roseborough and Breton 1968, Baer and Curtis 1984).

Another point to consider when trying to understand people's attitudes about achievement and its causes concerns the important mechanisms through which our beliefs and ideas are acquired and sustained. These mechanisms are the primary socialization, teaching, and idea-transmission apparatuses of our society, especially the media, the government, and the educational system. As was mentioned at the beginning of this chapter, there is reason to assume that the values fostered by these organizations will generally be consistent with the values favoured by dominant groups. Thus, some of the tendency for Canadians to see a society of considerable individual opportunity, regardless of their own personal social status rankings, may be traced to the pervasive influence of these ideological mechanisms.

An additional issue of note is the role of everyday life in shaping people's values. In the world of work, for example, most of us have probably observed situations in which either individual achievement or social background factors helped to determine who gets ahead and who does not. While such observations can sometimes provide important insight, they are unavoidably limited and incomplete in most cases. In other words, in contrast to social researchers who have the luxury of access to numerous and usually more representative sources of evidence when studying questions such as individual opportunity and achievement, most other people must form their attitudes on the basis of anecdotal experiences and impressions. One speculation we would offer is that, in this process, individual achievement may well be *more visible* or more prominent in most people's perceptions. When a person sees, for example, that relatively few high level managers, doctors, or judges are women and Blacks, but that *at least some are* women and Blacks, that person may be apt to conclude that gender and race are becoming less and less important factors for achievement these days. Thus, many members of the public, including those occupying lower status positions themselves, may conclude that, because there are evident exceptions to the rule, the rule no longer applies. If this type of thinking occurs, it would help explain why the dominant ideological view of individual opportunity for achievement is so widespread in the Canadian population.

Of course, one final possibility is that most Canadians are understandably happy with the chances for achievement in their society, because their country is, indeed, a land of opportunity. After all, for several years now, Canada has consistently been named by the United Nations as the best country in the world in which to live, primarily because of our relatively high level of material affluence and quality of life. Thus, perhaps the high level of support we have seen for the dominant ideology of individual achievement is to be expected. Even so, the clear evidence of structurally-based inequalities and injustices to be found in existing research on Canada (including most of the chapters appearing in this volume) means there is considerable room for skepticism on this issue. It also means there is ample room for improving the situation of the disadvantaged, in Canada as in virtually every nation of the world.

NOTES

1. The questions asked concerning these social statuses should be self-explanatory, with the exception of "social class self-identification." Here the question was: "Some people consider themselves to be a member of a specific social class. Of the following groups, would you consider yourself a member of the working class, lower middle/upper working class, middle class, upper middle class, upper class [don't know, can't choose; none of these classes]." See Table 27-3 for responses according to these categories of self-identification, and for the categories for the other measures of social status.

REFERENCES

Abercrombie, Nicholas, Stephen Hill, and Bryan S. Turner 1980 *The Dominant Ideology Thesis* London: George Allen and Unwin.

Allahar, Anton 1995 *Sociology and the Periphery* (2nd ed.) Toronto: Garamond.

Baer, Douglas, James Curtis, Edward Grabb, and William Johnston 1996 "What values do people prefer in children? A comparative analysis of survey evidence from fifteen countries." pp. 299–328 in Clive Seligman, James Olson, and Mark Zanna (eds.) *The Psychology of Values: The Ontario Symposium,* Volume 8 Mahwah, NJ: Lawrence Erlbaum.

Baer, Douglas and James Curtis 1984 "French Canadian-English Canadian value differences: national survey findings." *Canadian Journal of Sociology*, 9, 4, 405–28.

Baer, Douglas and James Curtis 1988 "Differences in the achievement values of French Canadians and English Canadians." pp. 476–84 in J. Curtis et al. *Social Inequality in Canada: Patterns, Problems and Policies* (1st ed.) Scarborough, Ont.: Prentice- Hall Canada.

Bobo, Lawrence and Vincent Hutchings 1996 "Perceptions of racial group competition: extending Blumer's theory of group position to a multiracial social context." *American Sociological Review* 61: 951–972.

Cairns, Alan and Cynthia Williams 1985 *Constitutionalism, Citizenship, and Society in Canada* Toronto: University of Toronto Press.

Dogan, M. and D. Pelassy 1984 *How to Compare Nations* Chatham, NJ: Chatham House Publishers.

Feldman, Stanley 1988 "Structure and consistency in public opinion: the role of core beliefs and values." *American Journal of Political Science* 82: 773–778.

Frizzell, Alan 1996 "The ISSP and international research: an introduction." pp. 1–7 in Alan Frizzell and Jon Pammett (eds.) *Social Inequality in Canada* Ottawa: Carleton University Press.

Giddens, Anthony 1990 *The Consequences of Modernity* Stanford: Stanford University Press.

Giddens, Anthony 1994 *Beyond Left and Right* Stanford: Stanford University Press.

Grabb, Edward 1994 "Democratic values in Canada and the United States: some observations and evidence from past and present." pp. 113–139 in Jerry Dermer (ed.) *The Canadian Profile* (2nd ed.) North York: Captus Press.

Gregg, Allan 1995 "Now and then. A nation transformed." *Maclean's*, Volume 108, No. 1 (January 8): 20–22.

Hampden-Turner, Charles and Alfons Trompenaars 1993 *The Seven Cultures of Capitalism* New York: Doubleday.

Hofstede, Geert 1980 *Culture's Consequences* Beverley Hills, CA: Sage.

Huber, Joan and William Form 1973 *Income and Ideology* New York: The Free Press.

Inglehart, Ronald 1990 *Culture Shift in Advanced Industrial Society* Princeton: Princeton University Press.

Inkeles, Alex 1997 *National Character. A Psycho-Social Perspective* New Brunswick, NJ: Transaction Publishers.

Johnstone, John C. 1969 *Young People's Images of Canadian Society* Studies of the Royal Commission on Bilingualism and Biculturalism, No. 2. Ottawa: Queen's Printer.

Kluegel, James and Lawrence Bobo 1993 "Opposition to race-targeting: self-interest, stratification ideology, or racial attitudes?" *American Sociological Review* 58: 443–464.

Kluegel, James and Eliot Smith 1982 "Whites' beliefs about blacks' opportunity." *American Sociological Review* 47: 518–531.

Kluegel, James and Eliot Smith 1986 *Beliefs about Inequality* New York: Aldine de Gruyter.

Kohn, Melvin (ed.) *1989 Cross-National Research in Sociology* Newbury Park, CA: Sage.

Li, Peter 1988 *Ethnic Inequality in a Class Society* Toronto: Wall and Thompson.

Lipset, S.M. 1967 "Values, education, and entrepreneurship." pp. 3–60 in S.M. Lipset and A. Solari (eds.), *Elites in Latin America* New York: Oxford University Press.

Lipset, S.M. 1996 *American Exceptionalism* New York: Norton.

Maclean's 1998 "Taking the pulse of a nation." Volume 110, 52, January 5.

Mann, Michael 1970. "The social cohesion of liberal democracy." *American Sociological Review* 35: 423–439.

Marchak, Patricia 1988 *Ideological Perspectives on Canada* (3rd ed.) Toronto: McGraw-Hill Ryerson.

Marx, Karl and Friedrich Engels 1846 *The German Ideology*. In *Marx Engels Collected Works*, Vol. 5. New York: International Publishers, 1976.

Marx, Karl and Friedrich Engels 1848 *The Communist Manifesto* New York: Washington Square Press, 1970.

Mizruchi, Ephraim 1964 *Success and Opportunity* New York: The Free Press.

Nevitte, Neil 1996 *The Decline of Deference: Canadian Value Change in Cross-National Perspective* Peterborough: Broadview Press.

Nevitte, Neil and Roger Gibbins 1990 *New Elites in Old States* Toronto: Oxford University Press.

Pammett, Jon 1996 "Getting ahead around the world." pp. 67–86 in Alan Frizzell and Jon Pammett (eds.) *Social Inequality in Canada* Ottawa: Carleton University Press.

Parkin, Frank 1973 *Class Inequality and Political Order* London: Paladin.

Perlin, George 1997 "The constraints of public opinion: diverging or converging paths?" pp.71–149 in Keith Banting, George Hoberg, and Richard Simeon (eds.) *Degrees of Freedom: Canada and the United States in a Changing World* Montreal and Kingston: McGill-Queen's University Press.

Robinson, Robert and Wendell Bell 1978 "Equality, success, and social justice in England and the United States." *American Sociological Review* 43: 125–143.

Rodman, Hyman 1963 "The lower-class value stretch." *Social Forces* 42: 205–215.

Roseborough, Howard and Raymond Breton 1968 "Perceptions of the relative economic and political advantages of ethnic groups in Canada." pp. 604–628 in B. Blishen, F. Jones, K. Naegele, and J. Porter (eds.) *Canadian Society: Sociological Perspectives* (3rd ed.) Toronto: Macmillan.

Sniderman, Paul, Joseph Fletcher, Peter Russell, and Philip Tetlock 1996 *The Clash of Rights: Liberty, Equality, and Legitimacy in Pluralist Democracy* New Haven: Yale University Press.

Williams, Robin M., Jr. 1960 *American Society* New York: Alfred Knopf.

Williamson, Linda 1997 "It's still a failure to communicate." In the *London Free Press*, Friday, December 12, p. A19.

Wright, Erik Olin, Andrew Levine, and Elliott Sober 1992 *Reconstructing Marxism* London: Verso.

Chapter 28

THE EXPERIENCE OF UNEMPLOYMENT

Patrick Burman

(Abridged from the author's "The self," Chapter IV in *Killing Time, Losing Ground: Experiences of Unemployment*, by Patrick Burman. Toronto: Wall & Thompson, 1988. Copyright, Thompson Educational Publishing. Reprinted by permission of the publisher.)

INTRODUCTION

Any generalizations about the temporal patterning of the self's experience throughout the jobless spell are risky because of the latter's sheer variety. The literature suggests that the first stage is often shock and immobilization. Shortly thereafter, there may be some optimism and minimization of the problem, as the person defines the inactivity as a kind of holiday. Then, as the months draw on with no success finding a job, there is a second broad stage characterized by emotional turmoil, depression, and withdrawal. Here the belief that "things will be all right" is undermined, and one's identity comes under strain. With prolonged unemployment, a third stage emerges, involving the scaling down or readjustment of hopes. The individual starts to accept the fact that the standards of the employed past are not going to be [a] reliable basis for evaluating achievements in the present. There is less active distress at this stage, with the emotional trajectory slightly rising and stabilizing.

Our treatment here will look at the *initial reaction* to the termination of employment, and then the *later phases* of the lengthening unemployment spell. The pivotal figure is the unemployed self, and how the generally changed social identity following job loss affects *personal* identity.

INITIAL REACTION

Of the 41 "job losers" in my sample, 10 informants expressed shock when their employment was terminated. Norma, 24, had been working for five months as a bus driver at the London Transit. Late one night, in an act of horseplay, she had climbed through the window of her parked bus into the bus driven by a friend of hers which had pulled up alongside. A passenger spotted it and reported her. After being asked for an explanation by management, she was fired three days later. She was in her fifth month of a six-month probationary period within which management could dismiss employees more easily. At a time when women L.T.C. bus drivers formed only 1% of its work-force, Norma was thinking of challenging the dismissal on grounds of sexual discrimination. Similar horseplay by men—she knew a man who drove occasionally with a foot out of the window—had resulted in only a fine or suspension.

When asked how she felt at the time: "I was in shock, I couldn't believe it ... He asked, 'Do you have anything to say for yourself? and I said 'No.' Like, I couldn't believe what happened ... I went out of there laughing." She went over to some other drivers and told them and they laughed, hardly believing anything so ridiculous. "But the day after, it hit me. And I was crying like anything." She stayed inside, away from her friends, and had little motivation to look for a job. The only thing she had ever wanted to do was drive a bus.

Bernard, waiting for a good job which would let him fly his fiancée to Canada to begin their family, was laid off from his labourer's job at a tree farm. "I was so set back ... I kept in bed, slept the whole day. Then watched television through the night ... I got into serious drinking, trying to drown my problem." A similar reaction was expressed by Lorne, fired from a dishwashing job: "I didn't want to be talked to, didn't want to be seen ... It's like I lost my best friend." He had been called on the phone by the employer and told not to bother to come in that day, that his work had been too slow. "I was in shock; I didn't say anything, just OK."

Being suddenly banished from a familiar environment left the self feeling wounded and out of place. Monica had been given a poor evaluation as a receptionist by a supervisor who allegedly did not know her work, which had been praised by others who did. The oral report of the evaluation was made to her in about four minutes:

> She told me everything on it [the three-page evaluation] in about four seconds flat. Her mouth was going a mile a minute. She gave an evaluation. And I remember being so shaken up by it that I couldn't talk ... .

And then she said, "Do you have any questions?" Well, I couldn't speak ... I was so shocked. And then she said, "OK, then, that's it." And she stood up to walk out, and I felt like saying "Don't open the door." Because I was crying, and there were all counsellors outside ... Like, we were in there a good four minutes. That was the evaluation, four minutes. Rather a rushed thing, because she had other things to do. As if my job ... It was my job that was on the line. And then, she had left."

She sat there and took some deep breaths. Others had gone into a meeting and she was supposed to answer the phones. "I was so upset that I couldn't work anymore, I couldn't think. If the phone rang, I didn't even know it was the phone. You know, all I could think about was my child ... You know, I had done this for two years. It was my routine, and I enjoyed it. I enjoyed the students." While the counsellors were in a meeting, she sat typing, not really knowing what she was doing. Yet she must have looked stricken, because when a couple asked where a room was, they took one look at her face, apologized and left.

The worker, as a factor in the productive process, worked. But the worker's *self* on the job wanted to do more than work. It wanted to "appropriate" the job into its identity-formation, to use it as a vehicle for communicative and craftlike purposes. So offices, machines, and work areas, while nominally owned by the company, were often felt by the workers to be their own personal possessions and territories—a kind of ownership-by-involvement. Being laid off, then, for some, was to be deported from a fellowship and a personal territory. Not surprisingly, a few of the informants compared being laid off to losing a best friend.

Warren's last job, sponsored by the Welfare Department, had been with a demolition company. Every dollar earned was a dollar taken off benefits. Though the work was dirty, involving cleaning and wrecking, and the pay insufficient, Warren valued it:

> Dirty, tough, but I tell you, I felt a hell of a lot good. I came home. I could sleep good at night, the wife and I got along really great ... We had a little bit of money to go out, wasn't much, maybe she'd go to Bingo, I'd go to a movie ... and we had a little bit of money to spend for the kids.

With every expectation of continued employment, Warren was quietly handed an envelope containing holiday and severance pay; the boss had not said a word. He described his reaction as "nauseous," as though someone had dropped a twenty-pound weight on his stomach.

> I just kinda felt like, like there was a void in your stomach ... Like wow, you had work and all of a sudden, it's not there. Like a friend, you know, like a real close friend, and he moves away and you feel, wow man, that's gone.

Back in the home, he was fighting with his wife again. While employed, his marriage had been "great"; now, "we just live, that's it."

The initial phase of shock experienced in a sudden layoff was not undergone by all the job losers in the sample. Some experienced anger, some saw the layoff coming and were resigned to it. Another reaction, reported by several informants, was a feeling of *relief* at having been set free from the previous job. In a few cases the job had involved working nights, which disrupted normal family routines. Simon, fired from his job, felt that the night work was dead-end and poorly paid anyway. Brenda, a waitress at a donut shop, quit, partly because she was required to work at night and partly because of the refusal of the boss to put her on full-time rotation. For a time she briefly experienced that sense of being on a holiday ("I was having a ball") which was sometimes associated with the early phase of unemployment. But now, jobless and on Mother's Allowance for a year, she was bored and restless and wanted full-time employment.

Some people reported being glad to be free of the constraining aspects of the job. Fran quit her job as office manager and secretary-receptionist at an office rental agency. She had become dissatisfied: the original owners were not involved anymore, there was too much pressure, and she wanted to do less typing and more headwork. While upset at quitting, she quickly felt much better at the widening of options. She did some job searching, then went back to school, and was using her intelligence more actively. Knowing that she did not have to stay where she was excited her. She was not as tired as when working, and had a more energetic and pleasant social life. She was on employment benefits, and had the wholehearted support of her family. ("I'm very lucky.")

If the job was hated, unemployment could come as a relief. Some of the younger men, supported by parents and their peer group, were glad they were not doing kitchen work. As Herb remarked:

> Why should I have a job doing something I don't want to do? Because that would definitely lower self-esteem, as far as I'm concerned ... There's too many people working and all they do is complain about, "I hate my job." So why don't you quit, do something else?

In some cases, however, the relief could be short-lived. Gail had stood up to an emotionally abusive boss who screamed at the top of his lungs for her to sit down as he prepared to tongue-lash her, unjustly in her view. She simply turned heel and left his office. That act gave her "one half second of satisfaction and a lot of woe after." She was relieved to be out from under his authority, but, as a 50-year-old divorcee living alone, with few prospects after five months of unemployment, she wondered about the wisdom of her act. Chainsmoking, anxious, she bitterly contemplated the high price she had paid for the exercise of her autonomy.

The comparisons between the "shocked" and the "relieved" were instructive. The "relieved" more often had quit their jobs, hence had controlled the timing and prepared emotionally for the event. Except for Gail (above), the other "relieved" persons had some financial and social support, such as an employed spouse or a parental home and income to draw on. These people had options and resources.

By contrast, the "shocked" and immobilized were more likely to have been involuntarily deprived of paid employment, and thus lacked emotional preparedness or control over time. Their job loss shattered their time frames rather than being integrated into them. More of them were unattached individuals, or single parents, possessing fewer resources of financial or social support. Four of the ten were from out of town, having extended kin in Exeter (60 miles away), other parts of Canada, the United States, and Kenya.

To sum up, those with financial and social (especially familial) support could choose a living situation which enabled them to pursue personal goals. People without such resources also lacked the accompanying freedoms—for them the job's enabling characteristics were desperately clung to. The job was more pivotal in their search for community, for self-esteem, and for an income. Being deprived of that job involuntarily, suddenly, was a profoundly threatening experience.

LATER PHASES

The cross-sectional rather than longitudinal design of the study makes generalizations about temporal effects on job search rather tentative. It may still be possible, however, to determine effects over time by grouping the sample into segments according to *duration of unemployment*. Were there significant differences in attitude and behaviour regarding job search among the various groupings?

My findings, as in the case of the initial impact of unemployment, partly corroborated and partly complicated the pattern sketched in the literature. For the long-term unemployed, there was considerable flattening of affect and morale, with resigned hopelessness replacing more active distress. In addition, new assumptions about one's relation to the environment and to the future appeared in seminal and developed form in the long-term unemployed. What was unexpected were the similarities which appeared across the board.

For those *unemployed three months or less*, there was some buoyancy expressed about the job search. Brenda, with her small retarded child, was energized, even possessed, by the job search. It served as a welcome contrast to being in the home. For married Tony, the job search was, for now, a relaxed and self-fulfilling adventure. His wife supported him financially and emotionally in his desire to find exactly what he wanted, and he had not yet been rejected that often. But in some of the accounts of those unemployed three months or less, there appeared a pessimism, a defeatedness, an attitude of coasting—which were usually associated with more prolonged unemployed spells. What explained it? This "premature" sense of defeatism seemed to possess those who had experienced unemployment and the frustrations of the job search in the past, often more than once. Their past employment had been sporadic; as they began their test job search their attitude was part dread and part resignation—"Here we go again."

In those *unemployed four to six months*, the theme of "being dragged down," of experiencing a loss of enthusiasm and confidence, was more pronounced. There was still an alternation of emotional "highs" and "lows." But the "lows" were starting to have a cumulative, qualitative impact on the job search. This was expressed by Simon, unemployed five months:

> Every letter of rejection hurts in a sense, you know, it's one more disappointment, and [I] feel kind of, almost used to it ... like you kind of expect it, and so the next time I do a letter of application, I kind of feel, well, I'm just going through the process, I'm really not going to get the job.
>
> The longer I'm without work, the more letters of rejection I get, the less likely I am to apply for the next job and the less confident I feel about it. And I'm sure that that colours the interview that I have, if I'm lucky enough to get an interview.

Over time the job search was becoming an empty ritual, devoid of meaning and personal implication. The self recoiled from it, partly out of protection, partly because, *as work*, repeated job-hunting offered no consummation, no result.

In the group *unemployed seven to twelve months*, we noticed a number of patterns, some of which will appear in mature form in the long-term unemployed. One of them was dread and anxiety about the future, with an accompanying desperate sense that one must hold on. This was particularly evident among those in a disadvantaged market position, especially older women. The end of work seemed to bring home thoughts of one's mortality. Gail talked about clinging to life: you simply could not allow yourself to die, or crawl into a shell. Joanne had an almost paralyzing vision of her own contingency:

> There are times when I am so scared that I'm not going to find a job. I think, "What the hell is wrong with me?" Even if I can't find a job in the field that I want, I can always work as a temp, and stay busy. My head knows this, OK?—but my guts go like that, and they just start wringing and I can get scared to death ... I'll have periods of insomnia. I'll get very short-tempered with my husband and with the children.

As she continued, notice how Joanne's realistic anxiety about her market position veered into self-disparagement and a fear that her life would unravel: "Sometimes I think there is something wrong with me, I ask myself: 'Why are you permitting this anxiety to come into your life?' And yet I seem powerless to stop it."

As the job search lengthened, the sense of oneself as a worker—which is central to our social identity—tended to weaken. Fran, unemployed for 10 months, remarked:

> I don't think I've ever been unemployed as long before. So it's getting used to seeing yourself as unemployed too. Like you always looked at yourself as a worker.

One woman said that one looked over the jobs on offer and began thinking, "I can't do that, I can't do that." People started settling for less, hence their talents came to be under-used even if they did find work. Debbie put it clearly:

> I think you tend to have a defeatist attitude about yourself and about the kind of jobs you can do, so you start looking for things that aren't as demanding. And also if you haven't been working, employers are less likely to hire you, if you haven't been involved with some kind of job.

"At the beginning," commented Beth, "I was feeling so good about myself that that was a lot easier ... Towards the end I was feeling like such a loser ... You portray this, it's written all over your face: 'Nobody wants me, please take me,' so that makes the communication and everything else ... You're almost begging for a job. That's humiliating."

In those *unemployed more than one year*, we see a kind of entrenched adjustment to unemployed conditions, both tender- and tough-minded. The "tender-minded" spoke in a resigned, muted tone when talking about the prospects of finding employment. Several could no longer believe that their unemployment would end. Connie, single, laid off from an advertising firm, had the attitude of "why bother, I'm not going to get it anyway." Her job-hunting had fallen off in frequency. She had also considered suicide. There was a suicidal hint in the words of Agnes, unemployed 27 months:

> I'm terribly depressed. I wonder if there is anything ahead, or should I just depart? [Laughs] Really, you do get to that point. I mean there's absolutely nothing ahead for me. Remarriage—that would be the only thing that would do something for me right now. And there's not too many men my age that I could live with ... I think our whole system is in very big trouble. And I am just one of the victims.

All five informants who had hinted at suicidal intentions at one time or another were longer-term unemployed. Monica talked of a phase when she did "self-destructive things."

> I'd be driving and I'd drive real fast and hope to hit a bridge or something. Then I'd say, "Come on! Your son's in the back seat."

The long-term unemployed were represented in all the categories of pathological behaviour. Of those informants who had explicitly mentioned depression as a problem, who had complained of anxiety, who had mentioned blaming self, who had admitted to excessive sleeping, who had had problems with drinking or desiring to drink as an escape—in all these distressed categories, those unemployed six months or more predominated.

Having so little leverage on their future, some long-term unemployed assumed religious postures. The question of whether they would find employment shifted to "is there a role for me in the social order?" The responses to the question ranged from faith to agnosticism to plain existentialist waiting. Martha, when asked what advice she would give to a newly-unemployed person, replied: "I guess in some cases religion. You've got to believe. A lot of people get strength from religion. I just think that better things are to come. There's got to be something out there for me." A few were skeptical that they would ever find decent work, adopting a certain resignation.

The tough-minded response was not to look to the future, but to live existentially. Faced with a future that seemed indeterminate and fateful, people relaxed their attempts to influence or anticipate it—in effect, lowering their expectations of life. Young Peter stated that he did not plan, but just looked "forward to what might happen. I don't have specifics, but I just look forward to continued life." Gord, unemployed for over two years, had given up the idea of a family. He had abandoned planning, figuring it would be a long haul which would not get any better, so he had best find a calm way of coping with it. The various expressions had a similar ring:

> I take the day as it comes. No use planning because you don't got the money to plan with.
> (Dick)

> What's the sense in setting a time-table, because I'm not going anywhere. (Matthew)
>
> I don't make plans. I just sit at home, waiting for a letter to arrive or a phone call that will have some good news, but it never seems to come.
> (Andrew)

Colleen, though not long-term unemployed, has waited a long time for even the chance at a good job. She offered a sort of parody of planning. "I sit down, have a cup of tea and my cigarette, and think about what I'm not going to do today." The woman suggested, more seriously, that her life was lived within each day, not the longer time spans. "You try to do something. Either go to the bank, make some kind of outing. Go to the store." As the unemployment dragged on, people who used to plan veered to the opposite of the planned state and lived intuitively—as if spurning the future that had been taken from them: "It comes and goes ... Whatever my mind swings to, I'll do that. No, I don't have any fixed periods of time." (Matthew)

Some adjustments were more focused than others. Nancy, 28 and single, laid off as a sales representative, and unemployed for 18 months, was looking forward to a course for women in trades. She talked of the effect of her long-term unemployment as involving "a total change of attitude ... Go with the flow." She and one other long-term unemployed woman drew *radical* not quietest conclusions from this, however. Having tried so hard, taken the right courses, "paid her dues" and still not found work, she concluded that the fault was not hers and she must not blame herself. On the strength of this, she worked with the local Union of Unemployed Workers to help the unemployed make their just claims on society. "Go with the flow" meant that the self should cease its long struggle against a society which overburdened selves with undeserved blame, and join itself with forces that sought to change society.

Most were not so fortified, however. A few spoke of adjusting themselves to a new order, wherein high technology provides little full-time work. Gord felt that his underemployment was a harbinger of tough times to come. He continually made a virtue of his necessity. He compared

> sitting and reading for four hours, and doing some job that's useless, that there's no need for, that's not helping anyone, or not helping yourself either. Just the idea of keeping your hands busy, to me it's senseless. I'd rather sit down and read. You're not screwing up the environment, making a mess.

His defense of his odd-jobs way of life seemed partly genuine, but also fueled by resentment. Gord resented the fact that his unemployment and poverty made him unattractive to women—so he criticized the women of today as shallow (as though *he* were rejecting *them*). Having been rejected by his family during some drinking years, he posited the view that one should never get close to one's family.

His ambivalence at being on the margin was caught in this passage:

> Well, I've resigned myself to the fact that I'll never meet anyone and have a family ... And I have a kind of resentment against that ... Maybe my feeling of self-worth has gone down ... I probably wouldn't meet anyone and have one or two children. I've resigned myself that will never happen.
>
> To be honest, I don't really give a shit ... It doesn't really matter.

Plainly it did matter, but he had to find some way to live with his unsheltered position in the marginal work world, as well as social rejection. Gord's "coming to terms" with those probabilities which hedged him in was chiefly the consequence of his marginalization but also partial contributor to his predicament.

TRANSCENDING UNEMPLOYMENT

Those who seemed to weather the atomizing, a-socializing effect of unemployment—and even occasionally to rise above it—were those insulated by one or more of the following factors: non-stigmatizing financial backing, social support, education, and collectivist ideology. We will review each in turn.

Non-stigmatizing financial backing could come from a number of sources. It might have been a disability allowance, an adequate employment insurance benefit, room and board in the parent's home, savings, or a sharing of the spouse's income. If it was a social wage, what made it non-stigmatizing was the clear understanding of the informant that it was his or hers by *right*, and that, far from resulting in a reduced, dependent existence, it was a "ramp" to a fuller life in the community. Whether disabled or on employment insurance benefits, such people were freed from some of the constraints of poverty to take courses, to move about in the job search, to explore contacts and opportunities in a community that was still theirs. If the support was from a spouse or parent, what made it non-stigmatizing in some cases was the trust invested in it. There seemed to be an understanding, sometimes unstated, that human life was worth more that its productivity or marketability, that there were times in life when a proper orientation to the public realm required a period of reflection and relief from its demands.

Social support came from many quarters—from spouses or partners, from friends, relatives, parents, fellow volunteers, other unemployed people in the intermediate organizations. The acceptance by these people of the unemployed person helped to reconnect the ligatures that were broken by the jobless condition. By continually treating the informant as a *person*—not atomized or abstracted, but as a concrete being capable of a life extending beyond the present—these supportive others reminded the person of the humanity which the public realm could not apprehend. By interacting with supportive others, and seeing that others were in a similar situation, one's social identity was preserved from collapse into self-blame. Laurie came out of her "ruts" by reminding herself that this was a *social* experience she was undergoing:

> There's more to life than this, and this is not the end of my life. A lot of other people are hoeing the same row and I don't need to feel so inferior, and ... degenerate and lazy and no good—because it's a worldwide condition anyway. And we just need to cope with it together.

Though *education* did not conclusively deter the negative impacts of unemployment, it did provide the analytical tools to generalize about the condition. Those without these tools felt personally distressed and powerless, as did Erica:

> The man on the street can't do anything because he can't understand it. I can't understand it. There's got to be an answer. Who is going to provide the answer? ... I don't think people are going to ask why, I don't think they know where to start. Why? Why aren't I working? Are there less jobs now than there were 20 years ago? Are there more people?

The response to this complexity, Erica thought, was the blaming of self.

The educated, by contrast, had a better chance to address the problem intellectually. Colleen, with a psychology degree, matter-of-factly distilled the problem of unemployment in a few sentences. She thought governments were holding the reins on social spending, and employers were taking advantage of the oversupply of labour by demanding high experience and qualifications for low pay. Another university graduate, Tony, looked at the situation as a personal problem but a structural issue:

> I'm the only one who's going to get myself out of this ... but I also see it as a structural problem which society has to deal with. There are 150 people looking for work and 100 jobs. It doesn't matter if the 50 people are working like mad to get a job. If it's not there, it's not there. No one's going to give it to you.

He felt that a post-industrial revolution would decrease the number of jobs, taking jobs from the blue-collar area and adding them to the white-collar area but in smaller numbers. "We have to look in radically new direction," he concluded.

Finally, those holding a *collectivist ideology*—the main variants being participatory socialism and Marxist analysis—were intellectually fortified against the misplaced egoism of self-blame. The holders of this perspective believed that the major responsibility for the high unemployment lay with business and government. According to the most articulate spokesman of this view, Jim, the roots of the present crisis lay in the objective contradictions between capitalism's world-wide search to maintain its rate of profit and the interests of communities and the working class. Subjectively, business and government were using the unemployed as a tool to "*reduce the price of labour payout, of forcing those who are working to work for less*."

> To the extent to which they can demoralize the unemployed, they have a potential scab ... and a capacity to intimidate workers ... [There are] large numbers of people who are scared, looking for work, not ever knowing what is expected of them.

It was in the interests of big business and government to have "*broken-down individuals as opposed to collective forces*." Not only in their analysis, but in their organizing and egalitarian practice, the leftist informants tried to counter this atomization, refusing (in Jim's words) to be "pushed around and carried by blind forces."

The leftists seemed determined to stand united against the assault on the working class represented by unemployment. Jim's advice to the unemployed was also aimed at the unemployed *person*, who had to be armoured against the marginalizing currents of capitalism:

> The essential thing I come back to is a sense of your person. Don't let them grind you down. Don't let them give you the impression you are all alone, don't let them atomize you ... You didn't make the situation, but you can have a hand in changing it.

These analytical tools were not just theories, but were an indispensable part of radical practice. Only such an analysis of the whole situation, it was thought, would prevent the unemployed from being crushed by their sufferings. And only in the collective struggle which followed from the analysis would the self come into its own—not in the private absorption or psychologism of liberal-capitalist society.

CONCLUSION

In the socially-conditioned practices of the unemployed self there were two idioms—that of the wheel or cycle of marginalization, and that of the "jagged edges." We will take each in turn.

The marginalization of the unemployed self meant that the personal identity had lost its mooring to the social identity. Cut off from significant personal agency in the social world, the practices left to the self to "right" became even more circumscribed. Introspecting, disconnected from active social roles or contents upon which it could reflect, it became increasingly self-referencing and subjectivized. Communal ties, even thoughts of the outside world, became fewer. Social injuries were transmuted into personal hurts. The mind cast back to past events which became exaggerated in their present influence.

Over time the self lost its sense of entitlement to the future. No longer acting in the future perfect, one prepared for a long accommodation in the present. The goal now was self-maintenance. The view of society became more cynical, and one kept a well-rationalized distance from others. The extreme situation to which entrenched unemployment drove the self left it the author of its own practices, but those practices did not enter the collective making of the society outside one's door. Marginalization had finally reached into the self and become reproduced in the self's own processes.

The idiom of those who were able to *transcend* unemployment, on the other hand, was determinedly active or at least self-protective—whether it was based on the confidence of a sense of entitlement, of intellectual comprehension, of active collective opposition, or of income. The key here was support, willingly offered and received, which was the lifeline that sustained a sense of agency in a community. Whether the others were family, friends, contacts or fellow unemployed, with them one was able to turn modest resources into rich returns in the community. By fighting for a place in the social order—as well as in the future—one not only improved the prospects of finally being employed, but also resisted the hypothesis of self-blame. The personal identity was turned outward to its social identity, and to how it might connect with the collective life of its time and place.

PREJUDICE AND DISCRIMINATION TOWARD MINORITIES IN CANADA AND THE UNITED STATES

Chapter 29

Jeffrey G. Reitz and Raymond Breton

(Abridged from Chapter 4, "Prejudice and discrimination," In *The illusion of Difference: Realities of Ethnicity in Canada and the United States*: Toronto: C.D. Howe Institute, 1994, pp. 64–89. Reprinted with permission.)

INTRODUCTION

How do Canadians and Americans compare in terms of racial and ethnic prejudice and discrimination? In this chapter, we shall attempt to answer this question, using not only measures of overt prejudice, but also measures of the extent to which people in the two countries uphold negative stereotypes of minorities, seek to maintain "social distance" between themselves and members of other groups (in this context, our analysis will consider attitudes toward immigration, minorities as neighbours, and intermarriage), and withhold support for government action against discrimination.

Prejudice is a matter of attitudes; discrimination is a matter of behaviour. Both things are difficult to measure. Our purpose here is not to resolve the problems of measurement. Rather, it is to see whether the standard indicators of prejudice and discrimination, which are perhaps flawed, suggest in any way that there is a difference between the level of prejudice and discrimination in Canada and the level in the United States. The familiar Canadian assumption that the level in Canada is lower can, we believe, be meaningfully addressed in this way.

TRENDS WITHIN EACH COUNTRY

In both Canada and the United States, a range of indicators of racial attitudes shows certain positive trends. The National Academy of Sciences report, *A Common Destiny: Blacks and American Society* (Jaynes and Williams 1989), gleaned data from dozens of national opinion polls conducted between 1942 and 1983. These polls show growing and now virtually universal verbal commitment to the principle of racial equality. White preferences for "social distance" from Blacks in various settings have declined significantly. Although popular support for government policies and programs to assist Blacks remains low and has shown no consistent trend over time, there has been no major White "backlash."

In Canada, race is less salient, and there is less research. Without doubt the climate in Canada too has improved since the Second World War, when racially exclusionary immigration policies were still in effect. For its study, *The Economic and Social Impact of Immigration*, the Economic Council of Canada assembled data from existing surveys of intolerance (Swan et al. 1991, 111–113). The council reported a "positive" trend among anglophones on an index of "tolerance." However, the study did not present specific quantitative results, and the index included items on gender as well as race.

These parallel attempts at trend analysis invite several observations. First, data on racial attitudes in Canada are so much less plentiful than data on attitudes in the United States that clear comparisons are difficult. Second, the existence of positive trends in racial attitudes in both countries may be a point of similarity between them, even if in some ways these changes prove superficial. Definitive comparison must focus on specific key areas, an approach that, as we shall show, yields interesting results. And third, the comparative data are very time-sensitive. One cannot meaningfully compare US data from the 1960s with Canadian data from the 1970s and 1980s. In fact, our goal here is really to measure the trajectory of change in the two countries. One might say that what is at issue is not the extent of cross-national differences, but the approximate number of years (if any) that one country may be ahead of the other in terms of changes in racial attitudes.

OVERT RACISM AND NEGATIVE RACIAL STEREOTYPES

US survey research clearly shows that overt racism, by which we mean the explicit assertion of innate White superiority, is now expressed only by a small minority. Schuman, Steeh, and Bobo (1985, 125) show that, as recently as the 1940s, only 50 to 60 percent of Americans outside the South—and even fewer in the South—endorsed the innate equality of Blacks, agreeing that "Negroes are as intelligent as White people" and can "learn things just as well if they are given the same education and training." Since the 1950s, the proportion has been at least 90 percent.

A survey conducted in 1990 by Decima Research Ltd. permits a comparison of the two countries. The Canadians in the survey were, overall, slightly less overtly racist than the Americans, but only slightly: 90 percent of the Canadians, and 86 percent of the Americans agreed that "all races are created equal" (*Maclean's* 1990). This difference is insubstantial. Large majorities in both countries deny overt racism.

The denial of overt racism in both countries is also reflected in the fact that few people support organizations with explicitly racist philosophies. The 1989 National Academy of Sciences study (Jaynes and Williams 1989) found that, in the United States, support for the Ku Klux Klan had increased somewhat during the late 1960s and 1970s but was still marginal. KKK groups in Canada and indigenous organizations with racist messages, such as the Western Guard or the Heritage Front, also have few members (Barrett 1987; Sher 1983; and see Schoenfeld 1991). Actually, many supporters of groups such as the KKK deny that they are racists. One-third of the respondents in a survey conducted in and near Chattanooga, Tennessee, had favourable views of the KKK. Many of them cited the KKK as a "charitable" organization and as one that supported law and order; they may have been dissembling their knowledge of its racial views (Selzter and Lopes 1986, 95). In both countries, some mainstream politicians, too, have been accused of appealing to hidden racial feelings, though as a rule they deny this intention.

How widespread are hidden racist attitudes? Is there more hidden racism in one country than the other?

US attitude surveys show that some of those who deny racism in fact have racist views that are easily brought to the surface. For example, when Americans are asked to explain why so many Blacks are poor, many of them refer to innate racial inferiority. The General Social Surveys (GSS) for 1988 and 1989 asked the following question:

> On the average Blacks have worse jobs, income, and housing than White people. Do you think that these differences are ... (a) mainly due to discrimination, (b) because most Blacks have less in-born ability to learn, (c) because most Blacks don't have the chance for education that it takes to rise out of poverty, and (d) because most Blacks just don't have the motivation or will power to pull themselves out of poverty? (Kluegel 1990, 514.)

The proportion of respondents who chose the explanation "Blacks have less in-born ability," either alone or in combination with other explanations, was 20.8 percent (Kluegel 1990, 517). Thus, although few Whites explicitly challenge the proposition (put forward in the 1990 Decima survey, for example) that all races are created equal, a significantly larger proportion refer to inherent racial inferiority when asked to explain Black poverty. Some people explain Black disadvantage as "God's plan" (Kluegel and Smith 1986, 188).

Many Americans, in shifting away from overtly racist views, have embraced what Kluegel calls "individualistic" explanations for Black-White inequality (Kluegel 1990, 515). They say that Blacks lack motivation or have an inferior culture. They deny "structuralist" explanations—that Blacks lack educational and employment opportunity or experience discrimination. In the 1977 GSS, the proportion of respondents who explained Black poverty by reference to innate Black inferiority was 26 percent (Kluegel and Smith 1986, 188; see also Sniderman and Hagen 1985, 30). In 1988–89, as we have shown, it was about 21 percent. Through this period, most endorsed individualist explanations, and only about 25 to 30 percent believed that Blacks experienced any significant discrimination. In fact, the 1977 GSS showed that the same proportion felt that Blacks were given preference—that there was discrimination against Whites (Kluegel 1985, 768). "Young and old Americans alike appear to believe that discrimination in the work force *currently* does not function to limit opportunity for Black workers to any substantial degree" (Kluegel 1985, 771).

What are the comparable Canadian attitudes? Canadian explanations for minority-group disadvantage are not, of course, strictly comparable with American explanations. Asking Canadians about minorities in Canada is obviously not necessarily the same as asking Americans about minorities in the United States. Nevertheless, in the 1987 Canadian Charter Study about 70 percent of the respondents agreed that "immigrants often bring discrimination upon themselves by their own personal attitudes and habits," 25 percent disagreed, and the remaining 5 percent gave various qualified responses or "don't know" (Sniderman et al. 1991). The proportion of those who cited an "individualistic" explanation—70 percent—is about the same as the proportion in the United States. Thus, Canadians, like Americans, frequently deny that the minorities in their respective countries are the victims of racial discrimination. Of course, what is in fact the case in each country is arguable. We examine data relevant to the actual comparative extent of discrimination below. For now, we simply note that Canadians and Americans seem to be alike in tending to prefer individualistic explanations of minority disadvantage to explanations that cite discrimination.

ANTI-SEMITISM

In both countries, the Jewish group is long-established and largely urban, accounts for 1 to 2 percent of the population, and has high average levels of educational and occupational attainment and earnings (Lieberson and Waters 1988; Li 1988; Leitz 1990). Because of this similarity, comparisons of negative attitudes and behaviour toward Jews provide a particularly good indication of relative predisposition toward ethnic tolerance. For Jews, unlike Blacks, the issue of relations with the other groups arises in a very similar way in the two countries.

Studies that measure the prevalence of negative stereotypes of Jews have produced remarkably similar aggregate results in the United States and Canada. We compared results from the Charter Study in Canada in 1987 (Sniderman et al. 1992; 1993) with those from a US survey reported by Martire and Clark (1982, 17) in 1981. In three of the four comparisons, about one Canadian in five and one American in five gave a response that described the Jewish group in a negative way. Canadians were more likely than Americans, however, to agree that Jews are "pushy."

There are positive stereotypes of the Jewish group as well as negative ones. Smith (1990, 9), using GSS data, found that in the United States, the general population rates Jews above "Whites" in relation to the descriptive tags "rich," "hard-working," "not violent," "intelligent," and "self-supporting."

In both countries, anti-Semitic stereotypes have their greatest currency within certain other minority groups. The frictions between Jews and these other minorities are secondary ethnic conflicts, derived from broader patterns of ethnic disadvantage. In Canada, French-Canadian attitudes toward Jews are more negative than those of any other group (Sniderman et al. 1991). However, French-Canadian attitudes toward other minorities are also more negative. At the same time, there is greater pressure toward conformity—including ethnic assimilation—in Quebec than there is in the rest of the country. These are classic patterns in group conflict: suspicion of outsiders and closing of ranks among insiders.

In the United States, there is a roughly parallel tension between Jews and Blacks. This tension is at least in part the result of a reactive response among Blacks, rather than an indication that Blacks have a greater predisposition to anti-Semitism than other groups. The position of Blacks in the United States has also led to tensions between Blacks and other minorities, including Asians and Hispanics (Oliver and Johnson 1984; Johnson and Oliver 1989; Rose 1989).

One can compare anti-Semitic behaviour in the United States and Canada by using the "audit of anti-Semitic incidents" that B'nai Brith, the Jewish service organization, publishes in each country. The Anti-Defamation League of B'nai Brith in the United States reported 1 879 incidents in 1991 (A'DLBB 1991, 29). In Canada, the equivalent organization is the League of Human Rights of B'nai Brith, whose more positive-sounding name suggests a less conflictful or more tolerant setting. Nevertheless, the number of incidents reported in Canada in 1991 was 251 (LHRBB Canada 1991, 4), more than might be expected given the roughly 10-to-1 US-Canadian population ratio. The totals for 1982 to 1992, however, uphold the ratio—there were 12 665 incidents in the United States and 1 191 in Canada. The year-to-year figures fluctuate not quite in lock step, responding similarly to events such as the Persian Gulf war, which seemed to provoke increases in anti-Semitic incidents—and anti-Muslim incidents as well—in both countries.

Thus, attitudes and behaviour reflect very similar patterns of anti-Semitism in the two countries. This case, free from some of the methodological complexities that affect other comparisons, does not support the hypothesis that Canadians are more tolerant than Americans.

SOCIAL DISTANCE

Social distance is a measure of dominant-group tolerance for social relations with members of a given minority. For a given minority, social distance is greater when the majority is unwilling to tolerate not only close relations such as marriage and family membership but also more distant relations. Thus, the majority may be unwilling to tolerate members of the minority as neighbours, as co-workers, or even as immigrants.

US data show that social distances from the dominant English-origin group are greatest for Blacks and other racial minorities, less for southern Europeans, and least for northern Europeans (Bogardus 1958, 1967). Surveys of university social science students conducted since the 1920s have shown that social distance for a variety of minority groups has declined over the years, but that the rank-order of racial groups has remained fairly stable (see Owen, Eisner, and McFaul 1981; and Sinha and Barry 1991). Table 29-1 shows how racial and ethnic groups in the United States have been ranked in various years. Sinha and Barry (1991), who have applied the concept of social distance to groups such as intravenous drug users, AIDS victims, people who have attempted suicide, and homosexuals, find that ethnic and racial groups are now less socially distant from the dominant groups than are these other groups. They suggest that race and ethnicity are becoming less important than behaviour as a basis for discrimination.

Comparable Canadian data are available for national samples as well as student populations. The national data describe the "social standing" of ethnic and racial groups, which is presumably akin to social distance or group prestige. In a national survey on ethnic social standing, English- and French-Canadian respondents placed group names in ranked categories. The results in Table 29-2 show a rank-order similar to the rank-order for US minorities in Table 29-1. Racial minorities, including Blacks and Asians, are at the bottom, southern Europeans rank higher, and northern Europeans higher still (Berry Kalin, and Taylor 1977; Pineo 1977, and Angus Reid Group Inc. 1991). Driedger and Mezoff (1981) derive similar results from data on Manitoba university students (see also Dion 1985).

Calculations of social distance index values on the basis of student samples yield similar results for the two countries. The 1977 figure for Blacks in the United States was 2.03 and a comparable figure for Blacks in Canada was 2.12; for West Indians it was 2.46 (Driedger and Mezoff 1981). For Chinese, the 1977 US figure was 2.29, and the 1981 Canadian figure was 2.33. For Mexicans, the US and Canadian figures were, respectively, 2.40 and 2.38; for Japanese, they were 2.38 and 2.40. There is one major discrepancy: the index value for American Indians in 1977 was 1.84, whereas the value for Native Indians in Canada, or at least in Manitoba, was substantially higher, 2.70.

No one has calculated precise index values for social distance between Whites and specific minorities in both countries on the

Table 29-1 Mean social distances of ethnic and racial groups in the United States, 1926–90 (as measured on the Bogardus social distance scale)

	1926	1946	1956	1966	1977	1990
Groups included in the Bogardus scale						
Americans (US White)	1.10	1.04	1.08	1.07	1.25	1.13
English	1.06	1.13	1.23	1.14	1.39	1.15
Canadians	1.13	1.11	1.16	1.15	1.42	1.19
Italians	1.94	2.28	1.89	1.51	1.65	1.36
French	1.32	1.31	1.47	1.36	1.58	1.37
Germans	1.46	1.59	1.61	1.54	1.87	1.39
American Indians	2.38	2.45	2.35	2.18	1.84	1.59
Poles	2.01	1.84	2.07	1.98	2.11	1.68
Jews	2.39	2.32	2.15	1.97	2.01	1.71
Blacks	3.28	3.60	2.74	2.56	2.03	1.73
Chinese	3.36	2.50	2.68	2.34	2.29	1.76
Japanese	2.80	3.61	2.70	2.41	2.38	1.86
Russians	1.88	1.83	2.56	2.38	2.57	1.93
Koreans	3.60	3.05	2.83	2.51	2.63	1.94
Mexicans	2.69	2.89	2.79	2.56	2.40	2.00
Groups not included in the Bogardus scale						
Israelis	–	–	–	–	–	2.63
Palestinians	–	–	–	–	–	2.78
Iranians	–	–	–	–	–	3.03
Spread	2.54	2.57	1.75	1.49	1.38	1.90
Change in spread	+0.03	–0.82	–0.26	–0.11	+0.52	

Note: The Bogardus social distance scale ranges from a low of 1.00 to a high of 7.00. The figures are based on mean ratings of the degree of distance that respondents would prefer to maintain between themselves and members of each group. The available responses are: acceptance "into my family through marriage or cohabitation" (1.00), acceptance "as close friends or room mate" (2.00), acceptance "in my dorm" (3.00), acceptance "as a co-worker or class mate" (4.00), acceptance "as speaking acquaintance only" (5.00), acceptance "as visitors only to my country" (6.00), and "would not accept into my country" (7.00).

Source: Sinha and Berry 1991, 7.

basis of national or even general-population data, let alone data collected at comparable points in time. As Table 29-2 has shown, Jaynes and Williams (1989, 122–123) summarized US national survey data to demonstrate that White social distances from Blacks have declined. These and other potentially comparable data address specific components of social distance, such as acceptance of minorities as neighbours, or as family members through intermarriage, rather than social distance generally. The following subsections consider four of these specific components.

Table 29-2 Social standing of minority groups in English and French Canada

	Social Standing as Ranked by:	
Minority Group	**English Canada**	**French Canada**
Own group	83.1	77.6
English	82.4	77.6
Italians	43.1	51.3
French	60.1	72.4
Germans	48.7	40.5
Canadian Indians	28.3	32.5
Poles	42.0	38.0
Jews	46.1	43.1
Blacks	25.4	23.5
Chinese	33.1	24.9
Japanese	34.7	27.8
Russians	35.8	33.2

Note: The categories are placed in order of the comparable groups in Table 29-1; some groups are not included.

Source: Pineo 1977, 154.

Immigration

One component of social distance is attitudes toward specific groups as immigrants. Canadians favour immigration more than Americans do, despite the fact that racial-minority immigration is currently greater in Canada. In the 1990 Decima survey, 58 percent of Americans wanted less immigration and only 6 percent wanted more (*Maclean's* 1990, 52). By contrast, 39 percent of Canadians wanted less immigration and 18 percent wanted more. Whether these more positive Canadian attitudes apply to "new" racial-minority immigrants is not clear. Nevertheless, in a 1976 Gallup poll, 63 percent of Canadians opposed racial restrictions and only 27 percent favoured them. In 1981, only 10 percent supported "cutting off all non-White immigration to Canada.

American attitudes toward immigration appear to have turned negative as immigration increased after the 1960s. In a series of comparable polls, the proportion of Americans who wanted less immigration increased from 33 percent in 1965 to 61 percent in 1993. There appears to be a nearly comparable trend in Canada. Angus Reid Group Inc. (1989, 4–5) reported that the proportion of Canadians who think too many immigrants are coming to Canada increased from 30 percent in May 1988 to 31 percent in February 1989 and 43 percent in August 1989. An Ekos Research Associates Inc. poll showed that this proportion had risen to 53 percent by February 1994 (*Globe and Mail* [Toronto], March 10, 1994, p. A1). On the other hand, Environics polls conducted in 1986 and 1989 showed a decline in agreement with the statement that "there is too much immigration to Canada," from 66 percent to 57 percent (Angus Reid Group Ltd. 1989, 5).

Canadians' somewhat more positive attitudes may reflect their country's different historical and institutional context, rather than cultural predisposition. Postwar Canadian immigration, mostly European in origin, has been a major element of economic and social development policy. Reimers and Troper (1992) argue that, in the United States, immigration has ceased to be a development policy and is now perceived as social welfare, and that public support has declined accordingly. Like Americans, and perhaps for similar reasons, Britons support racial minority immigration less than Canadians do. British immigration has been an obligation to former colonial territories in the Commonwealth, rather than a program of national development (see Reitz 1988a, 1988b).

At the same time, there are signs that growing unease with immigration among White Canadians as well as among White Americans is, in fact, related to race, not just to numbers or to immigration goals. In a 1979 survey in Toronto (Breton et al. 1990, 204), 63 percent of "majority Canadians" agreed that "present immigration laws make it too easy for certain groups to come to Canada." In identifying these "certain groups," respondents mentioned racial minorities three times more often than they mentioned other immigrant groups. European-origin immigrants shared these concerns. In the United States, a recent *Newsweek* poll asked a comparable question in a national sample: "Should it be easier or more difficult for people from the following places to immigrate to the US?" About half of the respondents said that it should be more difficult for people from China or other Asian countries to immigrate to the United States, and 61 percent said it should be more difficult for people from the Middle East to immigrate to the United States. These results from the two countries seem to be roughly parallel.

Community and Neighbourhood Residence

There has long been a significant cross-national difference in responses to racial minorities as neighbours. Comparative Gallup data assembled by Michalos (1982, 169, 206) indicate that in 1963 only 3 percent of Canadians said that they would definitely move "if coloured people came to live next door" and 91 percent said that they would stay put. In the United States at that time, 20 percent said that they would move and only 55 percent said that they would stay.

Things have changed since the 1960s, of course. Although racial preferences for neighbours are still significant and strong in the United States, feelings have relaxed noticeably over time. In the late 1960s, US movers declined to 12 percent and stayers rose to 65 percent. In 1978, only 10 percent would move if a Black moved next door (Schuman, Steeh, and Bobo 1985, 106–108). As late as 1981, however, a majority of northerners preferred a mostly White neighbourhood and one in four preferred and all-White neighbourhood (Schuman, Steeh, and Bobo 1985, 67). In the South, two-thirds preferred a mostly White neighbourhood and the preference for an all-White neighbourhood varied between 38 and 51 percent. Openness to Black neighbours varies with the numbers of Blacks mentioned in the question. Whereas only 46 percent of White Americans said they would not move if Blacks came into their neighbourhood in "great numbers," about 85 percent said they would not move if Blacks moved in "next door" or onto the "same block."

Canadian attitudes may not be markedly different, but in recent available surveys the same questions have not been asked. Replies to the most closely comparable questions do not suggest extreme cross-national differences. In the 1978–79 Ethnic Pluralism Survey in Toronto, two-thirds of the respondents said that they were willing to have a West Indian as a next-door neighbour "if you were completely free to decide yourself" (Breton et al. 1990, 200). The proportion that responded positively to having Chinese, Italian, or Portuguese neighbours was about 85 percent.

Acceptance into Social Clubs

A willingness to accept racial minorities into private clubs would seem to indicate an even greater tolerance than does a willingness to accept them into neighbourhoods. Yet the data for both countries show more support for open membership than for open neighbourhoods. In a 1987 Gallup poll, only 15 percent of Americans and 12 percent of Canadians thought private clubs should have the right to exclude prospective members of the basis of race. The exclusion of minorities from social clubs may be regarded as a symbol of overt racism and may therefore be rejected even if there is a desire to exclude.

Intermarriage

Both Canadians and Americans have become more tolerant of racial intermarriage in recent decades, but Canadians continue to lead Americans in this regard. In Canada, disapproval of Black-White marriages declined from 52 percent in 1968 to 35 percent in 1973 (Michalos 1982, 205), and those who disapprove are now only a small minority—16 percent, according to a 1988 Gallup National Omnibus Newspaper poll. In 1988, according to the same poll, 72.5 percent of Canadians approved of Black-White marriages. Lambert and Curtis (1984) show that English-Canadian disapproval declined from 60 percent in 1968 to 24 percent in 1983; there was less disapproval in Quebec.

In the United States, disapproval of Black-White marriages declined from 72 percent in 1968 to 60 percent in 1972 (Michalos 1982, 205). Yet, in 1983, only 40 percent of Americans approved of marriages between Whites and non-Whites (Schuman, Steeh, and Bobo 1985, 74–76). The 1988 GSS showed that 25 percent of Americans think Black-White marriages should actually be outlawed (Niemi, Mueller, and Smith 1989, 170). This figure represents a decline from earlier decades, but clearly the social climate in the United States is different from the social climate in Canada. The 1989 Decima poll confirms the difference: 32 percent of the American respondents, but only 13 percent of the Canadians, said that they would be unhappy if one of their children "married someone from a different racial background." Only 15 percent of the Americans, but 25 percent of the Canadians, said that they would be "happy" (*Maclean's* 1989).

To put the differences in the context of change, attitudes in the United States today are like those in the Canada of a decade or more ago. The Canadian data cited above show a change of about 2 percentage points per year. The US data in Jaynes and Williams (1989, 122) show a change of 1.5 points per year. In the matter of opposition to intermarriage, two of the data sources cited above indicate a difference between the two countries of about 20 points. Given a rate of 1.5 or 2 points per year, therefore, Canada may be ten or a dozen years ahead of the United States in the trend toward acceptance of interracial marriages.

COLLECTIVE AND GOVERNMENT ACTION AGAINST DISCRIMINATION

Americans have at times regarded race relations as one of their country's leading problems, a perception that has led to pressure for government action. A poll conducted in 1963, after a decade of growing racial unrest, showed that 52 percent of the US population considered racial problems to be the most important facing the country; only 25 percent gave priority to the threat of war with the Soviet Union. Later, the prominence of the race issue receded, but it continues to be more significant in the United States than it has ever been in Canada (Michalos 1982, 189–201).

In the context of race, accordingly, Americans have been more likely than Canadians to favour government action. In 1970, 25 percent of Americans, but only 11 percent of Canadians, put "reducing racial discrimination" among the top three government priorities for the future (Michalos 1982, 202). And, of course, the US government has indeed taken more action (Jain and Sloane 1981; Jain 1989). The Canadian federal government has avoided US-style legislation to mandate equal employment, on the grounds that the problem is less serious in Canada (Reitz 1988b).

The higher priority that Americans have placed on racial discrimination is attributable in part to the higher level of racial conflict in the United States; it does not necessarily indicate a greater underlying predisposition to favour government action against discrimination. Indeed, as racial conflict has declined, Americans' willingness to invoke government action against discrimination seems to have declined somewhat as well, even though racial tolerance has increased. Even as racial attitudes and social-distance scores improved in the 1970s and 1980s, Whites became more supportive of policies to assist Blacks only in the area of housing and accommodations, and less supportive of such policies in other areas, including schools.

Kluegel (1990) uses GSS data for 1986, 1988, and 1989 to probe Americans' attitudes toward assisting Blacks to achieve equality. The GSS respondents were asked the following:

> Some people think that Blacks have been discriminated against for so long that the government has a special obligation to help improve their living standards. Others believe that the government should not be giving special treatment to Blacks ... .Where would you place yourself on this scale, or haven't you made up your mind on this?

Pooling the surveys, Kluegel finds that only 13.8 percent agreed that the government was obligated to help Blacks; 59.3 percent stated that the government had no such obligation, and 26.9 percent took a position in between. Pooled analysis of these surveys, plus others conducted in 1977 and 1985, showed that the US population was evenly split between those who thought the government was doing too much—26.8 percent—and those who thought it was doing too little—24.7 percent. Kluegel makes this point:

> The only substantial change between 1977 and the late 1980s in how Whites view the Black-White socio-economic gap is a decline in the attribution of that gap to inborn ability differences. This decline parallels the trend of declining traditional prejudice ... .The abatement of perhaps the most invidious explanation for the Black-White status gap has not been accompanied by any noteworthy increase in attributions that favour efforts to provide equal opportunity for Black Americans. (Kluegel 1990, 523).

Smith's (1990, 7) analysis of the 1990 GSS data shows that negative images of Blacks in the context of work and welfare have had a direct effect on support for affirmative action for Blacks. Thus, although the explanations that Americans give for racial disadvantages have changed, there is a persistent reluctance to identify discrimination as a major cause of these disadvantages, and hence resistance to policies intended to offset discrimination. Bobo (1988, 109) offers a group-conflict interpretation of this resistance, suggesting that Whites oppose "change that might impose substantial burdens on Whites."

In Canada, no survey has asked if the government has an obligation to secure equal opportunity for Blacks. The 1987 Charter Study, however, did ask respondents if the government has an obligation to ensure equal opportunity in general. The statement "while equal opportunity to succeed is important for all Canadians, it's not really the government's job to guarantee it" elicited agreement from 63.3 percent of the respondents and disagreement from 33.7 percent. By contrast, as we noted above, only 13.8 percent of Americans approved of government intervention to assist Blacks. Of course, Canadian opinions might be different if racial minorities were targeted as beneficiaries. Support for government action to ensure equal opportunity might not translate into support for government action to assist a particular group.

Sniderman and Hagen (1985) show that American rejection of government intervention is linked to "individualism," and suggest that individualist values militate against collective solutions. If this is true, then Canadians, who are less committed to individualism than Americans are, might be more willing to support government intervention. However, the causal relation between values and policy may work the other way: opposition to government assistance to Blacks may reinforce individualism, which, in turn, may be invoked to legitimate racial inequality.

Thus, although discrimination has been a bigger political issue in the United States than it has been in Canada, and although more government intervention has occurred in the United States, Americans are not more likely than Canadians to favour collective responses to discrimination. Given their greater individualism, they may be less likely. Earlier, we showed that Canadians and Americans seem to be equally uncomfortable with the idea that discrimination is an explanation for inequality. The fact that social distances are less great in Canada may not mean that Canadians are more open to government intervention to ensure racial equality.

CONCLUSION

The findings reviewed here suggest that, despite the historical differences between race relations in Canada and race relations in the United States, Canadians and Americans are roughly similar in their attitudes and behaviour toward racial minorities. In both countries, blatant racism is marginal and the social distance between racial minorities and other groups is diminishing. The incidence of anti-Semitic attitudes and behaviour is about the same in each country. A majority of both Canadians and Americans feel that minorities are responsible for their own inequality, that discrimination is not a major cause of inequality, and that government should not intervene to ensure equality.

Although the social distance between the majority and the racial minorities has declined in both countries, it has consistently been smaller in Canada, especially in relation to intermarriage. Depending on the dimension of social distance in question, Canadian attitudes may be either comparable to American attitudes or a decade or more ahead of them.

One likely reason why social distance between the races is greater in the United States is that economic distance is greater as well. Another likely reason is that racial minorities constitute a much larger proportion of the total population in the United States than they do in Canada. Thus, there may be a sense among White Americans that exclusion is necessary to maintain a degree of racial homogeneity that White Canadians take for granted.

REFERENCES

Angus Reid Group Inc. 1989 *Immigration to Canada: Aspects of Public Opinion* Report prepared for Employment and Immigration Canada. Winnipeg: Angus Reid Group Inc.

Angus Reid Group Inc. 1991 *Multiculturalism and Canadians: Attitude Study 1991* (National Survey Report) Report submitted to Multiculturalism and Citizenship Canada.

Anti-Defamation League of B'nai Brith 1991 *1991 Audit of Anti-Semitic Incidents* New York: Anti-Defamation League of B'nai Brith.

Barrett, Stanley R 1987 *Is God a Racist? The Right Wing in Canada* Toronto: University of Toronto Press.

Berry, John W., R. Kalin, and D.M. Taylor 1977 *Multiculturalism and Ethnic Attitudes in Canada* Ottawa: Supply and Services Canada.

Bobo, Lawrence 1988 "Group conflict, prejudice, and the paradox of contemporary racial attitudes." In *Eliminating Racism: Means and Controversies*, Phyllis A. Katz and Dalmas A. Taylor (eds.), 85–114. New York: Plenum.

Bogardus, Emory S. 1958 "Racial distance changes in the United States during the past thirty years." *Sociology and Social Research* 43: 127–135.

Breton, Raymond, et al. 1990 *Ethnic Identity and Inequality: Varieties of Experience in a Canadian City.* Toronto: University of Toronto Press.

Dion, Kenneth L. 1985 "Social distance norms in Canada: effects of stimulus characteristics and dogmatism." *International Journal of Psychology* 20: 743–749.

Driedger, Leo and Richard Mezoff 1981 "Ethnic prejudice and discrimination in Winnipeg high schools." *Canadian Journal of Sociology* 6: 1–17.

Jain, Harish 1989 "Racial minorities and affirmative action/employment equity legislation in Canada." *Industrial Relations* 44, 3: 593–613.

Jain, Harish and P.J. Sloane 1981 *Equal Employment Issues: Race and Sex Discrimination in the United States, Canada, and Britain* New York: Praeger.

Jaynes, Gerald David and Robin M. Williams, Jr. 1989 *A Common Destiny: Blacks and American Society* Washington, DC: National Academy Press.

Johnson, James H. and Melvin L. Oliver 1989 "Interethnic minority conflict in urban America: the effects of economic and social dislocations." *Urban Geography* 10, 5: 449–463.

Kluegel, James R. 1985 "'If there isn't a problem, you don't need a solution': the basis of contemporary affirmative action attitudes." *American Behavioral Scientist* 28: 761–84.

Kluegel, James R. 1990 "Trends in Whites' explanations of the Black-White gap in socioeconomic status, 1977–1989." *American Sociological Review* 55, 4: 512–525.

Kluegel, James R. and Eliot R. Smith 1986 *Beliefs about Inequality: Americans' Views of What Is and What Ought to Be* New York: Aldine de Gruyter.

Lambert, Ronald and James Curtis 1984 "Québécois and English Canadian opposition to racial and religious intermarriage, 1968–1983." *Canadian Ethnic Studies* 16, 2: 30–46.

League of Human Rights of B'Nai Brith Canada 1991 *1991 Audit of Anti-Semitic Incidents* Downsview, Ont.: The League.

Lieberson, Stanley and Mary Waters 1988 From *Many Strands: Ethnic and Racial Groups in Contemporary America* New York: Russell Sage Foundation.

Li, Peter S. 1988 *Ethnic Inequality in a Class Society* Toronto: Wall and Thompson.

Maclean's 1989 "Portrait of Two Nations: The Dreams and Ideals of Canadians and Americans." July 3, 23–82.

Maclean's 1990 "Portrait of Two Nations: Should the Two Countries Become One?" June 25, 37–52.

Martire, Gregory and Ruth Clark 1982 *Anti-Semitism in the United States: A Study of Prejudice in the 1980s* New York: Praeger.

Michalos, Alex C. 1982 *North American Social Report: A Comparative Study of the Quality of Life in Canada and the USA from 1964 to 1974*, Vol. 5, *Economics, Religion and Morality* Dordrecht, Netherlands: D. Reidel.

Niemi, Richard G., John Mueller, and Tom W. Smith 1989 *Trends in Public Opinion: A Compendium of Survey Data* New York: Greenwood Press.

Oliver, Melvin L. and James H. Johnson, Jr. 1984 "Inter-ethnic conflict in the urban ghetto: the case of Blacks and Latinos in Los Angeles." *Research in Social Movements, Conflict and Change* 6: 57–94.

Owen, Carolyn, Howard C. Eisner, and Thomas R. McFaul 1981 "A half-century of social distance research: national replication of the Bogardus' studies." *Sociology and Social Research* 66, 1: 80–98.

Pineo, P. 1977 "The social standing of ethnic and racial groupings." *Canadian Review of Sociology and Anthropology* 14: 147–57.

Reimers, David M. and Harold Troper 1992 "Canadian and American immigration policy since 1945." In *Immigration, Language and Ethnicity: Canada and the United States* Barry R. Chiswick (ed.), 15–54. Washington, DC: AEI Press.

Reitz, Jeffrey G. 1980a "Immigrants, their descendants, and the cohesion of Canada." In *Cultural Boundaries and the Cohesion of Canada*, Raymond Breton, Jeffrey G. Reitz, and Victor Valentine (eds.), 329–471. Montreal: Institute for Research on Public Policy.

Reitz, Jeffrey G. 1988a "The institutional structure of immigration as a determinant of interracial competition: a comparison of Britain and Canada." *International Migration Review* 22, 1: 117–146.

Reitz, Jeffrey G. 1988b "Less racial discrimination in Canada, or simply less racial conflict? implications of comparisons with Britain." *Canadian Public Policy* 14, 4: 424–441.

Reitz, Jeffrey G. 1990 "Ethnic concentrations in labour markets and their implications for ethnic inequality." In Raymond Breton, Wsevolod Isajiw, Warren E. Kalbach and Jeffrey G. Reitz *Ethnic Identity and Inequality: Varieties of Experience in a Canadian City* Toronto: University of Toronto Press.

Rose, Harold M. 1989 "Blacks and Cubans in metropolitan Miami's changing economy." *Urban Geography* 10, 5: 464–486.

Schoenfeld, Stuart 1991 "Hate groups, hate propaganda and racial conflict." Unpublished manuscript.

Schuman, Howard, Charlotte Steeh, and Lawrence Bobo 1985 *Racial Attitudes in America: Trends and Interpretations* Cambridge, Mass.: Harvard University Press.

Seltzer, Rick and Grace M. Lopes 1986 "The Ku Klux Klan: reasons for support or opposition among White respondents." *Journal of Black Studies* 17, 1: 91–109.

Sher, Julian 1983 *White Hoods: Canada's Ku Klux Klan* Vancouver: New Star Books.

Sinha, Murli M. and Brian Berry 1991 "Ethnicity, Stigmatized groups and social distance: an expanded update of the Bogardus scale." Paper presented at the annual meetings of the American Sociological Association, Cincinnati, August 23–27.

Smith, Tom W. 1990. "Ethnic images." GSS Topical Report no. 19, National Opinion Research Center, University of Chicago.

Sniderman, Paul M. 1993. "Psychological and cultural foundations of prejudice: the case of anti-Semitism in Quebec." *Canadian Review of Sociology and Anthropology* 30, 2: 242–270.

Sniderman, Paul M. and Michael G. Hagen 1985 *Race and Inequality: A Study in American Values* Chatham, NJ: Chatham House.

Sniderman, Paul M. et al. 1991 "Political culture and the problem of double standards: mass and elite attitudes toward language rights in the Canadian Charter of Rights and

Freedoms." *Canadian Journal of Political Science* 22, 2: 259–284.

Sniderman, Paul M. et al. 1992 "Working papers on anti-Semitism in Quebec." Toronto: York University Institute for Survey Research.

Swan, Neil et al. 1991 *Economic and Social Impacts of Immigration: A Research Report Prepared for the Economic Council of Canada* Ottawa: Supply and Services Canada.

Chapter 30

PUBLIC PARTICIPATION, PROTEST, AND SOCIAL INEQUALITY

James Curtis, Edward Grabb, and Tina Chui

(An original chapter written for this volume.)

INTRODUCTION

In the popular media and public discussions, Canada is normally portrayed as a free and democratic society, in which all citizens have the right to influence political decisions, and in which everyone is encouraged to engage in different forms of community participation or collective action. In such a society, we might expect that people are relatively similar in their levels of involvement in the formal political process, and in the "parapolitics" that occurs among local community interest groups. Presumably, then, most Canadians should participate to about the same degree in such activities as voting, discussing politics, trying to influence others, joining political parties and community interest groups, making public protests, and supporting social movements.

In other words, we might think that, for these types of behaviours, members of more privileged status groups do not have an advantage over other people. In fact, we might even reason that the disadvantaged have more to protest about than other people and, therefore, are more highly represented than the advantaged in public protest activities, such as signing petitions or joining in demonstrations.

Some social scientists have questioned, however, whether there really is such a broad base to political and community group participation in Canada and other democratic countries. In particular, these researchers have doubted that individuals who rank lower on various social status dimensions have as great an opportunity or inclination to participate in these types of behaviours. This question is clearly an important one for students of social inequality to consider, because political action and interest group involvement are normally seen as fundamental to our basic human rights and civil liberties.

Research in Canada and other societies, especially extensive work in the United States, has shown that there is in fact a relationship between achieved and ascribed statuses and level of involvement in both politics and community organization activities (see, e.g., Curtis 1971; Smith 1975; Curtis and Lambert 1976; Milbrath and Goel 1977; McPherson and Lockwood 1980; Palisi and Palisi 1984; Knoke 1986; Kay et al. 1987; Curtis et al. 1989; Curtis, Grabb, and Baer 1992; Chui, Curtis, and Grabb 1993). These studies have found, for example, that persons with higher occupational status, education, and income are more likely than other people to join and participate in voluntary organizations of various kinds. Some studies also indicate that disadvantaged racial and ethnic groups, such as American Blacks, for example, are less likely to be involved in voluntary associations than are groups higher in the ethnic stratification system. However, other research also suggests that these ethnic or racial differences may be partially the result of socio-economic inequalities, rather than racial or ethnic differences *per se* (e.g., Smith 1975, p.253; Grabb and Curtis 1992). Along similar lines, other research indicates that males are more likely to participate in voluntary organizations than are females, and middle-aged people are more likely to do so than are older and younger people (e.g., Curtis 1971; Smith 1975; Cutler 1976; McPherson and Lockwood 1980; Edwards et al. 1984; Palisi and Palisi 1984; Knoke 1986; Curtis, Grabb, and Baer 1992). Similar patterns have been shown for participation in formal politics, such as voting, political party membership, political interest, and so on (e.g., Curtis and Lambert 1976; Milbrath and Goel 1977; Chui, Curtis, and Grabb 1993).

These differences have been explained in a variety of ways. One well-known explanation has suggested that these patterns are largely accounted for by the "relative centrality" of different groups in society (see, e.g., Milbrath and Goel 1977; Chui, Curtis, and Grabb 1993). According to this perspective, some people are more centrally located in important social networks. Persons from the higher socio-economic strata and from the more privileged or established racial, ethnic, gender, and age groupings are perhaps the best examples. These individuals generally have more power and resources at their disposal than others do. They also tend to have greater knowledge, information, and awareness of how various organizations operate in their community and elsewhere. For these reasons, it is argued, people of higher rank or social status are more likely to be active participants in the political processes that help to shape their society.

Involvement and interest in politics or other community activities can stem from various motivations. A belief in the value of individual participation in a free society and a wish to contribute to the welfare and progress of one's community and country are two examples. It is likely, however, that the tendency for members of more prosperous and powerful status groups to engage in such activities also reflects their own private interests (e.g., Olson 1965). In particular, people from advantaged groups may participate out of a desire to maintain their superior position in the stratification system, by working in and having greater control over those organizations that help decide upon important policies in the community or the wider society.

In this paper, we examine recent information dealing with the question of relative centrality and political involvement in Canada. More specifically, we consider the relationship between people's positions on different dimensions of social inequality, on the one hand, and different types of political and community organization participation, on the other hand.

DATA SOURCE AND PROCEDURES

Data Source

Our data come from a national sample survey of adult Canadians. The data were collected as part of the larger World Values Survey in 1991–93, an international survey of more than 40 countries conducted by Ronald Inglehart and associates (for details, see Inglehart et al. 1994). The present analyses are limited to the Canadian respondents aged 21 and older. Some younger respondents, aged 18 to 21, were in the sample but were excluded from the analyses because many were still in school and, therefore, may not have been able to give as much time to political activities as older people.

Measures of Respondent's Political and Organization Activities

Five measures of political activities were used: *discussing politics,*[1] *attempting to persuade people* on issues,[2] *interest in politics,*[3] *expecting to vote*[4] in the next election, and *political group activity.*[5] Table 30-1 shows the response categories for each of these types of activity.

In addition, we used a measure of public protest activity, based on responses to the following questions:

> Now I would like you to look at this card. I'm going to read out some different forms of political action that people can take, and I would like you to tell me, for each one, whether you have actually done any of these things, whether you might do it, or would never, under any circumstances, do it: *signing a petition, joining a boycott, attending lawful demonstrations, joining strikes,* or *occupying buildings or factories.*

The responses for each of these activities were given scores as follows: "have actually done" = 3, "might do it = 2" and "would never" = 1. These scores were then summed for each respondent to give her or him a measure of *participation in public protest activity.* This measure ranged from 6 (low protest activity) to 18 (high protest activity).

The survey also yielded information on the respondent's stated *support for social movements*, whether or not she/he was a member of organizations working for these movements. Respondents were asked:

> There are a number of groups and movements looking for public support. For each of the following movements which I read out can you tell me whether you approve or disapprove of this movement? : *ecology or nature protection* movement; *anti-nuclear energy* movement; *disarmament* movement; *human rights* movement (at home and abroad); *women's* movement; and *anti-apartheid* movement.

For present purposes, the response categories for each of the six movements were assigned scores as follows: "approve strongly" = 4, "approve somewhat" = 3, "disapprove somewhat" = 2, and "disapprove strongly" = 1. Then the respondents' support ratings for the six social movements were summed for a measure with a range of 6 (low support) to 24 (high support).

The six social movements asked about are what have been termed by others, "new social movements." Although some of these movements are tied to causes or issues that are not precisely new (e.g., women's rights and equality), they are called "new" because they typically have enjoyed renewed prominence in recent years. In addition, they are also seen to operate outside of or independently from more traditional movements, such as the labour union and early suffrage movements, for example (see Carroll 1992; Larana et al. 1994).

Finally, we also used a measure that gauged the *voluntary organization activity* of respondents. First, each respondent reported his or her memberships in community organizations, in answer to the following question: "Which, if any, of the following do you belong to?" A checklist of 16 possible organization categories was supplied: charities and social welfare, churches or religious organizations, education or arts groups, trade unions, political parties or groups, community action groups, human rights organizations, conservation or environmental groups, animal welfare groups, youth work groups, sport and recreation organizations, professional associations, women's groups, peace groups, health organizations, and "others". People were also asked, "And do you currently do any unpaid voluntary work for any of them?" Each respondent was given a score of one for each organization in which she or he was a member only, and a score of two for each working membership. These scores were then summed across all types of organizations, to produce a scale of voluntary organization activity. The measure ranged from 0 (no involvement) to 32 (high involvement).

Social Status Measures

Nine different measures of inequality or social status were examined for their possible relationship to the political and community activity measures. Tables 30-4 and 30-5 provide details on the exact categories used for each of the social status variables. Because of the international nature of the World Values Survey, *education* had to be measured using an indirect indicator, which was the respondent's age at completion of schooling; the ten values for this measure ranged from finished school "at 12 years of age or earlier" to finished school "at 21 years of age or older." Respondent's *occupational status* was measured using a set of 11 different categories that was roughly rank-ordered from high to low status. *Age* was grouped into six categories, with values ranging from younger (age 21–29) to older (70 or more). *Gender* was divided simply into female versus male. *Household income* had ten levels, from a low of under $5 000 per year to a high of $50 000 or more. *Language group* was divided into English versus French. The available *race* measure produced a four-fold classification: Whites, Blacks, Chinese, and All Others. Respondents were also divided into two categories according to *nativity* or country of birth: Canadian-born versus foreign-born. *Region* was a seven-category measure, running east to west, from the Atlantic region to British Columbia.

RESULTS

Overall Involvement in Political and Organizational Activities

Tables 30-1, 30-2, and 30-3 show the overall involvement of the respondents in the various political and organizational activities. Starting with Table 30-1, we see that a relatively large proportion of people, close to 72 percent, indicated that they would vote if an election were held tomorrow. This proportion is very similar to the voter turnouts in recent Canadian elections; these ranged from 69 to 75 percent in the 1980–1993 period, for example (Elections Canada 1993, Table 30-4). In addition, almost 60 percent said that they were either "very" interested (20 percent) or "somewhat" interested (39 percent) in politics. Close to 20 percent discussed politics "often," and another 57% did so "occasionally." However, only 14 percent tried regularly to persuade fellow workers, friends,

Table 30-1 Levels of involvement in various types of political and organizational activities: overall national adult sample

Type of Activity and Level of Involvement	Percentage of Sample	Type of Activity and Level of Involvement	Percentage of Sample
Discuss Politics		**Political Group Involvement**	
Often	19.7	None	92.2
Occasionally	57.1	Member, No Work	4.6
Never	23.2	Working Member	3.3
(N=)	(1618)	(N=)	(1620)
Persuade Friends		**Voting**	
Often	13.9	No	28.5
Time to Time/Rarely	73.0	Yes	71.5
Never	13.1	(N=)	(1625)
(N=)	(1619)		
		Voluntary Organization Involvement	
Political Interest		Member of None	35.9
Very	20.2	One	20.8
Some	39.3	Two	16.4
Not Very	26.2	Three Plus	26.9
Not at All	14.3	(N=)	(1625)
(N=)	(1619)	Working for None	56.7
		One	20.1
		Two	11.4
		Three Plus	11.8
		(N=)	(1625)

or family members concerning political issues. If we consider involvement in groups that are identified by the respondent as "political parties or groups," only 8 percent reported such involvement, with 5 percent saying they were simply a member of such a group, and another 3 percent also doing volunteer work for the group.

If we look at the other end of the scale, non-involvement, we see that 13 percent of the sample said they "never" attempted to persuade others of their views; almost one-quarter (23 percent) of the respondents never discussed politics; about 40 percent reported that they were "not very" interested or "not at all" interested in politics; 28 percent did not intend to vote; and 92 percent were not involved in political groups in any way.

When we turn to participation in all types of voluntary groups in the community (Table 30-1), we find that 64 percent had one or more memberships, and about 43 percent were doing work in one or more organizations. About 43 percent had multiple memberships, and about 23 percent were working in more than one organization.

Table 30-2 Levels of involvement in five types of public protest activity: overall national adult sample

Level of Involvement	Types of Protest Actions				
	Sign Petition	Join Boycott	Attend Demonstration	Join Strike	Occupy Facility
	%	%	%	%	%
Have Done	77.3	24.1	21.6	7.3	3.0
Might Do	14.4	41.8	42.0	26.4	18.6
Would Never Do	8.3	34.1	36.4	66.3	78.4
Total	100%	100%	100%	100%	100%

(N = 1625)

Overall, then, we find little evidence of mass involvement in political activity in Canada. It is true that a sizeable majority of Canadians vote federally, express some political interest, and at least occasionally engage in political discussion. However, very few are members of political parties or politically-oriented organizations, and even fewer do volunteer work for such organizations. There is stronger evidence of community participation if we look at the proportion of people who belong to at least one voluntary organization of whatever type, though even here the proportion of people who are not only members, but are also actively involved, is less than half of the total sample.

In Table 30-2 we consider rates of involvement in the various types of public protest actions. Here we see, once more, that involvement levels are generally low, with the exception of signing petitions. Seventy-seven percent of respondents report signing a petition, while another 14 percent think they might do so sometime in the future, and only 8 percent say they would never do so. However, for joining a boycott, only about one-quarter (24 percent) have ever done this, and 34 percent say they never would do so. For attending demonstrations the parallel figures are 22 percent ("have done") and 36 percent ("would never do"). The rates of involvement are even lower for

Table 30-3 Levels of approval for six social movements: overall national adult sample

Social Movement	Approval Level					
	Approve Strongly	Somewhat	Disapprove Somewhat	Strongly		
	%	%	%	%	(N)	Total
Ecology	53.5	41.3	3.9	1.3	(1590)	100%
Anti-nuclear	32.3	41.8	19.9	6.0	(1549)	100%
Disarmament	39.3	39.8	14.8	6.1	(1555)	100%
Human Rights	57.8	35.7	5.1	1.3	(1579)	100%
Women's	35.8	48.1	12.7	3.4	(1577)	100%
Anti-apartheid	46.5	36.8	11.5	5.2	(1439)	100%

"joining a lawful strike," with only 7 percent doing this, and 66 percent saying they would never do it. Finally, only 3 percent have occupied facilities, and 78 percent would never do so. If we sum the responses across these activities, to create an Index of Public Protest Activities ranging from 8 to 15, the overall sample has an average score of only 9.07.

In Table 30-3 we see that reasonably large proportions of respondents express support for each of the six new social movements. Well over one-half of the sample approve "strongly" or "somewhat" each social movement. The "strong" support ranges from a high of 58 percent for the human rights movement and 54 percent for the ecology movement to 47 percent for anti-apartheid, 39 percent for disarmament, 36 percent for the women's movement, and 32 percent for the anti-nuclear movement. When we sum the responses across all six types of social movement, producing an Index of Social Movement Support with a range of 6 to 24, we find a high average score for the overall sample of 19.6.

Social Status and Political Activity

We now turn to the key question of whether or not social status is related to level of involvement in the various political and community activities. In other words, do all categories of Canadians get involved more or less equally, or do people from more advantaged groups get involved more than others?

Table 30-4 provides data on the relationship between the five forms of political participation listed in Table 30-1 and the nine different measures of social status. Based on the relative centrality perspective, we would expect the following groups to be higher in political involvement than their less advantaged or less "central" counterparts: the more highly educated, those with higher incomes, those with higher occupational status, English-speakers, Whites, the native-born, males, the middle-aged, and those living in the more economically powerful regions of the country, especially Ontario.

Overall, the findings confirm many, though not all, of these expectations. As predicted, education and income have statistically significant relationships with all five measures of political participation, and in the expected direction. That is, the more highly educated respondents and those with higher incomes are more likely than other people to vote, to be involved in political groups, to show interest in politics, to discuss politics, and to attempt to influence others concerning political issues.

Age, occupation level, and region are significantly related to four of the five political activity measures. As expected, the middle-aged are more involved in voting, express greater political interest, discuss politics more, and attempt to influence the opinions of others more, at least as compared to younger people and (particularly) older people. Occupational status is related in the expected way to all the political activities except voting, where there is no statistically significant pattern. As for region, residents of the powerful or more prosperous regions, especially Ontario and the Western provinces, tend to be higher on political interest, discussing politics, and voting. Respondents from the Western regions also show higher levels of political group involvement.

Moving on to other ascribed statuses listed in Table 30-4, we see that language group is related to discussing politics, political interest, and voting, with English-speakers higher than French-speakers, as predicted using the relative centrality hypothesis. One caution here, though, is that voting pertains to the *federal* election and not the *provincial* election. If the voting question dealt with provincial elections, it is likely that the proportions of French-speakers and Quebecers

Table 30-4 Social statuses and average scores for involvement in five types of political activities

Social Status Categories	Type of Activity					
	N	Discuss Politics	Persuade Friends	Political Interest	Voting	Political Group Activity
Total Sample	1625	(1.96)	(2.01)	(2.65)	(.72)	(0.11)
Years of Schooling						
<12 years	32	1.84	1.97	2.35	.66	.06
13	20	1.85	1.80	2.40	.50	.05
14	73	1.68	1.88	2.45	.62	.05
15	82	1.73	1.87	2.93	.59	.04
16	170	1.77	1.86	2.42	.66	.08
17	172	1.87	2.00	2.52	.76	.05
18	297	1.90	1.99	2.61	.72	.12
19	137	1.91	2.04	2.58	.69	.10
20	93	2.04	2.02	2.74	.78	.09
21+years	519	2.18	2.10	2.88	.76	.15
eta		(.25)	(.17)	(.18)	(.13)	(.10)
significance		***	***	***	**	*
Occupational Level						
Owner>10employees	47	2.17	2.32	3.13	.75	.38
Owner<10employees	63	2.06	2.05	2.83	.71	.05
Professional.	289	2.20	2.07	2.90	.74	.18
Middle Maager	143	2.12	2.08	2.86	.76	.12
Lower Manager	191	1.88	1.94	2.52	.70	.05
Supervisor	39	2.14	2.08	2.95	.73	.15
Skilled Lab	117	1.85	1.93	2.53	.76	.07
Semi-skilled	234	1.81	1.97	2.47	.68	.09
Unskilled	228	1.78	1.97	2.38	.68	.07
Farmers	79	2.04	2.03	2.84	.75	.19
All Others	175	1.87	1.94	2.54	.69	.07
eta		(.25)	(.15)	(.23)	(.06)	(.16)
significance		***	***	***	n.s.	***
Income Level						
<$5000	71	1.75	1.96	2.27	.62	.03
$5–10,000	90	1.99	1.97	2.69	.74	.10
10–15,000	98	1.88	1.94	2.55	.69	.04
15–20,000	109	1.88	1.99	2.53	.63	.02
20–25,000	152	1.89	1.97	2.58	.70	.14
25–30,000	224	1.99	1.99	2.66	.77	.14
30–35,000	189	1.96	2.04	2.71	.75	.09
35–40,000	173	2.07	2.03	2.78	.84	.11
40–45,000	103	2.19	2.05	2.83	.82	.17
50,000+	178	2.19	2.16	2.92	.79	.19
eta		(.17)	(.13)	(.16)	(.15)	(.13)
significance		***	**	***	***	**

Table 30-4 continued

Social Status Categories	N	Discuss Politics	Persuade Friends	Political Interest	Voting	Political Group Activity
		Type of Activity				
Age						
21–29	308	1.81	2.03	2.44	.70	.08
30–39	457	1.95	2.02	2.58	.73	.11
40–49	315	2.01	2.05	2.70	.73	.14
50–59	207	2.03	2.02	2.84	.76	.15
60–69	191	2.11	1.95	2.90	.71	.09
70 & over	147	1.93	1.88	2.67	.60	.09
eta		(.14)	(.09)	(.15)	(.09)	(.05)
significance		***	**	***	*	n.s.
Gender						
Male	807	1.95	2.02	2.75	.73	.14
Female	818	1.94	2.00	2.56	.70	.09
eta		(.05)	(.03)	(.10)	(.04)	(.06)
significance		n.s.	n.s.	***	n.s.	**
Language Group						
English	1251	1.98	2.00	2.71	.74	.11
French	374	1.90	2.04	2.46	.62	.10
eta		(.05)	(.03)	(.11)	(.11)	(.02)
significance	n.s.	0	n.s.	***	***	n.s.
Race						
Whites	1499	1.96	2.01	2.67	.73	.11
Blacks	15	2.13	2.00	2.47	.53	.13
Chinese	48	1.83	1.98	2.51	.56	.13
All Others	63	1.90	1.95	2.33	.54	.11
eta		(.05)	(.02)	(.08)	(.11)	(.01)
significance		n.s.	n.s.	*	***	n.s.
Nativity						
Not Born in Canada	281	2.09	2.01	2.79	.69	.12
Born in Canada	1344	1.94	2.01	2.63	.72	.11
eta		(.09)	(.01)	(.06)	(.03)	(.02)
significance		**	n.s.	**	n.s.	n.s.
Region						
AT	133	1.81	1.88	2.37	.64	.15
QU	403	1.93	2.04	2.50	.63	.11
ON	611	1.99	2.01	2.74	.75	.09
MA	59	1.90	2.03	2.50	.69	.15
SK	74	1.97	1.97	2.82	.74	.12
AB	171	2.02	2.03	2.70	.74	.20
BC	174	2.04	2.02	2.88	.74	.05
eta		(.09)	(.08)	(.16)	(.14)	(.09)
significance		**	**n.s.**	***	***	**

Note: n.s. = not a statistically significant difference.
* = significant at p<.05
** = significant at p<.01
*** = significant at p<.001

voting would be more similar to those of other Canadians. Race appears to be related to only two of the five measures of political activity; for political interest and voting, Whites, as expected, are more active than other groups. Finally, in the case of nativity, we find no evidence of the expected pattern: the native-born are *less* involved than the foreign-born in political interest and political discussions, and there are no significant differences by place of birth on the other three political activity measures.

In Table 30-5, we relate the nine social status variables to three different indexes of activity: *political protest*, *social movement support*, and *community organization involvement*. Most of the relationships in Table 30-5 are statistically significant, and in the expected direction. In general, advantaged groups tend to be more involved in the three types of activity. The exceptions are that race and nativity are not significantly related to public protest and social movement support, and income is related to public protest and organization involvement, but not to support for social movements. As we would expect, those higher in education are more involved in public protest, in community interest groups, and in supporting social movements than are their less-educated counterparts. The same is true for males compared to females, the middle-aged compared to other age groups, and those with higher incomes and occupational statuses compared to others. One possible exception in the case of occupation is the skilled labour category which, despite relatively low occupational status (but perhaps because of links to labour organizations), has higher involvement levels on the three activity indexes than might otherwise be expected.

In the case of language group and region, the results are not entirely consistent with the relative centrality hypothesis. We find that the French and Quebecers are relatively high in public protest activity and social movement support, although residents of Alberta and British Columbia rank high on both of these measures as well. The results for voluntary association activity more closely follow the predicted pattern, with the English and people from Ontario being comparatively high on this measure.

We also conducted some multivariate analyses, using a technique called multiple classification analysis. This technique allowed us to look at the relationship between any one of the social status variables and the activity measures, while simultaneously controlling for the effects of all the other social status variables. These analyses are not reported in tables here, to conserve space. However, the results are largely the same as those shown in Tables 30-4 and 30-5. These results suggest that the patterns found in Tables 30-4 and 30-5 do not change in direction, even with the inclusion of controls, although some of the relationships are no longer statistically significant after controls. Thinking of the relationships in Table 30-4, first, we find that, with controls, one of the effects of occupational status (for political discussions) is no longer significant. The effect before controls may have been largely due to the strong joint effect of educational status on both occupation and the political discussion measure. The same change occurs for the effects of income on both political discussion and political persuasion. These findings appear to have resulted mainly from the effects of educational status differences. Also, one effect of race (upon political group involvement), one effect of language group (upon voting), and one effect of nativity (upon political group involvement) are not statistically significant after controls for the effects of education, occupation, and income, suggesting that there are differences resulting from these three achieved characteristics that make for the differences in political involvement by the ascribed characteristics.

Table 30-5 Social statuses and involvement in public protest, social movements, and voluntary community organizations

Social Status Categories	Average Level of Involvement					
	N	Public Protest	N	Support Movements	N	Community Groups
Total Sample	1625	9.07	1625	19.60	1625	2.66
Years of Schooling						
<12 years	29	6.83	19	17.90	32	1.75
13	20	8.35	13	17.31	20	2.45
14	67	7.66	48	19.13	73	1.60
15	75	7.91	67	18.76	82	2.15
16	153	8.19	138	19.25	170	1.69
17	158	8.46	143	19.69	172	2.23
18	271	9.12	251	19.55	297	2.48
19	120	9.23	114	19.65	137	2.42
20	89	9.35	86	19.95	93	2.77
21+years	479	9.96	460	19.93	519	3.56
eta		(.33)		(.12)		(.21)
significance		***		**		***
Occupational Level						
Ow.>10em	45	9.64	44	19.43	47	3.98
Ow.<10em	59	9.10	57	19.58	63	1.94
Professional	265	10.15	259	20.06	289	4.03
Mid.Manager	131	9.32	124	19.17	143	3.04
Low.Manager	175	8.79	151	19.66	191	2.36
Supervisor	54	8.98	48	18.44	59	2.41
Skilled Lab	107	9.42	94	19.06	117	2.09
Semi-skilled	219	8.90	193	19.83	234	2.10
Unskilled	211	8.61	198	19.38	228	3.27
Farmers	73	8.47	66	18.08	79	2.21
All Others	161	7.99	132	18.96	175	(.23)
eta		(.25)		(.18)		***
significance		***		***		
Income Level						
<$5000	62	7.77	53	19.57	71	1.94
$5–10,000	82	8.37	70	19.56	90	2.27
10–15,000	89	7.91	77	19.21	98	1.63
15–20,000	100	8.68	86	19.76	109	2.31
20–25,000	145	8.86	124	19.23	152	2.88
25–30,000	211	9.03	192	19.28	224	2.65
30–35,000	177	9.52	170	19.58	189	2.94
35–40,000	163	9.77	154	19.63	173	2.73
40–45,000	95	9.88	94	19.87	103	3.21
50,000+	170	10.04	161	19.91	108	3.76
eta		(.28)		(.08)		(.17)
significance		***		n.s.		**

Table 30-5 continued

Social Status Categories	Average Level of Involvement					
	N	Public Protest	N	Support Movements	N	Community Groups
Age						
21–29	275	9.35	255	20.16	308	2.19
30–39	423	9.65	392	20.18	457	2.67
40–49	288	9.51	278	19.72	315	3.11
50–59	196	8.56	173	19.34	207	3.02
60–69	172	8.05	165	`8.21	191	2.69
70 & over	136	7.32	103	18.15	147	2.34
eta		(.21)		(.24)		(.11)
significance		***		***		**
Gender						
Male	757	9.34	701	19.22	807	2.57
Female	733	8.78	665	19.97	878	2.79
eta		(.09)		(.13)		(.03)
significance		***		***		n.s.
Language Group						
English	1142	8.95	1058	18.33	1251	2.80
French	348	9.44	308	20.47	374	2.28
eta		(.12)		(.17)		(.08)
significance		***		***		**
Race						
Whites	1385	9.08	1261	19.59	1499	2.69
Blacks	11	8.00	14	21.00	15	2.00
Chinese	40	8.63	40	19.70	48	3.33
All Others	54	9.09	51	19.06	63	2.14
eta		(.09)		(.08)		(.06)
significance		n.s.		n.s.		.n.s.
Nativity						
Not Born in Canada	254	8.96	240	19.46	281	2.83
Born in Canada	1236	9.08	1126	19.62	1344	2.65
eta		(.03)		(.02)		(.06)
significance		n.s.		n.s.	.	.n.s.
Region						
AT	125	8.08	112	19.63	133	2.61
QU	374	9.51	332	20.48	403	2.36
ON	564	8.78	526	19.70	611	2.70
MA	50	9.16	47	19.21	39	3.45
SK	69	8.86	68	18.25	74	2.61
AB	150	9.25	127	18.68	171	2.19
BC	158	9.69	154	19.73	174	2.67
eta		(.22)		(.20)		(.09)
significance		***		***		*

Note: n.s. = not a statistically significant difference.
* = significant at $p<.05$
** = significant at $p<.01$
*** = significant at $p<.001$

Controls produce few changes in the statistical significance of the results reported in Table 30-5 for the indexes of public protest, support of social movements, and involvement in community groups. The exceptions are involvement in public protest and community organizations by language group, where the language group differences are found not to be significant after controls; however, the pattern of higher involvement by Quebec residents persisted with controls.

CONCLUSIONS

We have examined recent Canadian data on the question of who participates in political and community affairs in Canadian society. Drawing from previous research and theory on the subject, we began with the premise that those groups with more power or "relative centrality" in our society, such as those with higher education and socioeconomic status, the English language group, males, the Canadian-born, and the middle-aged, would have higher levels of political and community organization activity than other people. This premise receives partial support in the results. The strongest support is found for education, occupational status, income, and age. For some types of activity, there is support for the effects of gender and language group.

The patterns of results for race and nativity are much less consistent with, and sometimes even contradict, the relative centrality or relative power argument. Moreover, controlled analyses show that some of the effects of race and nativity, before controls, occur because of differences in education, occupation, and income across these two characteristics. However, this latter set of findings may not so much call into question the relative centrality argument per se, as suggest a specification of it. Namely, the results may demonstrate that power and resource differences that are rooted in achieved statuses such as socio-economic status and education (particularly the latter) are the key explanations for the correlation of such ascribed statuses as race and nativity with political activity. The findings appear to cast doubt on any *comprehensive* claims that political and community participation are easily understood or explained as simply consequences of the relative centrality of all social statuses. Instead, a more complex set of processes seems to be at work in accounting for the likelihood that individuals will join and participate in various political and community activities.

The patterns for region were also more complex than suggested by our working hypothesis, and do not lend themselves to easy generalizations. Perhaps our finding of higher involvement of Ontarians and people from the Western provinces can be traced to relatively greater socio-economic advantages in these regions, in which case there may be some support here for the relative centrality thesis. On the other hand, Quebecers were found to be somewhat more involved in political protests and support for new social movements than other Canadians, yet Quebec is a relatively disadvantaged province, judging by most economic indicators. The Quebec results, however, could represent a special set of circumstances, because of the typically higher levels of political unrest in that province, stemming from issues such as Quebec separatism or sovereignty and the debate over Canada's constitution.

In general, we have found that, apart from voting in federal elections and a few other exceptions, it is rare that a majority of Canadians becomes involved in various types of social action or political activity. Perhaps the low level of involvement in such behaviours as public protest activity is an indication that most Canadians are relatively happy with the way things are in their country and, therefore, feel no strong need to participate in political or social change. Nevertheless, to the extent that political and community activities are structured by social status, it is apparent, as well, that those who are *higher* in social status also tend to be the people who are *most* involved in such actions. Because we would assume that these individuals should be *happier* about the status quo than those who are lower in social status, this pattern may seem surprising. One possibility is that such actions on the part of those in advantaged situations are mainly directed toward helping and promoting the interests of others less fortunate than themselves. An alternative interpretation for the greater political and community involvement of more privileged groups is that they have a stronger desire to protect their own interests through such activities, and also possess the material and other resources necessary for participation.

We also should consider the possibility that power or relative centrality may explain some kinds of political and organizational involvement better than others. To some theorists, the existence of a wide range of voluntary political and community activities, as well as broad involvement by less powerful groups, may be indicative of a democratic and "pluralist" power structure in our society (e.g., Dahl 1982). A different view, however, must also be considered: it may be that people with greater power or centrality are simply being strategic and selective when deciding which activities they choose to pursue and which organizations they choose to join. Some writers argue that voluntary organizations serve as the representatives of competing or conflicting interest groups, some of which have a much greater capacity than others to ensure that their particular policy preferences are implemented (e.g., Hayes 1978, 1983). From this perspective, we would expect that people with higher social status or relative centrality, in pursuing their own desire to have access to power, would concentrate on truly influential organizations and activities, rather than on the whole range of activities.

Evidence from other research does suggest that such a pattern may be at work. For example, individuals with higher social status are significantly more likely than other people to run for political office. Moreover, they are even more likely to be successful in being elected to parliament, and even more likely still to serve as senior ministers in government (see, e.g., Forcese and de Vries 1977; Guppy et al. 1988). Those with higher social status are also far more likely to occupy powerful positions in Canada's system of "elites," both in public or government organizations and in the private economic and social spheres (e.g., Porter 1965; Clement 1975, 1977; Olsen 1980; Nakhaie 1997). Thus, while the present study gives some indication of a relatively broad base to political and community group involvement in Canada, the findings do not mean that those with privileged social statuses are rivalled by less advantaged groups or individuals in the overall power structure.

NOTES

1. "When you get together with your friends, would you say you discuss politics frequently, occasionally, or never?"
2. "When you, yourself, hold a strong opinion, do you ever find yourself persuading relatives or fellow workers to share your views? If so, does it happen often, from time to time, or rarely?"
3. "How interested would you say you are in politics—very interested, somewhat interested, not very interested, or not at all interested?"
4. "If there were a general election tomorrow, which party would you vote for?" Responses were divided into "would vote" and named choice versus "would not vote."
5. "Please look carefully at the following list of voluntary organizations and activities and say which, if any, do you belong to—political parties or groups—and which if any are you currently doing unpaid voluntary work for."

REFERENCES

Carroll, William (ed.) 1992 *Organizing Dissent: Contemporary Social Movements in Theory and Practice* Toronto: Garamond.

Clement, Wallace 1975 *The Canadian Corporate Elite* Toronto: McClelland and Stewart.

Clement, Wallace 1977 *Continental Corporate Power* Toronto: McClelland and Stewart.

Chui, Tina, James Curtis, and Edward Grabb 1993 "Who participates in community organizations and politics?" pp. 524–538 in James Curtis, Edward Grabb, and Neil Guppy, (eds.), *Social Inequality in Canada: Patterns, Problems and Policies* Scarborough: Prentice-Hall, (2nd ed.).

Curtis, James 1971 "Voluntary association joining: a cross-national comparative note." *American Sociological Review* 36:872–80.

Curtis, James, Edward Grabb, and Douglas Baer 1992 "Voluntary association membership in fifteen developed countries: a comparative analysis." *American Sociological Review* 57:139–152.

Curtis, James and Ronald Lambert 1976 "Voting, political interest, and age: national survey findings for French and English Canadians." *Canadian Journal of Political Science* 9:293–307.

Curtis, James, Ronald Lambert, Steven Brown, and Barry Kay 1989 "Affiliating with voluntary associations: Canadian-American comparisons." *Canadian Journal of Sociology* 14:143–161.

Cutler, Steven T. 1976 "Age differences in voluntary association membership." *Social Forces* 55:43–58.

Dahl, Robert 1982 *Dilemmas of a Pluralist Democracy* New York: Oxford University Press.

Edwards, Patricia K., John N. Edwards, and Alan DeWitt Watts 1984 "Women, work, and social participation." *Journal of Voluntary Action Research* 13:7–22.

Elections Canada 1993 *Official Voting Results: 35th General Election* Ottawa: Elections Canada.

Forcese, Dennis and John de Vries 1977 "Occupational and electoral success in Canada: the 1974 federal election." *Canadian Review of Sociology and Anthropology* 14:331–40.

Grabb, Edward and James Curtis 1992 "Voluntary association activity in English Canada, French Canada and the United States: multivariate analyses." *Canadian Journal of Sociology* 17:371–88.

Guppy, Neil, Sabrina Freeman, and Shari Buchan 1988 "Economic background and political representation." pp. 394–404 in *Social Inequality in Canada: Patterns, Problems, Policies* (1st ed.) J. Curtis, E. Grabb, N. Guppy, and S. Gilbert (eds.).

Hayes, M.T. 1978 "The semi sovereign pressure croups: a critique of current theory and an alternative typology." *Journal of Politics* 40:134–61.

Hayes, M.T. 1983 "Interest groups: pluralism or mass society?" pp.110–25 in *Interest Group Politics* A.J. Cigler and B.A. Loomis (eds.). Washington:CQ.

Inglehart, Ronald et al. 1994 *World Values Survey, 1991–92: Individual and Aggregate Level Codebook* Ann Arbor: University of Michigan, Institute for Social Research.

Kay, Barry, Ronald Lambert, Steven Brown, and James Curtis 1987 "Gender and political activity in Canada: 1965–84." *Canadian Journal of Political Science* 20:851–63.

Knoke, David 1986 "Associations and Interest groups." *Annual Review of Sociology* 12:1–21.

Larana, Enrique, Hank Johnston, and Joseph Gusfield (eds.) 1994 *New Social Movements: From Ideology to Identity* Philadelphia: Temple University Press.

McPherson, J.M. and W.G. Lockwood 1980 "The longitudinal study of voluntary association memberships: a multivariate analysis." *Journal of Voluntary Action Research* 9:74–84.

Milbrath, Lester and M.L. Goel 1977 *Political Participation* (2nd ed.) Chicago:Rand McNally.

Nakhaie, M. Reza 1997 "Vertical mosaic among the elites: the new imagery revisited." *Canadian Review of Sociology and Anthropology* 34:1–24.

Olsen, Dennis 1980 *The State Elite* Toronto: McClelland and Stewart.

Olson, Marvin E. 1965 *The Logic of Collective Action* Cambridge, Mass.: Harvard University Press.

Palisi, Bartolomeo J. and Rosalie J. Palisi 1984 "Status and voluntary associations: a cross-cultural study of males in three metropolitan areas." *Journal of Voluntary Action Research* 13:32–43.

Porter, John 1965 *The Vertical Mosaic* Toronto: University of Toronto Press.

Smith, David Horton 1975 "Voluntary action and voluntary groups." *Annual Review of Sociology* 1:247–70.

FOR FURTHER REFERENCE: CONSEQUENCES OF SOCIAL INEQUALITY

Allahar, Anton and James Cote 1998 *Richer and Poorer: The Structure of Inequality in Canada* Toronto: Copp Clark. The authors use a framework that centres on the role of dominant ideology to examine social inequality in Canada, with a special focus on issues of class, gender, age, and race/ethnicity. A key claim in this analysis is that Canadians are in a state of denial about the existence of major inequalities in their society.

Canadian Social Trends This journal is published four times per year by Statistics Canada. Each issue contains several brief and straight-forward presentations of up-to-date information on social problems, health, income and jobs, education, and demographic processes. Frequently the pieces show how people's achieved and ascribed social statuses are related to the issue in question.

Curtis, James and Lorne Tepperman (eds.) 1994 *Haves and Have-nots: An International Reader on Social Inequality* Englewood Cliffs, N.J.: Prentice-Hall. This volume presents research on patterns, explanations, and consequences of social inequality from numerous countries around the world.

Dunk, Thomas W. 1991 *It's a Working Man's Town* Montreal and Kingston: McGill-Queen's University Press. This is an interesting participant observation study of male working-class culture in Northern Ontario. The volume includes a thoughtful discussion of theories of class consciousness.

Hagan, John and Bill Mccarthy 1997 *Mean Streets: Youth Crime and Homelessness* Cambridge: Cambridge University Press. The authors present information on the (1) lives of homeless youth on the street, (2) how the youths came to be there, and (3) how they leave the streets. The social class dimensions of these phenomena are explored, along with other factors. Theories put forward in the previous literature are critiqued, and alternative theoretical interpretations are offered. The study is based on qualitative data gathered in two Canadian cities.

Johnson, Holly 1996 *Dangerous Domains: Violence against Women in Canada* Toronto: Nelson. This book presents results from several data sources including a Statistics Canada study of violence against women. The latter provides information on characteristics of the victim and her circumstances, and characteristics of the perpetrator of the violence. Also discussed are various individual-level and societal-level explanations of violence, and problems of measurement.

Marchak, M. Patricia 1988 *Ideological Perspectives on Canada* (3rd ed.) Toronto: McGraw-Hill Ryerson. The author provides an analysis of major political ideologies in Canada and their shifting currents over time. The ideologies are liberalism, socialism, conservatism, and a new "corporatism." The policy implications for social inequality of each ideology are discussed.

National Council Of Welfare 1990 *Health, Health Care and Medicare* Ottawa: National Council of Welfare. This brief monograph presents data on patterns of social inequalities in health care, health, and life expectancy in Canada. It provides, too, a systematic set of proposals for ways of reducing the inequality and improving the levels of health of Canadians.

Reitz, Jeffrey G. and Raymond Breton 1994 *The Illusion of Difference: Realities of Ethnicity in Canada and the United States* Toronto: C.D. Howe Institute. The authors give clear and concise comparisons of information from the two countries on: beliefs about levels of ethnic/racial inequality; attitudes toward retention of minority cultures; the extent of ethnic culture retentions; prejudice and discrimination; and the economic incorporation of minority groups.

Tepperman, Lorne 1994 *Choices and Chances* (2nd ed.) Toronto: Holt, Rinehart & Winston. This introductory-level books gives interesting discussions of what is known about patterns in people's desires around education, careers, and various aspects of lifestyles.

Index